Defensor pacis

RECORDS OF WESTERN CIVILIZATION

Marsilius of Padua

DEFENSOR PACIS

Translation and Introduction
by Alan Gewirth

With an afterword and bibliography
by Cary J. Nederman

COLUMBIA UNIVERSITY PRESS
NEW YORK

Columbia University Press
Publishers Since 1893
New York   Chichester, West Sussex

Copyright © 1956, 2001 Columbia University Press

Library of Congress Cataloging-in-Publication Data
Marsilius of Padua, d. 1342?
    [Defensor pacis. English]
    Defensor pacis / Marsilius of Padua ; translation and introduction by Alan
Gewirth ; with an afterword and updated bibliography by Cary J. Nederman.
        p. cm. — (Records of Western Civilization)
    Originally published by Columbia University Press in 1956 as v.2 of Marsilius
of Padua, the defender of peace.
    Includes bibliographical references and index.
    ISBN 0–231–12354–X (cloth) — ISBN 0–231–12355–8 (paper)
    1. Church and state. 2. State, The. 3. Political science—Early works to
1800. I. Gewirth, Alan. II. Nederman, Cary J. III. Title. IV. Series.
JC121 .M3213 2001
320.1 —dc21   2001028824

Casebound editions of Columbia University Press books are printed on
permanent and durable acid-free paper.
Printed in Canada

c 10 9 8 7 6 5 4 3 2 1
p 10 9 8 7 6 5 4 3 2

RECORDS OF WESTERN CIVILIZATION is a series published under the auspices of the Interdepartmental Committee on Medieval and Renaissance Studies of the Columbia University Graduate School. The Western Records are, in fact, a new incarnation of a venerable series, the Columbia Records of Civilization, which, for more than half a century, published sources and studies concerning great literary and historical landmarks. Many of the volumes of that series retain value, especially for their translations into English of primary sources, and the Medieval and Renaissance Studies Committee is pleased to cooperate with Columbia University Press in reissuing a selection of those works in paperback editions, especially suited for classroom use, and in limited clothbound editions.

Records of Western Civilization

The Art of Courtly Love, by Andreas Capellanus. Translated with an introduction and notes by John Jay Parry.

The Correspondence of Pope Gregory VII: Selected Letters from the Registrum. Translated with an introduction by Ephraim Emerton.

Medieval Handbooks of Penance: The Principal Libri Poenitentiales and Selections from Related Documents. Translated by John T. McNeill and Helena M. Gamer.

Macrobius: Commentary on The Dream of Scipio. Translated with an introduction by William Harris Stahl.

Medieval Trade in the Mediterranean World: Illustrative Documents. Translated with introductions and notes by Robert S. Lopez and Irving W. Raymond, with a foreword and bibliography by Olivia Remie Constable.

The Cosmographia *of Bernardus Silvestris*. Translated with an introduction by Winthrop Wetherbee.

Heresies of the High Middle Ages. Translated and annotated by Walker L. Wakefield and Austin P. Evans.

The Didascalicon *of Hugh of Saint Victor: A Medieval Guide to the Arts*. Translated with an introduction by Jerome Taylor.

Martianus Capella and the Seven Liberal Arts.
Vol. I: *The Quadrivium of Martianus Capella: Latin Traditions in the Mathematical Sciences*, by William Harris Stahl with Richard Johnson and E. L. Burge.
Vol. II: *The Marriage of Philology and Mercury*, by Martianus Capella. Translated by William Harris Stahl and Richard Johnson with E. L. Burge.

The See of Peter, by James T. Shotwell and Louise Ropes Loomis.

Two Renaissance Book Hunters: The Letters of Poggius Bracciolini to Nicolaus de Niccolis. Translated and annotated by Phyllis Walter Goodhart Gordan.

Guillaume d'Orange: Four Twelfth-Century Epics. Translated with an introduction by Joan M. Ferrante.

Visions of the End: Apocalyptic Traditions in the Middle Ages, by Bernard McGinn, with a new preface and expanded bibliography.

The Letters of Saint Boniface. Translated by Ephraim Emerton, with a new introduction and bibliography by Thomas F. X. Noble.

Imperial Lives and Letters of the Eleventh Century. Translated by Theodor E. Mommsen and Karl F. Morrison, with a historical introduction and new suggested readings by Karl F. Morrison.

An Arab-Syrian Gentleman and Warrior in the Period of the Crusades: Memoirs of Usāmah ibn-Munqidh. Translated by Philip K. Hitti, with a new foreword by Richard W. Bulliet.

De expugnatione Lyxbonensi (The Conquest of Lisbon). Edited and translated by Charles Wendell David, with a new foreword and bibliography by Jonathan Phillips.

Defensor pacis. Translated with an introduction by Alan Gewirth, with an afterword and updated bibliography by Cary J. Nederman.

CONTENTS

THE DEFENDER OF PEACE

DISCOURSE ONE

DISCOURSE TWO

DISCOURSE THREE

APPENDICES

PREFACE

THIS VOLUME presents the first complete translation of the *Defensor pacis* into any modern language. A partial translation was made into French some time before 1363, and this was in turn translated into Italian in 1363. The second and third discourses were translated into German in 1545. And an English translation by William Marshall, omitting about one-fifth of the work, appeared in 1535, when it was intended to be of help to King Henry VIII. I have consulted this translation in photostatic reproduction at the Columbia University Library and the University of Chicago Library.[1]

I hope that this volume may encourage others to translate some of the other monumental works of political thought of the late middle ages, not only for strictly scholarly purposes, but because the study of these works can help toward a deeper understanding of our political traditions in their relevance for the contemporary world.

The present translation was made from the text of the *Defensor pacis* edited by C. W. Previté-Orton, Cambridge University Press, 1928. Emendations of this text have been adopted from two sources: the edition of the *Defensor pacis* by Richard Scholz, in the *Fontes juris Germanici antiqui* of the *Monumenta Germaniae historica*, Hanover, 1932, and the review article on Previté-Orton's edition by Dino Bigongiari, "Notes on the Text of the *Defensor Pacis*," *Speculum*, Volume VII (1932), pages 36–49. I have indicated all departures from Previté-Orton's text in my footnotes, where "Scholz" and "Bigongiari" refer to the edition and article just mentioned.

Some of the footnote references to sources of Marsilius' citations are derived directly from the Previté-Orton and Scholz editions of the *Defensor pacis*. I have also used their many other historical references. The present translation, however, adds a considerable number of references not found in either of these editions.

Marsilius quotes extensively from Aristotle and the Bible. His quotations from Aristotle are in the Latin translations made by William of Moerbeke, and his quotations from the Bible are in the Vulgate translation made by St. Jerome. In translating Aristotle-Moerbeke, I have sought

---

[1] Marshall's translation, while pithy and forceful, is often inaccurate; as Previté-Orton says, it "was badly done and severely edited in the interests of monarchy" (*Proceedings of the British Academy*, XXI [1935], 163). See also Vol. I, p. 195, n. 105.

help both from the original Greek and from the Oxford and Loeb translations of Aristotle, but I have usually made my own translation. In translating the Vulgate Bible, I have followed in some cases the Douai translation, in others the King James Version; and at some points where I have felt that neither of these was close enough to the text as given and interpreted by Marsilius, I have made my own translation. Some of the chief problems of translating Marsilius, including his Aristotelian and Biblical quotations, are discussed in the last section of the Introduction.

The Introduction is intended to help the reader cope with the structure, basic ideas, and vocabulary of Marsilius' treatise. For a fuller analysis of Marsilius' political philosophy in its relation to medieval and modern thought, I may refer the reader to Volume I of the present work, *Marsilius of Padua and Medieval Political Philosophy*.[2] I have taken the liberty of giving footnote references in the translation to this first volume at points where important ideas or doctrines of the *Defensor* are discussed.

I am very grateful to Professor Dino Bigongiari for his help with the translation. He checked a large portion of it and gave me the benefit of his unsurpassed philological and stylistic sense. I also acknowledge with thanks the help of Professor Austin P. Evans, who also went over the translation and made many helpful suggestions. It need hardly be added that neither of these scholars is responsible for any errors which may still remain in the translation. I am indebted to Professor Charner M. Perry for many kinds of invaluable aid. I also wish to thank Professors Richard P. McKeon and Herbert W. Schneider for their help in regard to the publication of this work; the Department of Philosophy of Columbia University, for a subvention to help pay for the typing of the translation; the staff of the Columbia University Press, especially Miriam L. Bergamini, Edwin N. Iino, and Helen L. Stroop, for their editorial work on these volumes; and Mrs. Florence Field, for typing the Introduction.

This volume is dedicated to my children.

A.G.

[2] This is to appear shortly in an Italian translation to be published by Giangiacomo Feltrinelli Editore, Milan.

INTRODUCTION

STRUCTURE AND GENERAL ARGUMENT

MARSILIO DEI MAINARDINI was born between 1275 and 1280. He was rector of the University of Paris in 1313, and was associated there with Peter of Abano and other leading Averroists. He finished the *Defensor pacis* in 1324 (fifty years after the death of Thomas Aquinas, and three years after the death of Dante). In 1326 papal condemnation of the work forced him to flee to the court of Ludwig of Bavaria in Nuremberg. He died in 1342.

We know a few further facts about Marsilius' life.[1] But, perhaps more than in the case of most authors, these facts are slight by comparison with the history of the one major work he ever wrote.[2] The impact of the *Defensor pacis* reverberated during the following centuries, both from hearsay description of its conclusions and from actual reading of it. It was a book at which solid men of the age shuddered. When popes, cardinals, and writers simply concerned with preserving the social order wished to condemn heretics—Wyclif, Hus, Luther, among others—they charged them with having gotten their ideas from the "accursed Marsilius."[3] To be a Marsilian was regarded as subversive in a way similar to that which, centuries later, attached to being a Marxist. The analogy between Marsilius and Marx is not entirely without point, in this crucial respect: both men consciously set themselves in opposition to dominant institutions and ideas of their respective eras, and both gave expression to forces which wreaked havoc with those institutions.

The study of the *Defensor pacis* can, then, enlighten us on sources and leading characteristics of modern life and political thought. Yet at first scrutiny the book is not very impressive. It begins with imprecations against medieval papalism, but at once subsides into what seems like an equable commentary on Aristotle's *Politics*. Then, having developed a conception of what is apparently intended to be an ideal state, it accuses the papacy of being the cause which hinders this ideal from being realized, and launches into a prolonged discussion of ecclesiastic politics with fre-

---

[1] On Marsilius' life, see Vol. I, pp. 20–23, including the works cited at p. 20, n. 1.

[2] While Marsilius was associated with John of Jandun in flight and in subsequent papal condemnations, Marsilius was sole author of the work. Cf. my paper, "John of Jandun and the *Defensor Pacis*," *Speculum*, XXIII (1948), 267–72.

[3] For some references, see Vol. I, p. 302, nn. 1, 2, 5.

quent references to the New Testament, concluding, as it began, with imprecations.

It would be unfortunate, however, if the reader were not to venture beyond these initial impressions. Beneath the invective and the zealous commentary is an analysis of the human condition, of the problems it raises and how they are to be solved. The analysis involves a balancing of the respective rôles of men's values, their conflicts, their power relationships, and the ways in which these are to be brought into some sort of equilibrium. These problems have always been central to political thought. Marsilius' contribution consists in the fact that he not merely said something new about them, nor even that what he said was prophetic of the directions which historical development was actually to take, but also that his analysis can help us to understand and to cope with the perennial problems at issue. In the second and third parts of this Introduction an attempt is made to state what, in this broader perspective, Marsilius' political philosophy is. But first the reader deserves some help in wading through the complicated structure of Marsilius' treatise.

Scholars have sometimes asserted that the *Defensor pacis* lacks coherent structure. There are doctrinal and terminological disparities between Discourses I and II, and these have been considered so extreme that some commentators have declared it impossible that the same man could have written both discourses. And within the second discourse it has been pointed out that there are many excrescences and repetitions, to which has been added the charge that the discourse gives little evidence of systematic organization.[4]

Some of the more extreme of these criticisms have been disproved in recent years.[5] That the second discourse is repetitious cannot be denied; yet frequently the repetitions present different aspects of the same subject. That there are inconsistencies between the first and second discourses is also true; but they can be explained by means internal to the general plan of the treatise itself, particularly by the different contexts of the two discourses.[6] The work as a whole has a much clearer organization than the major charges of planlessness and incoherence would suggest.[7]

[4] See, e.g., H. Otto, "Marsilius von Padua und der *Defensor Pacis,*" *Historisches Jahrbuch,* XLV (1925), 206.

[5] See, e.g., R. Scholz, "Zur Datierung und Uberlieferung des *Defensor Pacis* von Marsilius von Padua," *Neues Archiv der Gesellschaft für ältere deutsche Geschichtskunde,* XLVI (1927), 499–500.

[6] See Vol. I, pp. 28–84, 248–59, and below, pp. xxi–xxii.

[7] Important aid in following the organization of the *Defensor* is provided by Marsilius' programs for subsequent chapters or paragraphs. In the footnotes to the translation, the programs outlined in each of these paragraphs have been correlated with the various chapters

Let us begin with the main divisions of the treatise. Of its three "discourses" (*dictiones*), the third is a brief summary of conclusions. The first and second discourses are distinguished from one another in two complementary ways. The first is in terms of the difference between a general and a singular causal analysis. Both discourses are concerned with the causes of civil peace and strife.[8] But the first discourse treats of the "usual" and "general" causes, while the second discourse treats of an "unusual" and "singular" or "special" cause, namely, the acts and pretensions of the papacy deriving from its claim to plenitude of power.[9] Thus the first discourse is concerned with the general structure and functioning of any state as such, while the second discourse examines the "singular" threat to that functioning within Christian states which arises from the papacy's claim to universal hegemony. Consequently, the first discourse is also related to the second as the normal to the pathological: the first discourse treats the "usual" operations of human nature and reason in the state, while the second, particularly in its latter phases, treats the "impediment" to those operations deriving from the papal pretensions.[10]

From this difference between the two discourses there follows a second difference, with respect to method. The first discourse presents demonstrations based on human reason, with support from Aristotle, while the second discourse "confirms" the first by the authority of the New Testament.[11] The general causes of civil peace and strife require no reference to the supernatural, and can thus be known by the unaided reason without support from revelation. On the other hand, the analysis of the sense in which the papacy is the "singular cause" of civil strife, while it involves the application of the general analysis to the particular case, also involves recourse to the materials of faith and revelation in order to explain the setting in which the papal claims arose and to provide the basis for evaluating those claims by reference to the proper religious function and political status of the priesthood. In this respect, reason and revelation, Aristotle and the New Testament, are in complete agreement, for all declare that neither the priesthood nor any other part of the state must interfere with the functioning of the ruling part.

---

or paragraphs of the treatise in which each part of the program is carried out. For the convenience of the reader, a list of these "program" paragraphs is here appended: I. i. 8; I. iii. 1; I. ix. 3; I. x. 2; II. i. 3–5; II. iv. 3; II. xvi. 1; II. xvii. 1; II. xvii. 3; II. xviii. 8; II. xxi. title; II. xxiii. 2.

[8] See, e.g., the opening sentence of III. iii.

[9] For this distinction, see I. i. 3, 7; I. xix. 1, 3; II. xxvi. 19; III. i.

[10] See I. i. 3; I. xix. 1–3; and Vol. I, pp. 12–13, 59.

[11] See I. i. 3.

The inconsistencies between the two discourses arise from the fact that, apart from the question of the political subordination of the priesthood to the government, the two methods and sources differ strongly in the doctrines to which they lead concerning the content of ethical values, the basis of religion, and the specific nature and limitations of political authority. The oppositions on these matters are the reflection of that contrariety which Marsilius, like the other Averroists, maintains as to the relation between reason and faith, and which he applies to the sphere of the practical.[12]

The following synoptic tables are presented in order to exhibit more fully the structure and argument of each discourse.

DISCOURSE I: THE GENERAL CAUSES OF CIVIL PEACE AND STRIFE AS SHOWN BY THE NORMAL STRUCTURE OF THE STATE ESTABLISHED BY REASON

A. *Introductory* (Chaps. I–II).
    a. The aim of the work: the peace of the state (Chap. I).
    b. Definitions of "state" and "peace" (Chap. II).
B. *Origin and Final Cause of the State* (Chaps. III; IV, paras. 1–2).
    a. Origin (Chap. III).
    b. Final cause (Chap. IV, paras. 1–2).
C. *The Parts of the State* (Chaps. IV–VII).
    a. Their final cause (Chaps. IV–VI).
      α. In general (Chap. IV).
      β. In particular (Chaps. V–VI).
        1. Of the parts other than the priesthood (Chap. V, paras. 1–9).
        2. Of the priesthood (Chaps. V, paras. 10-*fin.;* VI).
          i. From the standpoint of the pagan philosophers (Chap. V, paras. 10-*fin.*).
          ii. From the standpoint of the Christian revelation (Chap. VI).
    b. Their other causes (Chap. VII; continued in Chap. XV, paras. 4-*fin.*).[13]
D. *The First Part of the State: The Government and the Law by Which It Governs* (Chaps. VIII–XVI).

[12] See Vol. I, pp. 77 ff., 249 ff.
[13] In Chap. VII, para. 4, the efficient cause of the parts of the state is indicated briefly and in general terms. The detailed discussion of this efficient cause in Chap. XV, paras. 4-*fin.*, is possible only after the legislator has been set forth as the "efficient cause" of the government in Chap. XV, paras. 1–3; and this in turn requires the antecedent discussion of who is the legislator in Chaps. XII–XIII.

a. The kinds of government (Chap. VIII).

b. The causes of government (Chaps. IX–XVI).[14]

  α. The efficient cause of government (Chaps. IX; XV, paras. 1–3; XVI).

    1. The rightful efficient cause (Chaps. IX; XV, paras. 1–3).

      i. General: election (Chap. IX).

      ii. Specific: the legislator as efficient cause of election (Chap. XV, paras. 1–3).

    2. The erroneous efficient cause: hereditary succession (Chap. XVI).

  β. The formal cause of government, viz., the law (Chaps. X–XIV).

    1. The formal cause or definition of law (Chap. X).

    2. The final cause of law (Chap. XI).

    3. The efficient cause of law, i.e., the legislator (Chaps. XII–XIII).

    4. The material cause of law, which is also the material cause of government, i.e., the qualities of the perfect ruler (Chap. XIV).[15]

E. *The Government in Relation to the State as a Whole* (Chaps. XV, XVII–XIX).

  a. Government as efficient cause of the parts of the state and as the principle of the order of the state (Chap. XV, paras. 4-*fin.*).

  b. Unity of the state as deriving from unity of government (Chap. XVII).

  c. Correction of the government: pathological case where material cause (government) violates formal cause (law) (Chap. XVIII).

  d. Peace of the state as the effect of the government function (Chap. XIX).

Put most succinctly, the argument of Discourse I is as follows. The state exists in order to enable men to achieve a "sufficient life," wherein their various actions and passions are properly proportioned. To achieve this end, the state has various functional "parts," which are distinguished and defined by the contribution which their functions make to such proportioning.

---

[14] Although only the efficient and formal causes of the government are explicitly listed under this heading, it should be noted that the final cause has been listed above, under section C (Chap. IV, para. 5; Chap. V, para. 7). The material cause of the government is identical with the material cause of the law (which is listed below [Chap. XIV]), since both consist in the persons who perform the governmental function and who are the "subject matter" on whom the law, as form, is directly imposed, in the sense that the acts of the government must be in accordance with the law. Thus government is to law as matter to form: the government is the material cause of the law, while the law is the formal cause of the government; see Discourse I. x. 1, 2; I. xiv. 10; I. xv. 3; I. xviii. 2.

[15] See above, n. 14.

Peace is that order of the state wherein each of its parts performs its proper function without interfering with the rest. Hence peace is necessary to the endurance of the state and the achievement of the sufficient life. The government is that part of the state which maintains such peace. It does so by judging disputes which arise among the citizens, by assigning different citizens to different functions, and by regulating the performance of those functions. But in order that the government may not pervert this authority to its own private interests, it must be regulated in its functioning by law, and the law must be made by the people, the whole body of citizens. If these conditions are fulfilled, then the government will indeed maintain peace; and any interference with the governmental function will in turn impede the achievement of peace, thus threatening the destruction of the state and loss of the sufficient life. Consequently, the government must be "one" in the sense that all the governmental acts and commands emanate ultimately from one source. For if there were a plurality of governments, each equally supreme and not ordered under a single head, the resulting jurisdictional confusion would cripple and destroy the governmental function, and thereby the state would be destroyed.

DISCOURSE II: THE SINGULAR CAUSE OF CIVIL STRIFE— THE CLAIM OF THE PAPACY TO PLENITUDE OF POWER

A. *Introductory* (Chaps. I–II).
    a. General procedure of the discourse (Chap. I).
    b. Definition of important terms: "church," "spiritual," "temporal," "judge" (Chap. II).
B. *The Priesthood and Secular Political Power: The Powers of the Priests in Relation to Laymen in General and to Secular Rulers in Particular* (Chaps. III–XIV).
    a. Arguments *a contrario* to prove that the pope is supreme ruler over all men (Chap. III, paras. 2–9: arguments from Scripture; paras. 10–15: "quasi-political" arguments).
    b. What powers and status belong to the priesthood (Chaps. IV–XIV).
        α. The priests have no coercive power, and must be subject to the coercive power of secular rulers (Chaps. IV–V).
            1. Proved by the statements of Christ (Chap. IV).
            2. Proved by the statements of the apostles (Chap. V).
        β. The priests have the power to administer the sacraments, but this power is not coercive (Chaps. VI–X).

α. In ecclesiastic affairs (Chap. XXIV).

β. In civil affairs (Chap. XXV).

γ. In particular relation to the Roman empire and its ruler (Chap. XXVI).

E. *Final Objections and Replies* (Chaps. XXVII–XXX).

    a. Objections to the conclusions of Chapters XV–XXVI (Chap. XXVII).

    b. Replies to these objections (Chap. XXVIII).

    c. Replies to the scriptural arguments of Chapter III (Chap. XXIX).

    d. Replies to the "quasi-political arguments of Chapter III (Chap. XXX).

The argument of Discourse II "confirms" that of Discourse I by showing that the priesthood must rightfully be subject to the coercive authority of secular law and government, and that its own functions entail no coercive authority. Thus, just as Discourse I had proved that peace requires the unification of all coercive authority in the government and the law by which it governs, so Discourse II proves that the papal claim to plenitude of power disrupts such peace and leads to civil strife by destroying that unification, and is hence unjustified. The proof proceeds by explicit citation of the words and acts of Christ and the apostles, and by examination of the proper functions and organization of the priesthood.

Three major phases of this argument may be distinguished, bearing on: (1) the general political position of the priesthood as one of the parts of the state (Chapters IV–V); (2) the religious, sacramental function of the priesthood (Chapters VI–XIV); (3) the institutional aspects of the priesthood within the church (Chapters XV–XXIII). (1) Just as Discourse I had proved that peace requires the obedience of all the other parts of the state to the secular law and government, so Discourse II shows that this same obedience was enjoined on the priesthood in particular by Christ and the apostles, being necessary both for temporal peace and for eternal salvation. This point has as its corollary that secular rulers govern not only by election of the people but also by divine right. But as a consequence, where Discourse I placed rulers under severe limitations of human law, Discourse II, through the impact of quotations from the apostles and the church fathers, tends to remove all restrictions from rulers save the necessity of not violating divine law. (2) Moreover, the essential functions of the priesthood consist only in the performance of the sacraments and teaching of the means to salvation, and these can involve no coercive authority. This conclusion is established through the difference between religious obligation, which is voluntary, and political obligation, which is subject to coercion, and the parallel distinctions between human law and divine law, political authority and priestly authority, the sufficient life of this world and eternal salvation in the next world. (3) In addition to these conclusions as to the religious and sacramental aspects of the priesthood, involving sharp distinctions between the spiritual and the temporal, Marsilius also reinforces his earlier unificatory subsumption of the spiritual under the temporal. He distinguishes between the priests' "essential," sacramental authority, which is from God and is equal in all priests, and their "accidental," institutional authority, whereby they are assigned to specific pastorates and have hierarchic gradations of rank within the priesthood itself. This latter authority, Marsilius insists, is not from God but from man. Just as he had upheld the necessity that the priesthood, as one of the parts of the state, be subject to secular government and law, so he goes on to provide that in all matters bearing on the institutional effectuation of the priestly function and "accidental" authority, the whole body of the faithful must be in ultimate control. But since this whole body is numerically identical with the whole body of citizens who constitute the legislator, the maker of human secular law, it follows that the institutional control of secular and religious affairs rests with the same agency, and for the same reasons. Thus the whole body of the believers, and not the priesthood alone, must control excommunication, the designation of priests to particular posts, the filling of ranks in the priestly hierarchy, including the office of "head bishop" or pope, the distribution of benefices and other economic matters affecting the clergy, the election of general councils, and the enforcement of the councils' definitions of articles of faith.

From the above summary it can be seen that while the method of Discourse II involves reliance upon revelation, it also involves far more than quotations from Scripture and its "approved interpreters." Some of Marsilius' most important distinctions and arguments are presented in this discourse, although the explicit acceptance of the context of the Christian revelation in respect of the priesthood provides a scriptural basis distinct from the use of reason and Aristotle in the first discourse. Marsilius' use both of Scripture and of Aristotle is by no means a passive or servile repetition of texts. He bends them rather to the uses of his own independent doctrine, so that his citations of them are more properly viewed as developments and extensions of his own thought than as faithful interpretations of theirs.

The entire sequence of the second discourse, apart from the four concluding chapters containing objections and replies, culminates in the chapters of Section D which recount "how in particular the Roman bishop has used his assumed plenitude of power" in ecclesiastic affairs and in civil affairs, and even "more particularly" in relation to the ruler of the Romans. These chapters thus carry on the particularizing sequence of the treatise as a whole, for just as the subject matter of the second discourse is to that of the first as the "singular" to the "general," so the chapters just mentioned present the "particular" cases of the workings of the "singular cause" of civil strife. This particularizing sequence has two natural accompaniments: a concern with the literal history of events and institutions, and a large measure of polemical invective. To what extent such features have a place in a political philosophy is a fair subject for discussion. It may well be argued that a concern with historically particularized events removes the universality and timelessness which are properly characteristic of political philosophy. Yet the ultimate subject matter of politics, as of all practical disciplines, is particular acts, events, and institutions. However illuminating be the general principles of a political philosopher, his task is not completed until he has brought those principles to bear on the particular issues by reference to which they must finally be tested. To be sure, a concern with particulars alone yields not political philosophy but annals or journalism or propaganda. The *Defensor pacis,* however, is far closer to being a complete political philosophy for its concern with particulars than it would be had it remained solely at the level of the general.

It is also true, however, that Marsilius, like many other political thinkers, is too obsessively concerned with the exigencies of one particular issue. As a consequence, he ignores important problems which confront his own doctrine, including especially the way in which the people's legislative authority is to be carried on. He ignores, for the most part, the issues posed by the departures from republicanism among the north Italian cities, including Padua, at the very time at which the *Defensor* was being written. No political philosopher, however, is completely free of such limitations. If the *Defensor* lacks the encyclopedic sweep of Aristotle's *Politics,* the latter gives no suggestion of the drastic political changes which, at the time of its composition, were being effected by Alexander the Great, and which would have severely conditioned its discussions of both ideals and actualities. Moreover, in his monistic concentration on the papacy as the sole cause of civil strife, while ignoring all mitigating factors and concomitant causes, Marsilius' procedure is similar to Plato's castigations of the sophists, Augustine's fulminations against the "city of man," and Marx's berating of the bourgeois capitalists. It is perhaps inevitable that critical periods in human history, as seen from the purview of an all-embracing political philosophy, take the form of such dualistic clashes wherein one side is evil and the other good, and each side is viewed as a homogeneous unit.

The polemical invective with which Marsilius castigates the papacy through part of Discourse II is also the inevitable accompaniment of this particularizing approach. The expression of passion by a political philosopher is often the logical culmination of his exposition of the specific conditions which his general doctrine of moral and political values has shown to be evil and unjust. Reason of itself moves nothing, and without passion even moral evaluation may perhaps be impossible.

THE BASIC THEMES: REASON, POWER,
AND THE PEOPLE'S WILL

THE PERENNIAL philosophic significance of the *Defensor pacis* consists not only in its conclusion but in its premises. These premises are presented in Discourse I. Our primary question now is this: By what doctrinal means, through what premises, did Marsilius overthrow not only the doctrine of the papal plenitude of power to which the dialectic of medieval Christendom seemed inevitably to be led, but even the Gelasian doctrine of a parallelism between the spiritual and temporal powers? What root assumptions of those doctrines did he deny, which ones did he modify, what assumptions did he put in their place, and how did these latter ones lead to a doctrine so subversive of the orthodox papalist position?

When we come to seek out the answers to these questions, we find that the *Defensor* presents a body of argument which exhibits a striking conceptual complexity. Its premises combine seemingly divergent and even incompatible theories. At least, their various parts belong to what have usually been regarded as different and opposed philosophic traditions. It is precisely from this complex structure, however, that there follow the revolutionary conclusions of the treatise in the sphere not only of ecclesiastic but also of general politics.

An initial indication of the diversities of approach exhibited in the treatise may be given in the three following propositions which represent the basic themes of the *Defensor:* (1) the state is a product of reason and exists for the end of men's living well; (2) political authority is primarily concerned with the resolution of conflicts and is defined by the possession and structure of coercive power; (3) the sole source of legitimate political power is the will or consent of the people. These three propositions concerning the basis and legitimacy of political authority have in some sense been found in many political philosophies. The *Defensor* is particularly noteworthy, however, for the ways in which it interprets and develops each of the three, and for the devices which it exhibits for making them consistent with one another.

Each of these propositions, taken by itself, marks an approach to political problems which sets apart a whole school of political philosophy usually considered as antithetical to each of the other two. The first proposition represents the theme characteristic of that perennial tradition of political philosophy which has been designated by such terms as "rationalistic" and "idealistic": the state is explained by the rational moral ends which it enables men to achieve, so that both it and the political authority exercised in it are at once products of and limited by reason. The second proposition, on the other hand, represents the "positivistic" and "legalistic" theme which usually figures in a tradition opposed to the first: the state is now viewed not as the vehicle and embodiment of ideal rational ends or values but as the scene and the regulator of strife, so that the mark of the state and of political authority comes to be the structuring of the coercive power which controls and settles conflicts. Thus, whereas in the full development of the first theme only that political authority is legitimate which conforms to the moral demands of reason by leading men to a life of virtue, in the full development of the second theme any political authority is legitimate so long as it in fact settles conflicts and preserves society, so that not supreme virtue but supreme power is the mark of political authority. The third proposition, which in Marsilius' doctrine provides the dialectical mediation between the first two extremes, itself represents a tradition which has historically been opposed to each of the others: the "voluntaristic" and "republican" theme whereby the state and its authority are defined neither by rational ends nor by coercive power but rather by the people's will.

The familiar oppositions among these three themes penetrate to every sphere of political philosophy. And it is their copresence in Marsilius' doctrine which accounts for the similarities which have been found in it, now to the idealist tradition, now to the school of Machiavelli and Hobbes, and finally to the theories of Rousseau and the French Revolution. Thus, with respect to the ground of political obligation, the first theme places this ground in the moral ends or values which political authority enables men to achieve; the second, in the settlement of conflicts and the consequent removal of the insufferable conditions which unresolved conflict engenders; the third, in the consent of the governed. Similarly, with respect to the nature of law, for the first theme law is reason and justice; for the second, it is the command of the sovereign and the equilibrium which that command establishes among conflicting forces in society; for the third, it is the will of the people. Again, in the first theme sovereignty belongs to the best and wisest men; in the second, to those who are strongest with respect to all the senses of "power"; in the third, to the whole people. A statement of the main lines of the development of each of these themes in the *Defensor,* and of the ways in which they are related to one another, should help to present more specifically not only the central argument of the treatise but also its contribution to the understanding of the basic problems of political philosophy. The separate statement of these themes will inevitably involve a certain distortion of Marsilius' thought; but this distortion should be minimized when we come to present their relations to one another.

(1) *Reason and human values.* The state is initially conceived by Marsilius, following Aristotle, as existing for the sake of men's living well, the "sufficient life." A state is a "perfect" or complete community in that, as a result of a historical development, it comprises various functional "parts" which by their different functions are collectively able to provide for the human needs in whose fulfillment the sufficient life consists. This fulfillment involves the proper "moderating" or "proportioning" of man's diverse actions and passions; and while the beginnings of such proportioning derive from nature, the parts of the state are established by reason to bring this process to completion. Thus each part of the state is defined by its caring for a different human function: the farmers for the nutritive function; the mechanic artisans for the sensitive function; the government for the "transient" acts emerging from the cognitive and appetitive functions so far as they affect the sufficient life in the present world; and the priesthood for both "immanent" and "transient" acts emerging from the cognitive and appetitive functions so far as they affect the sufficient life in the future world. The two remaining principal parts of the state, the military and the financial, are required to assist the parts already mentioned.

Since the various parts of the state are defined by these functions which comprise the good life, it is of first importance that each part perform its proper operation without interfering with the others; indeed, the "peace" of the state, like the "justice" of Plato's *Republic,* consists precisely in this ordered interrelation whereby each part of the state "can perfectly perform the operations belonging to it according to reason and its establishment." [1] For the assurance of such order, however, regulation or "establishment" is needed; and this regulative function properly falls to the government, since its "moderating" of individual men's transient acts is but another phase of such over-all regulation of men's interaction in the state. The proper performance of this regulative function requires that it be done justly, that is, in such manner as to "reduce" men's transient acts to "equality or due proportion," so that it will lead to the

[1] I. ii. 3.

sufficient life for each citizen and thus to the common benefit of the whole. A good or "well-tempered" government, therefore, is distinguished from a bad or "diseased" one by the criterion of whether it aims at the common benefit or at the private benefit of the ruling class; hence the rule of one man (kingship), of a few (aristocracy), or of all (polity) may each be good, the choice among them being determined solely by particular circumstances, and not by differences of basic principle. However, not all the parts of the state make an equal contribution to the sufficient life, for food, shelter, and money are necessary preconditions rather than constitutive conditions of such life. Consequently, the farmers, mechanic artisans, and financiers, who are collectively called the "common mass" (*vulgus*), must not individually carry as much weight as the members of the other three functional parts, who are collectively called the "honorable class" (*honorabilitas*), so that democracy, defined as government by the *vulgus* alone, is an unjust form of government.

Since a just government is one which aims at the common benefit, the governmental function must itself be regulated by law, which is the "standard" or "measure" of human transient acts with respect to their attainment of the sufficient life; [2] that is, it is the universal science or doctrine of civil justice and the common benefit. [3] This science is the result of the "inquiry" carried on by prudent men who have sufficient leisure and experience to discover the true conditions of the just and the beneficial. [4] But in addition, since law, being universal, cannot adequately decide all cases, the ruler should have the virtues of prudence, justice, and equity to supplement the law; and he should have a general benevolence toward the state. Thus the sufficient life and the common benefit will be achieved by men leading a tranquil existence under the guidance of a beneficent government.

The above summary of the first basic theme of Marsilius' politics presents a portrait of the state which is closely similar to the central orientation of most of medieval political thought. The orientation is rational, objective, and teleological: the state is necessary to the full "proportioning" of man's powers, and political authority is justified because it provides the means to that proportioning in accordance with objective norms of justice. The state, government, and law are all products of reason, conforming to rational norms for rational ends. The parts of the state fulfill a suppletive function in relation to human actions and passions similar to that which Aristotle had assigned to "right reason" in the *Nicomachean Ethics*. Nor is this theme restricted to the naturalistic

---

[2] II. viii. 4, 5.   [3] I. x. 3.   [4] I. xii. 2.

and rational context of the Aristotelian politics. Just as we have remarked its similarity to the ideal state of Plato, so it likewise bears a structural affinity to the theocratic church-states developed in the medieval papalist tradition, save that the priesthood, divine law, and revelation hold the controlling position which Marsilius assigns to the government, human law, and reason, because of the higher end subserved by the former.

This very difference, however, emphasizes the fact that the rationalistic-finalistic theme is not maintained by the Paduan throughout his political philosophy. For if the attainment of the highest ends possible to man were the sole preoccupation of politics, then the class or part of the state which most fully provided the constitutive conditions of these ends should have been assigned the highest political authority. It was on this principle of distributive justice that Aristotle and the papalists upheld the political hegemony, respectively, of the most virtuous men and of the pope. Since Marsilius himself, in a few scattered contexts, admits that eternal life in the future world is man's highest end,[5] he too would have had to admit the papal supremacy. And even apart from this super-natural aspect, if he, like the other Aristotelians, upheld the superiority of the intellectual life over the practical life,[6] on this ground too he would have had to make the priesthood the holder of highest political authority, for he classes philosophy and the sciences among the disciplines the pursuit of which falls under the priestly office.[7] But, apart from all the other considerations which Marsilius adduces against this facile sequence proceeding from ends, or from the cognitive experts or the official representatives of ends, to the possession of political authority, the constitutive features of the ends themselves receive little further development in the *Defensor*. Despite his initial dedication of the state to the sufficient life, apart from its "moderating" of man's actions and passions, he presents no detailed specification of the "liberal functions such as derive from the virtues of both the practical and the theoretic soul."[8] No delineation is given of men actually enjoying or pursuing these values. Instead, Marsilius shifts his emphasis to the specifically political problems which must be solved before these ends can be attained. The characteristics of this shift from the constitutive features to the political pre-conditions of values mark the difference between the orientation of Marsilius and that of his predecessors, and lead to the second basic theme of the Marsilian politics.

[5] I. vi. 2; II. xvii. 12; II. xxvi. 16, 19.   [6] Cf. I. xvi. 23; II. xxx. 1; also Vol. I, p. 64.
[7] I. vi. 9. For the basis of this in Aristotle, see *Metaphysics* I. 1. 981b 23; *Nicomachean Ethics* VI. 7. 1141b 1 ff.; *Politics* VII. 9. 1329a 7 ff.
[8] I. iv. 1.

(2) *Conflict and coercive power*. The seemingly innocent description of the governmental function as consisting in the regulation or "proportioning" of men's transient acts in accordance with the law is actually far more portentous than it at first appeared. Transient acts are not simply another phase of human operations like nutritive and sensitive functions; far from being merely a question of smooth and equable interaction, the regulation of transient acts involves a precariousness and an imperativeness of the first magnitude. Men's propensity for strife is inveterate. The governmental regulation must "endure at every hour or minute," [9] for if it were to cease even for an instant, the unresolved quarrels and disputes among men will reach such proportions that the very association of men in the state will be endangered and soon destroyed.[10] Also, far from performing their own functions in accordance with reason and law, men will seek soft berths in other parts of the state, especially the priesthood, and will interfere with one another's functions; thus, both as individuals and as members of functional groups, men quarrel incessantly and tend to separate into warring factions, with the destruction of the state as the inevitable outcome. It is such quarrelling which is the characteristic social or "civil" activity of men;[11] consequently, the governmental function comprises not placid regulation but the imposition of coercive controls which, by threatening or actually giving punishment, enforce men's adherence to peace and hence the preservation of the state.

Now this conception of the governmental task as growing out of particularist strife and the need for curbing it is, of course, to be found in all political philosophies. Thus Thomas Aquinas gives the following explanation of the need for government, which evokes reminders of that other Thomas who wrote the *Leviathan* four centuries later: "Where there are many men together and each one looks out for what suits himself, the multitude would be broken up into diverse parts unless there were someone to watch out for that which concerns the good of the multitude."[12] And it was similarly Aquinas who set forth as a consequent function of the ruler that "through his laws and commands he is to coerce the men subject to him by punishments and rewards, forcing them away from iniquity and leading them to virtuous deeds."[13] Throughout the middle ages, indeed, the Augustinian doctrine was standard that government is made necessary by man's sinfulness which requires the forceful curbing of lust and greed. But it is a question of

---

[9] i. xv. 13.   [10] Cf. Vol. I, pp. 61–62, 106–9.   [11] Cf. i. ii. 4; and Vol. I, pp. 61, 87.

[12] *De regimine principum* i. i. This statement is repeated by John of Paris *De potestate regia et papali* cap. i.

[13] *De reg. princ.* i. xv.

basic explanatory direction and emphasis. A political philosopher may turn rather quickly from these lower depths to the rational and divine ends by which they are to be evaluated and to which men must ultimately be led; or else he may dwell on the depths themselves and tailor his concepts and recommendations to the dimensions proximate to them. The former was characteristic of the medieval tradition; the latter was to become central in the doctrine of Machiavelli, on the one hand, and in the Hobbesian portrait of the state of nature and the social contract, on the other. It is similarly here that Marsilius dwells; and a good part of the revolution he effected in political philosophy is based on this reorientation. Throughout the *Defender of Peace,* in every context where a crucial doctrine is being proved, the unchanging emphasis is that if this doctrine does not in fact receive institutional embodiment the result will be "fighting and separation, and finally the destruction of the state." [14]

The extent to which this emphasis overshadows, if it does not supersede, the rationalist theme of supreme values and the common benefit described above may be seen by noting the preferences evinced by Marsilius in a few crucial contexts where he is laying down basic definitions. Law, we noted before, is "the universal science or doctrine of civil justice and the common benefit." Yet this definition demands a significant addition which at once becomes a preferred alternative; for law as thus defined may be considered in two ways: "in one way in itself, insofar as it *only shows* what is just or unjust, beneficial or harmful; and as such it is called the science or doctrine of right. In another way it may be considered according as with regard to its observance there is given a command coercive through punishment or reward to be distributed in the present world . . . ; *and considered in this way it most properly is called, and is, a law.*" [15] Yet this is not all; for not only does law require coerciveness, but the other aspect, that of being a "science or doctrine of justice," may itself be absent: "*false* cognitions of the just and the beneficial become laws, when there is given a command to observe them." [16] Thus, in contrast to the entire medieval tradition which insisted that a law which is not just—a "false cognition of justice"—is not a law at all,[17] Marsilius makes the positivist aspect of coerciveness basic. Correlatively, what constitutes the "legislator" is not possession of the expert knowledge required to "inquire" into and to "discover" the "science of justice and benefit," but rather possession of the authority to make the coercive commands in which law properly consists.[18] And in parallel fashion, the ruler is to be defined not by his prudence, justice, equity, and benevo-

---

[14] I. xvii. 5. For a list of such passages, see Vol. I, pp. 106–7, nn. 95–105.
[15] I. x. 4.   [16] I. x. 5.   [17] See Vol. I, p. 134.   [18] I. xii. 2.

lence, but by his coercive authority whereby he is able "to judge concerning the just and the beneficial in accordance with the laws or customs, and to command and execute through coercive force the sentences made by him." [19] Prudence and justice constitute a ruler merely "in proximate potentiality"; only coercive authority makes a ruler "in actuality," [20] even without prudence and the moral virtues. There is no need to multiply examples of this Marsilian emphasis on coercive power as the definitive characteristic of political institutions. The very description of the difference between the household, the village, and the city-state—a difference which the other Aristotelians had put in finalistic terms of comparative degrees of approximation to the sufficient life consisting in the practice of the virtues—is presented by Marsilius as a process of gradual differentiation of degrees of coerciveness leading to the establishment of full-fledged coercive law and government in the state.[21]

The peace, the order, the unity of the state are all defined in similar terms of coerciveness. The peace which consists in each part of the state performing its proper function "in accordance with reason and its establishment" requires that the government exercise coercive control over all the parts of the state, with respect both to the individuals who become members of each of these functional parts and to their performance of their functions; for otherwise the seeking of preferred berths and the interference of one part with another, including the impeding of the governmental function itself of judging disputes, will endanger the existence of the state. The government, therefore, is the efficient cause of peace.[22] The order of the state consists not, as in the medieval tradition, in men's relation to their supreme moral and theological end and in their consequent subordination to the earthly representatives of this end, but rather in the subordination of the other parts of the state to the coercive authority of the government, because of the supreme necessity of the governmental judicial function for the preservation of the state.[23] And the unity of the state, which is particularly important, involves that all coerciveness be centered in the government and the law it executes, so that no other part of the state, and no other "law," can be coercive. For otherwise, if there were a multiplicity of centers of coercion and these were not ultimately ordered or reduced to a single source, the resulting confusion would lead to strife among the coercive authorities themselves and a breakdown of the governmental regulative functions.[24]

This second Marsilian theme is the forerunner of the doctrines of

[19] II. ii. 8.　　[20] I. xv. I.　　[21] I. iii. 4. See Vol. I, pp. 86–88.　　[22] I. xix. 3.
[23] I. xv. 14; I. xvii. 7.　　[24] I. xvii. 3 ff.

politics centered in considerations of power and stability which have been so characteristic of modern political thought. The orientation is legalistic and positivistic rather than rationalistic and finalistic; it proceeds in terms of the statics and dynamics of forces rather than ideal objective values or ends. In this phase of the doctrine political authority is justified because it maintains peace and order viewed simply as barriers to worse evils, not as means to higher goods; and there is even a strong tendency to drop all questions of justification and to hold that political authority must be obeyed because of the legal-constitutional structure as such. The state now emerges not as a community dedicated to a life of virtue but rather in two other ways: first, as a group of men pursuing their own particular interests and thereby engaging in conflict, and second, in consequence, as a legal-judicial order of coercive authority emanating from a single source. Political philosophy, as a result, no longer has the task of depicting an ideal state presided over by selfless men devoid of passion; it takes on the far more modest project of indicating the means whereby the social fabric may be preserved amid the conflicting claims of individuals and groups. In relation to the church-state controversy, this theme has the consequence that the papalists' claim to hegemony on the basis of the higher end subserved by the priesthood is readily turned aside, since the decisive consideration in the allocation of political superiority is not the relative dignity of different values subserved by different groups but rather the requirements for the effective use of coercive power for resolving conflicts and preserving the state. Politics becomes sharply distinguished from morals and religion, so far as concerns the criteria of authority.

(3) *Will and popular sovereignty.* The oppositions between the first two basic themes of the *Defensor pacis* are resolved by its third and final theme: that the sole source of legitimate political authority is the will or consent of the people. In most general terms, this resolution is effected by making the people's will at once the infallible test of the ends which the first theme had made basic and the exclusive legitimating principle of the coercive power which the second theme had made basic. Just as the concepts of law and the legislator had moved from the first theme, wherein legislation is the cognitive process of "discovering" what is just and beneficial for the community, to the second theme, wherein legislation is the giving of a coercive command, so by the third theme it is the people which alone gives this command.[25] Similarly, just as the concept of government had moved from the first theme, wherein government consists in the regulation of transient acts in accordance with

[25] I. xii. 3.

prudence, justice, and equity, to the second theme, wherein government consists in the possession and exercise of the coercive power to make binding judgments in accordance with coercive law, so by the third theme it is the people which, by "establishing" or electing the government, is the sole source of this authority.[26] The primacy of the people's will thus provides the ultimate explication and reconciliation of the factors involved in both the other themes.

This reconciliation of basic oppositions involves many problems. We shall best be able to grasp how Marsilius deals with these if we initially consider the relation of this third theme to the second theme of coercive power, and then to the first theme of rational ends.

Viewed abstractly, the republican theme is along quite different lines from the theme of coerciveness. According to the latter, coerciveness as such is the essence of political authority; but according to the former, coerciveness has no political authority unless it derives from the will of the people. Thus, whereas the essence of law had previously been put in its being a coercive command, in subsequent definitions it is stated to be "the command of the whole body of citizens." [27] But this addition marks a highly important qualification. It means that political authority is no longer to be looked for simply wherever coerciveness is exercised, either potentially or actually; for unless this coerciveness emanates from the people's will it is neither "political" nor authoritative, but rather "usurped," as Marsilius frequently puts it in his arguments against the papalists. In the light of this republican theme, then, what becomes the status of his conceptions of political authority as essentially consisting in coercive power? It might seem that the two themes can be made completely consistent only if the ground on which Marsilius upholds his republican position is that the people alone can in fact give to political authority that coerciveness without which its judgments on disputed matters cannot be binding. And indeed at one point Marsilius explicitly says this. After declaring that the legislative authority must belong only to those who can cause the laws to be observed, he argues as follows: "The power (*potestas*) to cause the laws to be observed belongs only to those men to whom belongs *coercive force* (*potentia coactiva*) over the transgressors of the laws. But these men are the whole body of the citizens or the weightier part thereof. Therefore, to them alone belongs the authority (*auctoritas*) to make laws." [28] Hence it would be simply because the people alone has the coercive force which is the essence of political power that such power belongs exclusively to it.[29]

---

[26] I. xv. 2.   [27] *Defensor minor* i. 4.   [28] I. xii. 6.
[29] Cf. Peter of Auvergne *In octo libros Politicorum Aristotelis commentarium* Lib. III.

This argument is not, however, merely an appeal to the *de facto* possession of coercive force as such. It involves also the recognition that when it is a question of long-range observance of laws, the will of the people supplies an added independent variable, which cannot be reduced to or equated with the mere exertion of force. In order to be effective, political authority must be coercive, that is, it must be able to make good its commands and prohibitions; otherwise, these have no political authority. But the possession of such coerciveness, far from requiring an order of fear or compulsion, is best guaranteed in the long run when it derives from the will of the people and accords with their conceptions of justice. Thus Marsilius' theme of coerciveness involves not only force (*potentia*) but also power (*potestas*) and authority (*auctoritas*); and Marsilius does not simply equate the first with the other two.[30] It is a question not only of who is strongest but of legitimacy, as to who has the *right* to coerce.[31] His emphasis on coerciveness as the mark of political authority derives from his overwhelming concern with the second theme—the requirements of the maintenance of peace and the preservation of the state. But he also stresses that those requirements consist not merely in the *de facto* imposition of force but also in its impartiality and in its being based on the consent of the people. Thus the coercive and republican themes are reconciled not only by the assimilation of the latter to the former but also by the *de jure* character of the former itself. Whatever be the case in Machiavelli and Hobbes, the doctrine of coerciveness does not rest on the positivism of pure power in the sense of coercive force. The supreme potentiality for the exercise of force does indeed coincide with the supreme political authority; but the essence of the latter is not simply reducible to that of the former. This insight is one of the most significant results of the juncture of Marsilius' coercive and republican themes.

Let us now turn to the relation of the republican theme to the first theme, that of rational ends. Viewed abstractly, these two themes appear to be quite diverse and even opposed to one another. The rationalist theme appeals to objective ends as the ground of political obligation and authority, as against the seeming relativism and positivism whereby political authority and obligation depend solely on what the people wills. But this opposition is at once removed by Marsilius' emphatic argument

---

Lect. 9: "duo exiguntur in regimine politiae. Unum est recta ratio; hoc autem habet ista multitudo per illos sapientes. Aliud est potentia, ut possit coercere et punire malos; hoc autem habet per populum."

[30] See below, p. lxxxvii.   [31] Cf. Vol. I, p. 143.

that the people's will, far from being subject to the vagaries of shifting appetites and partisan advantage, is inevitably directed to the common benefit. Republicanism is the necessary and indeed the only means of assuring the attainment of the common benefit; no other way is safe, for any individual and any group smaller than the whole people, if entrusted with supreme political authority, will almost inevitably pervert such authority to its own selfish interest.[32] Thus the republicanism of Marsilius' third theme is the indispensable means of achieving the ends of his first theme.

This basic aspect of the voluntarist doctrine also throws further light on Marsilius' second theme of coercive power. For it is from the wills of individuals or groups pursuing their own particular interests that arise the inevitable conflicts, which threaten the destruction of the state, and for whose resolution the coerciveness of binding judgments is needed. The wills of individuals or groups, then, are inevitably directed to their private advantage and lead to strife, while the will of the whole people is just as inevitably directed to the common benefit and assures peace. This contrast is fraught with momentous consequences. It involves the denigration of the "part" and of individualism, and the exaltation of the "whole" and of corporatism: only if individual wills are placed in a political context such that they are limited and modified by the wills of all the other members of the community is there an assurance of justice. But on this ground, too, any social institution or organization which can in any way affect the welfare of the community must come under the control of the whole people. To be sure, the "justice," "welfare," and "common benefit" here referred to are more "legal" than "moral," in that they primarily consist not in affirmative moral development and inculcation of virtue, which for the medieval tradition as for Aristotle was the essential function of political authority, but rather in the general equilibrium and adjustment of disputes which assures peace and order. Yet this doctrine still entails an absolutism whereby any value, group, or institution can be brought under the authority of the people's will.

This result also serves, however, to clarify the apparent opposition between the voluntarism of Marsilius' republican doctrine and the coerciveness which his second basic theme declares to be essential to political authority. For while the coercive and the voluntary are opposed, it is only the wills of individuals and partial groups which undergo the coercion of law and government when they transgress its commands

[32] I. xii–xiii *passim.*

and prohibitions, but it is the will of the whole people which is the source
of this coercion. Consequently, entirely apart from any question of voluntary obedience to the laws, political authority is at once coercive and
voluntary, in that the will of the whole imposes coercively binding
commands on the individuals and parts of that whole.

The relation between the voluntarist-republican theme and the theme of
rational ends is not exhausted in that aspect of it which has been so far
discussed, whereby the people's will is the only means of achieving the
end of the common benefit. Marsilius holds that the people's will must
be the sole source of political authority for a further reason quite distinct
from its necessary rôle in the attainment of the common benefit. The
nature of this reason can be grasped at points where crucial definitions
are being laid down. At several such points Marsilius compares the
finalistic factor of the common benefit with the factor of the people's
will as ultimate determinants of political value and authority. For example, Marsilius, like all the other medieval Aristotelians, declares that
the criterion of a good or well-tempered government is its aiming at
the common benefit; but—and this is unique to Marsilius—a further
criterion is added: that the government must be "in accordance with
the will or consent of the subjects." [33] Moreover, he then goes on to
declare that of these two criteria, common benefit and consent, the one
which distinguishes good from bad governments "absolutely or in greater
degree" is the consent of the subjects.[34] What can be the basis of this
preference? Marsilius purports to have arrived at it inductively through
a survey of the five kinds of monarchy described by Aristotle.[35] Yet
Aristotle himself had made the common benefit the primary distinguishing criterion of good government, introducing the factor of consent only
peripherally.[36] Marsilius declares further that elected governments are
preferable to the nonelected, in that the former "are over more voluntary subjects"; they rule by laws which are more conducive to the common benefit; they are generically more permanent in that when hereditary succession or some other nonelective method of choosing a ruler fails,
recourse must be had to election; and finally, the method of election yields
the best rulers.[37] In a long chapter comparing hereditary succession with
election these points are made in much fuller detail.[38] Yet, clearly, if the
will, consent, or election of the subjects is the primary criterion of good
government only because it yields a ruler who governs for the common

---

[33] I. viii. 3, 4.   [34] I. ix. 5.
[35] I. ix. 4. Cf. Aristotle *Politics* III. 14. 1284b 35 ff.
[36] Cf. *Politics* III. 6–7. 1279a 17 ff.; and Vol. I, p. 241, n. 37.
[37] I. ix. 6, 7.   [38] I. xvi.

benefit, it would seem that the common benefit rather than consent is the primary criterion of the value of governments, consent being but a means thereto.

There is, however, a further basis of the espousal of consent as the primary criterion. It emerges clearly in Marsilius' arguments in support of the people as the supreme legislative authority. We have already noted that among these arguments is the same means-end relation just considered with respect to elective government—that the will of the whole body of citizens is the surest means to laws which shall be for the common benefit.[39] Yet there is also another argument of a different kind: that the people must be the legislator even if the laws which it makes be "less useful" than those made by some partial group, because otherwise the citizens would not be "free," and such other laws, "however good," would be obeyed either reluctantly or not at all.[40] Here the volitional, consensual factor is shown to be an end in itself: to obey only a law which one has oneself made and willed is an absolute good, even if its consequences for the common benefit be otherwise less valuable. Thus the wills of the citizens acquire an autonomy overbalanced by no other consideration save that these wills must be comprised in a collective whole such that the freedom of each entails the freedom of all. This emphasis on freedom as an absolute good is the final political consequence of Marsilius' voluntarism.

Having come this far in the direction of the primacy of the will, does Marsilius' doctrine go still further? Does the voluntarist theme not only attain a position of absolute value independent of the finalistic theme but even subsume the latter itself? Does the relation between human social ends or values and the people's will extend beyond an instrumental one: is this will the essential or constitutive or causal condition of the value of the ends themselves? Are these ends good only because the people will them, or have they an "objective" goodness independent of that will? Three things must be said with regard to this question: First, Marsilius does not explicitly discuss it as an issue, as did scholastic philosophers and theologians seeking the foundation of moral values. Secondly, if we turn to the more subtle clues to be found in his use of language, we note that his mention of the "sufficient life" as an "end" is almost invariably accompanied by a reference to the fact that such a life is "desired" by men.[41] This would strongly suggest that Marsilius' voluntarism extends to ends as well as means. Thirdly, it must also be

---

[39] I. xii. 5.　　　　　　　　　　　[40] I. xii. 6.
[41] For a partial list of such quotations, see Vol. I, p. 60, n. 50.

noted that he does give "objective" specifications of the sufficient life as an end and a good, as consisting in the "moderating" and "tempering" of man's actions and passions through means discovered by reason.[42] But he does not discuss whether it is such "moderating" which constitutes the goodness of the end, or whether that goodness is constituted rather by the fact that the end is desired.

The significance of these points is that even if it is the fact of being desired by the people, or by all or most men, that essentially constitutes ends as goods for Marsilius, it still remains true that the means to these ends are "objective" in that they can and must be determined by reason. And since it is with these means that human law and government are directly concerned, Marsilius' republican doctrine that the will of the people is necessarily for good laws is not merely a tautology. For although he who wills the end also wills the means, this is true only in general, since it still requires knowledge and reason to ascertain what are the specific means which are to be willed. Nor is it only intellectual error which may break the continuity between the desire for ends and for the means thereto; for affectional and similar factors may lead to a failure to desire the means even when their relation to the end is clearly understood, because those means may appear too arduous, or may conflict with prejudice, or may otherwise impinge negatively on men's emotions. Thus although Marsilius defines law as the command of the people, and regards the sufficient life as being defined or at least determined by natural desire, this does not mean that the justice of the laws is itself essentially constituted by their being willed by the people.[43]

One further point should be made about Marsilius' theme of the people's will. This will is placed in a context of natural necessity which guarantees that the desire for the end, the sufficient life, will lead to a desire for the justice and law which are means to the end. If there were not this continuity of desire, then "there would occur deformity in nature and art in most cases; the impossibility of which is assumed from natural science."[44]

---

[42] I. v. 2–7.

[43] The qualifications here indicated are perhaps not sufficiently taken account of in such an interpretation as the following by A. P. d'Entrèves, *Natural Law* (London, 1951), p. 75: "Rousseau had a striking and untimely forerunner in a medieval writer. Marsilius of Padua, a fourteenth century Italian, had stated in so many words a theory of the general will in his *Defensor Pacis* (1324). According to him, not only are laws the expression of the will of the people, but it is because they are the expression of the will of the people that laws are good and just." On this question, see also below, pp. lvi–lviii.

[44] I. xiii. 2. See Appendix II, below.

The upshot, then, is that the people's will is unchallenged as the possessor of supreme authority. Doctrines of popular control were by no means foreign to medieval political thought. The Roman law tradition of the derivation of the emperor's power from the people, the Germanic tradition of the basis of law in immemorial popular custom, as well as the development of medieval institutions themselves, all pointed in this direction. Yet in no previous medieval work had this tendency been given so complete, explicit, and extensive a statement as in the popular sovereignty of Marsilius.

RELIGION AND POLITICS

a. THE BACKGROUND

MEDIEVAL LIFE was pervaded by religious concerns, and as a consequence medieval political thought was intensely preoccupied with the problem of the relation between the church and the state, between religion and politics. In its most general form the problem was the same for all thinkers: what should be the respective powers of the secular and the ecclesiastic authorities, the *regnum* and the *sacerdotium?* But in another sense the problem itself received widely differing interpretations at the hands of different thinkers, and these interpretations were integrally related to different conclusions. The nature of the "priesthood" and the "Church," the nature of religious and secular concerns, were themselves involved in dispute.

In the *Defender of Peace* the problem is initially broached in two different ways in Discourse I. These ways involve two different conceptions of the nature and function of religion and the priesthood. On the one hand, religion is viewed as a set of fictitious beliefs devised by "philosophers" in order to curb men's wrongdoing, through the myth of an avenging deity who punishes men in a future life for their crimes in the present life. The priesthood is the class appointed to teach these myths and perform the corresponding rites, and all this for the purpose of curbing men's disputes and conflicts and thereby preserving "the peace or tranquillity of states and the sufficient life of men for the status of the present world." [1] In this form, then, religion and the priesthood are definitely put in the service of secular values and the secular authority. But on the other hand, these "gentile" kinds of religion and priesthood are distinguished from the "true" religion and priesthood, that of Christianity. Marsilius accepts, on grounds of faith rather than reason, the doctrine that God is the creator of the world, that eternal life with God is man's "best end," and that the Christian priesthood has been appointed by God to teach men how to attain this end and to perform the related sacraments. This doctrine receives almost no explicit attention in the development of the leading themes of Discourse I, although it is stated

---

[1] i. v. 6. For the relation of this view of religion to the Averroist tradition, and references to Averroes, John of Jandun, and Siger of Brabant, see Vol. I, p. 84, n. 45.

there.[2] But in Discourse II this religious doctrine provides the context around which the entire discussion is centered.

The context of Discourse II is thus strikingly different from that of Discourse I. It is supernatural rather than natural, based primarily on faith rather than on reason, supported by the Bible rather than Aristotle, guided by divine providence rather than natural desire, and directed to a future life in another world rather than to the goods of this world. In its general form, this religious context was one with the orientation accepted by all medieval political thinkers. But its inevitable consequence seemed to be the acceptance of the political supremacy of the priesthood and papacy as the divinely appointed teacher and guardian of the supreme religious values. This papalist position underwent many vicissitudes during the eight centuries from St. Augustine and Emperor Valentinian III to St. Thomas Aquinas and Emperor Frederick II. But the canonist Pope Innocent IV, who excommunicated and deposed Frederick in 1245, and the canonists and philosopher-publicists who came after him, stabilized the doctrine of the papal "plenitude of power" in the extreme form in which it was made to follow from the religious orientation accepted by all political thinkers.

The general papalist argument was that since spiritual or religious ends are superior to temporal or secular ones, which are but means to the former, it follows that the pope as minister of the spiritual is superior in political authority to the secular rulers. Jesus' distinction between the things that are Caesar's and the things that are God's, and Pope Gelasius' distinction between "the sacred authority of the pontiffs and the royal power" as "the two things by which principally this world is ruled," were thus shown to be distinctions not between equals but between unequals falling into a hierarchic order of superior and inferior. The pope, as vicar of Christ, was held to be supreme ruler and judge over all men in both temporal and spiritual affairs.

This did not mean, however, that the pope always exercises temporal power directly. The papalists distinguished two different aspects of power: on the one hand, the primary authority of control (*auctoritas, imperium, directio*); on the other, the immediate execution (*executio*). The former belongs to the pope in both spiritual and temporal affairs, while the latter in temporal affairs is entrusted by the pope to the temporal or secular ruler, who must, however, effect it as the pope commands.[3]

The fullest attempt to refute this papalist doctrine prior to Marsilius

---

[2] I. vi. 1 ff.; I. xix. 4 ff.

[3] Egidius of Rome *De ecclesiastica potestate* III. v, vii (pp. 173, 180). James of Viterbo

was made by John of Paris at the beginning of the fourteenth century. John set forth an interesting and complex interpretation of the "indirect power" of the pope in temporal affairs; and it is worth examining the bases and consequences of his interpretation, not only because it sheds light on Marsilius' problem, but also because, like Marsilianism, it still has great relevance to contemporary issues as to the relation between religion and politics.[4]

In reply to the papalist insistence that the end for which the secular state exists is but a means to the religious end for which the spiritual power exists, John maintained, explicitly following Aristotle, that the end of the secular state is living in accordance with virtue, and this end is good intrinsically and not as a means to some further end: "it has in itself the essence of the good and is desirable in itself."[5] And in reply to the papalists' Augustinian doctrine that moral virtues are genuine virtues only if they are Christian or religious and thus based on belief in God, so that only a Christian state is truly just, John held that "the acquired moral virtues can be perfect without the theological virtues, nor are they perfected by them except by an *accidental* perfection." Hence, "even without Christ as ruler there is the true and perfect justice which is required for the state, since the state is ordered to living in accordance with acquired moral virtue, *to which it is accidental that it be perfected by any further virtues.*"[6] Thus the relation between religion and politics, between being a Christian and being a ruler, is merely an "accidental" one. John was here maintaining in a radical manner the Christian Aristotelians' autonomy of nature and morality in relation to grace and religion; the state was sufficiently justified by the former, and hence required no "perfecting" by the latter.

In terms of the three themes which we distinguished in Marsilius' general political philosophy, it can be seen that the papalists made the full weight of their doctrine rest on the first theme, that of supreme values or ends. It was from the relation between religious and secular ends that they deduced the relation between the political authorities of the papacy and the *regnum*. The rejoinder of John of Paris, as we

---

De regimine Christiano II. viii (pp. 250–51). Augustinus Triumphus *Summa de ecclesiastica potestate* qu.1. aa.1, 7. Alexander of St. Elpidius *Tractatus de ecclesiastica potestate* II. vi (in *Bibliotheca maxima pontificia*, ed. J. T. Roccaberti [Rome, 1698–99], II, 21).

[4] That "the contemporary doctrine and practice of the Church [is] orientated in the sense of the concept of the indirect power represented in the medieval tradition of John of Paris" is maintained by J. C. Murray, S.J., "Contemporary Orientations of Catholic Thought on Church and State in the Light of History," *Theological Studies*, X (1949), 212.

[5] *De potestate regia et papali* cap. xvii (p. 227).

[6] *Ibid.* cap. xviii (p. 229).

have thus far considered it, was that secular ends were not as lacking in moral dignity as the papalists had made them out to be. Yet he did not hold that secular and religious ends were totally disparate. On the contrary, he admitted that the secular end is "inferior" to the religious; it "is ordered to a higher end which is the enjoyment of God," and consequently the *sacerdotium* is "superior in dignity" to the *regnum*.[7] Yet this moral superiority, John insisted, does not entail political superiority. By an intricate series of arguments he undertook to establish a set of distinctions whereby this crucial entailment in the papalist doctrine was denied. We may summarize his arguments in terms of three closely related distinctions.

(1) *The distinction between the order of values and the order of authority.* An order of superiority and inferiority in value or dignity may be consistent with a parallelism or equality of the authority of the agents leading men to the respective values. The fact that one end is less noble than, or is ordered to, another end does not necessarily require that he who guides men to the latter end must be the source of the authority of him who guides men to the former end; rather, both "guiders" may derive their authority from some superior power. Thus, for example, the teacher of literature guides the members of a household to a nobler end than does the physician; yet from this it does not follow that the latter derives his authority from the former or that he is subject to the literary teacher in the preparation of his medicines; rather, both are subject to the head of the family, who hired them. Similarly, the pope and the secular ruler are both instituted directly by God, and not the secular ruler by the pope.[8]

(2) *The distinction between technical direction and political authority or dominion.* Even if we grant that the pope must be concerned with the functioning of the secular ruler because the latter's end is ordered to the former's, it still does not follow that such concern must take the form of political authority or "dominion." An order of superiority in any value entails only such a mode of "command" of one man over another as is directly involved in this superiority. But such command may require nothing more than moral or intellectual direction or instruction, and not at all an act of political authority or dominion. Thus, for example, the pharmacist's end is ordered to the physician's; but this entails only that the latter "commands" the former *per modum dirigentis*, in that he guides the pharmacist and judges whether he has compounded his pre-

---

[7] *Ibid.* cap. v (pp. 183–88). Cf. *ibid.* cap. ii (p. 178).
[8] *Ibid.* cap. v (p. 184). Cf. *ibid.* cap. xvii, xviii (pp. 225, 229–30).

scriptions properly. But he does not "command" the pharmacist *per modum auctoritatis*, i.e., by controlling his entry into his profession and his removal therefrom; rather, this is done by the king or lord of the city, who has superior authority over both physician and pharmacist. Similarly, it is God who holds this relation to both the pope and the secular ruler.[9] By this distinction between "dominion" and "instruction" John does away with such papalist assimilations as are found in Egidius of Rome's contention that just as "theology is lord (*domina*) over all other sciences and uses them for its purposes," so does the spiritual power "dominate" (*dominatur*) the temporal;[10] and in James of Viterbo's argument that the papacy has supreme "judiciary power" because it is "teacher" of the temporal power, and "he who is taught is in some way made subject to him who teaches, but one is subjected to another through the power of jurisdiction."[11] The specificity of the relation of political "authority," its irreducibility to the orders found among other values, clearly emerges.

(3) *The distinction between the essential and the accidental aspects of values and functions.* When one end is inferior to and ordered toward another, he who guides men to the inferior end must be subject to him who guides men to the superior end only in that essential respect in which such superiority consists. But this respect may be accidental to the function of him who guides men to the inferior end. For example, the teacher of literature directs the physician not *qua* physician but only "accidentally," i.e., insofar as it "happens" (*accidit*) that the physician wishes to be made a cultivated man. This direction bears not on the essentials of the art or science of medicine but only on a circumstance extrinsic thereto, so that the physician's functioning as such is left untouched by the literary teacher. Similarly, the pope does not direct the king "essentially," insofar as he is king, but only "accidentally," insofar as the king is a believer; hence the king "is established by the pope with respect to faith and not with respect to governance."[12] Conversely, the superior function has "command" over the inferior one only to the extent to which such command is necessary to the end for which the superior function exists: "the art to which pertains the superior end moves and commands the art to which pertains the inferior end, not indeed absolutely but only to the extent to which it is necessary to it for the realization of that ultimate end."[13] But for its end of leading

[9] *De potestate regia et papali* cap. xvii (p. 227). Cf. *ibid.* cap. xix (p. 234).
[10] *De eccl. pot.* ii. vi (p. 64).   [11] *De reg. Christ.* ii. iv (p. 195).
[12] *De pot. reg. et pap.* cap. xvii (pp. 225–26).   [13] *Ibid.* cap. xvii (p. 227).

men to eternal life the papacy does not need to have any political authority over the secular ruler. Thus in both directions there must be a specificity of the relation between powers and ends.

These distinctions of John went far toward breaking the theological monism and universalism of the papalists. His emphasis on the specificity both of politics and of religion meant that the latter lost its pervasive control over all aspects of life, and that the relation of political superiority and inferiority could no longer be identified with or deduced from the relation of superiority and inferiority in respect of religious and secular values. A pluralism of values and of kinds and loci of authority was substituted for the papalists' hierarchic dualism.

Yet to the medieval mind these distinctions seemed to be in danger of leading to an immoralizing of politics. If the relative order of political authorities was not to be determined by the order of moral ends, then what moral justification could the political order have? Now John's distinctions, as we have seen, did not go so far as to make either morals independent of religion, or politics independent of morals. Consequently, the combination of the distinctions and the dependence raised serious internal difficulties in his doctrine. Since the end which constituted the state's whole reason for being was admittedly "ordered to" the end of the priesthood, how could it be maintained that the secular and the priestly powers were "of diverse order or genus," [14] and that their relation was only "accidental"? The tension between these two considerations emerged in other parts of John's doctrine. For while he insisted that the papal authority is confined to the spiritual realm of man's theological end, and can give only "spiritual" penalties for sinning against that end, he went on to recognize that such penalties could include the pope's excommunication of the ruler and of all his subjects who persisted in obeying him. To be sure, in such case the pope would only "accidentally" depose the ruler; the people would do so "directly." Moreover, the ruler could himself "indirectly excommunicate and accidentally depose" a criminal pope by inciting the people to depose him.[15] But this process of excommunication was available far more readily to the pope than to the secular ruler; and its dangers for civil strife were clear, particularly since the papacy regarded itself as the final judge of sin. Thus, despite his obviously conciliatory intention, there was nothing in John's doctrine which prevented a frequent interference of the spiritual power with the temporal, of religion with secular politics.[16]

[14] *Ibid.* cap. xvi (p. 224).   [15] *Ibid.* cap. xiv (p. 214).
[16] These practical consequences of John's doctrine seem to be insufficiently taken account of

b. MARSILIUS' SOLUTION

The ecclesiastic politics of Marsilius may be viewed as taking its point of departure from the situation in which John of Paris had left the problem. But Marsilius' solution was far more radical; it ensured that the priesthood and papacy would in no way be able to challenge the political supremacy of the secular state. This solution was accomplished without any explicit denial of the superiority of religious over secular ends. There were two main phases to the solution. In the first, attention was centered not on the relative superiority of different ends but on the specifically political means of carrying on the functions required for the preservation of the state, i.e., for the endurance of men's associated living. In the second phase, the superiority of religious over secular ends was granted, but it was held that in all the institutional aspects of religion the whole people, the *universitas fidelium,* was a more trustworthy guardian of these ends than was the priesthood alone. Consequently, the papalist argument from the superiority of religious ends to the papal supremacy was answered by two main counterarguments. The first was that the endurance of any organized human society requires a monopoly of coercive power in the hands of the government, i.e., the secular officials charged with the police and judicial functions needed to quell disputes and quarrels. The second was that the whole people is better able to control the institutional aspects of organized religion than is the priesthood alone. Thus in the former line of argument, questions of the the relative dignity of ends or values were brushed aside as irrelevant

---

by Murray, *op. cit.* (above, n. 4). Dante in the *Monarchia* (III. xvi) made a point similar to John's, and its polemical outcome is similarly instructive. Just as John defended the intrinsic goodness of secular life, so Dante maintained that the goods at which the temporal and the spiritual powers aim, the "happinesses" of the present life and of eternal life, are *both* "ultimate ends" of man. These ends are like "diverse conclusions" of syllogisms; hence they are attained by "diverse means," the former through philosophic teachings in accordance with the moral and intellectual virtues, the latter through spiritual teachings in accordance with the theological virtues. Consequently, the emperor who directs men to their temporal end through the former means must similarly be distinct from the pope who directs men to their eternal end through the latter means; the emperor derives his authority immediately from God, not from the pope. Yet, despite his declaration that both ends are "ultimate," Dante then went on, like John of Paris, to admit that the mortal happiness of this life is "in some way ordered to" the immortal happiness of the next, so that in this way the emperor is "subordinate" to the pope and owes him the same "reverence" as an eldest son owes to his father. The consequence of this admission was drawn by Guido Vernani in his "reproof" of Dante: man is ordered not to two "ultimate ends" but only to one, eternal happiness, because this alone can "terminate and satisfy man's desire"; consequently, the temporal power must similarly be "ordered" by the spiritual (*De reprobatione Monarchiae compositae a Dante* III, ed. T. Käppeli, in *Quellen und Forschungen aus italienischen Archiven und Bibliotheken, herausg. vom Deutschen Inst. in Rom,* XXVII [1937–38], 123–46).

to the question of the allocation of political power; while in the latter line of argument it was held that even when such questions of ends were admitted, it was the whole people rather than the priesthood or papacy alone which was the most trustworthy guardian of the superior ends.

Now these two phases of Marsilius' doctrine were applications of what we have called the second and third themes of his general political philosophy—the themes of coercive power and of republicanism—to the problems of ecclesiastic politics. But the second theme exerted a pervasive influence even over the application of the third, for the grounds on which Marsilius elicited the need for republican controls, even in religious and ecclesiastic affairs, were precisely those which the emphasis on coercive power made central.

The application of the theme of the need for coercive power takes many interrelated forms in Discourse II. Just as Marsilius had distinguished, within the meanings of "law," between justice and coerciveness, with the latter being made the essence of political law,[17] so he likewise distinguishes, within the meanings of "judgment," between the intellectual discernment of cognitive experts and the coercive commands of rulers.[18] This distinction guarantees that arguments from the expertness of the priestly "judgments" in religious affairs will not validly conclude to the priests' rightful possession of coercive authority. Moreover, it is emphasized that Christ and the apostles, despite the superiority of their ends, wielded and wanted to wield no coercive authority and urged submission to the secular rulers, who thereby govern by divine as well as human right. By the same token, divine law as such has no coercive authority in this world, and is, properly speaking, not a "law" at all but rather a "doctrine."

These and similar arguments emphasize the need for a monopoly of coercive power in the hands of the secular rulers in order to ensure the unimpeded functioning of law and government.[19] But in addition they invoke the religious consideration that spiritual values must be voluntary, so that the use of coercion to enforce them would negate their very essence. By this consideration coercive authority is even further removed from the priesthood. But this in turn reintroduces questions of ultimate ends. In coping with them, Marsilius applies his republican theme exalting the people's will as the sole proper custodian of religious as well

[17] I. x. 4. See above, p. xxxvi.   [18] II. ii. 8.
[19] Cf., e.g., II. iv. 5: "For when there are two coercive dominions in respect of the same multitude, and neither is subordinated to the other, they impede one another, as was shown in Chapter XVII of Discourse I."

as secular values. In the previous phase of his ecclesiastic politics the realms of the spiritual and the temporal, religion and politics, were sharply separated so far as they involved *values or ends,* by making questions of ultimate values irrelevant to secular politics. But at the same time these realms were brought together under the supremacy of the temporal so far as they involved *persons,* by subjecting even the priesthood to the laws and jurisdiction of the secular power in all matters affecting the preservation of the state. And now in this further republican phase Marsilius unites these realms still more, in that the "people" or "whole body of citizens" (*universitas civium*), which controls secular politics as the maker of the laws and elector of governments, is numerically identical with the "church" or "whole body of believers" (*universitas fidelium*), which controls all the institutional aspects of religion. This *universitas civium fidelium* or *legislator fidelis* controls excommunication and other punishments for violations of divine law, it appoints the priests to their posts, including the "head bishop," it elects the general council which defines articles of faith and other ecclesiastic matters, and it gives coercive enforcement to the council's decisions. And the grounds of this supreme ecclesiastic authority of the people are the same as were employed in Marsilius' general politics: the people's freedom and its volitional and intellectual superiority over all its "parts," including the priesthood. In all these functions, moreover, the government or "ruling part" of the state acts as the executive agent of the people, just as it does in the nonecclesiastic sphere.[20]

The complete doctrine of the *Defensor pacis* thus sets up a unified church-state, with a single identical supreme authority in both state and church. The structural similarity to the doctrine of the upholders of the papal plenitude of power is obvious. We may well ask, then, whether, apart from the substitution of the people for the pope as possessor of the supreme power, there is any difference in principle between the two doctrines. Each doctrine is monistic and absolutistic so far as concerns the possession and extent of power. Moreover, each defends this monistic absolutism by an appeal to the same values. Far from denying the supreme value of the future life, Marsilius' insistence is rather that this value can be achieved with far greater certainty through the whole people's control of the institutional affairs listed above than if they are controlled by the pope or priesthood alone. Similarly, Marsilius explicitly

---

[20] As for what is to be done by believers in cases where the majority of the people or the ruler is not Christian, i.e., where *fideles* and *cives* do not completely or largely coincide, see II. xvii. 15; II. xxii. 12–15; and Vol. I, p. 296.

accepts the same theological cosmogony as do the papalists: political power derives ultimately from God and serves a divine function. Just as for the papalists it is the pope who is the divinely appointed holder of supreme authority over both spirituals and temporals, so for Marsilius it is the people and its elected government which are the objects of such ultimate appointment by God as their "remote cause." Here faith supports reason: the government rules both by human and by divine right, for obedience to it is commanded both by human and by divine law, and the rulers not only are established by the authority of the people but also are sent by God.

In what sense, then, can one maintain the usual interpretations of Marsilius as an upholder of "secularism," and as having made the "temporal power" supreme over the "spiritual power," the "state" over the "church"? The discussion of these problems of ecclesiastic politics is complicated by the ambiguity of the crucial terms: "church," "spiritual," "religious"; "state," "temporal," "political." It is safe to say that the papalists tried to expand the meanings of the first three terms to the point where they tended to absorb the last three.[21] But in Marsilius the case is much less clear. One might be tempted to say that he did the reverse of the papalists. And in fact he did insist on sharp distinctions between the "spiritual" and the "temporal."[22] But just as the papalists emphasized the "spiritual" aspects of "temporal" functions, so Marsilius pointed out the "temporal" consequences of "spiritual" functions.[23] Yet his sovereign people, *fidelis* as well as *civilis,* holds supreme authority over spirituals as well as over temporals for spiritual as well as temporal reasons.[24] Thus, the issue between Marsilius and the papalists, so far as it concerns fundamental questions of the relation between religion and politics, is far less capable of facile statement than their explicit opposition might suggest; for each had developed a monistic system of argument in which all the axiological claims of the other appeared to be absorbed. Indeed, the conclusion to which in all strictness we might seem to be led by these considerations is that the people which holds sovereign power in both church and state is "spiritual" as well as "temporal," so that, far from having subjected the spiritual power to the temporal, Marsilius has unified them in a manner even more obvious than was the case with the papalists, since the pope, after all, was directly only a "spiritual" and not a "temporal" power. Nevertheless, this very change in the locus of authority, as Marsilius develops its grounds and

---

[21] Cf. Vol. I, pp. 101–2.   [22] II. ii. 4–7.   [23] Cf. Vol. I, pp. 294–95.
[24] See II. xvii. 8, 11–12, 15; II. xx. 4, 7; II. xxi. 4; II. xxviii. 15.

consequences, involves crucial differences with respect to issues of basic principle in political philosophy.

To begin with, it must be noted that despite the supreme authority of the "faithful people" in both state and church, there is a point at which this supremacy stops. For Marsilius admits that the priesthood as such is peculiarly divine in origin; the priests alone have the "character" imprinted on each of them directly by God, and thereby they alone have the authority to teach the Gospel and administer the sacraments. In this respect, then, there is no confusion of laity and clergy, people and priesthood; the priests are not laymen, nor do they derive their priestly character from laymen, nor is it the case, as it was later to be for King Henry VIII and for Hobbes, that the ruler of the state is also the "head bishop" or "chief pastor" of the church. Moreover, the Gospel which the priests teach is itself divine in origin, and the human civil laws made by the people can in no way alter its content; on the contrary, if human law contradicts divine law, the former must not be obeyed.[25] These aspects of the priestly function, and these alone, are properly "spiritual," not "temporal."

By what doctrinal means, then, and in what respect, does the "faithful people" come to exercise supreme authority over "spiritual" affairs as well as over "temporal" ones? It is not because Marsilius explicitly holds temporal values to be superior to spiritual ones; on the contrary, as we have seen, the explicit presumption is that the people, being "faithful," is at least as much concerned with spiritual values as with temporal ones. The point involves, rather, a kind of distinction which his second basic theme, that of the need for coercive power, made peculiarly important, and which represents the specifically Marsilian emphasis. This is the distinction between what we may call the "internal" and the "external" aspects of religious values, between the conditions of the soul or of divine ordainment which essentially constitute those values as such, and the institutional, this-worldly conditions of their determination and control, enforcement, or application.

The immediate foundations of this distinction were laid in many phases of Marsilius' general politics, two of which may be mentioned here. One was the distinction between two different aspects of the functional parts of the state: on the one hand, each such part may be considered insofar as it consists in a certain mental quality or "habit of the soul" which renders its possessor fit to perform that function; on the other hand, each such part may be considered insofar as it is an officially "established"

[25] For references, see Vol. I, p. 162, n. 69.

part of the state, whose members have the authority or "licence" to
practice that function.[26] A second, closely related point was the distinction between the "material" and the "formal" aspects of law, i.e.,
between its content expressing certain doctrines as to what is just or
unjust, beneficial or harmful, and the coercive command which is attached to that content.[27] It is of the essence of the Marsilian political
philosophy that it concentrates nearly all its detailed attention on the
latter half of each of these distinctions, on official political authority
rather than ideal mental qualities and on the sanctions which emanate
from and in large measure constitute such authority rather than on
their ethical contents or ends. Terms like "prudence" and "justice" do
figure in the *Defensor pacis;* but Marsilius insists that they are not essential to political authority,[28] and the only specifications he gives of
them is as formal instrumentalities, not as having contents intrinsic to
ethical ends.

By these distinctions Marsilius is enabled to proceed from his admis-
sions of the divinity of the priesthood and of divine law, and of the
supreme value which they thereby possess, to his insistence on the people's
political authority over them. Thus the priestly "character" or "habit of
soul," and the sacraments which that character equips men to administer,
are indeed divine; but as such they are distinct from the authority to
practice the priestly function in any particular place. This authority,
Marsilius holds, can come only from the people to whom the priest is to
minister. Similarly, the Gospels are indeed divine; but as such they are
distinct from the authority to determine precisely what they mean in respect of all the doubtful problems of this-worldly belief and action; and
they are distinct too from the authority to determine the manner and
degree of required adherence to them. The former authority, Marsilius
holds, can belong only to a general council composed of both priests and
laymen and elected by the whole people, which alone, moreover, has the
latter authority to require adherence to any of the council's conclusions.
Thus, while Marsilius maintains the distinction between the divine and
the human, the spiritual and the temporal, the priests and the laity, he
elicits with unfailing sensitivity those aspects of each of the former which
are amenable to external control. And these aspects fall under the authority of the whole people rather than of the priesthood alone, not only
because of their temporal or secular consequences, but because, with respect

---

[26] I. vi. 10; I. vii; II. xv. 2 ff.   [27] I. x. 3, 4.

[28] On this point in relation to law, see I. x. 4, 5; I. xii. 2; in relation to government, see I.
xv. 1; II. ii. 8; in relation to the priesthood, see II. xv. 6–10; II. xvii. 1, 8.

both to their temporal and their spiritual aspects, the whole is more trustworthy morally and intellectually than the priests taken alone.

This same point is also characteristic of Marsilius' approach to natural law and justice. He treats these values in Aristotelian terms as the "common benefit"; and they are objective insofar as their *content* is determined by reason from consideration of the natural powers and acts of man and the institutions required to preserve and to "moderate" or "proportion" them. But with these values as with religious ones, the politically decisive question involves not their definition nor their deduction or justification from prior principles, but rather the conditions of their practical determination and control.

Now this distinction between the intrinsic definition and the external "political" determination of values was not, in general, original with Marsilius.[29] But what is unique is the specific form he gave to it and the extensive application he made of it to the problems of both general and ecclesiastic politics. It was calculated to destroy the argument—which had been denied by no previous antipapalists except, in a quite different form, by Gregory of Catino[30] and the anonymous author of the *York Tracts*[31] at the beginning of the twelfth century—whereby the papalists moved from the acknowledged premise that the priests were the official "representatives" or "experts" in respect of religious values to the conclusion that the priests were entitled to supreme authority in respect of the institutional effectuation of these values. As such, the general distinction involved four different but successive aspects: (1) the distinction between *values* and *knowledge:* between the intrinsic or constitutive conditions of values and the means of knowing those conditions; (2) the intra-cognitive distinction between *discovery* and *judgment:* between the ability to know or discover the general conditions of values and the ability to judge their applicability or appropriateness in the given cases; (3) the distinction between *knowledge* and *volition:* between knowing what is good and being willing to practice or apply it; (4) the distinction between the *non-coercive* and the *coercive:* between the existence of values as psychological or spiritual traits known, willed, and possessed by individuals or groups and the political authority to determine and enforce such values for the community as a whole.

Marsilius' arguments place emphasis now on one, now on another

---

[29] Cf. Thomas Aquinas' distinction between the two ways—as conclusions and as determinations—in which human laws are "derived" from the objective principles of natural law (*Summa theologica* II. 1. qu.95. a.2. Resp.).

[30] *Orthodoxa defensio imperialis* cap. ii ff. (MGH, *Libelli de lite*, II, 536 ff.).

[31] *Tractatus Eboracenses* IV (MGH, *Libelli de lite*, III, 665 ff.).

of these distinctions. But ultimately the arguments come down to the fourth distinction, in that supreme coercive authority with respect to all aspects of religious values which are amenable to social control belongs only to the people, and not to the priesthood. (1) Sometimes the argument is that those who officially represent religious values may yet not know how to ascertain what those values are when doubts arise, so that, for example, the priests' possession of the "character" whereby they can administer the sacraments is no guarantee that they can best determine doubtful meanings of divine law, or who should be appointed to particular pastorates. (2) Sometimes the argument is that those who can discover or ascertain what the values are may yet be less able to judge their application to particular cases than those who are to be affected by such application. (3) Sometimes, again, the argument is that those who know what the religious values are may yet, through vicious emotions, act contrary to them, so that coercive authority belongs not to the priests, who are the cognitive "experts" in matters of religion, but to the whole people as not being subject to such viciousness. (4) Sometimes, finally, the argument is that religious values, including faith, insofar as they are dealt with in divine law are intrinsically voluntary and not subject to coercion, so that any coercion which may be exercised in connection with them can derive its authority only from human law, not from divine law, and can be exercised only by the government as executive of human law, not by the priesthood as minister of divine law.

c. LIBERTARIANISM AND SECULARISM

One of the important limitations of Marsilius' doctrine is that he does not also apply such cautionary distinctions to his own allocation of political authority to the people. His confidence in the people's virtues and his ignoring of the difficulties which may arise both from giving unlimited power to the people and from making the secular government the unquestioned "executive" of the people's will are as extreme as the corresponding doctrines of the papalists in relation to the pope. In this respect as in others William of Ockham was far more cautious. But his pluralistic emphasis on the need for limiting all political power was not calculated to subject the priesthood so completely to the secular government as in Marsilius' doctrine or to remove all coercive power so completely from the papacy. Marsilius' conception of political power is monistic, unilinear, and ultimately unlimited; Ockham's is pluralistic, circular, and ultimately limited. The modern theory of sovereignty, in its extreme Hobbesian and Rousseauian form, derives from Marsilius; the modern theory of separation of powers and limited political authority derives from Ockham and the natural law tradition of which, in this respect, he was the summarizer and systematizer.

These features of Marsilius' doctrine account for the contrary characteristics which have been attributed to his ecclesiastic politics. It is now skeptical, now dogmatic; now a herald of freedom and toleration, now an exponent of authoritarian control and repression; now invincibly secular, with the temporal power in omnicompetent control over the spiritual, now involved in a pervasive and inseparable intermingling of spiritual and temporal concerns, with supreme authority belonging to a *populus fidelis,* a "church-legislator," which is as much spiritual as it is temporal. Each of these characterizations is to some extent justified. On the one hand, Marsilius' use of the distinction between the coercive and the non-coercive entails that no coercive authority attaches to the truth, as such, or, in particular, to law and its essential religious institutions of the priesthood, the sacraments, and the articles of faith. Here the Marsilian libertarian tendency with respect to religious toleration manifests itself, together with the seeming skepticism of the position that, even though the essential priesthood is divine, still the priesthood by itself cannot be trusted to determine either what shall be binding truth in religion or what shall be the socially binding institutions deriving from such truth. Here, too, Marsilius clearly projects a secular society in which, in the absence of any provision therefor by the secular power, religion and its institutions have no coercive political authority whatsoever, so that there may be a total separation of religion and politics, church and state. But on the other hand, the fact that the people has final authority over the external manifestations of religion involves in Marsilius the dogmatic and authoritarian doctrine that the people can certainly know what it is best to do with respect to the social, institutional aspects of religion, such as in the appointment of priests to particular posts, and also that the people can best make the arrangements whereby a general council can certainly determine what is religious truth. Here also Marsilius projects a society in which adherence to religious dogma as defined by councils of priests and laymen is made coercively binding on all men, with excommunication and other punishments for heretics and other infidels.

While each of these contrary characteristics can be found in Marsilius' total doctrine, there is nevertheless an important sense in which the libertarian and secular emphases are predominant. We can best grasp this sense by first adducing a certain general consideration concerning the value status of the doctrines argued for in political philosophies. These doctrines may be of four different kinds: they may be set forth either as *necessary* conditions of the state and society, or as *desirable but not necessary*, or as *admissible but neither necessary nor desirable*, or as *inadmissible*. To be sure, political philosophies differ in complexity, and in those which are more complex it is often not possible to indicate without serious qualifications what they regard as necessary, as desirable, and as admissible. Nevertheless, whatever the basis of the philosophy, these four different areas may be found in it by considering its basic definitions and evaluations; and the necessary, in particular, constitutes the essential emphasis of the philosophy as a whole. Thus, according to Aristotle, for example, a *necessary* condition of the state is that it pay some attention to virtue; an aristocratic constitution is *desirable but not necessary;* a democracy is *admissible but neither desirable nor necessary;* a tyranny is *inadmissible.* For Cicero, a *necessary* condition of the state is that it be just, as deriving from natural law; a "mixed" government is *desirable but not necessary;* a "popular state" is *admissible but neither desirable nor necessary.*

Now in Marsilius' general politics the respective areas of the necessary, the desirable, the admissible, and the inadmissible are quite clear. What is *necessary* is that the state have a government elected by the people,[32] that it rule by laws [33] made by the people,[34] that the supreme political authority be unified in the sense that there be no coercive authority in the state which does not derive from the people, its laws, and its government,[35] and that the government control the personnel and functioning of the other parts of the state.[36] What is *desirable but not necessary* is that the people be advised in legislation by those who have prudence and leisure [37] and that the ruler or rulers be prudent and just.[38] What is *admissible but neither necessary nor desirable* is variations in the numerical composition of the government and the particular modes of operation of the processes whereby the people makes the laws and elects the government.[39] What is *inadmissible* is the contradictories of all the features which are necessary. What, in these terms, is the status of Marsilius' ecclesiastic politics? To begin with, it is clear that Christianity is not a necessary condition of political legitimacy; in this Marsilius is one with the Christian Aristotelians. On the other hand, as we have seen, he follows an ancient tradition in holding that some kind

[32] I. xv. 2.
[33] I. xi.
[34] I. xii–xiii.
[35] I. xvii.
[36] I. xv. 4–10.
[37] I. xii. 2; I. xiii. 8.
[38] I. xiv; I. xv. 1.
[39] I. viii. 4; I. ix. 9–10; I. xv. 2.

of religion is "quasi-necessary" in the state because its threats of punishment in a future world for wrongdoing are powerful means of preserving peace.[40] That the religion be "true," i.e., Christian, is quite irrelevant to its fulfilling this secular function. But, given a state all or most of whose citizens are Christian—and this is what is assumed throughout most of Discourse II—what does Marsilius set forth as necessary, as desirable, and as admissible? It is quite clear that he regards as necessary all those propositions which follow from the necessary doctrines of his general politics, such as that the priesthood and divine law can have no coercive authority, and that the priests must obey the coercive authority of the secular government and its law. These propositions, which are particularized deductions from his general political doctrines concerning the peace and unity of the state as necessary conditions of its preservation, are also "confirmed" by the authority of the New Testament and its expositors. Another proposition which follows in the same way is that the legislator and ruler must control the numbers, personnel, and payment of the priesthood as of the other parts of the state.[41] But Discourse II also declares that on purely spiritual or religious grounds such popular control of the priestly personnel is even more necessary than the people's control over the election of the ruler, because eternal death, which a vicious priest might cause in his flock, is "graver" than temporal death.[42] On this ground, too, the legislator or ruler must compel the priests to administer the sacraments if for any reason they desist therefrom.[43] The same double ground of temporal and spiritual consequences is adduced to prove the necessity that doubts concerning the articles of faith be definitively resolved, and that such resolution be made by a general council composed of both laymen and priests and elected by all the believers.[44]

This list of the "necessary" controls of the legislator and ruler to be exercised in ecclesiastic and religious affairs is impressive. But it is to be noted that one important kind of act is not included therein: the infliction of excommunication and other punishments and compulsions for heresy and other violations of divine law. Despite the fact that Marsilius has said that the definitive determination of articles of faith is itself "necessary" to preserve the unity of the faith,[45] the most that he says with respect to the *coercive enforcement* of these determinations is that the authority over this enforcement, *"if it be lawful,"* belongs only to the

[40] I. v. 11. See Vol. I, pp. 83–84.   [41] II. viii. 9; II. xvii. 16, 17; II. xxi. 11–14.
[42] II. xvii. 12.   [43] II. xvii. 8, 12, 15.   [44] II. xx. 1, 4–8.   [45] II. xx. 1.

human legislator.[46] But at no point does he say that it is necessary or even desirable that this authority be put into effect for either temporal or spiritual reasons; on the contrary, he frequently contemplates with equanimity the possibility and even the actuality of the nonpunishment of heretics, and his repeated insistence that coercion in matters of religion is contrary to the spirit and purpose of divine law shows the direction of his own doctrinal preferences. In this respect Marsilius differs sharply from such a thinker as Aquinas, according to whom punishment of heretics is necessary and the killing of them is desirable.[47]

This point is of more general significance for the question of Marsilius' secularism. On the one hand, as we have seen, the coercive controls whose exercise by the legislator and ruler Marsilius regards as necessary extend to such spiritual affairs as the appointment of priests, their performance of the sacraments, and the determination of articles of faith—and for spiritual reasons of eternal life as well as for temporal reasons. But, on the other hand, these necessary controls are exercised only over priests, not over laymen, except insofar as both priests and laymen may require compulsion to attend general councils to which they have been elected.[48] What this means is that despite the large bulk of the *Defensor pacis* which Marsilius devotes to ecclesiastic politics and spiritual affairs, there is lacking in the treatise any suggestion of that necessary impingement of religious concerns on laymen and on all phases of secular life which, in different though related ways, was set forth by the papalists in Marsilius' day and, some two centuries later, by Calvin. To be sure, such a ubiquitous infiltration of the religious into the secular is *possible* for Marsilius, for he does not rule it out in principle. In this respect, his position is not that of Locke who declared that "I esteem it above all things necessary to distinguish exactly the business of civil government from that of religion, and to settle the just bounds that lie between the one and the other." [49] The Marsilian legislator can, *if it wishes,* set penalties compelling the observance of the general council's decisions not only concerning articles of faith and church ritual but also "concerning other human acts, such as fasting, the eating of meat, abstinences, the canonization and veneration of saints, prohibition or exclusion from mechanical or any other work, marriage within certain degrees of relationship, approval or disapproval of religious orders or groups, and other similar

[46] II. v. 7; II. xxi. 4–8. See Vol. I, pp. 160, 165–66, 312–13.
[47] *S. theol.* II. II. qu.10. a.8. Resp.; a.9; qu.11. a.3. Resp.; qu.39. a.4.
[48] II. xx. 3.
[49] *Letters concerning Toleration,* I (London, 1870), 5.

matters which divine law allows or permits." [50] But Marsilius is so far from regarding such coercive regulation as either necessary or desirable that he does not recur to it except in his list of conclusions, [51] where the insistence is again that the authority of coercive enforcement with respect to these matters belongs to the legislator or ruler—but not that this authority *must* be exercised. Such coercion is for Marsilius neither necessary nor desirable, but only admissible.

In final analysis, then, the Marsilian church-state is far more a state than a church. The coercive authority which is necessarily exercised in it in religious affairs is exercised almost exclusively over the priests. The area of religious indifference—to which no necessary coercion attaches—is far larger than the area of such coercion. In the absence of positive provision therefor by the people-legislator, complete religious freedom obtains: "individuals must be permitted to teach what they wish concerning the faith." [52] Marsilius does not go so far as to say that such freedom is itself necessary, although his repeated insistence on the incompatibility of faith and coercion, and on the non-coerciveness of divine law, buttressed by quotations from the apostles and other saints, points in that direction.

It is these considerations which make it legitimate to refer to Marsilius' basic position as secularism. Despite his explicit avowals of concern for the future life, and his scattered assertions of the greater importance of that life than the happiness of the present world, the final outcome of his doctrine is to place by far the major share of emphasis on the "necessary" political arrangements required for "civil peace," i.e., for the preservation of the state and the this-worldly sufficient life which it makes possible. The aspects of religion with which he deals are all such as were involved in the papal "impediments" to civil peace, whereas, on the other hand, he does not deal at all with even institutional aspects of religion not so involved—for example, the sacraments other than penance, order, and marriage (the last only in the *Defensor minor* and in a small tract excerpted therefrom, occasioned by difficulties concerning the marriage of Ludwig of Bavaria's son). To be sure, these omissions may be explained on the ground that they raised no issues of ecclesiastic politics. But the very fact that they did not do so for Marsilius is itself indicative that his basic concern is not religious but secular. The ubiquitous employment to which Egidius of Rome, for example, puts the sacrament of baptism as a necessary condition of legitimate authority is just as absent from Marsilius' doctrine as are Aquinas' insistence on the punishment

[50] II. xxi. 8. [51] III. ii. 34. [52] II. xxviii. 17.

of heretics and John of Paris' provisions for the pope's excommunication of a sinful ruler.

What Marsilius did by his exaltation of the people was to shift the whole cast of the traditional medieval church-state debate. Where that debate had been between two different groups or authorities in society, each representing a different set of values—*regnum* and *sacerdotium,* temporal power and spiritual power—Marsilius subsumed both of these under a *universitas* which was at once *civilis* and *fidelis,* secular and religious, state and church, and equally infallible in both spheres, so that it was a single all-inclusive locus and determiner of both spiritual and temporal values. Thereby, also, the discussion of the comparative value of secular and religious goals was no longer relevant. But then, having assigned supreme institutional authority in both secular and religious affairs to this *universitas,* Marsilius could allow its "natural desires" free play, and these were almost exclusively in a secular rather than in a religious direction.[53] And, in addition, the "secular" government, as exc¹ ¹sive coercive agent of the will of the *universitas,* attained a far greater triumph over the quondam "spiritual power" than had been possible for earlier antipapalists who had confined their discussions to the conflict between the two powers themselves, without fitting them into a larger whole as did Marsilius.

[53] See Vol. I, pp. 54 ff., 78 ff.; also, e.g., II. ix. 12, last sentence.

LANGUAGE AND TRANSLATION

MANY DIFFERENT problems of language are posed by the *Defender of Peace*. There are problems concerning the meanings of its chief terms, and problems concerning the translation of these terms from Latin into English. Underlying each of these problems are further, more general problems: ontological ones as to the kinds of objects referred to by the terms in question, and logical ones as to the kinds of meaning, in addition to referential or designative meaning, had by these terms. And in addition to these problems about terms, there are problems about the logical structure of the work, especially as to the relation between its initial propositions concerning man and society, on the one hand, and its practical recommendations or prescriptions for action, on the other.

To go into these problems adequately insofar as they pertain to the *Defender of Peace* would require a treatise as long as the *Defender* itself.[1] In what follows I shall confine myself exclusively to the specific problems of the meanings of the *Defender's* terms, both in the original Latin and in their English translation. The chief aim will be to clarify these for the English reader not versed in scholastic Latin and in the technical philosophical, theological, and legal concepts used by Marsilius.

It should be pointed out, to begin with, that the present translation is in many respects a double one. I have tried to render Marsilius' fourteenth-century Latin into twentieth-century English. This involves the difficulty which translators in all ages have invoked, that "Many words in every language have associations, echoes, and overtones, which no translation

---

[1] Some of them have been discussed in Vol. I, pp. 44 ff., 67 ff. Problems of the language of political theory have been discussed extensively in recent writings, among which are: M. Macdonald, "The Language of Political Theory," *Proceedings of the Aristotelian Society*, XLI (1940–41), 91–112; *id.*, "Natural Rights," *ibid.*, XLVII (1946–47), 225–50; H. L. A. Hart, "The Ascription of Responsibility and Rights," *ibid.*, XLIX (1948–49), 171–94; T. D. Weldon, *The Vocabulary of Politics* (London, 1953); H. D. Lasswell, *Language of Politics* (New York, 1949); H. D. Lasswell and A. Kaplan, *Power and Society* (New Haven, 1950); A. I. Melden and W. Frankena, "The Concept of Universal Human Rights," *American Philosophical Assn., Eastern Division*, I (1952), 167–207; and several papers by R. McKeon, esp. "Development of the Concept of Property in Political Philosophy," *Ethics*, XLVIII (1938), 297–366; "Discussion and Resolution in Political Conflicts," *Ethics*, LIX (1944), 235–262. The papers of McKeon show an unusual grasp of the concepts, structures, and interrelations of historical political philosophies; the writings of Macdonald and Weldon are exceptionally deficient in this regard.

can convey." [2] And it should be added that, besides these "associations, echoes, and overtones," many words in one language have literal referents which are not had by words in another language, especially when the words refer to socio-political institutions and the two languages have been used at different times in history. In medieval political writings a word like *civitas*, in its relation to the word "state," furnishes an obvious example. But in addition, Marsilius' Latin is itself in many respects a translation, so that in translating him we are also translating translations. Three such respects may be mentioned. The first is that he uses in Discourse I the *Politics* of Aristotle in the Latin translation by William of Moerbeke. Thus Marsilius' *civitas*, as he uses the term, is a translation of Aristotle's πόλις, and so we in using the term "state" are translating not only Marsilius' term but also Aristotle's. Consequently the differences, historical, philosophical, and other, between our "state" and Marsilius' *civitas* are compounded by the differences between the latter and Aristotle's πόλις. Secondly, Marsilius uses in Discourse II the New Testament in the Vulgate translation of St. Jerome. Here again there is a double shift from Greek into Latin and from Latin into English. Thus Marsilius' use of *regnum* in Discourse II is often a translation of the New Testament's βασιλεία, and hence involves all the difficulties of the distinction between "kingdoms" which are and are not of this world.[8] Here again there are multiple differences, historical, philosophical, and other, between the referents and connotations of the Greek, the Latin, and the English words. In the third place, less obviously but just as importantly, when Marsilius quotes, as he frequently does, St. Augustine and other commentators on the New Testament, as well as other theologians, a "translation" is involved. Even though they, like Marsilius, wrote in Latin, the meanings are often strikingly different. A word like *dominari* or *dominatio*, for example, will have for Augustine a meaning far more closely related to the Roman absolutist "domination" than to the Marsilian "rulership" or "governance." Consequently, to translate Marsilius' quotations from these authors, and his own subsequent comments thereon, involves translating not only Marsilius' own meanings but the meanings which he in turn, and sometimes mistakenly, attributed to these authors. We must translate Marsilius; but Marsilius himself has first "translated" these authors in a sense not too different in principle from that in which William of Moerbeke translated Aristotle, and Jerome the New Testament.

[2] E. Barker, *The Politics of Aristotle* (Oxford, 1948), p. lxiii.
[8] John 18:36; cf. *Defender of Peace* II. iv. 4 ff.

These difficulties complicate the problem of translating an author like Marsilius. The aim of what follows in this section is to clarify these difficulties insofar as they affect the important terms used by Marsilius. I shall follow a roughly logical order, proceeding from logical, metaphysical, and physical terms to psychological and moral terms, and finally to social and political terms. I shall avoid repeating the discussion of leading terms which was presented in Volume I.[4] Since Marsilius uses William of Moerbeke's translation of Aristotle, I shall frequently indicate the Greek term side by side with the Latin which translated it.

"Equivocation (*aequivocatio, ὁμωνυμία*); "ambiguity" (*ambiguitas*). A word is "equivocal"[5] when it has more than one meaning (*multiplicitas nominum*)[6] or a variety of uses (*varietas usus*).[7] Marsilius held that the papalist arguments had particularly exploited the equivocations of words like "law," "spiritual," "church," and "judgment"; hence his attempts to distinguish the meanings of these and others terms.[8] When words are equivocal they lead to "ambiguity,"[9] which consists in a diversity of interpretation of statements and a resulting confusion.

"Demonstration" (*demonstratio, ἀπόδειξις*). A demonstration in the strict sense is a syllogism whose middle term signifies the essence of its subject or minor term, and whose predicate or major term is proved to belong to the subject through that essential middle term. The middle term thus signifies the "cause" of the fact stated in the conclusion, and this cause "necessitates" the conclusion not merely formally, as in any syllogism, but also as a "necessary" truth.[10] Marsilius holds that his own treatise consists in "demonstrations," at least in Discourse I,[11] so that it involves "certainty."[12]

"Cause" (*causa, αἴτιον*). Following Aristotle[13] Marsilius distinguishes four kinds of cause.[14] The "material cause" (*causa materialis*) is the

---

[4] See the discussions of "natural desire" (Vol. I, pp. 56 ff.), "impediment" (p. 59), "immanent" and "transient" acts (p. 61), "faith" (pp. 67 ff.), "humility" and "magnanimity" (pp. 79 ff.), "perfect community" (pp. 86 ff.), "peace" (pp. 94 ff.), "unity" (pp. 115 ff.), "province," "monarchy," "empire" (pp. 126 ff.), "human law" (pp. 136 ff.), "rule of law" (pp. 139 ff.), "natural law" (pp. 147 ff.), "divine law" (pp. 152 ff.), "citizen" (pp. 175 ff.), "people" (pp. 180 ff.), "weightier part" (pp. 182 ff.), "quantity and quality" (pp. 185 ff.), "freedom" (pp. 219 ff.), "judgment" (pp. 226 ff.), "church" (pp. 260 ff.), "essential" and "accidental" powers (pp. 270 ff.).

[5] See II. x. 11; II. xii. 8; II. xxx. 3. Cf. Aristotle *Categories* 1. 1a 1 ff.

[6] See I. ii. 2; I. x. 3; II. ii. 1, 8; II. x. 11.   [7] See II. xii. 2.

[8] I. x. 3 ff.; II. ii. 1–3, 5–8; II. ix. 3. See Vol. I, pp. 46–47, 154, 226–28, 260–63.

[9] I. ii. 2; II. ii. 1, 8; II. xii. 2.   [10] Cf. Aristotle *Posterior Analytics* I. 2. 71b 9 ff.

[11] See I. i. 8; I. v. 2; I. xi. 1; I. xiii. 5 ff.; I. xiii. 2; I. xv. 2. Cf. Vol. I, pp. 48 ff.

[12] I. i. 8; I. ix. 2.

[13] Cf. *Metaphysics* I. 3. 983a 25 ff.; v. 2. 1013a 24 ff.; *Physics* II. 3. 194b 23 ff.

[14] See esp. I. vi. 10; I. vii. 1–3 (causes of the parts of the state); I. x. 2 (causes of the law); I. xix. 2 (causes of peace).

components of which a thing consists, and hence the preconditions for its being the kind of thing that it is. The "formal cause" (*causa formalis*) is the form or arrangement of these components, which makes the thing the kind of thing that it is and therefore constitutes the essence of the thing. The "efficient cause" (*causa efficiens*) is that which initiates a movement or change, hence that which "effects" or "makes" something. The "final cause" (*causa finalis*) is the end or purpose of a thing, event, or movement.

Marsilius uses several different expressions for the efficient cause besides *efficiens*: [15] *movens* [16] ("moving cause"), *agens* [17] ("acting cause"), *factiva* [18] ("productive cause," i.e., that which makes), *effectiva* [19] ("effective cause," that which effects). All of these have usually been translated as "efficient cause," since this is the traditional way of referring to the concept in question.

"Necessity" (*necessitas, ἀνάγκη*). The "necessary" as Marsilius uses it is that which follows inexorably from some cause. Thus the state and its parts or functions are "necessary" because of the final cause—living and living well—which is desired by men, and also because of the material cause—the natural condition of men.[20] The existence of laws in the state is likewise "necessary."[21] Strife and scandal arise "necessarily" among men who live together.[22] In addition, Marsilius uses "necessity" to characterize the relation between premises and conclusion in a demonstration;[23] this necessity, however, is not merely formal but is dictated by the nature of the subject-matter.[24] At one point, "necessary" is also used in the sense of that which provides the preconditions or means, as against fulfilling the constitutive conditions or ends, or living well.[25] This derives from Aristotle's distinction between the merely "necessary" and the "noble."[26]

"Nature (*natura, φύσις*). Aristotle defines "nature" as "a principle or cause of motion and rest in that to which it belongs primarily and essentially."[27] The two adverbs in this definition imply that different species of things have different natures, i.e., different kinds of internal principles of motion and rest. What is "natural" to a kind of thing is thus the specific mode of operation deriving from the fact that the thing is of that kind.

---

[15] I. vi. 10; I. xvii. 4; I. xix. 3.   [16] I. vii. 2, 3; I. ix. 3.
[17] I. ix. 1; I. x. 2; I. xix. 2.
[18] I. vii. 3; I. xvii. 1; I. xvii. 5, 8; I. xix. title and 2, 3.
[19] I. x. 1; I. xii. 1; I. xiv. 1.
[20] I. ii. 5; I. iv. 2, 3, 4, 5; I. v. 2, 3, 7, 8, 9, 10, 11; I. vi. 1.
[21] I. xi. 1.   [22] I. xv. 6.   [23] E.g., I. xii. 2.
[24] See Vol. I, pp. 48–51, 62–63, 208–9.   [25] I. v. 1.
[26] *Politics* vii. 809. 1328a 22 ff. See Vol. I, p. 190 and n. 61.
[27] *Physics* II. 1. 192b 21.

Marsilius seems to use the term in this sense as signifying the specifically human when he refers to what "all men" "naturally believe" and "naturally desire,"[28] as well as what "all men shun in accordance with nature."[29] However, Marsilius also tends to assimilate human "nature" to all other natures, and thereby, in Aristotelian terms, to the material cause rather than to the formal and final causes.[30] He derives many of his principles about man from Aristotle's theoretic "natural sciences," in which Aristotle deals not only with man but with other animals.[31] Thus Marsilius distinguishes "nature" from "reason" and "art";[32] and while he repeats the Aristotelian formula that "all men have a natural impulse toward the state,"[33] he does not repeat the other formulae that "the state exists by nature" and that "man is by nature a political animal."[34] However, in saying that the state exists "by nature," Aristotle uses "nature" in the sense of the final cause, not in the sense of the efficient cause, as does Marsilius.

"Deformity" (orbatio, πήρωμα), "deformed" (orbati, πεπηρωμένοι). Used by Aristotle to mean an abnormality in some organism, in that some aspect of it falls short of the "nature" of the species.[35] Used by Marsilius three times to refer to abnormality of some men's natures in respect of their desires,[36] and once to refer to abnormality in general.[37]

"Soul" (anima, ψυχή). Used by Marsilius in two senses: Aristotelian and Augustinian. (1) Aristotle defines the soul as "the first actuality of a natural body having life potentially in it";[38] hence the soul is the proximate principle of all the living functions of an organism. In this sense one may speak of different "souls"—nutritive, sensitive, appetitive, locomotive, rational—corresponding to the chief different powers or functions of organisms. Thus Marsilius says that in one sense "life is nothing other than soul,"[39] and he refers to the "vegetative soul" of plants,[40] the "nutritive part of the soul,"[41] "that which is ensouled in accordance with the nutritive faculty,"[42] as well as to "the virtues of both the practical and the theoretic soul,"[43] and the "rational and appetitive soul."[44] (2) For Augustine too the soul is that whereby bodies have life; but he distinguishes between nonrational souls and rational souls (some-

---

[28] I. iv. 2; cf. I. xii. 2.   [29] II. ix. 12.   [30] Cf. Physics II. 1. 192b 21.

[31] See I. iv. 3, where the natural condition of man is described from what "has been said in scientia naturarum."

[32] I. ii. 2; I. v. 2, 3; I. vii. 1.   [33] I. iv. 3; I. xii. 2. Aristotle Pol. I. 2. 1253a 30.

[34] Pol. I. 2. 1252b 31, 1253a 2. Cf. Vol. I, pp. 88-90.

[35] For references, see Vol. I, p. 58, nn. 35-37.

[36] I. iv. 2; I. xii. 5; I. xiii. 2.   [37] I. xvi. 23.   [38] De anima II. 1. 412a 28.

[39] I. v. 2.   [40] II. xii. 4.   [41] I. v. 4, 5.   [42] II. xxx. 1.

[43] I. iv. 4.   [44] II. xxx. 1.

times calling the former *anima* and the latter *animus*), and he tends to emphasize the latter, which he holds to be immortal and made in God's image.[45] Hence in general there is a much sharper distinction between soul and body in the Augustinian tradition than in the Aristotelian. Marsilius refers to the Augustinian conception in his discussions of Christian doctrine,[46] especially in connection with commentaries on the New Testament.[47] He refuses to accept the Augustinian distinction between soul and body, however, when this is put to polemical use to differentiate the priesthood from secular rulership; at such points he insists on the Aristotelian interpretation of the relation between soul and body.[48]

"Habit" (*habitus*, ἕξις). According to Aristotle, a habit is a firmly established quality, and a quality is "that in virtue of which people are said to be such and such." [49] Habits, then, are firmly ingrained conditions or qualities or "possessions" [50] of soul or body. Among habits are the moral virtues and vices; and these, unlike natural potentialities, are generated not by nature but by "habituation" (ἔθος, ἐθισμός).[51] Habits are intermediate between *powers* and *acts:* powers are relatively indeterminate potentialities which can be turned in several different directions of operation; habits are the relatively fixed results of one such turning; acts are operations of powers which may or may not have undergone habituation, but the acts may reflect habits.[52] In this sense, habits regulate acts. Marsilius uses the word *habitus* in this Aristotelian context of interpretation. Thus he refers to "habits of the human body or soul," [53] and he says that they "fulfill or perfect the human inclinations which exist by nature." [54] The moral and intellectual virtues are habits.[55] Similarly he refers to the military habit [56] and other "practical habits," [57] as well as the "habit of the first philosopher"; [58] the priestly character is a habit; [59] and rules and measures, like laws, which regulate human acts as to their mode of operation are habits.[60]

---

[45] See *De immortalitate animae, passim; De civitate Dei* VI. xii; VII. xxiii; XII. xxiii; *De libero arbitrio* I. vii. 16.

[46] E.g., I. vi. 2; I. xix. 5; II. iii. 10; II. vi. 2, 4.

[47] See esp. II. v. 4.   [48] II. xxx. 1. Cf. Vol. I, pp. 100–1.

[49] *Categories* 5. 8b 26 ff. Cf. *Metaphysics* v. 20. 1022b 10.

[50] As a "possession" which is "had," a habit is distinguished from a "privation" (*privatio, στέρησις*), which is a "lack" of what is normally had. See I. xvi. 23; II. xii. 2; and Aristotle *Categories* 9. 11b 33 ff.; *Metaphysics* v. 22. 1022b 22 ff.

[51] *Nicomachean Ethics* II. 1. 1103a 16 ff.; II. 5. 1105b 19 ff.

[52] Cf. II. xii. 18, where Marsilius refers to the "habit or act of charity."

[53] I. vi. 10.   [54] I. vii. 2.   [55] I. xiv. 2.   [56] I. vi. 10.

[57] I. x. 3; I. xv. 8; II. xxx. 4.   [58] II. xxx. 4.

[59] II. xv. 2.

[60] II. viii. 4. The rendition of *habitus* (as it occurs in scholastic philosophers) as "habit" is condemned by the translators (Y. R. Simon, J. J. Glanville, G. D. Hollenhorst) of *The*

"Virtue (*virtus, ἀρετή*). Used by Marsilius in two senses. (1) Sometimes it means simply a natural power, such as the "locomotive virtues" [61] and the "generative virtue." [62] (2) More usually it means an excellent "habit" (*q.v.*) of some kind, whereby a power of man is so organized and perfected as to emerge in the excellent functioning or operation of that power.[63] Among these powers are those of the practical and the theoretic soul, involving the passions and thought, respectively; thus Marsilius refers to the "functions in which are exercised the virtues of both the practical and the theoretic soul." [64] These are the moral and the intellectual virtues. But although Marsilius frequently refers to "moral virtue," [65] especially justice, he does not use the phrase *virtus intellectualis* as does, for example, Thomas Aquinas,[66] although he frequently refers to "prudence," one of the intellectual virtues.[67] Marsilius also refers to the "theological virtues," such as faith, hope, charity, and evangelical poverty.[68] He defines these in terms of their end, Christ,[69] and says that they are acquired through habituation by performing the corresponding acts.[70] Marsilius does not use *virtus,* as Machiavelli after him was to use *virtù,* in a morally indifferent sense. Like Aristotle, Marsilius holds that prudence and moral virtue are inseparable.[71]

"Acts" (*actus*); "transient acts" (*actus transeuntes*); "immanent" (*immanentes*); "controlled acts" (*actus imperati*). (See below, I. v. 4, p. 16, n. 6, and texts cited there; also II. viii. 3 and p. 157, n. 1.)

Material Logic of John of St. Thomas (Chicago, 1955), pp. 611–12, on the ground that this confuses two different "grounds of steadiness—a repetition of acts in habit, an objective necessity in *habitus*," and thereby confuses the Humean and Aristotelian interpretations of science. Although the Aristotelian ἕξις or *habitus* is not precisely the same as Hume's or Dewey's "habit," it seems that little is to be gained by changing the traditional rendition of Aristotle's term as "habit." Etymologically and historically the terms are very closely related, while in respect of meanings "habit" does preserve the sense of firm possession of a quality from which emerge characteristic modes of operation. It is doubtful whether for Aristotle, let alone all the scholastics who used his terminology, the "steadiness" of art and the moral virtues "is guaranteed by objective necessity" as is that of science, as the abovementioned translators hold. And it is also doubtful whether Aristotle intends such a relation between ἕξις and essence as they uphold; this seems to confuse ἕξις with δύναμις. A *potentiality* may derive from a thing's essence, but this is not the case with ἕξις, which is confined to man and subject to the circumstances of his experience and habituation, intellectual as well as practical. On some of the difficulties and dangers of changing the traditional translations of Aristotelian terms, I may refer to my paper "Aristotle's Doctrine of Being," *Philosophical Review,* LXII (1953), pp. 579–80.

[61] I. v. 7.   [62] I. xv. 5.

[63] Cf. Aristotle *N. Eth.* I. 13. 1102a 5 ff.; II. 1–5. 1103a 14 ff.; VI. 1–2. 1139b 35 ff.

[64] I. iv. 1.   [65] I. xiv. 2, 6, 9, 10; I. xv. 7; I. xvi. 18.

[66] *Summa theologica* II. 1. qus.57–58.   [67] See below, p. lxxxvi.

[68] II. ii. 5; II. xiii. 18.   [69] II. xiii. 16 ff.

[70] II. xiii. 13 ff. Cf. Thomas Aquinas' discussion of the theological virtues, *S. theol.* II. 1. qu.62; II. II. qus.1–44.

[71] I. xiv. 2, 10. Aristotle *N. Eth.* VI. 13. 1144b 30 ff. But cf. Vol. I, p. 214, n. 14.

"Happiness" (*felicitas*, εὐδαιμονία) and related terms. Marsilius uses many different expressions for the supreme values of life, many of them taken from Aristotle. In addition to "happiness," there are *living well* (*bene vivere*, εὖ ζῆν),[72] *good life* (*bona vita*),[73] *sufficient life* (*vita sufficiens*),[74] *living sufficiently* (*vivere sufficienter*),[75] *sufficiency of life* (*sufficientia vitae*).[76] The last three expressions probably come from Aristotle's doctrine that "self-sufficiency" (αὐτάρκεια, translated *per se sufficientia* by William of Moerbeke) is one of the chief characteristics of happiness[77] and also of the state.[78] In similar fashion Marsilius refers also the "sufficiencies" (*sufficientiae*) which perfect human actions and passions.[79]

"Beatitude" (*beatitudo*). Marsilius uses this term exclusively to refer to the supreme end of the future life, as "eternal beatitude."[80] He uses *felicitas* and *beatitudo* interchangeably in this connection,[81] but also uses all the other expressions listed above together with *felicitas* as nouns for the end of the future life, usually either with "eternal" or "for the status of the future world." See also *civil happiness, common benefit.*

"Status" (*status*). This term means in general a "standing," an at least relatively fixed condition or position of man.[82] Marsilius uses the term in two connections: (1) in respect of the general condition of man in this world and in the future world; (2) in respect of a particular kind of condition. (1) He regularly distinguishes "the status of the present world" (*status praesentis saeculi*) from "the status of the future world" (*status futuri saeculi*).[83] He sometimes distinguishes, in each case, between "in the status" and "for the status," with respect to laws.[84] For example, divine law applies to what men do "in" the status of the present world, yet "for" the status of the future world.[85] (2) Marsilius also refers to the "status of innocence" before the fall of man;[86] the "status of perfection,"[87] which is also a "status of poverty and humility";[88] and the "status of the ruler" (*status principis*), which is "the status which befits him and which he bears."[89] The term "status" became the mod-

---

[72] I. iv. 5; I. v. 1, 2, 3. See *Pol.* I. 2. 1252b 30.

[73] I. iv. 2.

[74] I. i. 2; I. iv. 2; I. v. 7, 11; II. viii. 5.

[75] I. iv. 5.

[76] I. iv. 5; I. xii. 7; I. xiii. 2; II. viii. 7; III. iii.

[77] *N. Eth.* I. 7. 1097b 7. Moerbeke's translation of this work can be found in Thomas Aquinas *In decem libros Ethicorum Aristotelis ad Nicomachum expositio* I. Lectio 9, ed. A. M. Pirotta and M. S. Gillet (Turin, 1934), p. 34.

[78] *Pol.* I. 1. 1252b 29. See Vol. I, pp. 63 ff.

[79] I. vi. 10; I. vii. 1.

[80] E.g., III. iii.

[81] E.g., at I. vi. 4.

[82] Cf. Thomas Aquinas *S. theol.* II. II. qu.183. a.1. Resp.

[83] See, e.g., II. viii. 5.

[84] II. viii. 4.

[85] II. viii. 5; II. ix. 3. Cf. II. x. 8.

[86] I. vi. 1, 2.

[87] II. xi. 2.

[88] II. xii. 1.

[89] II. xi. 2, 7.

ern term "state" when this "status of the ruler" was identified with the authority of the whole of the society. See *state*.

"Office" (*officium*). In Cicero's *De officiis* this term means moral duty, but in Marsilius it refers to any function (*opus*), performed in the state which contributes to living or living well. Thus he refers to "men of one office," "offices of men," [90] "offices of the state," [91] all of these being equivalent to the functional "parts" of the state, which are called "offices" because "they are ordered to human service." [92] Since men's entry into and performance of these "offices" is controlled by the government of the state, which "establishes" these offices,[93] there is a sense in which these offices have an "official" status in the state. But Marsilius also uses the term "officials" (*officiales*) in a more restricted sense to refer to those who "assist the ruler" in his judicial and other functions.[94] At one point he refers to these as "public civil officials," [95] seeming to need both adjectives to differentiate what we would nowadays call public officials from those whose work is "private"—but in an important sense for Marsilius as for other medievals there is no separate category of the private. In similar fashion Marsilius refers to "ecclesiastic offices" [96] and "priestly offices," [97] as well as to "ecclesiastic officials." [98]

"Order (*ordo*). This term is used in several different ways by Marsilius, all of which seem to involve the relating of men to one another according to some principle. (1) "Orders of men." Here it is used interchangeably with "offices," [99] which are functional parts of the state *"ordered* to human service." [100] (2) "Holy orders." This refers to the power which priests receive through their "ordainment" (*ordinatio*) [101] whereby they can perform the sacraments.[102] These are also referred to as "ecclesiastic orders," [103] and are distinguished from "prelacies" [104] which Marsilius interprets as meaning all specific appointments to perform priestly functions in particular places, and other functions incident to such appointments. (3) "Religious orders." Corporate groups (*collegia*) of clergymen formed for general or specific religious purposes, including "orders of poverty." [105] (4) "Order of the parts of the state." This refers to the parts of the state being ordered by and to the government, in the sense

---

[90] I. iv. 5; I. v. 5.
[91] I. vi. 9, 10; I. vii. 1; I. xv. 6; II. xv. 1, 2.
[92] I. vii. 1.
[93] I. xv. 4, 6–10, 12. See Vol. I, pp. 111–14.
[94] I. xii. 4; II. xx. 6; II. xxv. 12.
[95] III. ii. 24.
[96] II. xi. 5; II. xxi. 11; II. xxv. 5; II. xxviii. 28.
[97] II. xv. 9.
[98] II. xi. 5; II. xix. 26.
[99] I. iv. 5; I. v. 5.
[100] I. vii. 1.
[101] II. xv. 8.
[102] II. xv. 7, 8, 10; II. xxviii. 28.
[103] II. xxiii. 3.
[104] II. xxv. 4. Cf. Vol. I, pp. 269–72, on the distinction between order and jurisdiction.
[105] II. xxi. 8; II. xxiv. 13; II. xxv. 8.

of their being subordinated to its commands.[106] (5) "Order of the church." This refers to the graduated articulation of the church in which authority should be decentralized, archbishops supervising bishops, bishops supervising priests, etc.[107] It is noteworthy that Marsilius does not use the concept of order in that cosmological and moral sense in which the medieval tradition, from Augustine on, interpreted the entire world and all its parts as an order of "peace" governed by God.[108]

"Assemblage" (*congregatio*). The term *grex* means "flock," so a *congregatio* is a "flocking together" or "assemblage." Marsilius uses the term to refer to men's "coming together" in the most general sense. Men "assemble" for the sake of living and living well; [109] there is also a "general assembly of the citizens" to make laws; [110] the general council is an "assembly"; [111] so too were the Greek *ecclesia* [112] and the meetings of the apostles and other believers.[113]

"Community" (*communitas*, κοινωνία) and related terms. The terms *communitas*, *communicatio*, *communicare*, and *commune conferens* obviously are all closely related. They have the central reference of that which is "common" (*commune*) as opposed to that which is "proper," "private," or "individual." A *communitas* is a group of men having something in common. A *communicatio* is either identical with a *communitas* [114] or else, like *communicare*, it is the act of carrying on that which constitutes the *communitas*. The *commune conferens* is the "common benefit" which results from and aids the *communicatio*. The obvious renderings of these terms might seem to be, respectively, "community," "communication," "communicate," and "common benefit." But while the first and fourth of these renditions have been maintained throughout this translation, the second and third present difficulties. We ordinarily use "communication" to refer to the mutual expression of thoughts or feelings. Marsilius, however, uses *communicatio* in a far more "external" sense. We do not ordinarily refer to men's "communicating necessities to one another" (*necessaria . . . sibi communicantes invicem*) [115] or to "their communication of their functions to one another" (*communicatio ipsorum invicem suorum operum*),[116] nor do we refer to the whole

[106] I. xv. 14; I. xvii. 7. Cf. Vol. I, p. 111.   [107] II. xxiv. 12–13.
[108] See Vol. I, pp. 14–19, 95–96.   [109] I. iv. 3, 4, 5.
[110] I. xiii. 8: "in universali civium congregatione." See also I. xiii. 6; I. xvii. 4; II. xxii. 14.
[111] II. xx. 3.   [112] II. ii. 2.
[113] II. xvi. 6; II. xxii. 13, 15.
[114] William of Moerbeke renders Aristotle's κοινωνία indifferently as *communitas* or *communicatio*. See, e.g., *Pol.* I. 1. 1252a 1, 7 (Sus. p. 1); I. 2. 1252b 7, 10, 13, 15 (Sus. pp. 2, 3).
[115] I. iv. 5.   [116] I. xix. 2.

broad interaction and association of men in a community as a "communication" (*fiunt per hominum communicationem;* [117] *per ipsorum invicem communicationem;* [118] *communicantes civiliter;* [119] *de partibus civitatis, in quarum actione ac communicatione . . .* [120]). Accordingly, the terms *communicatio, communicare, communicantes* have frequently been rendered as "association" or as "sharing." This is one of the cases where the centralized meaning of the sets of Greek and Latin terms is lost in the English.

The extension of "community" for Marsilius comprises the household (*communitas domestica*),[121] the village (*vicus*),[122] and the state (*civitas*).[123] Unlike Aristotle, however, he does not call the groupings of master-slave or husband-wife "communities." [124] Nor, significantly, does he call the church, as such, a community; rather, it is something more distributive, found in the whole body of believers and in "all the parts of this whole body." [125]

Marsilius also uses the term "common" in the sense in which it is opposed to "private property." [126] See also *common benefit*.

"State" (*civitas* or *regnum,* πόλις). Although, as Marsilius notes, his predecessors distinguished *civitas* from *regnum* both quantitatively (the *regnum* being composed of several *civitates*) and specifically (the *regnum* being a "temperate monarchy"), Marsilius uses the two terms interchangeably.[127] Frequently he uses them together: *civitas sive regnum* [128] (which I have translated as "city or state"). In Discourse I, when he wishes to refer to the monarchies for which his predecessors used *regnum,* he uniformly writes instead "royal monarchy" (*regalis monarchia*).[129] In Discourse II, however, he frequently refers to the Vulgate New Testament where *regnum* was used to translate βασιλεία; [130] here I have had to use "kingdom" as the correct translation.

The difficulties of translating the political terms of one age into those of another come to a head with this term. Marsilius, following Aristotle, defines the *civitas* as the "perfect community" in the sense that it provides all the functions needed for living and living well.[131] The state, then, is not only a "legal-political" entity but also an economic, a moral, and a re-

---

[117] I. iv. 2. [118] I. iv. 3. [119] I. iv. 4.
[120] I. v. 1. [121] II. ii. 3. [122] I. ii. 4.
[123] I. iii. 5; I. iv. 1. [124] See *Pol.* I. 2. 1252b 10. [125] II. ii. 3.
[126] II. xii. 25. [127] I. ii. 2. Cf. Vol. I, pp. 117, 126–27.
[128] I. ii. 3; I. xvii. 1–3, 7, 11–13; I. xix. 12, etc.
[129] I. viii. 3; I. ix. 4–6. In William of Moerbeke's translation of Aristotle's *Politics,* πόλις was rendered *civitas,* and *regnum* was used for βασιλεία, so that there was no danger of confusing the terms for the political community and royal government.
[130] E.g., II. iv. 4 ff. [131] I. iv. 1.

ligious one. In this sense it is much broader in scope than the modern state.

Scholars have devoted much attention to the relation between medieval and modern conceptions of the state. It is easy to oversimplify this relation, in the direction of either similarity or difference.[132] The term *status* meant for the medievals, as it had for Cicero, some kind of fixed or "stable" condition or "standing" of persons or groups, with no specific "political" connotation.[133] The modern "state" may be said to have come about when the *status* of the ruling power was identified with the whole community over which that power ruled, so that the ruler's *status*, in virtue of his political authority, was, politically speaking, the community itself. This meant that the "state" was now defined in legal and political terms: there was no human political authority above it, while it was above all other authorities within a definite territory ("sovereignty"); and when "it" acted or was otherwise involved in relations of any kind, this meant that it was the ruler who was thus involved ("personality").

These aspects of legal personality and sovereignty were not entirely absent from medieval conceptions. In particular, they were anticipated in the lawyers' concepts of *civitas sibi princeps*, and *universitas superiorem non recognoscens*, and *rex in regno suo est Imperator regni sui*.[134] There are also important approaches to the modern conception in Marsilius, as well as differences. He does not *define* the state as the supreme ruler or government. But since he holds that the government, whether one ruler or many, must execute the legal enactments of the community or "state," he says that "when the rulers do this, the entire community does it, since the rulers do it in accordance with the legal determination of the community."[135] Here the government is not the state; yet when the government acts, it is the state which acts through the government, in virtue of the government's constitutional subordination to the state. Marsilius never says that "the state" acts or does anything; nor does he explicitly identify the "state" with either the "legislator" or the *uni-*

---

[132] Cf. the judicious remarks by F. M. Powicke, "Reflections on the Medieval State," *Transactions of the Royal Historical Society*, 4th Series, Vol. XIX (1936), pp. 1–18.

[133] Cf., e.g., the three occurrences of *status* within a few lines of one another in Cicero *De re publica* I. xxvi. 42, 44: "rei publicae statum," "incerto statu," "suum statum tenentibus." Only in the first of these occurrences does *status* have any "political" meaning, and then because of the words *rei publicae* which precede it. See *status*, above, pp. lxxviii–lxxiv.

[134] Cf. O. von Gierke, *Political Theories of the Middle Age*, trans. F. W. Maitland (Cambridge, 1900), pp. 96–99; C. N. S. Woolf, *Bartolus of Sassoferrato* (Cambridge, 1913), pp. 70–72, 267, 295–96, 378–81; F. Ercole, *La Politica di Machiavelli* (Rome, 1926), pp. 65 ff.; id., *Da Bartolo all' Althusio* (Florence, 1932), pp. 70 ff.

[135] I. xv. 4.

versitas civium. Yet his aim of differentiating the priestly function from secular rulership carries him far in the direction of a specifically legal-political conception of the state, as for example, when he contrasts "Christ's kingdom (*regnum*) in this world" with "temporal dominion or judgment over contentious acts and its execution by coercive power." [136]

This point is also related to Marsilius' conception of what kind of a "community" the state is. For Aristotle, who is followed in this as in other regards by most of the medieval Aristotelians, the state is a "communication of living well" (ἡ τοῦ εὖ ζῆν κοινωνία, *ipsius bene vivere communicatio*),[137] a "communion of good actions," [138] involving friendship and political virtue. For St. Augustine and his followers, similarly, the state is a "concord." [139] Marsilius, on the other hand, views this "communication" rather as a network of external relations whereby what is "communicated" is the functions and products of the various parts of the state,[140] without the ethical aspects of "communion" or rapport. The Marsilian doctrine thus marks a long step toward the "impersonal" character of modern society, as against the strong commitments to internal rapport and friendliness on which Aristotle had insisted, and which his medieval continuators repeated. In addition, the supremacy of the legislator on which Marsilius insists involves full sovereignty.[141]

Besides these difficulties of meaning in the term "state" itself, there are linguistic complexities. Whereas the Greek language, and to a lesser extent the Latin, have a central stem around which many related words revolve (πολι . . . , *civi* . . .), the English is far less centralized, taking in many different Greek and especially Latin stems.[142] The following table indicates the resulting complexity of translation: [143]

πόλις	civitas	"state" or "city"
πολίτης	civis	"citizen"
πολιτεία	politia	"polity" ["constitution"] [144]
πολίτευμα	politeuma	"government"
πολίτικος	politicus [vir], civilis	"statesman," "political," "civil"
πολιτική [145]	civilis [146] [sc. scientia]	"civil"
πολιτεύειν	civiliter vivere	"live a civil life"

[136] II. iv. 7. [137] *Pol.* III. 10. 1280b 33 (Sus. p. 188).
[138] *Ibid*. Cf. Vol. I, pp. 97–98, 103–4.
[139] *De civitate Dei* I. xv; XIX. xiii. Cf. Vol. I, pp. 95–96.
[140] Cf. I. iv. 3, 5; I. v. 1; and esp. I. xix. 2. See *community*, above, pp. lxxv–lxxvi.
[141] See Vol. I, pp. 256–58. [142] Cf. Barker, *op. cit.*, pp. lxvi, 106.
[143] I use William of Moerbeke's Latin translations of the Greek terms of Aristotle.
[144] See below, p. lxxix.
[145] Aristotle uses this term for "political science," of which ethics is a part: *N. Eth.* I. 2. 1094a 27.
[146] William of Moerbeke's translation in the *Nicomachean Ethics;* printed with Thomas Aquinas' commentary, Lib. I. Lect. 2 (p. 7).

A few remarks on Marsilius' use of these terms must suffice:

Politia is never used by Marsilius in Aristotle's sense of a "constitution" defined as "the order of the state in respect of its ruling officials and especially of the dominant ruler." [147] Marsilius comes closest to this when he says that in one sense a "polity" is "something common to every genus or species of regime or government." [148] As such, "polity" is a general term akin to "government." But this is far from being Aristotle's whole meaning. The reason for this difference is that for Marsilius there is a definite group of persons—the legislator, the whole body of citizens —which controls the order of the ruling officials, including the government. Thus, whereas for Aristotle the constitution is the πολίτευμα (supreme government) [149] in the sense that the government determines what the political order and values of the state will be, for Marsilius the legislator, which is distinct from the government, makes this determination.[150] And whereas for Aristotle many different kinds of constitution are admissible, for Marsilius there is only one legitimate kind, so that he has no need to discuss different kinds of constitution.

Marsilius also uses the *politia* in the sense of a specific kind of government: that in which "each citizen participates in some way in the government . . ." [151]

Politeuma is used only once by Marsilius; [152] he seems not to have understood it. He interprets the phrase "those who are in the government" (*eos in politeumate*) to mean "rebellious, or not caring to live a civil life"! [153] See also *government*.

Civiliter is frequently used by Marsilius. In Roman law this term is regularly opposed to *criminaliter*, and is used to indicate the character of a "civil" as opposed to a "criminal" suit or action at law.[154] Marsilius sometimes uses it in this sense. It is important, however, to grasp the meaning of the term in its Marsilian context. He uses *civiliter* as the adverb corresponding to the noun *civitas* and the adjective *civilis*. Hence

---

[147] *Pol.* III. 6. 1278a 9.
[148] I. viii. 3.
[149] *Pol.* III. 6. 1278a 11.
[150] Cf. Vol. I, pp. 171–74.
[151] I. viii. 3. Cf. *Pol.* III. 5. 1279a 39.
[152] I. xiii. 2.

[153] See Appendix I. It is perhaps noteworthy that Thomas Aquinas refrains from using the word *politeuma* in his commentary on the passages of the *Politics* where Aristotle uses it. Cf. Thomas Aquinas *In octo libros Politicorum Aristotelis expositio* Lib. III. Lects. 5, 6 (Quebec, 1940), pp. 137, 140. William of Ockham uses the term *policernia*, and gives an admirable brief analysis of Aristotle's meaning: *Dialogus* Pars III. Tract. I. Lib. II. cap. vi (Goldast, *Monarchia*, II, 794). Cf. C. H. McIlwain, *The Growth of Political Thought in the West* (New York, 1932), p. 306, n. 3. The term πολίτευμα and its derivatives (πεπολίτευμαι, πολιτεύεσθε) also occur in the New Testament (Philippians 3:20, Acts 23:1, Philippians 1:27), and are rendered by Jerome as *conversatio, conversatus sum*, and *conversamini*, respectively. The Douai translation reads "conversation" and "conversed."

[154] E.g., *Corpus juris civilis, Codex* I. xxix. 2; I. xlix. 1, 8; IX. xxii. 1.

the adverb takes on all the meaning which Marsilius assigns to the various functions of the state. Prominent among these is that pertaining to litigation and judgment at law; hence Marsilius refers to "effecting by civil means (*civiliter*) the reduction of men's contentious acts to due equality or proportion." [155] Likewise, he refers to men's "civil acts" in the sense of acts involving litigation or strife; [156] and Roman law is for him the "science of civil acts." [157] (Sometimes he uses "political or civil acts." [158]) Also, more generally, he uses the phrase *communicantes civiliter:* [159] "those who participate in civil association" (literally, "those who associate [or communicate] civilly"). This phrase is probably from Moerbeke, who renders Aristotle's τινὲς καὶ πολιτεύονται τῶν πολιτευομένων ("some of those who engage in political activity pursue such activity . . .") as *quidam civiliter conversantium civiliter conversantur* . . . [160] Another phrase used much more frequently by Marsilius is *viventes civiliter,* meaning "those who live a civil life." [161] This phrase is again from Moerbeke, who renders Aristotle's πολιτεύονται as *civiliter vivunt.*[162] Another source is Aristotle's references, in the *Nicomachean Ethics,* to the "end of the political life" (τέλος τοῦ πολιτικοῦ βίου,[163] rendered by Moerbeke as *finis civilis vitae* [164]). Likewise Marsilius refers to "civil death" (*mors civilis*).[165] However, Aristotle's meaning in these phrases is somewhat more restrictive than Marsilius'. By πολιτεύειν or βίος πολιτικός Aristotle means the life of active participation in political functions, legislative, governmental, or judicial, aimed at by men desirous of honor, in contrast to the life of contemplation and other values attainable by living in the state. By *vivere civiliter,* on the other hand, Marsilius means not merely such specifically "political" activity but also all the values of secular association. Thus, on the one hand, it does not mean merely living in a state in a territorial sense; but, on the other hand, it does mean a secular life devoted to the pursuit of all those objects of natural desire for which the state exists and hence participating in the political functions which that pursuit involves. Thus the *viventes civiliter* are distinguished not only from beasts and slaves [166] but also

---

155 II. ix. 12.

156 I. iii. 4; I. ix. 7; I. x. 2, 7; I. xii. 1. See Vol. I, p. 61.

157 II. xii. 18, 21; II. xxi. 15.   158 I. x. 2.

159 I. iv. 4.

160 *Pol.* I. 11. 1259a 35 (Sus. p. 49). See also *Pol.* II. 4. 1262b 24 (Sus. p. 71): *qui sic civiliter conversantur =* τοῖς οὕτω πολιτευομένοις.

161 E.g., I. i. 2; I. xvi. 1; II. i. 5; II. ii. 20. Cf. G. de Lagarde, *Marsile de Padoue,* 2d ed. (Paris, 1948), pp. 55–56.

162 *Pol.* I. 7. 1255b 27 (Sus. p. 27).   163 *N. Eth.* I. 5. 1095b 22, 31.

164 In Thomas Aquinas' commentary, Lib. I. Lect. 5 (p. 19).

165 II. xxvi. 12.   166 I. iv. 1.

from the priesthood.[167] The medieval Aristotelians likewise use *vivere civiliter* and *vita civilis* in the more general sense of life in civil association,[168] but without Marsilius' emphases either on strife and litigation or on secularism. These emphases were resumed, however, with detailed technical implications also for political power relations, in Machiavelli's repeated use of the phrase *vivere civile*.[169]

"Civil happiness" (*civilis felicitas*, εὐδαιμονία πολιτική). This is the ultimate aim of human acts in the present world.[170] It comprises all the values which men derive from living in the state. For Aristotle and the other medieval Aristotelians, however, "civil happiness," like "practical happiness," is contrasted with "theoretic happiness," the life of contemplation; this latter is declared to be superior in value.[171]

"Common benefit" (*commune conferens*, κοινὸν συμφέρον). For Aristotle the aiming at the common benefit, as against the private (ἴδιον) interest of the rulers alone, is the chief criterion distinguishing just from unjust forms of constitution.[172] While criteria of the common benefit, in turn, differ from state to state, the chief criterion is virtue.[173] For Marsilius, aiming at the common benefit is only one criterion of a just government, and not the most important one;[174] nor does he specify the common benefit in terms of the virtues other than justice. It is to be noted that Marsilius follows William of Moerbeke's translation of the *Politics* in using the term *conferens*[175] rather than, like Aquinas and other scholastics, *bonum* as the noun which is modified by *commune*.[176] Also, Marsilius frequently uses the expression in the plural, sometimes coupled with *justa*: *justa et conferentia communia*,[177] which I have regularly translated "matters of justice and the common benefit."

"Government" (*principatus*, ἀρχή) and related terms. Just as ἀρχή

---

[167] Cf. ii. xx. 8; ii. xxiv. 1.

[168] Thomas Aquinas *In Eth. Lib. n. Lect. xvi* (p. 688) (the phrase here is "illi qui civiliter conversantur"). Egidius of Rome *De regimine principum* iii. i. 3. John of Paris *De potestate regia et papali* cap. iii (p. 180). Dante *Monarchia* i. v.

[169] *Discorsi sopra . . . Livio* i. iii; i. v; i. ix; i. xix; ii. ii; ii. xix; etc. Cf. also Machiavelli's related phrases "il vero *vivere politico* e la vera quiete d'una città" (*ibid.* i. vi; also ii. introd.). See the extensive discussion of Machiavelli's concept in F. Ercole, *La Politica di Machiavelli* (Rome, 1926), pp. 96 ff.

[170] i. i. 7.   [171] See Vol. I, pp. 63–64.

[172] *Pol.* iii. 6–7. 1278b 30 ff.   [173] *Ibid.* iii. 9. 1280a 8 ff.

[174] i. viii. 3; i. ix. 5–7. See Vol. I, pp. 60, 223, 241; also above, p. xlii.

[175] See Sus. pp. 178, 179, and *passim*. Cf. McIlwain, *op. cit.*, p. 298, n. 2.

[176] Cf., e.g., I. Th. Eschmann, "A Thomistic Glossary on the Principle of the Preëminence of a Common Good," *Mediaeval Studies*, V (1943), 123–65.

[177] i. v. 7, 9; i. x. 4, 5, 6; i. xi. 3; i. xii. 2; i. xiii. 6, 8; i. xiv. 3; i. xv. 7. In some of these passages, *civilia* is used instead of *communia*. Cf. Aristotle *Pol.* vii. 8. 1328b 14: κρίσιν περὶ τῶν συμφερόντων καὶ τῶν δικαίων (Moerbeke: *judicium de conferentibus et justis* [Sus. p. 274]).

means "beginning," that which is first in some order,[178] so *principatus*, deriving from *princeps*, means the "first head" which "initiates" or controls in the political order.[179] I have translated *principatus* sometimes as "government" and sometimes, when it is intended more abstractly, as "rulership." Marsilius also uses the phrase *pars principans* ("ruling part") [180] for the ruler of the state; this phrase is derived from Moerbeke's translation of Aristotle's ἄρχον as *principans* [181] and from Aristotle's conception of the government as one of the "parts" (μέρη) [182] of the state. However, where Aristotle uses ἀρχή for any kind of "rulership" or "governance" over humans, including that over slaves, over children, and over one's wife,[183] Marsilius restricts *principatus* to the government of the state, and uses the term *regimen* (which I have uniformly translated "regime") for the more general relation.[184] *Regimen*, in turn, derives from *regere* ("to rule") and *rectum* ("straight," "right"), with their meaning of "straightness" or "correctness"; [185] *regimen* is thus that which sets forth the "straight" path or "direction" to be followed by those who are subject to it. Related to *regimen*, besides *regere*, are the terms *regula* and *regulare*. Thus Marsilius says that the ruler's function is to "regulate (*regulare*) the civil acts of all the other men in the state." [186]

"Law" (*lex*, νόμος) is the "rule" or "standard" (*regula*) in accordance with which the ruler must effect such regulation of men's civil acts.[187] Such rules are "measures" or "habits" of human acts,[188] and when perfected the rules are the "science or doctrine or universal judgment of matters of civil justice and benefit and of their opposites." [189] Hence the ruler is himself "the standard (*regula*) and measure of every civil act" when he acts "in accordance with the law and the authority given to him." [190] The law is to the ruler as "form" to "matter." [191]

Marsilius gives extensive definitions and discussions of law in three contexts: I. x; II. viii–ix; II. xii. 3–12. In the second context the emphasis

---

[178] Cf. Aristotle *Metaphysics* v. 1. 1012b 34 ff.

[179] On this meaning of ἀρχή, cf. J. L. Myres, *The Political Ideas of the Greeks* (New York, 1927), pp. 139–66; Barker, *op. cit.*, p. lxvii.

[180] I. v. 7; I. ix. 1, 2; I. x. 2; I. xv. 14, and *passim*. Marsilius also frequently uses *principans* alone.

[181] E.g., Sus. pp. 3 (*Pol.* I. 2. 1253a 30, 32; 1252b 6), 261 (*Pol.* VII. 4. 1326b 14, 15).

[182] *Pol.* VII. 8. 1328b 2, 14–15. Cf. *ibid.* IV. 14. 1297b 37.

[183] *Ibid.* I. 2. 1252a 30 ff.; III. 6. 1278b 16 ff.

[184] E.g., I. ii. 4; II. xx. 13.

[185] Cf. Isidore of Seville *Etymologiae* IX. iii. 4 (PL 82. 342); Barker, *op. cit.*, p. lxix.

[186] I. ix. 7; I. xv. 13.

[187] I. x. 1, 2, 6, 7; I. xii. 8; I. xiv. 7; II. viii. 4, 5.

[188] II. viii. 4.   [189] I. x. 3, 4. Cf. I. xii. 2.   [190] I. xvii. 2.

[191] I. x. 2; I. xiv. 10; I. xv. 3; I. xviii. 2. Cf. I. vii. 2. See Vol. I, p. 230.

is primarily on the "matter" of law as consisting in measures of human acts and the science of civil justice. In the third context the emphasis is primarily on the "form" of law as consisting in commands or prohibitions to which coercive sanctions are attached. In the first context both emphases are present, but the coercive aspect is held to be more essential than the aspect of justice inasmuch as even "false cognitions of the just and the beneficial become laws, when there is given a command to observe them. . . ."[192] See also *justice, right.*

In virtue of the ruler's relation to law, Marsilius also refers to him as the "judicial part" (*pars judicialis* or *judicativa,* δικαστική) of the state.[193] The ruler's function is to "judge" (*judicare*) men's acts in accordance with the law, and such "judgment" (*judicium,* δίκη) requires prior inquiry as to (*a*) the nature of the act in question, (*b*) whether it is prohibited by law, and (*c*) whether the accused person has committed it.[194] On completing this inquiry the ruler hands down his judgment, which is a "sentence" of condemnation to or acquittal from punishment in accordance with the law. Such judgment, involving the authority to give such a sentence, is to be distinguished from the judgment which lacks this authority.[195] The former is "coercive" (*coactivum,* ἀναγκαστικόν),[196] the latter not, just as laws too may or may not be coercive.[197]

Following his sentence, the ruler gives a "command" (*praeceptum,* ἐπίταξις) that his sentence be executed, and then there follows "execution" (*executio,* πρᾶξις) of this command.[198] Thus the ruler has both "judicial" and "executive" functions.

At a few points Marsilius also refers to the ruler as the "deliberative part" (*pars consiliativa,* βουλευτική).[199] However, the ruler is not the "deliberative" in the sense in which, according to Aristotle, the deliberative part of the state makes the laws and other basic decisions,[200] but only in the sense that it "deliberates about some matters."[201] Aristotle

[192] I. x. 5.   [193] I. v. 7; I. vii. 1; I. viii. 1; II. vii. 6.

[194] II. x. 4. For a detailed discussion of Marsilius' concept of judgment, see Vol. I, pp. 226–30.

[195] II. ii. 8.

[196] William of Moerbeke uses *coactivum* to translate both ἀναγκαῖον ("necessary") and ἀναγκαστική ("necessitative," "compulsive") where Aristotle writes that "the paternal command does not have . . . coerciveness. . . . But law has coercive force . . ." (*N. Eth.* x. 9. 1180a 20, 22; Moerbeke's translation is found in Aquinas' commentary, Lib. x. Lect. 14, p. 679).

[197] I. x. 4–5; II. viii. 4. See Vol. I, pp. 134–39.

[198] For detailed references both to the *Defensor* and to the Aristotelian sources, see Vol. I, pp. 168–69, 231–33.

[199] I. v. 7, 13; I. vii. 1; I. viii. 3.   [200] *Pol.* IV. 14. 1298a 1 ff.

[201] *Ibid.* IV. 15. 1299a 26.

distinguishes three "parts of all constitutions": deliberative, governmental (ἀρχαὶ), judicial;[202] but this distinction is only a differentiation of functions, not necessarily of the persons who perform these functions. Marsilius does not differentiate the governmental function from the judicial; but he does distinguish both from the "deliberative" insofar as it is legislative.[203] Consequently, the Marsilian government is quite different from Aristotle's πολίτευμα, which is defined as "the dominant authority of states" (τὸ κύριον τῶν πόλεων)[204] and is thus the "dominant governmental body," identical with the "constitution" (πολιτεία).[205] The Aristotelian πολίτευμα has a supremacy which the Marsilian principatus lacks;[206] for the latter, unlike the former, does not make the laws but only enforces them.

"Justice" (justitia, δικαιοσύνη). Marsilius, like the other medievals, holds that the end of law and government is to do justice, and he echoes Aristotle's terminology and distinctions in Book V of the Nicomachean Ethics in his references to this. The recurrent formula is that by justice men's acts "are reduced to due equality or proportion."[207] The justice which reduces (or "brings back") acts to equality is rectificatory justice. The acts in question are "transactions between man and man," some of which are voluntary (like sales or loans), while others are involuntary (like theft and murder). Justice rectifies the inequalities or wrongs brought about by these acts, regarding the men involved as initially equal and restoring equality according to arithmetical proportion whereby what was taken by the act in question is returned or restored. On the other hand, distributive justice reduces acts to due proportion. The acts here in question have to do with the distribution of various common goods like honors or money; and justice distributes these according to merit or desert, thereby following geometrical rather than arithmetical proportion.[208]

The act of the judge in effecting justice Marsilius calls justificatio,[209] which I have usually translated as "bringing to justice." William of Moerbeke uses this term to translate Aristotle's δικαίωμα, which Aristotle defines as "the correction of an act of injustice."[210]

---

202 *Ibid.* IV. 14. 1297b 35 ff.　　203 See Vol. I, p. 231, n. 34, also pp. 172–74.
204 *Pol.* III. 7. 1279a 26 (Sus. p. 178).　205 *Ibid.* III. 6. 1278b 9–11 (Sus. p. 173).
206 Cf. McIlwain, *op. cit.*, p. 306.
207 I. v. 7; I. xii. 8; I. xv. 11; II. viii. 7; II. ix. 12; II. xii. 12.
208 *N. Eth.* v. 2–5. 1130b 30 ff.　　209 I. xvi. 8, 22; I. xix. 12; II. viii. 7; II. xxvi. 19.
210 *N. Eth.* v. 7. 1135a 10–14. Moerbeke's translation is found in Aquinas' commentary, Lib. v. Lect. 12, p. 339. St. Paul uses δικαίωμα and δικαίωσις in Rom. 3:20, 4:25, 5:16, 5:18, and the Vulgate likewise renders this as *justificatio*, while the Douai translation renders it as "justification."

"Right" (*jus*). Marsilius uses this term primarily in the context of his discussion of evangelical poverty; throughout the remainder of the *Defender* he uses rather *lex* ("law"). He distinguishes four meanings of *jus*, according to which it is either identical with *lex;* or an act, habit, or power which is in conformity with *lex;* or an act or habit of particular justice, wherein *jus* is identical with *justum*.[211] The first two of these meanings correspond to what has been called the distinction between "objective" and "subjective" right, i.e., between the norms which regulate human acts and the powers which men have in accordance with those norms. In modern times the term "right" is used primarily in the second, subjective sense, particularly since the French Revolution. Marsilius, as has been said, uses the term *jus* in both senses; so too does William of Ockham after him; whereas Thomas Aquinas uses it almost exclusively in the "objective" sense.[212] Aquinas defines *jus* as "the object of justice," and distinguishes *jus* from *lex* only in that *lex* is "some rationale of *jus*" (*aliqualis ratio juris*).[213] In Roman and canon law and other medieval sources *lex* is likewise made in various ways a species of *jus*, although in Cicero it is rather *lex* which is the basic term.[214] The distinction between *jus* as standard of justice and *lex* as positive law emerges in modern languages other than English in the distinctions *droit-loi, Recht-Gesetz, diritto-legge*. The translation of *jus* as "right" is notoriously misleading because of the modern "subjective" meaning of "right."

"Temperate (*temperatum*, κεκραμένον) and "diseased" (*vitiatum*, ἡμαρτημένον) government. This is Marsilius' fundamental normative distinction of kinds of government. It is derived from Aristotle, but with a difference. Aristotle's term for the good forms of government is usually "right" (ὀρθαὶ, translated *rectae* by Moerbeke),[215] and the primary criterion of rightness is the final cause: the government's aiming at the common benefit. Occasionally, however, Aristotle also uses the phrase "well tempered" (εὖ κεκραμέναι, *bene temperatae*);[216] this seems to refer primarily to the constitution's being a proper "blend" or "mixture" of the various parts of the community.[217] The contrary of these good forms of

---

[211] II. xii. 3–12.   [212] *S. theol.* II. II. qu.57.   [213] *Ibid.* II. II. qu.57. a.1. ad 2.

[214] *Corpus juris civilis, Institutiones* I. ii. 3, 4; Isidore of Seville *Etymologiae* v. ii. 3 (PL 82. 199); *Corpus juris canonici, Decretum Gratiani* Pars I. dist. 1. can. 1–3; dist. 2. can. 1; Cicero *De legibus* I. vi. 19. See also Vol. I, p. 145.

[215] *Pol.* III. 6. 1279a 18, 20 (Sus. p. 177); III. 7. 1279a 24, 29 (Sus. p. 178).

[216] *Ibid.* v. 8. 1307b 30 (Sus. p. 538); IV. 3. 1290a 26 (Sus. p. 384) (here the translation is *bene contemperatae*). See M. Guggenheim, "Marsilius von Padua und die Staatslehre des Aristoteles," *Historische Vierteljahrschrift,* VII (1904), 349.

[217] This is related to but not identical with the polity which is a "mixture" of democracy and oligarchy and to which Aristotle refers as "well mixed" (μεμιγμένη καλῶς, *mixta bene, Pol.* IV. 9. 1294b 35 [Sus. p. 413]).

government is the "diseased," ἡμαρτημέναι, meaning literally the "erroneous" (which Moerbeke renders *vitiatae*); they are also called παρεκβάσεις (*transgressiones*), "perversions" of or "deviations" from the right forms.[218] For Marsilius, the "temperate" or "well-tempered" government preserves the Aristotelian characteristic of reflecting the whole community, but it is primarily characterized by its efficient cause: the government's resting on the election or consent of the subjects.[219] However, other criteria enter in a secondary way, including both aiming at the common benefit and ruling according to law.[220]

"Prudence" (*prudentia*, φρόνησις). Marsilius follows Aristotle in viewing prudence as the virtue whereby men act and deliberate well with regard to human affairs.[221] Thus for Marsilius prudence is one of the qualities of the perfect ruler; [222] those men whom nature generates apt for prudence are the material causes of the "judicial and deliberative part" of the state.[223] Similarly, to make laws requires prudence; [224] hence Marsilius recommends that the preliminary inquiry into matters of justice be left to "those men who are able to have leisure, who are older and experienced in practical affairs, and who are called 'prudent men' . . ." [225] As this passage suggests, Marsilius couples the "prudent" with the "leisured" (*vacantes*, σχολάζοντες).[226] They comprise the "honorable class" (*honorabilitas*) as contrasted with "the common mass" (*vulgus*) who are occupied in "necessary" labor.[227] However, Marsilius also insists that "those who are less learned or who do not have leisure for liberal functions" must nevertheless share in political power, i.e., in "making" or controlling the regulations which become laws, since "they share in the understanding and judgment of practical matters." [228]

"Legislator" (*legislator*, νομοθέτης). For Aristotle the νομοθέτης is primarily a "law-giver" who sets up either laws alone or also a constitution, such as Solon or Lycurgus.[229] He may himself be a ruler.[230] One of the matters with which the "law-giver" who sets forth a constitution will deal is "legislation" (νομοθεσία), i.e., the making of laws within the framework of a constitution.[231] For Marsilius the "legislator" is that which determines what shall be the coercively binding laws of the state.

---

[218] *Ibid.* III. 6. 1279a 20 (Sus. p. 177); III. 7. 1279a 24, 31 (Sus. p. 178).
[219] I. ix. 5. See Vol. I, pp. 60, 223, 241; also above, p. xlii.
[220] I. viii. 2–3; I. ix. 4–6.   [221] *N. Eth.* VI. 5. 1140a 24 ff.
[222] I. xiv. 3–5.   [223] I. vi. 1.
[224] I. x. 4.   [225] I. xii. 1. See I. xiii. 8.   [226] Cf. I. xiii. 4; I. xvi. 21; I. xvii. 4.
[227] I. viii. 3; I. xii. 2; I. xiii. 4, 8; II. xx. 2.   [228] I. xii. 4. See Vol. I, pp. 190–96.
[229] *Pol.* II. 12. 1273b 27–35. Cf. also II. 7. 1266a 31 ff.; II. 8. 1268a 37; IV. 11. 1296a 18–21; VII. 7. 1327b 36; VII. 13. 1332b 9, and *passim*.
[230] *Ibid.* III. 13. 1283b 38; III. 15. 1286a 22.
[231] Cf. *ibid.* IV. 14. 1298a 17 (περὶ τε νόμων θέσεως); 1298a 21 (πρὸς τὰς νομοθεσίας).

He does not distinguish between constitution and laws. The legislator
need not be, like Aristotle's νομοθέτης, the "discoverer" of the laws, nor
is he the ruler who puts them into operation; rather, he decides by his
choice what the laws, in the sense of coercive ordinances, shall be.[232] The
legislator also has other functions, such as electing the ruler [233] and the
priest; [234] but these are all consequent on its primary "legislative" function. And this legislator, according to Marsilius, must be the people, the
whole body of citizens.

"Power" (*potestas*) and related terms. Marsilius does not make any
technical distinctions among the meanings of such terms as *potestas*
("power"), *auctoritas* ("authority"), *jurisdictio* ("jurisdiction"). He frequently employs them interchangeably.[235] In contexts in which right-
fulness has to be distinguished from mere force, he uses *auctoritas* rather
than *potestas*, e.g., where he is discussing the seat of legislative [236] or governmental [237] authority. But *potestas* too is distinguished from force;
for the latter, Marsilius uses *violentia* [238] or *potentia*.[239] Yet even *potentia*
is used in a neutral sense; sometimes it is analogized to a natural power
or "potentiality" (δύναμις).[240] The chief distinction with respect to all
these terms except *violentia* is not between the legal and the illegal, or
between the normative or *de jure* and the positive or *de facto*, but between the coercive and the non-coercive.[241] When Marsilius says that
someone "has" coercive power or authority or jurisdiction, or that this
"belongs" to him, he is referring to the whole context of arguments
from moral values and legal-political functions in terms of which his
doctrine proceeds to justify such "having" or "belonging."

"Plenitude of power" (*plenitudo potestatis*). Marsilius distinguishes
eight different meanings of this term.[242] These distinctions involve the
extent of the objects falling under the power, but the mode of power
remains constant: it is power which is "following every impulse of the
will," and is "limited by no law." [243] James of Viterbo, who upheld the
papal plenitude of power, listed six attributes of such power, including

[232] I. xii. 2–3. On the concept of the legislator, see Vol. I, pp. 168–75.
[233] I. xv. 2. See Vol. I, pp. 237 ff.   [234] II. xvii. 9. See Vol. I, p. 281.
[235] See, e.g., I. xix. 5, 8, 9; II. iv. 2, and *passim*.
[236] I. xii. 2.   [237] I. xv. 1.   [238] I. ix. 8.
[239] I. xii. 6; I. xiv. 8; II. ix. 9.
[240] See I. xv. 5–6. William of Moerbeke renders Aristotle's δύναμις as *potentia* (e.g., *Pol.*
IV. 15. 1300b 8, 9 [Sus. p. 451]) and ἐξουσία as *potestas* (*ibid.* III. 1. 1275b 18 [Sus. p. 155];
v. 11. 1315a 14 [Sus. p. 584]). The New Testament frequently couples ἐξουσία and δύναμις
(e.g., Luke 4:36, 9:1; I Cor. 15:24; Eph. 1:21; Rev. 17:13); the Vulgate uniformly renders
the former as *potestas* and the latter as *virtus*. *Potentia* is used to translate κράτος (e.g., Eph.
1:19).
[241] See above, p. xxxvi; also Vol. I, p. 138.   [242] II. xxiii. 3.   [243] See also I. xi. 8.

the following: every Christian is subject to it; it includes all power, both spiritual and temporal, given by God for the governance of believers; all power in the church is derived from it; no human power exceeds, judges, or limits it, but it exceeds, judges, and limits all others; it is not restricted by the laws posited by it.[244] Egidius of Rome defined plenitude of power in general as follows: "plenitude of power is in some agent when that agent can do without a second cause whatever it can do with a second cause." [245] In this sense, whereby the agent can dispense with all intermediaries in achieving its effects, Egidius says that the pope has plenitude of power within the church; [246] but subsequently he gives a list of attributes of plenitude of power much like that of James of Viterbo.[247] There is a distant connection between this conception and the *plena potestas* of Roman law whereby a principal gave to a deputy "full power" to act for him in some task or function (*Corpus juris civilis, Codex* II. xii. 10). In the later middle ages this *plena potestas* was generalized, particularly in England, to apply to the relation between communities and the representatives they sent to Parliament.[248] The papalists, in an analogous way, thought of the pope's relation to God as that of deputy to principal (*vicarius Dei*). But this very limitation meant that the pope was only a judge according to divine and natural law, not a full sovereign who could make his own laws without limitation.[249]

"Dominant" (*dominans,* κύριον) and related terms: *dominus, dominium, dominatio, dominari.* These terms are used in a variety of traditions echoed by Marsilius, and I have had to translate them in different ways, depending on the context: "dominant," "lord," "master," "ruler," "owner"; "have supreme authority," "dominate"; "dominion," "lordship," "ownership." In his technical discussion of the meanings of *dominium* Marsilius defines it as the "principal power to lay claim to some thing rightfully acquired." [250] But he also uses this and its related terms in other, political meanings which center generically around the concept of control or power. Three such meanings may be distinguished:

---

[244] *De regimine Christiano* II. ix (p. 273). A similar interpretation, with main emphasis on the unlimited character of plenitude of power, is found in St. Bernard *De consideratione* II. viii (PL 182. 752); quoted by Marsilius, II. xxviii. 11.

[245] *De ecclesiastica potestate* III. ix (p. 190).   [246] *Ibid.* III. ix (p. 191).

[247] *Ibid.* III. x (pp. 196–99). See Vol. I, p. 8.

[248] See J. G. Edwards, "The *Plena Potestas* of English Parliamentary Representatives," in *Oxford Essays in Medieval History Presented to H. E. Salter* (Oxford, 1934), pp. 141–54; and G. Post, "*Plena Potestas* and Consent in Medieval Assemblies," *Traditio,* I (1943), 355–408.

[249] See McIlwain, *op. cit.,* pp. 284–87; also Vol. I, pp. 170, 256.

[250] II. xii. 13.

(1) any kind of ruler or power; (2) supreme power; (3) despotic power.
(1) Marsilius sometimes uses *dominans* and *dominium* in the first sense
to refer to the ruler or government of the state.[251] Here he follows Aristotle, who sometimes refers to the ruler's relation to his subjects as κύριος,
which Moerbeke translates *dominans*. But since Marsilius' ruler, unlike
Aristotle's, never has supreme legislative authority, the meanings are
likewise different. (2) In the second sense Marsilius quotes frequently
the scriptural reference to Jesus, as supreme power, as "lord of lords." [252]
But in the main he follows Aristotle-Moerbeke; [253] and I have usually
rendered *dominans* here either as "dominant" or as "having supreme
authority," although sometimes I have had to use "govern." In these
contexts Aristotle is referring to the "dominance" of the laws or of the
"multitude" which should be supreme in authority, or to the ruler's supreme control in various matters. Translators of the *Politics* frequently
render κύριον as "sovereign," but I have avoided this because of its possible misleading connotations. Whether Aristotle's κύριον is sovereign
in anything like the modern senses found in Bodin or (differently) in
Hobbes is a disputed question; [254] since Aristotle insists that the laws
must be κύριαι,[255] this seems different from the modern legislative sovereign who is subject as such to no law, or at least no positive law. Marsilius' conception of the legislator, on the other hand, anticipates this
modern conception of sovereignty,[256] but he uses *auctoritas* and *potestas*
as well as *dominans* in referring to the legislator. (3) In the third sense,
where *dominatio* means despotic rule or "domination," Marsilius follows
mainly the patristic tradition, which echoes that of Rome,[257] although
this meaning is also found in Aristotle-Moerbeke.[258] In this sense,
dominatio implies *servitus* ("slavery") and hence the loss of liberty. This
is close to the sense in which Jesus says that "The kings of the gentiles

---

[251] i. viii. 2, 3; ii. iv. 3–5.

[252] Rev. 19:16 (κύριος κυρίων, Vulgate: *dominus dominantium*), quoted I. xix. 11; II. xiv.
5; II. xxi. 20; II. xxv. 18.

[253] I. xi. 4, quoting *Pol.* III. 11. 1282b 2 (Sus. p. 198) (κυρίους = *dominas*); I. xiii. 4,
I. xv. 2, quoting *ibid.* III. 11. 1282a 38 (Sus. p. 197); I. xiv. 5, quoting *ibid.* III. 11. 1282b 4
(Sus. p. 198) (κυρίους = *dominos*); I. xiv. 5, quoting *ibid.* III. 16. 1287b 16 (Sus. p. 231)
(κύριαι = *dominantes*); I. xiv. 6, quoting *ibid.* II. 11. 1272b 41 (Sus. p. 138).

[254] See, e.g., McIlwain, *op. cit.*, pp. 80–81; Barker, *op. cit.*, pp. lxvii–lxviii.

[255] *Pol.* III. 11. 1282b 2.   [256] See Vol. I, pp. 256–58.

[257] On the Roman interpretation of *dominatio*, see F. Schulz, *Principles of Roman Law*
(Oxford, 1936), pp. 140–44.

[258] In many passages of Book I of the *Politics* Moerbeke renders Aristotle's δεσπόζον,
δεσπότης, δεσπόζειν as *dominans, dominus, dominari* (e.g., I. 2. 1252a 32, 34; I. 3. 1253b 6;
I. 6. 1255b 7, 11 [Sus. pp. 3, 4, 11, 25]). In Book III, however, where κύριον is rendered
dominans, Moerbeke renders δεσπότης and δεσποτεία by *despotes* and *despotia* (III. 6. 1278b
33, 35 [Sus. p. 175]).

lord it (κατακυριεύουσιν, Vulgate *dominantur*) over them."[259] It is also in this sense that Marsilius quotes Origen's comment that secular rulers "are not content to rule their subjects, but try to exercise violent lordship (*violenter dominari*) over them,"[260] as well as Chrysostom's statement that "The rulers of the world exist in order to lord it (*dominentur*) over their subjects, to cast them into slavery . . ."[261] There is little trace in Marsilius of that use, found in Egidius of Rome's *De ecclesiastica potestate* and subsequently in Richard Fitzralph and John Wyclif, whereby *dominium* is analogized universally to signify all the relations of superiority and control in the entire universe.[262]

"Discretion" (*arbitrium*). Marsilius uses this term for the most part to mean the power or act of making decisions or judgments without any legal or other limitation. The term occurs most frequently in I. xi, where *lex* and the *arbitrium* of the ruler are the two alternatives considered as the bases of the ruler's judgments. Occasionally Marsilius uses *arbitrium* in a more general sense to mean any kind of human (as against divine) power of free decision; here I have translated it as "discretionary will" (I. ix. 2) or as "decision" (I. xii. 1).

"Religion" (*secta*). Marsilius uses this term regularly to refer to any system of religious law; in this sense he also uses the term "law" (*lex*) itself.[263] Thus at one point he writes: "such are divine laws for the most part, which are called by the common name 'religions' (*sectae*)."[264] This is the third meaning of "law" which Marsilius distinguishes, where the term means "the standard containing admonitions for voluntary human acts according as these are ordered toward glory or punishment in the future world. . . . In this sense of the term law all religions (*sectae*), such as that of Mohammed or of the Persians, are called laws in whole or in part. . . ."[265] This use of "law" is of course related to the whole Stoic-Christian tradition of divine law; but Marsilius, like the other Averroists, uses it in an "indifferentist" sense to refer to any system of religious law, true or false.[266] The term *secta* is likewise generalized by Marsilius. Thomas Aquinas uses *secta* to mean heresy,[267] although some-

---

[259] Matt. 20:25; Luke 22:24; Mark 10:47. Quoted by Marsilius, II. iv. 13; II. xvi. 10, 11; II. xxiv. 8; II. xxviii. 24.

[260] II. iv. 13.   [261] *Ibid.*

[262] There is a faint echo of this at II. xiv. 5, 23.

[263] I. v. 10, 11; I. x. 7; I. xix. 12; II. viii. 4–5; II. xxx. 4.

[264] II. viii. 4.   [265] I. x. 3.

[266] Cf. Vol. I, p. 84, n. 45; also Lagarde, *Marsile*, p. 90.

[267] *S. theol.* II. II. qu.11. a.1. ad 3; a.2. arg. 1; *Contra gentiles* I. vi. At two points (II. xvi. 17; II. xx. 1) Marsilius likewise uses *secta* in this sense; here I have rendered it "sect."

times he uses it for any school, like that of the Peripatetics.[268] According to Isidore of Seville, who also couples the term with heretical error, *secta* etymologically is derived from that which one follows and upholds.[269] Jerome translates St. Paul's αἵρεσις as *secta;*[270] but here Paul is using the term in a neutral sense to mean the path of faith which he has chosen.

[268] *S. theol.* II. 1. qu. 59. a.2. Resp.
[269] *Etymologiae* VIII. iii (PL 82. 296–97): "Secta a sequendo, et tenendo nominata."
[270] Acts 26:5; cf. *ibid.* 24:14.

LIST OF FREQUENT REFERENCES
AND ABBREVIATIONS

Aristotle. Works. Ed. I. Bekker. Berlin, 1831–70.

Augustinus Triumphus. Summa de ecclesiastica potestate. Augsburg, 1473.

Bigongiari = D. Bigongiari. "Notes on the Text of the *Defensor Pacis*," *Speculum*, VII (1932), 36–49.

Corpus juris canonici. Ed. E. Friedberg. Leipzig, 1879–81.

Corpus juris civilis. Ed. P. Kruger *et al.* Berlin, 1908.

Dante Alighieri. De monarchia. In E. Moore, ed., *Le opere di Dante Alighieri* (Oxford, 1924), pp. 339–76.

Defensor minor = Marsilius of Padua. Defensor minor. Ed. C. K. Brampton. Birmingham, 1922.

Egidius of Rome. De ecclesiastica potestate. Ed. R. Scholz. Weimar, 1929.

—— De regimine principum. Venice, 1498.

Goldast, *Monarchia* = Monarchia sancti Romani Imperii. Ed. M. Goldast. 3 vols. Frankfort, 1611–14.

James of Viterbo. De regimine Christiano. Ed. H. X. Arquillière. Paris, 1926.

John of Jandun. Quaestiones in duodecim libros Metaphysicae. Venice, 1525.

John of Paris. De potestate regia et papali. In D. J. Leclerq, ed., *Jean de Paris et l'ecclésiologie du XIII*ᵉ *siècle* (Paris, 1942), pp. 173–260.

Martinus Polonus. Chronicon pontificum et imperatorum. In MGH, *Scriptores,* Vol. XXII.

MGH = Monumenta Germaniae historica.

Peter Lombard. Collectanea in omnes D. Pauli Apostoli epistolas. In PL 191–92.

—— Sententiarum libri quatuor. In PL 192.

Peter of Auvergne. In Politicorum Aristotelis libros commentarium. In *Thomae Aquinatis opera omnia* (Parma, 1861), Vol. XXI. (Completion of Thomas Aquinas' commentary.)

PG = Patrologiae cursus completus, series Graeca. Ed. J. P. Migne. Paris, 1857–66.

PL = Patrologiae cursus completus, series Latina. Ed. J. P. Migne. Paris, 1844–64.

Previté-Orton = The *Defensor Pacis* of Marsilius of Padua. Ed. C. W. Previté-Orton. Cambridge, 1928.

Pseudo-Isidore = Decretales pseudo-Isidorianae. Ed. P. Hinschius. Leipzig, 1873.

Ptolemy of Lucca. De regimine principum. Ed. J. Mathis. Turin, 1924. (Completion of Thomas Aquinas' work of same name.)

Scholz = Marsilius von Padua, *Defensor pacis*. Ed. Richard Scholz. Hanover, 1932.

Sus. = Aristotelis Politicorum libri octo cum vetusta translatione Guilelmi de Moerbeka. Ed. F. Susemihl. Leipzig, 1872.

Thomas Aquinas. Catena aurea in quatuor evangelia. In *Opera omnia* (Parma, 1861), Vols. XI–XII.

—— De regimine principum. Ed. J. Mathis. Turin, 1924.

—— In decem libros Ethicorum Aristotelis ad Nicomachum expositio. Ed. A. M. Pirotta. Turin, 1934.

—— In Politicorum Aristotelis libros commentarium. In *Opera omnia* (Parma, 1861), Vol. XXI. (Also used: In octo libros Politicorum Aristotelis expositio seu De rebus civilibus. Quebec, 1940.)

—— Summa theologica. Turin, 1938.

Vol. I = A. Gewirth. Marsilius of Padua, The Defender of Peace. Volume I: Marsilius of Padua and Medieval Political Philosophy. New York, 1951.

William of Moerbeke. Latin Translation of Aristotle's *Nicomachean Ethics*. In Thomas Aquinas, *In decem libros Ethicorum* (see above).

—— Latin Translation of Aristotle's *Politics*. In Sus. (see above).

THE DEFENSOR PACIS
IN ENGLISH TRANSLATION

THE DEFENDER OF PEACE

DISCOURSE ONE

CHAPTER I: ON THE GENERAL AIM OF THE DISCUS-
SION, THE CAUSE OF THAT AIM, AND THE DIVISION OF
THE BOOK

Tranquillity, wherein peoples prosper and the welfare of nations is preserved, must certainly be desirable to every state. For it is the noble mother of the good arts. Permitting the steady increase of the race of mortals, it extends their powers and enhances their customs. And he who is perceived not to have sought for it is recognized to be ignorant of such important concerns.[1]

THE benefits and fruits of the tranquillity or peace of civil regimes were set forth by Cassiodorus in this passage of his first epistle. Exhibiting through these great goods the greatest good of man, sufficiency of life, which no one can attain without peace and tranquillity, Cassiodorus aimed thereby to arouse in men the desire to have peace with one another and hence tranquillity. In this aim he was in accord with what the blessed Job said in his twenty-second chapter: "Be at peace, and thereby thou shalt have the best fruits."[2] Indeed, it was for this reason that Christ, son of God, decreed that peace would be the sign and messenger of his rebirth, when he wanted the heavenly choir to sing: "Glory to God in the highest: and on earth peace to men of good will."[3] For this same reason, too, he often wished peace to his disciples. Whence John: "Jesus came and stood amid his disciples and said, 'Peace be to you.'"[4] Counseling them concerning the maintenance of peace with one another, he said, in Mark: "Have peace among you."[5] And he taught them not only to have peace among themselves, but also to wish it to others, whence in Matthew:

---

[1] Cassiodorus *Variae* I. i (MGH, *Auctores antiqui*, XII, 10).
[2] Job 22:21. [3] Luke 2:14. [4] John 20:19. [5] Mark 9:50.

"When you come into the house, salute it, saying: 'Peace be to this house.' " [6]
Peace, again, was the heritage which he bequeathed to his disciples at the
time of his passion and death, when he said, in the fourteenth chapter of
John: "Peace I leave with you: my peace I give unto you." [7] And like
Christ, his true heirs and imitators, the apostles, wished peace to the men
to whom they sent epistles containing evangelical lessons and admonitions,
for they knew that the fruits of peace would be the greatest goods, as was
shown from Job and more fully exhibited through Cassiodorus.

2. Since, however, "contraries are [essentially] productive of contraries," [8] from discord, the opposite of tranquillity, the worst fruits and
troubles will befall any civil regime or state. This can readily be seen, and
is obvious to almost all men, from the example of the Italian state. For
while the inhabitants of Italy lived peacefully together, they experienced
those sweet fruits of peace which have been mentioned above, and from
and in those fruits they made such great progress that they brought the
whole habitable world under their sway. But when discord and strife
arose among them, their state was sorely beset by all kinds of hardships
and troubles and underwent the dominion of hateful foreign nations.
And in the same way Italy is once again battered on all sides because of
strife and is almost destroyed, so that it can easily be invaded by anyone
who wants to seize it and who has any power at all. Nor is such an outcome astonishing, for, as Sallust attests, writing about Catiline: "By concord small things increase, by discord great things perish." [9] Misled
through discord into the bypath of error, the Italian natives are deprived
of the sufficient life, undergoing the gravest hardships instead of the quiet
they seek, and the harsh yoke of tyrants instead of liberty; and finally,
they have become so much unhappier than citizens of other states that their
ancestral name, which used to give glory and protection to all who appealed to it, is now, to their ignominy, cast into their teeth by the other
nations.

3. Into this dire predicament, then, the miserable men are dragged
because of their discord and strife, which, like the illness of an animal,
is recognized to be the diseased disposition of the civil regime. Although
strife has many original causes, almost all those which can emerge in the
usual ways were described by the foremost of the philosophers in his *Civil
Science*.[10] Besides these, however, there is one singular and very obscure
cause by which the Roman empire has long been troubled and is still

---

[6] Matthew 10:12.   [7] John 14:27.
[8] Aristotle *Politics* v. 8. 1307b 29.   [9] Sallust *Jugurtha* x. vi.
[10] See Aristotle *Politics* v, *passim*.

troubled. This cause is very contagious and prone to creep up on all other cities and states; in its greediness it has already tried to invade most of them. Neither Aristotle nor any other philosopher of his time or before could have discerned the origin and species of this cause. For it was and is a certain perverted opinion (to be exposed by us below) which came to be adopted as an aftermath of the miraculous effect produced by the supreme cause long after Aristotle's time; an effect beyond the power of the lower nature and the usual action of causes in things. This sophistic opinion, wearing the guise of the honorable and beneficial, is utterly pernicious to the human race and, if unchecked, will eventually bring unbearable harm to every city and country.

4. The fruits of peace or tranquillity, then, are the greatest goods, as we have said, while those of its opposite, strife, are unbearable evils. Hence we ought to wish for peace, to seek it if we do not already have it, to conserve it once it is attained, and to repel with all our strength the strife which is opposed to it. To this end individual brethren, and in even greater degree groups and communities, are obliged to help one another, both from the feeling of heavenly love and from the bond or law of human society. This admonition Plato also gives us, as Tully attests in the first book of his treatise *On Duties,* when he said: "We were not born for ourselves alone; to part of us our native land lays claim, and to part, our friends." To this sentence Tully adds: "And so, as the Stoics were wont to say, the things that grow in the earth are all created for the use of men; but men are born for the sake of men. In this we ought to follow the lead of nature, and to bring forth common utilities for all." [11] But it would be no small common utility, indeed it is rather a necessity, to unmask the sophism of this singular cause of wars which threatens no small harm to all states and communities. Hence, whoever is willing and able to discern the common utility is obliged to give this matter his vigilant care and diligent efforts. For while this sophism remains concealed, this pestilence can in no way be avoided, nor its pernicious effect be completely uprooted from states or cities.

5. This task should not be neglected by anyone because of fear or laziness or any other blemish. For, as it is written in the second epistle to Timothy, Chapter 1: "God has not given us the spirit of fear, but of power and of love": [12] the power and love, I say, of spreading the truth; whence the Apostle continues: "Be not thou therefore ashamed of the

---

[11] Cicero *De officiis* I. vii. 22. The reference to Plato is Epistle IX. 358A (generally regarded as spurious); see also *Laws* XI. 923A.

[12] II Timothy 1:7–8.

testimony of our Lord." This was the testimony of the truth, for the bearing of which Christ said he had come into the world when he stated, in the eighteenth chapter of John: "For this was I born and for this came I into the world, that I should give testimony to the truth": [13] that truth, namely, which leads the human race to eternal salvation. Following the example of Christ, therefore, we must strive to teach the truth whereby the aforesaid pestilence of civil regimes may be warded off from the human race, especially the worshipers of Christ—the truth which leads to the salvation of civil life, and which also is of no little help for eternal salvation. Such striving is all the more obligatory for that person in whom the giver of graces has inspired a greater understanding of these things; and he who has the knowledge and the ability for this, but yet, like an ingrate, neglects it, commits a grave sin, as James attested in the fourth chapter of his canonic epistle, when he said: "To him who knoweth to do good and doeth it not, to him it is sin." [14] For this evil, the common enemy of the human race, will not be completely cut down, nor will the pernicious fruits which it has thus far produced be arrested, unless the iniquity of its cause or root is first revealed and denounced. For by no other path can the coercive power of rulers safely enter upon the final rout of the shameful patrons and stubborn defenders of this evil.

6. And so I, a son of Antenor,[15] heeding and obeying the aforesaid admonitions of Christ, of the saints, and of the philosophers, moved also by the spirit of an understanding of these things (if any grace has been given me), and of confidence sent to me from above (for as James attests in the first chapter of his epistle: "Every best gift and every perfect gift is from above, coming down from the Father of lights"); [16] acting from reverence for the giver, from love of spreading the truth, from fervent affection for country and brethren, from pity for the oppressed, from a desire to save them, to recall the oppressors from the bypath of error, and to arouse the resistance of those who suffer such things when they can and should combat them; and beholding in you especially, most exalted Ludwig, emperor [17] of the Romans, God's servant, who shall give to this task that external fulfillment of it which you desire, and who by some special ancient birthright, as well as by your singularly heroic and outstanding virtue, have a firmly ingrained love of wiping out heresies, upholding and preserving the catholic truth and every other worthy discipline, uprooting vice, encouraging virtuous pursuits, extinguishing strife, and spreading and

---

[13] John 18:37.   [14] James 4:17.
[15] Antenor was the legendary founder of Padua. Cf. Virgil *Aeneid* i. 242–49.
[16] James 1:17.
[17] This is the only place in the *Defender* where Marsilius refers to Ludwig as emperor.

nourishing peace or tranquillity [18] everywhere—I have written down the sentences which follow, after a period of diligent and intense study, thinking that these may be of some help to your vigilant majesty, who bestows careful attention upon the above-mentioned problems and others which may occur, as well as upon all matters affecting the public welfare.

7. It is my purpose, therefore, with God's help, to expose only this singular cause of strife. For to reiterate the number and nature of those causes which were set forth by Aristotle would be superfluous; but this cause which Aristotle could not have known, and which no one after him who could know it has undertaken to investigate, we wish to unmask so that it may henceforth be readily excluded from all states or cities, and virtuous rulers and subjects live more securely in tranquillity. This is the desirable outcome which I propose at the beginning of this work; an outcome necessary for those who would enjoy civil happiness, which seems the best of the objects of desire possible to man in this world, and the ultimate aim of human acts.[19]

8. I shall divide my proposed work into three discourses. In the first I shall demonstrate my views by sure methods discovered by the human intellect, based upon propositions self-evident to every mind not corrupted by nature, custom, or perverted emotion. In the second discourse, the things which I shall believe myself to have demonstrated I shall confirm by established testimonies of the eternal truth, and by the authorities of its saintly interpreters and of other approved teachers of the Christian faith, so that this book may stand by itself, needing no external proof. From the same source too I shall refute the falsities opposed to my conclusions, and expose the intricately obstructive sophisms of my opponents. In the third discourse, I shall infer certain conclusions or useful lessons which the citizens, both rulers and subjects, ought to observe, conclusions having an evident certainty from our previous findings. Each of these discourses I shall divide into chapters, and each chapter into more or less paragraphs depending upon the length of the chapter. One advantage of this division will be ease for the readers in finding what they look for when they are referred from later to earlier discourses and chapters. From this will follow a second advantage: a shortening of the volume. For when we assume in later pages some truth, either for itself or for the demonstration of other things, whose proof or certainty has been sufficiently set forth in preceding sections, instead of trifling with the proof all over again,

---

[18] As this passage indicates, Marsilius conceives the ruler as the "defender of peace." See also below, I. xix. 3.

[19] This emphasis on secular happiness as the ultimate value is noteworthy. See Vol. I, p. 78.

we shall send the reader back to the discourse, chapter, and paragraph in which the proof was originally given, so that thus he may easily be able to find the certainty of the proposition in question.

CHAPTER II: ON THE FIRST QUESTIONS IN THIS BOOK, AND THE DISTINCTION OF THE VARIOUS MEANINGS OF THE TERM "STATE"

ENTERING upon our proposed task, we wish first to show what are the tranquillity and intranquillity of the state or city; and first the tranquillity, for if this be not clear, one is necessarily ignorant also of what is intranquillity. Since, however, both of these seem to be dispositions of the city or state (let this be assumed from Cassiodorus), we shall consequently make clear what must be revealed at the very outset; namely, what is the state or city, and why. Through this, the definitions of tranquillity and of its opposite will be more readily apparent.

2. Following the aforesaid order for the definition of the tranquillity of the city or state, we must notice, in order to prevent ambiguity from entering our project, that the term "state" (*regnum*) has many meanings. In one sense it means a number of cities (*civitatum*) or provinces contained under one regime; in which sense a state does not differ from a city with respect to species of polity but rather with respect to quantity. In another sense the term "state" signifies a certain species of temperate polity or regime, which Aristotle calls "temperate monarchy";[1] in this sense a state may consist in a single city as well as in many cities, as was the case around the time of the rise of civil communities, for then there was usually one king in a single city. The third and most familiar sense of this term is a combination of the first and the second. In its fourth sense it means something common to every species of temperate regime, whether in a single city or in many; it was in this sense that Cassiodorus used it in the passage we quoted at the beginning of this book, and this, too, is the sense in which we shall use the term in our discussions of the matters under inquiry.[2]

3. Now we must define tranquillity and its opposite. Let us assume with

---

[1] See Aristotle *Politics* III. 7. 1279a 34; cf. ibid. v. 8. 1307b 30.

[2] This decision to use the term *regnum* to mean "something common to every species of temperate regime" is unique among the medieval Aristotelians in two respects, for the others use the term in Marsilius' third sense alone, i. e., as signifying a *royal monarchy* composed of a *number of cities*. See Vol. I, pp. 117, 126–27.

Aristotle in his *Politics*, Book I, Chapter 2, and Book V, Chapter 3, that the state is like an animate nature or animal.[3] For just as an animal well disposed in accordance with nature is composed of certain proportioned parts ordered to one another and communicating their functions mutually and for the whole, so too the state is constituted of certain such parts when it is well disposed and established in accordance with reason. The relation, therefore, of the state and its parts to tranquillity will be seen to be similar to the relation of the animal and its parts to health. The trustworthiness of this inference we can accept from what all men comprehend about each of these relations. For they think that health is the best disposition of an animal in accordance with nature, and likewise that tranquillity is the best disposition of a state established in accordance with reason. Health, moreover, as the more experienced physicists describe it, is the good disposition of the animal whereby each of its parts can perfectly perform the operations belonging to its nature; according to which analogy tranquillity will be the good disposition of the city or state whereby each of its parts will be able perfectly to perform the operations belonging to it in accordance with reason and its establishment. And since a good definition consignifies contraries, intranquillity will be the diseased disposition of the city or state, like the illness of an animal, whereby all or some of its parts are impeded from performing the operations belonging to them, either entirely or to the extent required for complete functioning.[4]

In this analogical way, then, we have defined tranquillity and its opposite, intranquillity.

CHAPTER III: ON THE ORIGIN OF THE CIVIL COMMUNITY

HAVING defined tranquillity as the good disposition of the state for the functioning of its parts, we must now examine what the state is in itself, and why;[1] what and how many are its primary parts;[2] what is the function appropriate to each part,[3] their causes,[4] and their order in relation to one another.[5] For these are the main points required for the perfect determination of tranquillity and its opposite.

---

[3] See *Politics* I. 5. 1254a 31 ff.; V. 3. 1302b 34 ff. Cf. *ibid*. VI. 4. 1290a 24 ff.

[4] For the background of these definitions of tranquillity and intranquillity, and the uniqueness of Marsilius' interpretations of them, see Vol. I, pp. 95 ff.

[1] See below, I. iv. 1, 2. [2] I. iv. 3–4; I. v. 1. [3] I. v. 5–13; I. vi.
[4] I. vii. [5] I. viii. 1; I. xv. 14.

2. However, before discussing the state and its species or kinds, since the state is the perfect community we must first trace the origin of civil communities and of their regimes and modes of living. From the imperfect kinds, men have advanced to perfect communities, regimes, and modes of living in them. For from the less to the more perfect is always the path of nature and of its imitator, art.[6] And men do not think that they have scientific knowledge of each thing unless they "know its first causes and first principles down to the elements." [7]

3. Following this method, then, we must note that civil communities had small beginnings in diverse regions and times, and growing gradually came at length to completion, just as we said happens in every process of nature or of art. For the first and smallest combination of human beings, wherefrom the other combinations emerged, was that of male and female, as the foremost of the philosophers says in the *Politics,* Book I, Chapter 1,[8] and as appears more fully from his *Economics.*[9] From this combination there were generated other humans, who first occupied one household; from these, more combinations of the same kind were formed, and so great was the procreation of children that a single household did not suffice for them, but many households had to be made. A number of these households was called a village or hamlet, and this was the first community, as is also written in the above-cited treatise.[10]

4. So long as men were in a single household, all their actions, especially those we shall henceforth call "civil," were regulated by the elder among them as being more discerning, but apart from laws or customs, because these could not yet have been discovered. Not only were the men of a single household ruled in this way, but so too was the first community, called the village. However, in some villages the case was different. For although the head of a single household might have been allowed to pardon or to punish domestic injuries entirely according to his own will and pleasure, this would not have been allowed the head of the first community called the village. For in this community the elder had to regulate matters of justice and benefit by some reasonable ordinance or quasi-natural law,[11] because thus it seemed appropriate to all by a certain equity, not as a re-

---

[6] See Aristotle *Physics* II. 8. 199a 9 ff.   [7] *Ibid.* I. 1. 184a 13.

[8] Aristotle *Politics* I. 2. 1252a 26 ff.   [9] Pseudo-Aristotle *Economics* I. 3. 1343b 8 ff.

[10] *Politics* I. 2. 1252b 9 ff. Aristotle, however, does not say that the village is the "first community," for he calls both the family and its several component relationships "communities." He says only that the village is "the first community for the sake of more than daily needs."

[11] For a similar interpretation of *lex naturalis* in the sense of a "law" which is primitive and unwritten, see James of Viterbo *De regimine Christiano* II. vii (ed. H. X. Arquillière [Paris, 1926], p. 229). See also below, II. xii. 7–8.

sult of prolonged inquiry, but solely by the common dictate of reason and a certain duty of human society.

The cause of this difference of regime in a single household and in a village is and was as follows. If someone in the single and first household or domestic family had killed or otherwise offended his brother, then the head of the household, if he so desired, was allowed not to give the wrongdoer the extreme penalty without any dangerous consequences resulting therefrom, because the injury seemed to have been done to the father alone, who forgave it; and because of the paucity of men; and again because it was less unfortunate and sorrowful for the father to lose one son than two. Our first ancestor, Adam, seems to have acted in this way when his firstborn son, Cain, killed his brother Abel. For there is properly no civil justice of a father in relation to his son, as Aristotle wrote in Book IV of the *Ethics*, the treatise on justice.[12] On the other hand, in the first community, the village or hamlet, such procedure was not and would not be allowed, because the case here was different from that of the family; indeed, unless injuries were avenged or equalized by the elder, there would have arisen fighting and the separation of the villagers.[13]

Villages having multiplied and the community grown larger because of increasing procreation, they were still ruled by one man, either because of a lack of many prudent men or through some other cause, as is written in the *Politics*, Book III, Chapter 9.[14] The ruler, however, was the elder or the man who was regarded as better, although the regulations of these communities were less imperfect than those by which the single village or hamlet was ordered. Those first communities, however, did not have so great a differentiation and ordering of parts, or so large a quantity of necessary arts and rules of living, as were gradually to be found afterwards in perfect communities. For sometimes the same man was both ruler and farmer or shepherd, like Abraham and several others after him; but in perfect communities this was not expedient nor would it be allowed.

5. These communities having gradually increased, men's experience became greater, more perfect arts and rules and ways of living were discovered, and also the parts of communities were more fully differentiated. Finally, the things which are necessary for living and for living well were brought to full development by men's reason and experience, and there

---

[12] Aristotle *Nicomachean Ethics* v. 6. 1134b 9 ff. Cf. *ibid.* v. 1138b 6. Marsilius regularly refers to Book v of the *Ethics* as Book iv. It is to be noted that in the *Eudemian Ethics*, also probably by Aristotle, the same book on justice is Book iv.

[13] See Vol. I, pp. 86–88.

[14] Aristotle *Politics* iii. 14. 1285a 2 ff. Cf. *ibid.* iii. 15. 1286b 8 ff.

was established the perfect community, called the state, with the differentiation of its parts, to the discussion of which we shall now proceed.

Let this much suffice, then, concerning the rise of the civil community.

CHAPTER IV: ON THE FINAL CAUSE OF THE STATE AND OF ITS CIVIL [1] REQUIREMENTS, AND THE DIFFERENTIATION IN GENERAL OF ITS PARTS

THE state, according to Aristotle in the *Politics,* Book I, Chapter 1, is "the perfect community having the full limit of self-sufficiency, which came into existence for the sake of living, but exists for the sake of living well." [2] This phrase of Aristotle—"came into existence for the sake of living, but exists for the sake of living well"—signifies the perfect final cause of the state, since those who live a civil life not only live, which beasts or slaves do too, but live well, having leisure for those liberal functions in which are exercised the virtues of both the practical and the theoretic soul.

2. Having thus determined the end of the state to be living and living well, we must treat first of living and its modes. For this, as we have said, is the purpose for the sake of which the state was established, and which necessitates all the things which exist in the state and are done by the association of men in it. Let us therefore lay this down as the principle of all the things which are to be demonstrated here, a principle naturally held, believed, and freely granted by all: that all men not deformed or otherwise impeded naturally desire a sufficient life, and avoid and flee what is harmful thereto. [3] This has been acknowledged not only with regard to man but also with regard to every genus of animals, according to Tully in his treatise *On Duties,* Book I, Chapter III, where he says: "It is an original endowment which nature has bestowed upon every genus of living things, that it preserves itself, its body, and its life, that it avoids those things which seem harmful, and that it seeks and obtains all those things which are necessary for living." [4] This principle can also be clearly grasped by everyone through sense induction.

3. But the living and living well which are appropriate to men fall into

---

[1] Reading, with Scholz, *civilium* for *scibilium*.   [2] Aristotle *Politics* 1. 2. 1252b 27.

[3] Reading, with Scholz, *huic* for *hinc*. On the significance of this principle, see Vol. I, pp. 54 ff.

[4] Cicero *De officiis* I. iv. 11.

two kinds, of which one is temporal or earthly, while the other is usually called eternal or heavenly. However, this latter kind of living, the eternal, the whole body of philosophers were unable to prove by demonstration, nor was it self-evident,[5] and therefore they did not concern themselves with the means thereto. But as to the first kind of living and living well or good life, that is, the earthly, and its necessary means, this the glorious philosophers comprehended almost completely through demonstration. Hence for its attainment they concluded the necessity of the civil community, without which this sufficient life cannot be obtained. Thus the foremost of the philosophers, Aristotle, said in his *Politics,* Book I, Chapter 1: "All men are driven toward such an association by a natural impulse." [6] Although sense experience teaches this, we wish to bring out more distinctly that cause of it which we have indicated, as follows: Man is born composed of contrary elements, because of whose contrary actions and passions some of his substance is continually being destroyed; moreover, he is born "bare and unprotected" from excess of the surrounding air and other elements, capable of suffering and of destruction, as has been said in the science of nature.[7] As a consequence, he needed arts of diverse genera and species to avoid the afore-mentioned harms. But since these arts can be exercised only by a large number of men, and can be had only through their association with one another, men had to assemble together in order to attain what was beneficial through these arts and to avoid what was harmful.[8]

4. But since among men thus assembled there arise disputes and quarrels which, if not regulated by a norm of justice, would cause men to fight and separate and thus finally would bring about the destruction of the state, there had to be established in this association a standard of justice and a guardian or maker thereof. And since this guardian has to restrain excessive wrongdoers as well as other individuals both within and outside the state who disturb or attempt to oppress the community, the state had

---

[5] See Vol. I, pp. 69–70; also below, I. v. 10; I. ix. 2; I. xii. 1; II. xxx. 4.

[6] Aristotle *Politics* I. 2. 1253a 29.   [7] Aristotle *On the Parts of Animals* IV. 10. 687a 25.

[8] It will be noted that this paragraph proves the necessity of "society," just as the first sentence of paragraph 4 proves the necessity of government, so that the two paragraphs might be viewed as proving that man is, respectively, a "social" and a "political" animal, without any need for referring to a "contract" of society and of government, as was to be the case in the seventeenth century. However, Marsilius' proofs, with their emphasis on merely biological needs as generating society, and on the need for regulating disputes as generating government, are also departures from Aristotle. See Vol. I, pp. 88–91, 103 ff. There may, however, be an influence of Avicenna here; see Avicenna *De anima (Sextus naturalium)* v. i (*Avicenne perhypatetici philosophi . . . opera* [Venice, 1508], fol. 22rb). See also I. Th. Eschmann's notes in his edition of G. B. Phelan's translation of Thomas Aquinas *On Kingship* (Toronto, 1949), pp. 4, 94–95.

to have within it something by which to resist these. Again, since the community needs various conveniences, repairs, and protection of certain common things, and different things in time of peace and in time of war, it was necessary that there be in the community men to take care of such matters, in order that the common necessity might be relieved when it was expedient or needful. But beside the things which we have so far mentioned, which relieve only the necessities of the present life, there is something else which men associated in a civil community [9] need for the status of the future world promised to the human race through God's supernatural revelation, and which is useful also for the status of the present life. This is the worship and honoring of God, and the giving of thanks both for benefits received in this world and for those to be received in the future one. For the teaching of these things and for the directing of men in them, the state had to designate certain teachers. The nature and qualities of all these and the other matters mentioned above will be treated in detail in the subsequent discussions.

5. Men, then, were assembled for the sake of the sufficient life, being able to seek out for themselves the necessaries enumerated above, and exchanging them with one another. This assemblage, thus perfect and having the limit of self-sufficiency, is called the state, whose final cause as well as that of its many parts has already been indicated by us in some measure, and will be more fully distinguished below. For since diverse things are necessary to men who desire a sufficient life, things which cannot be supplied by men of one order or office, there had to be diverse orders or offices of men in this association, exercising or supplying such diverse things which men need for sufficiency of life. But these diverse orders or offices of men are none other than the many and distinct parts of the state.

Let it suffice, then, to have covered thus in outline what the state is, why there came about such an association, and the number and division of its parts.

[9] *Communicantes civiliter.* See Introduction, above, pp. lxxv–lxxvi, lxxix–lxxx.

CHAPTER V: ON THE DIFFERENTIATION OF THE PARTS
OF THE STATE, AND THE NECESSITY OF THEIR SEP-
ARATE EXISTENCE FOR AN END DISCOVERABLE BY
MAN

WE have now completely listed the parts of the state, in whose perfect action and intercommunication, without external impediment,
we have said that the tranquillity of the state consists. But we must now
continue our discussion of them, since the fuller determination of these
parts, with respect both to their functions or ends and to their other appropriate causes, will make more manifest the causes of tranquillity and of
its opposite. Let us say, then, that the parts or offices of the state are of
six kinds, as Aristotle said in the *Politics,* Book VII, Chapter 7: the agricul-
tural, the artisan, the military, the financial, the priestly, and the judicial
or deliberative.[1] Three of these, the priestly, the warrior, and the judicial,
are in the strict sense parts of the state, and in civil communities they are
usually called the honorable class (*honorabilitatem*). The others are called
parts only in the broad sense of the term, because they are offices necessary
to the state according to the doctrine of Aristotle in the *Politics,* Book VII,
Chapter 7.[2] And the multitude belonging to these offices are usually called
the common mass (*vulgaris*). These, then, are the more familiar parts
of the city or state, to which all the others can appropriately be reduced.

2. Although the necessity of these parts has been indicated in the preceding chapter, we wish to indicate it again more distinctly, assuming this
proposition as having been previously demonstrated from what is self-
evident, namely, that the state is a community established for the sake of
the living and living well of the men in it. Of this "living" we have previously distinguished two kinds: one, the life or living of this world, that
is, earthly; the other, the life or living of the other or future world. From
these kinds of living, desired by man as ends, we shall indicate the necessity
for the differentiation of the parts of the civil community. The first kind
of human living, the earthly, is sometimes taken to mean the being of living things, as in Book II of the treatise *On the Soul:* "For living things,
living is their being";[3] in which sense life is nothing other than soul. At

---

[1] Aristotle *Politics* VII. 8. 1328b 2 ff.
[2] *Ibid.* 1328a 2 ff. On this distinction, see Vol. I, p. 190.
[3] Aristotle *On the Soul* II. 4. 415b 14.

other times, "living" is taken to mean the act, the action or passion, of the soul or of life.[4] Again, each of these meanings is used in two ways, with reference either to the numerically same being or to the similar being, which is said to be that of the species. And although each of these kinds of living, both as proper to man and as common to him and to the other animate things, depends upon natural causes, yet we are not at present considering it insofar as it comes from these causes; the natural science of plants and animals deals with this. Rather, our present concern is with these causes insofar as they receive fulfillment "through art and reason," whereby "the human race lives."[5]

3. Hence, we must note that if man is to live and to live well, it is necessary that his actions be done and be done well; and not only his actions but also his passions. By "well" I mean in proper proportion. And since we do not receive entirely perfect from nature the means whereby these proportions are fulfilled, it was necessary for man to go beyond natural causes to form through reason some means whereby to effect and preserve his actions and passions in body and soul. And these means are the various kinds of functions and products deriving from the virtues and arts both practical and theoretic.

4. Of human actions and passions, some come from natural causes apart from knowledge. Such are those which are effected by the contrariety of the elements composing our bodies, through their intermixture. In this class can properly be placed the actions of the nutritive faculty. Under this head also come actions effected by the elements surrounding our body through the alteration of their qualities; of this kind also are the alterations effected by things entering human bodies, such as food, drink, medicines, poisons, and other similar things. But there are other actions or passions which are performed by us or occur in us through our cognitive and appetitive powers. Of these some are called "immanent" because they do not cross over (*non transeunt*) into a subject other than the doer, nor are they exercised through any external organs or locomotive members; of this kind are the thoughts and desires or affections of men. But there are other actions and passions which are called "transient" because they are opposed in either or in both respects to the kind which we have just described.[6]

5. In order to proportion all these actions and passions, and to fulfill them

---

[4] For this distinction between being and act, see *ibid*. II. 1. 412a 10 ff. It is the distinction between first and second actuality.

[5] Aristotle *Metaphysics* I. 1. 980b 27. Cf. *Politics* VII. 13. 1332b 3–6.

[6] On this distinction between immanent and transient acts, see also below, I. v. 11; II. ii. 4, 5; II. viii. 3; II. ix. 11; II. xvii. 8; and Vol. I, p. 61, n. 56, and pp. 101–4.

in that to which nature could not lead, there were discovered the various kinds of arts and other virtues, as we said above, and men of various offices were established to exercise these for the purpose of supplying human needs. These orders are none other than the parts of the state enumerated above. For in order to proportion and preserve the acts of the nutritive part of the soul, whose cessation would mean the complete destruction of the animal both individually and as a species, agriculture and animal husbandry were established.[7] To these may properly be reduced all kinds of hunting of land, sea, and air animals, and all other arts whereby food is acquired by some exchange or is prepared for eating, so that what is lost from the substance of our body may thereby be restored, and the body be continued in its immortal being so far as nature has permitted this to man.

6. In order to moderate the actions and passions of our body caused by the impressions of the elements which externally surround us, there was discovered the general class of mechanics, which Aristotle in the *Politics,* Book VII, Chapter 6, calls the "arts."[8] To this class belong spinning, leathermaking, shoemaking, all species of housebuilding, and in general all the other mechanic arts which subserve the other offices of the state directly or indirectly, and which moderate not only men's touch or taste but also the other senses. These latter arts are more for pleasure and for living well than for the necessity of life, such as the painter's art and others similar to it, concerning which Aristotle says in the *Politics,* Book IV, Chapter 3: "Of these arts some must exist from necessity, and others are for pleasure and living well."[9] Under this class is also placed the practice of medicine, which is in some way architectonic to many of the above-mentioned arts.

7. In order to moderate the excesses of the acts deriving from the loco-motive powers through knowledge and desire, which we have called transient acts and which can be done for the benefit or for the harm or injury of someone other than the doer for the status of the present world, there was necessarily established in the state a part or office by which the excesses of such acts are corrected and reduced to equality or due proportion. For without such correction the excesses of these acts would cause fighting and hence the separation of the citizens, and finally the destruction of the state and loss of the sufficient life. This part of the state, together with its subsidiaries, is called by Aristotle the "judicial" or "ruling" and "delibera-

[7] On the significance of this allocation of agriculture to caring for a part of the "soul," see Vol. I, pp. 100–101.

[8] Aristotle *Politics* VII. 8. 1328b 6.   [9] *Ibid.* IV. 4. 1291a 2–4.

tive" part, and its function is to regulate matters of justice and the common benefit.

8. In addition, since the sufficient life cannot be led by citizens who are oppressed or cast into slavery by external oppressors, and also since the sentences of the judges against injurious and rebellious men within the state must be executed by coercive force, it was necessary to set up in the state a military or warrior part, which many of the mechanics also subserve. For the state was established for the sake of living and living well, as was said in the preceding chapter; but this is impossible for citizens cast into slavery. For Aristotle the preeminent said that slavery is contrary to the nature of the state. Hence, indicating the necessity for this part, he said in the *Politics*, Book IV, Chapter 3: "There is a fifth class, that of the warriors, which is not less necessary than the others, if the citizens are not to be slaves of invaders. For nothing is more truly impossible than for that which is by nature slavish to be worthy of the name 'state'; for a state is self-sufficient, but a slave is not self-sufficient." [10] The necessity for this class because of internal rebels is treated by Aristotle in the *Politics*, Book VII, Chapter 6.[11] We have omitted the quotation of this passage here for the sake of brevity, and because we shall quote it in Chapter XIV of this discourse, paragraph 8.

9. Again, since in some years on earth the harvests are large, and in others small; and the state is sometimes at peace with its neighbors, and sometimes not; and it is in need of various common services such as the construction and repair of roads, bridges, and other edifices, and similar things whose enumeration here would be neither appropriate nor brief— to provide all these things at the proper time it was necessary to establish in the state a treasure-keeping part, which Aristotle called the "money class." This part gathers and saves monies, coins, wines, oils, and other necessaries; it procures from all places things needed for the common benefit, and it seeks to relieve future necessities; it is also subserved by some of the other parts of the state. Aristotle called this the "money" part, since the saver of monies seems to be the treasurer of all things; for all things are exchanged for money.

10. It remains for us to discuss the necessity of the priestly part. All men have not thought so harmoniously about this as they have about the necessity of the other parts of the state. The cause of this difference was that the true and primary necessity of this part could not be comprehended through demonstration, nor was it self-evident.[12] All nations, however, agreed that it was appropriate to establish the priesthood for the worship

---

[10] *Ibid*. IV. 4. 1291a 6.   [11] *Ibid*. VII. 8. 1328b 7.   [12] See above, I. iv. 3, n. 5.

and honoring of God, and for the benefit resulting therefrom for the status of the present or the future world. For most laws [13] or religions [14] promise that in the future world God will distribute rewards to those who do good and punishment to doers of evil.

11. However, besides these causes of the laying down of religious laws, causes which are believed without demonstration, the philosophers, including Hesiod, Pythagoras, and several others of the ancients, noted appropriately a quite different cause or purpose for the setting forth of divine laws or religions—a purpose which was in some sense necessary for the status of this world. This was to ensure the goodness of human acts both individual and civil, on which depend almost completely the quiet or tranquillity of communities and finally the sufficient life in the present world. For although some of the philosophers who founded such laws or religions did not accept or believe in human resurrection and that life which is called eternal, they nevertheless feigned and persuaded others that it exists and that in it pleasures and pains are in accordance with the qualities of human deeds in this mortal life, in order that they might thereby induce in men reverence and fear of God, and a desire to flee the vices and to cultivate the virtues. For there are certain acts which the legislator cannot regulate by human law, that is, those acts which cannot be proved to be present or absent to someone, but which nevertheless cannot be concealed from God, whom these philosophers feigned to be the maker of such laws and the commander of their observance, under the threat or promise of eternal reward for doers of good and punishment for doers of evil. Hence, they said of the variously virtuous men in this world that they were placed in the heavenly firmament; and from this were perhaps derived the names of certain stars and constellations. These philosophers said that the souls of men who acted wrongly entered the bodies of various brutes; for example, the souls of men who had been intemperate eaters entered the bodies of pigs, those who were intemperate in embracing and making love entered the bodies of goats, and so on, according to the proportions of human vices to their condemnable properties. So too the philosophers assigned various kinds of torments to wrongdoers, like perpetual thirst and hunger for intemperate Tantalus: water and fruit were to be near him, but he was unable to drink or handle these, for they were always fleeing faster than he could pursue them. The philosophers also said that the infernal regions, the place of these torments, were deep and dark; and they painted

[13] The use of the term "law" (*lex*) to mean a system of religion is not peculiar to Marsilius. See Introduction, above, pp. xc–xci.

[14] *Sectarum*. See Introduction, above, pp. xc–xci.

all sorts of terrible and gloomy pictures of them. From fear of these, men eschewed wrongdoing, were instigated to perform virtuous works of piety and mercy, and were well disposed both in themselves and toward others. As a consequence, many disputes and injuries ceased in communities. Hence too the peace or tranquillity of states and the sufficient life of men for the status of the present world were preserved with less difficulty; which was the end intended by these wise men in laying down [15] such laws or religions.[16]

12. Such, then, were the precepts handed down by the gentile priests; and for the teaching of them they established in their communities temples in which their gods were worshiped. They also appointed teachers of these laws or doctrines, whom they called priests (*sacerdotes*), because they handled the sacred objects of the temples, like the books, vases, and other such things subserving divine worship.

13. These affairs they arranged fittingly in accordance with their beliefs and rites. For as priests they appointed not anyone at all, but only virtuous and esteemed citizens who had held military, judicial, or deliberative office, and who had retired from secular affairs, being excused from civil burdens and offices because of age. For by such men, removed from passions, and in whose words greater credence was placed because of their age and moral dignity, it was fitting that the gods should be honored and their sacred objects handled, not by artisans or mercenaries who had exercised lowly and defiling offices. Whence it is said in the *Politics*, Book VII, Chapter 7: "Neither a farmer nor an artisan should be made a priest." [17]

14.[18] Now correct views concerning God were not held by the gentile laws or religions and by all the other religions which are or were outside the catholic Christian faith or outside the Mosaic law which preceded it or the beliefs of the holy fathers which in turn preceded this—and, in general, by all those doctrines which are outside the tradition of what is contained in the sacred canon called the Bible. For they followed the human mind or false prophets or teachers of errors. Hence too they did not have a correct view about the future life and its happiness or misery, nor about the true priesthood established for its sake. We have, nevertheless, spoken of their rites in order to make more manifest their difference from the true priesthood, that of the Christians, and the necessity for the priestly part in communities.

---

[15] Reading, with Bigongiari (p. 37), *ex positione* for *expositione*.

[16] For antecedents of Marsilius' view of the socio-political basis and use of religion, see Vol. I, pp. 83–84.

[17] Aristotle *Politics* VII. 9. 1329a 28.   [18] This paragraph division is from Scholz.

CHAPTER VI: ON THE FINAL CAUSE OF A CERTAIN
PART OF THE STATE, THE PRIESTHOOD, SHOWN
FROM THE IMMEDIATE TEACHING OR REVELATION
OF GOD, BUT INCAPABLE OF BEING PROVED BY HU-
MAN REASON

IT remains now to discuss the final cause for which the true priesthood
was established in communities of the faithful. This was in order to
moderate human acts both immanent and transient controlled by knowledge and desire, according as the human race is ordered by such acts toward the best life of the future world. Hence it must be noted that although the first man, Adam, was created principally for the glory of God,
just as were the other creatures, nevertheless, unlike the other species of corruptible things, he was created uniquely in God's image and likeness, so
that he might be capable of participating in eternal happiness after the
life of the present world. Also he was created in a state of original innocence or justice and also of grace, as is plausibly said by some of the
saints and certain leading teachers of the sacred Scriptures. Now if Adam
had remained in this status, the establishment or differentiation of civil
offices would not have been necessary for him or for his posterity, because
nature would have produced for him the advantages and pleasures of the
sufficiency of this life in the earthly or pleasurable paradise, without any
punishment or suffering on his part.[1]

2. But because Adam corrupted his original innocence or justice and
grace by eating of the forbidden fruit, transgressing thereby a divine commandment, he sank suddenly into guilt and misery, and was punished by
being deprived of eternal happiness, the end to which he had been ordered
with all his posterity by the beneficence of glorious God. His desert for
transgressing this commandment was to propagate all his posterity in
lust. Every man after him was conceived and born in lust, contracting
therefrom the sin which in the law of the Christians is called "original."
The only exception was Jesus Christ who, without any kind of sin or lust,
was conceived by the Holy Spirit and born of the Virgin Mary; which
came about when one of the three divine persons, the Son, true God in
the unity of his person, assumed a human nature. As a result of this trans-

[1] On the significance of Marsilius propounding of this Augustinian conception of the state
as a consequence of sin, see Vol. I, p. 91.

gression of its first parents, the whole posterity of mankind was weakened in soul and is born weak, whereas it had previously been created in a state of perfect health, innocence, and grace. It was also because of this guilt that the human race was deprived of its best end to which it had been ordered.

3. But it is proper to God to have compassion for the human race, which he made in his own image, and which he had foreordained to a happy and eternal life. Hence God, who "never does anything in vain and never is lacking in necessaries," [2] willed to remedy the human plight by giving certain commands which men were to obey and observe, and which would counteract the transgression and heal the disease of the guilt resulting from it. Like an expert physician, he proceeded in a very orderly manner from the easier to the more difficult steps. For he first commanded men to observe the rite of holocausts, sacrificing the first fruit of the earth and the first-born of the animals, as if he wanted to test human penitence and obedience. This rite the ancient fathers observed with reverence for God, with faith, obedience, and thankfulness, down to the time of Abraham. To him God gave an additional command, more difficult than the first: the circumcision of the whole male sex in the flesh of the foreskin. By this command God seemed again to be testing even more severely human penitence and obedience. These commands were observed by some men down to the time of Moses, through whom God handed down to the people of Israel a law wherein he set forth, in addition to the previous commands, further ones for the status of both the present and the future world; and he appointed priests and levites as ministers of this law. The utility of observing all the prior commands and the Mosaic law was that men would be purged of sin or guilt, both original and actual or freely committed, and would escape and be preserved from eternal and temporal sensory punishment of the other world, although by observing these commands they would not merit eternal happiness.

4. It was such happiness, however, to which merciful God had ordered the human race and which he wished to restore to it after leading it back from the fall, following the appropriate order. Hence, most recently of all, through his son Jesus Christ, true God and true man in unity of person, he handed down the evangelical law, containing commands and counsels of what must be believed, done, and avoided. By observance of these, not only are men preserved from sensory punishment, as they had been by observance of the prior commands, but also through God's gracious ordainment they merit, by a certain congruity, eternal happiness. And for

---

[2] Aristotle *De anima* III. 9. 432b 22. Cf. *De caelo* I. 4. 271a 34; *Politics* I. 1. 1253a 9.

this reason the evangelical law is called the law of grace, both because
through the passion and death of Christ the human race was redeemed
from its guilt and from the penalty of losing eternal beatitude which it
had incurred as a result of the fall or sin of its first parents; and also because, by observing this law and receiving the sacraments established with
it and in it, we are given divine grace, after it is given it is strengthened
in us, and when we lose it, it is restored to us. Through this grace, by the
ordainment of God and the passion of Christ, our works come by a certain
congruity (as we have said) to merit eternal happiness.

5. Through Christ's passion the grace whereby men merit a blessed life
was received not only by those who came after but also by those who had
observed the first commands and the Mosaic law. Before Christ's advent,
passion, death, and resurrection, they had been deprived of this beatitude in the other world, in the place called Limbus. But through Christ,
they received the promise given to them by God, although in the prior
commands of the prophets and of the Mosaic law such a promise had been
handed down to them in a veiled and enigmatic manner, for "all these
things happened to them in figure," [3] as the Apostle said to the Hebrews.

6. This divine procedure was very appropriate, for it went from the less
to the more perfect and finally to the most perfect [4] of the things appropriate to human salvation. Nor should it be thought that God could not
have bestowed immediately at the outset, had he so wished, a perfect
remedy for the fall of man. But he acted as he did because he so willed
it and it was fitting, as required by men's sin, lest a too easy pardon be the
occasion for further sinning.

7. As teachers of this law, and as ministers of its sacraments, certain
men in the communities were chosen, called priests and deacons or levites.
It is their office to teach the commands and counsels of the Christian
evangelical law, as to what must be believed, done, and spurned, to the
end that a blessed status be attained in the future world, and the opposite
avoided.

8. The end of the priesthood, therefore, is to teach and educate men
in those things which, according to the evangelical law, it is necessary
to believe, do, and omit in order to attain eternal salvation and avoid
misery.

9. To this office appropriately pertain all the disciplines, theoretic and
practical, discovered by the human mind, which moderate human acts

---

[3] I Corinthians 10:11. Marsilius refers here only to the general argument of the Epistle to
the Hebrews.
[4] Note that the same characterization is applied to nature and art, above, I. iii. 2.

both immanent and transient arising from desire and knowledge, and which make man well disposed in soul for the status of both the present and the future world. We have almost all these disciplines through the teaching of the admirable Philosopher and of other glorious men; [5] however, we have omitted to enumerate them here, both for the sake of brevity and because it is not necessary to our present consideration.

10.[6] With respect to this chapter and the one following, we must understand that the causes of the offices of the state, in respect of each kind of cause, differ according as they are offices of the state and according as they are habits [7] of the human body or mind. For according as they are habits of the human body or soul, their final causes are the functions which are immediately and essentially forthcoming from them. For example, the final cause of the shipbuilding part of the state is a ship; of the military part, the use of arms and fighting; of the priesthood, the preaching of the divine law and the administration of the sacraments in accordance with it; and so on with all the rest. But according as they are offices determined and established in the state, their final causes are the benefits and sufficiencies which perfect human actions and passions, and which are forthcoming from the functions of the aforesaid habits, or which cannot be had without them. For example, from fighting, which is the act or end of the military habit, freedom is forthcoming and is preserved for men in the state, and this freedom is the end of the acts and functions of the military. So too from the function or end of the housebuilding part, which is a house, there is forthcoming to men or to the state protection from the harmful impressions of the air, the hot, the cold, the wet, or the dry, which protection is the final cause for whose sake the housebuilding office was established in the state. In the same way, from observance of the divine law, which is the end of the priesthood, eternal happiness is forthcoming to men. Similar considerations apply to all the other parts or offices of the state. And the other kinds of causes of these offices—the material, formal, and efficient causes—are distinguished in the same or a similar manner, as will appear in the following chapter.[8]

[5] In thus placing philosophy within the function of the priesthood, Marsilius would seem to be following Aristotle; see *Metaphysics* I. 1. 981b 20–24; *Nicomachean Ethics* VI. 7. 1141b 1 ff.; x. 7. 1177b 25 ff.; *Politics* VII. 9. 1329a 26 ff. Most of the other medieval Aristotelians, however, distinguish secular philosophy from religion. On the other hand, John of Jandun holds that the philosopher attains a this-worldly "knowledge of God" and is therefore "presupposed" by the priest. See *Quaestiones in duodecim libros Metaphysicae* Lib. 1. qu.18 (Venice, 1525) fol. 15 J-K; also Vol. I, pp. 78–79, n. 8.

[6] This paragraph division is from Scholz.

[7] For the meaning of "habit" (*habitus*), see Introduction, p. lxxi.

[8] For similar distinctions between the proximate and the remote, or the functional and the social, ends and other causes of parts of the state, see Albert the Great *Ethica* Lib. 1. Tr. III. cap.

We have now finished our discussion of the number of the parts of the state, their necessity, and their differentiation through the sufficiencies which are their ends.

CHAPTER VII: ON THE OTHER KINDS OF CAUSES OF THE SEPARATE EXISTENCE OF THE PARTS OF THE STATE, AND THE DIVISION OF EACH KIND IN TWO WAYS RELEVANT TO OUR PURPOSE

WE must now discuss the other causes of the offices or parts of the state. First we shall speak about their material and formal causes; then we shall inquire into their efficient cause. And since in things completed by the human mind the matter actually exists prior to the form,[1] let us first discuss the material cause. The proper matter of the different offices, according as the offices mean habits of the soul, is men inclined from their generation or nativity to different arts or disciplines. For "nature is not lacking in necessaries,"[2] and is more solicitous for what is more noble;[3] among corruptible things, the most noble is the human species, which, perfected by different arts or disciplines, is the matter wherefrom must be established the state and its distinct parts necessary for the attainment of sufficiency of life, as was shown in Chapters IV and V of this discourse. Hence nature herself initiated this differentiation in the generation of men, producing some who in their natural dispositions were apt for and inclined toward farming, others toward military pursuits, and still others toward the other genera of arts and disciplines, but different men toward different ones. Nor did she incline only one individual toward one species of art or discipline, but rather many individuals toward the same species, to the extent necessary for sufficiency of life. Hence, she generated some men apt for prudence, since the judicial and deliberative part of the state must be composed of prudent men; some men apt for strength and courage, since the military part is appropriately composed of such men. So too she adapted the other men to the other genera of

---

x; Tr. vi. cap. i (*Opera omnia*, ed. A. Borgnet, VII [Paris, 1891], 42–43, 84–85); and Peter of Auvergne *In Politicorum Aristotelis libros commentarium* Lib. iv. Lect. 13 (*Thomae Aquinatis opera omnia*, XXI [Parma, 1866], 545–46). Marsilius' chief use of the distinction is in connection with the priesthood. See below, ii. xv. 2 ff.

[1] Aristotle *Metaphysics* vii. 7. 1032b 31.
[2] Aristotle *On the Soul* iii. 9. 432b 22. See above, i. iv. 3.
[3] Cf. Aristotle *On the Parts of Animals* iv. 10. 686a 25 ff.

practical and theoretic habits which are necessary or appropriate for living and living well, so that out of the diversity of the natural inclinations toward habits of diverse genera and species in all men, she perfected what was necessary for the diversity of the parts of the state.[4]

The material causes of the offices of the state, according as the offices mean parts of the state, are already apparent. For these are men habituated by the arts and disciplines of diverse genera and species, from whom the diverse orders or parts are established in the state for the sake of the sufficiencies or ends forthcoming from their arts and disciplines. Considered in this way, as having been established in the state for this purpose, the parts of the state are properly called offices, in the sense of services, for they are ordered toward human service.

2. The formal causes of the offices of the state, according as they are habits of the human mind, are none other than these very habits. For these habits are themselves the forms of those who have them; they fulfill or perfect the human inclinations which exist by nature. Hence it is said in the *Politics,* Book VII, last chapter: "Every art and discipline aims to supply what nature lacks."[5] On the other hand, according as the offices of the state are established parts of the state, their formal causes are the commands which the efficient cause has given to or impressed upon the men who are appointed to exercise determinate functions in the state.

3. The efficient or productive causes of the offices, according as they mean habits of the soul, are the minds and wills of men through their thoughts and desires, individually or collectively. Also, in the case of certain offices, an added principle is the movement and exercise of the bodily organs. But the efficient cause of the offices, according as they are parts of the state, is frequently and in most cases the human legislator, although formerly, rarely and in very few cases, the immediate efficient cause was God, without human determination, as will be said in Chapter IX of this discourse and as will appear more fully from Chapter XII of this discourse and Chapter XV of Discourse II.[6] With regard to the priesthood, however, there is a different manner of establishment, which will be sufficiently discussed in Chapters XV and XVII of Discourse II.[7]

In this way, then, we have discussed the parts of the state and the necessity of their establishment from the three other kinds of cause.

---

[4] It will be noted that this doctrine of different "natural aptitudes" does not lead Marsilius to a doctrine of natural slaves and natural rulers, as it does Aristotle and the other medieval Aristotelians. See Vol. I, pp. 177–78.

[5] Aristotle *Politics* VII. 17. 1337a 1.

[6] Reading, with Scholz, "2e" after "15º." The passages referred to are I. ix. 2; I. xii. 1; II. xv. 2 ff.

[7] See below, II. xv. 2 ff.; II. xvii. 2 ff.

CHAPTER VIII: ON THE GENERA OF POLITIES OR REGIMES, THE TEMPERATE AND THE DISEASED, AND THE DIVISION OF THEIR SPECIES

WE must now show with greater certainty what was already shown to some extent above, that the establishment and differentiation of the parts of the state are brought about by an efficient cause which we have previously called the legislator. The same legislator establishes these parts, and differentiates and separates them as nature does with an animal, by first forming or establishing in the state one part which in Chapter V of this discourse we called the ruling or judicial part,[1] and through this the other parts, as will be indicated more fully in Chapter XV of this discourse.[2] Hence we must first say something concerning the nature of this ruling part. For since it is the first part of the state, as will appear below, the appropriate procedure will be to go from the indication of its efficient cause to the indication of the efficient cause which establishes and differentiates the other parts of the state.

2. There are two genera of ruling parts or governments, one well tempered, the other diseased.[3] With Aristotle in the *Politics*, Book III, Chapter 5,[4] I call that genus "well tempered" in which the ruler governs for the common benefit, in accordance with the will of the subjects; while the "diseased" genus is that which is deficient in this respect.[5] Each of these genera, again, is divided into three species: the temperate into kingly monarchy, aristocracy, and polity; the diseased into the three opposite species of tyrannical monarchy, oligarchy, and democracy. And each of these again has sub-species, the detailed discussion of which is not part of our present task. For Aristotle gave a sufficient account of them in Books III and IV of his *Politics*.

3. To obtain a fuller conception of these species of government, which is necessary for the clear understanding of what follows, let us define each species in accordance with the view of Aristotle. A *kingly monarchy*, then, is a temperate government wherein the ruler is a single man who rules for

---

[1] I. v. 7.   [2] I. xv. 2 ff.

[3] On these terms, see Introduction, above, pp. lxxxv–lxxxvi.

[4] Aristotle *Politics* III. 7, 8. 1279a 17 ff.

[5] Although the reference to the will or consent of the subjects is not entirely absent in the *Politics*, Marsilius' use of it as a basic and even primary criterion of a just or "well-tempered" government (see esp. I. ix. 5) is a departure from Aristotle and from the medieval Aristotelian tradition. See Vol. I, pp. 241–42; also pp. 60, 170, 220–23.

the common benefit, and in accordance with the will or consent of the subjects. *Tyranny,* its opposite, is a diseased government wherein the ruler is a single man who rules for his own private benefit apart from the will of his subjects. *Aristocracy* is a temperate government in which the honorable class (*honorabilitas*) alone rules in accordance with the will or consent of the subjects and for the common benefit. *Oligarchy,* its opposite, is a diseased government in which some of the wealthier or more powerful rule for their own benefit apart from the will of the subjects. A *polity,* although in one sense it is something common to every genus or species of regime or government, means in another sense a certain species of temperate government, in which every citizen participates in some way in the government or in the deliberative function in turn according to his rank and ability or condition, for the common benefit and with the will or consent of the citizens.[6] *Democracy,* its opposite, is a government in which the masses (*vulgus*) or the multitude of the needy establish the government and rule alone, apart from the will or consent of the other citizens and not entirely for the common benefit according to proper proportion.[7]

4. As to which of the temperate governments is best or which of the diseased governments is worst, and the relative goodness or badness of the other species, the discussion of these points is not part of our present concern.[8] Let it suffice to have said this much about the division of governments into their species and the definition of each.

CHAPTER IX: ON THE METHODS OF ESTABLISHING A KINGLY MONARCHY, AND WHICH METHOD IS THE MORE PERFECT;[1] ALSO ON THE METHODS OF ESTABLISHING THE OTHER KINDS OF REGIME OR POLITY, BOTH TEMPERATE AND DISEASED

HAVING determined these points, we must now discuss the methods of effecting or establishing the ruling part of the state. For from the better or worse nature of these methods, viewed as actions[2] emerging from that nature to the civil regime, we must infer the efficient cause by

---

[6] On the meanings of "polity," see Vol. I, pp. 236 ff.

[7] On this conception of "democracy," see Vol. I, pp. 190–91, 195.

[8] On the basis and significance of this indifference as to the relative merits of monarchy, aristocracy, and polity, see Vol. I, pp. 117–18, 172–73. See also below, I. ix. 9.

[1] Reading, with Bigongiari (p. 39) and MSS, *perfectioris* for *perfectionis.*

[2] Reading, with Bigongiari (p. 40) and MSS, *actionum* for *actionibus;* hence also *provenientium* for *provenientibus.*

which these methods and the ruling part established by them will emerge more advantageously to the polity.

2. In this book we are considering the causes and actions by which the ruling part must in most cases be established. First, however, we wish to indicate the method and cause by which this part has been established in the past, although rarely, in order to distinguish this method or action, and its immediate cause, from those by which the government must regularly and in most cases be established, and which we can prove by human demonstration. For of the former method no certain comprehension can be had through demonstration. This method or action, with its immediate cause, by which the ruling part and other parts of the state, especially the priesthood, were formed in the past, was the divine will commanding this either through the determinate oracle of some individual creature or else perhaps immediately through itself alone. It was by this method that the divine will established the government of the people of Israel in the person of Moses and of certain other judges after him, and also the priesthood in the person of Aaron and his successors. With respect to this cause and its free action, as to why it did or did not operate in one way or another, we can say nothing through demonstration, but we hold it by simple belief apart from reason.[3] There is, however, another method of establishing governments which proceeds immediately from the human mind, although perhaps remotely from God as remote cause, who grants all earthly rulership, as is said in the nineteenth chapter of John,[4] and as the Apostle clearly states in the thirteenth chapter of the epistle to the Romans,[5] and St. Augustine in *The City of God,* Book V, Chapter 21.[6] However, God does not always act immediately; indeed in most cases, nearly everywhere, he establishes governments by means of human minds, to which he has granted the discretionary will for such establishment. And as for this latter cause, what it is, and by what kind of action it must establish such things, this can be indicated with human certainty from what is better or worse for the polity.

3. Omitting, then, that method of which we cannot attain certain knowledge through demonstration, we wish first to present those methods of establishing governments which are effected immediately by the human will;[7] next we shall show which of these is the more certain and the simpler.[8] Then, from the better nature of that method we shall infer the efficient cause from which alone it must and can emerge.[9] From these points, consequently, will appear the cause which must move to the best establish-

[3] See above, I. iv. 3, n. 5.   [4] John 19:11.   [5] Romans 13:1.
[6] St. Augustine *De civitate Dei* v. xxi (PL 41. 167).   [7] I. ix. 4–6.
[8] I. ix. 7.   [9] I. xv. 1–3. Cf. I. x. 1; I. xiv. 1.

ment and determination of the other parts of the state.[10] Finally we shall
discuss the unity of the government,[11] through which it will also be apparent what is the unity of the city or state.[12]

4. In pursuit of this program, then, we shall first enumerate the methods
of establishing kingly monarchy, by speaking of their origins. For this
species of government seems rather kindred to us, and directly connected
with the rule of the family, as is clear from what we said in Chapter III.
After the determination of this point, the methods of establishing the other
divisions of government will be made clear.

There are five methods of establishing kingly monarchies, according to
Aristotle's *Politics,* Book III, Chapter 8.[13] One is when the monarch is
appointed for one determinate function with respect to the ruling of the
community, such as the leadership of the army, either with hereditary succession or for his own lifetime only. It was by this method that Agamem-
non was made leader of the army by the Greeks. In modern communities
this office is called the captaincy or constabulary.[14] This leader of the army
had no judicial power in time of peace, but when the army was fighting a
war he had the supreme authority to kill or otherwise punish transgressors.

Another method is that whereby certain monarchs rule in Asia; they
receive their dominating authority through hereditary succession, and
while they rule according to law, this law is like that of despots, being for
the monarch's benefit rather than completely for the community's. The
inhabitants of that region endure such rule "without protest," [15] because
of their barbaric and slavish nature and the influence of custom. This rule
is kingly in that it is native to the country and is over voluntary subjects,
because, for example, the monarch's ancestors had been the first inhabitants
of the region. But it is also in a sense tyrannical, in that its laws are not
completely for the common benefit but for that of the monarch.

A third method of kingly government is when the ruler receives his
authority through election rather than hereditary succession, but governs
according to a law which is not completely for the common benefit but
rather for that of the monarch, like the law of tyrants. Aristotle, therefore,

---

[10] I. xv. 4–10.   [11] I. xvii. 1–9.   [12] I. xvii. 11.

[13] Aristotle *Politics* III. 14. 1284b 35 ff.

[14] Marsilius' terms are *capitaneatus* and *constabiliaria.* The former meant a position of army
leadership; for a large number of references to the medieval use of this and cognate terms, see
Du Cange, *Glossarium mediae et infimae Latinitatis,* s.v. *capitaneatus, capitaneus.* Du Cange
has no entry for *constabiliaria,* but for the seemingly related terms *constabularia* and *contes-
tabiliaria* (the latter found in some MSS of the *Defensor* instead of *constabiliaria*), Du Cange
refers to *comes stabuli,* meaning the custodian of the royal stable, and gives a large number of
citations, s.v.

[15] *Politics* III. 14. 1285a 23. See also Ptolemy of Lucca *De regimine principum* III. xi (*fin.*)
(ed. J. Mathis [Turin, 1924], p. 63b).

called this species of government an "elective tyranny," [16] a tyranny because the law was despotic, and elective because it was not over involuntary subjects.

A fourth method is that whereby a ruler is elected with subsequent hereditary succession, and governs according to laws which are completely for the common benefit; this method was used "in heroic days," [17] as Aristotle says in the chapter previously mentioned. Those days were called "heroic" either because the stars then produced men who were believed to be "heroes," that is, divine, on account of their exceeding virtue; or because such men and not others were named rulers on account of their exceeding virtues and beneficial deeds, in that they brought together a scattered multitude and assembled it into a civil community, or they freed the region of oppressors by fighting and strength of arms, or perhaps they bought the region or acquired it by some other appropriate method and divided it among the subjects. At any rate these men were made rulers with subsequent hereditary succession, because of their bestowal of great benefits or their excess of virtue over the rest of the multitude, as Aristotle also said in the *Politics, Book V, Chapter 5.*[18] Under this species of monarchy, Aristotle perhaps included that in which someone is elected only for his own lifetime or a part of his lifetime; or else he designated it through the combination of this fourth species and the one called elective tyranny, because it shares features of both.

There is and was a fifth method of kingly monarchy, whereby the ruler is made lord (*dominus*) over everything in the community, disposing of things and persons according to his own will, just as the head of a family disposes at will of everything in his own household.[19]

5. To make clearer these concepts of Aristotle, and to summarize all the methods of establishing the other kinds of government, we shall say that every government is over either voluntary or involuntary subjects. The first is the genus of well-tempered governments, the second of diseased governments. Each of these genera is divided into three species or kinds, as was said in Chapter VIII. And since one of the species of well-tempered government, and perhaps the more perfect, is kingly monarchy, let us resume our previous statements about its various kinds or methods, by saying that the king or monarch either is named by the election of the inhabitants or citizens, or duly obtains the rulership without their election. If without the election of the citizens, this is either because he or his ancestors first inhabited the region, or because he bought the land and jurisdic-

---

[16] *Politics* III. 14. 1285a 32.   [17] *Ibid.* 1285b 4.   [18] *Ibid.* v. 10. 1310b 10 ff.
[19] See *ibid.* III. 16–17. 1287a 1 ff.

tion, or acquired it by a just war or by some other lawful method, such as by gift made to him for some great service. Each of these kinds of monarchy participates so much the more in true kingship, the more it is over voluntary subjects and according to law made for the common benefit of the subjects; and it savors so much the more of tyranny the more it departs from these features, that is, the consent of the subjects and law established for their common benefit. Hence it is written in the *Politics*, Book IV, Chapter 8: "These," that is, monarchies, "were kingly because they were according to law, and ruled voluntary subjects; but they were tyrannical because they ruled despotically and in accordance with their," that is, the monarchs', "own judgment." [20] These two features, then, distinguish temperate from diseased government, as is apparent from the clear statement of Aristotle, but absolutely or in greater degree it is the consent of the subjects which is the distinguishing criterion.[21] Now if the ruling monarch is elected by the inhabitants, it is either with all his posterity succeeding him or not. If the latter, this may be in several ways, as he is named either for his own lifetime alone, or for his own lifetime and that of one or more of his successors, or not for the whole lifetime either of himself or of any of his successors but only for some determinate period, such as one or two years, more or less. Again, he is named to exercise either every judicial office, or only one office such as leading the army.

6. The elected and the non-elected kingly monarchs agree in that each rules voluntary subjects. They differ, however, in that the non-elected kings rule less voluntary subjects, and by laws which are less politic for the common benefit, as we said before in the case of the barbarians. The elected kings, on the other hand, rule more voluntary subjects, and by laws which are more politic, in that they are made for the common benefit, as we have said.

7. From these considerations it is clear, and will be even more apparent in the sequel, that the elected kind of government is superior to the non-elected. This is also the view of Aristotle in that passage of the *Politics*, Book III, Chapter 8, which we cited above with reference to those who were made rulers in the heroic days.[22] Again, this method of establishing governments is more permanent in perfect communities. For at some time or other it becomes necessary to have recourse to this from among all the other methods of establishing governments, but not conversely. For example, if hereditary succession fails, or if for some reason the multitude

[20] *Ibid.* IV. 10. 1295a 15.
[21] On this important statement, see above, I. viii. 2, n. 5, and pages of Vol. I cited there.
[22] *Politics.* III. 14. 1285b 2; above, para. 4.

cannot bear the excessive malice of that family's rule, they must then turn
to the method of election, which can never fail so long as the generation
of men does not fail.[23] Moreover, by the method of election alone is the best
ruler obtained. For it is expedient that the ruler be the best man in the
polity, since he must regulate the civil acts of all the rest.[24]

8. The method of establishing the other species of temperate government is usually election; in some cases the ruler is chosen by lot,[25] without
subsequent hereditary succession. Diseased governments, on the other
hand, are usually established by fraud or force or both.[26]

9. Which of the temperate governments is better, monarchy or one of the
other two species, aristocracy or polity; and again, which of the monarchies is better, the elected or the non-elected; and moreover, which of
the elected monarchies, that established with hereditary succession ensuing
or that in which one man alone is named without such succession; which
in turn is divided into the further alternatives of whether it is better to
name the ruler for a whole lifetime, either of himself alone or of some
of his successors also, or only for some determinate period, such as one or
two years, more or less—in all these questions there is room for inquiry
and reasonable doubt.[27] It must be held without doubt, however, in accordance with the truth and the manifest view of Aristotle, that election is
the more certain standard of government, as will be more fully shown in
Chapters XII, XVI, and XVII of this discourse.[28]

10. We must not overlook, however, that different multitudes in different times and places are inclined toward different kinds of polity and
government, as Aristotle says in the *Politics,* Book III, Chapter 9.[29] Legislators and institutors of governments must hearken to this fact. For just
as not every man is inclined toward the best discipline or study, whereupon it is appropriate that he be directed toward the acquisition not of that
discipline but of some other good one for which he is more fitted, so too
a multitude in some time or place may perhaps not be inclined to accept
the best kind of government, and therefore recourse must first be had to
that kind of temperate government which is more appropriate to it. For
example, before the monarchy of Julius Caesar, the Roman people were
for a long time unwilling to accept any definite monarch, either with

---

[23] There is a suggestion here of the Averroist doctrine of eternal generation. See below, I.
xvii. 10, and texts cited in note thereto.

[24] This is a marked ignoring of the papalist claims of superior virtue. See also below, I. xv. 3.

[25] Cf. Aristotle *Politics* II. 6. 1266a 9; VI. 2. 1317b 21, 1318a 2.

[26] Cf. *ibid.* v. 4. 1304b 8.   [27] See above, I. viii. 4.

[28] Below, I. xii. 3; I. xvi. 11 ff.; I. xvii. 11.

[29] Aristotle *Politics* III. 14. 1284b 39, 1285a 19.

hereditary succession or even one who was named only for his own life-time. The reason for this was perhaps that there was a large number of heroic men worthy of rulership among them, both families and individuals.

11. From these conclusions, then, it emerges clearly that those who ask which monarch is better for a city or state, the one who rules through election or the one who rules through hereditary succession, do not put the question in the proper way.[30] What they must correctly ask first is, which monarch is better, the elected or the non-elected. And if the elected, again which, the one who is named with hereditary succession ensuing or the one who is named without hereditary succession. For although a non-elected monarch almost always transmits the rulership to his heir, not every elected monarch does so, but only the one who is named to rule with hereditary succession ensuing.

Let these, then, be our conclusions about the methods of establishing governments, and that the absolutely better method is election.

CHAPTER X: ON THE DISTINCTION OF THE MEANINGS OF THE TERM "LAW," AND ON THE MEANING WHICH IS MOST PROPER AND INTENDED BY US

SINCE we have said that election is the more perfect and better method of establishing governments, we shall do well to inquire as to its efficient cause, wherefrom it has to emerge in its full value; for from this will appear the cause not only of the elected government but also of the other parts of the polity. Now a government has to regulate civil human acts (as we demonstrated in Chapter V of this discourse),[1] and according to a standard (*regulam*) which is and ought to be the form of the ruler, as such. We must, consequently, inquire into this standard, as to whether it exists, what it is, and why. For the efficient cause of this standard is perhaps the same as that of the ruler.

2. The existence of this standard, which is called a "statute" or "custom" and by the common term "law," we assume as almost self-evident by induction in all perfect communities. We shall show first, then, what law

---

[30] Among those who put the question in this way are Egidius of Rome *De regimine principum* Lib. III. Pars II. cap. v; Augustinus Triumphus *Summa de ecclesiastica potestate* qu.35. aa.6–7.

[1] See above, I. v. 7.

is; [2] next we shall indicate its final cause or necessity; [3] and finally we shall demonstrate by what person or persons and by what kind of action the law should be established; [4] which will be to inquire into its legislator or efficient cause, to whom we think it also pertains to elect the government, as we shall show subsequently by demonstration. [5] From these points there will also appear the matter or subject of the aforesaid standard which we have called law. [6] For this matter is the ruling part, whose function it is to regulate the political or civil acts of men according to the law.

3. Following this procedure, then, we must first distinguish the meanings or intentions of this term "law," in order that its many senses may not lead to confusion. For in one sense it means a natural sensitive inclination toward some action or passion. This is the way the Apostle used it when he said in the seventh chapter of the epistle to the Romans: "I see another law in my members, fighting against the law of my mind." [7] In another sense this term "law" means any productive habit and in general every form, existing in the mind, of a producible thing, from which as from an exemplar or measure there emerge the forms of things made by art. This is the way in which the term was used in the forty-third chapter of Ezekiel: "This is the law of the house . . . And these are the measurements of the altar." [8] In a third sense "law" means the standard containing admonitions for voluntary human acts according as these are ordered toward glory or punishment in the future world. In this sense the Mosaic law was in part called a law, just as the evangelical law in its entirety is called a law. Hence the Apostle said of these in his epistle to the Hebrews: "Since the priesthood has been changed, it is necessary that there be a change of the law also." [9] In this sense "law" was also used for the evangelic discipline in the first chapter of James: "He who has looked into the perfect law of liberty, and has continued therein . . . this man shall be blessed in his deeds." [10] In this sense of the term law all religions, [11] such as that of Mohammed or of the Persians, are called laws in whole or in part, although among these only the Mosaic and the evangelic, that is, the Christian, contain the truth. So too Aristotle called religions "laws" when he said, in the second book of his *Philosophy:* "The laws show how great is the power of custom"; [12] and also in the twelfth book of the same work: "The other doctrines were added as myths to persuade men to obey the laws, and for the sake of expediency." [13] In its fourth and most familiar

---

[2] I. x.   [3] I. xi.   [4] I. xii–xiii.   [5] I. xv. 2.   [6] I. xiv; I. xv. 3.
[7] Romans 7:23.   [8] Ezekiel 43:12–13.   [9] Hebrews 7:12.   [10] James 1:25.
[11] *Sectae;* see above, I. v. 10, and Introduction, pp. xc–xci.
[12] Aristotle *Metaphysics* II. 3. 995a 4.   [13] *Ibid.* XII. 8. 1074b 3.

sense, this term "law" means the science or doctrine or universal judgment of matters of civil justice and benefit, and of their opposites.[14]

4. Taken in this last sense, law may be considered in two ways. In one way it may be considered in itself, as it only shows what is just or unjust, beneficial or harmful; and as such it is called the science or doctrine of right (*juris*). In another way it may be considered according as with regard to its observance there is given a command coercive through punishment or reward to be distributed in the present world, or according as it is handed down by way of such a command; and considered in this way it most properly is called, and is, a law.[15] It was in this sense that Aristotle also defined it in the last book of the *Ethics*, Chapter 8, when he said: "Law has coercive force, for it is discourse emerging from prudence and understanding." [16] Law, then, is a "discourse" or statement "emerging from prudence and" political "understanding," that is, it is an ordinance made by political prudence, concerning matters of justice and benefit and their opposites, and having "coercive force," that is, concerning whose observance there is given a command which one is compelled to observe, or which is made by way of such a command.

5. Hence not all true cognitions of matters of civil justice and benefit are laws unless a coercive command has been given concerning their observance, or they have been made by way of a command, although such true cognition is necessarily required for a perfect law. Indeed, sometimes false cognitions of the just and the beneficial become laws,[17] when there is given a command to observe them, or they are made by way of a command. An example of this is found in the regions of certain barbarians, who cause it to be observed as just that a murderer be absolved of civil guilt and punishment on payment of a fine. This, however, is absolutely unjust, and consequently the laws of such barbarians are not absolutely perfect. For although they have the proper form, that is, a coercive command of observance, they lack a proper condition, that is, the proper and true ordering of justice.

6. Under this sense of law are included all standards of civil justice and benefit established by human authority, such as customs, statutes, plebiscites, decretals,[18] and all similar rules which are based upon human authority as we have said.

---

[14] On these four senses of "law," see Vol. I, p. 133.

[15] This conception of coerciveness as the essence of law is a noteworthy departure from the medieval tradition's emphasis on reason as the essence of law. See Vol. I, pp. 133–34.

[16] Aristotle *Nicomachean Ethics* x. 9. 1180a 21.

[17] On Marsilius' uniqueness on this point in relation to the medieval tradition, see Vol. I, p. 134.

[18] See, however, below, I. xiii. 5; II. xxviii. 29.

7. We must not overlook, however, that both the evangelical law and the Mosaic, and perhaps the other religions as well, may be considered and compared in different ways in whole or in part, in relation to human acts for the status of the present or the future world. For they sometimes come, or have hitherto come, or will come, under the third sense of law, and sometimes under the last, as will be shown more fully in Chapters VIII and IX of Discourse II. Moreover, some of these laws are true, while others are false fancies and empty promises.

It is now clear, then, that there exists a standard or law of human civil acts, and what this is.

CHAPTER XI: ON THE NECESSITY FOR MAKING LAWS (TAKEN IN THEIR MOST PROPER SENSE); AND THAT NO RULER, HOWEVER VIRTUOUS OR JUST, SHOULD RULE WITHOUT LAWS

HAVING thus distinguished these various meanings of "law," we wish to show the end or necessity of law in its last and most proper sense. The principal end is civil justice and the common benefit; the secondary end is the security of rulers, especially those with hereditary succes. on, and the long duration of governments. The primary necessity of the law, then, is as follows: It is necessary to establish in the polity that without which civil judgments cannot be made with complete rightness, and through which these judgments are properly made and preserved from defect so far as it is humanly possible. Such a thing is the law,[1] when the ruler is directed to make civil judgments in accordance with it. Therefore, the establishment of law is necessary in the polity. The major premise of this demonstration is almost self-evident, and is very close to being indemonstrable. Its certainty can and should be grasped from Chapter V, paragraph 7 of this discourse. The minor premise will now be proved in this way: To make a good judgment, there are required a right emotion of the judges and a true knowledge of the matters to be judged; the opposites of which corrupt civil judgments. For if the judge has a perverted emotion, such as hate, love, or avarice, this perverts his desire. But such emotions are kept away from the judgment, and it is preserved from them, when the judge or ruler is directed to make judgments according to the

---

[1] On the relation of this exaltation of law to the view taken in the preceding chapter (para. 5) that laws may be unjust, see Vol. I, pp. 139 ff.

laws, because the law lacks all perverted emotion; for it is not made useful for friend or harmful for foe, but universally for all those who perform civil acts well or badly. For all other things are accidental to the law and are outside it; but they are not similarly outside the judge. Persons involved in a judgment can be friendly or inimical to the judge, helpful or harmful to him, by making him a gift or a promise; and in other ways too they can arouse in the judge a desire which perverts his judgment. Consequently, no judgment, so far as possible, should be entrusted to the discretion of the judge, but rather it should be determined by law and pronounced in accordance with it.

2. This was also the view of the divine Aristotle in the *Politics*, Book III, Chapter 9, where he asks whether it is better for a polity to be ruled by the best man without law or by the best laws; and he replies as follows: "That is better," that is, superior for judging, "which entirely lacks the passionate factor," that is, the emotion which may pervert the judgment, "than that to which passion is natural. But law does not have this," that is, passion or emotion, "while every human soul must necessarily have it"; [2] and he said "every," not excepting anyone, however virtuous. He repeats this view in the *Rhetoric*, Book I, Chapter 1: "Most of all" is this required, that is, that nothing be left to the discretion of the judge, to be judged apart from the law, "because the judgment of the legislator," that is, the law, "is not partial," that is, it is not made on account of some one particular man, "but is concerned with future and universal matters. Now the judge and the magistrate judge about present and determinate matters, with which love and hate and private benefit are often involved, so that they cannot sufficiently see the truth, but instead have regard in their judgments to their own private pleasure and displeasure." [3] He also makes this point in Book I, Chapter 2 of the same treatise: "We do not render the same judgments when we are pleased as when we are pained, when we love as when we hate." [4]

3. A judgment is also corrupted through the ignorance of the judges, even if they be of good emotion or intention. This sin or defect is removed and remedied by the law, for in the law is determined well-nigh perfectly what is just or unjust, beneficial or harmful, with regard to each human civil act. Such determination cannot be made so adequately by any one man, however intelligent he may be. For no single man, and perhaps not even all the men of one era, could investigate or remember all the civil acts determined in the law; indeed, what was said about them by the

---

[2] Aristotle *Politics* III. 15. 1286a 17.   [3] Aristotle *Rhetoric* I. 1. 1354b 4 ff.
[4] *Ibid*. I. 2. 1356a 14. See Vol. I, pp. 140–41, 206, 218.

first investigators and also by all the men of the same era who observed such acts was meager and imperfect, and attained its completion only subsequently through the additions made by later investigators. This can be sufficiently seen from experience, in the additions, subtractions, and complete changes sometimes made in the laws in different eras, or at different times within the same era.

Aristotle also attests to this in the *Politics*, Book II, Chapter 2, when he says: "We must not ignore that attention must be paid to the long time and many years of the past, in which it would not have remained unknown if these things were good," [5] that is, the measures which are to be established as laws. He says the same thing in the *Rhetoric*, Book I, Chapter 1: "Laws are made after long study." [6] This is also confirmed by reason, since the making of laws requires prudence, as we saw above from the definition of law, and prudence requires long experience, which, in turn, requires much time. Hence it is said in the sixth book of the *Ethics*: "A sign of what has been said is that while youths may become geometers, and be learned and wise in such sciences, they do not seem to become prudent. The cause is that prudence is of singular things which become known through experience; but a youth is not experienced, for experience requires a long time." [7] Consequently, what one man alone can discover or know by himself, both in the science of civil justice and benefit and in the other sciences, is little or nothing. Moreover, what is observed by the men of one era is quite imperfect by comparison with what is observed in many eras, so that Aristotle, discussing the discovery of truth in every art and discipline, wrote as follows in the *Philosophy*, Book II, Chapter 1: "One man," that is, one discoverer of any art or discipline "contributes to it," that is, discovers about it by himself alone, "little or nothing, but by the contributions of all a great deal is accomplished." [8] This passage is clearer in the translation from the Arabic, in which it reads as follows: "Each of them," that is, each of the discoverers of any art or discipline, "comprehends little or nothing about the truth. But when a collection is made from among all who have achieved some comprehension, what is collected will be of considerable quantity." [9] This may especially be seen in the case of astrology.[10]

It is in this way, then, by men's mutual help and the addition of

---

[5] Aristotle *Politics* II. 5. 1264a 1.   [6] Aristotle *Rhetoric* I. 1. 1354b 3.
[7] Aristotle *Nicomachean Ethics* VI. 9. 1142a 12.   [8] Aristotle *Metaphysics* II. 1. 993b 2.
[9] For the Latin translation from the Arabic, see *Aristotelis opera*, ed. Manardus (Venice, 1560), Vol. IV, fol. 47v.
[10] Marsilius' special mention of "astrology" here may have been occasioned not only by his long acquaintance with Peter of Abano but also by the work he himself had done in the subject. See Vol. I, p. 20 and p. 22, n. 17.

later to earlier discoveries, that all arts and disciplines have been perfected. Aristotle indicated this figuratively with regard to the discovery of music in the same place cited above, when he said: "If there had been no Timotheus, we should be lacking much melody; but if there had been no Phrynes, there would have been no Timotheus"; [11] that is, Timotheus would not have been so accomplished in melody if he had not had the melodies previously discovered by Phrynes. Averroes expounds these words as follows in the second book of his *Commentary:* "And what he," that is, Aristotle, "says in this chapter is clear. For no one can discover by himself the larger part of the practical or considerative," that is, theoretic, "sciences, because these are completed only through the assistance which an earlier investigator gives to the one following him." [12] And Aristotle says the same thing in the second book of the *Refutations,* last chapter,[13] concerning the discovery of rhetoric and of all other disciplines, whatever the case may have been with regard to the discovery of logic, whose complete development he ascribed to himself alone without the discovery or assistance of any predecessor; in which he seems to have been unique among men. He also makes the same point in the *Ethics,* Book VIII, Chapter 1: "Two persons are better able to act and to understand" [14] (supply: than one alone). But if two, then more than two, both simultaneously and successively, can do more than one man alone. And this is what Aristotle says with regard to our present subject in the *Politics,* Book III, Chapter 9: "It will appear most unreasonable if one man should perceive better, judging with only two eyes and two ears and acting with only two hands and feet, than many persons with many such organs." [15]

Since, then, the law is an eye composed of many eyes, that is, the considered comprehension of many comprehenders for avoiding error in civil judgments and for judging rightly, it is safer that these judgments be made according to law than according to the discretion of the judge. For this reason it is necessary to establish the law, if polities are to be ordered for the best with regard to their civil justice and benefit; for through the law, civil judgments are preserved from the ignorance and perverted emotion of the judges. This was the minor premise of the demonstration

---

[11] Aristotle, *Metaphysics* II. 1. 993b 15; inserting, with Bigongiari (p. 42), *non* before *Phrynes.*

[12] Averroes *Commentarius in Aristotelis Metaphysicam* Lib. II. cap. i, in *Aristotelis opera,* ed. Manardus (Venice, 1560), Vol. IV, fol. 49r.

[13] Aristotle *On Sophistical Refutations* 34. 183b 34 ff.

[14] Aristotle *Nicomachean Ethics* VIII. 1. 1155a 16.

[15] Aristotle *Politics* III. 16. 1287b 26. Aristotle himself uses this consideration as an argument for having many rather than few judges in cases not covered by the law, and not, like Marsilius, as an argument for the determination of judgments by law rather than by the discretion of the judges.

by which we have tried from the beginning of this chapter to prove the necessity of the laws. As to the method by which a dispute or civil law-suit is to be decided or judged when it is not determined by law, this will be discussed in Chapter XIV of this discourse.[16] Laws, therefore, are necess. y in order to exclude malice and error from the civil judgments or sentences of the judges.

4. For these reasons, Aristotle counseled that no judge or ruler should be granted the discretionary power to give judgments or commands without law, concerning those civil affairs which could be determined by law. Hence he said in the *Ethics,* Book IV, Chapter 5, the treatise on justice: "We must not allow man to rule, but" in accordance with "reason," [17] that is, law; and Aristotle indicated the cause which we pointed out above, the perverted emotion which can be had by man. In the *Politics,* Book III, Chapter 6, he said: "The first question shows plainly above all that laws rightly made should govern," [18] that is, that rulers should govern in accordance with laws. Again in the same treatise, Book III, Chapter 9, he said: "He who orders the mind to rule seems thereby to order God and the laws to rule; but he who orders man to rule," that is, without law, according to his own discretion, "instigates a beast"; [19] and shortly there-after he indicated the ground for this: "Hence the law is reason without desire," [20] as if to say that the law is reason or knowledge without emo-tion. He repeated this view also in the *Rhetoric,* Book I, Chapter 1: "It is best, therefore, for rightly made laws to determine as many matters as possible and to entrust as little as possible to the judges"; [21] giving the reasons adduced above, the exclusion from civil judgments of the judges' malice and ignorance, which cannot arise in the law as they do in the judge, as we have shown above. And even more clearly Aristotle says in the *Politics,* Book IV, Chapter 4: "Where the laws do not govern," that is, where rulers do not govern in accordance with the laws, "there is no polity," that is, none which is temperate. "For the law should govern all things." [22]

5. It still remains to show another reason why all rulers should govern according to law and not without it, and especially those monarchs who rule with hereditary succession: namely, in order that their governments

---

[16] See below, I. xiv. 3–6.

[17] Aristotle *Nicomachean Ethics* v. 6. 1134a 35. The expression "in accordance with" (*secun-dum*) is added by Marsilius. Note his other similar interpolations in this paragraph, all moti-vated by his literal conception that only man can "rule" or "govern," not reason or law. See Vol. I, pp. 139–40.

[18] Aristotle *Politics* III. 11. 1282b 1.   [19] *Ibid.* III. 16. 1287a 28.

[20] *Ibid.* 1287a 32.   [21] Aristotle *Rhetoric* I. 1. 1354a 32.

[22] Aristotle *Politics* IV. 4. 1292a 32. By "polity" in this passage Aristotle himself means a constitution of any kind, whether "temperate" or "diseased."

may be more secure and longer lasting. This was the second reason for the
necessity of laws which we indicated at the beginning of this chapter.
For when rulers govern according to law, their judgments are preserved
from the defect which is caused by ignorance and perverted emotion.
Hence the rulers are regulated both in themselves and in relation to their
citizen subjects, and they suffer less from sedition and from the consequent destruction of their governments which they would incur if they
acted badly according to their own discretion, as Aristotle clearly says in the
Politics, Book V, Chapter 5: "For a kingdom is destroyed least of all by
external forces: its destruction most usually comes from within itself. It
is destroyed in two ways: one is when those who share the ruling power
quarrel among themselves, the other is when they try to govern tyrannically,
by controlling more things, and contrary to the law. Kingdoms no longer
occur these days, but if monarchies occur, they are rather tyrannies." [23]

6. Someone will raise an objection about the best man, who lacks ignorance and perverted emotion.[24] As for us, however, we reply that such a
man happens very rarely,[25] and that even when he does he is not equal in
virtue to the law, as we proved above from Aristotle, from reason, and from
sense experience. For every soul sometimes has a vicious emotion. We can
readily prove this through the thirteenth chapter of Daniel; for it is there
written that "two elders came full of wicked device against Susanna, to
put her to death." [26] Now these were old men and priests and judges
of the people that year: nevertheless they bore false witness against her because she would not acquiesce to their vicious lust. If, then, old priests,
about whom it would least be expected, were corrupted by carnal lust,
what should be thought of other men, and how much more will they be
corrupted by avarice and other vicious emotions? Certainly no one, however virtuous, can be so lacking in perverted passion and ignorance as is
the law. Therefore, it is safer that civil judgments be regulated by the
law than that they be entrusted to the discretion of a judge, however
virtuous he may be.

7. Let us assume, however, although it is most rare or impossible, that
there is some ruler so heroic that in him neither passion nor ignorance finds
a place. What shall we say of his sons, who are unlike him and who, ruling
in accordance with their own discretion, will commit excesses which result in their being deprived of the rulership? Someone may say that the
father, who is the best of men, will not hand over the government to such

[23] *Ibid.* v. 10. 1312b 38.
[24] Cf. *ibid.* III. 13. 1284a 3 ff.; III. 17. 1288a 15 ff. Cf. also Dante *De monarchia* I. xi, xiii.
[25] See Vol. I, pp. 205–8, and n. 22. Also below, I. xvi. 17.   [26] Daniel 13:28.

sons. This reply, however, is not to be granted, for two reasons: first, because it is not in the father's power to deprive his sons of the succession, since the rulership is a hereditary possession of his family, and second, because even if it were in the father's power to transfer the rulership to whomever he wanted, he would not deprive his sons of it no matter how vicious they were. Hence, Aristotle answers this objection as follows in the *Politics,* Book III, Chapter 9: "It is difficult to believe this," that is, that the father will deprive his sons of the rulership, "as it would require a greater virtue than human nature is capable of." [27] For this reason it is more expedient for rulers that they be regulated and limited by law, than that they make civil judgments according to their own discretion. For when they act according to law, they will do nothing vicious or reprehensible, so that their rule will be made secure and longer lasting.

8. This was the counsel which the distinguished Aristotle gave to all rulers, but to which they pay little heed. As he said in the *Politics,* Book V, Chapter 6: "The fewer things the rulers control," that is, without law, "the longer must every government endure, for they," that is, the rulers, "become less despotic, they are more moderate in their ways and are less hated by their subjects." [28] And then Aristotle adduces the testimony of a certain very prudent king called Theopompus, who gave up some of the power which had been granted to him. We have thought it appropriate to quote Aristotle's words here because of this ruler's uniqueness and his outstanding virtue, almost unheard of in anyone else throughout the ages. This is what Aristotle said: "Theopompus exercised moderation," that is, he lessened his power, which may perhaps have seemed excessive, "among other ways by establishing the office of the ephors: for by diminishing his power he increased his kingdom in time," that is, he made it more durable; "hence in a way he made it not smaller but greater. When his wife asked him whether he was not ashamed to give his children a smaller kingdom than he had received from his father, he replied, 'Not at all, for the power I give to them will be more lasting.' " [29] O heroic voice, proceeding from Theopompus' unheard-of prudence, a voice which should be heeded by all those who wish to wield plenitude of power over their subjects apart from laws! Many rulers, not heeding this voice, have been destroyed. And we ourselves have seen that from lack of attention to this voice not the least of kingdoms in modern times almost underwent a revolution, when its ruler wished to impose upon his subjects an unusual and illegal tax.[30]

---

[27] Aristotle *Politics* III. 15. 1286b 26.   [28] *Ibid.* V. 11. 1313a 20.   [29] *Ibid.* 1313a 26.
[30] This is a reference to the leagues formed in France to protest against Philip the Fair's new taxation in 1314.

It is clear, then, from what we have said, that laws are necessary in polities if they are to be ordered with entire rightness and their governments are to be longer lasting.

CHAPTER XII: ON THE DEMONSTRABLE EFFICIENT CAUSE OF HUMAN LAWS, AND ALSO ON THAT CAUSE WHICH CANNOT BE PROVED BY DEMONSTRATION: WHICH IS TO INQUIRE INTO THE LEGISLATOR. WHENCE IT APPEARS ALSO THAT WHATEVER IS ESTABLISHED BY ELECTION DERIVES ITS AUTHORITY FROM ELECTION ALONE APART FROM ANY OTHER CONFIRMATION

WE must next discuss that efficient cause of the laws which is capable of demonstration. For I do not intend to deal here with that method of establishing laws which can be effected by the immediate act or oracle of God apart from the human will, or which has been so effected in the past. It was by this latter method, as we have said, that the Mosaic law was established; [1] but I shall not deal with it here even insofar as it contains commands with regard to civil acts for the status of the present world. I shall discuss the establishment of only those laws and governments which emerge immediately from the decision of the human mind.

2. Let us say, to begin with, that it can pertain to any citizen to discover the law taken materially and in its third sense, as the science of civil justice and benefit.[2] Such inquiry, however, can be carried on more appropriately and be completed better by those men who are able to have leisure, who are older and experienced in practical affairs, and who are called "prudent men," [3] than by the mechanics who must bend all their efforts to acquiring the necessities of life. But it must be remembered that the true knowledge or discovery of the just and the beneficial, and of their opposites, is not law taken in its last and most proper sense, whereby it is the measure of human

---

[1] See above, i. ix. 2; also i. vi. 3.

[2] See above, i. x. 3. This is really the first subdivision of the fourth sense of law.

[3] This seems to refer both to Aristotle's conception of "prudence" (e.g., *Nicomachean Ethics* vi. 8. 1141b 23 ff.) and to the *prudentes* of the Italian communes. Scholz cites Dino Compagni *Cronica* i. iv; ii. viii (*Scriptores rerum Italicarum*, Vol. IX, Part 2, pp. 16 f., 99, and n. 3).

civil acts, unless there is given a coercive command as to its observance, or it is made by way of such a command, by someone through whose authority its transgressors must and can be punished.[4] Hence, we must now say to whom belongs the authority to make such a command and to punish its transgressors. This, indeed, is to inquire into the legislator or the maker of the law.

3. Let us say, then, in accordance with the truth and the counsel of Aristotle in the *Politics*, Book III, Chapter 6,[5] that the legislator, or the primary and proper efficient cause of the law, is the people or the whole body of citizens, or the weightier part thereof, through its election or will expressed by words in the general assembly of the citizens, commanding or determining that something be done or omitted with regard to human civil acts, under a temporal pain or punishment. By the "weightier part" I mean to take into consideration the quantity and the quality of the persons in that community over which the law is made.[6] The aforesaid whole body of citizens or the weightier part thereof is the legislator regardless of whether it makes the law directly by itself or entrusts the making of it to some person or persons, who are not and cannot be the legislator in the absolute sense, but only in a relative sense and for a particular time and in accordance with the authority of the primary legislator. And I say further that the laws and anything else established through election must receive their necessary approval by that same primary authority and no other, whatever be the case with regard to certain ceremonies or solemnities, which are required not for the being of the matters elected but for their well-being, since the election would be no less valid even if these ceremonies were not performed. Moreover, by the same authority must the laws and other things established through election undergo addition, subtraction, complete change, interpretation, or suspension, insofar as the exigencies of time or place or other circumstances make any such action opportune for the common benefit. And by the same authority, also, must the laws be promulgated or proclaimed after their enactment, so that no citizen or alien who is delinquent in observing them may be excused because of ignorance.

4. A citizen I define in accordance with Aristotle in the *Politics*, Book III, Chapters 1, 3, and 7, as one who participates in the civil community in the government or the deliberative or judicial function according to his

---

[4] See above, I. x. 4-5.   [5] Aristotle *Politics* III. 11. 1281a 39 ff.

[6] The words *personarum et qualitate* were omitted from a younger group of manuscripts and from early printed versions, thereby leading to a mistaken interpretation of Marsilius' position as purely majoritarian. On the sources and meaning of his concept of "weightier part" (*valentior pars*), see Vol. I, pp. 182-99.

rank.[7] By this definition, children, slaves, aliens, and women are distinguished from citizens, although in different ways. For the sons of citizens are citizens in proximate potentiality, lacking only in years. The weightier part of the citizens should be viewed in accordance with the honorable custom of polities, or else it should be determined in accordance with the doctrine of Aristotle in the *Politics,* Book VI, Chapter 2.[8]

5. Having thus defined the citizen and the weightier part of the citizens, let us return to our proposed objective, namely, to demonstrate that the human authority to make laws belongs only to the whole body of the citizens or to the weightier part thereof. Our first proof is as follows. The absolutely primary human authority to make or establish human laws belongs only to those men from whom alone the best laws can emerge. But these are the whole body of the citizens, or the weightier part thereof, which represents that whole body; since it is difficult or impossible for all persons to agree upon one decision, because some men have a deformed[9] nature, disagreeing with the common decision through singular malice or ignorance. The common benefit should not, however, be impeded or neglected because of the unreasonable protest or opposition of these men. The authority to make or establish laws, therefore, belongs only to the whole body of the citizens or to the weightier part thereof.

The first proposition of this demonstration is very close to self-evident, although its force and its ultimate certainty can be grasped from Chapter V of this discourse. The second proposition, that the best law is made only through the hearing and command of the entire multitude, I prove by assuming with Aristotle in the *Politics,* Book III, Chapter 7, that the best law is that which is made for the common benefit of the citizens. As Aristotle said: "That is presumably right," that is, in the laws, "which is for the common benefit of the state and the citizens." [10] But that this is best achieved only by the whole body of the citizens or by the weightier part thereof, which is assumed to be the same thing, I show as follows: That at which the entire body of the citizens aims intellectually and emotionally is more certainly judged as to its truth and more diligently noted as to its common utility. For a defect in some proposed law can be better noted by the greater number than by any part thereof, since every whole, or at least every corporeal whole, is greater in mass and in virtue than any

[7] *Politics* III. 1. 1275a 22, 1275b 19; III. 3. 1277b 33; III. 13. 1283b 42. See Vol. I, pp. 175–79.

[8] *Politics* VI. 3–4. 1318a 3 ff. See Vol. I, pp. 198–99.   [9] See Vol. I, pp. 58–59, 186–87.

[10] *Politics.* III. 13. 1283b 40. The word "presumably" is owing to William of Moerbeke's having translated Aristotle's ἴσως as *forte* instead of as *aequaliter;* for Aristotle's own meaning is, "That is equally right. . . ."

part of it taken separately.[11] Moreover, the common utility of a law is better noted by the entire multitude, because no one knowingly harms himself.[12] Anyone can look to see whether a proposed law leans toward the benefit of one or a few persons more than of the others or of the community, and can protest against it. Such, however, would not be the case were the law made by one or a few persons, considering their own private benefit rather than that of the community. This position is also supported by the arguments which we advanced in Chapter XI of this discourse with regard to the necessity of having laws.

6. Another argument to the principal conclusion is as follows. The authority to make the law belongs only to those men whose making of it will cause the law to be better observed or observed at all. Only the whole body of the citizens are such men. To them, therefore, belongs the authority to make the law. The first proposition of this demonstration is very close to self-evident, for a law would be useless unless it were observed. Hence Aristotle said in the *Politics,* Book IV, Chapter 6: "Laws are not well ordered when they are well made but not obeyed." [13] He also said in Book VI, Chapter 5: "Nothing is accomplished by forming opinions about justice and not carrying them out." [14] The second proposition I prove as follows. That law is better observed by every citizen which each one seems to have imposed upon himself. But such is the law which is made through the hearing and command of the entire multitude of the citizens. The first proposition of this prosyllogism is almost self-evident; for since "the state is a community of free men," as is written in the *Politics,* Book III, Chapter 4,[15] every citizen must be free, and not undergo another's despotism, that is, slavish dominion. But this would not be the case if one or a few of the citizens by their own authority made the law over the whole body of citizens. For those who thus made the law would be despots over the others, and hence such a law, however good it was, would be endured only with reluctance, or not at all, by the rest of the citizens, the more ample part. Having suffered contempt, they would protest against it, and not having been called upon to make it, they would not observe it. On the other hand, a law made by the hearing or consent of the whole multitude, even though it were less useful, would be readily observed and endured by every one of the citizens, because then each would seem to have set the law upon himself, and hence would have no protest against it, but would rather tolerate it with equanimity.[16] The second proposition of

[11] On this argument, see Vol. I, pp. 212–19.   [12] Cf. i. xii. 8 and note 20 thereon.
[13] *Politics* iv. 8. 1294a 3.   [14] *Ibid.* vi. 8. 1322a 5.   [15] *Ibid.* iii. 6. 1279a 21.
[16] On this argument, and the conception of freedom which it involves, see Vol. I, pp. 218–23. The point that those who "have some part in government" will "love" it and will work

the first syllogism I also prove in another way, as follows. The power to cause the laws to be observed belongs only to those men to whom belongs coercive force over the transgressors of the laws. But these men are the whole body of citizens or the weightier part thereof. Therefore, to them alone belongs the authority to make the laws.[17]

7. The principal conclusion is also proved as follows. That practical matter whose proper establishment is of greatest importance for the common sufficiency of the citizens in this life, and whose poor establishment threatens harm for the community, must be established only by the whole body of the citizens. But such a matter is the law. Therefore, the establishment of the law pertains only to the whole body of the citizens. The major premise of this demonstration is almost self-evident, and is grounded in the immediate truths which were set forth in Chapters IV and V of this discourse. For men came together to the civil community in order to attain what was beneficial for sufficiency of life, and to avoid the opposite. Those matters, therefore, which can affect the benefit and harm of all ought to be known and heard by all,[18] in order that they may be able to attain the beneficial and to avoid the opposite. Such matters are the laws, as was assumed in the minor premise. For in the laws being rightly made consists a large part of the whole common sufficiency of men, while under bad laws there arise unbearable slavery, oppression, and misery of the citizens, the final result of which is that the polity is destroyed.

8. Again, and this is an abbreviation and summary of the previous demonstrations: The authority to make laws belongs only to the whole body of the citizens, as we have said, or else it belongs to one or a few men.[19] But it cannot belong to one man alone for the reasons given in Chapter XI and in the first demonstration adduced in the present chapter; for through ignorance or malice or both, this one man could make a bad law, looking more to his own private benefit than to that of the community, so that the law would be tyrannical. For the same reason, the authority to make laws cannot belong to a few; for they too could sin, as above, in making the law for the benefit of a certain few and not for the common benefit, as can be seen in oligarchies. The authority to make the laws be-

---

harder for the common good is made by Thomas Aquinas *S. theol.* II. i. qu.105. a.1. Resp.; *De regimine principum* I. iv (ed. J. Mathis [Turin, 1924], pp. 6–7); see also Ptolemy of Lucca *De regimine principum* II. viii (ed. J. Mathis [Turin, 1924], p. 90), and John of Paris *De potestate regia et papali* cap. xix (ed. D. J. Leclercq, *Jean de Paris et l'ecclésiologie du xiii⁰ siècle* [Paris, 1942], pp. 236–37). In none of these authors, however, is this point made with Marsilius' insistence that the supreme legislative authority can belong only to the people.

[17] See Introduction, above, pp. xxxix–xl, lxxxvii.

[18] On this famous maxim, see Vol. I, pp. 223–24.

[19] Reading, with Scholz, full stop after *pauciores*.

Marsilius says Democracy bad form of gov't but all his arguments are emblematic of this system.

longs, therefore, to the whole body of citizens or to the weightier part thereof, for precisely the opposite reason. For since all the citizens must be measured by the law according to due proportion, and no one knowingly harms or wishes injustice to himself,[20] it follows that all or most wish a law conducing to the common benefit of the citizens.

9. From these same demonstrations it can also be proved, merely by changing the minor term, that the approval, interpretation, and suspension of the laws, and the other matters set forth in paragraph 3 of this chapter, pertain to the authority of the legislator alone. And the same must be thought of everything else which is established by election. For the authority to approve or disapprove rests with those who have the primary authority to elect, or with those to whom they have granted this authority of election. For otherwise, if the part could dissolve by its own authority what had been established by the whole, the part would be greater than the whole, or at least equal to it.

The method of coming together to make the laws will be described in the following chapter.

CHAPTER XIII: ON SOME OBJECTIONS TO THE STATE-MENTS [1] MADE IN THE PRECEDING CHAPTER, AND THEIR REFUTATION, TOGETHER WITH A FULLER EXPOSITION OF THE PROPOSITION

OBJECTIONS will be made to our above statements, to the effect that the authority to make or establish laws does not belong to the whole body of the citizens.[2] The first objection is that those who for the most part are vicious and undiscerning should not make the law. For these two sins, malice and ignorance, must be excluded from the legislator, and it was to avoid them in civil judgments that we upheld the necessity of law in Chapter XI of this discourse. But the people or the whole body of citizens have these sins; for men for the most part seem to be vicious and stupid: "The number of the stupid is infinite," as it is said in the first chapter of Ecclesiastes.[3] Another objection is that it is very difficult or impos-

---

[20] Cf. J. J. Rousseau *Contrat social* II. vi: "nul n'est injuste envers lui-même." Cf. also *ibid.* I. vii. See Vol. I, p. 211, n. 34.

[1] Reading, with Scholz, *ad dicta* for *addicta*.

[2] For antecedents and possible sources of these objections, see Vol. I, pp. 199–203.

[3] Ecclesiastes 1:15.

sible to harmonize the views of many vicious and unintelligent persons; but such is not the case with the few and virtuous. It is more useful, therefore, that the law be made by the few than by the whole body of the citizens or the exceeding majority of them. Again, in every civil community the wise and learned are few in comparison with the multitude of the unlearned. Since, therefore, the law is more usefully made by the wise and learned than by the unlearned and uncultivated, it seems that the authority to make laws belongs to the few, not to the many or to all. Furthermore, that which can be done by fewer persons is needlessly done by more. Since, therefore, the law can be made by the wise, who are few, as has been said, the entire multitude or the greater part of it would needlessly be occupied therein. The authority to make the laws does not belong, therefore, to the whole body of the citizens or to the weightier part thereof.

2. From what we assumed above as the principle of all the things to be demonstrated in this book, namely, that all men desire sufficiency of life and avoid the opposite,[4] we demonstrated in Chapter IV the civil association of men, inasmuch as through such association they can attain this sufficiency, and without it they cannot. Hence too Aristotle says in the *Politics*, Book I, Chapter 1: "There is in all men a natural impulse toward such a community,"[5] that is, the civil community. From this truth there necessarily follows another, which is presented in the *Politics*, Book IV, Chapter 10, namely, that "that part of the state which wishes the polity to endure must be weightier than the part which does not wish it."[6] For nothing is desired by the same specific nature in most of its individual members and immediately at the same time as the thing's destruction, since such a desire would be futile. Indeed, those who do not wish the polity to endure are classed among the slaves, not among the citizens, as are certain aliens. Hence Aristotle says in the *Politics*, Book VII, Chapter 13: "Everyone in the country unites with the subjects in the desire to have a revolution," and then he adds: "It is impossible that there be so many persons in the government," that is, rebellious, or not caring to live a civil life, "that they are stronger than all the others,"[7] that is, than those who wish to carry on a political life (*politizare*). Why this is impossible is obvious; for it would mean that nature errs or is deficient for the most part. If, therefore, the weightier multitude of men wish the state to endure,

---

[4] See above, I. iv. 2.   [5] Aristotle *Politics* I. 2. 1253a 29.

[6] *Ibid*. IV. 12. 1296b 14. It will be noted how Marsilius' interpretation of this statement in terms of biological necessity removes the hypothetical character which it has for Aristotle.

[7] *Ibid*. VII. 14. 1332b 29 ff. It will be noted that Marsilius' interpolations are precisely contrary to the meaning of Aristotle. Perhaps he misunderstood the term for "government" (*politeumate*). On this term, see Introduction, pp. lxxviii–lxxix; and on Marsilius' misinterpretations of Aristotle in this paragraph, see Appendix, pp. 433–34.

as seems to have been well said, they also wish that without which the state cannot endure. But this is the standard of the just and the beneficial, handed down with a command, and called the law; for "it is impossible for the best-ruled state," that is, the state governed according to virtue, "not to be well ordered by laws," as is said in the *Politics,* Book IV, Chapter 7,[8] and as we demonstrated in Chapter XI of this discourse. Therefore, the weightier multitude of the state wishes to have law, or else there would occur deformity [9] in nature and art in most cases; the impossibility of which is assumed from natural science.[10]

With these manifest truths I again assume that common conception of the mind, that "every whole is greater than its part," which is true with respect both to magnitude or mass and to practical virtue and action. From this it clearly follows of necessity that the whole body of the citizens, or the weightier multitude thereof, which must be taken for the same thing, can better discern what must be elected and what rejected than any part of it taken separately.

3. Now that we have laid down these obvious truths, it is easy to refute the objections whereby one might try to prove that the making of the law does not pertain to the whole body of the citizens or the weightier multitude thereof but rather to a certain few. As for the first objection, that the authority to make laws does not belong to those who in most cases are vicious and undiscerning, this is granted. But when it is added that the whole body of citizens is such, this must be denied. For most of the citizens are neither vicious nor undiscerning most of the time; all or most of them are of sound mind and reason and have a right desire for the polity and for the things necessary for it to endure, like laws and other statutes or customs, as was shown above. For although not every citizen nor the greater number of the citizens be discoverers of the laws, yet every citizen can judge of what has been discovered and proposed to him by someone else, and can discern what must be added, subtracted, or changed. Hence in the major premise's reference to the "undiscerning," if what is meant is that because most of the citizens cannot discover the law by themselves, therefore they ought not to establish the law, this must be denied as manifestly false, as is borne out by sense induction and by Aristotle in the *Politics,* Book III, Chapter 6. By induction we can see that many men judge rightly about the quality of a picture, a house, a ship, and other works of art, even though they would have been unable to discover or produce them.

---

[8] *Politics.* iv. 8. 1293b 42.   [9] *Orbatio.* On this term, see Vol. I, pp. 58–59.
[10] Cf. Aristotle *Physics* ii. 8. 199a 9 ff.; *Nicomachean Ethics* i. 9. 1099b 20–24. On this argument from the non-futility of natural desire, and its relation to the Averroist doctrine of the unity of the intellect, see below, Appendix, pp. 435 ff. See also Vol. I, pp. 57 ff., 208–12.

Aristotle also attests to this in the place just cited, answering the proposed objection with these words: "About some things the man who made them is not the only or the best judge." [11] He proves this in many species of arts, and indicates that the same is true for all the others.

4. Nor is this position invalidated by those who say that the wise, who are few, can discern what should be enacted with regard to practical matters better than can the rest of the multitude. For even if this be true, it still does not follow that the wise can discern what should be enacted better than can the whole multitude, in which the wise are included together with the less learned. For every whole is greater than its part both in action and in discernment. This was undoubtedly the view of Aristotle in the *Politics,* Book III, Chapter 6, when he said: "The multitude is justly dominant in the more important matters," that is, the multitude or the whole body of citizens or the weightier part thereof, which he here signifies by the term "multitude," should justly be dominant with respect to the more important matters in the polity; and he gives this reason: "The people is composed of many persons including the council and the judiciary and the honorable class, and all of these together are more ample than any single person or group, including the few rulers who hold high governmental offices." [12] He means that the people, or the multitude composed of all the groups of the polity or city taken together, is more ample than any part of it taken separately, and consequently its judgment is more secure than that of any such part, whether that part be the common mass, which he here signified by the term "council" (*consilium*), such as the farmers, artisans, and others of that sort; or whether it be the "judiciary," that is, those officials who assist the ruler in judicial functions, as advocates or lawyers and notaries; or whether it be the "honorable class," that is, the group of the best men, who are few, and who alone are appropriately elected to the highest governmental offices; or whether it be any other part of the state taken separately. Moreover, even if we assume what is indeed true, that some of the less learned do not judge about a proposed law or some other practical matter equally as well as do the same number of the learned, still the number of the less learned could be increased to

[11] Aristotle *Politics* III. 11. 1282a 17.

[12] *Ibid.* 1282a 38 ff. Marsilius' misinterpretation of this passage is owing to the fact that he, like the other medieval Aristotelians, interprets *honorabilitas* (William of Moerbeke's translation of Aristotle's τίμημα) to mean "the honorable class," rather than "assessed property." See Vol. I, p. 180, n. 7, and pp. 189–99. In William of Moerbeke's translation as found in Susemihl (p. 197), there is a full stop after *praetorium* ("judiciary") and no comma after *honorabilitas,* so that, without Marsilius' misinterpretations, the English translation should read: "and the assessed property of all of these together is greater than that of the persons who either as individuals or as members of small groups hold high governmental offices."

such an extent that they would judge about these matters equally as well as, or even better than, the few who are more learned. Aristotle stated this clearly in the place cited above when he undertook to confirm this view: "If the multitude be not too vile, each member of it will indeed be a worse judge than those who have knowledge; but taken all together they will be better judges, or at least not worse."[13]

As for the passage quoted from the first chapter of Ecclesiastes that "the number of the stupid is infinite," it must be replied that by "stupid" was meant those who are less learned or who do not have leisure for liberal functions, but who nevertheless share in the understanding and judgment of practical matters, although not equally with those who have leisure. Or perhaps the wise author, as Jerome says in his commentary thereon, meant by "stupid" the unbelievers who, however much they may know the worldly sciences, are stupid in an absolute sense, in keeping with the statement of the Apostle in the first epistle to the Corinthians, Chapter 3: "The wisdom of this world is stupidity with God."[14]

5. The second objection carries little weight, for even though it be easier to harmonize the views of fewer persons than of many, it does not follow that the views of the few, or of the part, are superior to those of the whole multitude, of which the few are a part. For the few would not discern or desire the common benefit equally as well as would the entire multitude of the citizens. Indeed, it would be insecure, as we have already shown, to entrust the making of the law to the discretion of the few. For they would perhaps consult therein their own private benefit, as individuals or as a group, rather than the common benefit, as is quite apparent in those who have made the decretals of the clergy, and as we shall make sufficiently clear in Chapter XXVIII of Discourse II.[15] By this means the way would be opened to oligarchy, just as when the power to make the laws is given to one man alone the opportunity is afforded for tyranny, as we showed above in Chapter XI, paragraph 4, where we quoted from the fourth book of Aristotle's *Ethics,* the treatise on justice.

6. The third objection can be easily refuted from what we have already said: for although the laws can be better made by the wise than by the less learned, it is not therefore to be concluded that they are better made by the wise alone than by the entire multitude of citizens, in which the wise are included. For the assembled multitude of all of these can discern and desire the common justice and benefit to a greater extent than can any

---

[13] *Politics* III. 14. 1282a 15 ff.

[14] I Corinthians 3:19. Cf. Peter Lombard *Collectanea* on I Corinthians (PL 191. 1543–44, 1563). See also Haimo *Expositio in epistolas s. Pauli* on I Corinthians 1 (PL 117. 515 ff.).

[15] See below, II. xxviii. 29.

part of that multitude taken separately, however prudent that part may be.

7. Hence those do not speak the truth who hold that the less learned multitude impedes the choice and approval of the true or common good; rather, the multitude is of help in this function when it is joined to those who are more learned and more experienced. For although the multitude cannot by itself discover true and useful measures, it can nevertheless discern and judge the measures discovered and proposed to it by others, as to whether they should be added to, or subtracted from, or completely changed, or rejected. For many things which a man would have been unable to initiate or discover by himself, he can comprehend and bring to completion after they have been explained to him by someone else. For the beginnings of things are the most difficult to discover; as Aristotle says in the second book of the *Refutations,* last chapter: "Most difficult is it to see the beginning," [16] that is, of the truth proper to each discipline. But when this has been discovered, it is easy to add the remainder or to extend it. Hence, while only the best and most acute minds can discover the principles of the sciences, the arts, and other disciplines, nevertheless when these principles have been discovered, additions can be made to them by men of humbler mind. Nor should the latter be called undiscerning because they cannot discover such principles by themselves; on the contrary, they should be numbered among good men, as Aristotle said in the *Ethics,* Book I, Chapter 2: "That man is best who has achieved an understanding of all things by himself. But he too is good who hearkens to the wise words of another," [17] that is, by listening to him attentively and not contradicting him without reason.

8. It [18] is hence appropriate and highly useful that the whole body of citizens entrust to those who are prudent and experienced the investigation, discovery, and examination of the standards, the future laws or statutes, concerning civil justice and benefit, common difficulties or burdens, and other similar matters. Either some of these prudent and experienced men may be elected by each of the primary parts of the state enumerated in Chapter V, paragraph 1, according to the proportion of each part; or else all these men may be elected by all the citizens assembled together. And this will be an appropriate and useful method whereby to come together to discover the laws without detriment to the rest of the multitude, that is, the less learned, who would be of little help in the investigation of such

[16] Aristotle *On Sophistical Refutations* 34. 183b 24.

[17] Aristotle *Nicomachean Ethics* 1. 2. 1095b 10, quoting Hesiod *Works and Days* 293.

[18] Scholz, in his note to this passage, points out that in MS C (15th century) there is a note to this passage reading: "sic regulantur consilia anglicorum" ("the councils of the English are regulated in this way").

standards, and would be disturbed in their performance of the other functions necessary both to themselves and to others, which would be burdensome both to each individual and to the community.

After such standards, the future laws, have been discovered and diligently examined, they must be laid before the assembled whole body of citizens for their approval or disapproval, so that if any citizen thinks that something should be added, subtracted, changed, or completely rejected, he can say so, since by this means the law will be more usefully ordained. For, as we have said, the less learned citizens can sometimes perceive something which must be corrected in a proposed law even though they could not have discovered the law itself. Also, the laws thus made by the hearing and consent of the entire multitude will be better observed, nor will anyone have any protest to make against them.

These standards, the future laws, will thus have been made public, and in the general assembly of the citizens those citizens will have been heard who have wanted to make some reasonable statements with regard to them. Then there must again be elected men of the qualities, and by the method, indicated above, or else the aforesaid men must be confirmed; and they, representing the position and authority of the whole body of the citizens, will approve or disapprove in whole or in part the afore-mentioned standards which had been investigated and proposed, or else, if it so wishes, the whole body of the citizens or the weightier part thereof will do this same thing by itself. After this approval, the aforesaid standards are laws and deserve to be so called, not before; and after their publication or proclamation, they alone among human commands make transgressors liable to civil guilt and punishment.[19]

We think we have adequately shown, then, that the authority to make or establish the laws, and to give a command with regard to their observance, belongs only to the whole body of the citizens or to the weightier part thereof as efficient cause, or else to the person or persons to whom the aforesaid whole body has granted this authority.

[19] As Previté-Orton points out, the procedure here set forth by Marsilius corresponds well with that of the Italian communes of his day. See also Vol. I, pp. 23, 197, 254.

CHAPTER XIV: ON THE QUALITIES OR DISPOSITIONS
OF THE PERFECT RULER, THAT IT MAY BE KNOWN
WHAT KIND OF PERSON SHOULD BE NAMED TO
THE RULERSHIP. WHENCE THERE APPEARS ALSO
THE APPROPRIATE MATTER OR SUBJECT OF HU-
MAN LAWS

WE must next discuss the efficient cause of the ruling part of the
state. This will be to show by demonstration who has the authority
to elect this part, and consequently to establish the other parts of the state.
The establishment of the non-elected ruling part has been sufficiently discussed above in Chapter IX, paragraph 5. We shall begin, however, by determining what kind of person should appropriately be elected or promoted to the rulership. For from this we shall proceed with greater certainty to the authority which effects his election or establishment.

2. The man who is to be a perfect ruler should have two intrinsic habits
which cannot exist separately, namely, prudence and moral virtue, especially justice.[1] Prudence is required in order that his understanding may
be guided in ruling. As it is said in the *Politics,* Book III, Chapter 2: "Prudence alone is the virtue proper to a ruler, for it seems appropriate that
the other virtues be common to rulers and subjects."[2] The other habit,
moral virtue, especially justice, is required in order that the ruler's emotion
be right. As Aristotle says in the fourth book of the *Ethics,* the treatise on
justice: "The ruler is the guardian of justice."[3]

3. Prudence, then, is necessary for the man who is to be a ruler because
it makes him magnificently capable for his proper function, the judgment
of matters of civil benefit and justice. For in those civil human acts where
the act itself or its manner is not determined by law, the ruler is guided
by prudence in his judgment of the act or its manner or both, as well as in
his execution of the judgment, whereas without prudence he might err.
To take an example from Sallust's *Catiline,*[4] when the accomplices of
Catiline, powerful Roman citizens, conspired against the republic and
hence were liable to the death penalty, if Cicero the consul had punished
them according to the law in the customary time, place, and manner,

---

[1] On the background and significance of Marsilius' doctrine of the "perfect ruler," see Vol.
I, pp. 243-44.
[2] Aristotle *Politics* III. 4. 1277b 25.   [3] Aristotle *Nicomachean Ethics* v. 6. 1134b 1.
[4] Sallust *De conjuratione Catilinae* cap. lv.

there would very likely have arisen civil war destructive of the polity because of the sedition which these conspirators had incited among the people against the consul and the other rulers. Cicero, the consul or ruler of the city, avoided this danger through his prudence; for he handed the accused men over to the executioners and commanded that they be killed in the prison which perhaps for this reason is called "Tullian."

4. Prudence, then, guides deliberations concerning practical affairs, so that Aristotle in the *Ethics*, Book VI, Chapter 4, said that prudence is "a true reasoned habit of action with regard to the goods and evils of man," [5] insofar as he is man. The reason for this is that the human laws in accordance with which the ruler must regulate human civil acts deal for the most part with practical affairs, and it does not always seem possible to determine by law all such affairs at once, or the manners or circumstances in which they are involved, because these vary and differ with time and place. This is clearly taught by experience, and Aristotle attests to it in the *Ethics*, Book I, Chapter 1: "Political science deals with the good and the just; but there is such great difference and variation among these that they seem to exist by law alone, not by nature," [6] that is, because men wish thus to legislate concerning them, and not because the nature of the practical affairs themselves is so determined that one thing is just and something else unjust.[7] Aristotle also expressed the same point more fully in the *Politics*, Book III, Chapter 9: "But since some things can be comprehended under the laws and other things cannot, it is these latter which make men doubt and question whether it is preferable for the best law rather than the best man to rule. For it is impossible that the things about which they," that is, men, "deliberate be decided by law" [8] (supply: in all cases).

5. For these reasons it was necessary to entrust to the discretion (*arbitrio*) of rulers the judgment of certain aspects of men's civil acts, that is, those aspects which were not determined in themselves, or as to some manner or circumstance, by law. For in those aspects which have been determined by law, the ruler's duty is to follow that legal determination. This was the view of Aristotle in the *Politics*, Book III, Chapter 6: "The ruler, whether one man or many, must have the supreme authority in those cases concerning which the laws cannot speak with certainty, because it is difficult for laws universally to determine about all things." [9] He repeated this view in Chapter 9 of the same book: "There are even now some magistrates, such as judges, who are dominant in judging those cases which the law

<hr />

[5] Aristotle *Nicomachean Ethics* VI. 5. 1140b 5.

[6] *Ibid*. I. 3. 1094b 14.

[7] It is to be noted that Marsilius does not himself endorse this conventionalist position here.

[8] Aristotle *Politics* III. 16. 1287b 19.   [9] *Ibid*. III. 11. 1282b 3.

cannot determine, since no one doubts that in those which it can, the law commands best." [10] Prudence, therefore, is necessary to the ruler in order to judge such cases which cannot be determined by law. This view of Aristotle, which is almost self-evident, can be seen to be certainly true by anyone who cares to demonstrate it through what we said above in Chapter XI.

6. Also necessary to the ruler is moral goodness, that is, virtue, especially justice; for if the ruler be perverted in moral character, the polity will be greatly harmed, however much it be formed by laws. For we have already said that it is difficult or impossible to determine all things at once by laws, but some matters must be entrusted to the discretion of the ruler; and in these matters he can harm the polity if he be of perverted emotion. This was also the view of Aristotle in the *Politics,* Book II, Chapter 8: "Men who are dominant in important matters do much harm if they are villainous," that is, morally vicious; "and they have already harmed the Chalcedonian state." [11] And since they are preserved from this by moral virtue, especially justice, it is therefore appropriate, if we may call "appropriate" what is necessary, that no one who is to be a ruler lack moral virtue, especially justice.

7. It is also appropriate that the future ruler have a certain virtue called equity (*epieikeiam*) by which the judge is guided, especially with respect to his emotions, in those cases where the law is deficient. As Aristotle said in the fourth book of the *Ethics,* the treatise on justice: "This is the nature of equity, that it is a rectification of the law when it fails because of the particular." [12] This, I think, is what the jurists mean by "fairness" (*aequitas*). For it is a benign interpretation or moderation of the law in some case which the law comprehends under rigorous universality, and in which the law is said to be deficient because it does not except that case from the universality of the standard rule, although it would have done so either entirely or with some moderation if it had foreseen its occurrence.[13]

Also, together with these virtues the future ruler is required to have an outstanding love or benevolence for the polity and the citizens. For by this love the ruler's actions will be directed with solicitude and goodness toward the benefit of the community and of the individuals in it.

8. Besides these habits and dispositions the ruler must necessarily have a certain external organ, namely, a definite number of armed men, through whom he can execute his civil sentences upon rebellious and disobedient men by coercive force. As Aristotle said in the *Politics,* Book VII, Chapter 6: "For those who are associated with one another," that is, in civil

[10] *Ibid.* iii. 16. 1287b 15.   [11] *Ibid.* ii. 11. 1272b 41.
[12] Aristotle *Nicomachean Ethics* v. 10. 1137b 27.
[13] Cf. *Corp. jur. civ., Digest* i. iii. 18.

association, "it is necessary to have arms," that is, a multitude of armed men, "because of those who disobey the government," [14] that is, to punish those who disobey the rulers; for the laws and civil judgments would be useless unless they could be carried into execution. But this armed force of the ruler must be determined by the legislator, like the other civil functions: it must be so great that it exceeds the force of each individual citizen separately and of some of the citizens taken together, but not that of all or the majority of the citizens taken together, for otherwise it might happen that the ruler would attempt or be able to violate the laws, and to rule despotically without them or contrary to them. As Aristotle says in the *Politics*, Book III, Chapter 9: "The ruler must have a force which is so great that it is larger than that of a single individual or of several taken together, but smaller than that of the multitude." [15] The phrase "several taken together" (*simul plurium*) must be understood not in a comparative sense, as meaning "majority," but in a positive sense, according as it is derived from "plural number" in the sense of some multitude, but not the weightier part of the citizens. For if it were not understood in this way, Aristotle's words would be self-contradictory. Also, it is not necessary that the future ruler have this coercive power before his election to the rulership, unlike his intrinsic dispositions about which we spoke above. For otherwise, virtuous poor men would never attain to the rulership.[16] The opposite of this was desired by Aristotle himself, when he said in the *Politics*, Book II, Chapter 8: "The very first thing which it is necessary to provide is that the best men be able to have leisure and not be dishonored in any way, not only when in office but also when living as private persons." [17]

9. Let us now summarize the qualities of rulers and the other things necessary to them. Before election, prudence and moral virtue are necessary to the man who is to be elected ruler—or to the men, if there are to be several rulers, as in an aristocracy. Also, to the ruler who holds the highest governmental office of the city or state armed force is necessary as an instrument or external organ for executing his sentences made according to the laws; however, he is not to have this force before his election, but it is to be bestowed on him at the same time as the rulership. Furthermore, out-

---

[14] Aristotle *Politics* VII. 8. 1328b 7.   [15] *Ibid.* III. 15. 1286b 35.

[16] This point helps to throw into its true light Marsilius' combination of quantity with quality in respect of the legislator (above, I. xii. 3); it harmonizes with his defense of the *vulgus* in I. xii–xiii, as against his classification of democracy, where the *vulgus* "rules alone," among the diseased kinds of government (I. viii. 3). The question whether poor men should be made rulers was discussed in detail by Ptolemy of Lucca on the basis of some texts of Aristotle; his answer is mainly in the negative: *De regimine principum* IV. xv, xx (ed. J. Mathis [Turin, 1924], pp. 99–100, 105–6). Cf., however, Aristotle *Politics* III. 11. 1281b 30.

[17] *Politics* II. 11. 1273a 32. See also below, I. xvi. 21.

standing love or benevolence for the state and the citizens adds to the goodness and solicitude of the ruler's civil actions, although this quality is not so necessary a requirement for him as are the others which have been mentioned.

10. Aristotle also upholds these views in the *Politics,* Book V, Chapter 9: "Those who are to rule in the supreme governmental offices must have three qualifications: first, love for the established polity; second, power for the chief tasks of the government; third, virtue and justice"; [18] by "virtue" meaning prudence, which is the bond and mistress of all the virtues. As it is said in the *Ethics,* Book VI, last chapter: "If a man have the one virtue of prudence he will at the same time have all the moral virtues." [19] Aristotle placed prudence and moral virtue together because they do not exist separate from one another. Such seems to have been his view when he wrote in the same book and chapter: "This therefore is clear from what we have said, that it is impossible to be good in the full sense without prudence, or prudent without moral virtue." [20] In the passage from the fifth book of the *Politics* quoted above, Aristotle named the qualifications which we said should belong to the future ruler perhaps in the opposite order of their necessity.

From what we have said, the proper subject or matter of human laws is apparent. For this is the ruler when he will have been sufficiently prepared through prudence and moral virtue, especially justice. In this way, then, have we determined what kind of person the ruler of the city or state should be, and what things are necessary and appropriate to him.

---

[18] *Ibid.* v. 9. 1309a 33. For Aristotle the term which is here translated "power" means ability rather than physical force.

[19] Aristotle *Nicomachean Ethics* VI. 13. 1145a 1.   [20] *Ibid.* 1144b 30.

CHAPTER XV: ON THE EFFICIENT CAUSE OF THE BEST METHOD OF ESTABLISHING THE GOVERNMENT; FROM WHICH THERE ALSO APPEARS THE EFFICIENT CAUSE OF THE OTHER PARTS OF THE STATE

I T now remains to show the efficient cause of the ruler, that is, the cause by which there is given to one or more persons the authority of rulership which is established through election.[1] For it is by this authority that a person becomes a ruler in actuality, and not by his knowledge of the laws, his prudence, or moral virtue, although these are qualities of the perfect ruler. For it happens that many men have these qualities, but nevertheless, lacking this authority, they are not rulers, unless perhaps in proximate potentiality.[2]

2. Taking up the question, then, let us say, in accordance with the truth and the doctrine of Aristotle in the *Politics,* Book III, Chapter 6,[3] that the efficient power to establish or elect the ruler belongs to the legislator or the whole body of the citizens,[4] just as does the power to make the laws, as we said in Chapter XII. And to the legislator similarly belongs the power to make any correction of the ruler and even to depose him, if this be expedient for the common benefit.[5] For this is one of the more important matters in the polity; and such matters pertain to the entire multitude of the citizens, as we concluded in Chapter XIII of this discourse, paragraph 4, from the statements of Aristotle in the *Politics,* Book III, Chapter 6. For "the multitude is dominant in the more important matters,"[6] as was said there by Aristotle. The method of coming together to effect the aforesaid establishment or election of the ruler may perhaps vary according to the variety of provinces. But in whatever ways it may differ, this must be observed in each case, that such election or establishment is always to be made by the authority of the legislator, who, as we have very frequently said, is the whole body of the citizens, or the weightier part thereof. This proposition can and should be proved by the same demonstrations

---

[1] It will be noted that Marsilius distinguishes, at least analytically, between election and the control of election. He has already shown that "election is the more certain standard of government" (1. ix. 9); but he must now show who effects or controls that election.

[2] See Vol. I, p. 244. [3] Aristotle *Politics* III. 11. 1281b 31 ff.

[4] See Vol. I, pp. 237–38, 244–45. [5] See below, I. xviii.

[6] *Politics* III. 11. 1282a 38.

whereby we concluded, in Chapter XII above, that the making of the laws, the changing of them, and all other acts regarding them pertain to the whole body of the citizens. Only the minor term of these demonstrations need be changed, by substituting the term "ruler" for the term "law."

3. This proposition and its truth are very probable, if we may call "probable" what is necessary. For to whomever it pertains to generate some form, it also pertains to determine the subject of that form, as may be seen in all the productive arts. As Aristotle says in the *Physics,* Book II, Chapter 4: "It pertains to the same science to know both the form and the matter to a certain extent, as the physician knows both health and also the bile and phlegm in which health exists, and the builder knows both the form of the house and the matter, that is, wood and bricks." [7] This is also apparent by manifest induction in other natural and artificial objects. The reason for this is that the forms with their operations are the ends for whose sake the matters exist or are generated, as Aristotle says in the same book and chapter. Since, therefore, it pertains to the whole body of the citizens to generate the form, that is, the law, according to which all civil acts must be regulated, it will be seen that it pertains to the same whole body to determine this form's matter, that is, the ruler, whose function it is to order, according to this form, the civil acts of men. And since this is the best of the forms of the civil community, there ought to be determined for it the subject with the best qualities; [8] which we also concluded by probable reasoning in the preceding chapter. Hence it seems that it can appropriately be inferred that the ruler who is elected without hereditary succession is put at the head of the polity by a method which is absolutely superior to that which operates in the case of non-elected rulers, or of rulers named with hereditary succession ensuing.

4. Having shown the efficient cause of this part of the state, we must now discuss, in accordance with our frequently announced plan, the efficient cause which establishes and determines the other parts or offices of the state. Now the primary efficient cause we say is the legislator; the secondary, as it were the instrumental or executive cause, we say is the ruler through the authority granted to him for this purpose by the legislator, in accordance with the form which the legislator has given to him. This form is the law, in accordance with which the ruler must always, so far as possible, perform and regulate civil acts, as was shown in the preceding chapter. For although the legislator, as the primary and proper cause, must determine which persons must exercise what offices in the state, the execution of such matters, as also of all other legal provisions, is com-

---

[7] Aristotle *Physics* II. 2. 194a 22   [8] Cf. above, I. ix. 7 and n. 24 thereto.

manded, or as the case may be, prohibited, by the ruling part of the state. For the execution of the legal provisions is effected more conveniently by the ruler than by the entire multitude of the citizens, since in this function one or a few rulers suffice, whereas the entire community would needlessly be occupied therein,[9] and would be distracted from the other necessary functions. For when the rulers do this, the entire community does it, since the rulers do it in accordance with the legal determination of the community, and, being few or only one in number, they can execute the legal provisions more easily.

5. In this respect human arrangements appropriately imitated nature. For the state and its parts established according to reason are analogous to the animal and its parts perfectly formed according to nature, as is apparent from Aristotle's *Politics*, Books I and V, Chapter 2.[10] The action of the human mind in appropriately establishing the state and its parts was proportionate, therefore, to the action of nature in perfectly forming the animal. This proportion, from which the efficient and determining cause of the parts of the state will appear more fully, we shall undertake to describe following Aristotle in the sixteenth chapter of his treatise *On Animals*[11] and also Galen in a certain book of his called *On the Formation of the Foetus*,[12] together with the more expert of their successors. By a certain principle or moving cause, whether it be the form of the matter or separate from it, or something else having the power to generate the animal and its parts, there is formed first in time and in nature a certain organic part of the animal itself. In this part there is a natural virtue or power, together with some heat as an active principle; and this power and heat have a universal active causality for forming and differentiating each of the other parts of the animal. This first-formed part is the heart, or something analogous to the heart, as Aristotle said in the above-mentioned text, and as is also said by the other more expert philosophers. These men should be believed because of their experience in this field, and we must now assume what they say without proof, since to demonstrate it does not pertain to our present inquiry. Now this first-formed part of the animal is nobler and more perfect in its qualities and dispositions than the other parts of the animal. For in generating it, nature established in it a power and instrument by which the other parts of the animal are formed from suitable matter, and are separated, differentiated, ordered with respect to

---

[9] On this "razor" argument, see Vol. I, pp. 235–36.

[10] Aristotle *Politics* I. 5. 1254a 31 ff.; v. 3. 1302b 38.

[11] See Aristotle *De partibus animalium* III. 4. 665a 29 ff.

[12] See Galen *De formatione foetus* cap. iv (in *Opera*, ed. R. Chartier [Paris, 1679], V, 292 ff.).

one another, conserved in their dispositions, and preserved from harm so far as nature allows. Also, lapses from their nature because of illness or other impediment are repaired by the power of this part.

6. The state appropriately established according to reason must be considered in an analogous manner. For by the soul of the whole body of citizens or of its weightier part, there is first formed or should be formed in that whole body a part which is analogous to the heart. In this part, the soul of the whole body of citizens establishes a certain virtue or form with the active power or authority to establish the other parts of the state. This part is the government; its virtue, universal in causality, is the law; and its active power is the authority to judge, command, and execute sentences concerning civil justice and benefit. Because of this, Aristotle said in the *Politics,* Book VII, Chapter 6, that this part is "the most necessary of all" [13] in the state. The reason for this is that the sufficiency which is had through the other parts or offices of the state could, if they did not exist, be had sufficiently from some other source, such as through shipping and other kinds of commerce, although not so easily. But without the existence of the government the civil community cannot endure, or endure for long, since "it is necessary that scandals arise," [14] as it is said in Matthew. These "scandals" are men's contentions and injuries toward one another, and if they were not avenged or measured by a standard of justice, that is, the law, and by the ruler whose function it is to measure such things in accordance with the law, there would result the fighting and separation of the assembled men and finally the destruction of the state and loss of the sufficient life. [15]

7. This part of the state must be nobler and more perfect in its qualities, prudence and moral virtue, than the other parts of the state. As Aristotle said in the *Politics,* Book VII, Chapter 12: "If some men were as different from others as we believe gods and heroes to differ from men, in the first place being much superior in body, and then in soul, so that the superiority of the rulers over their subjects would be manifest beyond a doubt, it would clearly be better for the former to rule and the latter to be ruled once and for all," [16] that is, for life. Also the efficient cause of the state, that is, the soul of the whole body of citizens, establishes in this first part a certain virtue universal in causality, the law, and also the authority or power to make civil judgments, to command and to execute them, and all this in accordance with the law, not otherwise. This can be seen again from our analogy. The innate heat of the heart, through which the heart or its form

---

[13] Aristotle *Politics* VII. 8. 1328b 13.
[15] See Vol. I, pp. 108 ff.
[14] Matthew 18:7.
[16] Aristotle *Politics* VII. 14. 1332b 16 ff.

fulfills all its functions, is guided and measured in its functioning through the form or virtue of the heart; otherwise it would not function toward its proper end. Also, the warmth which is called "spirit" and which is like an instrument for fulfilling its functions, is ruled throughout the whole body by the same virtue, for otherwise neither of these heats would function toward its proper end, since fire acts "in a manner inferior to instruments," [17] as it is said in the second book of the treatise *On Generation* and also in the treatise *On the Soul*.[18] In a similar way, the authority of rulership which is given to some man, and which is analogous to the heat of the heart, and also his armed or coercive instrumental power which is analogous to the warmth which we called "spirit," must be regulated by the law in judging, commanding, and executing matters of civil justice and benefit, for otherwise the ruler would not act toward his proper end, the conservation of the state, as was demonstrated in Chapter XI.

8. Furthermore, in accordance with the aforesaid virtue, the law, and the authority given to him, the ruler must establish and differentiate the parts and offices of the state from the appropriate matter, that is, from men having the arts or habits appropriate to the offices. For such men are the proximate matter of the parts of the state, as was said in Chapter VII.[19] For this is the norm or law of well-established polities, to appoint to the offices of the state men who have the functional habits appropriate to the offices, and to ordain that those who do not have such habits, that is, youths, shall learn those habits to which they are naturally more inclined. This was the view of the eminent Aristotle in the *Ethics*, Book I, Chapter 1: "What disciplines there should be in states, and which one each person should learn, is ordained by this," [20] that is, by political or legislative prudence, and consequently by the ruler, who arranges the polity in accordance with the law. Aristotle also said this in the *Politics*, Book VII, Chapter 13: "The statesman making laws should therefore consider all these things, with respect both to the parts of the soul and to their passions." [21] He says this also in Book VIII of the same treatise, Chapter 1: "No one will doubt that the legislator must greatly concern himself with the education of the young. For where this is not done the polities are harmed." [22] From the aforesaid, therefore, it is apparent that it pertains to the legislator to determine or establish the parts and offices of the state, and that the judgment,

---

[17] Aristotle *De generatione et corruptione* II. 9. 336a 13.
[18] Aristotle *De anima* II. 7. 418b 11 ff.   [19] Cf. above, I. vii. 1.
[20] Aristotle *Nicomachean Ethics* I. 2. 1094a 28. On the similarities and differences between Marsilius' use of this statement and that of the other medieval Aristotelians, see Vol. I, pp. 112 ff.
[21] Aristotle *Politics* VII. 14. 1333a 37.   [22] *Ibid.* VIII. 1. 1337a 11.

command, and execution of that determination pertain to the ruler in accordance with the law.

9. This could be proved by the same demonstrations as we used in Chapter XII and earlier in this chapter with respect to the making of the laws and the naming of the ruler, simply by changing the minor term of the syllogisms.

10. As a consequence, no one, especially aliens, is allowed to assume an office in the state at his own pleasure. For no one must or reasonably can undertake at will the exercise of the military or priestly function, nor must the ruler permit this, for the result would be an insufficiency to the state of those things which it is necessary to procure through the other offices. Rather, the ruler must determine the persons, the quantity and the quality of these parts or offices of the state, with respect to their number, their ability, and other similar considerations, in order that the polity may not be destroyed through an immoderate excess of one part in relation to the others.[23] For this reason Aristotle said, in the *Politics,* Book V, Chapter 2: "Revolutions of polities also occur because of disproportionate increase. The body is composed of many parts, and it must grow in due proportion to preserve its symmetry; if this be not done the body will be destroyed, if it increases disproportionately not only in quantity but also in quality. Similarly, the state is composed of many parts, increase in some of which is often unnoticed, like the number of poor in democracies," [24] and like the priesthood in the law of the Christians. Aristotle said the same thing in Book III, Chapter 7 of the *Politics,*[25] but I omit to quote it here for the sake of brevity.

11. Again, this part, the ruler, by his authority in accordance with the law, must command the just and the honorable and prohibit their contraries, both in word and in deed, by affecting with rewards or punishments the merits or demerits of those who observe or transgress his legal commands. In this way the ruler will conserve in its proper being each part of the state, and preserve it from harm and injury. For if any part should do or suffer injury, he who inflicts the injury must be cured through the action of the ruler, by sustaining punishment. For punishment is like medicine for a delict. Hence it is said in the *Ethics,* Book II, Chapter 2: "Punishments are given because of this," that is, because of the pleasures which are had in wrongdoing, "for they are kinds of medicine." [26] He on whom the injury has been inflicted will be cured by receiving com-

---

[23] See Vol. I, pp. 112 ff.   [24] *Politics* v. 3. 1302b 33 ff.
[25] *Ibid.* III. 12–13. 1282b 14 ff.   [26] Aristotle *Nicomachean Ethics* II. 2. 1104b 17.

pensation; so that in this way all things will be brought back to due equality or proportion.

12. Moreover, this ruling part of the state conserves the other parts and assists them in the performance of both their proper and their common functions. Their proper functions are those which have to emerge from their own proper offices, while their common functions are their inter-communications with one another. Both kinds of function would be disturbed if the ruler's action were to cease correcting men who do violence.

13. Consequently, the action of the ruler in the state, like that of the heart in the animal, must never cease. For although the actions of the other parts of the state may at some time cease without harm to any individual, group, or community—such as the action of the military part in time of peace, and similarly with the other parts of the state—the primary action of this ruling part and of its virtue can never cease without harm. For the command and the common guardianship of the things which are lawful and prohibited in accordance with the law must endure at every hour or minute, and whenever anything unlawful or unjust is done, the ruler must compl. .ely regulate such acts or must perform the preliminary steps toward such regulation.

14. From what we have said, it can be sufficiently clear what is the order of the parts of the state in relation to one another. For all the other parts are ordered by and toward the ruler as the first of all the parts for the status of the present world.[27] For in the civil community that part is first which has to establish, determine, and conserve the others in and for the status of the present world or the civil end. But such is the part which rules in accordance with human law, as we have already concluded by probable and demonstrative reasoning. Therefore, it is the first of all the parts of the state, and the others are ordered to it.

Such, then, are our conclusions concerning the efficient cause of the election of the ruling part, the establishment of the other parts of [28] the state, and their order in relation to one another.

---

[27] See Vol. I, p. 111.   [28] Omitting, with Scholz, et after partium.

CHAPTER XVI: WHETHER IT IS MORE EXPEDIENT
FOR THE POLITY TO APPOINT EACH MONARCH IN-
DIVIDUALLY BY A NEW ELECTION, OR TO ELECT
ONE MONARCH ALONE WITH ALL HIS POSTERITY,
WHICH IS USUALLY CALLED HEREDITARY SUCCES-
SION

WITH respect to what we have said there is a recognized problem:
whether, for those who live a civil life and who elect a single man
to be their ruler, it is more expedient to appoint this monarch to rule with
all his posterity, which is usually called hereditary succession, or to appoint
him ruler for his own lifetime alone and to hold a new election whenever
he has died or has otherwise been justly deprived of the rulership. To some,
the former procedure seems preferable for certain apparent reasons.[1] First,
because the monarch who succeeds a member of his own family will take
better care of the commonwealth, regarding it as his private hereditary
property, whereas this is not the case with a monarch who is not sure that
his own heir will be the next ruler. As Aristotle said in the *Politics*, Book
II, Chapter 1: "That receives least care which is common to most men;
for men take the greatest care of what is their own, but less care of what
is common to them all, and then only when it concerns them individually."[2] And later on in the same chapter Aristotle says: "There are two
things which make men solicitous and loving: what belongs to them and
what is dear to them."[3] In Chapter 5 he says: "And also with respect to
pleasure it is indescribable what a difference it makes for a man to feel that
something is his own."[4]

Another argument with respect to the principal question is that the
successors of the hereditary monarch will seem less despotic to their subjects than will rulers newly elected, because the former will have been
accustomed to the rulership and will not regard it as something new where-

---

[1] For sources of these arguments, see Egidius of Rome *De regimine principum* Lib. III. Pars.
II. cap. v; Peter of Auvergne *In Politicorum Aristotelis libros commentarium* Lib. III. Lects.
11, 13, 14 (*Thomae Aquinatis opera omnia*, XXI [Parma, 1866], 482, 490, 495). For other
sources, see Vol. I, p. 244, n. 58; also p. 88. See also the related discussions of the advantages
and disadvantages of having "perpetual" rulers as against rulers for fixed periods only, in
Ptolemy of Lucca *De regimine principum* IV. vii, viii, xvi (ed. J. Mathis [Turin, 1924], pp.
88–91, 101), where many of Marsilius' arguments on each side are anticipated.

[2] Aristotle *Politics* II. 3. 1261b 33.   [3] *Ibid*. II. 4. 1262b 22.

[4] *Ibid*. II. 5. 1263a 40.

from to become exalted and disdainful toward their subjects. But when the monarchs are always newly elected, they very often become exceedingly proud, like the newly rich. As it is said in the *Rhetoric,* Book II, Chapter 24: "All may see with ease the character of those who acquire riches. For they become haughty and proud from the possession of wealth, as if they had all the good things." [5]

2. Furthermore, the subject multitude will be more obedient to those who succeed to the rulership by heredity, because it will have grown accustomed to obeying these rulers' predecessors. As it is said in the *First Philosophy,* Book II, last chapter: "We value that to which we are accustomed"; [6] and in the *Politics,* Book II, Chapter 5, near the end: "He will do less good by making changes than he will do harm by becoming accustomed to rebelling against the rulers." [7] To these words should be added our statements concerning custom in Chapter XVIII, paragraph 6.

3. Again, because some family may have bestowed such great benefits upon the rest of the multitude, or it may excel the other citizens so greatly in virtue, [8] or for both reasons, it will deserve always to rule and never to be ruled. Aristotle discusses this in the *Politics,* Book III, Chapter 8: "A fourth species of kingly monarchy, that of heroic times, was hereditary, over willing subjects, and in accordance with law. For the first rulers were benefactors of the people, in arts or in war; they either brought them together into a community or procured the land for them; thus they were made the kings of voluntary subjects, and their kingship was handed on to their descendants." [9] He makes this point still more clearly in Chapter 9 of the same book: "Whenever, therefore, it happens that a whole family or some individual is so outstanding in virtue as to excel all others in the community, then it is just for this family to be the royal family and supreme over all, or for this one man to be king." [10] He repeats this position in the *Politics,* Book V, Chapter 5: "A kingdom is formed to protect the better class from the people and the king is chosen by the better class from its own number, because either he himself or his family excels in virtue and virtuous actions." [11]

4. Moreover, a better ruler is obtained through hereditary succession because hereditary rulers are more inclined toward virtue, being born of more eminent parents. Thus Aristotle in the second book of the *Politics* quotes a certain poet, Theodectes, whose Helen says: "Who will dare to call a slave the person descended on both sides from divine forbears?"; [12]

[5] Aristotle *Rhetoric* II. 16. 1390b 31 ff.
[7] Aristotle *Politics* II. 8. 1269a 17.
[9] Aristotle *Politics* III. 14. 1285b 4.
[11] *Ibid.* v. 5. 1310b 9.

[6] Aristotle *Metaphysics* II. 3. 994b 32.
[8] Cf. above, I. ix. 4.
[10] *Ibid.* III. 17. 1288a 15.
[12] *Ibid.* I. 6. 1255a 36.

and a little further on Aristotle adds: "For they think it proper that, just as man descends from man, and beast from beast, so from good men a good man is born." [13] Again, the hereditary monarch is usually better nurtured; as Aristotle says in the *Rhetoric,* Book I, Chapter 13: "It is likely that good parents will have good children, and as a man has been nurtured, so will his character be." [14]

5. Again, the hereditary ruler does not undergo those difficulties which always beset the newly elected ruler. For in the case of the latter, there is the difficulty of having virtuous electors, whom it is necessary but difficult to have for a good election. Moreover, when such electors are found, it is difficult for them not to quarrel, and thus quarreling there is danger of leading the entire polity into sedition, as is shown by experience in the election of the ruler of the Romans. Also human minds are often prone to fall into evil,[15] and consequently, because of love or hate, money or entreaty, or hope of some other pleasure or profit, the electors will not always, but rather too rarely, name the better man as ruler.

6. Furthermore, the moral character of a hereditary monarch can be more easily known by the citizens and consuls, since he is a single determinate man, whereas he who is to be newly elected is not thus determinate. For very many are the citizens whom it is possible to elect ruler. But it is easier to know the moral character of one man than of many. And it is important to know the moral character of the ruler, who must be counseled, persuaded, and guided in some matters, however prudent he may be. As it is said in the *Rhetoric,* Book I, Chapter 11: "The moral character of each person provides the most effective means of persuasion." [16]

7. Again, having a hereditary monarch seems to prevent the subjects from ambitious striving for self-promotion, from being rash or presumptuous, and from incitement to sedition. For since the subjects know that the rulership is never owed to them and that they cannot obtain it lawfully, they do not aspire to it or become involved in sinister machinations to obtain it. On the other hand, when they can attain to the rulership lawfully, and believe that they can do so, as is the case where a new monarch is always elected, they spend their time plotting. As Cicero said, in the treatise *On Duties,* Book I: "It is very unfortunate that in the greatest and most brilliant minds there exists very often a desire for honor, power, command, and glory." [17] For, considering themselves worthy of rulership be-

---

13 *Ibid.* 1255b 1.   14 Aristotle *Rhetoric* I. 9. 1367b 29.

15 See Genesis 8:21. Also, for parallels in other medieval writers and in Machiavelli, see Vol. I, p. 201, n. 8.

16 Aristotle *Rhetoric* I. 8. 1366a 12.   17 Cicero *De officiis* I. viii. 26.

cause of some excellence or other, they obtain the votes of the electors by entreaty or bribery, or in some other illegal way.

8. Moreover, an elected monarch, not transmitting the rulership to his descendants, will not dare to bring powerful men to justice, especially by killing them or by other corporeal punishment, even though they transgress the law. For he will be afraid that hatred, bitter enmity, and injuries will result for his own heirs, who will perhaps not be rulers after him. But the hereditary monarch need not fear this, so that he will securely and completely exercise justice over any transgressors of the law.

9. Again, that method of naming the monarch is the more perfect which is in use in more regions, among more peoples, more of the time. For that which is more natural is more perfect; but that is more natural which is found in more cases: "For the nature of things is the nature which is in most of them most of the time," as it is written in the third book of the treatise *On Heaven and Earth* [18] and in the second book of the *Physics*,[19] and as is evident by induction. But the method of naming the monarch by hereditary succession bears this relation to the method of new elections, as is shown by induction in the majority of monarchs, regions, and peoples, and as is also clear from the events described by historians in most times.

10. Finally, the rule of the hereditary monarch is more similar to the governance or rule of the universe; for in the universe there is always, immutably, a single ruler, as it is said in the twelfth book of the *Philosophy,* last chapter: "One ruler let there be, because things do not wish to be ordered badly." [20] But such seems to occur where the son succeeds his father in the rulership, because of the unity of the family and because the father is deemed to be almost the same person as the son.

11. Now let us assume the conclusions set forth above in Chapter XIV: that every monarch must be prudent and good in moral virtue, especially justice, and excellently disposed toward the other citizens. Let us also accept what we said in Chapter IX, paragraph 10, concerning the diversity of inclinations and dispositions of peoples and regions toward different kinds of government. It must then be held, I believe, that for the sufficiency of civil life it is absolutely better for the commonwealth that each monarch be named by a new election rather than by hereditary succession. For this method, which we have called the preferable method of naming the monarch, will always, or with rare failures, operate to yield the best possible ruler; either a perfect one or at least an adequate one. For by the

[18] Aristotle *De caelo* III. 2. 301a 8.   [19] See Aristotle *Physics* II. 8. 198b 35 ff.
[20] Aristotle *Metaphysics* XII. 10. 1076a 3.

election of the human legislator the common benefit of the citizens is almost always aimed at and attained, rarely failing, as was shown in Chapter
XIII.[21] But an adequate monarch is almost the most important factor affecting the common benefit, as experience teaches and as was deduced by
reason in Chapter XIV. But hereditary succession, which depends upon
birth and is often fortuitous, cannot give such a man with such certainty,
as is plain by induction in those states which name the monarch in this
way.

12. Moreover, every good feature which is absolutely required in the
monarch, and which is furnished by hereditary succession, the method of
new election will likewise exhibit almost always, but the converse is not
true. For the civil multitude can elect the monarch's heir and successor if
he is virtuous and prudent; but if he is not of such character, a new election
will yield some other person who is virtuous and prudent. Hereditary succession, however, could not have yielded such a person in this case.

13. Again, because of the fact that the future monarch will be newly
elected, the present one will be made more diligent in his civil guardianship of the persons and things of the community: first, because he will be
virtuous, as we assume him to be by the fact of his having been elected;
second, because he will fear correction by the next ruler; and third, because he will want his children to be deserving of election in the future.
Hence too he will take greater care that they be virtuous and well educated;
and the children, considering this fact, will aim with greater effort at the
virtues and at the performance of their duties. Hence, it is very likely that
a son brought up to be similar to his father in virtue will be named to the
rulership because of his merit and the obedience customarily given to him,
so long as the son has such character. What we have here said is also the
view of the Philosopher in the *Politics,* Book I, Chapter 9; Book II, Chapter
8; Book III, Chapters 2 and 9; and Book VII, Chapter 12.[22]

14. Let us now undertake to refute the arguments to the contrary. As
for what was first adduced, that the hereditary monarch will take greater
care of the common benefit or of the commonwealth, since he will regard
it as his private hereditary property,[23] it must be replied that the monarch
who obtains his position by a new election will do this more, since it is
clear that he is more often prudent and good, as is plain from induction.
For when the son of a monarch turns out to be virtuous he can always
be elected to rule, although the converse is not true. This ruler will act in

---

[21] Cf. above, I. xiii. 2. See also Vol. I, pp. 57–58, incl. n. 34; pp. 218–19.
[22] See Aristotle *Politics* I. 12. 1259b 10 ff.; II. 11. 1272b 35 ff.; III. 4. 1277a 14 ff.; 15. 1285b
37 ff.; VII. 14. 1332b 12 ff.
[23] See the present chapter, para. 1.

accordance with his individual and civil virtue, for the sake of the best end in this world, deeds of virtue, and in order to obtain the resulting external honor and fame for himself, his memory, and his posterity.[24] He will, then, take care of the commonwealth or community equally as much as or more than will the hereditary monarch, who, knowing in advance that his descendants will succeed him in the rulership, very often pays no attention to such aims if he is not virtuous, and is less afraid of being corrected if he is delinquent.

15. And as for what was added, that the hereditary monarch will be less despotic than the elected one,[25] this must be denied. For he who ought to rule politically becomes despotic through imprudence, or malice, or both, especially when he hopes to be able to do wrong with impunity. But, now, he who is named monarch by a new election is usually more prudent and better than the hereditary one, so that he will abstain more from wrongdoing through virtue. Also he is less able to do wrong with impunity, and is more easily corrected than the ruler whose descendants will definitely succeed him in the rulership. The example adduced concerning the newly rich does not negate the present argument. For the newly rich, ignorant and morally vicious, feel disdain or contempt for others; riches come to them as an instrument wherewith to exploit their malice, although riches in their own nature are determined more toward the goodness and sufficiency of the life of this world than toward the opposite, as is plain from the *Politics*, Book I, Chapters 6, 7, and 8.[26] So it is with the rulership. Hence when these things come to prudent and virtuous men, such as will more often be had as rulers by a new election than by hereditary succession, the result will be not despotism and arrogance but praiseworthy deeds, which the virtuous ruler could not perform while lacking such instruments. We grant to our opponents that the subject multitude does sometimes happen to suffer despotism from the first elected ruler, but this comes with those who succeed him by inheritance. For since he was newly elected he did not inherit the rulership from his parents, and therefore, according to the reasoning of our opponents, he will show arrogance and contempt for his subjects because of being newly arrived, just as with the newly rich. In truth, however, our opponents should say rather the opposite of this; for it is because of the outstanding virtue of this first elected ruler, or

---

[24] See the present chapter, para. 1. This view of the ruler's personal end or reward as purely secular stands in sharp contrast with the traditional medieval doctrine that only the future life can give an adequate reward to the ruler. For references, see Vol. I, p. 78, n. 7.

[25] See the present chapter, para. 1.

[26] Aristotle *Politics* I. 8. 1256a 1 ff.; 9. 1256b 40 ff.; 10. 1258a 27 ff.; 11. 1258b 12 ff. On the contrast of this defense of "riches" with Marsilius' treatment of evangelical poverty (below, II. xi–xiv), see Vol. I, pp. 80–81.

the great benefits bestowed by him on the multitude, that the rulership is granted to his familial descendants as being virtuous because of him, so that it is he who is the more virtuous. For "always," according to the oracle of the wise Gentile, "the cause of an attribute's inhering in a subject, itself inheres in the subject to a greater degree than does that attribute." [27]

16. As for the argument concerning the obedience of the subject multitude,[28] although this must be paid special attention above all the others, it is not necessary to concede that the newly elected monarch is less excellent in this respect than the hereditary ruler. For although obedience is strengthened by custom, we nevertheless see that novelty gives rise to greater admiration and respect, especially when the newly elected ruler is from another region or province.[29] Again, the custom of obedience is directed absolutely to the laws and the government, and only in a relative sense to the person of the ruler. Whence we always see that all men respect the government and the laws in thought and in deed, although they sometimes despise the person of the ruler because of his inadequacy; but the converse is not true. Consequently, since the subject multitude is almost everywhere accustomed to obeying the laws and the governments, a change in the family of the person ruling does less harm than the adequacy of the newly elected ruler does good; and from the people's respect for him because of his virtue there results an even greater obedience to the government and the laws. A sign that obedience to the government and the laws is sufficient is what we see in the ecclesiastic household with regard to the Roman pope. For the subject multitude almost always gives him his due obedience, and even more than is due. We shall show the cause of this in the first chapter of Discourse II, paragraph 1. This obedience being very great, the ruler may at some time become despotic, when he hopes to go unpunished; we see that this has happened with certain of the aforesaid bishops. And as for what Aristotle said in the second book of the *Politics*, that "he will do less good by making changes," etc., this has reference to those who on any occasion, however slight, seek to change the law or the ruler.

17. As for what Aristotle said in the *Politics*, Book III, Chapter 9, that some family may be found so preeminent in virtue or in doing good for the rest of the multitude, that it will deserve to rule and not be ruled [30]— this might perhaps be true at some particular time and place, but one does

---

[27] Aristotle *Posterior Analytics* I. 2. 72a 28.   [28] See the present chapter, para. 2.

[29] As Previté-Orton points out, this seems to refer to the practice of the Italian communes in choosing a *podestà* from another city.

[30] Aristotle *Politics* III. 17. 1288a 15. Marsilius here paraphrases what he quoted above in the present chapter, para. 3.

not usually find such a family everywhere.[31] Whence Aristotle said in the *Rhetoric*, Book II, Chapter 24: "Nobility means not degenerating from the family nature. This is not usually found in persons of noble birth, who are mostly of little worth. For in the generations of men there is a varying crop as in the fruits of the fields; sometimes, if the family be good, there are born in it for a certain period extraordinary men," that is, men of exceeding virtue; "and then it deteriorates," that is, becomes deficient. "A family of fine nature will degenerate into insanity, as, for example, the descendants of Alcibiades and of the elder Dionysius";[32] that is, although these men, Alcibiades and the elder Dionysius, were illustrious, their descendants were degenerate. It must therefore be said that so long as a family continues to produce noble offspring and it seems expedient to the legislator, it can appropriately be ordained or established that a new ruler shall be obtained by election from this family alone, whenever the old ruler fails, so that a better man may be had from the same family. For it is not certain what kind of monarchs the sons will be, and especially the eldest son, who is almost always and everywhere made the ruler by those who use the method of hereditary succession.

Moreover, although some provinces may sometimes contain such a family of illustrious men, and at the time of the province's origin such a family may have been outstanding because there were then few prudent and virtuous men to elect and to be elected, nevertheless we do not always see this happening. Rather, when the community is reduced to its last resource, as with the Romans, it appears that the ruler must be named by a new election, as by a more certain and more perfect method. For although hereditary rule may seem suited to some regions, even to most, nevertheless this way of naming the ruler is not on that account more perfect than the method of holding a new election for each ruler; just as the artisan's habit or occupation, although it may be found in more regions or persons, is not thereby more perfect than the physician's.

18. Granting the proposition that he who is descended from virtuous parents is more frequently inclined to virtue, and is better nurtured,[33] we must say that the method of electing each new monarch is better in this respect than the method of hereditary succession, since the ruler who obtains his post by election is not merely inclined toward prudence and virtue, as is the hereditary monarch, but is already fully developed in virtue and actually practicing it. But it is better to receive to the ruler-

---

[31] See above, I. xi. 6.   [32] Aristotle *Rhetoric* II. 15. 1390b 23 ff.
[33] See the present chapter, para. 4.

ship such a man of actual ability and accomplishment; and he is not so frequently furnished by the method of hereditary succession.

19. Of the disadvantages which we cited against the method of new election,[34] the one which is especially to be feared and watched out for is the difficulty that arises from the lack of virtuous men by whom alone an election should be made. And even more, there is the disagreement of the electors, which threatens the polity or state with schism. A further difficulty arises if the electors are of evil emotion, for under its influence they or the weightier part of them may agree to elect a vicious ruler.

In reply to these objections it must be said that the election whereby the ruler is named to the rulership with all his posterity or succession suffers the first of these difficulties more than does the method of repeated election of each new monarch. For at the time of the origin of polities there was a lesser number of prudent men; [35] if they made an error in that first election because of their lack of ability, the state would be very greatly harmed, since it would be for a longer time. As for the objection about schism among the electors, although this must be heeded above all the other objections, it does not prove that the method of electing each new monarch is less excellent than the method of having a single election whereby a ruler is named with all his posterity. For election is always made for the common benefit, which the human legislator almost always wishes and attains,[36] as was demonstrated in Chapter XIII. And to the legislator also belongs the authority to make this election, as was proved with certainty in Chapter XII and in the chapter preceding this one. Again, let us assume, with our opponent, that to make this election pertains only to prudent and virtuous men. It is not likely nor true in most cases that they will quarrel among themselves, since they are prudent; nor will they become corrupted by their emotions since they are virtuous. This was the third difficulty presented above.

As for the example we adduced about the difficulty from which the Roman Empire suffers because it must hold a new election for each new monarch, it must be said that this difficulty does not come from election as the essential cause, but rather from the malice, ignorance, or both of certain men who impede the election and accession of the aforesaid ruler. We must skip over this point here, since these men, their actions, their past, present, and future methods, and their motives will be discussed in detail in

[34] See the present chapter, para. 5.
[35] See above, I. iii. 4; below, II. xvii. 7; II. xxii. 15.
[36] See above in the present chapter, para. 11 and n. 21.

Chapter XIX of this discourse and in Chapters XXIII to XXVI of Discourse II.

20. The objection that the hereditary monarch is guided with good counsel more easily and more surely than is the elected [37] has slight plausibility. For if the monarch is of vicious character, those measures should not be recommended to him by his counselors which are in accord with his moral character, or which he himself desires, but rather the opposite. But assuming that the monarch is the kind of man whom we have said to be expedient in our own assumptions and true proofs, his counselors, whom our opponent assumes with us to be prudent and virtuous men, must absolutely recommend to him the things which are for the common benefit of the polity. Indeed, it will be said that it is perhaps more expedient for the counselors not to know the moral character of the former kind of monarch, so that they may not consider his illegal wishes in order to obtain his grace or favor for themselves, but may instead counsel what is truly for the common benefit. However, since they have political prudence they know this sufficiently; hence it makes no difference in this respect what sort of moral character the monarch has, for they must always recommend to him what is more expedient for the polity.

Moreover, let us assume that knowledge of the monarch's moral qualities will be of some help to the counselors because they will be able to guide him with greater certainty. It must nevertheless be said that this knowledge is not of as much help as is the certainty of having almost always a virtuous and prudent monarch; and the moral character of this monarch, who is to be guided by counsel, must be considered the essential factor. This can be known sufficiently by any prudent counselor. But such a monarch is more certainly obtained by the method of new election than by hereditary succession, as we have frequently said. And it must also be noted that the ministers or counselors sometimes are more obedient to a bad hereditary monarch, and dare less to rebuke him or to attempt to correct him, because his offspring will rule after him. And as for what Aristotle says in the first book of the *Rhetoric,* that "the moral character of each provides the most effective means of persuasion," [38] this can be granted as true; for since each man's desires are in accordance with his moral character or inclination, he believes more firmly and readily the person who seeks to persuade him along such lines. However, if he has perverted desires, as we have said, what he desires should not be recommended to him.

---

[37] See the present chapter, para. 6.
[38] Aristotle *Rhetoric* I. 8. 1366a 12. See the present chapter, para. 6.

Moreover, it should not be overlooked, and we see it happening quite often, that the monarch if he is not virtuous follows the counsels of vicious rather than of virtuous men; hence the monarch should be named by new election, for in this way a virtuous ruler will be obtained with greater certainty.

21. As for the argument that under a hereditary monarch the citizens lose to a greater extent their arrogance or presumption and their undue ambition for rulership,[39] it must be replied that they lose not only what is undue, but also what is reasonably due to them, so that they are given grounds for sedition. For when most of the citizens observe that they are very frequently governed by men who are less worthy in virtue, and that they are always deprived of rulership, then either they have insufficient leisure for the virtues whereby they are worthy to rule, or else, having such leisure consistently but nevertheless being deprived of the rulership which is sometimes due them, they will justly engage in sedition.[40] But they will not attempt so to engage if they hope that they may in due time be elected to rule. Moreover, since they are prudent and virtuous they will not attempt to engage in sedition unless they have been gravely wronged; but such wrong will not be inflicted on them by the legislator, or by the virtuous ruler, such as we have said almost every elected ruler will be. For the virtuous ruler and legislator aim for the most part at what is just, as we have said in Chapters XIII and XIV. As for the contention of our opponent that it is undue ambition or presumption for the citizens to desire rulership, this is not true; for it is not undue ambition, pride, or presumption for a virtuous and thus well-deserving man to desire rulership in due time, but it is rather to desire a work of magnanimity and political virtue. Hence, Aristotle attests in the fourth book of the *Ethics* that it is not improper or contrary to virtue for the magnanimous man to desire great honors.[41] And as for the words of Cicero in the first book *On Duties,* that "it is very unfortunate that in the greatest and most brilliant minds there exists very often a desire for honor, power, command, and glory," [42] if this is true, it is only when such things are desired in undue quantity or quality or in other ways contrary to the norm and standard of reason.

22. As for the next argument, that the monarch, not transmitting the

---

[39] See the present chapter, para. 7.

[40] Cf. Aristotle *Politics* II. 5. 1264b 8; Ptolemy of Lucca *De regimine principum* IV. vii (p. 89).

[41] See Aristotle *Nicomachean Ethics* IV. 3. 1123a 34 ff. On the relation between this support of the Aristotelian "magnanimity" and the Christian "humility" which Marsilius upholds in Discourse II, see Vol. I, p. 81.

[42] Cicero *De officiis* I. viii. 26; cf. the present chapter, para. 7.

rulership to his heirs, will not dare to bring powerful men to justice or to punish them, at least by corporeal punishment or by death, because he will fear their ill will against his children,[43] it must be replied that the elected ruler, with the qualities we have said he will have, will not fear because he will be courageous in spirit. And if powerful men are brought to justice and punished in accordance with the law and their own demerit, they will feel little or no hatred for the monarch and his sons, and will not seek vengeance. For they will understand that justice must be done by that ruler or another one. However, if they do conceive hatred and a desire for vengeance because of their ignorance or malice or both, they will not dare to seek vengeance, for they will fear the legislator and the next ruler by whom they will expect to be punished again as they were by his predecessor in office.

23. As for the litigious argument that in most regions and times monarchs seem to be named through election with subsequent hereditary succession,[44] it must be said that this was perhaps not truly the case at most times. Let us assume, however, that it is as our opponent says. But as for what he adds, that this method of establishing governments is therefore more natural and more perfect, this must be denied. And when he adduces the testimony of Aristotle from the third book *On Heaven and Earth,* and the second book of the *Physics,* that "the nature of things seems to be what is in most of them most of the time," it must be said that it is true within the same species that what is found in most cases is more natural than the privation or deformity thereof. However, it is not more natural nor more perfect than any other thing diverse from it in species, for if it were, then the artisan would be more perfect than the first philosopher, and the artisan's function more perfect than first philosophy and any other theoretic discipline; yet this conclusion, as we have said before,[45] is neither necessary nor true. But now elective monarchy is not a privation of hereditary monarchy, nor conversely, but they are mutually disparate species, incapable of existing in the same person in respect of the same multitude or subject community. There are perhaps other errors in the aforesaid argument, which we have left for the consideration of the reader and have omitted to discuss here, for the sake of brevity.

24. As for the last argument, that the monarch who is elected with all his posterity is superior because the unity of his rule bears a greater similarity to the ruler of the universe,[46] it must be replied that the similarity of this unity, which is of a rather equivocal kind, must not be considered

[43] See the present chapter, para. 8.
[45] See the present chapter, para. 17.
[44] See the present chapter, para. 9.
[46] See the present chapter, para. 10.

so important as the conformity of perfection with respect to soul or habit of soul. For the latter is the outstanding reason why a man should be named to the rulership, not similitude of family, in which there is essentially considered only unity of corporeal dispositions, but not habit of soul which is the essential reason for which rulership is due to someone. And in respect to such unity or similarity of perfection, the monarch who is elected individually will be in conformity both with his virtuous predecessor and with the primary being or ruler of all beings, to a greater degree and with greater frequency than will the hereditary monarch who rules only because he belongs to a family in which someone else was once elected to rule. This is clear from our previous statements.

25. Other objections on each side with respect to what is better and worse for the polity will perhaps occur to whoever wishes to consider the matter. However, we have already stated those which we think more worthy of attention.

Let it suffice, then, to have discussed in this way the most-perfect method of appointing the monarch.

CHAPTER XVII: ON THE NUMERICAL UNITY OF THE SUPREME GOVERNMENT OF THE CITY OR STATE, AND THE NECESSITY FOR THAT UNITY; WHENCE THERE APPEARS ALSO THE NUMERICAL UNITY OF THE CITY OR STATE ITSELF, AND OF EACH OF ITS PRIMARY PARTS OR OFFICES

WE must now discuss the unity of the ruler or government.[1] To begin with, let us say that in a single city or state there must be only a single government; or if there is more than one government in number or in species, as seems expedient in large cities and especially in a state (*regno*) taken in its first sense,[2] then there must be among them one in number which is supreme, to which all the other governments are reduced, by which they are regulated, and which corrects any errors arising in them.

2. Now I maintain, with respect to this supreme government alone, that it must necessarily be one in number, not many, if the state or city is to be rightly ordered. And I say the same with regard to the ruler, not that

---

[1] On this whole chapter, see Vol. I, pp. 115-25.   [2] See above, I. ii. 2.

the ruler is to be one in number with respect to person but rather with respect to office. For there may be some supreme, well-tempered government which is one in number, but in which more than one man rules; such are the aristocracy and the polity, of which we spoke in Chapter VIII. These several men, however, are numerically one government with respect to office, because of the numerical unity of every action, judgment, sentence or command forthcoming from them. For no such action can emerge from any one of them separately, but only from the common decree and consent of them all or of their weightier part, in accordance with the laws established on such matters. And it is because of such numerical unity of the action thus forthcoming from them that the government is and is called one in number, whether it be ruled by one man or by many. Such unity of action is not, however, required in any of the other offices or parts of the state; for in each of them there can and must be forthcoming separately, from the diverse individuals in them, many actions similar or diverse in species. Indeed, such unity of action in these offices would be unbearable and harmful both to the community and to the individuals.[3]

3. Such being the meaning of the numerical unity of the government or ruler, we wish to prove that the government or ruler in the city or state is to be only one in number, or, if more than one, that the supreme government of them all is to be only one in number, not more. We shall demonstrate this first as follows. If there were several governments in the city or state, and they were not reduced or ordered under one supreme government, then the judgment, command, and execution of matters of benefit and justice would fail, and because men's injuries would therefore be unavenged the result would be fighting, separation, and finally the destruction of the city or state. But this consequence is the evil which is most to be avoided; and that it is a consequence of the given antecedent, that is, of a plurality of governments, can be clearly shown. For, in the first place, transgressors of the laws cannot reasonably be brought to justice unless they are called before the ruler for examination of the charges against them. But if we assume a plurality of governments not reduced to some one supreme government, as our opponent says, then no one called before the ruler will be able sufficiently to obey the summons. For suppose, as frequently happens, that because of some transgression of the law a man is called by several rulers not ordered one below another, to answer charges at the same time. One ruler is bound and able to summon the accused man for the same reason as the other ruler; and the man who is summoned is bound to appear before one of the rulers, lest he be regarded as being

[3] On this point, see also below, I. xvii. 12; II. viii. 9, *fin.*

in contempt, for the same reason as before the other ruler, or rulers, if there
be more than two. Either, therefore, he will appear before all the rulers at
once, or before none of them, or else before a certain one and not before
the other or others. But he will not appear before all the rulers at one
and the same time, since this is impossible by nature and by art, for the
same body cannot be in different places at the same time, or reply or
speak at the same time to many persons who are perhaps asking different
questions at the same time. Moreover, even though it is impossible, let
us assume that the person summoned does appear before several rulers,
and is silent or replies to different questions at the same time. Yet he will
perhaps be convicted by one ruler and be acquitted by another, of the
same crime; or if convicted by both, with different penalties. Hence he
will be both required and not required to make amends; or if required
by both, it will be to such a degree by one, and to a greater or lesser degree
by another, and thus both to such a degree and not to such a degree. Hence
he will either do contradictory things at the same time, or else will make
no amends at all. For he must obey one ruler's command for the same
reason as another's. He has no more reason for appearing before one
ruler than before the other or others. If, however, he appears before one
of them, ignoring the others, and is perhaps absolved by him of civil guilt
and punishment, he will nevertheless be convicted by the others for
contempt. Therefore the man summoned will neither appear before all the
rulers at once nor be able properly to appear before a certain one and
not before another. The only remaining course, consequently, is for the
man who is summoned to appear before no ruler at all; therefore justice
will be incapable of being done in his case. It is impossible, therefore, for
the city or state to have a plurality of such governments not subordinated
one to another, if civil justice and benefit are to be conserved.[4]

4. Moreover, if there were a plurality of such governments, the common
utility would be completely disturbed. For the rulers must frequently
command the assemblage of the citizens, especially of those who have
leisure, to inquire into and to decide matters relating to the common
benefit, or to avoid harmful impending dangers such as are presented by

---

[4] For antecedents of this argument, see Dante *De monarchia* I. x (where, however, it is
applied to the judgment not of subjects but of rival rulers themselves), and especially *Disputatio
inter militem et clericum* (in *Monarchia*, ed. Goldast, I, 14). For subsequent restatements of
the argument which seem definitely to have Marsilius as their source, see William of Ockham
Octo quaestiones de potestate papae III. i, xii (*Opera politica*, ed. J. G. Sikes [Manchester,
1940], I, 100–101, 110); Richard Hooker *Of the Laws of Ecclesiastical Polity* VIII. ii. 18, esp.
the last sentence (*Works*, ed. I. Walton [Oxford, 1865], II, 509); it should be noted, however,
that much of this paragraph of Hooker's work is a literal translation of Thomas Aquinas *De
regimine principum* I. i.

external or internal enemies who intend to oppress the community and to take away its freedom. Now the citizens or subjects who must obey the command of one ruler to assemble at a certain place and time must for the same reason obey the command of another ruler to assemble at the place and time which he selects; and each ruler might select the same time but different places; and again, what one of the rulers wishes to propose may perhaps be different from what the other wants. But it does not seem possible to be in different places at the same time, or to have different aims at the same time.

5. Again, from this there would result the division and opposition of the citizens, their fighting and separation, and finally the destruction of the state, for some of the citizens would wish to obey one government, and some another. There would also be strife between the governments themselves because one of them would want to be superior to the other; in addition, the governments would war against the citizens who refused to be subject to them. Moreover, when the rulers disagreed or quarreled among themselves, since they would lack a superior judge, the above-mentioned scandals would also arise.[5]

6. Again, if this plurality of governments is assumed, one of the greatest effects of human reason and art will be useless and superfluous. For all the civil utility which would be had from many supreme governments can be perfectly had through one government or one supreme government without the harms resulting from a plurality of them.[6]

7. Moreover, if such a plurality is assumed, no state or city will be one. For states are one, and are called one, because of the unity of the government to which and by which all the other parts of the state are ordered,[7]- as will appear also from what follows. And again there will be no order of the parts of the city or state, since they will be ordered to no first part, because they are required to be subjected to none, as is clear from the previous arguments. And there will be a confusion both of them and of the whole state; for each man will choose for himself whatever office he wishes, one or more, with no one regulating or separating such offices. So many are the evils which would follow upon this that it is difficult or impossible to enumerate them all.[8]

8. Furthermore, in the well-ordered animal the primary principle which commands it and moves it from place to place is one, as is apparent from the book *On the Motion of Animals*.[9] For if there were many of

[5] See Vol. I, p. 116, n. 6; p. 127, n. 6.
[6] For this "razor" argument, see also above, 1. xv. 4. Cf. Dante *De monarchia* 1. xiv.
[7] See above, 1. xv. 14.   [8] See above, 1. xv. 10; also Vol. I, pp. 111–13.
[9] Aristotle *De motu animalium* 1. 698a 15 ff.; 8. 702a 21 ff.

these principles and they gave contrary or different commands at the same time, the animal would either have to be borne in contrary directions or remain completely at rest, and it would have to lack those things, necessary and beneficial to it, which are obtained through motion. The case is similar in the state properly ordered, which we have said, in Chapter XV,[10] to be analogous to the animal well formed according to nature. Hence, just as in the animal a plurality of such principles would be useless and indeed harmful, we must firmly hold that it is the same in the state. The same thing can be seen, if one wishes to consider the question further, with respect to the first altering principle in the animal, just as with respect to that which moves it from place to place, and similarly in the whole order of movers and objects moved.[11] But let us omit these points, since they pertain rather to natural science; and what we have said about them thus far is sufficient for the present consideration.

9. Moreover, "in general art partly completes some things which nature cannot finish and partly imitates her," as it is written in the second book of the *Physics*.[12] Now since in the nature of things there is one primary ruler in number, not more, because "things do not wish to be ordered badly," as it is said in the twelfth book of the *First Philosophy*,[13] therefore the primary government established according to the reason and art of men will also be only one in number. Together with the reasons we have given, this can be seen to be true, expedient, and necessary by everyone's sense experience; for it is seen to be impossible for any place or province or assemblage of men to be well ordered in which there is lacking unity of government in the way we have said. This is clearly apparent to almost all men with respect to the Romans' state, and we gave some indications of it in our introductory remarks.[14]

10. As to whether it is advantageous to have one supreme government in number for all those who live a civil life in the whole world, or whether on the contrary it is at a certain time advantageous to have different such governments in different regions of the world which are almost necessarily separate from one another in place, and especially for men who use different languages and who differ widely in morals and customs—this ques-

10 See above, I. xv. 5-7.

11 Cf. Aristotle *De motu animalium* 5. 700a 26 ff. Marsilius is here referring to the Aristotelian distinctions of four kinds of motion: with respect to place (locomotion), quality (alteration), quantity (increase and decrease), and substance (generation and destruction). Cf. also Aristotle *Categories* 14. 15a 14 ff.; *Physics* III. 1. 201a 4 ff.

12 Aristotle *Physics* II. 8. 199a 16.

13 Aristotle *Metaphysics* XII. 10. 1076a 3. It should be noted that Marsilius used the same text above, I. xvi. 10, as an argument in favor of hereditary monarchy, which he subsequently refuted, I. xvi. 24.

14 See above, I. i. 2.

tion merits a reasoned study, but it is distinct from our present concern. The heavenly cause moves perhaps toward the latter alternative, in order that the procreation of men may not become excessive. For one might perhaps think that nature, by means of wars and epidemics, has moderated the procreation of men and the other animals in order that the earth may suffice for their nurture; wherein those who say that there is eternal generation would be very strongly upheld.[15]

11. But to return to our proposed aim, let us indicate, as is already somewhat apparent from our previous remarks, what is the numerical unity of the city or state. This [16] is a unity of order; it is not an absolute unity, but rather a plurality of men who are said to be some one thing in number not because they are one in number formally through some form, but rather because they are said to be related to one thing in number, namely, the government, toward which and by which they are ordered and governed. For the city or state is not one through some one natural form, such as by composition or mixture, since its parts or offices, and the persons or parts of these parts, are many in actuality and formally separate from one another in number, since they are separate in place and in subject. Hence they are not one through some one thing formally inhering in them, or touching [17] or containing them like a wall. For Rome, Sicily, and the other communities are one state or empire in number only because each of them is ordered by its will toward a supreme government which is one in number. In almost the same way, too, the world is said to be one in number, not many worlds, not because of some one numerical form which formally inheres in all beings; rather, all beings are said to be one world in number because of the numerical unity of the first being, since every being naturally is inclined toward and depends upon the first being. Hence the statement wherein all beings are said to be one world in number does not mean that some numerical unity is formally in all beings, or that some universal is predicated of them in consequence of one thing; rather it is a plurality of certain things, which plurality is called one because it is in relation to one thing and because of one thing. Similarly, the men of one city or province are called one city or state because they wish one government in number.

[15] On this discussion of world government, see Vol. I, pp. 126–31; also below, II. xxviii. 15. For the Averroist doctrine of eternal generation, to which Marsilius here refers, see P. Mandonnet, *Siger de Brabant et l'averroisme latin au XIIIe siècle*, 2d ed. (Louvain, 1911), I, 170 ff.; and Condemned Propositions of 1277, Nos. 138, 139 (*ibid.*, II, 186).

[16] This sentence and the one following lean very heavily on Thomas Aquinas *In decem libros Ethicorum Aristotelis ad Nicomachum expositio* Lib. I. Lect. I (ed. A. M. Pirotta [Turin, 1934], pp. 3–4, n. 5).

[17] Reading, with Bigongiari (p. 36) *per tangens* for *pertangens*.

12. However, men are not one part of the state in number for the same reason for which they are one state or one city in number. For although they wish one government in number, for which reason they are called one city or state, yet they are referred to this numerically one government through a different active and passive establishment, which is none other than the different command given to them by the ruler; and it is through this different command that they are appointed to different offices. From the difference of this command, too, they are formally different parts and offices of the state.[18] But each of the offices is said to be one in number or one part of the state in number, despite the numerical plurality of the persons in it, not because of some on: thing inhering in them all, but rather because they are referred to one active command of the ruler in accordance with the determination of the law.[19]

13. From what has been said in this chapter and in Chapters IX, XII, XIII, and XV, it can be concluded by evident demonstration that to no individual, of whatever dignity or rank he may be, and to no group, does there belong any rulership or coercive jurisdiction over anyone in this world, unless this authority shall have been granted to them immediately by the divine or the human legislator.

Let this much suffice with respect to the questions of what kind the unity of the government must be, what is the numerical unity of the city or state, and for what reason each of these is and is said to be one in number; and also concerning the numerical and specific unity of the parts or offices of the state, and their order, differentiation, and separation from one another.

[18] See above, I. vii. 2.

[19] This point obviates the papalist argument that the unity of the "church" requires that it have a single head as the source of all the authority exercised in it. The unity of the priesthood will hence derive not from the pope but from its being subject to the temporal ruler's command. See below, II. viii. 9 *fin.;* II. xxviii. 14, 15; and Vol. I, pp. 113, 121, 274–76.

CHAPTER XVIII: ON THE CORRECTION OF THE RULER, AND FOR WHAT CAUSE, HOW, AND BY WHOM HE MUST BE PUNISHED WHEN HE TRANSGRESSES THE LAW [1]

W E have previously stated that it pertains to the legislator to correct governments or to change them completely, just as to establish them.[2] In this connection, someone may well wonder whether it is expedient that rulers be corrected by coercive judgment and force; and if it is expedient, whether they should be corrected for every kind of excess, or only for some and not for others; also who should make such judgments against the rulers, and execute them by coercive force—for it was said above that it pertains to the rulers alone to issue civil sentences and to punish transgressors of the laws by coercive force.

2. Let us say that the ruler through his action in accordance with the law and the authority given to him is the standard and measure of every civil act, like the heart in an animal, as was sufficiently shown in Chapter XV.[3] Now if the ruler received no other form beside the law and the authority and the desire to act in accordance with it, he would never perform any action which was wrong or corrigible or measurable by someone else.[4] And therefore he and his action would be the measure of every civil act of men other than himself, in such manner that he would never be measured by others, like the well-formed heart in an animal. For since the heart receives no form that inclines it to an action contrary to the action which has to emerge from its natural virtue and heat, it always does naturally the appropriate action and never the contrary. Hence it regulates and measures, through its influence or action, the other parts of the animal, in such manner that it is not regulated by them nor does it receive any influence from them.

3. But since the ruler is a human being, he has understanding and appetite, which can receive other forms, like false opinion or perverted desire or both, as a result of which he comes to do the contraries of the things determined by the law. Because of these actions, the ruler is rendered measurable by someone else [5] who has the authority to measure or regulate him, or his unlawful actions, in accordance with the law. For otherwise

---

[1] On this chapter see Vol. I, pp. 238–40, 244–46, 250–51.
[2] See above, I. xii. 3, 9; I. xv. 2.   [3] See above, I. xv. 6, 7.
[4] Reading, with Scholz, *alio* for *aliquo*.   [5] Reading, with Scholz, *alio* for *aliquo*.

every government would become despotic, and the life of the citizens
slavish and insufficient.[6] This is an evil to be avoided, as is apparent from
our discussions in Chapters V and XI.

Now the judgment, command, and execution of any correction of the
ruler, in accordance with his demerit or transgression, must be done by
the legislator, or by a person or persons appointed for this purpose by the
authority of the legislator, as was demonstrated in Chapters XII and XV.
And it is well to suspend for some time the office of the ruler who is to
be corrected, especially in relation to the person or persons who must judge
of his transgression, because otherwise there would then be a plurality of
governments in the community, from which would result schism, agitation, and fighting; and also because he is corrected not as a ruler but as a
subject who has transgressed the law.

4. Coming now to the questions which were raised above, let us say that
the ruler's excess is either grave or slight; it may occur frequently or only
rarely; and it is among the things determined by law or it is not. If the
ruler's excess be grave, such as against the commonwealth or against a
notable or any other person, from failure to correct which there could
likely arise scandal or agitation among the people, then whether the excess
be one which occurs frequently or rarely, the ruler must be corrected for
it. For if the excess be not avenged, agitation might arise among the people, and upheaval and destruction of the polity. If the excess is determined
by law, it must be corrected according to the law; but if not, then it must
be corrected according to the sentence of the legislator; and it must be
determined by law as much as possible, as we showed in Chapter XI.

5. If the ruler's excess be small, then its occurrence and its commission
by the ruler may be either rare or frequent. If it is rarely committed or
rarely capable of being committed by the ruler, then it must be allowed
to pass and be glossed over rather than having the ruler corrected for it.
For if the ruler is corrected for every small and infrequent excess, he will
be made an object of contempt, which will result in no slight harm to
the community, since the citizens then exhibit less respect and obedience
for the law and the ruler. Again, since the ruler is unwilling to undergo
correction for every slight offense, because he will regard this as bringing
him into low repute, there will be a possibility of grave scandal. But such
a condition must not be stirred up in communities when no evident utility
can emerge therefrom, but rather harm.

6. Such was clearly the view of Aristotle on this question, in the *Politics*,
Book II, Chapter 4, where he said: "It is manifest that some errors of both

[6] Cf. Aristotle *Politics* II. 12. 1274a 14–18.

legislators and rulers should be allowed to pass. For one will do less good by making changes than one will do harm by becoming accustomed to rebelling against the rulers." [7] By "legislator" Aristotle meant an established law; and he says that if men have become accustomed to observing it, then it must not be changed in order to make a slight correction in it, but must rather be allowed to pass. For frequent changing of the laws saps their strength, which is the custom of obeying and observing what the laws command. As Aristotle said in the same book and chapter: "The law has no power for persuasion except that of custom," [8] that is, for the law to be observed by the subjects, the most important factor is custom. And the case is very similar with regard to respecting and obeying the ruler.

7. But if the ruler's excess, while slight in extent, is capable of frequent occurrence, then it must be determined by law, and the ruler who frequently commits the offense must be given the appropriate punishment. For an offense, however slight, would be of notable harm to the polity if it were frequently committed, just as "small expenses frequently incurred consume a fortune," that is, in riches. "For the whole sum is not small, although it is made up of small sums," as it is written in the *Politics,* Book V, Chapter 4. [9]

Such then are our conclusions concerning the correction of rulers, by whom it should be done, and for what reasons.

CHAPTER XIX: ON THE EFFICIENT CAUSES OF THE TRANQUILLITY AND INTRANQUILLITY OF THE CITY OR STATE, AND ON THAT SINGULAR CAUSE WHICH DISTURBS STATES IN AN UNUSUAL WAY; AND ON THE CONNECTION BETWEEN THE FIRST DISCOURSE AND THE SECOND

THE last remaining task of this discourse is to infer from our previous findings the causes of tranquillity and of its opposite in the city or state. For this was the principal aim which we set for ourselves from the outset. And first we shall show these causes in their common being, that is, those which emerge in the usual manner, assuming that outstanding discussion of them which Aristotle presented in the fifth book of the *Politics*. Then

---

[7] Aristotle *Politics* II. 8. 1269a 16.   [8] *Ibid.* 1269a 20.   [9] *Ibid.* v. 8. 1307b 33 ff.

we shall undertake a specific discussion of an unusual cause of the discord
or intranquillity of civil regimes, the one which we said in our introductory remarks [1] had long troubled, and still plagues even more, the Italian
state.

2. For this task we must repeat the definitions of tranquillity and of its
opposite given in Chapter II.[2] For tranquillity was the good disposition of
the city or state, whereby each of its parts can perform the functions appropriate to it in accordance with reason and its establishment. From this
definition the nature of tranquillity is clear. For when it is called a "good
disposition," there is noted its general intrinsic essence. And when it is said
that "through it each part of the state can perform the functions appropriate to it," there is signified its end, which also makes us understand its
proper essence or differentia. Since it is a certain form or disposition of
the city or state, and is no more one than we said the city or state to be one
in Chapter XVII, paragraphs 11 and 12, it has no formal cause; for to have
a formal cause is peculiar to composites. Its efficient or productive cause we
can grasp from what was said in Chapter XV, and from the various things
which necessarily follow from it in the city or state. These are the mutual
association of the citizens, their intercommunication of their functions
with one another, their mutual aid and assistance, and in general the
power, unimpeded from without, of exercising their proper and common
functions, and also the participation in common benefits and burdens according to the measure appropriate to each,[3] as well as the other beneficial
and desirable things expressed in the statement of Cassiodorus which we
placed at the beginning of this book.[4] The contraries of all these, and particularly of some, follow upon intranquillity or discord.

3. Since, therefore, the due action of the ruler is the efficient and con-
serving cause of all the aforesaid civil benefits, as was demonstrated in
Chapter XV, paragraphs 11 and 12, it will be the efficient cause of tranquillity;[5] and this was undoubtedly the view of the Apostle, when he said
in the first epistle to Timothy, Chapter 2: "I desire therefore first of all
that supplications . . . be made for . . . kings and for all that are in high
station, that we may lead a quiet and tranquil life."[6] And on the other
hand, from whatever has essentially impeded the action of this ruling part
of the state there will emerge, as from an efficient cause, intranquillity or
discord. A sufficient conception of the general character of this cause, as
well as of the many species and modes by which it is varied and the usual
actions from which they emerge, was provided by Aristotle in the fifth

book of his *Civil Science,* which we have called the *Politics.* There is, however, a certain unusual cause of the intranquillity or discord of cities or states, a cause which arose upon the occasion of the effect produced by the divine cause in a manner different from all its usual action in things; and this effect, as we recall having mentioned in our introductory remarks, could not have been discerned either by Aristotle or by any other philosophers of his time or before.[7]

4. This cause has for a long time been impeding the due action of the ruler in the Italian state, and is now doing so even more; it has deprived and is still depriving that state of peace or tranquillity, and of all the above-mentioned goods which follow thereon; it has vexed it continually with every evil, and has filled it with almost every kind of misery and iniquity. In accordance with our original aim, we must determine the specific nature of this cause which is such a singular impediment because of its customarily hidden malignity. Hence we must recall what we said in Chapter VI: that the son of God, one of the three divine persons, true God, assumed a human nature to redeem the sin of our first parents and the consequent fall of the whole human race. Long after the time of Aristotle, he became a true man, being at the same time God; called Jesus Christ, he is worshiped by faithful Christians. This Christ, blessed son of God, at once God and man in the same person, lived among the Jewish people, from whom he drew his fleshly origin. He began to teach and did teach the truth of what men must believe, do, and avoid in order to attain eternal life and avoid misery. Because of this having finally suffered and died from the malice and insanity of the Jews under Pontius Pilate, vicar of Caesar, he rose up from the dead on the third day after his death and ascended the heavens. Earlier, however, while he was still living a corruptible life, he selected, for the salvation of the human race, certain colleagues for the ministry of teaching the truth; these men are called the apostles, and Christ commanded them to preach throughout the entire world the truth which he had taught and in which he had instructed them. So in Matthew, Chapter 28, he said to them after his resurrection: "Go ye therefore and teach all nations, baptizing them in the name of the Father, the Son, and the Holy Ghost, teaching them to observe all things whatsoever I have commanded you."[8] By these apostles, whose names are well enough known among faithful Christians, and by certain other men, Christ wanted the evangelic law to be written, and so it was written, by their utterances as by certain instruments immediately moved and directed by divine virtue. Through this law, we should be able to comprehend the commands and counsels of

[7] See above, i. i. 3.   [8] Matthew 28:19 20.

eternal salvation in the absence of Christ and the apostles and evangelists. Also, in this law, Christ established and made known the sacraments which wash away original and actual sin, which produce and conserve divine grace, which recover it when it is lost, and which ordain the ministers of this law.

5. Christ also first ordained the afore-mentioned apostles as the teachers of this law and as ministers of the sacraments according to it, bestowing on them through the Holy Ghost the authority of this ministry, which authority is called "priestly" by faithful Christians. Through this authority he bestowed on these same men and on their successors in this office, and on no others, the power, under the form of certain words said by them collectively or individually, of transubstantiating bread and wine into his true body and blood. Together with this he granted them the authority to bind and loose men from sins, which is usually called the power of the keys, as well as the power of appointing other men in their place with the same authority. This authority the apostles also bestowed upon certain men, or God did it through the apostles when they prayed and laid their hands on other men. These others also received the power of so doing; and so they then did, and are doing, and will continue to do until the end of the world. In this way, also, the apostle Paul ordained Timothy, Titus, and several more, and taught them to ordain others. Whence he said in the first epistle to Timothy, Chapter 4: "Neglect not the grace that is in thee, which was given thee by prophecy, with the laying on of the hands of the priesthood." [9] And in the epistle to Titus, Chapter 1: "For this cause I left thee in Crete, that thou shouldest set in order the things that are wanting and shouldest ordain priests in every city, as I also appointed thee." [10] And this authority of the priesthood and of the keys, whether it be one or many, is a certain character or form of the soul impressed through the immediate action of God.

6. But besides this there is a certain other authority which was given to priests by man in order to avoid scandal after the number of priests had multiplied. This latter authority is the preeminence of one among them over the others in directing them in the proper performance of divine worship in the temple, and in ordering or distributing certain temporal things which were established for the use of the aforesaid ministers. The efficient cause of this authority, and whence it is derived, will be sufficiently discussed in Discourse II, Chapters XV and XVII; for this authority is not given immediately by God, but rather through the will and mind of men, like the other offices of the state.

[9] I Timothy 4:14.   [10] Titus 1:5.

7. And so, having thus repeated and made somewhat clear the origin of ecclesiastic ministers, and the efficient cause of their office, we must now note further that among the aforesaid apostles of Christ there was one named Simon, also called Peter, who first received from Christ the promise of the authority of the keys, as it is said in Augustine's gloss on the sixteenth chapter of Matthew, on that statement of Christ: "And I will give unto thee the keys of the kingdom of heaven." The gloss says: "He who avowed before the others," that is, that Jesus Christ is the true son of God, "is given the keys ahead of the others," [11] that is, before the others. And after Christ's passion, resurrection, and ascent into heaven, this apostle came to Antioch, and was there made bishop by the people, as is shown by his history. From that city, as the aforesaid history says, he went to Rome for an undetermined reason concerning which there are diverse views. At Rome he became bishop over the Christian faithful, and finally on account of his profession and preaching of Christ, he was beheaded, and with him at the same time and place the apostle Paul was also, according to the afore-mentioned history.[12]

8. Because of the prerogative which this disciple or apostle seemed to have over the others, inasmuch as he was given the keys before the others through the afore-mentioned words of the Scripture and certain other words spoken to him alone by Christ, which will also be mentioned below, some of the bishops who succeeded him in the apostolic or episcopal seat at Rome, especially after the time of the Roman emperor Constantine, declare and assert that they are over all the other bishops and priests in the world, with respect to every kind of jurisdictional authority. And some of the more recent Roman bishops make this claim not only with regard to bishops and priests, but even with regard to all the rulers, communities, and individuals in the world, although they do not apply it equally or express it so explicitly with regard to all the others as they do with regard to the ruler called emperor of the Romans and all the provinces, cities, and individual persons subject to him. And yet in truth, the singular expression of dominion or coercive jurisdiction over this ruler seems to have taken its form and origin from a certain edict and gift which certain men say that Constantine made to St. Sylvester, Roman pontiff.[13]

[11] Matthew 16:19, and *Glossa ordinaria, ad loc.;* see Bede *Homiliae* II. 16 (PL 94. 222).

[12] For the sources of this account, see Pseudo-Clement *Recognitiones* x. lxxi (PG I. 1473), and Pseudo-Isidore (Gelasius *Decretum . . . de apocryphis scripturis,* PL 130. 984). The latter is repeated by Martinus Polonus *Chronicon* (MGH, *Scriptores,* XXII, 409). See also below, II. xvi. 9, 16.

[13] The implied skepticism of Marsilius' "certain men say" with regard to the apocryphal donation of Constantine is noteworthy. For further discussion of the donation, see below, II. xi. 8; II. xvi. 9; II. xxii. 10, 19.

9. But because that gift or privilege did not state this clearly, or because it perhaps expired on account of later events, or even because, while being valid with regard to the other governments of the world, the force of that privilege or concession did not extend to the government of the Romans in all their provinces,[14] later bishops of the Romans therefore assumed for themselves this universal coercive jurisdiction over the whole world under another all-embracing title, "plenitude of power," [15] which they assert was granted by Christ to St. Peter and to his successors in the episcopal seat of Rome, as vicars of Christ. For Christ, as they truly say, was "king of kings and lord of lords," [16] and of all persons and things; yet from this there does not follow what they wish to infer, as will appear with certainty in our subsequent discussions. The meaning of this title among the Roman bishops, therefore, is that just as Christ had plenitude of power and jurisdiction over all kings, princes, communities, groups, and individuals, so too do those who call themselves vicars of Christ and of St. Peter have this plenitude of coercive jurisdiction, limited by no human law.

10. An evident sign that the Roman bishops intend this title of plenitude of power to have the meaning which we have stated is that a certain Clement, the fifth Roman bishop of that name, uses it in this way in a certain edict or decretal of his *On the Sentence and the Thing Judged,* in the seventh book,[17] in regard to Henry VII, of divine memory, the most recent emperor of the Romans. For in revoking a certain sentence of that happy Henry, he gave such an interpretation of the aforesaid title as we have said. We shall not cite this interpretation here, because it is well known, and for the sake of brevity; and also because we shall quote it more appropriately in Discourse II, Chapter XXV, paragraph 17. Since, therefore, Christ neither is nor was king and lord over the Roman emperor in greater degree than over any other king or ruler, but rather equally as much or more over the latter, because in the time of Christ the Roman ruler was monarch over all lands everywhere, it is evident that the meaning of this title extends to all governments by virtue of the same root. And that this is the meaning which the Roman bishops intend this title to have is also clearly shown to us by the belligerent attack of Boniface VIII against Philip the Fair of bright memory, the king of the French, and then by the subsequent decretal of the same Boniface, which we shall cite in Discourse

---

[14] Omitting, with Scholz, commas after *existens* and *provinciis.*

[15] On the concept of "plenitude of power," see II. xxi. 13; II. xxiii. 2 ff.; Vol. I, pp. 8, 170, 256–58; also above, Introduction, pp. lxxxvii–lxxxviii. The term "title" has a technical legal meaning for Marsilius.

[16] Revelation 19:16.   [17] *Corp. jur. can., Clem.* Lib. II. Tit. II. cap. 2.

II, Chapter XX, paragraph 8. In this decretal, he declares that it must be believed to be necessary for eternal salvation that "every human creature" be subject in coercive jurisdiction to the Roman pontiff.[18]

11. In this way, then, have the Roman bishops entered upon these affairs. First, under the guise of seeking peace among the Christian believers, they have excommunicated certain men who are unwilling to obey their decrees. Then they impose on them penalties both real and personal, more harshly against those who are less able to resist their power, such as communities and individuals among the Italians, whose state, divided and wounded in almost all its parts, can more easily be oppressed; but more mildly against those, like kings and rulers, whose resistance and coercive power they fear. On these latter, however, they are gradually creeping up in the attempt to usurp their jurisdictions, not daring to invade them all at once. Hence their stealthy double-dealing has hitherto been concealed even from the Roman rulers and the peoples subject to them. For the Roman bishops have gradually seized one jurisdiction after another, especially when the imperial seat was vacant; so that now they finally say that they have total coercive temporal jurisdiction over the Roman ruler. Most recently and most obviously, the present bishop has written that he has supreme jurisdiction over the ruler of the Romans, both in the Italian and the German provinces, and also over all the lesser rulers, communities, groups, and individuals of the aforesaid provinces, of whatever dignity and condition they may be, and over all their fiefs and other temporalities. This bishop openly ascribes to himself the power to give and transfer their governments, as all can clearly see from certain writings of this bishop, which he calls "edicts" or "sentences." [19]

12. This wrong opinion of certain Roman bishops, and also perhaps their perverted desire for rulership, which they assert is owed to them because of the plenitude of power given to them, as they say, by Christ— this is that singular cause which we have said produces the intranquillity or discord of the city or state.[20] For it is prone to creep up on all states, as was said in our introductory remarks, and by its hateful action it has for a long time distressed the Italian state, and has kept and still keeps it from tranquillity or peace, by preventing with all its force the appointment or institution of the ruler, the Roman emperor, and his functioning in the said empire. From lack of this function, which is the just regulation of

---

[18] *Corp. jur. can., Extravag. commun.* Lib. i. Tit. 8. cap. i (*Unam sanctam*).

[19] See the bulls of Pope John XXII, July 16, 1317, March 31, 1318, and especially those against Ludwig of Bavaria, Oct. 8, 1323, and March 23, 1324; in MGH, *Constitutiones*, Vol. V, Nos. 443, 792, 881, pp. 367, 616, 692.

[20] See above, I. i. 3.

civil acts, there readily emerge injuries and contentions, and these,[21] if not measured by a standard of justice or law because of the absence of the measurer, cause fights, whence there have resulted the separation of the citizens and finally the destruction of the Italian polities or cities, as we have said. With this opinion, therefore, and perhaps also with what we have called a desire for ruling, the Roman bishop strives to make the Roman ruler subject to him in coercive or temporal jurisdiction, whereas that ruler neither rightly ought to be, as we shall clearly show below, nor wishes to be subject to him in such judgment. From this there has arisen so much strife and discord that it cannot be extinguished without great effort of souls and bodies and expenditure of wealth.

For the office of coercive rulership over any individual, of whatever condition he may be, or over any community or group, does not belong to the Roman or any other bishop, priest, or spiritual minister, as such, as has been demonstrated in Chapters XV and XVII of this discourse. And this was what Aristotle held with respect to the priesthood in any law or religion, when he said in the fourth book of the *Politics:* "Hence not all those who are elected or chosen by lot are to be regarded as rulers. Consider the priests in the first place. These must be regarded as different from the political rulers," etc. "And of the superintendent functions," that is, offices, "some are political," etc. And a little below he adds: "And other offices are economic." [22]

13. Since this pernicious pestilence, which is completely opposed to all the peace and happiness of man, could well infect with a disease of the same corrupt root the other states of faithful Christians throughout the world, I consider it supremely necessary to repel it, as I said in my introductory remarks. This is to be done first by tearing away the mask of the afore-mentioned false opinion, as the root of the past and future evils; and then by checking, through external action if necessary,[23] its ignorant or unjust patrons or expositors and stubborn defenders. To these tasks all men are obligated who have the knowledge and ability to thwart this evil; and those who neglect or omit them on whatever grounds are unjust, as Tully attested in the treatise *On Duties,* Book I, Chapter V, when he said: "There are two kinds of injustice: one, of those men who inflict it; the other, of those who do not drive away the injury from those upon whom it is inflicted, if they can." [24] See, then, according to this notable statement of Tully, that not only those who inflict injury on others are unjust,

---

[21] Reading, with Scholz, *facile quae.*   [22] Aristotle *Politics* iv. 15. 1299a 16 ff.
[23] Marsilius thus clearly conceives his doctrine as a prelude to action.
[24] Cicero *De officiis* i. vii. 23. See also above, i. i. 4–6.

but also those who, while having the knowledge and ability to prevent men from inflicting injury on others, do not do so. For every man is obligated to do this for another by a certain quasi-natural law,[25] the duty of friendship and human society. And lest I myself, by knowingly transgressing this law, be called unjust at least to myself, I propose to drive away this pestilence from my brethren, the Christian believers, first by teaching, and then by external action so far as I may be able. For, as I seem indubitably to see, there has been given to me from above the power to discern and unmask the sophism which has sustained in the past, and by which they still strive to sustain, the wrong opinion, and perhaps also the perverted desire, of certain former Roman bishops and of the present one with his accomplices. It is this opinion and desire which is the parent of all the scanda.. mentioned above.

[25] See above, I. iii. 4; also I. i. 4.

DISCOURSE TWO

CHAPTER I: ON THREE IMPEDIMENTS OR MODES OF OPPOSITION TO THE TRUTHS CONTAINED IN THIS DISCOURSE; THE AIM OF THE DISCUSSION; AND THE METHOD OF PROCEDURE

AS I enter upon this arduous undertaking, I see that while there can undoubtedly be no opposition to it which is based on the truth, yet hostilities are being leveled against it by three dangerous enemies of that very truth. The first of these enemies is the persecution of the violent power of the Roman bishops and their accomplices. These will strive with all their might to defeat this undertaking and its truthful proclaimers, who squarely oppose their plan to seize and unjustly to possess temporal goods, and their ardent desire for rulership. To recall these men from their goal by truthful arguments, no matter how clear, will be difficult. But may merciful God in his grace deign to recall them, may he subdue their violent power, and may his believers do likewise—rulers and subjects alike, the peace of all of whom is threatened by these men.

Just as much by a second enemy, an old opponent of almost every truth, are hostilities being leveled against this undertaking: I mean by the habit of listening to and believing falsehoods, those falsehoods which for a long time have been disseminated by certain priests or bishops and their supporters, and which have taken root in the souls of most simple Christian believers. For these priests in their utterances and writings have enveloped divine and human doctrines concerning human acts, both individual and civil, in a motley entanglement which is very difficult to unravel. From this jumble of doctrines they proceed to infer, although invalidly, conclusions which have helped them to impose their unjust despotism upon Christian believers. And the latter, in their simplicity, are led by the misreasonings of these priests, and by the threat of eternal damnation, to believe that divine ordainment binds them to obey such written and spoken sophistries, in which the conclusion frequently does not follow from the premises. For the true doctrines concerning the matters under inquiry and dispute, and concerning their true and simple origins, have been effaced from men's minds, and in their stead falsehoods have been gradually inserted, so that now most men cannot distinguish the true from the false. For the custom of listening to falsehoods is troublesome and most subversive of the truth in every discipline, as Aristotle attests in the second book of the *Philosophy*, last chapter.[1] Because of this custom, readers and hearers of this work, especially those untrained in philosophy and in the holy Scriptures, will at the very outset be greatly impeded from grasping and fully believing the truths contained in this volume.

And finally, a third oppressive enemy of the truth will also be a great impediment to this doctrine of mine: I mean the envy of those who, while believing I have spoken the truth, will nevertheless oppose it with the slanderous fangs of surreptitious detraction or with the loud barks of arrogance, moved by the utterly vicious spirit of burning envy, because they will see that this true doctrine has been expressed by someone other than themselves.[2]

2. I shall certainly not desist from my plans through fear of the violent power of the priests, whom I address in these writings, and who have an ardent and undue desire for rulership; for as the psalmist says, "The Lord is my helper: and I will not fear what man can do unto me."[3] Nor will the railings of my invidious detractors prevent me from expressing what can be so beneficial to all when expressed, and so harmful when neglected. And since these men will be tormenting themselves, they will frustrate their own purposes with their malice; for "envy," as Uguccio well says, "reverts against him who is envious, since it is the torment of a soul wasting away because of the good of another."[4] As for that inimical custom of listening to falsehoods, it will be sufficiently thwarted by the evidence of the truths to be presented.

3. I shall begin this second discourse by adducing the authorities of the holy canon, together with certain fictitious and foreign interpretations of them made by certain men, whereby it might seem possible to prove that to the Roman bishop rightfully belongs the highest of all coercive jurisdictions or rulerships, especially in the Christian world, over the Roman ruler and all other governments, communities, groups, and

---

[1] Aristotle *Metaphysics* II. 3. 995a 4.

[2] With these three groups of Marsilian enemies may be compared the three groups of men whom Dante charged with opposing the truth: the supreme pontiff and other priests; the so-called "sons of the church"; and the "decretalists" or canonists. See *De monarchia* III. iii.

[3] Psalm 117:6 (King James Version, 118:6).

[4] Uguccio of Pisa, bishop of Ferrara, commentator on Gratian's *Decretum*. The quotation is not found in his edited work.

even individual laymen, and still more over priests or bishops and deacons, both groups and individuals, of whatever condition they may be.[5] For if by virtue of the words of the Scripture this conclusion applies to one of these lay or clerical groups or individuals, by the same necessity does it apply to all the rest.

Next, in support of this position I shall adduce some quasi-political arguments [6] which appear quite plausible once we assume certain scriptural truths, which latter all men must indeed assume to be harmoniously true. I shall adduce these arguments, as I say, so that I may then clearly refute them, lest some person be again deceived by them or by similar arguments and in order that their refutation may make more obvious the weakness of the above-stated belief to which they have for so long lent an appearance of probability.

4. And then, in opposition to these arguments, I shall set forth the truths of the holy canon, with the expositions of its holy interpreters, which are not fictitious, not foreign or false, but fitting and proper.[7] These clearly demonstrate that the Roman bishop called pope, or any other priest or bishop, or spiritual minister, collectively or individually, as such, has and ought to have no coercive jurisdiction over the property or person of any priest or bishop, or deacon, or group of them, and still less over any secular ruler or government, community, group, or individual, of whatever condition they may be; unless, indeed, such jurisdiction shall have been granted to a priest or bishop or group of them by the human legislator of the province. To demonstrate and confirm this proposition, there can and should be adduced, when the occasion arises, the political demonstrations whose proper principles are contained in Chapters XII, XV, and XVII of Discourse I. For we have arranged not to repeat these demonstrations, for the sake of brevity.

Following this, I shall show the nature and extent of the priestly power of the keys,[8] which Christ gave to the Roman bishop and to every other priest. For on the clarification of this matter depends the solution of many questions, which will show the way to the truth and the end which we are striving to bring forth.

5. Then it will be of advantage to discuss some questions arising from what we have said; [9] with these, too, we shall say something suitable for our proposed task concerning the privileges of the Roman rulers,[10] which were granted in the past to the Roman bishops. For from these privileges

[5] See below, II. iii. 1–9.   [6] See below, II. iii. 10–15.   [7] See below, II. iv–v.
[8] See below, II. vi–vii.   [9] See below, II. viii–xi.
[10] See below, II. xi. 8; II. xvi. 9; II. xviii. 7; II. xxii. 19.

arose the usurpations and seizures of coercive jurisdictions which the Roman bishops now ascribe to their own authority; and afterwards these usurpations were strengthened by custom, or rather abuse, especially when the imperial seat was vacant. For at the beginning it was these privileges of the Roman rulers, and nothing else, which sustained the Roman bishops in their acquiring and retaining of coercive jurisdiction. But later on, either because they were deservedly deprived of such jurisdiction, or to prevent the weakness of their pretexts and the truth about the jurisdiction wrongly assumed by them from becoming known and to conceal their ingratitude, or even perhaps, as we have shown to be likely in the last chapter of Discourse I,[11] because they are aiming at the seizure of coercive jurisdiction over all states, a step not supported by the afore-mentioned privileges, the Roman bishops substituted for the latter a different universal title, plenitude of power, in order to subject to themselves the rulers and all men who live a civil life. By this power, which Christ is said to have given to St. Peter as his vicar, every Roman bishop, as Peter's successor, claims to have supreme coercive jurisdiction over all men and provinces.

The closing chapters of this discourse will show, however, that the authorities of the sacred canon, adduced to controvert what we have called the doctrine of the truth and of the Scripture, do not support the above error, but rather oppose it, as will clearly appear from the expositions of the saints and of other approved teachers of the Christian faith.[12] Through these it will likewise be evident that the expositions, or rather fictions, of certain men who try to twist the Scripture into supporting the afore-mentioned false opinion, do violence to the Scripture and are foreign to it and distortions of it, and do not agree with the views of the saints and the more learned teachers of the Christian faith.

And last of all, I shall refute [13] the arguments which I have called "quasi-political," and which seem to lend some support to this oft-mentioned false opinion.

---

[11] See above, I. xix. 8 ff.   [12] See below, II. xxviii–xxix.   [13] See below, II. xxx.

CHAPTER II: ON THE DISTINCTION OF THE MEAN-
INGS OF THE WORDS OR TERMS WHICH COMPOSE
THE QUESTIONS TO BE DECIDED

BEFORE entering upon our proposed discussion, we shall distinguish
the meanings of the words which we shall use in the principal questions, lest the many meanings of these words cause the doctrines which we
wish to set forth to become ambiguous and confused. For as it is said in the
first chapter of the *Refutations:* "Those who are ignorant of the force of
names misreason both in their own discussions and when listening to others." [1] The words or terms whose many meanings we wish to distinguish
are these: "church," "judge," "spiritual," and "temporal"; for the purpose
of our inquiry is to know whether it pertains to the Roman or any other
bishop, priest, deacon, or group of them, who are usually called "churchmen," to be coercive judges over temporal or spiritual affairs, or both, or
whether they are such judges over neither of these.

2. And so, in pursuit of these aims, let us say that this term "church" is
a word used by the Greeks, signifying among them, in those writings
which have come down to us, an assembly of people contained under one
regime. Aristotle used it in this sense when he said, in the *Politics,* Book
II, Chapter 10: "All men share in the ecclesia." [2]

Among the Latins, this word according to colloquial and familiar usage
means, in one of its senses, a temple or house in which the believers worship together and most frequently invoke God. For thus the Apostle
spoke of the "church" in the first epistle to the Corinthians, Chapter 11:
"Have you not houses to eat and to drink in? or despise ye the church of
God?" [3] Whereon the gloss according to Augustine: "Despise ye the
church of God, that is, the house of prayer?", and a little below he adds:
"Daily usage has brought it about that one does not say 'to go forth or
take refuge in the church' unless one goes or takes refuge in a certain
place and building." [4]

In another sense this word "church" means all the priests or bishops,
deacons, and others who minister in the temple or the church taken in the

---

[1] Aristotle *On Sophistical Refutations* I. 165a 15.

[2] Aristotle *Politics* II. 10. 1272a 10. The point here made depends upon the fact that the
word for "church" (*ecclesia*) is the same as that which the Greeks used for a general assembly
(ἐκκλησία), and which William of Moerbeke translates *ecclesia*.

[3] I Corinthians 11:22.   [4] See Peter Lombard *Collectanea* (PL 191. 1639).

preceding sense. And according to this meaning, only clergymen or ministers are commonly called persons of the church or churchmen.

Again in another sense, and especially among the moderns, this word "church" means those ministers, priests or bishops and deacons, who minister in and preside over the metropolitan or principal church. This usage was long since brought about by the church of the city of Rome, whose ministers and overseers are the Roman pope and his cardinals. Through custom they have brought it about that they are called the "church" and that one says the "church" has done or received something when it is these men who have done or received or otherwise ordained something.

3. But the word "church" has also another meaning which is the truest and the most fitting one of all, according to the first imposition of the word and the intention of these first imposers, even though this meaning is not so familiar nor in accord with modern usage. According to this signification, the "church" means the whole body of the faithful who believe in and invoke the name of Christ, and all the parts of this whole body in any community, even the household.[5] And this was the first imposition of this term and the sense in which it was customarily used among the apostles and in the primitive church. Hence the Apostle, in the first epistle to the Corinthians, Chapter 1, wrote: "To the church of God that is at Corinth, to them that are sanctified in Christ Jesus, called to be saints, with all that invoke the name of our Lord Jesus Christ." [6] Whereon the gloss according to Ambrose: "Sanctified in baptism, and this in Christ Jesus." [7] And it was in accordance with this meaning that the Apostle spoke in the twentieth chapter of the Acts, to the Ephesian priests, when he said: "Take heed to yourselves and to the whole flock, wherein the Holy Ghost hath placed you bishops, to rule the church of God which he hath purchased with his own blood." [8] And therefore all the Christian faithful, both priests and non-priests, are and should be called churchmen according to this truest and most proper signification, because Christ purchased and redeemed all men with his blood. Thus too it is explicitly said in the gloss on the twenty-second chapter of Luke: "This is my body, which is given for you." [9] " 'For you,' " says the gloss, "does not mean that for the apostles alone was the body of Christ given and his blood shed, but for the sake of the whole of human nature." [10] Thus, then, the blood of Christ was not shed for the apostles alone; therefore it was not they

---

[5] On this definition, see Vol. I, pp. 260 ff.　　[6] I Corinthians 1:2.
[7] See Peter Lombard *Collectanea* (PL 191. 1535).　　[8] Acts 20:28.
[9] Luke 22:19.
[10] See Theophylact's gloss, in Thomas Aquinas *Catena aurea* (XII, 228).

alone who were purchased by him, nor consequently their successors in office, the priests or ministers of the temple, alone; therefore it is not they alone who are the "church" which Christ purchased with his blood. And for the same reason, those ministers, bishops or priests and deacons, are not alone the "church" which is Christ's bride, but they are rather a part of this bride, since it was for this bride that Christ gave himself. Hence the Apostle, in the epistle to the Philippians, Chapter 5, writes: "Husbands, love your wives, as Christ also loved the church, and delivered himself up for it." [11] But now Christ delivered himself up not for the apostles alone or their successors in office, the bishops or priests and deacons, but rather for the whole of human nature. Therefore it is not they alone or their congregation who are the bride of Christ, although a certain congregation of them, abusing the word in order to advance fraudulently their own temporal well-being to the detriment of others, calls itself exclusively the bride of Christ. This same sense can be derived from the words of the Apostle in the first epistle to the Corinthians, last chapter; the epistle to the Thessalonians, Chapter 1; the epistle to the Colossians, Chapter 4; and the epistle to Philemon, Chapter 1.[12] For in all these places the Apostle took "church" in what we have said to be its proper and truest meaning.

4. Now we must proceed to distinguish the meanings of the words "temporal" and "spiritual." [13] Beginning with that which is better known to us,[14] let us say that this term "temporal" in one of its more familiar senses refers to all corporeal things, natural and artificial, except man, which are in any way in man's power and are ordered toward his use, needs, and pleasures in and for the status of worldly life. In this way, also, more generally, "temporal" customarily refers to all that which begins and ends [15] in time. For these things, as it is written in the fourth book of the *Physics,* properly are and are said to be in time.[16]

In another sense, "temporal" refers to every human habit, action, or passion, whether in oneself or directed toward another by man for a purpose of this world or of the present life.

Less universally, this word "temporal" refers to those human actions · and passions which are voluntary and transient, resulting in benefit or

[11] Actually Ephesians 5:25.

[12] I Corinthians 16:1, 9; I Thessalonians 1:1; II Thessalonians 1:1; Colossians 4:15, 16; Philemon 1:2.

[13] On these distinctions, see Vol. I, pp. 100–104.

[14] See Aristotle *Posterior Analytics* I. 2. 72a 1; *Physics* I. 1. 184a 16; *Nicomachean Ethics* I. 4. 1095b 1.

[15] Reading, with Scholz, *desinit* for *defirit*.

[16] See Aristotle *Physics* IV. 12. 221a 3 ff.

harm to someone other than the agent.[17] It is with these actions and passions that the makers of human laws are mainly concerned.

5. Now I wish to distinguish the meanings or senses of the term "spiritual." In one sense it refers to all incorporeal substances and their actions.

In another sense it refers to every immanent action or passion of man's cognitive or appetitive power.[18] In this meaning, too, certain actions of corporeal things on the senses of animals are usually called spiritual and immaterial, such as the idols or phantasms and species of things, which are in some way the soul's means of knowing; in this class some place the actions of sensible things even on inanimate substances, like the generation of light and similar things.

Again, and more pertinently, this word "spiritual" refers to the divine law, and the teaching and learning of the commands and counsels in accordance with it and through it. Under this signification also come all ecclesiastic sacraments and their effects, all divine grace, all theological virtues, and the gifts of the Holy Spirit ordering us toward eternal life. For it was in this way, and appropriately, that the Apostle used this word in the epistle to the Romans, Chapter 15,[19] and in the first epistle to the Corinthians, Chapter 9, when he said: "If we have sown unto you spiritual things, is it a great matter if we reap your carnal things?"[20] Whereon the gloss according to Ambrose: "Spiritual things, that is, those things which vivify your spirit, or which were given by the Holy Spirit, namely, the word of God, and the mystery of the kingdom of the heavens."[21]

Moreover, in another sense this word is used for any voluntary human action or passion, whether in oneself or directed toward another, which is done for the purpose of meriting a blessed life in the future world. Such are the contemplation of God, love of God and of one's neighbors, abstinence, mercy, meekness, prayer, offerings for piety or divine worship, hospitality, pilgrimage, castigation of one's own body, contempt for and flight from worldly and carnal pleasures, and generally all similar actions and passions done for the aforesaid purpose.

Again, this word refers, although not so properly as in the second and third sense, to the temple or the church taken in its second sense; and to all the utensils and ornaments which serve therein for divine worship.

Most recently of all, very unsuitably and improperly, certain men ex-

---

[17] On this concept of "transient" acts, see texts cited above, I. v. 4, n. 6.
[18] On this concept of "immanent" acts, see texts referred to in preceding note.
[19] Romans 15:27.   [20] I Corinthians 9:11.
[21] See Peter Lombard *Collectanea* (PL 191. 1609), where the gloss is attributed to Ambrose as far as "spirit," the remainder to Augustine.

tend this word to signify the voluntary transient actions and omissions of priests or bishops, deacons, and other temple ministers, which are for the benefit or harm of someone other than the agent for the status of worldly life.

Again, and even more improperly, these men extend the same word to signify their possessions and temporal goods, mobile and immobile, as well as certain proceeds of these which they call tithes, so that under cover of this word they may be exempted from the regulation of the civil laws and rulers.[22]

6. But it is quite clear that they abuse the word in giving it such meanings contrary to the truth and the intention and usage of the Apostle and the saints, who called such things not spiritual, but carnal and temporal. Hence in the fifteenth chapter of the epistle to the Romans it is written: "For if the Gentiles have been made partakers of their spiritual things, their duty is also to minister unto them in carnal things." [23] And again, more explicitly, in the first epistle to the Corinthians, Chapter 9: "If we have sown unto you spiritual things," wrote the Apostle, "is it a great thing if we shall reap your carnal things?" [24] Whereon the gloss according to Ambrose: "For 'if we have sown unto you spiritual things,' that is, those things which vivify your spirit, or which were given by the Holy Spirit, namely, the word of God and the mystery of the kingdom of the heavens, 'is it a great thing if we shall reap' for sustenance 'your carnal things,' that is, those temporal things which have been bestowed for life and the needs of the flesh?" [25] Note these external goods, whereby the preachers of the gospel were to be sustained in food and clothing, are here explicitly called "carnal" and "temporal" by the Apostle and by Ambrose, as in truth they are, whether they be tithes or estates, contributions or alms, or collections. And Ambrose gave the reason, for they "have been bestowed for life and the needs of the flesh," that is, for corruptible life.

7. The same view must also undoubtedly be held concerning certain actions of priests, bishops, and deacons. For not all their acts are or should be called spiritual; on the contrary, many of them are civil, contentious, and carnal or temporal. For these men can lend at interest, deposit, buy, sell, strike, kill, steal, commit adultery, rob with violence, betray, deceive, bear

---

[22] For writers who use "spiritual" in the last two senses, see Egidius of Rome *De ecclesiastica potestate* III. viii (pp. 168, 171–72); and James of Viterbo *De regimine christiano* II. viii (ed. H. X. Arquillière [Paris, 1926], p. 254).

[23] Romans 15:27.   [24] I Corinthians 9:11.

[25] See Peter Lombard *Collectanea* (PL 191. 1609); attributed to Ambrose as far as "Holy Spirit," the rest to Augustine.

false witness, defame, fall into heresy, and commit other outrages, crimes, and contentious acts such as are perpetrated also by non-priests.[26] Hence it is appropriate to ask them whether such acts as these, of which we have said they are capable, are spiritual or should be so called by anyone of sound mind. And it is clear that the answer is no, but rather carnal and temporal. Hence the Apostle, in the first epistle to the Corinthians, Chapter 3, speaking to all men about such actions, said: "For whereas there is among you envying and contention, are you not carnal and walk you not according to man?"[27] Since, therefore, undoubted experience demonstrates that from the afore-mentioned acts and other similar ones there arise envying and contentions among priests, both among themselves and toward laymen, it is manifest that such acts of priests are carnal or temporal and should not in truth be called spiritual.

A sign that what we have said is true, even according to the views of clergymen, is that the Roman pontiffs, to settle such contentions, have given forth many human ordinances, which they call "decretals," and before these there were the laws of the Roman rulers dealing with the same acts. For the deacons and priests or bishops can and do perform many voluntary transient actions which redound to the benefit or harm and injury of someone else for and in the status of the present life. And therefore the human law must be the measure of such actions, as was said in Chapter XV of Discourse I,[28] and as will be said still more pertinently in Chapter VIII of this discourse.[29]

8. It now remains to distinguish the meanings of the words "judge" and "judgment," which signifies the action of the judge.[30] For these are among the terms which have many meanings, and that multiplicity introduces ambiguity which impedes the determination of questions. In one sense, "judge" means anyone who discerns or knows, especially in accordance with some theoretic or practical habit; and so the word "judgment" means such men's knowledge or discernment. In this sense, the geometer is a judge, and judges concerning figures and their attributes; and the physician judges concerning the healthy and the sick, and the prudent man concerning what should be done and what should be avoided, and the housebuilder concerning how to build houses. Thus, every knower or expert is called a judge, and judges about things which can be known or done by him. It was in this sense that Aristotle used these

---

[26] Most of the items in this list of contentious acts are found in Aristotle *Nicomachean Ethics* v. 2. 1131a 4 ff., where they are given as examples of the transactions between man and man which are dealt with by rectificatory justice.

[27] I Corinthians 3:3.

[28] See above, I. xv. 3 ff.

[29] See below, II. viii. 5 ff.

[30] On these distinctions, see Vol. I, pp. 226–29.

words in the *Ethics,* Book I, Chapter 1, when he said: "Everyone judges well the things which he knows, and is a good judge of them." [31]

In another sense, this word "judge" means the man who has the science of political or civil law, and who is usually called an "advocate," although in many provinces, and particularly in Italy, he is called a "judge."

In a third sense, this word "judge" means the ruler, and "judgment" means the sentence of the ruler who has the authority to judge concerning the just and beneficial in accordance with the laws or customs, and to command and execute through coercive force the sentences made by him. In this sense, a certain book is called Judges, being one part of the holy canon or Bible. It was in this sense, too, that Aristotle spoke of the judge or ruler in the *Rhetoric,* Book I, Chapter 1, when he said: "But the magistrate and the judge make judgments concerning the present and the determinate." So too, referring to the judgment of the ruler, he continues: "They," that is, the magistrate or judge, "are often involved in personal likes and dislikes, so that they cannot see the truth sufficiently well, but instead have regard in their judgments to their own pleasure and displeasure." [32]

There are perhaps other meanings of the above words; we think, however, that we have indicated those which are more familiar and more necessary for our proposed inquiry.

CHAPTER III: ON THE CANONIC STATEMENTS AND OTHER ARGUMENTS WHICH SEEM TO PROVE THAT COERCIVE RULERSHIP BELONGS TO BISHOPS OR PRIESTS AS SUCH, EVEN WITHOUT THE GRANT OF THE HUMAN LEGISLATOR, AND THAT THE SUPREME OF ALL SUCH RULERSHIPS BELONGS TO THE ROMAN BISHOP OR POPE

HAVING thus distinguished the meanings of these terms with which the largest part of our inquiry will deal, we now enter more securely upon our principal task. First of all, we shall adduce the authorities of the holy Scripture which might lead someone to think that the Roman bishop called pope is the supreme judge, in the third sense of "judge" or "judgment," over all the bishops or priests and other ecclesiastic ministers in the

---

[31] Aristotle *Nicomachean Ethics* I. 1. 1094b 28.   [32] Aristotle *Rhetoric* I. 1. 1354b 6 ff.

world, and also over all rulers, communities, groups, and individuals of this world, of whatever condition they may be.

2. Let us first quote the passage of Scripture in the sixteenth chapter of Matthew, where Christ says to St. Peter: "And I will give to thee the keys of the kingdom of heaven: and whatsoever thou shalt bind on earth, it shall be bound also in heaven: and whatsoever thou shalt loose on earth, it shall be loosed also in heaven." [1] For through this passage, certain Roman bishops have assumed for themselves the authority of the supreme jurisdiction mentioned above. For by the "keys" given to St. Peter by Christ, they wish to understand plenitude of power over the whole regime of men; just as Christ had this plenitude of power over all kings and rulers, so did he grant it to St. Peter and his successors in the Roman episcopal seat, as Christ's general vicars in this world.

3. A second passage of Scripture in support of the same position is taken from the words of Christ in the eleventh chapter of Matthew, when he said: "All things are delivered to me by my father"; and again in the twenty-eighth chapter when he said: "All power is given to me in heaven and in earth." [2] Since, therefore, St. Peter and his successors in the episcopal seat at Rome were and are Christ's vicars, as they say, it seems that all power or plenitude of power has been given to them, and consequently jurisdictional authority over everyone.

4. A third passage to the same effect is taken from the eighth chapter of Matthew and the fifth chapter of Mark, where it is written: "And the devils besought him," that is, Christ, "saying, If thou cast us out hence, send us into the herd of swine. And he said to them, Go. But they going out went into the swine: and, behold, the whole herd ran violently down a steep place into the sea, and they perished in the waters." [3] From these words it appears that Christ disposed of temporal things as if they were all his own; for otherwise he would have sinned in destroying the herd of swine. But it is wrong to say that Christ, whose flesh did not see corruption, sinned. Since, therefore, St. Peter and his successors the Roman bishops are and were the special vicars of Christ, as some say, they can dispose of all temporal things as judges in the third sense of the word, and they, like Christ, have plenitude of power and dominion over them all.

5. Again, the same is shown by what is written in the twenty-first chapter of Matthew, the eleventh of Mark, and the nineteenth of Luke: "Then Jesus sent two disciples, saying to them, Go ye into the village that is over against you, and immediately you shall find an ass tied, and a colt

---

[1] Matthew 16:19. [2] Matthew 11:27; 28:18.
[3] Matthew 8:31, 32. Cf. Mark 5:12, 13.

with her"; or, "a colt tied, upon which no man yet hath sat," as in Mark and Luke. "Loose them and bring them to me." [4] From these words the same conclusion can be reached, and by the same mode of deduction, as from the passage quoted immediately above.

6. Moreover, the same point is proved from the twenty-second chapter of Luke, where these words are found: "Behold, here are two swords," said the apostles, replying to Christ. "And he," that is, Christ, "said to them: It is enough." [5] By these words, according to some men's interpretation, it must be understood that there are in the present world two governments, one ecclesiastic or spiritual, the other temporal or secular. Since, therefore, Christ said to the apostles: "It is enough," namely, for you to have these two swords, he seems to have meant that both swords should belong to the authority of the apostles, and particularly to St. Peter as the leading apostle. For if Christ had not wanted the temporal sword to belong to them, he should have said: It is too much.

7. Again, it seems that the same must be believed from the twenty-first chapter of John, where Christ spoke to St. Peter as follows: "Feed my sheep, feed my lambs, feed my sheep," [6] repeating the same phrase three times, just as we have quoted. From these words some draw the following interpretation: that St. Peter and his successors the Roman bishops ought absolutely to be in charge over all of Christ's faithful sheep, that is, the Christians, and especially over the priests and deacons.

8. Moreover, this clearly seems to be the view of St. Paul in the first epistle to the Corinthians, Chapter 6, where he writes: "Know ye not that we shall judge angels? how much more secular things?" [7] Therefore, judgments in the third sense over secular things seem to pertain to priests or bishops, and especially to the first of them, the Roman bishop. Again, the Apostle seems to have thought the same in the first epistle to the Corinthians, Chapter 9, when he said: "Have not we power to eat," [8] etc. And the same in the second epistle to the Thessalonians, Chapter 3.[9] In these passages he seems explicitly to hold that God gave him power over the temporalities of the faithful, and consequently jurisdiction over them.

9. The same is again shown from the first epistle to Timothy, Chapter 5, where the Apostle wrote to Timothy: "Against a priest receive not an accusation, but under two or three witnesses." [10] From this, then, it seems that the bishop has jurisdiction at least over priests, deacons, and other ministers of the temple, inasmuch as it pertains to him to hear accusations against them.

[4] Matthew 21:1, 2. Cf. Mark 11:1, 2; Luke 19:29, 30.
[5] Luke 22:38.   [6] John 21:15–17.   [7] I Corinthians 6:3.
[8] I Corinthians 9:4.   [9] II Thessalonians 3:8, 9.   [10] I Timothy 5:19.

We shall omit to quote proofs in support of the proposed conclusion and its opposite from the Old Scripture or Testament, for a reason which we shall indicate in Chapter IX of this discourse.[11]

And so, from the aforesaid authorities of the holy Scripture, and other similar ones, and from such interpretations of them, someone might be led to think that the highest of all rulerships belongs to the Roman bishop.

10. Following upon these, it is fitting to adduce some quasi-political arguments which might perhaps lead men to fancy and believe the aforesaid conclusion. The first of these arguments is as follows. As the human body is to the soul, so is the ruler of bodies to the ruler of souls. But the body is subject to the soul with respect to rule. Therefore too the ruler of bodies, the secular judge, must be subject to the rule of the judge or ruler of souls, and especially of the first of them all, the Roman pontiff.[12]

11. Again, another argument from almost the same root: As corporeals are to spirituals, so is the ruler of corporeals to the ruler of spirituals. But it is certain that corporeals are by nature inferior and subject to spirituals. Therefore the ruler of corporeals, the secular judge, must be subject to the ruler of spirituals, the ecclesiastic judge.

12. Moreover, as end is to end, and law to law, and legislator to legislator, so is the judge or ruler in accordance with the one of these to the judge or ruler in accordance with the other. But the end toward which the ecclesiastic judge, the priest or bishop, directs, the law by which he directs, and the maker of that law, are all superior to and more perfect than the end, the law, and the maker to which and by which the secular judge directs. Therefore the ecclesiastic judge, bishop or priest, and especially the first of them all, is superior to every secular judge. For the end toward which the ecclesiastic judge directs is eternal life; the law by which he directs is divine; and its immediate maker is God, in whom neither error nor malice can lodge. But the end toward which the secular judge aims to direct is sufficiency of this worldly life; the law by which he directs is human; and the immediate maker of this law is man or men, who are subject to error and malice. Therefore, the latter are inferior to and less worthy than the former. Therefore, too, the secular judge, even the supreme one, is inferior to and less worthy than the ecclesiastic judge, the supreme priest.[13]

13. Moreover, a person or thing is absolutely more honorable than another when the action of that first person or thing is absolutely more honorable than the action of the second. But the action of the priest or bishop,

---

[11] See below, II. ix. 10. See also Vol. I, pp. 72–73.

[12] For upholders of this argument, see Vol. I, p. 100, n. 54.

[13] For upholders of this argument, see Vol. I, pp. 104–5, nn. 85, 88.

the consecration of the blessed body of Christ, is the most honorable of all the actions which can be performed by man in the present life. Therefore, any priest is more worthy than any non-priest. Since, therefore, the more worthy should not be subject to the less worthy, but rather above it, it seems that the secular judge should not be above the priest in jurisdiction, but rather subordinate to him, and especially to the first of them all, the Roman pontiff.

14. The same is again shown with more specific reference to the Roman ruler, called emperor. For any person who has the authority to establish this ruler's government and to transfer it at pleasure from nation to nation is superior to this ruler in judgment, in the third sense of "judgment." But the Roman pontiff proclaims that he is such a person, inasmuch as he transferred the Roman empire from the Greeks to the Germans, as was set forth in the seventh of his decretals, *On Oaths;* [14] and the same is stated even more explicitly by the modern so-called bishop of the Romans, in an edict of his addressed to Ludwig, duke of Bavaria, elected king of the Romans.[15]

15. Another argument to the same effect is that a great difficulty seems to arise if we assume that Christ's vicar, the Roman bishop, and the other bishops who are successors of the apostles, are subject to the sentence of any secular ruler. For since the secular ruler may sin against divine and human law, whereupon he must be corrected, as was said in Chapter XVIII of Discourse I,[16] and since he, being supreme over all laymen, does not have a superior or an equal, inasmuch as a plurality of governments was rejected in Chapter XVII of Discourse I, it will seem that coercive jurisdiction over him belongs to the Roman bishop, and not conversely.[17]

By the above, therefore, it might seem possible to prove that bishops or priests have coercive jurisdiction, and that to the supreme Roman pontiff belongs the supreme rulership of all in this world. We seem adequately to have set forth both the authorities of the holy Scripture and certain quasi-political and human arguments in support of this position.

[14] *Corp. jur. can., Clem.* Lib. II. Tit. 9. *De jurejurando* (Romani Principes). See also Egidius of Rome *De ecclesiastica potestate* I. iv; II. vi (pp. 12, 55); and Alvarus Pelagius *De planctu ecclesiae* I. xxxvii (*Bibliotheca maxima pontificia,* ed. J. T. Roccaberti [Rome, 1698–99], III, 49).

[15] This is the monitorium of John XXII, Oct. 8, 1323 (MGH, *Constitutiones,* V, No. 792, pp. 616–19).

[16] In I. xviii, Marsilius referred to the ruler's transgression of human law alone, not divine law. See also Vol. I, pp. 250–51.

[17] This argument is found in Egidius of Rome *De ecclesiastica potestate* III. viii (p. 187); and in James of Viterbo *De regimine Christiano* II. vii (ed. H. X. Arquillière [Paris, 1926], pp. 243–44).

CHAPTER IV: ON THE CANONIC SCRIPTURES, THE
COMMANDS, COUNSELS, AND EXAMPLES OF CHRIST
AND OF THE SAINTS AND APPROVED DOCTORS WHO
EXPOUNDED THE EVANGELIC LAW, WHEREBY IT IS
CLEARLY DEMONSTRATED THAT THE ROMAN OR
ANY OTHER BISHOP OR PRIEST, OR CLERGYMAN,
CAN BY VIRTUE OF THE WORDS OF SCRIPTURE CLAIM
OR ASCRIBE TO HIMSELF NO COERCIVE RULERSHIP
OR CONTENTIOUS JURISDICTION, LET ALONE THE
SUPREME JURISDICTION OVER ANY CLERGYMAN OR
LAYMAN; AND THAT, BY CHRIST'S COUNSEL AND
EXAMPLE, THEY OUGHT TO REFUSE SUCH RULER-
SHIP, ESPECIALLY IN COMMUNITIES OF THE FAITH-
FUL, IF IT IS OFFERED TO THEM OR BESTOWED ON
THEM BY SOMEONE HAVING THE AUTHORITY TO DO
SO; AND AGAIN, THAT ALL BISHOPS, AND GENERALLY
ALL PERSONS NOW CALLED CLERGYMEN, MUST BE
SUBJECT TO THE COERCIVE JUDGMENT OR RULER-
SHIP OF HIM WHO GOVERNS BY THE AUTHORITY OF
THE HUMAN LEGISLATOR, ESPECIALLY WHERE THIS
LEGISLATOR IS CHRISTIAN

WE now wish from the opposite side to adduce the truths of the holy
Scripture in both its literal and its mystical sense, in accordance
with the interpretations of the saints and the expositions of other approved
doctors of the Christian faith, which explicitly command or counsel that
neither the Roman bishop called pope, nor any other bishop or priest, or
deacon, has or ought to have any rulership or coercive judgment or jurisdiction over any priest or non-priest, ruler, community, group, or individual of whatever condition; understanding by "coercive judgment" that
which we said in Chapter II of this discourse to be the third sense of "judge"
or "judgment." [1]

[1] See above, ii. ii. 8.

2. The more clearly to carry out this aim, we must not overlook that in this inquiry it is not asked what power and authority is or was had in this world by Christ, who was true God and true man, nor what or how much of this power he was able to bestow on St. Peter and the other apostles and their successors, the bishops or priests; for Christian believers have no doubts on these points. But we wish to and ought to inquire what power and authority, to be exercised in this world, Christ wanted to bestow and in fact (*de facto*) did bestow on them, and from what he excluded and prohibited them by counsel or command. For we are bound to believe that they had from Christ only such power and authority as we can prove to have been given to them through the words of Scripture, no other.[2] For it is certain to all the Christian believers that Christ, who was true God and true man, was able to bestow, not only on the apostles but also on any other men, coercive authority or jurisdiction over all rulers or governments and over all the other individuals in this world; and even more perhaps, as for example the power to create things, to destroy or repair heaven and earth and the things therein, and even to be in complete command of angels; but these powers Christ neither bestowed nor determined to bestow on them. Hence Augustine, in the tenth sermon *On the Words of the Lord in Matthew,* wrote the following: " 'Learn of me' not how to make a world, not how to create all visible and invisible things, nor how to do miracles in the world and revive the dead; but: 'because I am meek and humble of heart.' "[3]

3. Therefore for the present purpose it suffices to show, and I shall first show,[4] that Christ himself came into the world not to dominate men, nor to judge them by judgment in the third sense, nor to wield temporal rule, but rather to be subject as regards the status of the present life; and moreover, that he wanted to and did exclude himself, his apostles and disciples, and their successors, the bishops or priests, from all such coercive authority or worldly rule, both by his example and by his words of counsel or command. I shall also show [5] that the leading apostles, as Christ's true imitators, did this same thing and taught their successors to do likewise; and moreover, that both Christ and the apostles wanted to be and were continuously subject in property and in person to the coercive jurisdiction of secular rulers, and that they taught and commanded all others, to whom they preached or wrote the law of truth, to do likewise, under pain of eternal damnation. Then I shall write a chapter [6] on the power or authority of the keys which Christ gave to the apostles and their successors in office,

---

[2] See Vol. I, p. 77.   [3] St. Augustine *Sermo LXIX* on Matthew 11:28–29 (PL 38. 441).
[4] II. iv. 4 ff.   [5] II. v.   [6] II. vi.

bishops and priests, so that it may be clear what is the nature, quality, and extent of such power, both of the Roman bishop and of the others. For ignorance on this point has hitherto been and still is the source of many questions and damnable controversies among the Christian faithful, as was mentioned in the first chapter of this discourse.

4. And so in pursuit of these aims we wish to show that Christ, in his purposes or intentions, words, and deeds, wished to exclude and did exclude himself and the apostles from every office of rulership, contentious jurisdiction, government, or coercive judgment in this world. This is first shown clearly beyond any doubt by the passage in the eighteenth chapter of the gospel of John. For when Christ was brought before Pontius Pilate, vicar of the Roman ruler in Judaea, and accused of having called himself king of the Jews, Pontius asked him whether he had said this, or whether he did call himself a king, and Christ's reply included these words, among others: "My kingdom is not of this world," that is, I have not come to reign by temporal rule or dominion, in the way in which worldly kings reign. And proof of this was given by Christ himself through an evident sign when he said: "If my kingdom were of this world, my servants would certainly fight, that I should not be delivered to the Jews," as if to argue as follows: If I had come into this world to reign by worldly or coercive rule, I would have ministers for this rule, namely, men to fight and to coerce transgressors, as the other kings have; but I do not have such ministers, as you can clearly see. Hence the interlinear gloss: "It is clear that no one defends him." And this is what Christ reiterates: "But now my kingdom is not from hence," [7] that is, the kingdom about which I have come to teach.

5. Expounding these evangelic truths, the saints and doctors write as follows, and first St. Augustine:

If he had answered Pilate's question directly, he would have seemed to be answering not the Jews but only the Gentiles who thought this of him. But after answering Pilate, he answered the Jews and the Gentiles more opportunely and fitly, as if to say: Hear ye, Jews and Gentiles, I do not impede your rule in this world. What more do you want? Through faith approach ye the kingdom which is not of this world. For what is his kingdom but those who believe in him? [8]

This, then, is the kingdom concerning which he came to teach and order, a kingdom which consists in the acts whereby the eternal kingdom is attained, that is, the acts of faith and the other theological virtues; not,

---

[7] John 18:36, and *Glossa interlinearis, ad loc.*
[8] See Thomas Aquinas *Catena aurea* (XII, 442).

however, by coercing anyone thereto, as will be made clear below. For when there are two coercive dominions in respect of the same multitude, and neither is subordinated to the other, they impede one another, as was shown in Chapter XVII of Discourse I.[9] But Christ had not come to impede such dominion, as Augustine said. Hence on the passage in the same chapter of John: "Thy own nation and the chief priests have delivered thee up to me. What hast thou done?"[10] Augustine wrote: "He sufficiently shows that the act is looked upon as a crime, as if to say: If you deny you are a king, what then have you done to be delivered up to me; as if it would not be strange if he who called himself king were delivered up to the judge to be punished."[11] So, then, Augustine thought that it would be nothing strange if Christ had been punished, had he called himself secular king, especially before those who did not know he was God; and that he denied he would be a king of such a kingdom or with such authority, namely, to coerce transgressors of the law. Hence on the words in the same chapter of John: "Sayest thou this thing of thyself, or did others tell it thee of me?"[12] Theophylact wrote: "Christ spoke to Pilate as if to say: If you say this on your own, show the signs of my rebellion, but if you have heard it from others, then make the ordinary inquiry."[13] But if the opinion of our adversaries were correct, Christ should never have said what Theophylact states, namely, that Pilate should make the ordinary inquiry about him; indeed, were they correct, he should rather have said that it did not pertain to Pilate to make this inquiry, inasmuch as he, Christ, of right (*de jure*) was not and did not wish to be subject to him in jurisdiction or coercive judgment.

6. Again, on the words, "my kingdom is not from hence," Chrysostom says: "He does not deprive the world of his providence and leadership, but he shows that his kingdom is not human or corruptible."[14] But every kingdom which is coercive over anyone in this world is human and corruptible. Moreover, on the words in the same chapter of John: "Thou sayest that I am a king,"[15] Augustine wrote: "He spoke in this manner not because he feared to admit that he was king, but so that he might neither deny he was a king nor affirm that he was such a king whose kingdom is thought to be of this world. For he said, 'Thou sayest,' as if to say: You, a carnal man, speak carnally,"[16] that is, about carnal rule over contentious and carnal temporal acts, taking "temporal" in its third sense; for the

---

[9] See above, I. xvii. 3–5.   [10] John 18:35.
[11] See Thomas Aquinas *Catena aurea* (XII, 442).   [12] John 18:34.
[13] See Thomas Aquinas *Catena aurea* (XII, 442).   [14] See *ibid.*
[15] John 18:37.   [16] See Thomas Aquinas *Catena aurea* (XII, 442).

Apostle called such acts "carnal" in the first epistle to the Corinthians, Chapter 3.[17]

From the above it appears, therefore, that Christ came into the world to dispose not about carnal or temporal rule or coercive judgment, but about the spiritual or heavenly kingdom; for almost always it was only about this latter that he spoke and preached, as is plain from the gospel in both its literal and its mystical sense. And hence we most often read that he said: "Like is the kingdom of heaven," etc., but very rarely did he speak of the earthly kingdom, and if he did, he taught that it should be spurned. For he promised that in the heavenly kingdom he would give rewards and punishments according to the merits or demerits of the agents, but never did he promise to do such things in this world, but rather he does the contrary of what the rulers of this world do. For he most often afflicts or permits the affliction of the just and the doers of good, and thus he leads them to the reward of his kingdom.[18] For "all that have pleased God passed through many tribulations," as it is written in the eighth chapter of Judith.[19] But the rulers of this world, the judges of the worldly kingdom, do and ought to do the contrary, maintaining justice; for when they distribute rewards in this world to those who observe the laws, and punishments to perpetrators of evil, they act rightly; whereas if they did the contrary they would sin against human and divine law.[20]

7. Let us return to the principal question through what Christ showed by deed or example. For in the sixth chapter of John we read that "when Jesus therefore knew that they would come to take him by force and make him king, he fled again into the mountain, himself alone." [21] Whereon the interlinear gloss: "From this he descended to care for the multitude, teaching men to avoid the good fortunes of this world and to pray for strength to withstand them." [22] It is certain, therefore, that Christ avoided rulership, or else he would have taught us nothing by his example. This view is supported by the expositions of St. Augustine, who wrote that "the Christian faithful are his kingdom, which is now cultivated, now redeemed, by the blood of Christ. But his kingdom will be manifest when the clarity of his saints will be revealed after the judgment made by him. But the disciples and the crowds, believing in him, thought he had come to reign." [23] So, then, the saints never understood, by Christ's kingdom in

---

[17] I Corinthians 3:1-3.
[18] Cf. Augustine *De civitate Dei* i. viii, ix; xx. ii; and Augustinus Triumphus *Summa de ecclesiastica potestate* (Augsburg, 1473) qu.6. a. 1.
[19] Judith 8:23.   [20] See Vol. I, p. 81.   [21] John 6:15.
[22] *Glossa interlinearis, ad loc.*   [23] See Thomas Aquinas *Catena aurea* (XII, 330).

this world, temporal dominion or judgment over contentious acts and its execution by coercive power against transgressors of the laws in this world; but by his kingdom and governance in this world they understood, rather, the teaching of the faith, and governance in accordance with it toward the heavenly kingdom. This "kingdom," says Augustine,[24] will indeed be "manifest after his judgment" in the other world. He repeatedly states that to think Christ then reigned as the crowds thought was to "ravish him," that is, to have a wrong assumption and opinion of him. Whereon Chrysostom also: "And the prophet," that is, Christ, "was now among them, and they wanted to enthrone him as king," that is, because he had fed them. "But Christ fled, teaching us to despise worldly honors." [25]

8. Moreover, the same is shown very evidently by Christ's words and example in the following passage of the twelfth chapter of Luke: "And one of the multitude said to him, Master, speak to my brother, that he divide the inheritance with me. But he," that is, Christ, "said to him, Man, who hath appointed me judge or divider over you?" [26] As if to say: I did not come to exercise this office, nor was I sent for this, that is, to settle civil disputes through judgment; but this, however, is undoubtedly the most proper function of secular rulers or judges. Now this passage from the gospel contains and demonstrates our proposition much more clearly than do the glosses of the saints, because the latter assume that the literal meaning, such as we have said, is manifest, and have devoted themselves more to the allegorical or mystical meaning. Nevertheless, we shall now quote from the glosses for a stronger confirmation of our proposition, and so that we may not be accused of expounding Scripture rashly. These words of Christ, then, are expounded by St. Ambrose as follows: "Well does he who descended for the sake of the divine avoid the earthly, and does not deign to be judge over disputes and appraiser of wealth, being the judge of the living and the dead and the appraiser of their merits." And a little below he adds: "Hence not undeservedly is this brother rebuffed, who wanted the dispenser of the heavenly to concern himself with the corruptible." [27] See, then, what Ambrose thinks about Christ's office in this world; for he says that "well does he avoid the earthly," that is, the judgment of contentious acts, "who descended for the sake of the divine," that is, to teach and minister the spiritual; in this he designated Christ's office and that of his successors, namely, to dispense the heavenly or spiritual; that spiritual of which Ambrose spoke in his gloss on the first epistle to the

[24] *Ibid.*   [25] *Ibid.*   [26] Luke 12:13-14.
[27] See Thomas Aquinas *Catena aurea* (XII, 145).

Corinthians, Chapter 9, which we quoted in Chapter II of this discourse under the third meaning of this word "spiritual." [28]

9. It now remains to show that not only did Christ himself refuse rulership or coercive judgment in this world, whereby he furnished an example for his apostles and disciples and their successors to do likewise, but also he taught by words and showed by example that all men, both priests and non-priests, should be subject in property and in person to the coercive judgment of the rulers of this world. By his word and example, then, Christ showed this first with respect to property, by what is written in the twenty-second chapter of Matthew. For when the Jews asked him: "Tell us therefore, what dost thou think? Is it lawful to give tribute to Caesar, or not?" Christ, after looking at the coin and its inscription, replied: "Render therefore to Caesar the things that are Caesar's, and to God the things that are God's." [29] Whereon the interlinear gloss says, "that is, tribute and money." [30] And on the words: "Whose image and inscription is this?" [31] Ambrose wrote as follows: "Just as Caesar demanded the imprinting of his image, so too does God demand that the soul be stamped with the light of his countenance." [32] Note, therefore, what it was that Christ came into the world to demand. Furthermore, Chrysostom writes as follows: "When you hear: 'Render to Caesar the things that are Caesar's,' know that he means only those things which are not harmful to piety, for if they were, the tribute would be not to Caesar but to the devil." [33] So, then, we ought to be subject to Caesar in all things, so long only as they are not contrary to piety, that is, to divine worship or commandment.[34] Therefore, Christ wanted us to be subject in property to the secular ruler. This too was plainly the doctrine of St. Ambrose, based upon this doctrine of Christ, for in his epistle against Valentinian, entitled *To the People,* he wrote: "We pay to Caesar the things that are Caesar's, and to God the things that are God's. That the tribute is Caesar's is not denied." [35]

10. The same is again shown from the seventeenth chapter of Matthew, where it is written as follows: "They that received the didrachmas came to Peter, and said, Doth not your master pay the didrachmas?" and then, a little below, is written what Christ said to Peter: "But that we may not scandalize them, go to the sea and cast in a hook, and that fish which shalt

---

[28] See above, II. ii. 5.

[29] Matthew 22:17, 20–21.

[30] *Glossa interlinearis, ad loc.*

[31] Matthew 22:20.

[32] *Glossa ordinaria, ad loc.* See Thomas Aquinas *Catena aurea* (XI, 410), where an earlier form of this gloss is cited from Jerome, with no mention of Ambrose.

[33] See Thomas Aquinas *Catena aurea* (XI, 253).

[34] For a list of other passages to the same effect, involving the limitation of secular government by divine law, and a discussion of their significance, see Vol. I, pp. 162–63, and n. 69.

[35] St. Ambrose *Sermo contra Auxentium de basilicis tradendis* cap. xxxv (PL 16. 1061).

first come up, take: and when thou hast opened its mouth, thou shalt find a piece of money: take that, and give it to them for me and thee." [36] Nor did the Lord say only, "Give it to them," but he said, "Give it to them for me and thee." And Jerome on this passage says: "Our Lord was in flesh and in spirit the son of a king, whether we consider him to have been generated from the seed of David or the word of the Almighty Father. Therefore, being the son of kings, he did not owe tribute." And below he adds: "Therefore, although he was exempt, yet he had to fulfill all the demands of justice, because he had assumed the humility of the flesh." [37] Moreover, Origen on the words of Christ: "That we may not scandalize them," spoke more to the point and in greater conformity to the meaning of the evangelist, as follows: "It is to be understood," that is, from Christ's words, "that while men sometimes appear who through injustice seize our earthly goods, the kings of this earth send men to exact from us what is theirs. And by his example the Lord prohibits the doing of any offense, even to such men, either so that they may no longer sin, or so that they may be saved. For the son of God, who did no servile work, gave the tribute money, having the guise of a servant which he assumed for the sake of man." [38]

How, then, is it possible, on the strength of the words of the evangelic Scripture, that the bishops and priests be exempt from this tribute, and from the jurisdiction of rulers generally, unless by the rulers' own gratuitous grant, when Christ and Peter, setting an example for others, paid such tribute? And although Christ, being of royal stock in flesh, was perhaps not obliged to do this, yet Peter, not being of royal stock, had no such reason to be exempt, just as he wanted none. But if Christ had thought it improper for his successors in the priestly office to pay tribute and for their temporal goods to be subject to the secular rulers, then without setting a bad example, that is, without subjecting the priesthood to the jurisdiction of secular rulers, he could have ordained otherwise and have made some arrangement about those tax collectors, such as removing from them the intention of asking for such tribute, or in some other appropriate way. But he did not think it proper to do so, rather he wanted to pay; and from among the apostles, as the one who was to pay with him the tribute, he chose Peter, despite the fact that Peter was to be the foremost teacher and pastor of the church, as will be said in Chapter XVI of this discourse, in order that by such an example none of the others would refuse to do likewise.

11. The passage of Scripture which we quoted above from the seven-

[36] Matthew 17:23, 26.   [37] See Thomas Aquinas *Catena aurea* (XI, 209).
[38] See *ibid*.

teenth chapter of Matthew is interpreted in the way we have said by St. Ambrose in the epistle entitled *On Handing Over the Basilica,* where he writes as follows: "He," that is, the emperor, "demands tribute, it is not denied. The fields of the church pay tribute." And a little further on he says, more to the point: "We pay to Caesar the things that are Caesar's, and to God the things that are God's. The tribute is Caesar's, it is not denied." [39] Expressing more fully this which we have called the meaning of the above-quoted passage of Scripture, St. Bernard in an epistle to the archbishop of Sens wrote as follows: "This is what is done by these men," namely, those who suggested that subjects rebel against their superiors. "But Christ ordered and acted otherwise. 'Render,' he said, 'to Caesar the things that are Caesar's, and to God the things that are God's.' What he spoke by word of mouth, he soon took care to carry out in deed. The institutor of Caesar did not hesitate to pay the tax to Caesar. For he thus gave you the example that you should do likewise. How, then, could he deny the reverence due to the priests of God, when he took care to show it even for the secular powers?" [40]

And we must note what Bernard said, that Christ, in taking care to pay the tax to the secular powers, showed "due," and therefore not coerced, "reverence." For everyone owes such tax and tribute to the rulers, as we shall show in the following chapter from the words of the Apostle in the thirteenth chapter of the epistle to the Romans, and the glosses thereon of the saints and doctors; although perhaps not every tax is owed everywhere by everyone, such as the entry tax [41] which was not owed by the inhabitants, although the custodians or collectors sometimes wrongly demanded and exacted it from simple inhabitants or natives, such as were the apostles. And therefore, in agreement with Origen, who I believed grasped the meaning of the evangelist on this point better than did Jerome, I say that it seemed customary and was perhaps commonly established in states, especially in Judaea, that entry taxes were not to be paid by inhabitants or natives, but only by aliens. And hence Christ said to Peter: "Of whom do the kings of the earth receive tribute?" etc.,[42] by "tribute" meaning that entry tax which the tax collectors were demanding. For Christ did not deny that the children of the earth, that is, natives, owe "tribute," taking the word as a common name for every tax; on the contrary, he later said

---

[39] St. Ambrose *Sermo contra Auxentium* cap. xxxiii (PL 16. 1060–61).

[40] St. Bernard *De moribus et officio episcoporum* cap. viii (PL 182. 829).

[41] This is the *pedagium,* a tax paid to the ruler of a territory by those who came into the territory from outside. See the many references in Du Cange, *Glossarium mediae et infimae Latinitatis,* s.v. *pedagium.*

[42] Matthew 17:24.

of it, excepting no one: "Render to Caesar the things that are Caesar's"; and this was also expressed by the Apostle in agreement with Christ, when he said, in the thirteenth chapter of the epistle to the Romans: "For this cause also you pay tribute," that is, to rulers, "for they are the ministers of God." [43] By "children," therefore, Christ meant the children of kingdoms, that is, persons born or raised therein, and not the children of kings by blood; otherwise his words would not seem to have been pertinent, for very often he spoke in the plural both for himself and for Peter, who was certainly not the child of such kings as those discussed by Jerome. Moreover, if Christ was of David's stock in flesh, so too were very many other Jews, although not perhaps Peter. Again, the tribute was not then being exacted by David or by anyone of his blood; why, therefore, should Christ have said, "The kings of the land . . . then the children are free," [44] saying nothing about the heavenly king? But it is certain that neither Christ nor Peter was a child of Caesar, either in flesh or in spirit. Moreover, why should Christ have asked the above question? For everyone certainly knows that the children of kings by blood do not pay tribute to their parents. Jerome's exposition, therefore, does not seem to have been as much in agreement with Scripture as was Origen's. But the above words of Scripture show that Christ wanted to pay even undue tribute in certain places and at certain times, and to teach the Apostle and his successors to do likewise, rather than to fight over such things. For this was the justice of counsel and not of command which Christ, in the humility of the flesh which he had assumed, wanted to fulfill and to teach others to fulfill. And the Apostle, like Christ, also taught that this should be done. Hence, in the first epistle to the Corinthians, Chapter 6: "Why do ye not rather take wrong? why do ye not rather suffer yourselves to be defrauded?" [45] than to quarrel with one another, as he had said before.

12. Moreover, not only with respect to property did Christ show that he was subject to the coercive jurisdiction of the secular ruler, but also with respect to his own person, than which no greater jurisdiction could be had by the ruler over him or over anyone else, for which reason it is called "capital jurisdiction" (*merum imperium*) by the Roman legislator. [46] That

---

[43] Romans 13:6.

[44] Matthew 17:24-25. The complete text, required to make sense of the fragment quoted by Marsilius, is as follows: "The kings of the earth, of whom do they receive tribute or custom? Of their own children, or of strangers? And he said: Of strangers. Jesus said to him: Then the children are free."

[45] I Corinthians 6:7. See Vol. I, p. 81.

[46] For this untranslatable phrase see *Corp. jur. civ., Digest* ii. i. 3: "Capital jurisdiction is to have the power of the sword to punish criminal men, which jurisdiction is also called power" (*Merum est imperium habere gladii potestatem ad animadvertendum facinorosos*

Christ was thus subject can be clearly shown from the twenty-seventh chapter of Matthew; for there it is written that Christ allowed himself to be seized and brought before Pilate, who was the vicar of the Roman emperor, and he suffered himself to be judged and given the extreme penalty by Pilate as judge with coercive power; nor did Christ protest against him as not being a judge, although he perhaps indicated that he was suffering an unjust punishment. But it is certain that he could have undergone such judgment and punishment at the hands of priests, had he so desired, and had he deemed it improper for his successors to be subject to the secular rulers and to be judged by them.

But since this view is borne out at great length in the nineteenth chapter of John, I shall here adduce what is written there. When Christ had been brought before Pilate, vicar of Caesar, to be judged, and was accused of having called himself king of the Jews and son of God, he was asked by Pilate: "Whence art thou?" But having no reply from Jesus, Pilate spoke to him the following words, which are quite pertinent to our subject; here is the passage: "Pilate therefore saith to him, Speakest thou not to me? Knowest thou not that I have power to crucify thee, and I have power to release thee? Jesus answered: Thou shouldst not have any power against me, unless it were given thee from above." [47] See, then, Jesus did not deny that Pilate had the power to judge him and to execute his judgment against him; nor did he say: This does not pertain to you of right (*de jure*) but you do this only in fact (*de facto*). But Christ added that Pilate had this power "from above." How from above? Augustine answers: "Let us therefore learn what he," that is, Christ, "said, and what he taught the Apostle," that is Paul, in the epistle to the Romans, Chapter 13.[48] What, then, did Christ say? What did he teach the Apostle? "That there is no power," that is, authority of jurisdiction, "except from God," whatever be the case with respect to the act of him who badly uses the power. "And that he who from malice hands over an innocent man to the power to be killed, sins more than does the power itself if it kills the man from fear of another's greater power. But God had certainly given to him," that is, Pilate, "power in such manner that he was under the power of Caesar." [49]

The coercive judicial power of Pilate over the person of Christ, therefore, was from God, as Christ openly avowed, and Augustine plainly

---

homines, quod etiam potestas appelatur). See the discussion of this concept in T. Mommsen, *Römisches Staatsrecht*, 2d ed. (Leipzig, 1876), I, 182–87; II, 259–60; also Pauly-Wissowa, *Realenzyklopädie* (Leipzig, 1894–1939), s.v. *imperium merum;* M. P. Gilmore, *Argument from Roman Law in Political Thought, 1200–1600* (Cambridge, Mass., 1941).

[47] John 19:9–11.   [48] Romans 13:1–7.

[49] See Thomas Aquinas *Catena aurea* (XII, 445).

showed, and Bernard clearly said in his epistle to the archbishop of Sens: "For," as he wrote, "Christ avows that the Roman ruler's power over him is ordained of heaven," [50] speaking of Pilate's power and with reference to this passage of Scripture. If, then, the coercive judiciary power of Pilate over Christ was from God, how much more so over Christ's temporal or carnal goods, if he had possessed or owned any? And if over Christ's person and temporal goods, how much more over the persons and temporal goods of all the apostles, and of their successors, all the bishops or priests?

Not only was this shown by Christ's words, but it was confirmed by the consummation of the deed. For the capital sentence was pronounced upon Christ by the same Pilate, sitting in the judgment seat, and by his authority that sentence was executed. Hence in the same chapter of John this passage is found: "Now when Pilate had heard these words, he brought Jesus forth, and sat down in the judgment seat"; and a little below is added: "Then therefore he delivered him," that is, Jesus, "to them to be crucified." [51] Such was the Apostle's view regarding Christ, when he said in the third chapter of the epistle to the Galatians: "But when the fulness of the time was come, God sent his son, made of a woman, made under the law," [52] and therefore also under the judge whose function it was to judge and command in accordance with the law, but who was not, however, a bishop or a priest.

13. Not only did Christ wish to exclude himself from secular rulership or coercive judicial power, but he also excluded it from his apostles, both among themselves and with respect to others. Hence in the twentieth chapter of Matthew and the twenty-second chapter of Luke this passage is found: "And there was also a strife among them," that is, the apostles, "which of them should seem to be the greater. And he," Christ, "said to them, The kings of the Gentiles lord it over them, and they that have power over them are called beneficent." (But in Matthew this clause is written as follows: "And they that are the greater exercise power upon them.") "But you not so: but he that is the greater among you, let him become as the younger; and he that is the leader, as he that serveth." [53] "But whosoever will be the greater among you, let him be your minister. And he that will be first among you shall be your servant: even as the Son of man is not come to be ministered unto, but to minister," [54] that is, to be a servant in the temporal realm, not to lord it or rule, for in spiritual ministry he was first, and not a servant among the apostles. Whereon Origen comments: "'You know that the princes of the Gentiles lord it over them,' that is,

[50] St. Bernard *De moribus et officio episcoporum* cap. ix (PL 182. 832).
[51] John 19:13, 16.   [52] Actually Galatians 4:4.   [53] Luke 22:24-27.
[54] Matthew 20: 25-28.

they are not content merely to rule their subjects, but try to exercise violent lordship over them," that is, by coercive force if necessary. "But those of you who are mine will not be so; for just as all carnal things are based upon necessity, but spiritual things upon the will, so too should the rulership of those who are spiritual rulers," prelates, "be based upon love and not upon fear." [55] And Chrysostom writes, among other remarks, these pertinent words:

The rulers of the world exist in order to lord it over their subjects, to cast them into slavery and to despoil them [namely, if they deserve it] and to use them even unto death for their [that is, the rulers'] own advantage and glory. But the rulers [that is, prelates] of the church are appointed in order to serve their subjects and to minister to them whatever they have received from Christ, so that they neglect their own advantage and seek to benefit their subjects, and do not refuse to die for their salvation. To desire the leadership of the church is neither just nor useful. For what wise man is there who wants to subject himself of his own accord to such servitude and peril, as to be responsible for the whole church? Only he perhaps who does not fear the judgment of God and abuses his ecclesiastic leadership for secular purposes, so as to change it into secular leadership.[56]

Why, then, do priests have to interfere with coercive secular judgments? for their duty is not to exercise temporal lordship, but rather to serve, by the example and command of Christ. Hence Jerome: "Finally he," that is, Christ, "sets forth his own example, so that if they," the apostles, "do not respect his words they may at least be ashamed of their deeds," [57] that is, wielding temporal lordship. Hence Origen on the words: "And to give his life a redemption for many," [58] wrote as follows:

The rulers of the church should therefore imitate Christ, who was approachable, and spoke to women, and placed his hands upon the children, and washed the feet of his disciples, so that they might do the same for their brethren. But we are such [he is speaking of the prelates of his day] that we seem to exceed even the worldly rulers in pride, either misunderstanding or despising the commandment of Christ, and we demand fierce, powerful armies, just as do kings.[59]

But since to do these things is to despise or be ignorant of Christ's commandment, the prelates must first be warned about it, which is what we shall do in this treatise, by showing what authority belongs to them; then,

---

[55] See Thomas Aquinas *Catena aurea* (XI, 234). It will be noted how Marsilius' interpolation, while supporting his own position, falsifies that of Origen.

[56] *Ibid*. Here again it will be noted how Marsilius' interpolation ("if they deserve it") falsifies the meaning of Chrysostom by blurring the latter's condemnation of secular rulers.

[57] *Ibid*. Marsilius' misinterpretation of Jerome's meaning necessitates a mistranslation of this passage. What Jerome says is that the apostles "may at least be shamed to deeds" (*erubescant ad opera*), i.e., deeds such as Christ wanted them to perform, not the "wielding temporal lordship" with which Marsilius taxes them.

[58] Matthew 20:28.   [59] See Thomas Aquinas *Catena aurea* (XI, 234).

if they disregard this, they must be compelled and forced by the secular rulers to correct their ways, lest they corrupt the morals of others. These, then, are the comments made on the passage in Matthew. On Luke, Basil writes: "It is fitting that those who preside should offer bodily service, following the example of the Lord who washed the feet of his disciples." [60]

Christ, then, said: "The kings of the Gentiles lord it over them. But you," that is, the apostles, "not so." So Christ, king of kings and lord of lords, did not give them the power to exercise the secular judgments of rulers, nor coercive power over anyone, but he clearly prohibited this to them, when he said: "But you not so." And the same must consequently be held with respect to all the successors of the apostles, the bishops or priests. This too is what St. Bernard clearly wrote to Eugene, *On Consideration,* Book II, Chapter IV, discussing the above words of Christ: "The kings of the Gentiles lord it over them," etc. For Bernard wrote, among other things:

What the apostle [Peter] has, this did he give, namely, the guardianship, as I have said, of the churches. But not lordship? Hear him. "Neither as lording it over the clergy," he says, "but being made a pattern of the flock." And lest you think he spoke only from humility, but not with truth, the voice of the Lord is in the gospel: "The kings of the Gentiles lord it over them, and they that have power over them are called beneficent." And he adds: "But you not so." It is quite plain, then, that lordship is forbidden to the apostles. Go, then, if you dare, and usurp either the apostolate if you are a lord or lordship if you are an apostle. You are plainly forbidden to have both. If you wish to have both at once, you shall lose both. In any case, do not think you are excepted from the number of those about whom God complains in these words: "They have reigned, but not by me: they have been princes, and I knew not." [61]

And so from the evangelic truths which we have adduced, and the interpretations of them made by the saints and other approved teachers, it should be clearly apparent to all that both in word and in deed Christ excluded and wished to exclude himself from all worldly rulership or governance, judgment, or coercive power, and that he wished to be subject to the secular rulers and powers in coercive jurisdiction.

[60] *Ibid.* (XII, 229).
[61] St. Bernard *De consideratione* ii. vi (PL 182. 748). The first citation is from I Peter 5:3, the last from Hosea 8:4.

CHAPTER V: ON THE CANONIC UTTERANCES OF THE APOSTLES AND THE EXPOSITIONS OF THE SAINTS AND DOCTORS, WHICH CLEARLY PROVE THE SAME AS IN THE PRECEDING CHAPTER

IT now remains to show that Christ's foremost apostles held this same view and doctrine: and first Paul, who in the second epistle to Timothy, Chapter 2, warned the man whom he had appointed priest or bishop not to meddle in worldly affairs. For he said: "No soldier of God entangleth himself with secular affairs." [1] Whereon the gloss according to Ambrose: "For no one who is in spiritual things a soldier of God entangles himself in any secular affairs whatsoever, since God cannot be divided by two contrary servants, just as no man can serve two masters." [2] And Ambrose said "whatsoever," making no exceptions. Since, therefore, the most secular of all affairs is government or the coercive judgment of contentious acts, inasmuch as it orders and regulates all the secular affairs or secular civil acts of men, as was demonstrated in Chapter XV of Discourse I, the Apostle teaches that this especially has to be avoided by the man who must serve God by ministering to spiritual affairs, as every bishop and priest must.

2. But this view, which we have said was that of the Apostle, is clarified by his words in the first epistle to the Corinthians, Chapter 6, where he said: "If then ye have judgments of things pertaining to this world, appoint them to judge who are the most despised in the church." [3] For the Apostle was here speaking to all the faithful and to the church most properly so called, according to its last meaning.[4] And these words of the Apostle are expounded by the gloss according to Ambrose and Augustine as follows: "If ye have judgments of things pertaining to this world, appoint them to judge who are the most despised in the church, that is, men who are wise, but yet of lesser merit," namely, than priests and teachers of the gospel. And the omission of ministers of the gospel is explained as follows: "For the apostles traveled too much to have time for such matters. Therefore he wanted that such affairs be judged by those wise men, faithful and holy, who remained at home, and not by those who roamed hither and thither to spread the gospel." [5] But another reason for this is given by the

---

[1] II Timothy 2:4.   [2] See Peter Lombard *Collectanea* (PL 192. 367).
[3] I Corinthians 6:4.   [4] See above, II. ii. 3.
[5] See Peter Lombard *Collectanea* (PL 191. 1577), there attributed to St. Ambrose down to "merit," the rest to St. Augustine.

gloss according to Gregory in the *Morals,* and in my judgment it correctly interprets the Apostle's meaning. For why should the "most despised," and not bishops or priests, be appointed to exercise secular judgments? Says Gregory: "In order that those men may try earthly disputes who have perceived the wisdom of exterior things," that is, of secular or civil acts. "But those who are endowed with spiritual gifts ought not to become entangled in earthly affairs, so that, not being compelled to deal with lesser goods, they may be able to serve greater ones." [6] See, then, that what we said about the office forbidden to priests by the Apostle was most clearly the meaning of the Apostle and the saints. Expressing the same view, Bernard writes as follows in his treatise to Eugene, *On Consideration,* Book I, Chapter 5, directing his words to the Roman and other bishops: "Therefore your power is over crimes, not over possessions; because of the former, and not because of the latter, did you receive the keys of the kingdom of the heaven; and so you will exclude those who lie, not those who have possessions. 'That you may know,' he says, 'that the Son of man hath power on earth to forgive sins.'" And a little below he adds: "For which seems to you to be the greater power and dignity, the forgiving of sins or the dividing of wealth? These lowly earthly affairs have their own judges, the kings and princes of the earth. Why do you invade foreign territory? Why do you extend your scythe to another's crop?" [7] It does not, therefore, pertain to the office of the bishop or priest to judge contentious carnal or temporal acts by coercive judgment; indeed, when bishops and priests mix in such affairs, "they invade alien territory," that is, they disturb someone else's office and "extend their scythe to another's crop," according to Bernard. The Apostle, therefore, wanted those persons to judge by coercive judgment who were not ordained to minister [8] the gospel and who perceived the science of exterior things, that is, of civil acts. Since, therefore, no criminal is exempt from such judgment, it is apparent that both priests and non-priests are subject to the coercive judgment of rulers.

3. And it must here be carefully noted that in writing to all the faithful of Corinth, as appears from his salutation, and mentioning the "most despised" in the church, that is, laymen, according to the interpretation of the glosses, the Apostle did not say: I appoint the most despised, or anyone else, to judge your secular affairs; nor did he even leave someone there in his place to judge such affairs or to appoint such judges. But if this had

---

[6] Gregory the Great *Moralia in librum Job* XIX. 25 (PL 76. 125), cited from Peter Lombard *Collectanea* (PL 191. 1577).

[7] St. Bernard *De Consideratione* I. vi (PL 182. 736). The text quoted is from Matthew 9:6.

[8] Reading, with Scholz, *ad ministrandum* for *administrandum.*

pertained to his office and authority, he would have done so or have had
to do so, just as he did in the case of priests and bishops. For he appointed
these in the places where the faithful lived, and he commanded or assigned
them to appoint others, as appears in the first epistle to Timothy, Chapter
3, and in the epistle to Titus, Chapter 1. For he wrote to Titus: "For this
cause left I thee in Crete, that thou shouldest set in order the things that
are wanting," that is, "the evils in sinners, and the furtherance of goodness," as the gloss says, "and shouldest ordain priests in every city." [9] But
concerning secular judges, since these have to be chosen by human election
in the way we indicated in Chapter XV of Discourse I, the Apostle said:
"Appoint ye," speaking in the plural to all the faithful, since to them belongs this authority; he did not say to some bishop or priest in the singular:
"Appoint thou," as he did in the case of priests; nor did he command that
secular acts be judged by bishops or priests, but rather he forbade it. Hence
Bernard wrote, in the place mentioned above:

But hear what the Apostle thinks on such matters. "Is it so, that there is not
a wise man among you," he says, "that shall be able to judge between his brethren?" And he adds: "I speak to your shame. Set them to judge who are the most
despised in the church." And so, according to the Apostle, you, a man of apostolic rank, usurp a lowly office, the rank of the "most despised." Hence too the
bishop [that is, the Apostle] instructed another bishop: "No soldier of God
entangleth himself with secular affairs." [And Bernard continues:] Do you
think these times would continue if the men who fight over earthly heritage
and ask you for judgment were answered by you with the words of the Lord:
"O men, who has made me a judge over you"? What kind of judgment would
soon be pronounced over you? Something like this: "What says this rustic, untutored man? You do not know your primacy, you dishonor your high, pre-emi-
nent seat, you lower the apostolic dignity." And yet they who would say this will
not, I think, show where any apostle ever sat as judge over men, or adjuster of
boundaries, or distributor of lands. For I have read that the apostles stood to
be judged themselves, but not that they sat to judge others. That will be in the
future, it did not so happen in the past. Does the slave lower his dignity so
greatly, if he does not wish to be greater than his master, or the disciple if he
does not wish to be greater than he who sent him, or the son if he does not
transgress the bounds set by his father? "Who has made me judge?" asks the
Master and Lord. And will the servant or disciple feel wronged unless he
judges all men?

Bernard said, therefore, that it is wrong for the successor of the apostles to
usurp judicial office. And again he adds these words: "But he does not
seem to me to be a good estimator of things, who thinks it wrong for the
apostles not to be judges of such affairs, to whom has been given authority

[9] Titus 1:5, and *Glossa interlinearis, ad loc.*

over greater things. Why should not those who will judge the angels in heaven despise judging the petty earthly possessions of men?" [10]

4. The holy Apostle also taught that all men alike, without exception, must be subject in coercive judgment to the secular judges or rulers, and that these must not be resisted unless they have commanded that something be done which is against the law of eternal salvation. Hence in the thirteenth chapter of the epistle to the Romans:

Let every soul be subject to the higher powers. For there is no power but of God: the powers that be are ordained of God. Whosoever resisteth the power, resisteth the ordinance of God: and they that resist shall receive to themselves damnation. For rulers are not a terror to good works, but to the evil. Wilt thou then not be afraid of the power? do that which is good, and thou shalt have praise of the same; for he is the minister of God to thee for good. But if thou do that which is evil, be afraid; for he beareth not the sword in vain. For he is the minister of God, a revenger to execute wrath upon him that doeth evil. Wherefore ye must needs be subject, not only for wrath, but also for conscience sake. For this cause pay ye tribute also: for they are God's ministers, attending continually upon this very thing. Render therefore to all their dues: tribute to whom tribute is due; custom to whom custom; fear to whom fear; honor to whom honor.[11]

I wish furthermore to quote the gloss of the saints and catholic doctors on these notable words of the Apostle, for the truth of our position is so clearly demonstrated by the statements of the Apostle and the glossator that no one of sound mind who reads these statements should have any further doubts. The Apostle, then, said: "Let every soul," etc., making no exceptions.[12] Whereon the gloss, first according to Augustine, and then at some points according to Ambrose, says the following:

And here he urges humility. For some men thought that the faithful should not be ruled by evil rulers, and especially infidels; and if the rulers were good and faithful, they should be equal to the good and faithful. But the Apostle here removes this pride from the superior part, that is, the soul, by which he signifies the whole man. For what is every soul but every man? As if to say: All the aforesaid things must be done, for although you may be perfect in the body of Christ, yet let every soul be subject, that is, let every man be subject. And I signify man by the word soul in order that you may be subject not only in body but also in will. Therefore let every soul be subject, so that man may be subordinate even in will to the secular powers, good or evil, namely, to kings, princes, tribunes, centurions, and other such rulers.

[10] St. Bernard *De consideratione* I. vi, vii (PL 182. 735-36).

[11] Romans 13:1-7.

[12] Cf. *Tractatus Eboracenses* ("York Tracts") IV (MGH, *Libelli de Lite*, III, 670): "If, therefore, the Apostle said 'every,' then the priest is not excepted" (*Si ergo "omnis," nec sacerdos excipitur*). On this work, see now G. H. Williams, *The Norman Anonymous of 1100 A.D.* (Cambridge, Mass., 1951).

See then what the Apostle meant by "the higher powers," namely, secular rulers. And then the gloss goes on:

For if your ruler be good, he is your nourisher; if he be evil, he is your tempter. And so accept your nourishment gladly, and let yourself be tested by the temptation. Be you therefore gold, and look upon the world as if it were the furnace of the goldsmith. Let every soul therefore be subject to the higher powers, that is, in that in which they are high, namely, in worldly affairs; or the reason is given when he says "higher," that is, because they are higher. For the phrase, "There is no" proves that they must be thus subjected; since all power is from God. But "the powers that be are ordained of God"; therefore the power has been ordained by God, that is, whoever has power has the ordainment of God. "And so whosoever resisteth the power, resisteth the ordinance of God." And this is what he says, as if the reason why they ought to be subject was that no man, whether he be good or evil, has any power unless it is given by God. Hence the Lord said to Pilate: "Thou shouldest not have any power against me, unless it were given thee from above." [13]

And this is repeated by Bernard in an epistle to the archbishop of Sens:

No one had a more worldly function than Pilate, before whom the Lord stood to be judged. "Thou shouldest not have any power over me," said the Lord, "unless it were given thee from above." He was already then saying and undergoing in his own case what he afterwards proclaimed in the churches through the apostles: "there is no power but of God"; and "whosoever resisteth the power resisteth the ordinance of God."

And a little below, Bernard adds: "For Christ avowed that even over himself the power of the Roman ruler had been ordained by heaven." [14]

And in the gloss there follows:

"The powers that be are ordained of God," that is, they have been reasonably ordered by him. And so he who by force or deceit resists the power, that is, the man having the power, in those things namely which pertain to the power, such as tribute and the like, resists the ordinance of God, that is, the man who has the power through God's ordinance. Hence the person who thus resists does not act in accordance with the ordinance of God. Now as to the good power, it is obvious that God reasonably authorized it; but as to the bad, this can also be seen, since the good men are purified by it, the evil are punished, and it is itself brought to destruction. And note that by the word "power" is meant sometimes the power which was given by God, and sometimes the man having the power; these the careful reader will distinguish. "But whosoever resisteth the power"; as if to say: whosoever resists the power, resists the ordinance of God. But this is so grave that those who resist bring down damnation upon themselves. And hence one should not resist [that is, not anyone, or no one, should resist] but should be subject. If, however, the power commands that which you ought not to do, then soundly despise it in this case, from fear of

[13] See Peter Lombard *Collectanea* (PL 191. 1503-4).
[14] St. Bernard *De moribus et officio episcoporum* cap. ix (PL 182. 832).

a greater power. Take heed of the gradations of human affairs. Suppose the overseer commands what should not be done, suppose he gives orders against the proconsul? Again, if the proconsul orders one thing, and the emperor another, is it to be doubted that the latter [that is, the emperor] is to be obeyed, and the former [that is, the proconsul] disregarded? Hence if the emperor orders one thing and God another, God must be obeyed and the emperor disregarded.[15]

But Augustine did not say: If the emperor orders one thing, and the bishop or pope another; yet this is what he should have said if the pope were superior in jurisdictional rank. What Augustine meant was that if the emperor commanded that something be done against the law of eternal salvation, which is the immediate command of God, in this the emperor was not to be obeyed; in such a case the pope who gives a command in accordance with this law, that is, the divine (although he neither can nor should coerce anyone in this world according to it), must be obeyed rather than the emperor who commands that something be done contrary to divine law.[16] But when the pope commands something else in accordance with his decretals as such, he must not be obeyed against the command of the emperor or of his laws, as is here apparent and as will be more fully proved in Chapter IX of this discourse.[17]

Then the gloss continues:

As if to say, they deservedly incur damnation, for good or evil rulers "are not a terror to good works but to the evil," that is, they are not to be feared by those who do good, but by those who do evil. For if the ruler is good he does not punish the person who does well, but rather he rewards him. But if the ruler is bad, he does not harm the good man, but rather he purifies him. But the evil person ought to fear, because rulers are established to punish the evil. By "rulers" the Apostle means those who are appointed to correct life and ward off adversities, and these are in God's image in that the others are subordinate to one. And when he says "Wilt thou then," he means that the rulers are to be feared by evil-doers. "Wilt thou then not be afraid of the power," whichever it be, good or evil? "Do that which is good" and you have no cause to fear, on the contrary "you will have praise of the same," even if it be evil, inasmuch as then it will be a cause of a greater crown. So that if the power is just, "you will have praise from the same," for it will praise you; but if it is unjust, "you will have praise from the same," not because it will praise you, but because it will afford you the opportunity for being praised, so that truly you will have praise from it. "For he is the minister of God to thee for good," that is, he does good to you, whether he be good or evil, because he tests you or was given to you by God for your own good, in order to protect you and yours. For it is manifest that rulers were given by God so that no evil should be done to the good. "But if thou do evil," as if to say: the good man should not be afraid; "but if thou do

[15] See Peter Lombard *Collectanea* (PL 191. 1504–5).
[16] See Vol. I, pp. 162–63.   [17] See below, II. ix. 6–10.

evil, be afraid," and one must be afraid because "he beareth the sword," that is, he has judiciary power, "not in vain," but to punish the wicked. And the Apostle explains this, saying: "For he is the minister of God" that is, he avenges in place of God. He is a "revenger to execute the wrath" of God, that is, to avenge an offense to God, or to show what will be God's revenge, for this punishment falls more heavily on those who persist in evil. I say that he is a revenger, "upon him," that is, to correct and punish him, "that doeth evil," because he is the minister of God. "Therefore you must needs be subject" to him, as if to say that you must be subject of necessity or to necessity, that is, to the necessary ordinance; and this "not only" to avoid the "wrath" of the ruler or of God, but also for conscience sake, so that your mind may be clean by obeying him whom God has made ruler [that is, who thus rules through the ordainment of God]. For although all the faithful, insofar as they are faithful, are one in Christ, in whose faith there is no distinction between Jews, Greeks, masters, and slaves, and so on, yet in their mortal association there is a difference, and the apostles teach that its order must be preserved on the road of this life. For some things we maintain in the unity of the faith without any distinction, and others in the order of this life as on the way, lest the Lord's name and doctrine be blasphemed. "For this cause" this is the proof of your subjection, that is, of why you ought to be subject, since for this cause, that is, to show your subjection, "pay ye tribute," which is the sign of subjection. The Apostle does not say "give up" tribute, but rather "pay," as if to those who are going to repay it, because the rulers do repay it by rendering service in your defense when they fight for the country and do judgment. "Pay ye tribute," ye, I say, "attending" to God in "this very thing," that is, you attend to God because you give them tribute. Truly through this do you attend to God, for the rulers are the ministers of God, and for this were they established, to reward the good and punish the wicked. Or thus: for they are ministers, and hence you ought to pay tribute, because "they are ministers of God," and they are "attending upon" you, when they defend the country, "upon this very thing," that is, on account of this, namely on account of the tribute they attend to you in defending the country, and because they are ministers of God.[18]

5. And so by these words of the Apostle and by the expositions of the saints which we have quoted above, he who does not want to blaspheme the name and doctrine of the Lord as being unjust and as preaching against the civil laws, must hold beyond any doubt, as is said by Augustine's gloss here and in the first epistle to Timothy, Chapter 6,[19] that all men, of whatever status or condition they may be, must be subject in property and in person to the jurisdiction of the secular rulers, and must obey them in all things which do not contradict the law of eternal salvation, especially when they are in accordance with human laws or honorable and approved customs. For clearly it is about these rulers that the Apostle speaks when he says: "Let every soul be subject," etc., and that "not in vain" do they

[18] See Peter Lombard *Collectanea* (PL 191. 1505–6).
[19] I Timothy 6:1.

bear "a sword," and the other things which he wrote about them, both regarding their defense of the country and the paying of tribute to them, according to the expositions of the saints. But the Apostle never said these things about any bishop or priest. For the rulers whom we are obliged to obey in coercive jurisdiction are the ones who must defend the country by armed force, which in no way appertains to the bishop or priest. Hence St. Ambrose wrote as follows in his second epistle to Valentinian, entitled *To the People:* "I shall be able to weep, I shall be able to lament, I shall be able to grieve; against arms, soldiers, and Goths, my tears are my weapons, for such are the munitions of the priest; in any other way I neither can nor should resist." [20] Again, such rulers, whom we are obliged thus to obey, might be infidels, as the gloss said near the beginning; but infidels neither are nor can be bishops. And therefore it is plain to all that the Apostle was speaking not about priests or bishops, but rather about kings and princes, as Augustine said. And the Apostle excepted no one from this subjection since he said "every soul." If, then, they who resist such powers, even infidel and wicked ones, bring eternal damnation on themselves, how much greater is the indignation of almighty God, and of Peter and Paul his apostles, which is incurred by those who in contempt of this teaching of God and of the apostles have so long harassed and still harass faithful kings and princes, and especially and inexcusably the ruler of the Romans? For the rulers "are ministers of God," as the Apostle said; nor did he say: they are our ministers, or Peter's, or any other apostle's; and therefore they are not subject to the coercive judgment of any bishop or priest, but rather conversely. This was set forth also by the gloss according to Augustine, when he wrote: "Hence if the emperor orders one thing, and God another," etc., naming no bishop or archbishop or patriarch as having such jurisdiction; yet this is what he would or should have done if Christ, "king of kings and lord of lords," [21] had granted to himself this power over the emperor, as they fancifully say in their decretals, which in truth are nothing but oligarchic ordinances which the Christian faithful as such are in no wise obliged to obey, as was demonstrated in Chapter XII of Discourse I and as will be shown more specifically in what follows.

6. By the above words, however, we do not mean that reverence and obedience are not owed to an ecclesiastic teacher or pastor in those matters whose observance he commands or teaches in accordance with the evangelic law, but not differently or in contrariety to that law, as is sufficiently clear

[20] St. Ambrose *Sermo contra Auxentium* cap. ii (PL 16. 1050).
[21] Revelation 19:16.

from the twenty-third chapter of Matthew and Jerome's gloss thereon.[22] Also, however, the ecclesiastic pastor or teacher neither should nor can compel anyone to such observance in this world by any pain or punishment in property or in person; for we do not read that such power to coerce and govern anyone in this world was given to him by the evangelic Scripture, but rather that it was forbidden by counsel or command, as is clear from the present chapter and the preceding one. For such power in this world is given by the human laws or legislators; [23] and even if it were given to the bishop or priest to coerce men in those matters which relate to divine law, it would be useless. For those who were thus coerced would not be helped at all toward eternal salvation by such compulsion.[24] And this was plainly the mind of the Apostle when he said, in the second epistle to the Corinthians, Chapter 1: "Moreover, I invoke God as witness upon my soul, that to spare you I came not as yet unto Corinth; not because we exercise dominion over your faith, but we are the helpers of your joy; for by faith ye stand." [25] Whereon the gloss according to Ambrose:

"I invoke God as witness" not only against my body but also "upon," that is, against, "my soul," if I lie in what I say: "that I came not as yet unto Corinth," that is, after I left you. And I did this "to spare you," that is, lest I grieve many persons by the harshness of my correction, which he spared them lest by too great harshness they be moved to sedition. Hence he wants them to be assuaged first, and for this reason he refrained from carrying out his designs, not because of carelessness or carnal thought. For a spiritual person abstains from carrying out a design when he plans something more beneficial for salvation. And lest they resent what might appear almost as dominion, in that he had said "to spare you I did not come," he adds: But I do not say "to spare you," "because we exercise dominion over your faith," that is, because your faith undergoes dominion and coercion, for faith is of the will, not of necessity; but I say it rather because "we are the helpers," if you wish to cooperate, "of your joy" eternal, or of the joy of your correction, because they rejoice who are corrected. Well did I say "over your faith," for "by faith," which works through choice, "ye stand," not by dominion.[26]

This same interpretation of the above words of the Apostle was made and clearly expressed for all by St. John Chrysostom in his book of *Dialogues,* also entitled *On the Priestly Dignity,* for in Book II, Chapter 3, after quoting from the Apostle: "We do not exercise dominion over your faith, but we are your helpers," etc., he wrote: "They who are judges outside," that is, secular judges, "when they have subdued wicked men, wield very great

[22] Matthew 23:3. See *Glossa ordinaria, ad loc.,* and Thomas Aquinas *Catena aurea* (XI, 259).
[23] Reading, with Scholz, *legislatoribus humanis.*
[24] See Vol. I, pp. 155–56.   [25] II Corinthians 1:23.
[26] See Peter Lombard *Collectanea* (PL 192. 16–17).

power over them and suppress the depravity of their earlier ways against their will. But in the church, one must be converted to better ways not through coercion but with acquiescence, for the laws give us no such power to keep men from sin by the authority of our sentence." And he speaks in the person of all priests, giving first the reason already stated as to why they cannot coerce anyone, namely, because they have no coercive authority over anyone in this world, for this had not been given to them by "the laws," that is, by the legislators in those days, or in those places or provinces. Then he gives another reason: "Even if it," that is, such power, "were given, we," that is, bishops or priests, "would not have wherein to exercise such power, since our God," Christ, "will reward not those who are by necessity," that is, violence, "removed from sin, but rather those who abstain of their own will." [27]

7. By these considerations, however, we do not wish to say that it is inappropriate that heretics or those who are otherwise infidel be coerced, but that the authority for this, if it be lawful to do so, belongs only to the human legislator.[28]

Coercive power does not, therefore, belong to any priest or bishop, but they as well as the rest must in this respect be subordinate to the secular judges, as we have said. Hence the Apostle again said, in the first epistle to Timothy, Chapter 2: "I exhort, therefore, that first of all supplications, prayers, intercessions, and giving of thanks be made for all men, for kings, and for all that are in authority, that we may lead a quiet and peaceful life." [29] Whereon the gloss: "Directing these words to Timothy, he gave to the church a universal example." [30] And then the gloss according to Augustine adds: " 'For all men,' that is, for men of every race, and especially 'for kings,' even if they be wicked, and for 'all that are in authority' established, such as dukes and counts, even though they be wicked"; [31] but the Apostle and Augustine name no bishop or priest as being among those who are in authority or who have such judiciary power, but only secular rulers. "But he," that is, the Apostle, "gives the reason," Augustine says, "as to why he wishes to pray for kings and for men in authority, even though they be wicked, for he says that this will help us 'that we may lead a quiet and peaceful life' free from persecution; 'and peaceful,' that is, undisturbed." [32] See then this testimony to what we said in the last chapter of Discourse I,[33] namely, that the cause which produces

---

[27] St. Chrysostom De sacerdotio II. iii (PG 48. 634).
[28] On this point, see Vol. I, pp. 158 ff.
[29] I Timothy 2:1-2.
[30] See Peter Lombard Collectanea (PL 192. 335-36), cited from Haimo.
[31] Ibid. (336), cited from Augustine.   [32] Ibid.   [33] See above, I. xix. 3.

and preserves tranquillity is the proper and unimpeded action of the ruler. And then Augustine adds these pertinent words:

Hence the Apostle admonished the church to pray for kings and for all men in authority, inspired by the same holy spirit as was Jeremiah, who sent a letter to the Jews in Babylon telling them to pray for the lives of King Nebuchadnezzar and his sons and for the peace of the state, saying: 'because in their peace will be your peace.' But this symbolically signified that the church in all its saints, who are citizens of the heavenly Jerusalem, was to serve under the kings of this world. And therefore the Apostle warns the church to pray for the kings, that it might lead a quiet life.[34]

So, then, it was undoubtedly the view of the Apostle and of Augustine that the church or all the Christian faithful must be subject to secular rulers, especially faithful ones, and must obey those of their commands which are not contrary to the law of eternal salvation. But if the Apostle had meant that bishops or priests must rule and have coercive judgment over men's property or persons in and for the status of the present life, he would have said to Timothy, whom he had made a bishop: "I exhort . . . for all kings and bishops, that are in authority."

8. Moreover, in the epistle to Titus, Chapter 3, the apostle said: "Warn them," that is, those to whom you preach, "to be subject to the princes and powers."[35] Nor did the Apostle say: Warn secular persons only; nor again did he say: Warn them to be subject to us and to princes. For the Apostle well knew that neither he nor other priests or bishops ought to rule or to judge others by litigious judgment over secular acts; rather, he had called them away from all secular affairs, let alone the governing or judging of them, when he said, in the second epistle to Timothy, Chapter 2: "No soldier of God entangleth himself in secular affairs." Hence Ambrose wrote: " 'Warn them' etc., as if to say: Although you have spiritual powers," that is, to command about spiritual things, "yet 'warn them to be subject to the princes,' namely, the kings and dukes, 'and to the' lesser 'powers' ";[36] because "the Christian religion deprives no one of his right."[37] Ambrose said this for the reason that the Apostle wanted and taught that the faithful should be subject even to infidel or wicked lords and rulers, just as he says in the last chapter of the first epistle to Timothy: "Let as many servants as are under the yoke,"[38] etc. Whereon the gloss according to Augustine:

It should be known that some men had been preaching that liberty is common to all in Christ, which is true about spiritual liberty, but not about carnal liberty, as they meant it. Hence the Apostle here speaks against them, ordering

[34] See Peter Lombard *Collectanea* (PL 192. 337).
[35] Titus 3:1.
[36] See Peter Lombard *Collectanea* (PL 192. 392).
[37] Ambrose *Super epistolam ad Titum* (PL 17. 502).
[38] I Timothy 6:1.

the servants to be subject to their masters. Let not Christian servants therefore demand, as is said with respect to Hebrews, that they should be set free after serving six years; for this is mystical. And the Apostle tells why he gives this counsel, saying: "lest both the name of the Lord be blasphemed" as interfering in things not belonging to him, and also the Christian "doctrine" as being unjust and preaching against the laws [39] [that is, the civil laws].

How, then, and by what conscience according to God does any priest, whoever he be, wish to absolve subjects from the oath by which they are bound to faithful rulers? For this is manifest heresy, as will appear more fully below. Therefore the Apostle said: "Warn them to be subject to the princes"; he did not say that laymen only should be subject, but made no distinctions, because according to him "every soul" is "subject" to the rulers in coercive or contentious judgment. If this is not so, then tell me why he said, "Let every soul be subject," etc. For if they ought to have been in this respect subject to Timothy and Titus, in vain would he have said, "Warn them," etc. Again, if he wanted that some men be warned to be subject to the secular powers, and some men not, he would have spoken inadequately, not making this distinction, which will never be found in his writings, but rather the opposite. For he said: "Let every soul be subject," etc. But if some men were to have been exempted from such subjection, the Apostle would here have spoken improperly and falsely, which is unthinkable.

This was likewise the view and doctrine of St. Peter the apostle in his first epistle, Chapter 2, where he said: "Submit yourselves for the Lord's sake to every human creature," that is, who is established in rulership. That he meant the rulers is clear from the examples which he added immediately after, when he said: "Whether it be to the king as supreme, or to governors as sent by him for the punishment of evil-doers, and for the praise of them that do well; for so is the will of God." [40] I have not quoted the glosses of the saints on this passage, because everything which they say here is contained in the gloss which we quoted above on the words of the Apostle in the epistle to the Romans, Chapter 13. So then, St. Peter and St. Paul agree in saying that kings and dukes are sent by God "for the punishment of evil-doers," that is, to take revenge upon them in this world by coercive force; but neither these apostles nor the saints expounding their words ever said that bishops and priests were sent for this purpose, but rather the opposite, as was especially clear from the words of Chrysostom quoted above.[41] Since, therefore, priests as well as non-priests may be evil-doers and

---

[39] See Peter Lombard *Collectanea* (PL 192. 357). The reference to the Hebrews is Exodus 21:2.

[40] I Peter 2:13–15.   [41] See above, para. 6 of this chapter.

commit all the transgressions which we enumerated in Chapter II of this discourse,[42] it necessarily follows that they must be subject to the coercive judgment of kings, dukes, or other secular rulers, who, as we showed in Chapter XV of Discourse I, are to be established by the authority of the human legislator. For God has sent these rulers "for the punishment of evil-doers, and for the praise of the good," as St. Peter said; for "so," that is, that they be obeyed, "is the will of God," as he said in that passage.

9. Again, St. Paul confirmed this both by words and by the manifest example of his deeds, for in the Acts, Chapter 25, it is read of him that he avoided the coercive judgment of the priests, and openly said: "I appeal unto Caesar"; and again: "I stand at Caesar's judgment seat, where I ought to be judged"; says the interlinear gloss: "for here is the place of judgment." [43] Thus avoiding the judgment of the priests, he avowed that he was subject to the coercive jurisdiction of Caesar. But it should not be thought that when the Apostle said that there is "where I ought to be judged," that is, before Caesar, he was speaking insincerely, from fear of death, for he had already chosen and determined to die for the truth, as is to be seen from the Acts, Chapter 21, when he said: "For I am prepared not only to be bound but also to die at Jerusalem for the name of the Lord Jesus" [44] Christ. Who then will be so senseless as to think that the Apostle, for the sake of prolonging his life, would with his words have committed so great a crime as to authorize, by his example and his teaching, the wrong subjection of the whole priesthood to the jurisdiction of lay rulers, if he had considered this to be improper and wrong? For it would have been better for him, who was not under compulsion from anyone, not to have gone to Jerusalem, rather than to go and tell lies against himself and his neighbor. And hence, because it is wrong to think this of him, it is apparent that he thought in mind just as he spoke by word of mouth, and in imitation of his master, Christ, to whom he did not wish to be superior, and who recognized not only Caesar, but even Pilate his vicar, as his earthly judge, when he said, in the nineteenth chapter of John: "You would not have any power over me unless it had been given you from above," that is, by the celestial ordinance of God, as Augustine said above in his gloss on the epistle to the Romans, Chapter 13: "because no man, good or bad, has any power unless it is given by God"; which was also expressed more fully by Bernard in his epistle to the archbishop of Sens, which we quoted in paragraph 4 above.

Since, therefore, coercive jurisdiction or power over anyone in this world

[42] See above, II. ii. 7.   [43] Acts 25:10, with *Glossa interlinearis, ad loc.*
[44] Acts 21:13.

has been granted to no bishop by divine law, but has rather been forbidden by counsel or command, as has been clearly shown in the present chapter and the preceding one, and since such power does not belong to priests or bishops as such by hereditary succession,[45] it necessarily follows that they are subject in this to the secular judges, as was clearly apparent from the words of the apostles Peter and Paul and the other saints, and as can be proved by demonstrative reasoning from what we said in Chapters XV and XVII of Discourse I; nor does any bishop or pope have coercive jurisdiction over any priest or non-priest in this world, unless it shall have been granted to him by the human legislator, who always has the power to revoke this jurisdiction for a reasonable cause, the full determination of which is known to pertain to the same legislator,[46] especially in communities of the faithful.

We think, therefore, that by the evangelic truths, the eternal testimonies, and by the interpretations or expositions of the saints and the other approved teachers of the Christian faith, we have clearly shown that Christ renounced rulership or coercive jurisdiction over anyone in this world, that by counsel or command he forbade it to his apostles and their successors, the bishops or priests, that he willed that he and his apostles be subject to the coercive jurisdiction of the secular rulers, and that he and his foremost apostles, Peter and Paul, taught both by word and by deed that this must be observed.

CHAPTER VI: ON THE AUTHORITY OF THE PRIESTLY
KEYS, AND WHAT KIND OF POWER THE PRIEST OR
BISHOP HAS IN EXCOMMUNICATION

WE must next show what power and authority and what kind of judgment over the believers Christ wanted to grant, and did in fact grant, to these same apostles and their successors by virtue of the words of the holy Scripture. Among the passages which seem to have the most explicit bearing on this question are Christ's words to Peter in Matthew, Chapter 16, when he said: "I will give unto thee the keys of the kingdom of heaven"; [1] also Christ's words to all the apostles, in Matthew, Chapter 18, and John, Chapter 20: "Whatsoever ye shall bind on earth, shall be

---

[45] Cf. Thomas Aquinas *Summa theologica* II. 1. qu.105. a.1. ad 4; Augustinus Triumphus *Summa de ecclesiastica potestate* (Augsburg, 1473) qu.10, qu.11.

[46] See Vol. I, p. 299.   [1] Matthew 16:19.

bound in heaven"; [2] and: "Whosesoever sins ye remit, they are remitted unto them," [3] etc. For it was from these words especially that the opinion and title of plenitude of power, which the Roman bishop ascribes to himself, drew its origin.

2. In order to have a more certain understanding and knowledge of these matters, we must recall some of the statements made in the last chapter of Discourse I, namely, that Christ, true God and true man, "came into this world to bear witness unto the truth," as he said in John, Chapter 18; the truth, I say, concerning what must be believed, done, and avoided in order that mankind may attain eternal life. And this truth he taught by words and showed by example, and finally he recorded it in the writings of the evangelists and of his apostles, so that in the absence of himself and of his apostles we might be guided by these Scriptures in matters pertaining to eternal salvation. And this was the office which he entrusted to his successors the apostles, when he said to them after his resurrection, as a last bidding in the twenty-eighth and last chapter of Matthew: "Go ye therefore and teach all nations, baptizing them in the name of the Father, the Son, and the Holy Ghost, teaching them to observe all things whatsoever I have commanded you." [4] By the administration of baptism, which Christ commanded to be done by his apostles, he had them understand also the administration of the other sacraments which he instituted for the sake of the eternal salvation of mankind. Among these other sacraments is that of penance, whereby the actual mortal and venial guilt of the human soul is destroyed, and God's grace, corrupted by the guilt, is restored to the soul; without this grace human works, so God ordains, would not be deserving of eternal life. Hence in Romans, Chapter 6: "Life eternal by the grace of God." [5]

3. And so the ministers of this sacrament, as of all the others, are the priests as successors of Christ's apostles; the words of Scripture quoted above prove that to all these priests, in the person of Peter and the other apostles, was given the power of the keys or of bestowing the sacrament of penance, that is, the power of loosing or binding men to sins, which is the same thing. Hence on the words of Matthew, Chapter 16: "And I shall give unto thee the keys of the kingdom of heaven," [6] Jerome writes as follows:

The same judiciary power is indeed held by the other apostles, to whom he said after the resurrection: "Receive ye the Holy Ghost. Whosesoever sins ye remit, they are remitted unto them; and whosesoever sins ye retain, they are

---

[2] Matthew 18:18.   [3] John 20:23.   [4] Matthew 28:19 20
[5] Romans 6:23.   [6] Matthew 16:19.

retained." Every church in its priests and bishops has this power, but Peter especially received it, so that all might understand that whoever has separated himself from the unity and society of the faith can neither be absolved from sin nor enter heaven.[7]

And Jerome said, "from the unity of the faith," and not from the unity of Peter or of the Roman bishop, since some of these might be heretics or otherwise vicious, and such bishops have in fact been found. And according to Jerome and Augustine on the same passage, this judiciary power is the authority of the keys, concerning which Augustine wrote: "The keys are the knowledge and power of discerning whereby the worthy must be admitted into the kingdom and the unworthy excluded," [8] that is, by the priest. But how he can admit and how exclude will appear below; and from this will also appear the nature and extent of the power of these keys which Christ granted to Peter and the apostles.

4. But first we must note that, in the soul of him who commits a mortal sin, guilt is generated and the divine grace which had been bestowed on him is destroyed. This guilt binds the sinner to a debt of eternal damnation for the status of the future life. If he persists in this guilt, he is cut off from the society of the faithful in this world by a certain form of correction called, among the Christian faithful, "excommunication." And on the other hand we must note that by repenting of his sin and by making an external confession to the priest—both of which, together and separately, are called by the name "penance"—the sinner obtains a three-fold benefit: first, he is cleansed of his internal guilt and the grace of God is restored in him; second, he is absolved from the debt of eternal damnation, to which his guilt had bound him; and third, he is reconciled to the church, that is, he is or should be reunited to the society of the faithful. To accomplish these things, then, in the sinner, namely, to loose him from or bind him to guilt or the debt of eternal damnation, which has to be done somehow by the power of the keys granted to the priest, as will be said below, is to minister the sacrament of penance.

5. Having made these preliminary remarks, we now advance to the main thesis; and in accordance with the mind of the Master of the Sentences, or rather of the Scripture and of the saints by whose authority he speaks in Book IV, Distinction 18,[9] and also in accordance with the view of Richard in a book of his entitled *On the Power of the Priestly Keys*,[10]

---

[7] *Glossa ordinaria, ad loc.* See Peter Lombard *Libri sententiarum* Lib. iv. dist. 19. cap. iii (PL 192. 890).

[8] *Glossa ordinaria, ad loc.* See Peter Lombard *Sent.* Lib. iv. dist. 18. cap. iii (PL 192. 885).

[9] Peter Lombard *Sent.* Lib. iv. dist. 18 (PL 192. 885–89).

[10] Richard of St. Victor *De potestate ligandi et solvendi* (PL 196. 1159–78).

let us say that for true penance or the true reception of the sacrament of penance it is required, first, that the sinner feel internal contrition or sorrow for the delict committed. Secondly, there is required the intention and act of confessing the delict, by expressing or revealing it in words to the priest, if a priest be available; if he be not at hand, it suffices that the person who is thus penitent or contrite have the firm intention of confessing his guilt to the priest at the first opportunity.

6. And by this they mean that in the sinner who is truly penitent, that is, who is contrite and has the intention of confessing, God alone performs certain things before the confession and before all action on the part of the priest. These things are the expulsion of guilt, the restoration of grace, and the forgiving of the debt of eternal damnation. That these are accomplished by Christ alone the Master proves in Book IV, Distinction 18, Chapter IV,[11] by the authorities of the Scripture and of the saints: and first by the authority of the psalmist,[12] who says in the person of God: "I alone am he that blotteth out the transgressions and sins of the people." [13] Again, by the authority of Ambrose, who says: "The word of God cancels sins, and the priest is judge. The priest performs his office, but exercises the rights of no power." [14] And once more Ambrose says the same thing: "He alone cancels sins, who alone died for our sins." [15] Augustine too says this: "No one removes sins except Christ alone, who is the lamb removing the world's sins." [16] But that God does this before all action on the part of the priest, the Master deduces from the words of Augustine on the psalm, "Whose sins are covered." [17] For "by these words," says the Master,

it is clearly shown that God himself absolves the penitent from the debt of punishment; and he does this when by internal illumination he inspires true contrition of the heart. This view is upheld by reason, and supported by the authorities. For a man with a contrite and humble heart has compunction for his sin only in charity. But he who has charity is worthy of life. But no one is worthy of life and death at the same time. Therefore, he is not then bound to a debt of eternal death, for he ceased to be a child of wrath when he began to love and repent. From then on, therefore, he is loosed from wrath, which remains not with respect to him who believes in Christ, but with respect to him who does not believe. Therefore it is not the priest, to whom he later confesses, who frees him from the eternal wrath wherefrom he has already been freed by the Lord, by saying: I shall confess. It is God alone, therefore, who cleanses man from the internal stains of sin, and frees him from the debt of eternal punishment.

---

[11] Peter Lombard *Sent.* Lib. IV. dist. 18. cap. iv (PL 192. 886).
[12] Reading, with Scholz and mss., *psalmistae* for *prophetae.*   [13] Isaiah 43:25.
[14] Ambrose, in Peter Lombard *Sent.* Lib. IV. dist. 18. cap. iv (PL 192. 886).
[15] *Ibid.* (but missing in PL 192. 886).   [16] Augustine, *ibid.*   [17] Psalm 32:1.

And then the Master recites the authorities of the psalmist and of the saints adduced above, after which he says in epilogue: "These and many other witnesses teach that God alone cancels sins. And just as he cancels some men's sins, so does he retain the sins of others." [18]

7. However, as we said above, God requires that the penitent have the intention of confessing his sins to the priest at the very first opportunity, just as the Master says in Book IV, Distinction 17, Chapter IV, where he asks "whether it is sufficient to confess one's sins to God alone," [19] and decides, by the authorities of the Scripture, that the answer is in the negative, if a priest be available. But if a priest be not available, it is sufficient to have made a confession to God alone, but always with the intention of confessing if one can. And Richard, agreeing with the Master, also held this view in his book mentioned above,[20] and from his discussions in various chapters it is concluded that before all ministry on the part of the priest, God removes the guilt from the person who is truly penitent, that is, contrite, about his sin, and frees him from the debt of eternal death, but under the condition that he must then confess his crime to a priest at the first opportunity. This condition the Master called the "firm intention" of confessing one's sins, when a priest was available. And the Master reached the same conclusion in Book IV, Distinction 18, Chapters V and VI, answering therewith the reasonable question as to why the action or office of the priest is required in penance, if God alone, before all ministry on the priest's part, wipes out the guilt and the debt of eternal damnation. Said the Master: "Amid such great diversity," for both the saints and the doctors seemed to disagree on this point, although they do not in truth disagree, "what must be held? This much we can well say and think, that God alone cancels and retains sins. And yet he bestowed upon the church," that is, the priests, who in one sense are called the church, as was seen in Chapter II of this discourse, "the power of binding and loosing. But he binds and looses in one way, and the church," that is, the priests, "in another. For he by himself so cancels the sin, that he cleanses the soul of its internal stain, and relieves it from the debt of eternal death. This power, however, he did not grant to the priests, but he gave them the power of binding and loosing, that is, of showing men to be loosed or bound." [21] In this passage, the Master set forth for what purpose the office or ministry of the priest is required in penance, and then he went on to clarify it:

Hence the Lord himself first restored the leper to health and then he sent him to the priests, by whose judgment it was to be shown that the leper was cleansed.

[18] Peter Lombard *Sent.* Lib. IV. dist. 18. cap. iv (PL 192. 886).

[19] *Ibid.* Lib. IV. dist. 17. cap. iv (PL 192. 881 f.).

[20] Richard of St. Victor *De potestate ligandi et solvendi* cap. vi–viii (PL 196. 1163–65).

[21] Peter Lombard *Sent.* Lib. IV. dist. 18. cap. v–vi (PL 192. 887).

Thus too he sent Lazarus, who had already been brought to life, to his disciples to be loosed, for although one may be loosed in the eyes of God, yet in the eyes [that is, in the knowledge] of the church one is not regarded as being loosed except through the judgment of the priest. Hence in loosing or retaining sins the ecclesiastic priest acts and judges just as the rabbi once did with regard to those who had been contaminated with leprosy, which signifies sin.[22]

This view is reiterated towards the close of Chapter VI, and is confirmed by the authority of Jerome. On the passage in Matthew, Chapter 16: "And I shall give unto thee the keys of the kingdom of heaven," Jerome writes: "The evangelic priests have that right and duty which rabbis once had under the law in the treatment of lepers. They cancel or retain sins when they judge and show that these sins have been canceled or retained by God." Hence, "in Leviticus lepers are commanded to show themselves to the priests, who do not make them leprous or clean, but discern who are clean and who are unclean." [23] For this reason, therefore, is the priest's office required for the penitent, namely in order to show, in the eyes of the church, whose sins God has retained or canceled.[24]

8. There is also something else which God does for the sinner not without the ministry of the priest, as the same Master and Richard [25] thought. This is the commutation of the temporal penalty of purgatory, which the sinner was to have undergone for his crimes (no matter how much he may have repented or confessed), into some this-worldly satisfaction, like fasting, prayer, alms-giving, pilgrimage; and it is with regard to this that the priest exercises the rights of power over the sinner. Hence the Master writes as follows in Distinction 18, Chapter VII: "And it is to be noted that when they bind men with some penitential satisfaction, by that very fact they show that these men are loosed from their sins, for penitential satisfaction is not imposed on anyone unless the priest considers him truly penitent; but on another man the priest does not impose this satisfaction and by that very fact he judges that this man's sins are retained by God." [26] And also the priest commutes the sinner's due penalty of purgatory into some this-worldly satisfactions, and then he reconciles him to the church, that is, to the communion of the faithful; in this he likewise exercises power over sinners, but only if he acts with discernment. Hence the Master writes, in the place cited above:

The priests also bind men when they impose a penitential satisfaction on those who make confessions; they loose men when they cancel a part of it, or when they admit to the communion of the sacraments those who have been purified by it. This way [that is, of loosing or binding] was noted by Leo above. It is

[22] *Ibid.* cap. vi (PL 192. 887).   [23] *Ibid.*
[24] On this discussion of the priest's function in penance, see Vol. I, pp. 266–67.
[25] Richard of St. Victor *De potestate ligandi et solvendi* cap. viii, xxiv (PL 196. 1165, 1176).
[26] Peter Lombard *Sent.* Lib. IV. dist. 18. cap. vii (PL 192. 888).

in this way that priests are said to cancel or retain sins. Hence Augustine said above: "Those whom they pardon, God pardons," etc. For they perform an act of justice for the sinners when they bind them by a just punishment; they perform an act of mercy when they relax the punishment somewhat, or reconcile sinners to the communion of the sacraments; other acts for sinners they cannot perform.[27]

From this too it can be seen that guilt or punishment in accordance with the merits of sinners can be no more relaxed by the Roman bishop than by any other priest.

9. From these authorities of the saints, the Master, and Richard, it is thus clear that God alone removes the guilt and the debt of eternal damnation from the truly penitent sinner, without any prior or concomitant action on the part of the priest, as was shown above. Of this I also wish to give an infallible demonstration in accordance with the Scripture and the words of the saints and teachers. For it is God alone who cannot be ignorant as to whose sin is to be pardoned and whose retained; and it is God alone who neither is affected by vicious emotions nor renders unjust judgments over anyone. But such is not the case with the church or the priest, whoever he be, even the Roman bishop. For any one of these priests and bishops may sometimes err, or be swayed by vicious emotions, or both; as a result, if a truly penitent person who duly intended to confess, or had even actually confessed, were not forgiven his sin or guilt and his debt of eternal damnation because of the priest's ignorance, malice, or both, then Christ's evangelic promise, which is an object of faith, that he would give rewards of eternal glory to the good and the punishments of Gehenna to the wicked, would frequently come to naught. Hence, suppose, as frequently occurs, that some sinner has falsely and wrongly made a confession of his sins, and as a result, due to the priest's ignorance, malice, or both, he has received absolution and benediction; or suppose, as also frequently occurs, that some other person has properly and adequately confessed his sins to the priest, and has been refused absolution and benediction due to the priest's ignorance, malice, or both. Are then the sins of the first, the one who made a false confession, canceled, and those of the second, the true penitent, retained? This question must firmly and undoubtedly be answered in the negative.[28] And hence on the words of John, Chapter 20: "Receive ye the Holy Ghost, and whosesoever sins ye remit," etc., Chrysostom wrote as follows: "For neither the priest, nor the angel or archangel, can accomplish anything in those things which have been given by God. The priest gives indeed his benediction and his hand; for it is not just that those who come

to the faith should be harmed through another's malice with respect to the symbols of our salvation." [29] And on the words of Matthew, Chapter 16: "And I shall give unto thee the keys of the kingdom of heaven," etc., Jerome wrote in the same vein, as follows: "Some men, not understanding this passage, adopt the supercilious attitude of the Pharisees, thinking that they can condemn the harmless and acquit the harmful, when with God it is not the sentence of the priests but rather the lives of the accused parties that are inquired into." [30] To these words the Master, in Distinction 18, Chapter VI, adds this noteworthy statement: "Thus it is here clearly shown that God does not (always) follow the judgment of the church, which sometimes judges with malice and ignorance"; [31] "of the church," that is, of the priests in it. And in Chapter VIII the Master adds: "For sometimes he who is sent out," that is, he is judged to be outside the church by the priest, "is within; and he who is outside," that is, in accordance with the truth, "is seen to be kept within," namely, by the false judgment of the priests.

10. Summing up this view of the power of the priestly keys, which we have gathered and quoted above from the words of the saints and doctors, the Master writes as follows in Book IV, Distinction 18, Chapter VIII: "It has already been shown how the priests cancel or retain sins. But God has kept for himself a special power of canceling or retaining, in that he alone lifts the debt of eternal death and purifies the soul from within." [32] The same thing is said by the Master in Chapter IX of the same distinction: "Hence the soul's lack of resemblance to God resulting from sin, and the consequent increase of our estrangement from him, is understood to be the stain of the soul, of which it is purged in penance. But this purging is done by God alone, who alone revives and illuminates the soul; this the priests cannot do, although they are the physicians of souls." [33]

11. But "there is another method of binding and loosing," for which the action of the priest is similarly required, namely, through excommunication. This occurs, as the Master says in Book IV, Distinction 18, Chapter VII, when some person

who has been thrice called upon in accordance with the canonic discipline to correct his manifest guilt, and who fails to give satisfaction, is cut off by the sentence of the church from the place of prayer, the communion of the sacraments, and the company of the faithful, so that he may feel shame and, converted by the disgrace of his crime, may become penitent, so that his spirit is saved. If he professes penance and submits, he is admitted to the denied com-

---

[29] See Thomas Aquinas *Catena aurea* (XII, 457).

[30] See Peter Lombard *Sent.* Lib. IV. dist. 18. cap. vi (PL 192. 887).

[31] *Ibid.* (PL 192. 887). The word "always" is omitted in Marsilius' text, but see below. para. 12.

[32] *Ibid.* (PL 192. 888 f.).   [33] *Ibid.* cap. ix (PL 192. 889).

munion and reconciled to the church. Now this is the anathematization of the church; it inflicts this penalty upon those who are deservedly smitten, in that God's grace and protection is taken away from them even more and they are abandoned to themselves, so that they are free to fall into sin and the devil is given greater power for violence over them. And it is also thought that they are not helped by the prayers of the church nor by the suffrage of blessings and deserts.[34]

12. With regard to the above, in order that it may be known to whom belongs the power of excommunication, and in what way, we must note that in excommunication the accused is judged as to his punishment for the status of the future life, by a certain judgment which will be discussed more explicitly in Chapter IX of this discourse; and also a grave penalty is inflicted on him for the status of the present life, in that he is publicly defamed and the company of other persons is forbidden to him. Hence too he is deprived of civil communion and benefits. And although the infliction of the first penalty, on a person who is undeservedly smitten, does no harm for the status of the future life, because "God does not always follow the judgment of the church," that is, of the priests, namely, when they judge someone unjustly, as was sufficiently shown above; yet a person who was thus unjustly smitten by the priest would be harmed most gravely for the status of the present life, because he is defamed and deprived of civil association. And for this reason [35] it must be said that although the words and action of the priest are required to promulgate such a judgment, yet it does not pertain to some one priest alone or to a group of priests alone to give a coercive judgment and command about who is to be excommunicated or acquitted. But the appointment of such a judge—that is, one who is to summon, examine, and judge the accused person, and acquit him or condemn him to be thus publicly defamed or cut off from the company of the faithful—pertains to the whole body of the faithful in that community in which the defendant is to be judged by such a judgment, or to the superior of that whole body, or to a general council.[36] However, the examination of the imputed crime, as to whether or not it be such as merits excommunication, ought to be made by such a judge with the help of a group of priests or of a determinate number of the more experienced from among them, in accordance with the established laws or customs.

For the priests must discern or judge, by a judgment in the first sense, about the crimes for which, according to the evangelic law, a person must be cut off from the company of the faithful lest he infect others; just as a physi-

[34] *Ibid.* cap. vii (PL 192. 888).
[35] On the emphatic character of this secular "reason," see Vol. I, p. 294.
[36] See Vol. I, pp. 158–60, 283.

cian or a group of physicians has to judge, by a judgment in the first sense, about the bodily diseases for which a diseased person, such as a leper, must be separated from the company of others lest he infect them. And again, the crime must be such as can by sure testimony be proved to have been committed by someone. Consequently, just as it does not pertain to any physician or group of physicians to make a judgment or to appoint a judge having coercive power to expel lepers, but rather this pertains to the whole body of faithful citizens or to the weightier part of them, as was demonstrated in Chapter XV of Discourse I, so too in the community of the faithful it pertains to no one priest or group of priests to make a judgment or to appoint a judge having coercive power to expel persons from the company of the community because of a disease of the soul, such as a notorious crime, although such a judgment ought to emerge from the counsel of the priests, inasmuch as they are held to know the divine law wherein are determined the crimes because of which the criminal must be denied the society of the crimeless believers. "For the lips of the priest shall keep knowledge, and they shall seek the law at his mouth," from Malachi, Chapter 2.[37]

But whether the person who is charged with such a crime has committed it, must be judged not by the bishop or priest alone but by the whole body of the faithful in that community, or by that body's superior, as we have said, or by a judge whom it has appointed for this purpose, either a priest or non-priest; but the judgment must be based upon the proofs which are brought forth. And if the defendant be convicted by witnesses, and the crime be such as merits excommunication—which is the only question on which it is necessary to stand by the judgment of the college of the priests or of the sounder part [38] thereof—then the sentence of excommunication must be pronounced upon the criminal by the afore-mentioned judge appointed for this purpose by the whole body of the faithful in that community, and this sentence must be executed by the command of the judge and the words of the priest, insofar as it affects the criminal for the status of the future life also.

13. The truth of what we have said is demonstrated by the Scripture, whence this species of correction seems to have arisen; namely, in Matthew, Chapter 18, when Christ said:

If thy brother shall trespass against thee, go and tell him his fault between him and thee alone. If he shall hear thee, thou has gained thy brother. But if he will not hear thee, then take with thee one or two witnesses, so that every word may be established in the mouth of two or three witnesses. And if he shall

---

[37] Malachi 2:7.   [38] *Sunioris partis.* See Vol. I, pp. 193–94.

neglect to hear them, tell it unto the church; but if he neglect to hear the church, let him be unto thee as heathen and publican.[39]

Christ said, then: "Tell it unto the church"; he did not say: unto the apostle or the bishop or priest or any group of them alone. And by "church" Christ there meant the multitude of the faithful, or the judge appointed for this purpose by its authority; for it was in this sense that the term was used by the apostles and the primitive church, as was fully shown in Chapter II of this discourse.[40] And that it was in this sense that Christ understood the word "church," that is, as the whole body of the believers or faithful, and that it pertains to this whole body to appoint such a judge or to make such judgments over contumacious persons and other such criminals, I demonstrate through the Apostle, in the first epistle of the Corinthians, Chapter 5, where, following and explaining the meaning of Christ's words, he showed most explicitly the cause for which such judgment should be made over someone, the form and manner in which it should be made, and who should make it, when he said: "For I verily, absent in body, but present in spirit, have judged already as though I were present, concerning him that hath so done this deed, in the name of our Lord Jesus Christ, when we are gathered together, and my spirit, with the power of our Lord Jesus, to deliver unto Satan such a person," [41] namely, a certain criminal who had carnally known his father's wife. Whereon the gloss according to Augustine: "In this way have I judged that you, gathered together into one body without dissension, aided by my authority and the power of Christ which will cooperate with you, shall deliver to Satan such a person." [42] See, then, for what reason, by whom, and how someone must be excommunicated, according to the view and doctrine of the Apostle, whose injunction is perhaps to be considered a counsel rather than a command, even according to divine law; for even if men had indulgently tolerated such a criminal to associate with them (although not without scandal and the danger that some of them might be infected), they could nonetheless have been saved and have performed meritorious deeds.

Moreover, even if the Apostle's words were strictly viewed as a command according to divine law, yet it was not commanded that this action be taken only by the priest or bishop or a group of them alone.[43] And therefore, when the Apostle said: "I as absent in body, but present in spirit, have judged already," etc., it must be understood as a judgment in the first sense, not the third, because of what he adds: "When ye are gathered together,

[39] Matthew 18:15–17.   [40] See above, II. ii. 3.   [41] I Corinthians 5:3–5.
[42] See Peter Lombard *Collectanea* (PL 191. 1571). Augustine is not named.
[43] See Vol. I, pp. 158–59.

and my spirit." Thus he handed down to them the form of procedure whereby contention over this question might be prevented from arising among them, for it was to be made by them "gathered together into one body," especially if it was to be by means of a coercive judgment; for which reason Augustine said: "That you, gathered together into one body, without dissension," that is, the judgment is to be made by your common consent, or by a judge appointed for this purpose by your common consent, which is the same thing. And therefore the Apostle did not command that some one priest make this judgment, nor did he write to some priest or bishop that he should make it, although he then sent Timothy, who was a bishop, to these people, as is plain from the fourth chapter of his epistle; yet this is what the Apostle would have done, had he thought this judgment to pertain to the authority of the priest alone, as he had done in other cases. We have also proved this by quotations from the first epistle to Timothy, Chapter 3, and the epistle to Titus, Chapter 1, in the preceding chapter.[44]

Furthermore, this view which we hold could be plausibly confirmed by reason in accordance with Scripture. For such a judgment, as we have said, is made with greater certainty and with more freedom from suspicion than that made only by the will of a single priest or of a group of priests alone, whose judgment would more readily be perverted by love or hate or consideration of private advantage than would the judgment of the whole body of the faithful, to which one always comes to appeal. However, as we have said, such sentence must be executed by the priest insofar as the divine virtue is invoked herein to inflict on the criminal some punishment in this world which could not be imposed by the power of man, such as the torture of the demon; and also because the criminal is similarly judged with respect to punishment for the status of the future world, and is deprived of the suffrages of the church, which God perhaps decreed was to be done by the action of the priest alone.

Moreover, if it pertains to any bishop or priest, either alone or together with a group of clergymen, to excommunicate any person without the consent of the whole body of the faithful, then from this it follows that priests or groups of them can remove all states and governments from the kings or rulers who have them. For when any ruler is excommunicated, the multitude subject to him will also be excommunicated if it wishes to obey the excommunicated ruler; and thus the power of every ruler will be broken. But the opposite of this condition was desired by the teacher of the Gentiles in Romans, Chapter 13 and I Timothy, Chapter 6, and by Augustine in his gloss thereon, as we showed in Chapter V of this dis-

[44] See above, II. v. 3.

course, paragraphs 7 and 8. The objections which might seemingly be made to this conclusion will be easily refuted by what we shall say in Chapters IX, X, XIV, and XVII of this discourse.

14. The priests have also a certain other authority, whereby bread and wine are transubstantiated into the blessed body of Christ at the utterance of a prayer by the priest after he has spoken certain words. This authority is a character of the soul, like the authority of the keys, and it is called the power of performing the sacrament of the eucharist. Some theologians hold that it derives from the same character as the power of the keys, which we discussed above, while others say that it derives from a different character, and that Christ bestowed it upon the apostles at another time, and by other words, such as those which he spoke in Matthew, Chapter 26, in Mark, Chapter 14, and in Luke, Chapter 22: "This is my body, which is given for you, do this in remembrance of me"; [45] "do this," that is, have the power to do this. But whatever be the truth regarding this disagreement, it is not important for the present consideration; for we think that for our purposes we have sufficiently reviewed what can be proved from the holy Scripture concerning the authorities or powers which Christ bestowed upon the priests or bishops.

CHAPTER VII: SUMMARY OF THE STATEMENTS MADE IN THE PRECEDING CHAPTER, AND THEIR CLARIFICATION AND CONFIRMATION

LET us now summarize what was said concerning the power or authority of the priestly keys which Christ gave to the apostles. In the sinner who is truly penitent, that is, sorrowing for his sin, some things are performed by God alone without any previous ministry on the part of the priest; these are the illumination of the mind, the purging of the guilt or blemish of the sin, and the remitting of eternal damnation. Other things, however, God performs in the same sinner not by himself alone, but through the ministry of the priest, such as, for example, showing in the eyes of the church which persons are to be regarded as being loosed or bound from sins both in this world and in the other world, that is, of which persons God has retained or dismissed the sins. Again, there is something else which God accomplishes with respect to the sinner through the ministry of the priest, namely, the commutation of the penalty of purga-

---

[45] Matthew 26:26; Mark 14:22; Luke 22:19. The passage quoted is from Luke.

tory, which was owed to the sinner for the status of the future life, into some temporal or this-worldly satisfaction. For the penalty is relaxed in whole or in part according to the satisfactions imposed and the condition of the penitent person, all of which must be done by the priest with the key of power in accordance with his discernment. Thus too the priest excludes the contumacious from the communion of the sacraments, and admits those who repent in the manner described near the end of the preceding chapter.

2. This was the view of the Master in Book IV, Distinction 18, Chapter 8, when he said:

With respect to these methods of binding and loosing, it is necessary to understand the sense in which these words are true: "Whatsoever ye shall loose on earth, shall be loosed in heaven; and whatsoever ye shall bind on earth, shall be bound in heaven." For sometimes they [that is, the priests] show persons to be loosed or bound who are not so with God, and sometimes they bind to or loose from the penalty of having to give satisfaction persons who do not deserve it, and they admit the undeserving to the sacraments and exclude the deserving. But their binding and loosing must be understood with respect to those persons whose deserts demand that they be bound or loosed. Therefore, whatever persons they loose or bind while applying the key of discernment to the merits of the parties concerned, these are loosed or bound in the heavens, that is, with God, because the divine judgment approves and confirms the priest's sentence when it proceeds in this manner.

And then the Master said, as it were in epilogue: "This then is the nature and extent of the use of the apostolic keys." [1]

3. To make this even more evident, we shall draw a rather familiar example or comparison to it, which seems closely to fit the words and meaning of Christ and of the saints whose authorities we cited above, and especially Ambrose. For Ambrose said that "the word of God cancels sins, the priest is judge. The priest performs his office, but exercises the rights of no power." [2] Now let us say that in freeing the sinner, the priest, as the turnkey of the heavenly judge, is analogous to the turnkey of the earthly judge. For just as the criminal is condemned to or absolved from civil guilt and punishment by the word or sentence of the judge of this world, namely, the ruler; so by the divine word is a person absolutely bound to or loosed from guilt and the obligation of damnation or punishment for the status of the future world. And just as no one is condemned to or released from civil guilt or punishment by the action of the turnkey of the earthly ruler, but by his action in opening or closing the prison the

---

[1] Peter Lombard *Sent.* Lib. IV. dist. 18. cap. viii (PL 192. 888).
[2] *Ibid.* (PL 192. 886). See also above, II. vi. 6.

criminal is merely shown to be released or condemned; so too no one is loosed from or bound to guilt or an obligation of eternal damnation by the action of the priest, but it is shown in the eyes of the church which person is regarded as being loosed or bound by God, when that person receives the priest's benediction and is admitted to the communion of the sacraments, in the manner stated toward the close of the preceding chapter. And hence, while the turnkey of the earthly judge performs his office by opening or closing the prison, he nevertheless exercises the rights of no judiciary power of acquittal or condemnation; for even though he might in fact open the prison for some criminal whom the earthly judge had not acquitted, and might proclaim to the people that he was acquitted, yet this criminal would not on that account have been released from civil guilt or punishment. And on the other hand, if the turnkey were to refuse to open the prison and were to announce that some person, whom the judge's sentence had really acquitted, was not acquitted but condemned, nevertheless this person would not on that account be liable to civil guilt or punishment. In an analogous way, the priest, the turnkey of the heavenly judge, performs his office by making a verbal announcement of acquittal or condemnation or malediction. But if the priest, from ignorance, malice, or both, were to announce that persons were or would be absolved who really were or would be condemned by the heavenly judge, or the reverse, nevertheless the former would not on that account be absolved nor the latter condemned, since the priest would not have applied with discernment the key or keys to the merits of the persons under trial. And hence he "performs his office," as Ambrose said, but he "exercises the rights of no power," since the priests sometimes announce to the church that persons who are or will be loosed with God, are or will be bound for the future world, and the reverse, as we said above by the authority of the saints and of the Master in Book IV, Distinction 18, Chapter VIII.[3] And therefore the priest does not exercise the rights of power. For if he did, the divine justice and promise might sometimes perish.

4. He alone, therefore, exercises the rights of power in these matters and is the judge having coercive power, who alone cannot be deceived about human thoughts and deeds, for as it is written in Hebrews, Chapter 4: "All things are bare and open to his eyes," [4] and who alone has no vicious desire, for "thou art just, O Lord, and all thy judgments are just, and all thy ways are merciful and true and just," as it is written in Tobias, Chapter 3; [5] and therefore there is only one such judge. Hence in James, Chapter 4, it is written: "There is one lawgiver and judge, that is able to

---

[3] See above, II. vi. 12.   [4] Hebrews 4:13.   [5] Tobias 3:2.

destroy and to deliver"; [6] which James said neither about himself nor about any of the apostles, although he was one of those three "who seemed to be pillars" of the church, as the Apostle said in Galatians, Chapter 2.[7] But such sentences as Christ made or would make in the other world, he wanted to have announced by the priests by a judgment in the first sense, as it were in prediction, so that by this judgment sinners in this world might be frightened and diverted from crimes and sins to penance, for which purpose the priestly office is much needed and valuable. In this way, if the physician of bodily health, to whom the power to teach and practice the art of medicine has been given by decree of the human judge or legislator, were to promulgate to the people a judgment in accordance with the science of medicine concerning those who were going to be healthy or to die, so that through this judgment men might lead sober lives and be diverted from intemperance in order to maintain or acquire bodily health, then he would also give commands or instructions about such matters, and as physician he would command that they be observed, and would judge that those who observed them would be healthy and those who transgressed them would be ill or would die. These persons, however, would be made healthy or ill not primarily by the physician but by the action of the nature of man, although the physician would be of some service. Nor, again, could the physician by his own authority compel a healthy or a sick person to do certain things no matter how conducive these things might be to bodily health, but he could only exhort, teach, and frighten men by his predictive judgment in the first sense, by making it known to them that health would follow from the observance of certain precepts, and illness or death from their transgression. So too, in an analogous way, the physician of souls, that is, the priest, judges and exhorts about those matters which lead to the soul's eternal health or to its eternal death or temporal punishment for the status of the future world. Yet with reference to these matters the priest neither can nor should compel anyone in this world by a coercive judgment, as we proved by the authority of the Apostle in II Corinthians, Chapter 2, and by the words of Ambrose thereon, together with the explicit statement of Chrysostom which we quoted in Chapter V of this discourse, paragraph 6.

5. For this reason, the priest with respect to his office should not be likened to a judge in the third sense, but rather to a judge in the first sense, that is, to one who has the authority to teach and practice, like the physician, but has no coercive power over anyone. For it was in this way that Christ called himself a "physician," not a ruler, when in Luke, Chapter

[6] James 4:12.   [7] Galatians 2:9.

5, he said of himself: "They that are well do not need a physician, but they that are sick"; [8] nor did he say: they need a judge, for he had not come into the world to exercise coercive judgment over litigants, as we showed from Luke, Chapter 12, in Chapter IV of this discourse, paragraph 8. But by such coercive judgment Christ will judge the living and the dead on that day about which the Apostle said in the last chapter of the second epistle to Timothy: "Henceforth there is laid up for me a crown of righteousness, which the Lord, the righteous judge, shall give me at that day." [9] For at that time Christ by coercive judgment will inflict penalties on those who in this world have transgressed the law made immediately by him. And this was the reason why Christ symbolically said to Peter: "I shall give unto thee the keys of the kingdom of heaven"; but he did not say: I shall give unto thee the judgment of the kingdom of heaven. And hence, as we have already said, the turnkey neither of the earthly nor of the heavenly judge has coercive judgment, which we called judgment in the third sense, because neither turnkey exercises the rights of such power, as Ambrose plainly said concerning the priest and as has also been sufficiently shown by the authority of other saints.

And so let this be our conclusion concerning the authority of the priests or bishops, and the power of the apostolic keys which Christ granted to them.

CHAPTER VIII: ON THE DIVISION OF HUMAN ACTS, AND HOW THEY ARE RELATED TO HUMAN LAW AND THE JUDGE OF THIS WORLD

EVERY coercive judgment is concerned with human voluntary acts in accordance with some law or custom, and with these acts insofar as they are ordered either toward the end to be attained in this world, that is, sufficiency of worldly life, or toward the end to be attained in the future world, which we call eternal life or glory. Hence, in order to make clearer the distinction between those who judge or ought to judge with regard to each of these ends, and between the laws in accordance with which, the judgments by which, and the manners in which they must respectively judge, let us discuss the differences between the acts themselves. For the determination of these points will be of no little help toward the solution of the earlier questions.

[8] Luke 5:31.   [9] II Timothy 4:8.

2. Let us say, therefore, that of human acts arising from knowledge and desire, ome arise without any control by the mind, and others arise through the control of the human mind. Of the first kind are cognitions, desires, affections, and pleasures which arise from us and in us without any control or command being given about them by the intellect or the appetite; such are the cognitions and emotions which we have when we are aroused from sleep, or which arise in us in other ways without any control by our mind. But these acts are followed by cognitions, feelings, and emotions which are concerned with continuing the prior acts, or with investigating and understanding some of them, as in the action which proceeds through recollection; and these are and are called "controls" or "commands" of the mind, because they are done or elicited by our control, or because certain other acts are elicited by them, such as pursuits and avoidances.[1]

3. But between controlled and uncontrolled acts there is this difference arising from what we have said, that over uncontrolled acts we do not have complete freedom or control as to whether or not they shall be done, but over controlled acts we do have this power, according to the Christian religion.[2] And I have said that we do not have complete power over the former kind of acts, because it is not in our power wholly to prohibit their occurrence, although by acts of the second kind, which are called "controls," and by what follows from them, we may so dispose the soul that it will not easily perform or receive acts of the first kind, that is, when each of us has become accustomed to commanding himself to desire or think about the opposites of these acts.

Of controlled acts some are and are called "immanent," and others "transient." [3] Immanent acts are controlled cognitions, emotions, and the corresponding habits made by the human mind; they are called "immanent" because they do not cross over into any subject other than the agent himself. Transient acts, on the other hand, are all pursuits of things de-

[1] For a possible source of this distinction between "uncontrolled" and "controlled" acts, see Thomas Aquinas *Summa theologica* II. I. qu.8. *init.* Marsilius' interpretation of the distinction, however, is not entirely the same as Thomas'. Thomas first distinguishes between "voluntary" and "involuntary" acts, and then distinguishes between two kinds of voluntary acts, the "elicited," which are acts immediately of the will itself (like willing and choosing), and the "controlled," which are acts of other powers moved by the will. Marsilius, on the other hand, identifies controlled, elicited, and voluntary acts, and then divides these into "immanent" and "transient" acts (see para. 3). It should be noted that the term here translated "controlled" is *imperatus;* the English term is used in order to avoid confusion with the important term *praeceptum,* which, following William of Moerbeke, who used *praecipere* to translate Aristotle's ἐπιτάττειν, is translated "command" or "commanded." See especially below, II. xii. 3; also Vol. I, pp. 169, 231.

[2] This reference to religion may indicate some skepticism as to whether such freedom is rationally demonstrable. See Vol. I, p. 57, text and n. 30.

[3] See above, I. v. 4; also Vol. I, p. 61.

sired, and the omissions thereof, in the manner of privations, and the motions produced by some of the body's external organs, especially of those which are moved in respect of place. Again, of transient acts some exist and are done without harm or injury to any individual, group, or community other than the agent; such are all the kinds of productive activity, and also the giving of money, pilgrimages, castigation of one's own body by scourging or beating or any other way, and other similar acts. Other transient acts, however, exist and are done with the opposite circumstances, that is, with harm or injury to someone other than the agent; such are flogging, theft, robbery, bearing false witness, and many others of various manners and kinds.

4. Now of all these acts which arise from the human mind, especially the controlled ones, there have been discovered certain standards or measures or habits whereby they arise and are done properly and correctly for the attainment of the sufficient life both in this world and in the next. Of these habits or standards there are some in accordance with which the acts of the human mind, both immanent and transient, are guided and regulated in their being done or omitted without any reward or punishment being given to the doer or omitter by someone else through coercive force; such are most of the operative disciplines, both those of action and those of production. But there are other standards in accordance with which such acts are commanded to be done or omitted with reward or punishment being given to the doers or omitters by someone else through coercive force. Of these coercive standards, again, there are some in accordance with which their observers or transgressors are rewarded or punished in and for the status of the present life; such are all human civil laws and customs. But there are other coercive standards in accordance with which doers are rewarded or punished in and for the status of the future life only; such are divine laws for the most part, which are called by the common name "religions," [4] among which, as we said in Chapter VI of Discourse I,[5] only that of the Christians contains the truth and the sufficiency of what must be hoped for the future world.

5. For the sufficient life or living of this world, therefore, there has been laid down a standard of controlled transient human acts which can be done for the benefit or harm, right or wrong, of someone other than the agent; a standard which commands and coerces transgressors by pain or punishment for the status of the present world alone. This standard we called by the common name "human law" in Chapter X of Discourse I; its final

---

[4] *Sectae.* See above, Introduction, pp. xc–xci.   [5] See above, I. v. 13; I. vi. 1, 7.

necessity and efficient cause we indicated in Chapters XI, XII, and XIII of Discourse I.

On the other hand, for the life or living in this world, but for the status of the future world, a law has been given and laid down by Christ. This law is a standard of controlled human acts, both immanent and transient, which are in the active power of our mind, according as they can be done or omitted rightly or wrongly in this world, but for the status or end of the future world.[6] This law is coercive and distributes punishments or rewards, but inflicts these in the future world, not in the present one, in accordance with the merits or demerits of those who observe or transgress it in the present life.

6. But since these coercive laws, both the divine and the human, lack a soul and a judicial and executive moving principle, they needed to have some animate subject or principle which should command and regulate or judge human acts in accordance with these laws, and which should also execute the judgments and coerce their transgressors. This subject or principle is called a "judge," in what we called the third sense of this term in Chapter II of this discourse.[7] Hence in Book IV of the *Ethics,* the treatise on justice, it is said that "the judge is like an animate justice." [8] It is necessary, then, to have a judge in accordance with human laws, a judge of the kind we have said, having the authority to judge, by a judgment in the third sense, about contentious human acts, to execute the judgments, and to punish by coercive force anyone who transgresses the law. For this judge "is the minister of God," and "a revenger to execute wrath upon him that doeth evil," as the Apostle said in the epistle to the Romans, Chapter 13; [9] he has been sent by God for this purpose, as it is said in the first epistle of Peter, Chapter 2.[10]

7. And the Apostle said: "him that doeth evil," whoever he be, understanding this to apply to all men without differentiation. Consequently, since priests or bishops and generally all ministers of temples, who are called by the common name "clergyman," can do evil by way of commission or omission, and since some (would that it were not most) of them do sometimes in fact harm and wrong other persons, they too are subject to the revenge or jurisdiction of the judges to whom belongs coercive power to punish transgressors of human laws. This was also clearly stated by the Apostle in the epistle to the Romans, Chapter 13: "Let every soul," he said, "be subject to the higher powers," namely, "to kings, princes, and

---

[6] Reading, with Scholz, comma after *seculi.*
[7] See above, II. ii. 8.
[8] Aristotle *Nicomachean Ethics* v. 4. 1132a 22.
[9] Romans 13:4.
[10] I Peter 2:14.

tribunes," according to the exposition of the saints.[11] For the same proper matter must undergo the action of the same agent which is naturally endowed and ordained to act upon it for the end for which it is apt, as is clear from the second book of the *Physics*. For as it is there written, "each thing is acted upon as it is naturally endowed to be acted upon," [12] and conversely. But the transgressor of the law is the matter or subject upon which the judge or ruler is naturally endowed and ordained to act by bringing it to justice in order to effect due equality or proportion for the purpose of maintaining peace or tranquillity and the living together or association of men, and finally for the sake of the sufficiency of human life. Consequently, wherever such matter or subject is found in a province subject to a judge, this judge must bring him to justice. Since, therefore, the priest can be such proper or essential matter, that is, a transgressor of human law, he must be subject to the judgment of this judge.[13] For to be a priest or non-priest is accidental to the transgressor in his relation to the judge, just as to be a farmer or house-builder; in the same way, to be musical or unmusical is accidental to the healthy or the sick man in his relation to the physician. For that which is essential is not removed or varied by that which is accidental; otherwise there would be infinite species of judges and physicians.[14]

Therefore, any priest or bishop who transgresses human law must be brought to justice and punished by the judge who has coercive power over transgressors of human law in this world. But this judge is the secular ruler as such, not the priest or bishop, as was demonstrated in Chapters XV and XVII of Discourse I, and in Chapters IV and V of this discourse. Therefore, all priests or bishops who transgress human law must be punished by the ruler. And not only must the priest or other minister of the temple be punished for a transgression as the layman is, but he must be punished all the more in proportion as he sins more gravely and unseemingly, since he whose duty it is to be better acquainted with the commands

---

[11] In Peter Lombard *Collectanea* (PL 191. 1503).

[12] See Aristotle *Physics* II. 8. 199a 9. Marsilius' text reads: *Sic agitur unumquodque sicut natum est agi.* This is a misquotation of William of Moerbeke's translation of this passage, which reads: *Ergo sicut agitur, sic aptum natum est: et sicut aptum natum est, sic agitur unumquodque* (in *Thomae Aquinatis opera omnia*, ed. Leonine [Rome, 1884], II, 92). Aristotle's Greek is as follows: Οὐκοῦν ὡς πράττεται, οὕτω πέφυκε, καὶ ὡς πέφυκεν, οὕτω πράττεται ἕκαστον. Moreover, Marsilius misinterprets the passage, which is rendered as follows in the Oxford translation of R. P. Hardie and R. K. Gaye: "Now surely as in intelligent action, so in nature; and as it is in nature, so it is in each action." However, Marsilius' misinterpretation is also found in Thomas Aquinas' commentary on the passage; see p. 93 of his commentary in the edition cited in this note.

[13] See Vol. I, pp. 120–21 and n. 34.

[14] This point is reminiscent of Aristotle's doctrine that the accidental attributes of a thing are infinite in number. Cf. *Metaphysics* IV. 4. 1007a 14 ff.; VI. 2. 1026b 6 ff.

of what must be done and avoided, has greater knowledge and ability to choose; and again, since the sin of the person whose duty it is to teach is more shameful than the sin of the person whose duty it is to be taught. But such is the relation of the priest's sin to that of the non-priest. Therefore, the priest sins more gravely, and should be punished more.

8. Nor must the objection be sustained which holds that injuries by word of mouth, or to property or person, and other deeds prohibited by human law, are spiritual actions when inflicted on someone by a priest, and that it does not therefore pertain to the secular ruler to take revenge on the priest for such acts. For such deeds as are prohibited by law, like adultery, beating, homicide, theft, robbery, insult, libel, treason, fraud, heresy, and other similar acts committed by the priest, are carnal and temporal, as is very well known by experience, and as we showed above in Chapter II of this discourse by the words of the Apostle in the first epistle to the Corinthians, Chapters 3 and 9, and in the epistle to the Romans, Chapter 15.[15] And so much the more must these actions be adjudged carnal and temporal, in proportion as the priest or bishop sins by them more gravely and shamefully than do the persons whom he must recall from such actions, for by his vicious example he gives them an opportunity and an excuse for doing wrong.

9. Therefore, like laymen, every priest or bishop is and ought to be subject to the jurisdiction of the rulers in those matters whose observance is commanded by the human law. The priest neither is himself exempt from the coercive judgment of rulers, nor can he exempt anyone else from it by his own authority. This I demonstrate, in addition to what was said in Chapter XVII of Discourse I, by deducing from its contradictory the greatest evil. For [16] if the Roman bishop or any other priest were thus exempt, so that he would not be subject to the coercive judgment of rulers but would himself be such a coercive judge without the authorization of the human legislator and could separate all ministers of temples, who are called by the common name of "clergymen," from the jurisdiction of rulers, and could subject them to himself, as is done by the Roman pontiffs in modern times, then it would necessarily follow that the jurisdiction of secular rulers would be almost completely annulled. This I believe would be a grave evil of serious import to all rulers and communities; for "the Christian religion deprives no one of his right," as we showed in Chapter V of this discourse from the words of Ambrose on the passage in the

---

[15] See above, II. ii. 6, 7. See also Vol. I, pp. 102–3.

[16] Scholz points out that the remainder of this chapter, to the middle of its penultimate paragraph, and most of the first two paragraphs of Chapter IX are repeated verbatim in Philippe de Mézières *Somnium viridarii* (1389) cap. cii (*Monarchia,* ed. Goldast, I, 91 f.).

epistle to Titus, Chapter 3: "Warn them to be subject to the princes and powers." [17]

The consequence of this evil I show as follows: In divine law one finds that for the priest or bishop to have a wife is not prohibited but rather allowed, especially if he have not more than one, as it is said in the first epistle to Timothy, Chapter 3.[18] But that which is decreed by the human law or constitution can be revoked by the same authority, as such. Therefore, the Roman bishop who makes himself legislator, or who uses his plenitude of power (if one grant that he has this), can allow all priests, deacons, and subdeacons to have wives, and not only them, but also other persons not ordained in the priesthood or diaconate or otherwise consecrated, who are called "clergy of the simple tonsure"; indeed, he can grant such permission even more fittingly to these latter, as Boniface VIII is seen in fact to have done, in order to increase his secular power. For all who had taken one virgin wife, and who were willing, he enrolled in the company of the clergy, and decreed that they should be so enrolled by his ordinances which are called "decretals"; [19] and not stopping there, these bishops have similarly exempted from human civil laws, duly made, certain laymen who are called "jolly friars" in Italy and Beguins elsewhere; on the same ground they have dealt and can deal at their pleasure with the Knights Templars, the Hospitallers, and many other such orders, like that of Altopascio and so on.[20] But if all such persons are thus exempted from the jurisdiction of rulers in accordance with these decretals, which also grant certain immunities from public or civil burdens to those who are thus exempted, then it seems very likely that the majority of men will slip into these orders, especially since both literate and illiterate persons are accepted indiscriminately. For everyone is prone to pursue his own advantage and to avoid what is disadvantageous.[21] But with the greater number or majority of men slipping into clerical orders, the jurisdiction and coercive power of rulers will become ineffective, and the number of those who have to bear the public burdens will be reduced to almost nothing; which is the gravest evil, and destructive of the polity. For he who enjoys civil honors and advantages, like peace and the protection of the human legis-

---

[17] See above, II. v. 8.   [18] I Timothy 3:2, 12.

[19] *Corp. jur. can., Sext.* Lib. III. Tit. 2 cap. 1 (*De clericis coniugatis*). This declares that married "clerks" who bear the tonsure and clerical garbs are not to be tried or condemned by the secular tribunal. See also Vol. I, pp. 26, 120–21.

[20] The "jolly friars" or Frati Gaudenti were the Knights of the Virgin founded in Bologna in 1261. The Beguins were associations of pious persons. The Knights Templars and Hospitallers were likewise lay orders, dating from the twelfth century. The canons or knights of Altopascio maintained hospitals for pilgrims (spreading from a township near Lucca). For the history and rules of some of these orders, see references in Scholz, p. 229, n. 2.

[21] See Vol. I, p. 61.

lator, must not be exempt from the civil burdens and jurisdiction without the determination of the same legislator.[22] Hence the Apostle said, in the epistle to the Romans, Chapter 13: And for this very reason "pay ye tribute." [23]

To avoid this eventuality it must be granted, in accordance with the truth, that the ruler by authority of the legislator has jurisdiction over all bishops or priests and clergymen, lest the polity be destroyed by having an unordered multiplicity of governments, as was shown in Chapter XVII of Discourse I; and the ruler must determine, in the province subject to him, the definite number of clergymen, as also of the persons in every other part of the polity, lest by their undue increase they be able to resist the ruler's coercive power, or otherwise disturb the polity, or deprive the city or state of its welfare by their insolence and their freedom from necessary tasks, as we showed from the *Politics,* Book V, Chapter 1, in Chapter XV of Discourse I.[24]

Thus, therefore, it is the human law and judge, in the third sense, which have to regulate transient human acts which affect the advantage or disadvantage, right or wrong, of someone other than the agent. To this coercive jurisdiction all men, lay and clergy, must be subject. But there are also certain other judges according to human laws, who have been called judges in the first or the second sense,[25] such as the teachers of these laws; but these judges have no coercive authority, and there is nothing to prevent that in any one community there be many of them, even when they are not subordinate to one another.[26]

CHAPTER IX: ON THE RELATION OF HUMAN ACTS TO DIVINE LAW AND TO THE JUDGE OF THE OTHER WORLD, NAMELY CHRIST; AND ALSO HOW THESE ACTS ARE RELATED TO THE TEACHER OF THE SAME LAW, THE BISHOP OR PRIEST, IN THIS WORLD

ACCORDING to this reasoning, therefore, there is also a certain judge who has coercive authority over transgressors of divine law, which we have called the coercive standard of some human acts both immanent and transient. But this judge is one alone, Christ, and no one else. Whence

---

[22] See Vol. I, pp. 26–27, and n. 32.   [23] See Romans 13:6.
[24] See above, I. xv. 10.   [25] See above, II. ii. 8.
[26] See above, I. xvii. 12, n. 19.

in the fourth chapter of James: "There is one lawmaker and judge, that is able to destroy and to deliver." [1] But this judge's coercive power is not exercised over anyone in this world, to punish or reward transgressors or observers of the law made immediately by him, which we have often called the evangelic law. For in his mercy Christ wished to give every person the opportunity to become deserving up to the very end of his life and to repent of sins committed against Christ's law,[2] as will be shown below by the authorities of the holy Scripture.

2. But there is also another judge according to the evangelic Scripture, who is analogous to the human law's judge in the first sense. This other judge is the priest, who is the teacher in this world of divine law and of its commands concerning what must be done or shunned in order to attain eternal life and avoid punishment. However, he has no coercive power in this world to compel anyone to observe these commands. For it would be useless for him to coerce anyone to observe them, since the person who observed them under coercion would be helped not at all toward eternal salvation, as we showed clearly in Chapter V of this discourse, paragraph 6, through Chrysostom, or rather through the Apostle. Hence this judge is properly likened to the physician, who is given the authority to teach, command, and predict or judge about the things which it is useful to do or omit in order to attain bodily health and avoid illness or death. It was for this reason, too, that Christ called himself a physician in and for the status of the present life, and not a ruler or a judge. Hence in the fifth chapter of Luke, which we also quoted in a preceding chapter, Christ spoke of himself to the Pharisees as follows: "They that are well do not need a physician, but they that are sick." [3] For Christ did not ordain that anyone should be forced to observe in this world the law made by him, and for this reason he did not appoint in this world a judge having coercive power over transgressors of this law.

3. Hence it must be noted that the evangelic law can stand in a twofold relation to men, over whom it was made by Christ. In one way, it can be related to them in and for the status of the present life; and in this way it has in its various parts the nature more of a doctrine, theoretic or practical or both, than of a law taken in its last and proper sense, although the word "law" can also be taken in other senses, like the second and the third, which we discussed in Chapter X of Discourse I.[4] And the reason for what we have said is that law, taken in its last and proper sense, is a coercive

---

[1] James 4:12.
[3] Luke 5:31. See above, II. vii. 5.

[2] See Vol. I, p. 157.
[4] See above, I. x. 3, 4.

standard, that is, a standard in accordance with which its transgressor is punished by the coercive force which is given to the man who must judge in accordance with it. But now the evangelic doctrine, or the maker of that law, does not command that anyone be compelled in this world to observe the things which it commands men to do or omit in this world. Consequently, in its relation to man's status in and for this world, it ought to be called a doctrine, not a law,[5] except in the way we have said. This was also the view of the Apostle in the second epistle to Timothy, Chapter 3, when he said: "All scripture divinely inspired is useful for teaching, for reproof, for correction, for instruction in righteousness." [6] But never did the Apostle say: for coercion or punishment in this world. Hence in the second epistle to the Corinthians, Chapter 1: "Not because we exercise dominion over your faith, but we are the helpers of your joy; for by faith ye stand." [7] Whereon Ambrose wrote what we quoted above in Chapter V of this discourse, and it bears repeating: "And lest they," that is, the Corinthians, "resent what might appear almost as dominion, in that he," the Apostle, "had said 'to spare you I did not come,' he," the Apostle, "adds: But I do not say 'to spare you' 'because we exercise dominion over your faith,' that is, because your faith undergoes dominion and coercion, for faith is of the will, not of necessity; but I say it rather 'because we are the helpers,' if you wish to cooperate." Note, then, they are helpers, that is, by teaching, and "if you wish to cooperate." "For 'by faith,' which works through choice, 'ye stand,' not by dominion." [8]

But the evangelic Scripture or law can also stand in another relation to men, for their status in the other world, in which alone, and not in this one, those men will be punished who have transgressed this law in the present life. And viewed in this other relation it is most properly given the name of law, and he who will then judge in accordance with it is most properly called a judge, in the third sense as having coercive power. But inasmuch as the priest or bishop, whoever he be, guides and regulates men in accordance with this law in the status of the present life alone, although with reference to the future life, and since the immediate maker of that law, Christ, has not granted to the priest the authority to coerce anyone in accordance with it in this world, it follows that the priest is not properly called a judge, in the third sense as having coercive power, and he neither can nor should coerce anyone in this world by such judgment through punishment in property or in person. Analogous to this is the relation of

[5] See Vol. I, p. 154.   [6] II Timothy 3:16.   [7] II Corinthians 1:23.
[8] See above, II. v, 6.

any practical teacher, such as a physician, to the judgment of men's bodily health, without coercive power over anyone, as we said near the beginning of this chapter.

4. In agreement with the mind of the Apostle in the second epistle to the Corinthians, Chapter 1, this was also clearly the view of St. John Chrysostom in his book of *Dialogues,* also entitled *On the Priestly Dignity,* Book II, Chapter III. For the sake of brevity, we shall not here repeat those of his remarks which we quoted in Chapter V of this discourse, paragraph 6, but shall here cite what he adds to the aforesaid passage. This, then, is what Chrysostom wrote:

There is great need of art, then, for this purpose, to help persuade men, when they are ill, to offer themselves willingly to the medicine of the priests, and not only this, but to be grateful for being cured. For a man will either break his bandages, which he certainly has free power to do, and will make his illness worse, or he will spurn the words which were to act as a surgical knife, and by his contempt will add to himself another wound, so that an opportunity for cure becomes the means of a worse disease. For there is no one who can cure a person against his will.

And then after several further remarks, which the pastor of souls ought to note in his corrective, although not coercive, function, Chrysostom continues:

If a man is led away from the right faith, great exhortation, industry, and patience are required of the priest, because he cannot lead the erring person back to the path by force, but will try to persuade him to return to the true faith, from which he originally strayed.[9]

See, then, how this saint separates the judgment of priests from that of rulers, in that the judgment of priests neither is nor ought to be coercive; and he gives the reasons which we have often stated: first, that coercive power is given by the laws or legislators, and was not granted to the priests of his time or province; and second, that even if coercive power were granted to them, in vain would they exercise it on their subjects, for coercion is of no spiritual help toward eternal salvation.[10] And Chrysostom said the same thing in writing on the words of the ninth chapter of Luke: "If anyone wishes to come after me, let him deny himself." [11] I have, however, omitted this passage here because the discussion has been sufficient, and for the sake of brevity.

5. This again was clearly the view of St. Hilary in his epistle to the emperor Constantine, wherein he wrote, among other things: "God taught rather than demanded knowledge of himself; in his precepts he counseled

---

[9] Chrysostom *De sacerdotio* II. iii, iv (PG 48. 634 f.).   [10] See II. v. 6; II. ix. 2.
[11] Luke 9:23.

that the heavenly works be admired, but he spurned the use of coercive authority to impose avowal of himself." See, then, that God wants men to be taught knowledge and avowal of himself, that is, by faith; he does not want anyone to be coerced, but spurns this. And the same point is reiterated a little below: "God does not require a forced avowal." And farther below Hilary says the same thing in the person of all priests: "I cannot accept anyone unless he is willing, hear anyone unless he prays, bless anyone unless he proffers himself." [12] God, then, does not want a forced avowal of himself, nor does he want anyone to be dragged thereto by the violent action or compulsion of someone else. Hence in Hilary's epistle against Auxentius, the bishop of Milan, whom he held to be an Arian and who, as he says, used armed force to make men profess his own opinion concerning, or rather contrary to, the catholic faith, Hilary, reproving him even if what he had taught had been true, writes as follows: "First we may grieve over the hardships of our age, and bemoan the stupid opinions of these times, whereby human institutions are believed to prop God's power, and one labors to protect the church of Christ by secular maneuvering." And again, in the same epistle: "But now—O sorrow!—earthly arguments are used to justify divine faith and Christ is indeed shown to be helpless when he is made dependent upon canvassing. The church frightens men with exile and imprisonment and uses coercion to induce belief in itself—that church which was once believed in amid exile and imprisonment." [13] And when Hilary speaks of the "church," he means the college of priests or bishops and the other ministers of the temple, who are called clergymen.

6. This too was clearly the view of Ambrose in his second epistle to the emperor Valentinianus, entitled *To the People,* when he said: "I shall be able to weep, I shall be able to lament, I shall be able to grieve; against arms, soldiers, and Goths, my tears are my weapons, for such are the munitions of the priest, in any other way I neither can nor should resist." [14] See, then, that the priest should not, even if he could, use weapons or coercive force against anyone, or command or urge that they be used, especially against the Christian faithful; but the whole world can observe that certain priests have followed the opposite course, against the teaching of the sacred canon and of the saints.

7. According to the truth, therefore, and the clear intention of the Apostle and the saints, who were the foremost teachers of the church or faith, it is not commanded that anyone, even an infidel, let alone a believer,

[12] St. Hilary of Poitiers *Epist. ad Constantium Augustum* 1. 6 (PL 10. 561).
[13] St. Hilary *Contra Auxentium* 3 (PL 10. 610).
[14] St. Ambrose *Sermo contra Auxentium* 2 (PL 16. 1050). See above, II. v. 5.

be compelled in this world through pain or punishment to observe the commands of the evangelic law, especially by a priest; and hence the ministers of this law, the bishops or priests, neither can nor should judge anyone in this world by a judgment in the third sense, or compel an unwilling person, by any pain or punishment, to observe the commands of divine law, especially without authorization by the human legislator; for such coercive judgment in accordance with divine law must not be exercised or executed in this world, but only in the future one. Hence in the nineteenth chapter of Matthew: "But Jesus said to them," that is, to the apostles: "Verily I say unto you, that ye which have followed me, in the regeneration when the son of man shall sit on the throne of his glory, ye also shall sit upon twelve thrones, judging the twelve tribes of Israel." [15] See, then, when it was that the apostles were going to sit with Christ as judges in the third sense, namely, in the other world, not in this one. Whereon the gloss: " 'in the regeneration,' that is, when the dead will rise up alive again." [16] Hence, according to the gloss: "There are two regenerations, the first from water and the holy spirit, the second in resurrection." [17] Hence "ye also shall sit," and the gloss according to Augustine says: "When he who was in the guise of a servant and who was judged," that is, Christ, who was in this world judged by coercive judgment, and did not himself judge, "will exercise judiciary power," that is, in the resurrection, "you shall be judges with me." [18] See, then, that according to Christ's words in the gospel and the exposition of the saints, Christ did not in this world exercise judiciary, that is, coercive, power, which we called judgment in the third sense, but rather, in the guise of a servant, he underwent such judgment by another man; and when he will exercise such coercive judiciary power in the other world, then, and not before, will the apostles sit with him to make such judgments.

8. Hence it is indeed to be wondered why any bishop or priest, whoever he be, assumes for himself greater or other authority than that which Christ or his apostles wanted to have in this world. For they, in the guise of servants, were judged by the secular rulers. But their successors, the priests, not only refuse to be subject to the rulers, contrary to the example and command of Christ and of the apostles, but they even claim to be superior to the supreme rulers and powers in coercive jurisdiction. Christ, however, said in the tenth chapter of Matthew: "And ye shall be brought before governors and kings for my sake"; [19] but he did not say: Ye shall

---

[15] Matthew 19:28.
[16] *Glossa interlinearis, ad loc.*
[17] *Glossa ordinaria, ad loc.*
[18] *Glossa ordinaria, ad loc.*
[19] Matthew 10:18.

be governors or kings. And further on he adds: "The disciple is not over his master, nor the servant above his lord." [20] Therefore, no coercive judgment, rulership, or dominion can or ought to be exercised in this world by any priest or bishop as such. This was also clearly the view of the famous Philosopher in the *Politics,* Book IV, Chapter 12, for he said: "Hence not all those who are elected or chosen by lot are to be regarded as rulers. Consider the priests in the first place. These must be regarded as different from the political rulers. And also there are the masters of choruses and heralds, and also ambassadors who are elected. And of the superintendent functions some are political, being exercised over all the citizens with regard to some action." And a little below he adds: "And other offices are economic." [21]

9. What we have said is also borne out by this, that if Christ had wanted the priests of the New Law to be judges according to it, in the third sense of judge, that is, with coercive judgment, settling by such verdicts men's contentious acts in this world, then he would have given in this law special commands about such acts, just as he did in the Old Law in the case of Moses, whom God, by his own utterance and not through man, made ruler and coercive judge of the Jews, as it is told in the seventh chapter of the Acts.[22] For this reason, also, God gave to Moses a law prescribing what must be observed in and for the status of the present life for the purpose of settling human disputes; a law which contained special commands about such matters, and was in this respect analogous to human law in some part of it. Accordingly, men were compelled and forced to observe these commands in this world through pain or punishment by Moses and by the coercive judges who took his place, but not by any priest, as is quite clear from the eighteenth chapter of Exodus.[23] But such commands were not given by Christ in the evangelic law; rather, he took for granted the commands which were or would be given in human laws, and he commanded every human soul to observe these and to obey the men who ruled in accordance with them, at least in those commands which were not opposed to the law of eternal salvation.[24] Hence in the twenty-second chapter of Matthew and the eleventh of Mark: "Render unto Caesar the things that are Caesar's," by "Caesar" signifying any ruler. So too the Apostle said in the thirteenth chapter of Romans, and it bears repeating: "Let every soul be subject to the higher powers." So too in the first epistle to Timothy, last chapter: "Even to infidel lords," and the gloss thereon according to Augustine, which we quoted in Chapter V of this discourse, paragraph 8.[25]

[20] Matthew 10:24.   [21] Aristotle *Politics* iv. 15. 1299a 16 ff. See above, i. xix. 12.
[22] Acts 7:35.   [23] Exodus 18:13–26.
[24] See Vol. I, p. 120, n. 31; pp. 162–63.   [25] See above, ii. iv. 9; ii. v. 4, 8.

From all these it is quite evident that Christ, the Apostle, and the saints held the view that all men must be subject to the human laws and to the judges according to these laws.

10. Moreover, from the above it is plain that the Christian faithful are not obliged to observe all the commands or counsels of the Old Law or Testament which the Jewish people were required to observe; indeed, they are forbidden to observe some of them, like the ceremonial commands, under pain of eternal perdition, as the Apostle teaches in the epistles to the Romans, Chapters 3 and 7; to the Galatians, Chapters 2, 3, and 5; to the Ephesians, Chapter 2; and to the Hebrews, Chapters 7 and 10. And following the doctrine of the Apostle, Saints Jerome and Augustine agree on this point in their eleventh and thirteenth epistles to one another, asserting that persons who observe or who pretend to observe such ceremonies after the promulgation of the evangelic law will be "cast unto the devil's abyss." [26] And similarly the Christian faithful are not obliged to observe the legal commands of the Old Law, as is apparent from the words of the Apostle quoted above, in the first epistle to Timothy, last chapter, and the gloss of Augustine thereon, when he said: "Therefore let not Christian servants demand," that is, because they cannot demand, "what is said with respect to the Hebrews," [27] etc. Since, therefore, no special commands are given in the law of grace to settle men's contentious acts in this world, it remains that such matters must be dealt with by the human laws alone and by the judges according to these laws who hold authority from the human legislator.

11. But there were also certain other commands in the Mosaic law which were to be observed for the status of the future world, like those relating to sacrifices or hostages or offerings for the redemption of sins, especially hidden ones, which are committed through immanent acts; and no one was compelled by pain or punishment of the present world to observe these commands.[28] Analogous to these commands are all the counsels and commands of the New Law, for Christ neither wanted nor commanded that anyone be compelled to observe them in this world, although he does give a general command that human laws be observed, but under pain or punishment to be inflicted in the other world upon transgressors. Hence the transgressor of human law most usually sins against divine law, although not conversely. For there are many acts of com-

---

[26] See St. Jerome Epist. 112 (PL 22. 916–31), and Epist. 116, Augustine's reply (PL 22. 936–51). See also Peter Lombard *Collectanea* on Galatians 2 and 5 (PL 192. 110–14, 153, 158), and on Hebrews 7 (PL 192. 454).

[27] See above, II. v. 8.

[28] On the significance of Marsilius' discussion of the Mosaic law, see Vol. I, pp. 152–53.

mission or omission whereby one sins against divine law, which gives
commands on those matters whereon human law would command in vain;
such are the acts which above we called "immanent," which cannot be
proved to be present or absent to anyone, but which nevertheless cannot be
concealed from God.[29] And therefore divine law, which is concerned with
the proper commission or omission of such acts, was appropriately handed
down for the betterment of men, both in this world and in the one to come.[30]

12. But someone will object that the evangelic law is imperfect, if, as we
have said, it cannot sufficiently regulate men's contentious acts in and for
the status of the present life. In reply let us say that we are sufficiently
guided by the evangelic law with respect to what we must do or avoid in
the present life, although for the status of the future life, for the attainment
of eternal salvation and the avoidance of eternal punishment. It was for
this purpose that the evangelic law was made, and not for the purpose of
effecting by civil means [31] the reduction of men's contentious acts to due
equality or proportion for the status or sufficiency of the present life, inasmuch as Christ came into the world to regulate such acts not for the
present life, but for the future life only. And for this reason there are diverse
standards of human temporal acts, which guide men toward these ends by
diverse methods. For one standard, the divine, in no way gives instructions
as to how disputes and claims are to be conducted, although it does not
prohibit these; and hence, as we have said, it hands down no special commands about such matters. But the other standard of human acts, the
human law, does give such instructions, and commands that transgressors
be punished. It was for this reason that Christ replied as follows, in the
twelfth chapter of Luke, to the man who asked him to render judgment
over his brother and himself: "Man, who made me a judge or a divider
over you?" [32] As if to say I have not come to exercise such judgment.
Whence the gloss. "He does not deign to be judge over quarrels and dispenser of riches, who has judgment over the living and the dead and is the
final examiner of their merits." [33] The evangelic law, therefore, could not
sufficiently measure human acts for the purpose of the present world. For
standards which measure such acts to the proportion which men want, and
lawfully, for the status of the present life are not given in the evangelic law,
but are rather assumed from human laws, either those which have already

[29] See above, I. v. 4; II. viii. 3.
[30] The same point concerning the difference between human and divine law is made by
Thomas Aquinas *Summa theologica* II. I. qu.91. a.4. Resp.; qu.100. a.2. Resp.; a.9. Resp.
Nevertheless, the end even of human law for Aquinas is internalistic; see Vol. I, pp. 101-2, 110.
[31] *Civiliter*. See above, Introduction, pp. lxxix–lxxx.   [32] Luke 12:14.
[33] See above, II. iv. 8.

been given or those which are going to be given.[34] Without these standards
lack of justice would cause men's quarrels or disputes to result in fighting,
separation, and insufficiency of human worldly life, which almost all men
shun in accordance with nature.

13. It cannot, therefore, be truly said that the evangelic law or doctrine
is imperfect, for it was not originated to have the perfection which it has
been shown not to have. For it was made to give us immediate guidance in
the things which are necessary for the attainment of eternal salvation and
the avoidance of misery, and on these matters it is indeed sufficient and
perfect. But it was not made for the purpose of settling litigious civil affairs
for the end which men want, and lawfully, in worldly life. For if it were on
this account called imperfect, it might with equal propriety be called imperfect because it does not enable us to heal bodily ills or measure magni-
tudes or sail the ocean. Yet that it is not absolutely perfect can soundly be
granted, for there is only one such being, God himself. And this view is
upheld as indubitably true by the gloss according to Gregory on I Corinthians, Chapter 6, where he writes as follows: " 'I speak to your shame':
namely, in order that those men may try earthly disputes who have perceived the wisdom of exterior things. But those who are endowed with
spiritual gifts ought not to become entangled in earthly affairs." [35] But if
by "the wisdom of exterior things" and of earthly disputes and quarrels,

---

[34] The same position on the relation between divine and human law is taken by Thomas
Aquinas *Summa theologica* II. 1. qu.108. aa.1–3. However, the difficulties of this sharp separation between the two laws, with which Marsilius does not here deal, arise from the fact that
to a certain extent the two laws deal with the same acts. According to Aquinas, the divine
law of the gospel is concerned with the interior acts in which the kingdom of God principally consists; but consequently it is also concerned with the necessary conditions of those
acts. Hence the evangelic law must prohibit "all the exterior acts which are repugnant to
justice, or to peace, or to spiritual joy" (*loc. cit.* a.1. ad 1). Thus, although the particular determination of justice may be a matter of indifference, to be left to human law (*ibid.* a.1.
Resp.; a.2. Resp.), there are moral commands found in the evangelic law which provide
the general principles to which the human law's regulation of secular life must conform.
Marsilius does not deny this doctrine, but he also does not, like Thomas, supply the specifying
detail as to the content of divine law which would clarify its affirmative relation to human law.
Instead, he emphasizes the non-coerciveness of divine law and the necessity that its doubtful
meanings be determined by general councils and enforced only by human legislators (see
Vol. I, pp. 62–63). And when in the *Defensor minor* (ed. C. K. Brampton [Birmingham,
1922], xiii. 5–6) he does deal specifically with the identity of the contents of human and
divine law, he also adds that human law itself enforces those contents (see Vol. I, pp. 163–64).
But the papalists could just as easily make divine law and its earthly representatives the en-
forcers of those common contents (see Vol. I, pp. 101–2, 104–5). In either case, the dualistic
relation of the two laws gave way to an actual political subordination of the one or the
other law so far as the enforcement of their common contents was concerned. The real
distinction, in other words, is not with respect to the *contents* of the two laws but rather with
respect to the conditions of their *enforcement*—and it is to this latter consideration that
Marsilius characteristically devotes the most attention.

[35] See above, p. 128.

Gregory had meant the holy Scripture, he would not have said that "those who are endowed with spiritual gifts," that is, the holy Scripture, "ought not to become entangled in earthly affairs"; nor would he have distinguished such persons from one another on the basis of these doctrines. Moreover, the Apostle and the saints, according to one interpretation, had called men who have such wisdom, that is, of exterior things, "the most despised" in the church, an opinion which neither the Apostle nor the saints expounding his words held concerning the men who were learned in the holy Scripture.

We think, then, that for our purpose we have sufficiently shown the number and kinds of legal human acts, and how they are to be regulated and corrected, that is, by what laws and judges, in what manner, at what times, and through what persons.

CHAPTER X: ON THE COERCIVE JUDGE OF HERETICS, NAMELY TO WHOM IT PERTAINS TO JUDGE HERETICS IN THIS WORLD, TO CORRECT THEM, TO INFLICT ON THEM PENALTIES IN PERSON AND IN PROPERTY, AND TO EXACT AND DISPOSE OF THESE PENALTIES

CONCERNING what we have said doubts may well arise. For if only the ruler by the legislator's authority has jurisdiction over all forms of compulsion in the present life, through coercive judgment and the infliction and exaction of penalties in property and in person, as was shown above, then it will pertain to this ruler to make coercive judgments over heretics or other infidels or schismatics, and to inflict, exact, and dispose of the penalties in property and in person. But this seems inappropriate. For it might seem that it pertains to the same authority to inquire into a crime and to judge and correct the crime; but since it pertains to the priest, the presbyter or bishop, and to no one else, to discern the crime of heresy, it would seem to follow that the coercive judgment or correction of this and similar crimes also pertains to the priest or bishop alone. Moreover, the judging and punishing of a criminal might seem to pertain to the person against whom or against whose law the criminal has sinned. But this person is the priest or bishop. For he is the minister or judge of divine law, against which essentially the heretic, schismatic, or other infidel sins, whether this sinner be a group or an individual. It follows, therefore, that this judgment pertains to the priest, and not to the ruler. And this clearly seems to be the view of St. Ambrose in his first epistle to the Emperor Valentinian; [1] but since he seems to adhere to this view throughout the whole epistle, I have omitted to quote from it for the sake of brevity.

2. But now let us say, in accordance with our previous conclusions, that any person who sins against divine law must be judged, corrected, and punished according to that law. But there are two judges according to it. One is a judge in the third sense, having coercive power to punish transgressors of this law; and this judge is Christ alone, as we showed by James, Chapter 4, in the preceding chapter.[2] But Christ willed and decreed that all transgressors of this law should be coercively judged and punished in the future world only, not in this one, as the preceding chapter made sufficiently clear. There is another judge according to this law, namely, the priest or bishop, but he is not a judge in the third sense, and may not correct any transgressor of divine law in this world and punish him by coercive force; this was clearly shown in Chapters V and IX of this discourse by the authority and the invincible reasoning of the Apostle and the saints. However, the priest is a judge in the first sense of the word, and he has to teach, exhort, censure, and rebuke sinners or transgressors of divine law, and frighten them by a judgment of the future infliction of damnation and punishment upon them in the world to come by the coercive judge, Christ, as we showed in Chapters VI and VII of this discourse, where the power of the priestly keys was discussed, and in the preceding chapter,[3] where we compared the physician of bodies with the priests, "who are the physicians of souls," as Augustine said by the authority of the prophet and as the Master repeats in Book IV, Distinction 18, Chapter IX.[4] Since, then, the heretic, the schismatic, or any other infidel is a transgressor of divine law, if he persists in this crime he will be punished by that judge to whom it pertains to correct transgressors of divine law as such, when he will exercise his judicial authority. But this judge is Christ, who will judge the living, the dead, and the dying, but in the future world, not in this one. For he has mercifully allowed sinners to have the opportunity of becoming deserving and penitent up to the very time when they finally pass from this world at death.[5] But the other judge, namely, the pastor, bishop or priest, must teach and exhort man in the present life, must censure and rebuke the sinner and frighten him by a judgment or prediction of future glory or

[1] St. Ambrose Epist. 21 (PL 16. 1045-49).   [2] See above, II. ix. 1.
[3] See above, II. vi. 9-13; II. vii. 3-5; II. ix. 3-5.
[4] Peter Lombard Sent. Lib. IV. dist. 18. cap. ix (PL 192. 889), citing Psalm 88:11.
[5] See above, II. ix. 1.

eternal damnation; but he must not coerce,[6] as is plain from the previous chapter.

3. Now if human law were to prohibit heretics or other infidels from dwelling in the region, and yet such a person were found there, he must be corrected in this world as a transgressor of human law, and the penalty fixed by that law for such transgression must be inflicted on him by the judge who is the guardian of human law by the authority of the legislator, as we demonstrated in Chapter XV of Discourse I. But if human law did not prohibit the heretic or other infidel from dwelling among the faithful in the same province, as heretics and Jews are now permitted to do by human laws even in these times of Christian peoples, rulers, and pontiffs, then I say that no one is allowed to judge or coerce a heretic or other infidel by any penalty in property or in person for the status of the present life.[7] And the general reason for this is as follows: no one is punished in this world for sinning against theoretic or practical disciplines precisely as such, however much he may sin against them, but only for sinning against a command of human law.[8] For if human law did not prohibit anyone from becoming drunk, or making and selling shoes according to his means or desires, or practicing medicine, or teaching, or working at other such functions as he pleased, then no one who became drunk, or who acted wrongly in any occupation, would be punished.[9]

4. It must therefore be noted that in any coercive judgment of this world, before the sentence of acquittal or conviction is pronounced, several pertinent questions must be investigated in due order. The first is whether the statement or deed of which the defendant is accused is such as it is said to be. This is to know the nature of what is said to have been committed. The second question is whether such an act is prohibited by human law. And the third, whether the accused did or did not commit it. After these questions have been investigated there follows the judgment or sentence of conviction or of acquittal for the defendant. For example, if a person is accused of being a heretic or a counterfeiter of golden vases or of some other metal, then before he is acquitted or convicted by coercive sentence, inquiry must be made, first, as to whether the statement or deed of which he is accused is heretical or not. Secondly, whether to say, do, or teach such a thing is prohibited by human law. Thirdly, whether such crime was or was not committed by the person who is charged with it. And finally,

---

[6] See Vol. I, p. 138.
[7] On the bearing of this position for religious freedom and toleration, see Vol. I, pp. 164–66.
[8] See Vol. I, pp. 119–20.   [9] See Vol. I, pp. 122–23, 313.

after the investigation of these questions, there follows the coercive judgment of acquittal or conviction.

5. Concerning the first of these questions, the truth must be ascertained by the ruler through the experts in each discipline, who have to consider the essence or nature of the statement or deed of which the defendant is accused; for these experts are judges in the first sense, as we said in Chapter II of this discourse, and they are held to know the nature of such things; to them the ruler has given the authority, which in liberal disciplines is usually called a "license," to teach or practice such things in the state. And this procedure is analogous to that of all the other productive or mechanical arts, as was demonstrated in Chapter XV of Discourse I.[10] For thus the physician has to know who are lepers and who are not through the condition of their bodies; thus too the priest has to know which statements or doctrines are heretical and which are catholic; thus the goldsmith or silversmith has to know about metals; thus too the expert or teacher of law has to know about loans and deposits and other such civil acts. For about such matters the ruler as such is not required to know, although according to the law, if the law be perfect, the nature of the various statements, deeds, and acts must be ascertained through those who teach or practice the various disciplines.[11]

6. And now I say, with reference to the question under discussion, that any person who is a teacher of the divine Scriptures, such as every priest is or ought to be, can and ought to judge, but by a judgment in the first sense, whether or not the crime of which someone is accused is heresy. Whence in Malachi, Chapter 2: "For the lips of the priest shall keep knowledge, and they shall seek the law," that is, the divine law, "at his mouth." [12] For such ought to be the priests or bishops, the successors of the apostles, to whom Christ said in Matthew, Chapter 28: "Go ye therefore and teach all nations . . . teaching them to observe all things whatsoever I have commanded you." [13] Thus too in I Timothy, Chapter 3: "He must" among other things "be a teacher," [14] that is, of the sacred law. Thus too in Titus, Chapter 1: "A bishop must hold fast the faithful word as he hath been taught, that he may be able by sound doctrine both to exhort and to convince the gainsayers. For there are many deceivers, whose mouths must be stopped." [15] With respect to the second question, as to whether or not such an act is prohibited by law, the ruler ought to ascertain this from the law,

---

[10] See above, i. xv. 8–11.

[11] This distinction between non-coercive legal experts and coercive judges is parallel to that found in the Italian communes, as Previté-Orton points out.

[12] Malachi 2:7.   [13] Matthew 28:19–20.   [14] I Timothy 3:2.

[15] Titus 1:7–11, abbreviated.

taken in its last and proper sense, in accordance with which he has to
rule by authority of the legislator. And as for the third thing which must
be known, as to whether or not the heretical word or deed has been spoken
or done by the person accused of such crime, this can be judged by both
the learned and the unlearned who are usually called "witnesses," through
their external and internal senses. And then, after these matters have
been ascertained, the ruler must deliver the judgment or sentence of conviction or acquittal, and exact or remit the penalty of the person who had
been accused of the crime.

7. For a person is not punished by the ruler solely for sinning against
divine law. For there are many mortal sins even against divine law, such as
fornication, which the human legislator knowingly permits,[16] and which
the bishop or priest does not, cannot, and should not prohibit by coercive
force. But if the heretic's sin against divine law is such as human law also
prohibits, then he is punished in this world as a sinner against human
law. For this latter sin is the precise or primary essential cause why a person
is punished in this life, for where this is given, the effect is given, and
where it is removed, so is the effect. And conversely, he who sins against
human law will be punished in the other world as sinning against divine
law, not as sinning against human law. For many things prohibited by
human law are nevertheless permitted by divine law; for example, if a
person does not repay a loan at the established date because of inability due
to accident, illness, forgetfulness, or some other obstacle, he will not be
punished for this in the other world by the coercive judge of divine law,
and yet he is justly punished for it in this world by the coercive judge of
human law. But if any person has sinned against divine law, he will be
punished in the other world regardless of whether or not his act, such as
fornication, is permitted by human law; and hence sinning against divine
law is the primary essential cause, which in philosophy is usually called the
cause "as such," [17] of the punishment which is inflicted for and in the
status of the future world; since where this cause is given, the effect is
given, and where it is removed, so is the effect.

8. Therefore, the judgment over heretics, schismatics, and other infidels,
and the power to coerce them, to exact temporal punishment from them,
and to assign the pecuniary mulcts to oneself or to the community, and

---

[16] See Thomas Aquinas *Summa theologica* II. ii. qu.69. a.2. ad 1, where the same illustration is given, with, however, an explanation not in Marsilius' legalistic terms but rather by
reference to the extent to which the virtues are had by the great majority of men, for whom
human law is made. See also *ibid*. II. i. qu.98. a.1. Resp., where the difference between the
commands of human and divine law is explained by the difference between their ends. See also
Vol. I, pp. 109–10.

[17] See Aristotle *Posterior Analytics* i. 5. 74a 12. See Vol. I, p. 48, n. 17.

not to anyone else, belongs only to the ruler by authority of the human legislator, and not to any priest or bishop, even though it be divine law which is sinned against. For although the latter is indeed a law in its relation to men in and for the status of the present life, yet it is not a law in the last sense as having coercive power over anyone in this world; this is evident from the preceding chapter and Chapter V of this discourse. It is, however, a law in the third sense, as was made clear in Chapter X of Discourse I.[18] And the priests are its judges, in the first sense of "judge," in this world, and they have no coercive power, as was shown in Chapter V of this discourse and in the preceding chapter by the words of the Apostle, Ambrose, Hilary, and Chrysostom. For if the priests were coercive judges or rulers over heretics because the latter sin against the discipline of which the priests are the teachers and the performers of certain operations upon others in accordance with it, then in similar fashion the goldsmith would be coercive judge and ruler over the counterfeiter of golden works, which is quite absurd; similarly too the physician would coerce those who act wrongly with respect to the art of medicine; and there would be as many rulers as there are functions or offices of the state against which it is possible to sin.[19] But the impossibility or uselessness of this multiplicity of rulers was shown in Chapter XVII of Discourse I. For persons who committed such sins against the offices of the state would not on that account be coerced or punished, unless something else intervened, namely, a command of human law or of the legislator. For if such sins were not prohibited by human law, then those who committed them would not be punished.

9. What we have said may be seen in a familiar example. Suppose that human law prohibits lepers from dwelling among the other citizens; will the physician, who alone can judge of their illness in accordance with his discipline, that is, as to whether or not they are lepers, be able to exclude them from the company of others by coercive force, resting upon his own authority as a teacher of the science of medicine? The answer is certainly no. The only person who can thus exclude them is the one to whom has been entrusted the guardianship of coercive human law, namely, the ruler. For no private individual or group is allowed to judge, coerce, or punish anyone, but only the ruler. However, in order to ascertain the nature of the crimes charged, either according to the determination of the law if it deals with this, as it will if it be perfect, or by his prudence if the law is silent on this point, the ruler should use and trust the judgment of the experts in the disciplines which treat the nature of such deeds, acts, or words,

---

[18] See above, I. x. 3.   [19] See Vol. I, pp. 119–20.

such as physicians when lepers or non-lepers are concerned, and theologians in cases involving criminals, who are symbolized by lepers in the holy Scripture, according to the exposition of the saints. Similarly, the ruler ought to rely upon the goldsmith in cases concerning counterfeit metal vases, and in like manner upon those who are learned in all the other kinds of production and action. Thus, therefore, the physician of souls, that is, the priest, should judge about heretics or other infidels, but by a judgment in the first sense, that is, by distinguishing the heretical from the non-heretical word or deed. But it pertains only to the ruler by human law to judge about these matters by a judgment in the third sense, that is, by convicting or acquitting the accused parties, by inflicting temporal punishment upon those who are convicted, and by forcing them to pay such penalty; and again, only the ruler may dispose of the penalties exacted if they be in property, just like the penalties which are exacted for other crimes, in accordance with the determination of the legislator or of the human law.

10. What we have said is borne out by the Scripture in the Acts of the Apostles, Chapter 25.[20] For when the Apostle was accused by the Jews of being a heretic, although falsely, his case was investigated, tried, appealed, and settled before and by the judge who had been named by the authority of the human legislator for this matter, just as for the other contentious or civil acts.

11. The arguments to the contrary [21] may be refuted without difficulty. For when it is said that he who has knowledge about the crime of heresy ought to judge the heretic, a distinction must be drawn owing to the ambiguity of this term "judge" or "judgment"; and in one way the statement is true, that is, if these terms are taken according to their first sense; but if they are taken in their third sense, then the statement is false. And hence our conclusion is in no way refuted by this misreasoning. As for the further argument that the person against whom or against whose law the criminal sins, ought to judge the criminal and inflict the penalty and dispose of it according to his will if it be in property; this is true if the person sinned against is understood to be the judge in the third sense, and if his law which 's sinned against is taken according to the last sense of "law," as coercive; and then, when it is assumed that the heretic sins against divine law, this argument must be granted. And accordingly, the heretic will be judged by the judge, in the third sense, of that law, namely, Christ, but only in the other world, not in this one, in accordance with the decree of the

---

[20] The reference is to the proceedings against Paul before Festus, in Acts 25.
[21] See above, para. 1 of this chapter.

legislator of that law, which thus provided. And by this judge the heretic also will be given punishment or reward in accordance with his observance or transgression of the commands and counsels of the law. But no bishop or priest is such a judge of this law, that is, the divine law, but he is a judge in the first sense only, like a teacher, especially with regard to the relation of this law to men in and for the status of the present life.

Again, let us assume the truth of the major premise of this syllogism, interpreting it in the way we have said, namely, that a transgressor must be judged by the coercive judge against whom or against whose law the transgressor sins, taking "law" only in its last sense. Then we must subsume this true proposition, namely, that the heretic sins only against the judge of this world, taking "judge" in its third sense, and only against the law of which he is guardian, taking "law" also in its last and proper sense, namely, as coercive, and not against any other coercive law or judge in this world. And therefore it is only by such a law and by such a judge that the heretic must be coercively judged in this world, if the maker of this law so ordains. And it is the same judge who must exact the penalty from such transgressor, and if the penalty be in property, it is this judge who must dispose of it in the manner which the human legislator has decreed in the law. Or else the question is to be settled by showing that there is equivocation in the terms of the major premise, and therefore distinctions are needed, as in the previous misreasoning.

12. Thus, therefore, it is not legitimate to infer as a necessary conclusion that because some person has to be condemned or coercively judged as a heretic in and for this world, and punished in property or in person or both, therefore this must be done by a priest or bishop. This conclusion is not legitimate unless, as we have said, "judgment" be taken in the first sense. Nor does it follow from this that therefore the condemned heretic's material or temporal goods, which are exacted from him as full or partial penalty for the crime, ought to be disposed of by some bishop or priest; just as it does not follow that because someone has to be judged as a counterfeiter of money, therefore he must be judged by the experts in money, unless perhaps we take "judge" in the first sense, but not in the third, as coercive; and also it does not follow that the temporal goods which are exacted from the counterfeiter in punishment must be disposed of by the monetary experts, either as a group or individually. But rather he must be coercively judged by the ruler, and the penalty must be applied in the way determined by human law.

13. As for St. Ambrose's epistle,[22] it must be replied that he understood

22 See above, para. 1 of this chapter.

"judgment" in the first sense, not in the third, when he said that the crime of heresy pertained to the judgment of priests or bishops. For in the days of the primitive church, none of the bishops or pontiffs ever exercised this latter form of judgment on their own authority, although later on they advanced occasionally to such exercise as a result of certain concessions made to them by the rulers. And hence to those who consider the true origins of such exercises of authority, which now from abuse seem to have the validity and form of right, they will appear as fantastic dreams.

Let these, then, be our conclusions concerning the judge, the judgment, and the coercive power over infidels and heretics.

CHAPTER XI: ON SOME SIGNS, TESTIMONIES, AND EXAMPLES FROM BOTH CANONIC AND HUMAN WRITINGS, WHICH SHOW THE TRUTH OF THE CONCLUSIONS REACHED IN CHAPTERS IV, V, VIII, IX, AND X OF THIS DISCOURSE WITH REGARD TO THE STATUS OF BISHOPS AND OF PRIESTS GENERALLY. AND WHY CHRIST SEPARATED THEIR STATUS, THAT OF POVERTY, FROM THE STATUS OF RULERS

IN the preceding chapters having demonstrated, both by the authorities of the canonic Scripture and by evident quasi-political arguments, that to no bishop or priest or other clergyman belongs coercive jurisdiction over anyone in this world, we now wish to show the truth of this by manifest signs and testimonies. This is evident, that we do not read that Christ or any of his apostles ever or anywhere appointed a judge or vicar to exercise such coercive rule or to make such judgments. Now since it seems likely that neither he nor his apostles were ignorant or negligent of something so necessary in human society, it follows that if they had thought that this pertained to their office, and if they had wanted that it be a concern of their successors, the bishops or priests, then they would have given some command or counsel with regard to it.[1] Indeed, they did hand down the form and method of appointing spiritual ministers, bishops, priests, and deacons; and that this pertains to their office is adequately seen from the words of the Apostle in I Timothy, Chapter 3, in Titus, Chapter 1, and in many other parts of Scripture.

[1] Placing full stop after *legimus*, and comma after *videatur*.

2. But Christ separated the office of priests or bishops from that of
rulers; yet if he had wanted to, he could have exercised both the status of
ruler and the office of priest, and he could have ordained that the apostles
do likewise. But such was not his will; to the contrary, he who disposed
all things absolutely for the better, wanted these offices to be distinguished
in person and in essence, as being the more proper arrangement. For Christ
had come to teach humility and contempt for this world, as the way to
deserve eternal salvation; hence, in order that he might teach humility and
contempt for the world or for temporal things by example rather than by
words, he entered this world in the utmost humility and contempt for
temporal things, well knowing that men are taught not less but rather more
by deed or example than by words.[2] Whence Seneca wrote in his ninth
epistle: "What is to be done must be learned from him who does it."[3]
Christ, therefore, willed to be born in the utmost humility and contempt
for the world, or poverty, in order that he might teach us sooner by his
example than by words. Whence in Luke, Chapter 2: "She," namely, the
Blessed Virgin, "wrapped him in swaddling-clothes, and laid him in the
manger."[4] Notice that it was in another's house, and in a manger, which
was the place for cattle and fodder; and likewise notice that the child was
wrapped in someone else's swaddling-clothes, because the Blessed Virgin
and Joseph were pilgrims and wayfarers there. Poor was Christ born, and
poor did he live, as he grew older; hence in speaking of his poverty, he
said, in Matthew, Chapter 8, and Luke, Chapter 9: "The foxes have holes,
and the birds of the air have nests; but the Son of man hath not where to
lay his head."[5] And this condition, as the status of perfection, Christ taught
those persons to choose who, having duly observed the other commands
and counsels, wish to be his closest disciples and imitators, and especially
his successors in the office which he had come into the world to exercise.
And hence, when someone asked him, in Matthew, Chapter 19, Mark,
Chapter 10, and Luke, Chapter 18: "Good master, what shall I do to possess
eternal life? Jesus said unto him: know the commandments: Thou shalt
not kill, etc. And he said: All these have I kept from my youth up. Hearing
this, Jesus said to him: Yet lackest thou one thing," or "If thou wilt be
perfect," as it is said in Matthew, "sell all that thou hast and distribute unto
the poor, and thou shalt have treasure in heaven."[6] And again Christ said

---

[2] Omitting *tam*, and placing comma after *doceret*, with Bigongiari (p. 46).

[3] See Seneca *Epist. 98* (Lib. xvi. Epist. 3) para. 17 (ed. O. Hense, in *Opera quae supersunt*
[Leipzig, 1914], III, 486).

[4] Luke 2:7.   [5] Matthew 8:20; Luke 9:58.

[6] Matthew 19:16-21; Mark 10:17-21; Luke 18:18-22. The quotation is from Luke, the
variant from Matthew.

to his disciples, in Luke, Chapter 14: "So likewise, whosoever he be of you that forsaketh not all that he hath, he cannot be my disciple." [7]

3. See, then, that the status of poverty and contempt for the world is that which befits every perfect man, especially the disciple and successor of Christ in the pastoral office; indeed, it is almost necessary for the man who must urge upon others contempt for the world, if he wishes to succeed in his teaching or preaching. For if such a person who teaches those whom he addresses to spurn riches and governmental office, nevertheless himself possesses and thirsts for these things, then he manifestly refutes his own words by his actions. Hence Chrysostom wrote against such persons in his book *On Compunction of the Heart:* "To say and not to do, not only is of no profit, but is a great evil. For the person who carefully composes his speech and is negligent in his life, is greatly to be condemned." [8] And the foremost of the philosophers echoes this in the *Ethics,* Book X, Chapter 1, saying: "For when they," that is, words, "disagree with what is perceived," that is, the speaker's deeds, which are perceived, "they destroy the truth of the speaker," that is, of the one who composes speeches. And shortly after he adds: "For when they," that is, words, "are in harmony with deeds, they are believed." [9] And hence, because he who knew how best to do all things, that is, Christ, wanted that words should be credible to those who are taught contempt for the world and the rejection and avoidance of carnal vanities and pleasures, he urged that deeds should conform to words. Hence in Matthew, Chapter 5, he spoke as follows to all the future teachers of such matters, in the person of the apostles: "Let your light thus shine before men," that is, your teaching, which is likened to light. "Thus," indeed, "let it shine so that they may see your good deeds." Whereon the gloss: "I look for deeds so that they may be seen, and so that teachings may thus be confirmed"; [10] for otherwise words and teachings are little believed. Whence on the words in Matthew, Chapter 10: "Do not possess gold or silver," the gloss, stating the reason for this, says: "If they possessed these, they would seem to be preaching for the sake not of salvation but of riches." [11]

4. For they who are teachers or pastors of others, and who possess such riches, do more to destroy men's faith and devotion by their contrary deeds and examples than they do to strengthen them by their words, for these

[7] Luke 14:33.   [8] Chrysostom *De compunctione* I. 10 (PG 47. 410).

[9] Aristotle *Nicomachean Ethics* x. 1. 1172a 36 ff. Marsilius reads *condenti* instead of *contempti,* which is William of Moerbeke's translation of Aristotle's καταφρονούμενοι. Hence, if the translation of Marsilius were faithful to Aristotle, it should read "and they are despised" after "truth," and "of the speaker" should be omitted.

[10] Matthew 5:16, and *Glossa ordinaria, ad loc.*

[11] Matthew 10:9, and *Glossa ordinaria, ad loc.*

latter are manifestly contradicted by their deeds, which men heed more than they do words. And it is greatly to be feared that the evil examples furnished by these men's deeds will finally make the faithful give up all hope of the future world. For what almost all the ministers of the church do— the bishops or priests and the other clergymen, but most obviously those who occupy the greater thrones of the church—is such that they seem in no way to believe in God's future judgment in the other world. For if the future just judgment of God in the world to come is indeed believed in by most of the Roman pontiffs and their cardinals and the other priests or bishops, who have been given the care of men's souls and put in charge of distributing ecclesiastic temporal goods to the poor, and similarly by all the rest, deacons and clergy, then by what conscience in accordance with God —let them answer, I beg—do they seize or steal, at every opportunity, all the temporal goods they can, which devout believers have bequeathed for the sustenance of gospel ministers and other poor persons, and donate or bequeath them to their relatives, or to any other persons not in need, obviously despoiling the poor thereby? And again—let them answer, I beg— by what conscience in accordance with the Christian religion do they consume the goods of the poor on so many unnecessary things—horses, estates, banquets, and other vanities and pleasures, open and concealed— when, according to the Apostle in the first epistle to Timothy, last chapter,[12] they ought to be content with food and shelter for ministering the gospel?

5. I pass over their corrupt methods of distributing ecclesiastic offices and benefices or temporalities. For the distributors or their intermediaries, ministers of Simon Magus, are motivated by the desire to obtain the favor or good will of wealthy laymen, or are given bribes, if it be fair to say this, and hence, as is obvious to everyone, ecclesiastic offices and benefices are bestowed upon ignoramuses, criminals, children, strangers, troublemakers, and persons who are clearly idiots. Such is the practice despite the command of the Apostle, in I Timothy, Chapter 3, that officials of the church must be known to be proved and perfect in their life or morals and in their doctrine. Whence the Apostle writes: "And he," that is, the priest or bishop, "must have a good report of them that are without"; how much more of them that are within the church? and a little below: "Likewise must the deacons be grave. And let these also be first proved; then let them use the office of deacon, being found blameless."[13] And yet it can be properly said that most of these men are indeed "proved," as the world knows, for they are proved with respect to their ability at bribing and soliciting.

[12] I Timothy 6:8.   [13] I Timothy 3:7, 8, 10.

6. But rather than attempt to enumerate every one of their corrupt practices, which would be impossible or at any rate very difficult, we shall make a general statement concerning the acts of almost all priests or bishops and other ministers of the temple. Invoking Christ's judgment if we lie, we testify before him that these bishops and almost all other priests in modern times practice in almost every instance the opposites of the gospel teachings whose observance they preach to others. For they have a burning desire for pleasures, vanities, temporal possessions, and secular rulership, and they pursue and attain these objectives with all their energies, not by rightful means, but by wrongdoing, hidden and open. And yet Christ and his true imitators the apostles spurned these things and taught other men to spurn them, especially if they are to preach before others the gospel of contempt for worldly things.

7. For if Christ had wanted to, if he had thought it proper for a preacher, he could have held the status of ruler in this world and could similarly have suffered in that status. But he fled to the mountain in order to reject and to teach the rejection of such a status, as we showed above in Chapter IV of this discourse from John, Chapter 6. For not this status befits men who preach contempt for it, but rather the status of subjects and of humble men, such as both Christ and his apostles held in this world. On the other hand, the status of external poverty and humility does not befit the ruler, for he should have a status which good subjects will respect and bad ones fear, and through which he will be able to use coercion, if necessary, upon rebellious transgressors of the laws; this he could not well do if he held the status of poverty and humility. And for this reason the preacher's office does not befit the ruler. For if the ruler were to urge upon the people the status of poverty and humility, and if he were to counsel turning the other cheek when smitten, and giving a cloak to the stealer of one's tunic rather than suing him,[14] such counsels would not readily be believed when spoken by the ruler, because by the status which befits him and which he bears he would deny his own words. Moreover, it would be inappropriate for the ruler to give and observe such counsels. For inasmuch as it is his function to punish wrongdoers even when those who suffer wrong do not demand that such punishment be given; it follows that if he were to preach that injuries should be forgiven he would furnish wrongdoers with an opportunity for further crime, and persons who were offended or wronged would come to question or to lose faith in the enforcement of justice. This was

[14] See Matthew 5:40. For the contrast between Marsilius' interpretation of the relation of the Sermon on the Mount to secular values, and that of Aquinas and others, see Vol. I, pp. 81-82.

why Christ, who always disposed all things for the best, wanted the offices of ruler and priest not to be joined in the same person, but rather to be separated. And this seems to be the explicit conviction of St. Bernard in his treatise addressed to Pope Eugene, *On Consideration,* Book II, Chapter 4, where he writes as follows: "Go, then, if you dare, and usurp either the apostolate if you are a lord or lordship if you are an apostle. You are plainly prohibited from having both. If you wish to have both at once, you shall lose both. In any case, do not think you are excepted from the number of those about whom God complained in these words: They have reigned, but not by me: they have been princes, and I knew not." [15]

8. What we have said is borne out by the decrees or histories of the Roman pontiffs. For these pontiffs there inscribed and assented to a certain privilege of the Roman emperor Constantine, whereby he granted to St. Sylvester, the Roman pontiff, coercive jurisdiction over all the churches in the world and over all other priests or bishops. And since all the Roman popes, as well as the other priests or bishops, admit that this grant was valid, they must consequently concede that the same Constantine originally had this coercive jurisdiction over them, especially since no such jurisdiction over any clergyman or layman is known to belong to the pope by virtue of the words of Scripture.[16] And this is what St. Bernard explicitly says in his epistle to Eugene *On Consideration,* Book IV, Chapter 4; for he there writes: "This is Peter, whom no one ever saw bedecked with gems or silks or garments of gold, or mounted on a white horse, or attended by a soldier, or guarded by pugnacious servants. Yet even without these he considered himself sufficiently well equipped to observe the commandment: 'If you love me, feed my sheep.' For in these things," that is, secular splendor and powers, "you have succeeded not Peter, but Constantine." [17] Therefore, the office of rulers is not the office of priests as such, nor conversely; but let it suffice to have reviewed in this way the difference between them.

---

[15] St. Bernard *De consideratione* II. vi. 11 (PL 182. 748). See above, II. iv. 13.

[16] The famous Donation of Constantine was included in Pseudo-Isidore's collection, and then in part in Gratian's *Decretum,* Pars I. dist. 96. cap. 13, 14. See also *Corp. jur. can., Sext.* Lib. I. Tit. 6. cap. 17.

[17] St. Bernard *De consideratione* IV. iii. 6 (PL 182. 776). The citation is from John 21:17.

CHAPTER XII: ON THE DIFFERENTIATION OF THE
MEANINGS OF CERTAIN TERMS NECESSARY FOR THE
DETERMINATION OF QUESTIONS CONCERNING THE
STATUS OF SUPREME POVERTY

WE have thus shown in outline that Christ and his wayfarers the
apostles taught and maintained the status of poverty and humility.
But now since the faithful must believe it as certain that all the teachings or
counsels of Christ and his apostles in some way make men deserving of
eternal life, we must accordingly inquire into the poverty of Christ and
his apostles, its nature, quality, and degree, in order that it may not be
obscure to wayfarers who wish to imitate them.

2. Undertaking this inquiry, then, we shall first discuss the nature of
what is called "poverty" or "being poor," and in how many senses the term
is used; and similarly with respect to "being rich." For these seem to be
opposed to one another sometimes as habit and privation, sometimes as
contraries.[1] Then we shall differentiate each of these terms into its various
senses, and shall give their definitions, so that if poverty have any merit,
and there be an order of relative perfection among its various kinds, the
supreme or first of these kinds may be made clear to us. Now all men
call a person "rich" when he has lawful or rightful power or ownership or
possession of temporal things, which are called "riches," whether owned
in private or in common or in both ways; and on the other hand, a
person is called "poor" when he lacks such goods. Hence, in order that
the doctrine which we wish to expound may not be rendered ambiguous by the varied usages of certain of the terms mentioned above, which
we shall have to employ in our discussion, we shall first distinguish their
meanings or senses. These terms are: "right," "ownership," "possession,"
"private," "common," "rich," and "poor."

3. We shall begin by distinguishing the meanings of "right" (*jus*), since
we shall need these in the distinctions and definitions of the other terms,
and not conversely. [i] "Right," then, in one of its senses means law taken
in the third and last sense of "law," which we discussed in Chapter X of
Discourse I.[2] This is twofold, one human, the other divine, and the latter

---

[1] On these two modes of "opposition," see Aristotle *Categories* 9. 11b 33 ff. Cf. also above,
I. xvii. 23; and Introduction, above, p. lxxi, n. 50.

[2] This was really the fourth sense of "law." See above, I. x. 3–4.

at a particular time and in a particular way comes under the last meaning of law, as has been said above.[3] The nature and quality of these laws, how they agree and how they differ, have been sufficiently discussed in Chapters VIII and IX of this discourse. But reconsidering them again in relation to our present purpose, let us say that these laws agree in this respect first of all, that each is a command or prohibition or permission of acts whose nature it is to emerge through the control of the human mind. But the laws differ in that the human is coercive in this world over those who transgress it, while the second, the divine, is not coercive in this world, but in the future world only. The word "command" also is used in two senses. In one sense it is used actively, referring to the act of the commander; it is in this sense that we say that the expressed will of a man who holds power, such as a king or other ruler, is a command. In another sense, "command" refers to what is willed by the act of the commander; in this sense we say that the servant has done the command of the master—not that the servant has done the master's act, which is to command or order, but that the servant has done what was willed by the master's act or command. And therefore, whenever this word "command" refers to the commander, it means the same as the act of commanding; whenever it refers to the subject, it means the same as what is willed by the act of commanding, and is then used passively.[4]

This word "command," then, taken actively and in the general sense, means the legislator's ordinance or statute, both affirmative and negative, obliging the transgressor to punishment. But in modern usage it is taken for an affirmative statute. For usage has brought it about that an affirmative statute does not have a specific name of its own, but has kept the general name of "command"; but a negative statute does have a specific name of its own, for it is called a "prohibition."

I call an "affirmative statute" one which orders something to be done; a "negative statute," one which orders something not to be done. If such an ordinance, which obliges the transgressor to punishment, be affirmative, it is called a "command"; if it be negative, and also thus obliges, it is called a "prohibition." Now "prohibition" is used in two senses, actively and passively, as is "command." These two ordinances, which oblige transgressors to punishment, are usually expressed in laws, either in their own proper

---

[3] See above, I. x. 7; II. viii. 5; II. ix. 3.

[4] The reason for Marsilius' emphasis on this distinction between the active and passive modes of law is that it is important for his project of distinguishing divine from human law. For the two laws may agree when viewed "passively," since what is commanded or prohibited in the one may also be commanded or prohibited in the other; but they differ when viewed "actively," since they have different "legislators" or "commanders" or efficient causes. See especially *Defensor minor* xiii. 5. (ed. C. K. Brampton [Birmingham, 1922], p. 40).

species or in a similar or analogous one.[5] But in another and stricter sense, "command" and "prohibition" are used in divine law to refer only to that affirmative or negative statute which obliges the transgressor to eternal punishment. It is in this sense that these words are used by theologians when they say that commands are "necessary for salvation," that is, that observance of them is necessary, if one is to be saved. Whence in Luke, Chapter 18: "If thou wilt enter into life, keep the commandments," [6] that is, the commands.

4. But there are certain other ordinances, both affirmative and negative, which are expressed or only implied in the laws, and which, whether referring to the same act or to a different one, do not oblige the man who does or omits the act to punishment. Very many acts are the objects of such ordinances, such as the performance or omission of an act of liberality. And it is such acts which are properly said to be "permitted by law," although this word "permission" is sometimes taken in a general sense to refer to statutes which oblige to punishment. For everything which the law commands to be done, it permits to be done, although not conversely; so too, what the law prohibits to be done, it permits not to be done. And again, of these permitted acts, taking "permitted" in its proper sense as that which does not oblige to punishment, some are meritorious according to divine law and are called "counsels," while others which are not thus meritorious are given the unqualified name of "permissions." And these terms, thus taken in their proper sense, are again used in two ways, actively and passively, as are prohibitions and commands. But these for the most part are not given specific expression in the laws, particularly in human laws, because their number is so large and a general ordinance concerning them is sufficient. For everything which is not commanded or prohibited by the law is understood to be permitted by the ordinance of the legislator. A "command" in accordance with the law, then, in its proper sense is an affirmative statute obliging its transgressor to punishment; a "prohibition" in its proper sense is a negative statute obliging its transgressor to punishment; a "permission" in its proper sense is an ordinance of the legislator obliging no one to punishment. We shall henceforth use these terms in these proper senses.[7]

[5] That is, an act may be commanded (or prohibited) in a law which deals either specifically with that act or with acts similar thereto.

[6] While the reference is to Luke 18:18, the passage cited is really Matthew 19:17.

[7] Marsilius' "formal" definitions of command, prohibition, and permission in terms solely of their respective sanctions are in keeping with his definition of law as coercive command; see above, I. x. 4, 5; II. viii. 4. See also Corp. jur. civ., Digest I. iii. 7. Thomas Aquinas, on the other hand, defines these concepts "materially," i.e., in terms of the ethical quality of the acts which are their objects or contents. See Summa theologica II. I. qu.92. a.2; qu.108. a.1. Resp.; a.4. Resp.; II. II. qu.124. a.3. ad 1; qu.184. a.3. See also Vol. I, pp. 135–36.

5. From the above, it can readily be seen what is meant by the term "lawful"; for everything which is done in accordance with the command or permission of the law, or which is omitted in accordance with the prohibition or permission of the law, is lawfully done or omitted, and can be called "lawful," while its opposite or contrary is "unlawful."

6. From the above, we can also see what is usually meant by the term "equitable" (*fas*). For in one sense the equitable is the same as the lawful, so that the two are used convertibly. In another sense, the equitable is that which the legislator is reasonably presumed to have permitted in some case, although such an act is generally or regularly prohibited; as, for example, it is equitable to pass through another's field sometimes, or to handle another's property without the owner's express consent, although it is not "right" taken regularly in any of the senses given above. For the handling of another's property is regularly prohibited; yet it is equitable in the case where the owner is reasonably presumed to give his consent, even though he does not expressly give it; for which reason there is sometimes need of equity (*epieikeia*) in such cases.[8]

Thus, then, in one sense right is the same as law, divine or human, or what is commanded or prohibited or permitted according to these laws.

7. There is also another division of right, and properly of human right, into natural and civil. Natural right (*jus naturale*), according to Aristotle in the fourth book of the *Ethics,* the treatise on justice, is that statute of the legislator with respect to which almost all men agree that it is honorable and should be observed.[9] Examples are that God must be worshiped, parents must be honored, children must be reared by their parents up to a certain age, no one should be injured, injuries must be lawfully repulsed, and the like.[10] Although these depend upon human enactment, they are metaphorically called "natural" rights because in all regions they are in the same way believed to be lawful and their opposites unlawful, just as the

---

[8] See above, I. xiv. 7. See also Aristotle *Nichomachean Ethics* v. 10. 1137a 32 ff.

[9] See Aristotle *Nicomachean Ethics* v. 7. 1134b. 19. Marsilius' definition is, however, quite different from that of Aristotle, who defines natural justice as "that which has everywhere the same validity, and does not depend upon men's thinking one way or another." Aristotle's natural justice thus has no such intrinsic connection with either positive enactment ("statute of the legislator") or universal agreement among men as has Marsilius'. See Vol. I, pp. 147–49.

[10] While similar examples of "natural law" are found throughout the medieval tradition, one important source goes back to Cicero, who develops the following six-fold list of "natural laws": "religionem, pietatem, gratiam, vindicationem, observantiam, veritatem" (*Rhetorici libri de inventione* II. xxii. 65). Albert the Great discusses Cicero's list in detail, and presents the following summary of it, which should be compared with Marsilius' examples: "deos verendos, parentes honorandos, socialiter vivendum cum aequalibus, melioribus meliorem cultum impendendum, unumquodque sicut se habet esse determinandum, et contrarium esse repellendum" (*Ethica* Lib. v. Ti. iii. cap. iii, in *Opera omnia,* ed. A. Borgnet, VII [Paris, 1891], 368).

acts of natural things which are devoid of will are everywhere uniform, like fire, which "burns here just as it does in Persia." [11]

8. However, there are some men who define natural right as the dictate of right reason in practical matters, which they place under divine right; [12] and consequently everything done in accordance with divine law and in accordance with the counsel of right reason is lawful in an absolute sense; but not everything done in accordance with human laws, since in some things the latter fall away from right reason.[13] But the word "natural" is used equivocally here and above.[14] For there are many things which are in accordance with the dictate of right reason, but which are not agreed upon as honorable by all nations, namely, those things which are not self-evident to all, and consequently not acknowledged by all.[15] So too there are some commands, prohibitions, or permissions in accordance with divine law which do not agree in this respect with human law; but since many cases of this are well known, I have omitted to cite examples for the sake of brevity.

9. And hence too, some things are lawful according to human law which are not lawful according to divine law, and conversely. However, what is lawful and what unlawful in an absolute sense must be viewed according to divine law rather than human law, when these disagree in their commands, prohibitions, or permissions.[16]

10. [ii] "Right" is used in a second sense to refer to every controlled human act, power, or acquired habit, internal or external, both immanent and transient or crossing over into some external thing or something pertaining thereto, like its use or usufruct, acquisition, holding, saving, or exchanging, and so on, whenever these are in conformity with right taken in its first sense. What the use or usufruct of a thing is, together with the other lawful or rightful ways of handling things, we shall assume for the present from the science of civil arts.

It is in this sense that we usually say: "This is someone's right," when he wishes or handles some thing in a manner which is in conformity with right taken in the first sense. Hence, such wish or handling is called right because it conforms to the command, prohibition, or permission of right;

[11] This illustration is from Aristotle *Nicomachean Ethics* v. 7. 1134b 25.

[12] The tradition to which Marsilius refers goes back at least to Cicero *De re publica* III. xxii. 33. See also *Corp. jur. civ., Instit.* I. ii. 11; Isidore of Seville *Etymologiae* v. ii. 1 (PL 82. 198); *Corp. jur. can., Decret. Gratiani* Pars I. dist. 1. See Vol. I, p. 149, n. 15.

[13] See Vol. I, p. 149 and n. 16.   [14] See Vol. I, pp. 150–51.

[15] See in this connection Thomas Aquinas' distinction, in his discussion of natural law, between two senses of "self-evident": "in itself" and "in relation to us," in *Summa theologica* II. I. qu.94. a.2. Resp. See also Duns Scotus *Opus Oxoniense* Lib. III. dist. 37. nn. 3–5; Lib. IV. dist. 17. n. 3.

[16] See Vol. I, pp. 135, 151, 162–64.

just as a column is called right (*dextra*) or left because it is situated nearer to the right or the left side of an animal. Right, then, taken in this second sense, is none other than what is willed by the active command, prohibition, or permission of the legislator, and this is what we called above the passive meaning of these three words.[17] And this too is what we previously called lawful.[18]

11. [*iii*] In another sense this term "right" means the sentence or judgments made by judges in accordance with the law or with right taken in its first sense. It is in this sense that men usually say: "The judge or ruler has done or rendered right to someone," when he has convicted or acquitted someone by a legal sentence.

12. [*iv*] "Right" is also used to refer to an act or habit of particular justice; in this sense we say that he wishes right or justice who wishes what is equal or proportional in exchanges or distributions.[19]

13. Next we must distinguish the meanings or senses of "ownership" or "lordship" (*dominium*).[20] [*i*] In its strict sense, this term means the principal power to lay claim to something rightfully acquired in accordance with right taken in its first sense; that is, the power of a person who knows about this and does not dissent therefrom, and who wants to allow no one else to handle that thing without his, the owner's, express consent, while he owns it. This power is none other than the actual or habitual will thus to have the rightfully acquired thing, as we have said; and it is called the "right" of some person because it conforms to right taken in the first sense, just as we have said that a column is right or left when it is nearer to the right or to the left side of an animal.

14. [*ii*] Again, this term is more commonly used for the aforesaid power, whether it be only over a thing, or only over the use or the usufruct of the thing, or over all of these at once.

15. [*iii*] The same term is also used for the aforesaid power, but as belonging to a person who does not know of it or consent to it but who yet does not explicitly dissent therefrom or renounce it. In this sense, an infant or a person who is absent or generally unaware thereof, but yet capable, can acquire, by himself or through another, a thing or something

---

[17] See above, para. 3.   [18] See above, para. 5.

[19] This concept of particular justice is derived from Aristotle, who distinguishes it from universal or political justice, in that the latter comprises all the virtues as prescribed or practiced in the political context, whereas particular justice is the special virtue of "fairness" or "equality" (*Nicomachean Ethics* v. 1–2. 1129a 32 ff.). Particular justice is divided into rectificatory and distributive, which regulate, respectively, exchanges or transactions and distributions of various common goods. The basis of the former is arithmetical equality; of the latter, geometric proportion (*ibid*. v. 2–5. 1130b 30 ff.). See above, Introduction, p. lxxxiv.

[20] See above, Introduction, pp. lxxxviii–xc.

pertaining thereto together with the ownership of it or the power to claim it before a coercive judge from any person who steals or wants to steal it. And we have said that this power belongs to a person who does not explicitly dissent; for one who does explicitly dissent, or who renounces a thing or something pertaining thereto, does not acquire such things, or ownership of them, or the power to lay claim to them. For anyone can lawfully renounce a right which is offered to him in accordance with human laws, nor is anyone compelled by any law to accept, against his will, the benefit of a right.[21] But the afore-mentioned kinds of ownership are legal, for they are acquired or may be acquired by ordainment of the law or of its legislator, and by men's choice.[22]

16. [*iv*] Again, this term "ownership" is used to refer to the human will or freedom in itself with its organic executive or motive power unimpeded. For it is through these that we are capable of certain acts and their opposites. It is for this reason too that man alone among the animals is said to have ownership or control of his acts; this control belongs to him by nature, it is not acquired through an act of will or choice.[23]

17. Next we must distinguish the meanings of "possession." [*i*] Taken broadly, it signifies in one sense the same as ownership in either of its first three senses, or some temporal thing in relation to a person who has and wishes to have it in the manner defined in the first two senses of ownership. Whence in Genesis, Chapter 13: "He was very rich in possession of gold and silver"; [24] and in Chapter 17 of the same book: "And I will give unto thee, and to thy seed after thee, all the land of Canaan, for an everlasting possession." [25]

18. [*ii*] In another sense, and more strictly, "possession" means the afore-mentioned ownership together with the actual corporeal handling of the thing or of its use or usufruct in the present or in the future; it is in this sense that this word is most often used in the science of civil acts.

19. [*iii*] Again, this term means the lawful corporeal handling of a thing whether it belongs to oneself or even to someone else; as in Acts, Chapter 4: "Neither said any of them that aught of the things which he possessed was his own; but they had all things common." [26]

20. [*iv*] "Possession" is also used, although improperly, to refer to the

---

[21] See *Corp. jur. civ., Digest* L. xvii. 69.

[22] The distinction herein implied between ownership and use, which is developed in the following two chapters, while it goes back to the earliest discussions of the theory of property, is set forth in terms similar to Marsilius' in the bull of Pope Nicholas III, *Exiit qui seminat* (Aug. 14, 1279, *Corp. jur. can., Sext.* Lib. v. Tit. 12. cap. 3). There may also be an influence of Ubertino da Casale, as Previté-Orton suggests.

[23] Cf. above, II. viii. 3.   [24] Genesis 13:2.   [25] *Ibid.* 17:8.

[26] Acts 4:32.

unlawful corporeal holding of a thing by oneself or through someone else, in the present or in the future.

21. And now we have to distinguish the meanings of the terms "private" or "proper" (*proprium*) and "common" (*commune*). [*i*] In one sense, "proper" or "property" is used to refer to ownership taken in its first meaning; it is in this sense that the term is used in the science of civil acts.

22. [*ii*] Again, more broadly, it is used for ownership taken in both its first and its second senses; this is the sense in which it is used by theologians, and also in much of the holy Scripture.

23. [*iii*] These words "private" or "proper" and "property" are further used among theologians to refer to the individuality of a person or thing or something pertaining thereto, when it belongs to one person alone, not with any other person. For it is in this sense that theologians take "private," contrasting it with "common," when they ask whether it is more perfect, or more deserving of eternal life, to have temporal things as private property, that is, individually, or to have such things in common with another person or persons.

24. [*iv*] Again, this term "proper" or "property" is used to refer to an accident which inheres essentially in a subject. Philosophers use the term in this sense, but more familiarly in the sense in which it means that which is convertible with the subject.[27]

25. Now the term "common," insofar as it is pertinent to our purpose, is taken in the senses opposite to the last two meanings of "private" or "proper."

26. It now remains for us to distinguish the meanings of the terms "poor" and "rich." [*i*] Most commonly, the term "rich" means a person who lawfully has an overabundance of temporal things, called "riches," for any particular time at once, present and future.

27. [*ii*] In another sense, "rich" means a person who lawfully has the aforesaid things only in sufficient quantities for any particular time at once, present and future.

28. Again, "rich" taken in a more proper sense has two other meanings. [*iii*] According to one, it means a person who has the aforesaid things in overabundance, as we have said, and who wishes thus to have them. [*iv*] According to the other, "rich" means a person who has the aforesaid things in sufficient amounts only as we said in the second meaning, and who wishes thus to have them.

29. "Poor" in some senses is used as the privative opposite of the first two meanings of "rich." [*i*] In one sense, it signifies a person who lacks

[27] See Aristotle *Topics* I. 5. 102a 17 ff.

only an overabundance of temporal things. [*ii*] In another sense, it signifies a person who does not even have a sufficient amount for any time at once.

30. [*iii*] In a third sense, "poor" is used as the contrary opposite of "rich," first to designate a person who freely wishes to be lacking in an abundance of temporal goods for any time.

31. [*iv*] In a fourth sense it signifies a person who does not wish to have even a sufficient amount of goods for any time at once, present and future, but who freely wishes to lack them at some time.

We must note, furthermore, that "rich" in the second and fourth senses is the same as "poor" in the first and third senses. Hence, not every sense of the term "poverty" or "poor" is opposed indifferently to every sense of the term "rich."

32. Nor must we fail to see that of voluntarily poor persons there are some who give up temporal goods for an honorable purpose and in appropriate manner, but there are others who seem to give up such things not for such a purpose, but for the sake of empty glory or for some other mundane error.

33. And it must also be noted that of the temporal things which are called "riches," there are some which, by their own nature and by men's common agreement, are consumable in a single act or use, like foods, beverages, medicines, and other such; and there are others which naturally endure to subserve more than one use, like field and house, axe and clothing, horse or servant.

Although the terms given above may perhaps have other meanings, we think that we have enumerated those which are more familiar and more pertinent for our purposes. Properly to distinguish and describe or define them is difficult because their usage varies among different authors and even in the same author, and there is also variation in different places and times. For "almost every word has many meanings," as it is said in the first book of the treatise *On Generation*.[28]

---

[28] Aristotle *De generatione et corruptione* i. 6. 322b 30.

CHAPTER XIII: ON THE STATUS OF SUPREME POV-
ERTY, WHICH IS USUALLY CALLED EVANGELICAL
PERFECTION; AND THAT THIS STATUS WAS HELD
BY CHRIST AND HIS APOSTLES

HAVING thus distinguished the senses and meanings of the terms given above, we shall now infer some conclusions. The first of these is that no one can lawfully handle, individually or in common with others, some temporal thing, whether his own or someone else's, or something pertaining thereto, like the use or the usufruct, without right or without having a right to the thing or to something pertaining thereto—taking "right" in its first and second senses. For every deed which is not commanded or permitted to be done by right is not lawful, as everyone can clearly see from the definition of "lawful"; nor must we linger to prove this, since it is almost self-evident to all men.

2. The second conclusion which we can infer from what we have said is that one can handle a thing, or something pertaining thereto, lawfully according to one law, such as the divine, and unlawfully according to another, such as the human; and likewise conversely; and again, one can do the same thing lawfully or unlawfully according to each law. This is not difficult to see, since the commands, prohibitions, and permissions in these laws sometimes differ and disagree with one another and sometimes agree. Consequently, when one acts in accordance with the command or permission of one kind of law, one acts lawfully according to it; but if this act is prohibited by the other kind of law, one does it unlawfully according to that other law; if it is permitted by both kinds of law, one acts lawfully according to both. But if it is prohibited by both, one does it unlawfully according to both laws. Whether anything which is permitted to be done or omitted by divine law, is commanded or prohibited by human law, and conversely, still remains to be considered; for it does not pertain to our present inquiry. It is, however, certain that many things are permitted by human law, like fornication, drunkenness, and other sins, which are prohibited by divine law.[1]

3. And now I wish to show that even apart from having any ownership, in the first three senses, of any temporal thing or of anything pertaining thereto, a person may lawfully handle it in private (in the third sense of

[1] Cf. above, II. x. 7.

"private") or even possess it in common with someone else (understanding the third sense of "possession"), and also lawfully destroy it. This is so, I maintain, regardless of whether that thing, or something pertaining thereto, be consumable in some one use or not; whether it be private to him (in the third sense of "private") or be common to him with another person or persons; whether it be his own, that is, rightfully acquired by him, or belong to someone else who, having rightfully (in the first sense) acquired it, consents to his handling it.

I demonstrate this proposition as follows. That temporal thing (or something pertaining thereto) which a person handles or holds apart from having ownership of it (in the first three senses of ownership), in accordance with divine law or human law or both, he can handle and destroy lawfully, apart from having ownership of it (in the above senses) whether in private or in common with others. But, regardless of whether a thing (or something pertaining thereto) be his own or belong to someone else who consents to his handling it, a person can, in accordance with these laws, handle the thing, as has been said, apart from having the aforementioned ownership of it. Therefore he can lawfully handle the thing without having ownership of it.[2]

The first proposition of this deduction is self-evident from the definition of "lawful." The second I prove by an argument taken from induction, first with regard to a thing which belongs to a person privately or in common with someone else, or which he has rightfully acquired through his own act or someone else's, as by gift or legacy, by hunting, or fishing, or by some other lawful labor or deed of his. For suppose that a person has thus acquired a thing. It is then certain that he can use and handle it in accordance with the laws, since acquisition of a thing in the aforesaid ways is in accordance with the law, as is plain from induction. Also it is clear that anyone who has the capacity can lawfully renounce a right introduced on his behalf, since, according to human and divine law, a benefit is not bestowed on an unwilling person.[3] Therefore, a person who can by his own or by another's deed acquire ownership of a thing, or of its use, will be able to renounce such ownership. Since, therefore, the same person, if he wants to, acquires both the power lawfully to use a thing and the power

---

[2] This argument involves an inference not from use "apart from" (*absque*) ownership to use "without" (*sine*) ownership, as Previté-Orton says (his edition, p. 224, n. 1), but rather from what can be done "in accordance with divine and human law" to what can be done "lawfully." The argument depends upon the definition of *lawful* given in II. xii. 5. The *simplex facti usus* and other concepts here indicated are found in the bull of Nicholas III referred to above, II. xii. 15, n. 22, *Exiit qui seminat* (Aug. 14, 1279, *Corp. jur. can., Sext. Lib.* v. Tit. 12. cap. 3).

[3] See *Corp. jur. civ., Digest* L. xvii. 69.

to claim it and to prohibit another person from it, he can lawfully renounce the power of laying claim to the thing (or something pertaining thereto) or of prohibiting another therefrom (which power is none other than ownership taken in its first three legal senses), without renouncing the power of using the thing (or something pertaining thereto). This latter power falls under right taken in its second sense, and is by some men called "simple use of a thing" (*simplex facti usus*) without the right of using (*jus utendi*), by "right of using" meaning "ownership" in any of its three senses given above.

4. Moreover, a thing which belongs to no one (*in nullius bonis est*) a person can lawfully use in accordance with the laws; but when someone has renounced the power to lay claim to a thing and to prohibit another person therefrom, that thing can then belong to no one; therefore a person can lawfully use it. Since, therefore, a person who renounces the aforesaid power does not have the aforesaid ownership of the thing, it is apparent that one can lawfully handle and use a thing apart from having any of the aforesaid legal ownership.

5. Again, those things are separate from each other, of which one can for any time be given up by lawful vow, and the other not. But the aforesaid ownership of a thing, or the power to lay claim to and prohibit from a temporal thing or something pertaining thereto, can be given up for any time by lawful vow; while the lawful having or simple use of a thing cannot by lawful vow be given up for any time. Therefore these two cases are properly separate from each other. The first proposition of this deduction is self-evident from the definition of "lawful"; for the same thing cannot at once be lawful and unlawful according to the same law. The second proposition I shall prove with respect to each part. And first, that to give up for any time the aforesaid ownership by vow is lawful: for that vow is lawful which can be derived from the counsel of Christ. But such giving up is what Christ counseled, when in Matthew, Chapter 20, he said: "And every one that hath forsaken house or lands . . . for my name's sake, shall receive an hundredfold, and shall inherit everlasting life." [4] The same counsel is to be found in Matthew, Chapter 5, and Luke, Chapter 6, when Christ said: "And him that taketh away thy cloak, forbid not to take thy coat also." [5] "And if any man will sue thee at the law, and take away thy coat, let him have thy cloak also." [6] Whereon Augustine: "If he gives this command with regard to necessary things," that is, he counsels that one should not sue at law, "how much more so with regard to

---

[4] Really Matthew 19:29, quoted from memory.   [5] Luke 6:29.
[6] Matthew 5:40, quoted from memory.

superfluities?" [7] And in accordance with this teaching of Christ, the Apostle said in I Corinthians, Chapter 6: "Now therefore there is utterly a fault among you, because ye go to law one with another. Why do ye not rather take wrong? Why do ye not rather suffer yourselves to be defrauded?" [8] (supply: rather than sue someone at law, even justly, in order to lay claim to a temporal thing?). Whereon the gloss according to Augustine, after quoting the above passages of the gospel, adds: "This," that is, to sue at law justly, "the Apostle tolerates in the weak, since such judgments have to be made among brethren in the church with brethren sitting as judges." [9] And then, because of some doubts regarding Augustine's meaning, the gloss adds:

Correctly to understand the above words of Augustine, where he says that "it is a sin to go to law with a brother," it must here be stated what is fitting for the perfect in such matters and what is not, and what is allowed to the weak and what is not. The perfect, then, are allowed to demand what is theirs simply, that is, without suit, litigation, or judgment; but it is not fitting for them to have recourse to a lawsuit before a judge. The weak, however, are allowed to demand what is theirs both by starting a lawsuit before a judge and by having judgments against a brother.[10]

Therefore, a lawful vow can be taken with respect to the giving up of ownership. But if it is not lawful for the perfect to sue before a coercive judge, then they do not have the power lawfully to lay claim to a thing, which power is the ownership discussed above; for they have renounced such power by a vow which they are allowed at no time to contravene, especially while it still stands.

And as for the other part of the second proposition, that the lawful having of a thing or of its use, or the simple use of a thing, cannot be given up for any time—this is clear enough: for nothing which is prohibited by divine law can lawfully fall under a vow. But such giving up is prohibited by divine law, because it is a species of homicide. For he who observed such a vow would knowingly kill himself from hunger or cold or thirst; which is explicitly prohibited by divine law, as in Matthew, Chapter 19, Mark, Chapter 10, and Luke, Chapter 18, where Christ, confirming some commands of the old law, says: "Thou shalt not kill," etc.[11] Therefore, the simple use of a thing, or the lawful having of it, is separate from all the afore-mentioned kinds of ownership, or the power of laying claim to and prohibiting from the thing or something pertaining thereto.

6. From this too it clearly follows of necessity that it is insane heresy to

[7] In Thomas Aquinas *Catena aurea* (XI, 73).
[8] I Corinthians 6:7.
[9] In Peter Lombard *Collectanea* (PL 191. 1578).
[10] *Ibid.*
[11] Matthew 19:18; Mark 10:19; Luke 18:20.

assert that a thing or its use cannot be had apart from the aforesaid owner-ship.[12] For he who says this thinks nothing other than that Christ's counsel cannot be fulfilled; which is an open lie and, as we have said, must be shunned as vicious and heretical.

7. Nor is any difficulty presented by the objection that, while one may lawfully vow to give up an *act* of litigation, yet one cannot thus vow to give up the *habit* or the active legal *power* to claim the thing and prohibit it from someone else before a coercive judge, which power we have called ownership. For this statement is false, since every habit or legal power, acquired or acquirable, the act of which can be given up by lawful vow, can itself be given up in the same way, as is apparent by induction in all objects of deliberation which fall under vows. For he who vows chastity or obedience gives up by his vow not only the acts, but also the lawful power to perform these acts which had previously belonged to him by right (taken in the first sense). Again, it is inconsonant with the truth to say that a person has lawful power to perform acts all of which are unlawful, since a power is not called lawful or unlawful, nor is the difference between these known, otherwise than through the lawfulness or unlawfulness of the acts which emerge or can emerge from that power. Since, therefore, all the acts which emerge from the lawful power which a person had before his vow, are unlawful after the vow has been taken, it is clear that the person taking the vow has retained no lawful power to perform these acts.

8. Next I show that apart from having any ownership (in the senses given above), a person can have lawful use of something which belongs to another man, even to the extent of consuming the thing itself, if he exercises this use with the consent of the owner. For since the thing is assumed to be entirely in the ownership (or power to claim) of another person, it is certain that such ownership is not transferred to anyone else except by the deed and the express consent of the owner, and with no dissent on the part of the person to whom such ownership (or power to claim) of such a thing or of its use is to be transferred. Suppose, therefore, that the owner does not wish to transfer such ownership of a thing or of its use to some other person. Suppose, too, that this other person dissents from receiving such ownership, as for instance, because he has given up the ownership of all temporal things by an explicit vow, as befits those who are perfect. Suppose, further, that an owner consents to have some perfect person use some thing of his, even to the extent of consuming the thing, and

---

[12] Marsilius here and in the following paragraphs is refuting the bull of Pope John XXII, *Ad conditorem canonum* (*Corp. jur. can., Extravag. Joh. XXII* Tit. 14. cap. 3, published Dec. 8, 1322), which revoked *Exiit qui seminat* (see above, p. 193, n. 22).

that the perfect person, who has given up ownership of every thing, wishes to use such thing with the owner's consent. I say, then, that the person who thus uses the thing, uses it lawfully, and that he nevertheless has no ownership whatsoever (in the senses given above) of the thing or of its use. That he has no ownership of the thing, or of its use, is apparent from the assumed conditions with regard both to the will of the owner and to the condition of the person who is to receive the use of the thing, who has completely given up such ownerships. That he uses the thing lawfully is apparent from the definition of "lawful," since everyone is permitted by law to use a thing belonging to someone else even to the extent of consuming it, if there intervenes the express consent of the owner of the thing.

9. Now if we take ownership or control in its last sense, as meaning the human will or freedom, with that natural motive power which is not acquired but innate in us, then I say that neither lawfully nor unlawfully can we freely handle a thing, or something pertaining thereto, without having such ownership or control, nor can we give up such ownership or control. And for the sake of brevity, I pass over this without proof, since it is almost self-evident, inasmuch as without these powers no one can continue to exist.

10. From these statements, then, it can be seen that not all lawful or rightful (in the first or second sense or both) power over a temporal thing or over its use is ownership, although conversely all lawful ownership (in the first three legal senses) of a thing or of its use or both, is lawful or rightful power. And hence, when one argues in this fashion: there is lawful or rightful power over a thing or its use, therefore there is lawful or rightful ownership of the thing or of its use—one makes an invalid inference. For a person can lawfully have and handle a thing, whether it is his in private or in common or whether it belongs to another—in which case the owner or the person who has lawfully acquired it must give his consent—without acquiring any legal ownership of it.

11. Having set forth these premises, we now enter more fully upon our main task. We say first that the existence of poverty or of poor persons is almost self-evident, and is found in many passages of Scripture, from which it will suffice to quote one, in Mark, Chapter 12, where Christ says: "Verily I say unto you, that this poor widow hath cast more in than all of them." [13]

12. Next I show similarly by Scripture that poverty is meritorious as a means toward eternal life, for the Truth has said, in Luke, Chapter 6:

[13] Mark 12:43.

"Blessed be the poor: for yours is the kingdom of God," [14] that is, you merit it, for in this life no one except Christ is actually blessed, but rather merits it.

13. And from this it necessarily follows that poverty is a virtue, if one becomes habituated thereto by many acts of thus willing to lack temporal goods; or else poverty is an act which is productive of a virtue or elicited from a virtue; for everything which is meritorious is a virtue or an act of virtue. Again, every counsel of Christ pertains essentially to virtue; but poverty is such a counsel, as is sufficiently clear from Matthew, Chapters 5 and 19 [15] and from many other passages of the evangelic Scripture.

14. From this it necessarily follows that the poverty to which we here refer as a virtue is that voluntary poverty which was defined in the third and fourth senses of poverty given above. For there is no virtue or deed of virtue without choice, and there is no choice without consent, as is sufficiently clear from the second and third books of the *Ethics*.[16] This can be confirmed by Matthew, Chapter 5, where Christ said: "Blessed are the poor in spirit," by "spirit" meaning will or consent, although some of the saints interpret "spirit" to mean pride, which interpretation is not, however, very appropriate, inasmuch as there immediately follow in the same chapter these words: "Blessed are the meek." [17] But whatever be the interpretation of this passage, there is no doubt, according to the views of the saints, that if poverty is deserving of the kingdom of the heavens, as Christ says, it must be not primarily the external lack of temporal goods, but an internal habit of the mind, whereby one freely wishes to be lacking in such goods for the sake of Christ. Whence on the words in Luke, Chapter 6: "Blessed are the poor," etc., Basil writes: "Not everyone who is oppressed by poverty is blessed. For there are many persons who are poor in means, but most avaricious in desire, and these are not saved by their poverty, but damned by their desire. For nothing which is involuntary can be blessed, since every virtue is marked by free will." [18] Poverty, then, is a meritorious virtue, and consequently voluntary. But external lack is not in itself a virtue, inasmuch as it does not lead to salvation without the proper desire; for a person might be lacking in temporal goods under coercion and against his will, and yet he would be condemned because of his inordinate desire for these goods. This was also the view of the Apostle on this subject, when in II Corinthians, Chapter 8, he said: "For if

[14] Luke 6:20.   [15] Matthew 5:3; 19:21–24, 29.

[16] See Aristotle *Nicomachean Ethics* III. 1–2. 1109b 30 ff.

[17] Matthew 5:3, 4. The saints referred to are Chrysostom and Augustine; in Thomas Aquinas *Catena aurea* (XI, 55).

[18] In Thomas Aquinas *Catena aurea* (XII, 70), on Luke 6:20.

there be first a willing mind, it is accepted according to that a man hath" [19] —"accepted," that is, meritorious.

15. Moreover, if this choice to be lacking in temporal goods is to be meritorious, it must be made for the sake of Christ. Hence the Truth says in Matthew, Chapter 19: "And everyone that hath forsaken houses . . . for my name's sake." [20] Whereon Jerome: "He who has forsaken carnal things for the sake of the Savior, will receive spiritual things, whose worth is to that of carnal things as the number one hundred is to a small number." And further on: "Those who because of faith in Christ have shunned all secular desires, riches, and pleasures in order to preach the gospel, will be benefited a hundredfold and will possess eternal life." [21]

16. Again, since that which is opposed to avarice is essentially meritorious, it is essentially a virtue; such is voluntary poverty for the sake of Christ; for avarice is a vice. This virtue of voluntary poverty bears an analogy to moral liberality, although it differs from it in its end and is of a more perfect species, at least so far as concerns the mean in the thing itself, as will be clear from what follows; and hence both of them cannot be placed in the same indivisible species. [22]

17. From these considerations, therefore, it can be seen that meritorious poverty is the virtue whereby a person wishes for the sake of Christ to be deprived of and to lack all the temporal goods, usually called riches, which are over and above what is necessary for his subsistence.

18. Whence too it manifestly follows that this virtue is not the habit or act of charity, as some seem to think. [23] For poverty is not the habit or act which is essentially and primarily opposed to the actual or habitual hatred of God, because if it were, then more than one thing would be primarily opposed to one thing. For although the vice which is opposed to each theological virtue is incompatible with charity, yet from this it does not follow that charity is every theological virtue, since such vices are not opposed to charity primarily.

19. Nor is any difficulty presented by the argument that the virtue whereby we tend toward God through love, and the virtue whereby we recede from an inordinate desire for temporal things, are essentially the

[19] II Corinthians 8:12.   [20] Matthew 19:29.

[21] Thomas Aquinas *Catena aurea* (XI, 228).

[22] For the indivisible species, see Aristotle *Posterior Analytics* II. 13. 96b 15 ff.; *Metaphysics* v. 10. 1018b 4. For the mean "in the thing itself," see Aristotle *Nicomachean Ethics* II. 6. 1106a 25 ff., where it is pointed out that the "mean" in which the moral virtues consist is a mean "relatively to us" rather than a mean in terms of the thing or object with which the virtue is concerned. For liberality as a moral virtue, see *ibid.* IV. 1. 1119b 21 ff.

[23] See Pope John XXII *Ad conditorem canonum*, at "Cum enim perfectio . . ." (*Corp. jur can., Extravag. Joh. XXII* Tit. 14. cap. 3).

same virtue, just as the motion whereby a thing leaves some terminus and
the motion whereby it tends in the opposite direction are essentially the
same motion; and that since by charity we essentially tend toward God,
therefore it is by this same virtue, and not by a different one, that we seem
to depart from the love of temporal things.

20. The weakness of this argument can be seen through our previous
statement. For although by charity we essentially and primarily tend toward
God through love, yet its opposite, from which we essentially and primarily
depart, is hatred of God, not the unlawful love of temporal things. This is
so even though this latter departure sometimes is a consequence of charity,
because when one departs from the love of temporal goods, there follows
virtuous poverty, which is essentially and primarily such a voluntary giving
up of temporal things as is necessarily followed by the departure from
what is opposed to it essentially and primarily, namely, the unlawful love of
temporal things. For if our opponent reasoned truly, the conclusion from
true premises would be as follows: that charity is well-nigh every virtue,
since charity is necessarily followed by most of the virtues, like faith and
hope, whereby we essentially and primarily depart from heresy and despair,
respectively.

21. Moreover, charity cannot fall under a vow, because it is a command.
But the afore-mentioned poverty, especially as taken in the fourth sense,
falls under a vow. Therefore, charity is not essentially virtuous poverty, nor
conversely, although poverty follows upon charity just as do most of the
other theological virtues.

22. Moreover, I say that the highest mode or species of this virtue is the
explicit vow of the wayfarer, whereby for the sake of Christ he renounces
and wishes to be deprived of and to lack all acquired legal ownership, both
in private and in common, or the power to claim and to prohibit another
from temporal things (called "riches") before a coercive judge. And by this
vow, also, the wayfarer wishes, for the sake of Christ, to be deprived of and
to lack, both in private and in common, all power, holding, handling, or
use of temporal things over and above what is necessary quantitatively and
qualitatively for his present subsistence. Nor does he wish at one time to
have such goods, however lawfully they may come to him, in an amount
sufficient to supply several of the future needs or necessities either of himself alone or of himself together with a determinate other person or persons in common. Rather, he wishes to have at one time only what is necessary for a single need, as the immediately actual and present need of
food and shelter; but with this sole exception, that the person who takes
this vow should be in such place, time, and personal circumstance that he

can acquire for himself, on each successive day, a quantity of temporal things sufficient to supply his aforesaid individual need, but only one at a time, not more. This mode or species of meritorious poverty is the status which is considered to be necessary for evangelical perfection, as will clearly be seen from what follows. And this mode of meritorious poverty, or this status of a person who does not have possessions in private (in the third sense) or even in common with another (in the sense of "common" which is opposed to the above sense of "private"),[24] we shall henceforth, for the sake of brevity, call "supreme poverty," and the person who wishes to have this status we shall call, in keeping with the custom of theologians, "perfect."

23. That this mode of meritorious poverty is the supreme one can be shown from this, that through it all the other meritorious counsels of Christ are observed. For in the first place, men give up by a vow all the temporal things which it is possible for a wayfarer to give up; secondly, most of the impediments to divine charity are removed for those who take this vow; thirdly, they are put in condition to endure many secular passions, humiliations, and hardships, and are willingly deprived of many secular pleasures and vanities; and in a word, they are put in the best condition to observe all the commands and counsels of Christ. That he who takes such a vow completely gives up temporal things to the extent that it is possible and lawful for the wayfarer to do so, is evident. For he wishes to have at one time nothing except what is necessary to supply a single present or almost present need of food and clothing; less than this no faithful wayfarer is allowed to have, since if he wished to have less than was necessary for sustenance of his life, he would knowingly be a homicide, which by divine law at least no one is allowed to be. Therefore, he who wishes to have temporal things in such quantity that he is not allowed to have less, wishes to have the minimum of them; and he who gives up such a quantity of them that he is not allowed to give up more, gives up the maximum. But this is what the wayfarer does in accordance with the aforesaid mode of meritorious poverty, which we have called the supreme mode. But that this is in accord with the counsel of Christ is evident. For he gave a counsel concerning this vow in Luke, Chapter 14, when he said: "So likewise, whosoever he be of you that forsaketh not all that he hath, he cannot be my disciple."[25]

24. That the person who takes this vow removes from his path most of the impediments to divine charity, is evident. For the love and will to save temporal things turns a man toward them, and consequently turns

---

[24] See above, II. xii. 23, 25.   [25] Luke 14: 33.

him so much the more away from love or affection for God. Whence the Truth in Matthew, Chapter 6: "Where your treasure is, there will your heart be also." [26] To no avail is the excuse that the person who has these things does not turn his love toward them. For listen to Christ, who in Matthew, Chapter 13, and Mark, Chapter 4, says that "the deceitfulness of riches chokes the word." [27] Whereon Jerome: "Riches are flatterers which do one thing and promise another." [28] And hence, Christ counseled complete renunciation of temporal things for the person who wishes to be perfect, in Luke, Chapter 18: "Sell all that thou hast, and distribute unto the poor." [29] Whereon Bede: "Whoever wishes to be perfect, then, must sell the things which he has: not partly, as Ananias and Sapphira did, but completely." [30] And on the same passage, Theophylact adds these pertinent words: "He urges supreme poverty. For if there remains anything," that is, any temporal things, "he is its slave," [31] namely, the person who saves such things for himself. For such things by their very nature move inordinately the emotions of their possessors. Expounding the same counsel of Christ in Matthew, Chapter 19,[32] Raban adds a remark in support of the same position which is quite pertinent. He writes: "There is a difference between having money and loving money. But it is safer neither to have nor to love riches." [33] For, as Jerome says on the same passage: "It is difficult to despise riches when one possesses them." [34] For "they are stickier than lime," as Thomas says,[35] discussing the same counsel of Christ in Luke, Chapter 18.[36] Therefore, the person who gives up riches so far as it is possible and lawful for the wayfarer to do so, removes from his path the greatest impediments to charity.

25. Also he exposes himself to many secular passions, humiliations and hardships; he willingly deprives himself of many worldly pleasures and advantages. While this is self-evident from experience, let us quote the wise Solomon in Ecclesiastes, Chapter 10: for "all things," he says, "obey money," [37] that is, the person who has money. And on the other hand, as it is written in Proverbs, Chapter 15: "All the days of the poor are evil"; [38] for the poor man "has many afflictions," [39] as the gloss thereon says. Again in Proverbs, Chapter 19: "Wealth maketh many friends; but the poor man is separated from his neighbor." [40] But that it is meritorious and advisable to bear sorrows in this world and to abstain from pleasures, is evident from

[26] Matthew 6:21.   [27] Matthew 13:22 (here quoted); Mark 4:19.
[28] Thomas Aquinas *Catena aurea* (XI, 169).   [29] Luke 18:22.
[30] *Catena aurea* (XII, 198).   [31] *Ibid.*   [32] Matthew 19:24.
[33] *Catena aurea* (XI, 225).   [34] *Ibid.*
[35] *Ibid.* (XII, 198); "Thomas" is a slip for Theophylact.   [36] Luke 18:25.
[37] Ecclesiastes 10:19.   [38] Proverbs 15:15.   [39] *Glossa ordinaria, ad loc.*
[40] Proverbs 19:4.

Matthew, Chapters 5 and 19, and Luke, Chapter 6, where it is written with regard to the bearing of sorrows: "Blessed are the poor," "Blessed are they that mourn," "Blessed are they which are persecuted," [41] "Blessed are ye that hunger," [42] together with the other statements there added; and with regard to abstinence from pleasures: "Everyone that hath forsaken houses and brethren," with the other things there listed, "shall receive an hundredfold, and shall inherit everlasting life." [43] This same position is expounded by the glosses of the saints thereon, which I have omitted to quote for the sake of brevity and because this matter is sufficiently well known. This too was the view of the Apostle, in Romans, Chapter 8: "For I reckon," he writes, "that the sufferings of this present time are not worthy to be compared with the glory which shall be revealed in us." [44] And therefore the adversities of this world are meritorious for those who willingly bear them. The same view was taken in II Corinthians, Chapter 1, when the Apostle said "that as ye are partakers of the sufferings, so shall ye be also of the consolation." [45] Whereon Ambrose: "For your hardships will be repaid with equal," that is, proportional, "glory." [46] But groups of persons who have ownership of temporal things in common do not entirely put themselves in condition thus to bear secular sufferings and hardships; indeed, they do so in lesser degree than do many poor secular married couples who sometimes have private possessions, and who nevertheless are more often in need of things required for sufficiency of life than are they who only possess such things in common.

26. Furthermore, that through this mode of meritorious poverty, which we have called the supreme mode, all the commands and counsels of Christ can be observed to the highest degree, will be apparent to anyone who reads the gospel, especially the chapters we have indicated. For how can a person who has chosen to endure such poverty be avaricious or proud, incontinent or intemperate, ambitious, pitiless, unjust, timid, slothful, or jealous; why should he be mendacious or intolerant, for what reason malevolent toward others? On the contrary, he who has put himself in this condition seems to have an open door to all the virtues, [47] and also to the serene fulfillment of all the commands and counsels. This is so plain to anyone who considers it that I omit the proof, for the sake of brevity.

27. Thus, therefore, the supreme mode or species of meritorious poverty is that which we have described above; for through it, all the commands and meritorious counsels of Christ can be more fully and more securely

[41] Matthew 5:3, 5, 10.   [42] Luke 6:21.   [43] Matthew 19:29.
[44] Romans 8:18.   [45] II Corinthians 1:7.
[46] In Peter Lombard *Collectanea* (PL 192. 11).
[47] Placing, with Scholz, comma after *videtur*.

observed. And from this description it is apparent, first, that the perfect person ought, by an explicit vow, to renounce temporal things so far as their ownership is concerned, both because this is the counsel of Christ, as we have shown above from Luke, Chapter 14, and because the perfect person by thus manifesting his poverty renders himself more contemptible in the sight of others and makes a fuller abandonment of secular honors. Whence in Luke, Chapter 9: "If any man will come after me, let him deny himself." [48] From this, moreover, it follows that no one can observe supreme poverty before attaining the complete use of reason. And from this description it also follows that the perfect person ought neither to have nor to acquire or save anything for himself, that is, for the purpose of supplying his future needs, but should look out only for the immediate present, except in the case which we have mentioned in the description above. Whence in Matthew, Chapter 7: "Take therefore no thought for the morrow: for the morrow shall take thought for the things of itself." [49] Whereon the gloss: " 'for the morrow,' that is, for the future; but he grants that thought must be taken with regard to the present. It is not proper to take thought for the future, since the divine ordinance provides for this; but gratefully accepting what the present offers, let us leave the care of the uncertain future to God, who takes care of us." [50] And the same counsel is given in Matthew, Chapter 7, when Christ said to his disciples: "Behold the fowls of the air: for they sow not, neither do they reap, nor gather into barns; yet your heavenly father feedeth them." And a little below he adds: "Therefore take no thought, saying, What shall we eat, or what shall we drink, or wherewith shall we be clothed? For after all these things do the Gentiles seek." [51]

28. Now when we said that the perfect person is not allowed to provide for himself for the morrow, we did not mean that if anything remained from his lawful daily acquisitions, he ought to throw it away and in no manner save it, but that he ought to save it only with the firm intention of properly distributing it to any poor person or persons he met who were more needy than he. Whence in Luke, Chapter 3: "He that hath two coats, let him impart to him that hath none: and he that hath meat, let him do likewise"; [52] understanding by "two coats" and "meat" that which remains over and above one's own present needs.

We said that the surplus must be given to *any* poor person; for a community of men who save or have goods for certain definite persons only, such as the community of monks, canons, and the like, is not a perfect com-

[48] Luke 9:23.   [49] Matthew 6:34.   [50] *Glossa ordinaria, ad loc.*
[51] Matthew 6:26, 31–32.   [52] Luke 3:11.

munity; [53] for the perfect community, like that of Christ and his apostles, extends to all the faithful, as is clear from the Acts, Chapter 4. And if it chanced to extend to infidels also, it would perhaps be still more meritorious, according to Luke, Chapter 6: "Do good to them which hate you." [54]

But the perfect person lawfully can and should keep surplus goods, so long as he has the firm intention of dealing with them as we have said. Whence in John, Chapter 6: "Gather up the fragments that remain, that nothing be lost. Therefore they gathered them together, and filled twelve baskets with the fragments of the twelve barley loaves." [55] This view was also expressed by the gloss on the words in Matthew, Chapter 18: "Take that piece of money"; for the gloss says: "So great was the poverty of the Lord that he did not have wherewith to give tribute. Judas had the common goods in the bags, but he said that it was wrong to convert to one's own uses the goods of the poor." [56] Which shows that what had been stored up belonged to the poor, that is, it was saved with that intention.

29. And from this it is clear that they are wrong who say that perfection is attained by vowing to accept nothing for distribution to the poor who are weak or otherwise incapable of acquiring for themselves the necessities of life.[57] For, as is clear from II Corinthians, Chapters 8 and 9, the Apostle acquired goods with this purpose,[58] and there is no doubt that he did so lawfully and meritoriously. And this is also apparent from the gloss on the words in John, Chapter 21: "Feed my sheep," etc.[59] But since the matter is quite evident, I omit to quote these passages, for the sake of brevity.

30. From our above description of supreme poverty it also necessarily follows that the perfect person neither can nor ought to save or keep in his power any real estate, like house or field, unless he has the firm intention of giving it away as soon as he can, or exchanging it for money or for something else which can immediately and conveniently be distributed to the poor.[?] For since house or field could not as such be conveniently distributed to the poor without incurring the difficulty of giving too much to some and too little to others, we must follow the counsel of Christ, and do what he advised when he said, in Matthew, Chapter 19, Luke, Chapter 8, and Mark,

[53] Contrast this conception of the "perfect community" with the Aristotelian conception which Marsilius quotes above, I. iv. 1. See Vol. I, p. 81, n. 20.

[54] Luke 6:27.   [55] John 6:12–13.

[56] Matthew 17:26, and *Glossa ordinaria, ad loc.*

[57] This view is implied by Thomas Aquinas *Summa theologica* II. II. qu.84. a.3; qu.86. a.3, as Previté-Orton points out. On the difference between Aquinas' and Marsilius' views of "perfection," see Vol. I, p. 82.

[58] The aid given to the Macedonians and Achaeans.

[59] *Glossa ordinaria* on John 21:15–17; see Alcuin, in Thomas Aquinas *Catena aurea* (XII, 462).

[60] See the bull of Nicholas III, *Exiit qui seminat* (*Corp. jur. can., Sext.* Lib. v. Tit. 12. cap. 3).

Chapter 10: "Go and sell." [61] Nor did Christ say: Give to the poor every-thing that you have; nor did he say: Throw away everything that you have; but rather he said: "Go and sell," for by selling the distribution of wealth can be more conveniently made. Such too was the counsel of the apostles, and those to whom they gave this counsel followed it out, wishing to distribute their goods to the poor conveniently. Whence in Acts, Chapter 4: "For as many as were possessors of lands or houses sold them, and brought the prices of the things that were sold. And distribution was made unto every man according as he had need." [62]

31. From the above it is also apparent that no perfect person can acquire the ownership (in the first, second, and third senses) of any temporal thing, as we have proved above from Matthew, Chapter 5, and Luke, Chapter 6. And we have confirmed this through the Apostle in I Corinthians, Chapter 6; and we made it sufficiently clear by the words of Augustine and the gloss on that scriptural passage. [63] Since the matter is evident, I have omitted to quote these passages for the sake of brevity.

32. Nor should we pay attention to the argument that perfect men may lawfully save real estate in order to distribute the annual income thereof to the poor. For it is more meritorious because of love of Christ and pity for one's neighbor to distribute at once to the poor both the real estate and the income thereof, rather than the latter alone; and besides, it is more meritorious to give away the real estate alone rather than its income alone. For in this way help can be given to many poor and needy persons at once, who might perhaps through want become ill or die before the income became available, or commit an act of violence, theft, or some other evil. Again, a person who kept the real estate might die before the time when the income was distributed, and thus he would never have the merit therefrom that he could have had.

Entirely the same view must be held with respect to any kind of chattels, which similarly, when thus kept, naturally affect to an inordinate degree the desire of the person who holds them. But if the virtue here considered is believed to be charity, as some seem to think, then undoubtedly this mode of charity, that is, with supreme poverty, is more perfect than having private or common ownership of a temporal thing, as is plain from the pre-ceding reasonings.

33. But now advancing to the principal proposition, we wish to show that Christ while he was a wayfarer observed the supreme species or mode

---

[61] Matthew 19:21; Luke 18:22; Mark 10:21.   [62] Acts 4:34-35, abbreviated.
[63] See above, para. 5 of this chapter.

of meritorious poverty.[64] For that which is first in each sphere is greatest; but Christ under the New Law was the first of the wayfarers who merited eternal life; therefore he was the greatest of all in perfection; therefore he observed this status with respect to temporal things, for without this it is impossible, according to the common law, to attain the greatest degree of meritoriousness. Again, if he had not observed this mode of poverty, then some other wayfarer could have been or might in the future be more perfect in merit than Christ according to the common law, which it is impious to believe. For Christ asserted that this status was required for perfection in merit, when he said: "If you wish to be perfect, sell all whatsoever that thou hast and distribute unto the poor"; [65] nor did he add: the things that thou hast in private or in common, but he meant this to be taken universally, so that he stressed its universal meaning by saying: "all whatsoever." For he who has the ownership or keeping of temporal things in common with another person or persons, in a way other than the one described by us, has not given up all the temporal things which it is possible to give up, nor is he exposed to so many secular sufferings or deprived of so many advantages as is he who renounces temporal things both as private property and in common, nor is he thus free from solicitude for these things, nor does he observe all the counsels of Christ equally as much as does he who completely gives us temporal things.

34. And now I wish to show that while Christ observed supreme poverty, he did have some possessions both as private property and in common. That he had private property (in the third sense) is shown by the passage in Mark, Chapter 2: "For there were many, and they followed him. And the scribes and sinners saw him eat with publicans and sinners." [66] Now it is certain that he lawfully had as private or individual property that which he put to his mouth and ate. Moreover, his clothes were his private or individual property, as is sufficiently clear from Matthew, Chapter 27, Mark, Chapter 15, Luke, Chapter 23, and John, Chapter 19. Whence in Matthew, in the chapter mentioned: "They took the robe off from him, and put his own raiment on him." [67] Thus too in John, in the chapter just mentioned: "Then the soldiers, when they had crucified Jesus, took his garments." [68] Thus too in Mark and Luke,[69] whose passages are omitted for the sake

[64] Marsilius here argues against the bull of John XXII, *Cum inter nonnullos,* of Nov. 12, 1323 (*Corp. jur can., Extravag. Joh. XXII* Tit. 14. cap. 4), which condemned the doctrine that Christ had absolute poverty. Marsilius' position on this and other issues is in turn condemned in John's bull, *Quia quorundam mentes,* of Nov. 10, 1324 (*ibid.* Tit. 14. cap. 5).
[65] Luke 18:22.   [66] Mark 2:15–16.   [67] Matthew 27:31.
[68] John 19:23.   [69] Mark 15:20; Luke 23:24.

of brevity. Christ, therefore, even while observing supreme poverty, lawfully or rightfully had temporal things as his private property, and wanted them and it was fitting that he want them; otherwise he would have sinned mortally, for being a true man he was subject to hunger, as is apparent from Matthew, Chapter 21, and Mark, Chapter 18,[70] and hence he needed food, which he had to take when he was able to do so, for otherwise he would have gravely sinned, by knowingly starving himself to death.

35. Christ also lawfully had some things in common while observing supreme poverty. Whence in John, Chapter 12: "This Judas said, not that he cared for the poor; but because he was a thief, and had the bags," [71] that is, the common belongings of Christ and the apostles and the other poor persons. That these were held in common is apparent from the fact that Christ ordered some of them to be distributed to the hungry crowds of the poor, as is sufficiently clear from Matthew, Chapter 14. The "bags" were the repositories wherein was kept the alms money which had been given to them. This is again shown by the fourteenth chapter of the same book: "For some of them thought that Judas had the bag." [72] Also it is shown by the gloss on the passage in Matthew, Chapter 18: "Take that piece of money," etc., whereon the gloss says: "Judas had the common goods in the bags." [73] Thus too the apostles, while observing supreme poverty, had belongings in common among themselves and with other poor persons, after the resurrection of Christ. Whence in Acts, Chapter 4: "But they had all things in common." [74] And similarly they had some things as private property, namely, their own food and clothing, which they applied for their private use, just as did Christ.

36. Next I wish to give a necessary proof of what constitutes the principal thesis of this chapter and the ones immediately preceding and following, namely, that Christ the wayfarer, giving a preeminent manifestation of the height of perfection, had no acquired ownership (in the first, second, or third sense), in private or in common, of any temporal thing or of its use. For if he had assumed for himself such ownership, he would not have observed all the counsels, and especially that form of poverty which is the highest one possible for the wayfarer. But Christ observed all these counsels in the most perfect manner of any wayfarer. Therefore, Christ did not have or want to have such ownership of temporal things, which the Scripture in many passages calls "possession," as in Luke, Chapter 14: "Whosoever he be of you that forsaketh not all that he possesseth"; [75] so too in Matthew,

---

[70] Matthew 21:18; Mark 11:12 (not Chapter 18).   [71] John 12:6.
[72] John 13:29.
[73] *Glossa ordinaria* on Matthew 17:26; see above, para. 28 of this chapter.
[74] Acts 4:32.   [75] Luke 14:33.

Chapter 10: "Possess neither gold, nor silver, nor brass in your purses," [76] that is, do not keep these unless perhaps for a lawful occasion, namely, for the purpose and needs mentioned above, such as for the sake of the powerless poor, as Paul did, or from urgent necessity of time, place, and personal condition; which cases will be made clearer in the following chapter. Although even in the afore-mentioned cases the person who has taken a vow of supreme poverty is not allowed to have ownership, for such ownership necessarily excludes the fulfillment of Christ's counsel regarding supreme poverty. Christ, therefore, did not have the aforesaid ownership of temporal things, nor can it be had by any imitator of him, that is, by anyone who wishes to observe supreme poverty.

37. In consequence of these considerations, I say that it cannot be proved from the holy Scripture that Christ, however condescending he may have been to the weak, had the aforesaid ownership or possession of temporal goods in private or in common, although some of the saints are believed to have held this view.[77] For by parity of reasoning one might conclude that Christ did everything which was permitted lest he should seem to have condemned the status of persons who did such things. If this argument were sound, Christ would have accepted and exercised secular rulership or contentious jurisdiction over litigation, whereas the opposite of this was irrefutably shown in Chapter IV of this discourse; so too, he would have married, would have engaged in lawsuits before a coercive judge, and would have done everything else that was permitted; but that Christ did these things no one can prove by Scripture, but rather the opposite. For it was not necessary or fitting for him to do such things in order that he should not seem to have condemned the status of those persons who did them, and who are called "weak." For it does not follow that because Christ was not married, therefore he seemed to be condemning the status of those who were married; and similarly in the other cases. For he himself sufficiently expressed the difference between the things which it is necessary to do or omit for salvation—the commands or prohibitions—and the things which are not necessary for salvation, which the saints call "supererogatory." For when someone asked Christ what things were necessary for eternal salvation, Christ replied: "If thou wilt enter into life, keep the commandments." And again when the person asked him what things were supererogatory, Christ did not reply: If thou wilt enter into life, but he said to

---

[76] Matthew 10:9.

[77] See the bulls of Nicholas III, *Exiit qui seminat* (*Corp. jur. can., Sext.* Lib. v. Tit. 12. cap. 3), and of John XXII, *Quia quorundam* (*Corp. jur. can., Extravag. Joh. XXII* Tit. 14. cap. 5), the latter of which quotes a statement of St. Augustine (in *Corp. jur. can., Decret. Gratiani* Pars II. can. 17. C. XII. qu.1) to the effect that Christ held property.

him: "If thou wilt be perfect." [78] In these words in Matthew, Chapter 19, Luke, Chapter 18, and Mark, Chapter 10, Christ explicitly showed that for eternal life the observance of the commandments was sufficient, for he made no reply, to the person asking about this, other than to say: "Keep the commandments, if thou wilt enter into life." And hence it was not necessary or fitting for Christ to do all the things that were permitted, in order that he should not seem to have condemned the status of persons who did such things, for he had already made it clear that men can be saved by observing only the commandments or commands, taking "command" in its more general sense as both affirmative and negative; but it was more fitting for Christ to observe the counsels, as for example to maintain supreme poverty and not to marry, in order to afford to all others an example of such observance; which, as we read in Scripture, he actually carried out both in word and in deed. For speaking of his poverty in Matthew, Chapter 8, and Luke, Chapter 9, he said: "The foxes have holes, and the birds of the air have nests; but the Son of man hath not where to lay his head." [79] Whereon the gloss: "I am so poor that I do not have a shelter of my own." [80] For "so great was the poverty of the Lord that he did not have wherefrom to give tribute," as the gloss says on the words in Matthew, Chapter 18: "Take that piece of money, and give to them for me and you." [81] But we never read that Christ had a castle or fields or treasure chests in order that he might not seem to be condemning the status of those who did have such things.

38. But if Christ had done things that were permitted, he could none the less have equally obeyed all the counsels, for he, who was the legislator, was able do such things in order that he should not seem to be condemning the status of those who did them. Hence he would not have wanted in an unqualified sense to do such things, as do the weak who want them for their own advantage; but he would have wanted to do such things for a different purpose, wanting them and at the same time, in a certain way, not wanting them, since he wanted them not for himself but for the aforesaid reason. But all other perfect men can in no way properly want such ownership, if they are to observe the counsels to the full. For they cannot want such ownership in order that they may not seem to be condemning the status of others, as it does not pertain to them to approve or condemn anyone's status, because they neither were nor are nor will be legislators. If therefore they wanted such ownership, they would want it as weak persons, not as perfect ones. So, then, it would have been lawful for Christ

---

[78] Matthew 19:17, 21; Mark 10:19–21; Luke 18:18–22.   [79] Matthew 8:20; Luke 9:58.
[80] *Glossa ordinaria* on Matthew 8:20.   [81] See above, para. 28 of this chapter.

to do these things that were permitted, if he had wanted to, while at the same time observing all the counsels to the full; but it can be lawful for no one else to do so, for the reason already stated.

39. But if it be asked who can be so perfect as to wish to have, at one time, only such an amount of temporal goods as is merely sufficient for one's own present or immediate need, I reply that Christ and other men did so desire, although such men are few, because "strait is the gate, and narrow is the way . . . and few there be that find it," as it is written in Matthew, Chapter 7.[82] And do you tell me, I beg: How many voluntary martyrs are there in these times, how many heroic men, how many Catos, Scipios, and Fabricii? [83]

CHAPTER XIV: ON SOME OBJECTIONS TO THE CONCLUSIONS OF THE PRECEDING CHAPTER, THE REFUTATION OF THESE OBJECTIONS, AND CONFIRMATION OF THE STATEMENTS MADE IN THAT CHAPTER

TO the statements made in the preceding chapter someone will object that if the ministers of the gospel, the bishops and priests, who wish to hold the status of perfection, can save nothing to supply their future needs but must save goods only with the desire and firm resolve to give them to the first poor person or persons they meet and in proportion to their need, together with the other conditions stated in our description of supreme poverty, then how will they be able to attend to preaching the word of God and at the same time to look after their daily livelihood, which seems necessary if they are allowed to save nothing for themselves for the future? For to do both these things at once seems difficult or even impossible. Whence in Acts, Chapter 6: "It is not reason that we should leave the word of God and serve tables"; [1] the apostles here indicate that both these things cannot be done at once. It is lawful, therefore, for the perfect to save temporal things to take care of their future needs. The same thing, moreover, is shown in a different connection; for on the words of John, Chapter 14, "For some of them thought, because Judas had the bag . . . in which offerings were saved," the gloss writes, "In this the church is shown the way to save necessaries." [2] Since, therefore, the word "church" in this passage means the perfect, especially the priests or bishops, it seems

---

[82] Matthew 7:14.   [83] Cf. Cicero De officiis III. iv. 16.   [1] Acts 6:2.
[2] Glossa ordinaria on John 13:29.

that they can lawfully save things which are necessary to them for the future. Again, on the words of Matthew, Chapter 7: "Take therefore no thought for the morrow," the gloss says: "But no one ought to be scandalized if he sees one of the just men procuring these goods which are necessary to himself and his people; do not judge that he is taking thought for the morrow, since it was with the purpose of giving an example of this that he who taught this and to whom the angels ministered, had the bags whence to supply necessaries for use." [3] The same is confirmed by John, Chapter 14, where it is written as follows: "For some of them thought, because Judas had the bag, that Jesus had said unto him, Buy those things that we have need of against the feast." [4] Christ and the apostles, therefore, had money saved with which they were able to buy such things. The same is again shown in another way; for on the words in Matthew, Chapter 6: "Behold the fowls of the air," etc., the gloss says: "He does not prohibit men to be provident and labor, but he does prohibit solicitude: so that all our hope may be in God." [5] The perfect, therefore, are allowed to provide for their future needs. The same is shown, moreover, from Matthew, Chapter 14, Mark, Chapters 6 and 8, and Luke, Chapter 10. For Christ said to the apostles: "How many loaves have ye? . . . They said: Seven." [6] But they had saved these beyond their present needs. Therefore the perfect are allowed to save temporal things for themselves for the future.

2. Next it is shown with necessity that the perfect, even while remaining perfect, have or can have private or common ownership (taken in the first, second, or third senses) of temporal things or of their use, and especially of things which are consumable in a single use. This is first shown from Luke, Chapter 22, when Christ says to the apostles: "And he that hath no sword, let him sell his garment, and buy one." But he who buys or sells something, transfers ownership of the thing or of its price to someone else. No one transfers to another what he did not have previously. Christ and the apostles, therefore, had the aforesaid ownership.

3. Next I show the same thing in another way, as follows: He who has had the lawful use of a thing whose use is inseparable from the aforementioned ownership of it, has necessarily had ownership of the thing. [7] But Christ and the apostles had the use of such things. Therefore they necessarily had ownership of them. The first proposition of this deduction is obvious. The second is proved by that use of consumable goods which

---

[3] *Glossa ordinaria* on Matthew 6:24.   [4] John 13:29.

[5] *Glossa ordinaria* on Matthew 6:26.

[6] Matthew 14:17; Mark 6:38, 8:5 (quoted); Luke 9:13.

[7] The inseparability of use from ownership in consumable things was stressed by John XXII in *Ad conditorem canonum* (*Corp. jur. can., Extravag. Joh. XXII* Tit. 14. cap. 3).

Christ and the apostles had. For they had the use of a thing which was either rightfully theirs or rightfully not theirs. If they had the use of a thing which was rightfully theirs, then they had ownership of the thing at the same time with its use. But if they had the use of a thing which was not theirs, then it was either someone else's or no one's before being used. If the thing was no one's, then this is what follows: a thing which is no one's is rightfully granted to him who occupies it; but Christ and the apostles necessarily occupied the thing prior to or concomitantly with their use of it; therefore they had ownership of the thing prior to or concomitantly with its use. But if the thing which they thus used was another's, then they used it either with or without the consent of the thing's owner. If without the consent, and especially if they consumed the thing in using it, or otherwise used it in such a way as the owner is presumed rightfully to have prohibited, then such use would have been unlawful, which it would be impious to say regarding Christ or the apostles. But if such use, which consumed the thing, was with the owner's consent, then the owner of the thing granted to the user either the use alone apart from ownership or the use together with ownership. If the use apart from ownership, then the use would have been unlawful, for such use deprives the owner of the ownership of his thing without any act on his part, which cannot lawfully or rightfully be done. But if the person who thus uses the thing has been granted the use together with the ownership by the owner, then it is quite evident that such user, even while being perfect, has necessarily had ownership of the thing together with its use.

4. Moreover, if the perfect person had no ownership of any temporal thing, then it would follow that the thing could lawfully, because rightfully, be taken away from him even while he was actually in need of it. For things which belong to no one can lawfully or rightfully be occupied by anyone. But things to which no one can lay claim belong to no one. And such are the things which the perfect person has, as is sufficiently clear from the antecedent hypotheses.

Moreover, persons who have to furnish hospitality must necessarily provide for the future and have ownership of some things. All the successors of the apostles, namely, the bishops, are obliged to furnish hospitality. Whence in I Timothy, Chapter 3 and Titus, Chapter 2: "A bishop must be given to hospitality." [8]

Furthermore, the holy fathers, the bishops, seem to have acted in this way; for they had ownership of fields and possessions, at least in common with other bishops and priests. Whence Ambrose in his epistle *On Handing*

[8] I Timothy 3:2 (quoted); Titus 1:7.

Over the Basilica writes: "The fields of the church pay tribute." [b] Therefore, fields and other real estate were possessed by perfect men, who also
are designated, or should be designated, by the name "church," especially
the priests.

5. This is also shown with regard to Christ in particular. For first of all,
according to the laws, even the human laws, a person who has redeemed
someone from death is made lord over him, and consequently lord or owner
of all his temporal goods.[10] But Christ redeemed us from death, not from
any death whatsoever, but from eternal death. Therefore he acquired lordship over our bodies and ownership of our temporal goods.[11] Again in
Revelation, Chapter 19, it is written of him, that he had "on the vesture
written: King of kings and lord of lords." Whereon the gloss: "On the
vesture, namely, of humanity." [12] Since, then, a king and lord has ownership of all things, it is clear that Christ had such ownership in temporal
things.

6. Now from our previous conclusions concerning supreme poverty and
the ownership of temporal things, we shall be able to make proper reply
to these objections of the present chapter, stating at the outset, however, in
accordance with the views of Christ and of the Apostle, that the ministers
of the gospel, the priests or bishops together with lower orders, must be
content with their daily bread and necessary clothing, if they wish to maintain the status of perfection or supreme poverty. Whence in I Timothy, last
chapter: "And having food and raiment let us be therewith content." [13]
Persons to whom the gospel is preached are therefore obligated, at least
according to divine law, to supply these things to the preachers. For in
Deuteronomy, Chapter 25, are these symbolic words: "Thou shalt not
muzzle the ox when he treadeth out the corn," [14] which Paul interprets,
in I Corinthians, Chapter 9, as having been said for the sake of future
teachers and ministers of the gospel, when he writes: "Doth God take care
for oxen? Or saith he it altogether for our sakes?" [15] The same is to be
seen from Matthew, Chapter 10, when Christ in this connection and to
this end said: "The workman is worthy of his meat." [16] Therefore those
who receive the gospel must, if they can, supply the preacher with his daily
bread and clothing. And such support, as being owed to them by divine law,
the preachers can lawfully demand, although not in a coercive judgment
of the present world; and persons to whom the gospel is ministered sin

[9] St. Ambrose *Sermo contra Auxentium* (PL 16. 1060).

[10] See *Corpus jur. civ., Instit.* I. i. iii. 3; *Digest* I. v. 4.

[11] This argument is found in Egidius of Rome *De ecclesiastica potestate* II. x (ed. R. Scholz
[Weimar, 1928], p. 95).

[12] Revelation 19:16, and *Glossa interlinearis, ad loc.*   [13] I Timothy 6:8.

[14] Deuteronomy 25:4.   [15] I Corinthians 9:9-10.   [16] Matthew 10:10.

against divine law if they refuse to give these necessities when they can afford them. Whence in I Corinthians, Chapter 9: "Even so hath the Lord ordained that they which preach the gospel should live of the gospel." Just as he who "feedeth a flock, eateth of the milk of the flock; and he who planteth a vineyard, eateth of the fruit thereof." [17] But on the other hand, no believer is obliged, according to Scripture, to give tithes or any other fixed part of his income to preachers.

7. But if persons to whom the gospel is ministered be so poor that they cannot give the preacher the necessary food and clothing, then they are not obliged to do so by divine law, but the preacher must seek out these necessities of life from another source, as by giving some other instruction or by engaging in some other operative art if he knows how, or in some other honorable and appropriate way. For this was what the Apostle did, in order that he might not become a burden on the poor people to whom he preached. Whence in Acts, Chapter 20, he speaks of himself as follows: "I have coveted no man's gold and silver, ye yourselves know; for these hands have ministered unto my necessities, and to them that were with me." [18] He said the same in the last chapter of II Thessalonians: "Neither did we eat any man's bread for nought, but wrought with labor and travail night and day, that we might not be chargeable to any of you." [19] But now that the number of devout believers has increased, and especially in these present times, it is not necessary for the ministers of the sacred doctrine to work with their hands or to beg. For in communities of the faithful, both the maker of human law and private individuals have established and set apart certain revenues of both movable and immovable things, by which the ministers of the gospel can sufficiently, nay abundantly, be supported.

8. But someone will ask: To whom belongs the ownership (in the above senses) of these temporal things, and especially the immovable ones, or the power to claim them before a coercive judge of the present world? For, according to the preceding chapter, such ownership cannot belong to gospel ministers while they are perfect. We shall answer that the ownership of temporal things which have been set apart for the support of gospel ministers belongs to the legislator or to deputies appointed for this purpose either by the legislator or by the donors, if they be private individuals, who have given and set apart such goods out of their own resources for the afore-mentioned use. Persons thus appointed to protect and lay claim to ecclesiastic temporal goods are usually called "patrons of churches." For in antiquity the saintly and perfect men who ministered the gospel desired to imitate Christ, and hence, not wishing to bring suit against anyone, they did not assume the ownership of temporal things, but

[17] I Corinthians 9:14, 7.   [18] Acts 20:33-34.   [19] II Thessalonians 3:8.

only that use of them which was necessary for their own immediate support and for that of the powerless poor. For if it had been in their power to give away immovable temporal things, even without owning them or intending to claim them, and if they had not given them away to the first poor persons that they met, then they would not have observed the counsel of Christ, wherein he said: "Go and sell all that thou hast, and give to the poor." [Hence, if, as some persons heretically hold, Christ as man owned all temporal things, then he sold them, or else he did not observe the counsel which he gave for perfection. If, then, he sold them, they cannot be claimed by the Roman or any other bishop, or priestly college, as being Christ's successors,] [20] or else they would have had such goods as private property or even in common.

However, it must not be thought that these patrons, who we said were owners empowered to lay claim to such goods, have the power to give them away or to convert them to other uses. For if they did so, they would sin against divine law at least, and perhaps against human law as well, since not for this purpose is ownership granted to them, but only for the purpose of laying claim to the goods before a coercive judge and protecting them against persons who steal or who want to steal or otherwise dispose of them. And consequently, if the custody and distribution of the proceeds be entrusted to one of the perfect men by the legislator or by a private individual having the power so to do, then I say that this perfect person, while observing supreme poverty, can lawfully, nay meritoriously, accept this charge out of love and compassion for his neighbor.

9. But someone else will say that the perfect person is thus providing for the morrow or for many morrows, since he receives and intends to receive his food and clothing throughout the year from the proceeds entrusted to him. It must be replied that such goods are entrusted to him for distribution with the condition that a sufficient quantity be kept to supply the preacher with appropriate food and clothing for his daily needs, the rest to be distributed to the poor. And inasmuch as the preacher is appointed or elected for the common utility of the faithful, to preach to a certain people in a certain determinate place in order that they may attain eternal salvation, he appropriately proposes, as preacher, to take at once only such a quantity of goods as is sufficient to supply his needs for a single day; but he would not propose to take many such supplies at once or successively from the same stock of goods, if he could have the time at once to earn his daily

---

[20] The passage in brackets, according to Previté-Orton and Scholz, is a later revision added by Marsilius. It seems to be directed against John XXII's bull, *Quia vir reprobus*, of Nov. 16, 1329, which in turn was an attack on Michael of Cesena, the Franciscan general (Raynaldus, *Annales ecclesiastici* [Lucca, 1750], an. 1329, paras. 22–68).

livelihood and to preach. But since he cannot have the time for both of these at once, he must aim to take many daily supplies of food and drink from the same stock of goods, but on successive days. For if he were to distribute to the poor what remains over and above one daily supply for himself, he would not have whence to take his supply for the next day; and thus, being forced to seek it out, he would necessarily have to give up the care of the people which he had taken on, whereupon he would commit a mortal sin by causing the common harm of souls, and also by distributing goods not belonging to him in a way inconsistent with, or rather contrary to, the intention of those who entrusted such goods to him for distribution. Therefore, since by the decree of the faithful, to whom belongs the authority to ordain this, it seemed expedient that a determinate people have a determinate minister of the gospel and the sacraments, who having to minister to them must be supported in these things by them, he does not save for the morrow, for his own sake and by his own intention, something which it is in his power to distribute. Again, since his circumstances are such that he cannot seek out for himself his daily livelihood, for the reason already stated, he can while continuing to remain perfect take many daily shares from the goods entrusted to his custody, but always with the intention of distributing what remains over and above his present needs, if it be in his power to acquire his future daily food and if he be in a position to do so, as we said in our description of supreme poverty.

10. A daily supply of food and clothing must, therefore, suffice to the gospel minister, which supply must be ministered to him by those who receive his ministry. And he can lawfully ask for this as being owed to him by divine right, although he must not claim it by human right before a coercive judge, even if this shall have been commanded by human right. Whence on the passage in II Timothy, Chapter 1: "No soldier of God," etc.,[21] the gloss according to Augustine declares as follows: "This then is what the Apostle says, writing to Timothy, that if Timothy were perhaps in need, and did not wish to be supplied with his daily food by those to whom he ministered the gospel, and could not do physical labor, then he should not engage in pursuits in which his intention might be thwarted,"[22] whence it remained that he must beg. Note, therefore, Augustine did not say that if they had been unwilling to supply Timothy with his food, they should have been compelled to do so, nor that Timothy should have demanded it before a coercive judge. For he who takes away "thy coat" must be given "thy cloak also" rather than be sued in contentious judgment "at the law," according to the counsel of Christ in Matthew, Chapter 5, and

---

[21] II Timothy 2:4.   [22] In Peter Lombard *Collectanea* (PL 192. 367–68).

Luke, Chapter 6.[23] And this was also what the Apostle said in II Corinthians, Chapters 8 and 9, asking them to support the poor: "I speak not by commandment," and further on: "Herein I give my advice," calling such alms by the name of "grace," so that he also signified that it was voluntary: "Every man according as he purposeth in his heart, so let him give, not grudgingly or of necessity." [24]

11. But now it remains to reply separately to each of the objections set forth at the beginning of this chapter. First, then, with regard to the quotation from Acts, Chapter 6: "It is not reason that we should leave the word of God," etc.,[25] it must be replied that the apostles said this not because they wished to acquire temporal goods and save them for the future, unless in the way we said in our description of supreme poverty, but rather because they wanted a supply to be acquired for them which would take care only of their present or immediately pressing need, since they could not do this by themselves while having at the same time to preach the gospel.

12. As for the other objection, taken from the gloss on John, Chapter 14, that "he shows the church the way to save necessaries," etc.,[26] I say that the church, that is, perfect men, are shown the way to save, both in private and in common, what remains over and above their present or almost present needs, if this excess comes to them lawfully, as by gift or as the earnings of their own physical labor. And the perfect are allowed to save for the reason and purpose stated in our description of supreme poverty, although they ought not to acquire on their own behalf anything in excess of their own present or almost present needs; however, rather than throw away superfluous goods which come to them lawfully, they ought to keep them or entrust them to such other men for safekeeping and distribution as they know to be most suitable for this purpose. Whence on the words in Matthew, Chapter 10: "The workman is worthy of his meat," [27] Jerome writes: "Take ye therefore only such an amount of necessaries as will enable you to have leisure to attend to eternal things." [28] And also on the same passage Augustine writes: "He," that is, Christ, "spoke these words to the apostles, so that they might be secure and not possess or carry the things necessary to this life, whether great or small; and he shows that the faithful owe all things to their ministers who make no excessive demands." [29] Consequently, if tithes are not necessary for their sustenance,

---

[23] Matthew 5:40; Luke 6:29.   [24] II Corinthians 8:7, 8, 10; 9:7.

[25] Acts 6:2. See above, para. 1 of this chapter.   [26] See above, para. 1 of this chapter.

[27] Matthew 10:10.   [28] *Glossa ordinaria, ad loc.*

[29] Thomas Aquinas *Catena aurea* (XI, 131 f.).

but are partly or wholly superfluous, then gospel ministers, according to the sacred Scripture, cannot exact that which is superfluous, nor are the Christian faithful obliged to give it.

13. But that Christ meant that the ministers can ask only for the food or clothing for which they have a present or almost present need, is apparent from Jerome's gloss on the words, "neither two coats." Whereon St. Jerome writes: "By 'two coats' he seems to me to mean a double supply of clothing; not that a man should be content with one coat in the Scythian regions of freezing glacial snow, but that, understanding by one coat one set of clothing, we are not to wear one and save another from fear of the future." [30] He prohibits, therefore, having two coats at once, that is, two sets of garments one of which is sufficient for the time being; and the same must be understood, and for the same reason, with regard to food, according to the statements of Scripture and the expositions of the saints adduced above.

14. It does not, therefore, befit the perfect, the successors of Christ and of the apostles, to keep fields, towns, or castles in their ownership for themselves; nor was the church, that is, the gospel ministers, ever given, by the deeds or example of Christ or the apostles, a model of having ownership of real estate or of keeping it in their power for the future. But the opposite of this we do indeed find in Scripture, by the counsel of Christ, when he said: "Go and sell." And again: "Do not possess gold," etc. And also in Acts, Chapter 4: "They sold them and brought the prices of the things that were sold." [31] The church, then, is given a model of keeping some movable things for the purposes stated above, but not immovable things, for immovables which were in its ownership or which it had absolute power to alienate should be sold at the first opportunity.

15. This was also the view of Bede in his exposition of the passage in Luke, Chapter 22: "When I sent you without purse," etc.[32]

The rule of living which he teaches his disciples [writes Bede] is not the same in time of persecution as in time of peace. Having sent his disciples to preach he commanded them not to take anything on the way, that is, bear anything along with them, ordering that those who preach the gospel should live by the gospel. With the pastor and flock in imminent danger of death and actually persecuted by the whole nation, he decrees a rule appropriate to the time, permitting them to take along their necessary food, until the rage of the persecutors be abated and the time for preaching return.[33]

[30] Thomas Aquinas *Catena aurea* (XI, 131). The gloss is on Matthew 10:10.
[31] See above, II. xiii. 30, 35, 36.   [32] Luke 22:35.
[33] Thomas Aquinas *Catena aurea* (XII, 231).

When this time does return, they do not need to bear or carry anything along for their future needs, because they must be supported by those who receive the gospel, and they can lawfully ask this of them daily. If, therefore, the apostles and their successors had been allowed at any time whatsoever to save goods which they might need for any time in the future, Christ would in vain and improperly have given them one rule for times of peace and another for times of persecution. And this is what we said in our description of supreme poverty, that the perfect are not allowed to save temporal things, if their circumstances of place, time, and personal condition are such that they can conveniently acquire on each day the food that they need.

16. As for the other objection based on the gloss on Matthew, Chapter 7, where it says: "But no one ought to be scandalized," etc.,[34] it must be said that the perfect person can lawfully procure the goods to supply his urgent or immediately urgent, almost present need; but the surplus, if there be any, he must save for the poor, without any intention of claiming ownership; thus to save it is more expedient and meritorious than to allow it to go to waste, for it is a deed of mercy and supererogation, whence in Matthew, Chapter 5: "Blessed are the merciful." [35]

And when the same gloss adds that "Christ had the bags whence to supply necessaries for use," this must be granted; but he had such goods saved in the bags either because conditions of time or place or other circumstances required him to do this, or in order that he might therefrom provide for poor persons whom he met. This is quite clear from the gloss on the words in Matthew, Chapter 18: "Take that piece of money," etc.; for the gloss says: "So great was the poverty of the Lord that he did not have wherewith to give tribute. Judas had the common goods in the bags, but he said that it was wrong to convert to one's own uses the goods of the poor." [36] So, then, the goods which had been saved were "of the poor," that is, for the sake of the poor; and by "the poor" we are to understand not only the apostles, but also any others, especially believers, to whom Christ together with the apostles gave food out of the goods which were saved, as is apparent from Matthew, Chapter 14, Mark, Chapters 6 and 8, and John, Chapter 6. Whence Christ said: "Give ye them to eat." [37] Thus too, as is there written, he commanded them to save surplus goods lest they be lost; whence in John, Chapter 6: "Gather up the fragments that remain, that nothing be lost. Therefore they," that is, the apostles, "gathered them together and filled twelve baskets."

---

[34] See above, para. 1 of this chapter.   [35] Matthew 5:7.
[36] See above, p. 209.   [37] Matthew 14:16–22; Mark 6:35–44, 8:1–8; John 6:5–12, 13.

17. As for the other objections, from the gloss on Matthew, Chapter 6, when it said: "He does not prohibit men to be provident and to labor"; from John, Chapter 14: "For some of them thought," etc.; and again from Matthew, Chapter 14, Mark, Chapters 6 and 8, and Luke, Chapter 9, when Christ said to the apostles: "How many loaves have ye," etc.; [38] all must be answered in like manner as was the immediately preceding objection.

18. We must now answer the objections whereby it was argued that the perfect person, even while observing supreme poverty, can have the afore-mentioned private or common ownership of temporal things. As for the first objection, which was based upon Luke, Chapter 22, that everyone who buys or sells, or who can buy or sell, some temporal thing, necessarily has ownership of the thing or of its price [39]—this I deny. And when it is proved by the assertion that every buyer or seller transfers the ownership of some thing or of its price, I deny this with respect to all perfect men. For although the thing is essentially transferred or exchanged by them law-fully for a price, or conversely, they do not on that account transfer to others, or themselves receive, the ownership of the thing, unless perhaps they be said to transfer the ownership accidentally, as because those to whom the thing is lawfully transferred become owners of it; but the essential transfer of ownership is from another source, as will be seen below.[40] But in no way do they receive or are they able to receive owner-ship, while remaining perfect.

But our opponent will say: He who buys a thing from a perfect man, or sells him a thing, receives that which is transferred by the perfect man, and nothing else; and similarly he transfers to the perfect man that which he had. Since, therefore, the buyer receives the ownership of the thing which he buys, and since the seller previously had, and now ceases to have, the ownership of the thing which he sells to the perfect man, it necessarily follows that the perfect man previously had ownership of the thing sold by him, or that he subsequently has ownership of the thing bought by him. The first proposition of this misreasoning I grant, if by "nothing else" is meant "no other thing"; and similarly I grant that the perfect man re-ceives the thing which someone else transfers to him, and ceases to have the thing which he sells. But when it is added that the buyer receives ownership of the thing, and that the ownership is therefore transferred from the perfect man to the buyer, there is committed the fallacy of "figure of speech," since to receive ownership of a thing, or a thing with ownership, is not to receive a substance,[41] but a mode thereof. Hence this misreason-

---

[38] See above, para. 1 of this chapter.   [39] See above, para. 2 of this chapter.
[40] Reading, with Bigongiari (p. 48), full stop after *patebit*.
[41] Reading, with Bigongiari (p. 38) and MSS, *quid* for *quod*.

ing is similar to the one which Aristotle presents in the second book of the *Refutations,* and is to be classed with that kind of sophistic argument called "figure of speech," which is illustrated by the following example: "You gave me only a penny; but you did not have only a penny; therefore you gave me what you did not have." [42] However, the former misreasoning differs from this one, in that in the present one a substance is changed into a relation,[43] whereas the converse happens in the one adduced by Aristotle. However, to do the question greater justice, now that the questioner's sophism has been exposed, and for the sake of those who are less learned in the sophistical art, I say that when the perfect man sells a thing by exchanging it for a price, he lawfully transfers the thing to someone else, since he has rightfully acquired it and has legally been empowered to dispose of it, although he has never had ownership of it. For in the preceding chapter it was shown that one may properly have lawful or rightful power (using "rightful" in the first and second senses) over a thing or over its use or over both at once, even to the point of consuming the thing, without yet having any ownership (taken in its three oft-mentioned senses); and hence one has lawful power to exchange the thing which one has rightfully acquired, provided no one else has ownership over it. But our objector will say: Whence does the buyer acquire the ownership of the thing? I reply that he acquires this ownership by permission of law or right taken in the first sense—both human and divine. For when things belong to no one, their ownership is granted to the person who, wanting them, occupies them. How much more, then, when things do belong to someone in a certain manner, as for example by right (in the first and second senses), but not with ownership—how much more, I say, can the ownership of such things be rightfully (in the first sense) acquired by a person who, wanting them, receives them by the grant and consent of the perfect man to whom they in some manner belonged and who effected the transfer, which transfer however was accidental so far as ownership was concerned? And conversely, I say that when a perfect man buys something, he receives lawful power over it, but not ownership, neither essentially nor accidentally, and thus the ownership passes out of the hands of the seller or anyone else.

19. But our opponent will say: From this it follows that a purchasable or any other thing can lawfully be taken away from a perfect man, even if he be in actual need of it, since it belongs to no one, in that no one has the ownership of it or the power to claim it; and similarly with its price or

---

[42] Aristotle *On sophistical refutations* 22.
[43] Reading, with Bigongiari (p. 38) and MSS, *ad aliquid* for *aliquid.*

the thing bought by it—all of which seems absurd. To this it must be replied that a thing which belongs to no one is rightfully granted to the person who occupies it. And when it is said that the thing which a perfect man has or holds, belongs to no one, since no one has ownership of it by right, especially by human right, there is here committed the fallacy of drawing an invalid conclusion; since it does not follow that because a thing is rightfully in the ownership of no one, therefore it rightfully belongs to no one; for, as we have said, a thing can rightfully (in the first sense) be acquired by someone apart from any of the aforesaid ownership of it. But if human rights or laws permitted this, namely, that a thing which was in the ownership of no one was to be understood to belong to no one, and consequently that it was rightfully granted to any person who occupied it, then I say that any thing which is in the hands of a perfect man may be seized by any person who is able to do so, and this person may lawfully make the thing his own in accordance with human right taken in its first sense, as is apparent from the definition of "lawful"; although if the perfect man does not give his consent, especially if he be needy, then that person may not lawfully seize the thing or make it his own in accordance with divine right, but rather he sins mortally in so doing, since he commits an act which divine law prohibits under pain of eternal damnation. But it can happen that something which is allowed by one law is at the same time prohibited by the other, as was shown from the preceding chapter. For fornication of unmarried persons is permitted by human law in order to avoid some greater evil, whereas it is prohibited by divine law with the aforesaid penalty.

20. As for the other objection, that when lawful use of a thing is inseparable with the ownership of it, he who had lawful use of it had necessarily the ownership of it; [44] this must be granted if the inseparability referred to is inseparability of ownership from use in the person of the user, in which sense "ownership" is meant actively, in such a way that ownership of a thing attaches itself to every person who uses it. But if this inseparability refers to the thing, in which sense "ownership" is meant passively, then there can surely be use and ownership of the same thing, but this does not necessarily mean that the owner and the user are the same person. For a person may lawfully use a thing which is not his own if the owner of the thing gives his consent, as was made plain in the preceding chapter; and hence in this sense the objection must be denied.

But granting the proposition in its first sense, in which our opponent seems to mean it, then the minor premise, that Christ and the apostles

[44] See above, para. 3 of this chapter.

had lawful use of some things whose ownership was not separated from their use, that is, in the user, I deny as being heretical, if we take "ownership" in its first three senses. And when it is defended by adding that they had the use of a thing which was either rightfully theirs or rightfully not theirs, I reply that they used things of both kinds: sometimes things which were rightfully theirs, and sometimes things that belonged to others—but the latter they used with the consent of the owners. And when it is said, moreover, that if they used things which were rightfully theirs, then they had ownership of them together with their use, the argument errs through drawing an invalid conclusion, as we said above. For it does not follow that because a person has rightfully acquired some thing or the use thereof, he therefore has rightfully acquired the ownership of it; although it does follow that because a person has rightfully acquired the ownership of a thing or of its use, therefore he has rightfully acquired the thing or its use. But if, on the other hand, it is said that he then uses a thing which is not his, and which therefore is either another's or belongs to no one, I reply that he may lawfully use things of both kinds, either simultaneously or successively.

And when our opponent destroys both parts of the consequent by taking first the second alternative and saying that a perfect man cannot use a thing which belongs to no one without acquiring ownership of it, because he must occupy the thing antecedently to or concomitantly with its use, and thus acquire ownership of it, I reply that the perfect man does occupy such thing antecedently, but when it is from this inferred that he therefore becomes owner of the thing, then an invalid conclusion is again drawn. For a perfect man might catch and eat a fish even though he had previously made an explicit vow never to lay contentious claim, before a coercive judge, to the aforesaid fish or to any other temporal thing. But our opponent will say: to the person who seizes a thing, ownership of it is granted. I reply that this is true when the person wants the ownership, but not when he does not want it, inasmuch as by divine and human law every person is permitted to refuse ownership, as is plain from the preceding chapter.

As for the first part of the consequent, namely, that when a thing belongs to someone else, a perfect man cannot have the use of it without having the aforesaid ownership of it, since, as our opponent shows, this use is had with the owner of the thing either granting it and giving his consent, or else refraining from so doing—it must be replied that the owner does indeed give his consent, for otherwise the use would be unlawful, especially if the owner dissented tacitly or expressly. But, then, says our opponent, if the owner gives his consent, he either grants or does not grant ownership of the thing to the perfect man. To which I reply that both cases can lawfully occur, even when the thing concerned is consumable in a single use of it. To which my opponent retorts: Conceding, then, that the use granted to a perfect man, which he exercises over the thing, is the use which consumes the thing; if, along with the use, he also uses the ownership granted to him, it follows that the perfect man has, together with the use, also the said ownership. To which conclusion I object by saying that again the fallacy of drawing an invalid inference is committed, since it does not follow that because a person grants to someone else the use and ownership of a thing, therefore he to whom the thing is granted is made owner of the thing; for he can accept one, namely, the lawful power of use, and decline the other, namely, the ownership, or he may have previously declined it by a vow. Our opponent, hence, will say: To whom, then, belongs the ownership of the thing? I reply, to the owner to whom it belonged before he had made the explicit grant to the perfect man, and which the latter refused to accept; or else the ownership belongs to no one. But if it be said that the owner of a thing has granted the use of his thing to a perfect man, even to the extent of consuming it, but without ownership of it, to this I reply that Christ and the apostles and every perfect man, while remaining in supreme poverty, can lawfully use that thing in such a way as to consume and destroy it. And when it is objected that such use is unlawful because it deprives the owner of the ownership of his thing without any act on his part, I answer that it must here be noted that the owner of a thing which is consumable in one use of it grants and can lawfully grant to the perfect man the use, with the intention of retaining for himself the ownership of the thing so long as the thing continues to exist; but, as soon as the thing ceases to exist, either in successive stages or completely, he does not intend to keep the ownership but renounces it, but only from then on, and not before. And this is what is done by those who grant alms to the perfect, lest vicious persons steal it from them because the perfect are deprived, although by their own will, of the power to demand such things at law or before a coercive judge. For if the owner of a thing intended always to have the ownership of his thing, he never would or should grant to the perfect man that use of it which would destroy it, unless he were insane, since no one can be owner of a thing which does not exist. Similarly, a perfect man would not accept such a grant of use, if he knew that such was the owner's intention. And hence I say that the owner of a thing is by his own act deprived of his ownership of it in successive stages or completely, when the thing is being consumed or has been completely consumed, because he wishes and explicitly says that he wishes to be thus deprived; and hence he suffers no injury. For this reason, also, when perfect men use things belonging to other men, and the owners of the things consent to such use, then this use is not unlawful, but rather holy and honorable, and yet the perfect men use these things lawfully without the aforesaid ownership.

21. The subsequent objection [45] has already been fully answered in the latter part of our refutation of the first objection. To the next objection, which took its origin from I Timothy, Chapter 3, and Titus, Chapter 1, "that the bishop must be given to hospitality," [46] my reply is as follows. Assuming that the bishop must always and everywhere be supremely poor or perfect if he is to be a perfect imitator of Christ and the apostles, I say that the words "the bishop must," or it is necessary that the bishop "be given to hospitality," can be understood in two senses in accordance with the mind of the Apostle: in one sense as being completely and absolutely necessary, in another sense as being hypothetically necessary; and further they can be understood as referring either to an emotional disposition by itself, that is, a firm intention, or to an emotional disposition together with its external effect. If, then, it be understood as absolutely necessary that the bishop be hospitable in his emotional disposition, I say that this is true and that this was the Apostle's meaning. But if the necessity be understood with reference to external effect, I say that the bishop must be or ought to be hospitable not in the sense of absolute necessity, but rather with hypothetical necessity, that is, if he has the means wherewith he can show hospitality. But if the bishop were absolutely obliged to show hospitality as an external effect, he would necessarily have to possess and to aim to save temporal things, and consequently he would have to lay claim to them at law and to own them. But his obligation to show hospitality as external effect is not absolute, but hypothetical. For the highest of pontiffs was sometimes not hospitable in external effect, for he said: "The Son of man hath not where to lay his head"; [47] and again, as we quoted above: "So great was the poverty of the Lord that he did not have wherewith to give tribute." [48] How, then, could Christ at that time have shown hospitality in external effect, even though he always maintained it in internal emotional disposition? And hence to the major premise of the syllogism we must reply that a person who must hypothetically show external hospitality, or absolutely have internal hospitality, must not become owner of any temporal thing; but the bishop must hypothetically

[45] See above, para. 4 of this chapter, first part.
[46] See above, para. 4 of this chapter, second part.
[47] Matthew 8:20.   [48] See above, para. 16 of this chapter.

provide or save for the future if he can, not for his own sake, however, but for the sake of the poor, as is clear from the gloss on the words in John, Chapter 21: "Feed my sheep." [49]

22. As for the further objection, that the holy bishops owned immovable goods, as was shown above from St. Ambrose's epistle *On Handing Over the Basilica;* [50] I reply that when the holy bishops, like Ambrose and the others, said that the fields and other things were "of the church," they did not mean that the bishops had ownership of them in private or in common, or had the power to sell them, give them away, or lay claim to them (the bishops are often denoted by the name "church," if they have maintained the status of supreme poverty, which we assume for the present). Rather, the fields are said to be "of the church" only because their proceeds had been dedicated to the worship of God and the support of gospel ministers and temples by an ordinance of the legislator or some other donor; in whose, that is, the ordainers', hands remained the ownership of these fields, or the power to protect and claim them from anyone else who wanted to seize them, as we said near the beginning of this chapter. And this was the meaning of the afore-mentioned saints; whence Ambrose, in the same epistle, writes after the above-quoted words as follows: "If the emperor desires the fields, he has the power to claim them; no one of us," that is, of the priests or bishops, "intervenes. What the people bestow can redound to the poor. Let there be no ill-will concerning the fields; let him take them if such is his pleasure; I do not give them to the emperor, but neither do I deny them." [51] But modern bishops would not speak in this way; and yet if Ambrose had thought he was committing a mortal sin by not defending the fields or denying them to the emperor, he would certainly have denied them to him, especially if he had been absolutely obliged to show external hospitality, as some men seem to have fancied, who yet are "masters in Israel" [52] and who should not be (nor perhaps are they) in ignorance on such matters; but they strive to please man rather than God.[53]

23. But as for what was shown with reference to Christ in particular, that according to the human laws a person who has redeemed someone from death is made lord over him and owner of his temporal goods, and that Christ redeemed all men from death; [54] to the first proposition I reply that it is not universally true, even according to the civil laws, unless

---

[49] See above, II. xiii. 29.   [50] See above, para. 4 of this chapter.

[51] St. Ambrose *Sermo contra Auxentium* cap. xxxiii (PL 16. 1060).

[52] John 3:10.

[53] This is a reference, as Previté-Orton points out (p. 261, n. 3), to such "servile experts" of Pope John XXII as Cardinal Berengar Fredoli (see F. Tocco, *La quistione della povertà nel secola XIV* [Naples, 1910], pp. 143–52).

[54] See above, para. 5 of this chapter.

the person is willing to receive such ownership. For even if it be granted that every redeemer of someone else is by right permitted to become lord over the person who is redeemed from death, and owner of his temporal goods, I still say that the redeemer does not necessarily become lord over the person redeemed, for example, if the redeemer does not wish such lordship or renounces it. And hence, even though Christ has thus redeemed all men from death, and can consequently become lord over them all, as the human laws say; nevertheless I declare that Christ, being perfect, was not a temporal lord, especially with human or acquired lordship or ownership, because Christ renounced all such ownership, both over persons and over things, as is sufficiently clear from Chapters IV and XIII of this discourse. Or else it must be said that Christ becomes lord over all for that status for which he redeemed us from death. But this is the status of the other world, and not of the present one; for he did not redeem us from this-worldly death, about which human laws speak. And hence by his act of redemption he did not acquire lordship over men or ownership of their temporal things for the status of the present world. For if he were owner of all the temporal goods of men, how could Christ have been speaking the truth when, in Matthew, Chapter 8, and in Luke, Chapter 9, he said of himself: "The Son of man hath not where to lay his head?" [55] Therefore, either he never acquired such ownership, as we said in the refutation of the second objection; or, if he could have acquired it, he did not wish it and renounced it, as could also be done by any other perfect man; or else he would have spoken an open lie, which it is impious to believe.

24. As for the final objection, from Revelation, Chapter 9, where it was said that Christ had "on the vesture written: King of kings," etc., and this "on the vesture of humanity," according to the gloss; [56] I say, that Christ had this written "on the vesture of humanity" because "the word of God" [57] was joined with a human garment, by reason of which that lordship belonged to him, just as the word was written on sheepskin, by reason of which this skin has something venerable about it, as signifying a branch of learning or some other truth. Or else it must be said that St. John was there thinking not of such lordship, that is, temporal, but rather of the lordship of the eternal kingdom or with reference to the eternal kingdom. Whence the gloss adds: "King of kings, that is, over all the saints." [58] And therefore, let not the Roman pope or any other bishop err, nor cause others to err with him; for if he seeks to possess and own temporal things, he can perhaps do this lawfully, even while being in a status of salvation, but not

[55] Matthew 8:20; Luke 9:58.   [56] See above, para. 5 of this chapter.
[57] See Revelation 19:13.   [58] *Glossa interlinearis* on Revelation 19:16.

while maintaining the status of supreme poverty or perfection, like Christ and the apostles.

We think, therefore, that we have adequately determined the nature of meritorious poverty, and what is its supreme mode or most perfect species, and that Christ and his imitators the apostles maintained this status while they were sojourners in this world.

CHAPTER XV: ON THE DIFFERENTIATION OF THE PRIESTLY OFFICE ACCORDING TO ITS ESSENTIAL AND ACCIDENTAL, SEPARABLE AND INSEPARABLE AUTHORITY; AND THAT NO PRIEST IS INFERIOR TO A BISHOP IN ESSENTIAL, BUT ONLY IN ACCIDENTAL DIGNITY

BUT these conclusions of ours raise a difficult question which it is very necessary to consider. For in Chapter XV of Discourse I we made a statement which we repeated at the end of Chapter VIII of this discourse: that the human legislator, by itself or through the ruler, is the efficient cause of the establishment of all the offices or parts of the state.[1] But we also recall having said, in the last chapter of Discourse I, that the priesthood or the priestly office of the New Law was first established by Christ alone,[2] who, however, renounced all secular rulership and temporal lordship (as we showed in Chapters IV, XI, XIII, and XIV of this discourse), and who was not the human legislator (as we showed in Chapters XII and XIII of Discourse I). Hence we seem to have said that that which establishes every office of the state is not the same as the human legislator or ruler. Hence it may well be wondered to whom belongs the authority to establish the priesthood, especially in communities of believers, since the above statements seem to contradict one another on this point.

2. Attempting to resolve this apparent contradiction, we shall first repeat what we said in Chapters VI and VII of Discourse I:[3] that each office of the state has one cause according as the office means a habit of the soul, and another cause according as the office is a part of the state established for the sake of the benefits to be derived therefrom; and this is to be noted with respect to the priesthood as well as with respect to the other offices of

---

[1] See above, I. xv. 4; II. viii. 9.   [2] See above, I. xix. 5.
[3] See above, I. vi. 9; I. vii. 1–3.

the state. For according as the priesthood means a certain habit of the soul, which the teachers of the holy Scripture call a "character," its immediate and essential efficient cause, or essential maker, is God imprinting this quality upon the mind, although by means of a certain human ministry which prepares the way, as it were. This ministry, in the New Law, drew its origin from Christ. For as a human priest, Christ, who was true God and true man, performed the ministry which succeeding priests have since performed; and as God he imprinted the character upon the souls of those whom he appointed as priests; in this way he appointed first the apostles, as his immediate successors, and then later all the other priests, but through the ministry of the apostles and of his other successors in this office. For when the apostles or the other priests lay their hands on others and utter the proper words or prayers, Christ, as God, imprints this priestly habit or character on those who are worthy and willing to receive it.

And a similar view must be taken with regard to the bestowal of the other orders whereby a certain character is imprinted on the soul of the recipient. This "priestly character," whether one or many, is the power whereby the priest can consecrate from bread and water the blessed body and blood of Christ by uttering certain words, and can minister the other ecclesiastical sacraments; and by this character also the priest can bind and loose men from sin.

3. According to the views of some men, this character or power was received by the apostles when Christ spoke to them the words written in Matthew, Chapter 26, Mark, Chapter 14, and Luke, Chapter 22. Because his words appear most completely in Luke, let us quote them as they are there found: "And he," Christ, "took bread, and gave thanks, and brake it, and gave unto them," the apostles, "saying: This is my body, which is given for you: this do in remembrance of me"; [4] "this do," that is, have the power of doing this. But other men have held that this authority was given to the apostles through the words written in John, Chapter 22, when Christ said to them: "Receive ye the Holy Ghost. Whosoever sins ye remit, they are remitted unto them; and whosoever sins ye retain, they are retained." [5] Others, again, say that this was done with the words found in Matthew, Chapter 16, when Christ said to the apostles in the person of Peter: "I will give unto thee the keys of the kingdom of heaven"; [6] or by the words which Christ spoke to them in Matthew, Chapter 18: "Verily I say unto you: whatsoever ye shall bind on earth shall be bound in heaven: and whatsoever ye shall loose on earth shall be loosed in heaven." [7] And

[4] Luke 22:19; Matthew 26:26–28; Mark 14:22–24.   [5] John 20:22–23.
[6] Matthew 16:19.   [7] Matthew 18:18.

still others say that there are two such priestly powers or authorities: one whereby the priests can perform the sacrament of the eucharist, and the other whereby they can bind or loose men from sins.[8] These two powers, it is said, were bestowed by Christ on the apostles at different times and with different utterances. However, it does not pertain to the present inquiry to determine which of these views is most probable. For regardless of the manner or time of the appointment of the apostles in this office, it is certain that this power was given to them by Christ, and that by their ministry and that of their successors this power is bestowed on other men who are received into this office. Whence in I Timothy, Chapter 4: "Neglect not the gift that is in thee, which was given thee by prophecy, with the laying on of the hands of the priest." [9] And in the same way the deacons receive their character by the laying on of the hands of the priest. Concerning these deacons it is written in Acts, Chapter 6: "They set these," that is, the men who were to become deacons, "before the apostles: and when they had prayed they laid their hands on them." [10]

4. Now with respect to this priestly character, whether one or many, which we have said to be the power of performing the sacrament of the eucharist or of consecrating Christ's body and blood, and the power of binding and loosing men from sins, which character we shall henceforth call the "essential" or "inseparable authority" of the priest insofar as he is a priest, to me it seems likely that this character is the same in kind among all priests, and that the Roman or any other bishop has no more of it than has any simple priest.[11] For with respect to this authority, regardless of whether it be one or many, the bishop does not differ from the priest; this is asserted not only by Jerome, but also by the Apostle, who openly holds this view, as will be seen below. For on the words in Matthew, Chapter 16: "Whatsoever ye shall bind on earth," etc., Jerome writes: "The same judiciary power" (supply. as Peter had) "is had by the other apostles, to whom he," Christ, "said after his resurrection: 'Receive ye the Holy Ghost. Whosesoever sins ye remit, they are remitted unto them,' etc. Every church has this power through its priests and bishops"; [12] and Jerome here names the priests first, because this authority belongs to the priest *qua* priest primarily and as such. Now with reference to the power of the sacrament of the eucharist, no one contends that every priest does not have it equally

---

[8] See Peter Lombard *Sent.* Lib. IV. dists. 8, 19, 24 (PL 192. 856–58, 889–92, 900–965); Thomas Aquinas *Summa theologica* III. qu.82; Suppl. qu.17.

[9] I Timothy 4:14.　　　　　　　　[10] Acts 6:6.

[11] This position is also upheld by John of Paris *De potestate regia et papali* cap. xii (ed. D. J. Leclercq, *Jean de Paris et l'ecclésiologie du XIIIe siècle* [Paris, 1942], p. 209). See also Vol. I, p. 270.

[12] *Glossa ordinaria* on Matthew 16:19.

with the Roman bishop. And hence it is to be wondered why some men obstinately but unreasonably assert that the Roman pontiff has from Christ a greater power of the keys than have the other priests; [13] for this cannot be proved from Scripture, but rather the opposite.

5. The more clearly to grasp this, we must not overlook the fact that these names "priest" and "bishop" were in the primitive church synonymous, although they were applied to the same man by virtue of different properties. For the name "priest" (*presbyter*) was applied to a man by virtue of his age, as being an elder; "bishop" (*episcopus*) was applied to him by virtue of his dignity or care over others, as being an overseer. And hence in an epistle of Jerome to Evander the priest, usually entitled *How the Priest and the Deacon Differ,* Jerome writes as follows: " 'Priest' is a name given for age, 'bishop' for dignity. Hence in the epistles to Titus and to Timothy, the ordination of bishops and deacons is discussed, but no mention is made of priests, because the priest is contained in the bishop." [14] This is also made clear by the words of the Apostle in Philippians, Chapter 1, when he wrote: "To all the saints in Christ Jesus which are at Philippi, with the bishops and deacons." [15] So, then, he named the priests not otherwise than as bishops. For it is certain that there were many bishops in one city only because there were many priests. This is again made clear by the Apostle's words in Titus, Chapter 1, when he wrote: "For this cause left I thee in Crete, that thou shouldest set in order the things that are wanting, and shouldest ordain priests in every city, as I also appointed thee, if any be blameless." And immediately he adds what quality must be had by a man who is to be ordained as priest: "For a bishop must be blameless, as the steward of God." [16] So, then, those who were to be ordained as priests he called by no other name than "bishop." And in Acts, Chapter 20, he speaks to the priests of one church, Ephesus, as follows: "Take heed therefore unto yourselves, and to all the flock, over which the Holy Ghost hath made you bishops, to feed the church of God, which he hath purchased with his own blood." [17] See, then, that the Apostle addressed many persons as bishops in the church of one city, Ephesus; this was only because there were many priests, all of whom were called "bishops," because they had to be overseers over the people, although this name "bishop" was in the later church reserved only for him who was appointed the first priest in

---

[13] See St. Bernard *De consideratione* II. viii (PL 182. 751–52); Thomas Aquinas *Summa theologica* Suppl. qu.20. a.1. ad 1; James of Viterbo *De regimine Christiano* II. iv, v (ed. H. X. Arquillière [Paris, 1926], pp. 194, 201, 216); Augustinus Triumphus *Summa de ecclesiastica potestate* (Augsburg, 1473) qu.20.

[14] St. Jerome Epist. 146, *Ad Evangelum* (PL 22. 1195).   [15] Philippians 1:1.

[16] Titus 1:5, 6, 7.   [17] Acts 20: 28.

a city or locality by the other priests and the people. But the Apostle called them bishops rather than priests in order to make them mindful of the care and solicitude which they had to exercise on behalf of the other believers. But himself he called "priest," not "bishop," out of humility, as is plain from the passage from I Timothy, Chapter 4, quoted above, when he said: "Do not neglect the gift that is in thee," etc.[18] So too Peter and John called themselves "elders" (*seniores*), that is, priests, because this name was given for age. Whence in I Peter, Chapter 5: "The elders which are among you I exhort, who am also an elder, and a witness of the sufferings of Christ." [19] And in II John, Chapter 1: "The elder unto the elect lady and her children." [20] And again in III John, Chapter 1: "The elder unto the well-beloved Gaius." [21] Indeed, wherever the Scripture has the words "elder" or "fellow elder," St. Jerome in his above-mentioned epistle has "priest" or "fellow priest," since the apostles used these words as synonyms.

6. But because the number of priests had markedly increased after the days of the apostles, the priests, in order to avoid scandal and schism, elected one of their number to guide and direct the others in the exercise of the ecclesiastic office and service, in the distribution of offerings, and in the proper arrangement of other matters, lest the household and service of the temples be disturbed because of conflicting desires, by each man's acting according to his own pleasure, and sometimes wrongly. Through later custom this priest, who was elected to regulate the other priests, retained for himself alone the name of "bishop," as being an overseer,[22] because he supervised not only the faithful people (for which reason all priests were in the primitive church called bishops), but also his fellow priests; and hence, antonomastically,[23] the overseer later kept for himself alone the name "bishop," while the others retained the simple name "priest."

7. But the aforesaid election or appointment made by man does not give to the person thus elected any greater essential merit or priestly authority or power, but only a certain power with regard to the ordering of the household in God's house or temple: namely, the power to direct and regulate the other priests, deacons, and officials, in the same way that the prior is today given power over monks. This power is not coercive unless the authority for such coercion shall have been granted by the human legislator to the person thus elected, as was demonstrated in Chapters IV and VIII

---

[18] I Timothy 4:14.   [19] I Peter 5:1.   [20] II John 1:1.
[21] III John 1:1.   [22] See Thomas Aquinas *Summa theologica* II. II. qu.183. a.1. ad 1.
[23] Reading, with Bigongiari (p. 38) and MSS, *antonomastice* for *Antiochiae*.

of this discourse, and as will appear more fully in the following chapter; nor does this power bestow any other, intrinsic dignity or authority on the person elected. This is similar to the way in which soldiers at war elect the captain, who in ancient times was called "commander" (*praeceptor*) or "imperator" (although this name "imperator" was transferred to a certain kind of royal monarchy, the highest of all, and the word is now used in this sense).[24] In this way, too, the deacons elect one of their number to be archdeacon, who is by this election given no essential merit or holy order greater than that of the diaconate, but only such human power as we have mentioned, to direct and regulate the other deacons. Hence the Roman bishop has no more essential priestly authority than has any other bishop, just as St. Peter had no more such authority than the other apostles. For they all received this same authority equally and immediately from Christ, as was shown above by the authority of Jerome writing on the words in Matthew, Chapter 16: "And I will give unto thee the keys of the kingdom of heaven," and as will be more fully shown in the following chapter.

8. This was clearly the view of St. Jerome in the afore-mentioned epistle where, after demonstrating by the authority of many apostles that in the primitive church, in the days of the apostles, the priest and the bishop were completely the same with respect to the essential dignity bestowed by Christ, he gives the reason, saying: "One man was elected and put over the rest in order to prevent schism from arising, lest the church of Christ be destroyed by each man's following his own will. For in Alexandria, from Mark the preacher to Hereidas and Dionysius the bishops, the priests always elected one of their number to fill the highest seat, and called him bishop; in this same way the army would choose an 'imperator,' " that is, a commander (*praeceptor*) or captain according to modern usage, but not an *imperator* in the sense of a monarch, as the word is used today, "or the deacons would elect one of their number whom they knew to be industrious, and would call him 'archdeacon.' For what acts, except those in a regulatory capacity (*ordinatione*), does the bishop perform which the priest does not perform?"[25] referring here to acts of essential authority. For by "regulatory capacity" Jerome did not mean the power or act of bestowing holy orders, for besides this the bishops, even in this day, did, and still do, many things which the priests do not do, although every priest has the divine power to bestow all the sacraments, just as has the bishop. But by

---

[24] For the use of *imperator* in the sense of captain, see Cicero *De officiis* II. viii. 28; II. xi. 40; III. xx. 79; III. xxvi. 99.

[25] St. Jerome Epist. 146, *Ad Evangelum* (PL 22. 1194).

"regulatory capacity" Jerome there meant the household power, which we mentioned above, given to the bishop immediately by man or men. And this position with respect to the priestly authority I confirm by reason as well as by the authority of Jerome: by reason, because many bishops have been elected by all the people, as were St. Clement, St. Gregory, St. Nicholas, and many other saints,[26] and yet the people, or even their fellow priests, certainly bestowed on these bishops no greater holy order or intrinsic character, but only the power to regulate church ritual and to guide persons in the performance of divine worship in the temple or house of God. And hence such bishops, elected to direct the other priests in the temple and to instruct the people in matters of faith, were by ancient lawmakers (like Justinian and the Roman people) called "reverend stewards," and the supreme one was called "most reverend steward." [27]

That the essential dignity of the bishop is not different from that of the priest, and that neither is greater than the other, Jerome also clearly showed in his afore-mentioned epistle, when he said:

Nor is the church of the city of Rome to be considered different from the church of the whole world. Gaul, Britain, Africa, Persia, the Orient, India, and all the barbaric nations, all worship one Christ, and observe one rule of truth. If authority be in question, the whole world is greater than the city. Wherever the bishops be, whether at Rome or Eugobius, Constantinople or Phegius, Alexandria or Rathanis, they are all of the same merit, and the same priesthood. The power of riches and the humility of poverty make the bishop either prouder or lowⁱⁱer. But otherwise, all are successors of the apostles.[28]

9. But there are certain other, non-essential appointments to priestly offices. Such is the election we mentioned above, whereby one of the priests is named to regulate or guide the others in matters pertaining to divine worship. Such too is the election and appointment of other priests to teach and minister the sacraments of the New Law to a specified people in a designated place of greater or lesser size, and to distribute both among themselves and among other poor persons the temporal things which have been set apart by the legislator or by individuals for the support of poor preachers in a certain province or community, and also for the support of other poor persons unable to provide for themselves on account of age, weakness, or other misfortune (but this latter bounty must come out of what remains over and above the needs of the preachers). These temporal

---

[26] See *Acta sanctorum* March 12 (II, 131); *Liber pontificalis*, ed. L. Duchesne (Paris, 1886–92), II, 152.

[27] See *Corp. jur. civ., Codex Justinianus* Lib. 1. Tit. iii. cap. 25, 41. Marsilius here confuses the bishop (*episcopus*) with the steward (*oeconomus*).

[28] St. Jerome Epist. 146, *Ad Evangelum* (PL 22. 1194).

things, thus set apart, are now called "ecclesiastic benefices," which we discussed in Chapter XIV of this discourse. For they are entrusted to ministers of temples to be distributed for the aforesaid purposes; the ministers have for these tasks been elected and appointed to a certain province, since the essential authority whereby they are successors of the apostles does not assign them to teach and minister the sacraments of the New Law to the people of one place rather than to the people of another, just as the apostles were given no definite territorial assignment. For Christ said to them, in the last chapter of Matthew: "Go ye therefore and teach all nations"; [29] he did not assign the apostles to definite places, but they later apportioned among themselves the peoples to whom and the provinces in which they were to preach the word of God or the evangelical law; and sometimes, also, they learned of their mission through divine revelation. Whence in Galatians, Chapter 2: "They," James, Cephas, and John, "gave to me and Barnabas the right hands of fellowship; that we should go unto the heathen, and they unto the circumcision." [30]

10. Thus, then, it is clear from the above what is the efficient cause of the appointment of the priesthood, according as it signifies a habit or character of the soul, and of the other orders which are called holy; for this cause is God or Christ, without mediation, although first there occurs a certain human, as it were preparatory, ministry, like the laying on of hands and the uttering of words, which perhaps effect nothing to this end but which thus precede by virtue of a certain pact or divine ordinance. And from what we have said it is also apparent that the above appointment is different from the human appointment whereby one priest is put at the head of the others and whereby too the priests are assigned to teach and instruct the peoples of particular provinces in the divine law, to minister the sacraments to them, and to distribute the temporal things which we have called ecclesiastic benefices.

From the above it is also clear that with respect to their primary authority, which we have from the outset called "essential," all the priests are equal in merit and in priesthood, as Jerome said in his epistle mentioned above, giving the reason that "all" bishops "are successors of the apostles." He here seems to indicate that all the apostles had equal authority, and that, consequently, no individual apostle had authority over any other apostle or apostles, either with respect to their essential appointment, which we have called primary, or with regard to their secondary appointments.

Hence, too, it seems that a similar view must be taken concerning the relation of the apostles' successors to one another; but it remains to determine what is the source of those appointments which we have said to be secondary and made by human authority, and what their efficient cause reasonably is.

CHAPTER XVI: ON THE EQUALITY OF THE APOSTLES IN EACH OFFICE OR DIGNITY BESTOWED ON THEM IMMEDIATELY BY CHRIST. WHENCE IS PROVED WHAT WAS SAID IN THE PRECEDING CHAPTER CONCERNING THE EQUALITY OF ALL THEIR SUCCESSORS; AND HOW ALL THE BISHOPS ARE ALIKE SUCCESSORS OF EVERY APOSTLE

AT the outset, then, we shall in this chapter show that no apostle had preeminence over the others with respect to the essential, that is, priestly, dignity which Christ gave to them; and then we shall show that there was no preeminence with respect to any other appointment, which we have called secondary, given to them immediately by Christ, and still less with respect to coercive jurisdiction—although this last has been adequately demonstrated in Chapters IV and V of this discourse. From these propositions we shall deduce as a necessary conclusion that no particular one of the bishops who are the successors of the apostles has any authority or power, of the kinds mentioned above, over his fellow bishops or priests, and that this, rather than the opposite, is what can be proved by the words of Scripture. And finally we shall deduce as a necessary consequence what is the main intention of this and the preceding chapters: that these appointments which we have frequently called secondary pertain to the faithful human legislator as their essential efficient cause, just as does the establishment of the other parts of the state.

2. The first proposition, then, is proved from Luke, Chapter 22. For when Christ gave to the apostles the power to administer the sacrament of the eucharist, he said to them: "This is my body, which is given for you: this do in remembrance of me," [1] that is, have the power to do this, but by uttering similar words whenever you have to perform this act, namely: "This is my body." Now Christ did not address these words to St. Peter more than to the others. For he did not say: Do thou this (*fac*) and give the other apostles the power to do this; but rather he said: "Do ye" (*facite*),

[1] Luke 22:19.

speaking in the plural, and to all the apostles alike. The same view must also be held concerning the power of the keys, regardless of whether this power was given to the apostles at the same or at a different time, and by the same words or by different ones, such as by the words which are found in John, Chapter 20. For later Christ said to the apostles: "As my father hath sent me, even so send I you. And when he had said this, he breathed on them and saith unto them: Receive ye the Holy Ghost. Whosesoever sins ye remit, they are remitted unto them; and whomsoever sins ye retain, they are retained." [2] Christ said, then: "As my father hath sent me, even so send I you"; nor did he say to Peter or to any other individual apostle: I send thee even as my father, etc., and thou art to send others. Nor, again, is it written that Christ breathed "on him," but rather "on them," not on one individual. Nor did Christ say to Peter: Receive thou the Holy Ghost and then give it to the others; but rather he said: "Receive ye," speaking in the plural, and to all the apostles alike. And this is also what is found in the last chapter of Matthew, when Christ said to the apostles: "Go ye therefore and teach all nations"; and he said, "Go ye," speaking in the plural and to all alike, and not to Peter alone: Go thou and send others.

3. The Apostle gives an even clearer statement of the solution of this question, which we quote in order that no one may believe that any apostle had such prerogative or authority over the others. Explicitly denying such authority to Peter, who would perhaps have seemed most likely to have it because of certain words which Christ addressed to him alone, and because he was older than the rest, Paul wrote as follows in Galatians, Chapter 2: "But of these who seemed to be somewhat, they added nothing to me. But contrariwise, when they saw that the gospel of the uncircumcision was committed unto me, as the gospel of the circumcision was unto Peter (for he that wrought effectually in Peter to the apostleship of the circumcision, the same was mighty in me toward the Gentiles); and when James, Cephas, and John, who seemed to be pillars, perceived the grace that was given unto me, they gave to me and Barnabas the right hands of fellowship." [3] He, then, who "wrought in Peter to the apostleship," wrought also in Paul; but this person was Christ; therefore Paul did not receive this office from Peter, nor, similarly, did the other apostles. Whereon the gloss according to Augustine, expressing this more fully, says: "Those 'who seemed to be somewhat,' namely, Peter and the others who had been with the Lord, 'added,' that is, imparted, 'nothing to me.' Wherein it is clear that they are not superior to me, who have been made perfect by the Lord

---

[2] John 20:21-23.   [3] Galatians 2:6-9.

so that there was nothing which they added to my perfection." [4] See, then, that Paul was not inferior to Peter or to the others. And in support of this view, the gloss adds: " 'When they saw that the gospel of the uncircumcision was committed unto me,' as a believer, with as great primacy 'as the gospel of the uncircumcision was unto Peter.' " [5] So, then, Paul was sent with an eminence equal to that of Peter, and not by Peter or by any other apostle, but immediately by Christ; and this was further made explicit by Paul in Galatians, Chapter 1, when he wrote: "Paul an apostle, not of men, neither by men, but by Jesus Christ, and God the Father." [6] Whereon the gloss according to Ambrose: " 'Paul an apostle, not' elected or sent 'by men,' that is, by Ananias, as some said, or by any others, as some men were elected and sent by the apostles." [7] And a little below, the gloss according to Augustine adds: "The other apostles seemed to be of greater importance, because they were the first; Paul seemed to be the least important, because the newest. But now he appears more worthy, because the first were ordained by Christ *qua* man, that is, mortal; but the newest apostle, Paul, was ordained by Christ as fully God, that is, completely immortal, and by God the Father who did this through his Son. And to make it clear why he said 'neither by man,' Paul adds, 'God the Father, who raised him from the dead.' And so he ordained me more eminently through the immortal Christ, than he did the others through the mortal Christ." [8]

4. The Apostle again confirms this in a paragraph further on in the same book and chapter: "I certify you, brethren, that the gospel which was preached of me is not after man; for I neither received it of man, neither was I taught it, but by the revelation of Jesus Christ." [9] Whereon the gloss according to Augustine: " 'I certify you, brethren, that the gospel which was preached of me is not after man,' that is, man did not teach or send me. And truly the gospel is not of man. 'For I neither received it of man,' that is, no man elected me or ordered me to preach the gospel, 'neither was I taught it' by a human teacher, 'but by the revelation of Jesus Christ.' " [10] So, then, neither Peter nor any other apostle or man elected, sent, or ordered Paul to preach the gospel. And the same must also be held with respect to the other apostles. Peter, then, held no power over the other apostles immediately from God, and still less coercive jurisdiction, neither to install them in the priestly office, nor to set them apart, nor to send them to their posts as preachers. The only point that can well be granted is this: that Peter was the first of the apostles in point of age, or perhaps in respect of length of time spent in service, or by the election

[4] In Peter Lombard *Collectanea, ad loc.* (PL 192. 107).   [5] *Ibid.* (108).
[6] Galatians 1:1.   [7] In Peter Lombard *Collectanea* (PL 192. 95).   [8] *Ibid.*
[9] Galatians 1:11–12.   [10] In Peter Lombard *Collectanea* (PL 192. 99).

of the apostles who properly revered him on this account; although such election cannot be proved from the Scripture.

5. A sign that what we have said is true, is that St. Peter is in the Scripture found to have assumed no special authority over the other apostles, but rather to have maintained equality with them. For he assumed for himself no authority to settle questions relating to the preaching of the gospel, with respect to doctrine; but these questions were settled through the common deliberation of the apostles and of other more learned believers, and not by Peter or any other apostle alone. And hence, in Acts, Chapter 25, when the preachers of the gospel disagreed as to whether the uncircumcised believers had to be circumcised in order to gain eternal salvation, some of the apostles arguing in the affirmative, and Paul and Barnabas protesting against this, "the apostles and elders came together for to consider of this matter." Peter and James said that such circumcision was not necessary, and the elders and the other apostles agreed with them. Whence it is added below: "Then pleased it the apostles and elders, with the whole church, to send chosen men of their own company to Antioch . . . and they wrote letters by them." And the manner of writing was in conformity with their manner of deliberating, thus: "The apostles and elders and brethren send greeting unto the brethren which are of the Gentiles in Antioch and Syria and Cilicia. . . ." The chapter continues in this vein when a little below it is written: "It seemed good unto us, being assembled with one accord, to choose men and send them unto you." And likewise, further below: "For it seemed good to the Holy Ghost, and to us, to lay upon you no greater burden." [11] The afore-mentioned questions relating to the faith were not, then, settled by Peter through the plenitude of power which is claimed for the Roman bishop by some idle dreamers, "masters in Israel," who in unwritten dogmas have declared (what Peter did not dare) that the Roman bishop by himself alone can settle questions of faith; [12] which is an open falsehood and clearly opposed to the Scripture. We shall discuss this at length in the following chapter and in Chapter XX of this discourse.

6. It was by the congregation of learned believers, therefore, that deliberations were conducted, and questions settled, and elections made, and documents written; and on this congregation's authority rested the validity of what was thus determined and commanded. For the congregation of the apostles was of greater authority than was Peter or any other apostle alone. Whence we read that it was this whole congregation that sent Peter to

---

[11] Acts 15:6, 22, 23, 25, 28.

[12] See Egidius of Rome *De ecclesiastica potestate* I. i; Augustinus Triumphus *Summa de ecclesiastica potestate* (Augsburg, 1473) qus.10, 11.

Samaria, as is shown in Acts, Chapter 8: "Now when the apostles which were at Jerusalem heard that Samaria had received the word of God, they sent unto them Peter and John." [13] Why, then, do certain sacrilegious flatterers take it upon themselves to say that any bishop has plenitude of power from Christ, even over clergymen, let alone over laymen, when St. Peter or any other apostle never presumed by word or deed to ascribe such power to himself? For those who make this assertion should be ridiculed, not believed nor feared, since what they say is opposed to the literal and manifest sense of the Scripture. For St. Peter never had such power over the apostles or over any other men, but rather, as we have said, he maintained equality with them in accordance with the command of Christ. Whence in Matthew, Chapter 23: "But be not ye called Rabbi: for one is your master," Christ, "and all ye are brethren," [14] that is, equal. And he said "all," making no exceptions. This view is confirmed by the Apostle in Galatians, Chapter 2, where he writes as follows: "I went up by revelation, and communicated unto them that gospel which I preach among the Gentiles." [15] Whereon the gloss according to Augustine: "I did not learn from them as from greater men," that is, from Peter and the other leading apostles, who will be mentioned below, "but 'I communicated unto them' as friends and equals." [16] The same is again found below in the same chapter, where the Apostle wrote: "But when Peter was come to Antioch, I withstood him to the face, because he was to be blamed, etc." [17] Whereon the gloss according to Jerome: "They communicated nothing unto me, but I communicated unto Peter." And then it is added: " 'I opposed him,' as an equal. For he would not have dared do this unless he had known that he was not unequal." [18] So, then, Paul was in office and in dignity equal, not inferior, to Peter, although Peter was older, and as a pastor was prior in time.

7. And it is likewise clear that neither St. Peter nor any other apostle had preeminence or power over the others in the distribution of the temporal offerings of the primitive church. Whence in Acts, Chapter 4: "For as many as were possessors of lands or houses sold them, and brought the prices of the things that were sold, and laid them down at the apostles' feet: and distribution was made unto every man according as he had need." [19] So, then, the church's temporal offerings were disposed of by the apostles together, and not by Peter alone. For it is not written that they "laid them down at the feet" of Peter, but "of the apostles." Nor is it written that Peter distributed them, but that "distribution was made."

---

[13] Acts 8:14.   [14] Matthew 23:8.   [15] Galatians 2:2.
[16] Peter Lombard *Collectanea* (PL 192. 103).   [17] Galatians 2:11.
[18] *Collectanea* (PL 192. 108).   [19] Acts 4:34-35.

8. Tell me, then, whence does the Roman bishop obtain the authority to distribute such things according to his own wishes, or to claim, as if they belonged to him alone, bequests left in men's wills for religious purposes, but which have been entrusted to others for saving or distribution? For the Roman bishop, whether alone or with anyone else, is not authorized by divine or human right to demand such things which have been placed in the trust or custody of other men in accordance with reasonable laws, such as by the will of the testators or of those who have made such arrangements. "For let the testator speak," that is, about something belonging to him, "and his words will be law," as it is written elsewhere.[20] For no support can be obtained from the holy Scripture on behalf of the contention that the afore-mentioned power belongs to the Roman or any other bishop; but rather the opposite. And if these bequests have been entrusted to the church of a determinate diocese for distribution, this distribution will pertain to the bishops who preside over that determinate diocese, and not to the Roman bishop. The reason for this is that the Roman bishop neither has nor had immediately from Christ any power or authority over his fellow bishops or priests: this was one of the propositions set forth at the beginning of this chapter. For just as Peter had no power over the other apostles, so too Peter's successors in the episcopal seat at Rome have no power over the successors of the other apostles. For Peter had no power to bestow the priesthood or the apostolate or the episcopate on the others, since they all received this power or authority immediately from Christ, and not through the ministry of Peter, as we have clearly proved above from the Scripture. This is also explicitly stated by Augustine, *On the Questions of the New and Old Testament,* Question 94, where he writes as follows: "On the same day," that is, Pentecost, "that the law was made, the Holy Ghost came down among the apostles, so that they might receive authority and know how to preach the evangelic law." [21]

9. Moreover, just as we read that Peter was elected bishop at Antioch by the multitude of believers,[22] not needing the confirmation of the other apostles, so too did the other apostles become administrators of the other provinces without any knowledge, appointment, or consecration on the part of Peter, for they had been sufficiently consecrated by Christ. Consequently, it must similarly be held that the successors of these apostles needed no confirmation by the successors of Peter; indeed, many of the

[20] See *Glossa ordinaria* on *Corp. jur. civ., Codex Justinianus* VI. xliii. 7; and *Corp. jur. civ., Authentic.* Coll. IV. Tit. i, *De nuptiis* (Nov. 22) cap. ii.

[21] St. Augustine *Quaestiones veteris et novi testamenti* qu.95 (PL 35. 2292).

[22] See above, I. xix. 7. According to Previté-Orton (p. 503, n. 24), the ultimate source of this view is Pseudo-Clement *Recognitiones* x. lxxi (PG 1. 1473).

successors of the other apostles were duly elected and appointed as bishops, and piously ruled their provinces, without any appointment or confirmation by the successors of Peter. And this practice was thus legitimately maintained until about the time of the emperor Constantine, who gave to the bishop and church of Rome a certain preeminence and authority over all the other churches, bishops, and priests in the world.[23] And that Peter and the other apostles were thus equal was shown by the Apostle in Galatians, Chapter 2, when he wrote: "They," James, Peter, and John, "gave to me and Barnabas the right hands of fellowship; that we should go unto the heathen, and they unto the circumcision" [24]—"the right hands of fellowship," and therefore "of equality," [25] as has been sufficiently shown above by the gloss according to Augustine, although the Apostle's statement on this point is so clear that it does not need the gloss. We have also proved this point through Jerome's epistle to Evander, which says that all bishops, "whether at Rome or" elsewhere, "are of the same priesthood" and "of the same merit" [26] or power bestowed immediately by Christ.

10. Now although some saints call St. Peter "the prince of the apostles," [27] they here use the term "prince" loosely and inappropriately. But if they mean "prince" in the strict sense of the term, then they are in open opposition to the thought and the words of Christ, who in Matthew, Chapter 20, and Luke, Chapter 22, says: "The princes of the Gentiles lord it over them, but you not so." [28] And hence it must be said that the saints called Peter "prince" not because of any power which had been given to him over the apostles immediately by Christ, but perhaps because he was the oldest, or because he was the first to avow that Christ was the true son of God, or because his faith was perhaps the most fervent and constant, or because he met with Christ and was most frequently called into conference and council. Whence the Apostle, in Galatians, Chapter 2: "James, Cephas," that is, Peter, "and John seemed to be pillars," [29] whereon the gloss according to Ambrose: "Because they were the most honored among the apostles, since they were always in conference with the Lord." [30] A convenient example of this kind of relation is afforded by secular princes none of whom is over the others in power, such as counts of the same kingdom none of whom is inferior to any other in jurisdiction or authority, but all of whom are immediately subject to the king; yet one or more of these princes are some-

---

[23] See the Donation of Constantine in Pseudo-Isidore *Decretales*, ed. Hinschius, p. 252.

[24] Galatians 2:6–9.   [25] Peter Lombard *Collectanea* (PL 192. 107).

[26] See above, II. xv. 8.

[27] See St. Jerome *De viris illustribus* (PL 23. 607). See below, II. xxviii. 22.

[28] Matthew 20:25–26; Luke 22:25–26.   [29] Galatians 2:9.

[30] Peter Lombard *Collectanea* (PL 192. 108).

times held in greater esteem because of their greater age or virtue, or because of their greater services to the king or kingdom, for which they are more loved and held in greater respect by king or people. And this is the way in which we ought to think about the relation of the apostles to one another and to Christ. For they were all under Christ's power and authority, receiving their priestly and apostolic appointment immediately from him, and not from one another, as is clearly proclaimed throughout the Scripture, as well as by the saints who came after. St. Peter, it is true, was held in greater honor among the apostles, but this was for the reasons we have already mentioned, and not because Christ had given him any power over the other apostles. For Christ forbade that any one of the apostles should have power over the others (as we have shown above from Matthew, Chapter 23) when he spoke to them these words, which are directly and immediately pertinent: "Be not ye called Rabbi; for one is your master, and ye are all brethren." [31]

11. Similarly, Peter had no coercive jurisdiction over the other apostles, any more than conversely, and consequently the successors of the apostles have no coercive jurisdiction over one another. For Christ utterly forbade them to have such jurisdiction, in Matthew, Chapter 20, and Luke, Chapter 22, where we find a passage which is of immediate pertinence: for when "there was a strife among them, which of them should be accounted the greatest, he," Christ, "said unto them: The kings or princes of the Gentiles lord it over them, and they that are the greater exercise power upon them. But you not so." [32] Christ could not have made this denial more clearly. Why, then, will anyone give greater credence, on this point, to a human statement, whether of a saint or non-saint, than to the clearest utterance of Christ? For Christ spoke against such statements in Mark, Chapter 7, when he made these directly pertinent remarks: "Howbeit in vain do they worship me, teaching the doctrines and commandments of men. For laying aside the commandment of God, ye hold the tradition of men." And a little below: "Full well ye reject the commandment of God, that ye may keep your own tradition." [33] This is what is done by those persons who teach human decretals stating that to the Roman bishop belongs power and ownership over the temporal goods not only of the church but even of the empire and kingdom; these persons "reject the commandment of God," as was demonstrated in Chapter XIV and as is quite clear from the present chapter, in order that they may "keep their own tradition" with regard to temporal goods, for their own advantage.

[31] Matthew 23:8.   [32] Matthew 20:25; Luke 22:24-26.
[33] Mark 7:7, 8, 9; see Matthew 15:3, 6.

12. But even if the apostles had chosen St. Peter to be their bishop or leader because of his age and his greater acquired holiness, as is maintained in a decree of the pope Anacletus, contained in the *Codex* of Isidore, as follows: "The other apostles received honor and power in equal fellowship with him," Peter, "and wanted him to be their leader"; [34] even if this were true, it would not follow that his successors in the Roman or some other seat, if he was bishop elsewhere, have this priority over the successors of the other apostles, unless they have been elected to such leadership by the successors of those others; for some of the successors of the other apostles have been of greater virtue than some of Peter's successors, although, properly, every bishop is alike the successor of every apostle in office, though not in territory. Again, why would this priority belong more to Peter's successors at Rome than to those at Antioch or Jerusalem or elsewhere, if he was bishop in many cities?

13. Moreover, every bishop is alike the successor of every apostle in intrinsic, that is, inseparable, dignity, and has the same merit or perfection in this dignity or character; for they have all received this character immediately from the one giver or efficient cause, namely, Christ, and not from the man who laid his hands on them. Nor does it make any difference which of the apostles laid on his hands. Whence in I Corinthians, Chapter 3: "Let no man glory in men. Whether Paul, or Apollo, or Cephas," etc.,[35] has baptized you or otherwise laid his hands on you, it makes no difference. Whence it is added: "And ye are Christ's," that is, you have the internal stamp from Christ. Whereon the gloss: " 'And ye are Christ's,' not man's, in creation or re-creation," [36] (supply: the re-creation which is through the sacraments).

14. Furthermore, the Roman bishop neither is nor ought to be called the particular successor of St. Peter on account of the laying on of hands, because the Roman bishop happens to be a man on whom St. Peter never laid his hands, either indirectly or directly; nor again is the Roman bishop St. Peter's particular successor because he occupies a certain seat or has been assigned a certain territory. For, in the first place, none of the apostles were assigned by divine law entirely to some one people or territory, for in the last chapter of Matthew these words are addressed to all the apostles: "Go ye therefore and teach all nations." [37] Moreover, we read that St. Peter was at Antioch before being at Rome. Again, even if Rome were to become uninhabitable, Peter's succession would not on that account cease.

---

[34] Pseudo-Isidore *Decretales,* Anacletus (2) cap. xxiv (ed. Hinschius, p. 79).

[35] I Corinthians 3:21–23.   [36] See Peter Lombard *Collectanea* (PL 191. 1564).

[37] Matthew 28:19. On this point, see Marsilius' critic, Alvarus Pelagius *De planctu ecclesiae* I. xxxvii (*Max.ma bibliotheca pontificia,* ed. J. T. Roccaberti [Rome, 1698–99], III, 35).

And besides, it cannot be proved by the divine law that Christ or any of the apostles decreed that the bishop of any determinate province or diocese is or ought to be called the special successor of Peter or any other apostle, and leader of the rest, however unequal in authority we might suppose the apostles to have been; but rather, the successors of St. Peter and the other apostles are, in a certain sense, that person or those persons who are most like them in their lives and holy morals. For if the blessed apostles were asked who their successors were, they would reply that it was such virtuous men, just as Christ their master replied in Matthew, Chapter 12, "to one who said unto him: Thy mother and thy brethren stand without, desiring to speak with thee. But Christ answered: Who is my mother? and who are my brethren? And he stretched forth his hand toward his disciples and said: Behold my mother and my brethren! For whosoever shall do the will of my Father which is in heaven, the same is my brother, and sister, and mother." [38] What priest or bishop, then, deserves most to be called the successor of the apostles? He, certainly, who imitates them most in morals and in deeds.

But if it be objected that a bishop becomes the particular and principal successor of St. Peter because he is elected bishop by the Roman clergy and perhaps by the rest of the people in addition, and that he thereby becomes the bishop of the universal church, although with particular regard for the Roman city so long as it stands, it must be replied that, although this statement can be convicted of many falsehoods, one charge will suffice to refute it: that it cannot be proved by the holy Scripture, but rather the opposite, as was shown above and as will be more fully shown in the following chapter. Hence it can be denied as easily as it is stated. But from what source and for what reason the Roman church and bishop receive, if they ought to receive, priority over the others, will be discussed at greater length in Chapter XXII of this discourse.

15. That the above-mentioned outmoded claims (for they will perhaps be seen to be most outmoded and unthinkable, if not false) are heard is all the more surprising because it can be proved by the certain testimony of the Scripture that the Roman bishops are, with reference to province and people, the successors of Paul rather than of Peter, especially in the episcopal seat at Rome; and again (which will appear even more surprising), because it cannot be directly proved through the Scripture that the Roman bishops are the particular successors of St. Peter in virtue of being assigned to a certain seat or province, but by this criterion it is rather the bishops at Antioch who are St. Peter's successors. The first assertion can be proved by

[38] Matthew 12:47–50.

this, that although St. Paul was sent to all nations in general, as was every other apostle (whence in Acts, Chapter 9: "He is a chosen vessel unto me, to bear my name before the Gentiles, and kings, and children of Israel" [39]), yet he was particularly and primarily the apostle to the Gentiles, just as Peter was to the Jews, in accordance both with revelation and with the arrangement of the apostles among themselves. Whence in Galatians, Chapter 2: "they," James, Peter, and John, "saw that the gospel of the uncircumcision was committed unto me, as the gospel of the circumcision," that is, the Jews, "was unto Peter" [40]; and Paul shows that although he and Peter were in charge of both these territories, for Peter could have preached to the Gentiles and Paul to the Jews if a cause or necessity for this had arisen, yet by dispensation Paul had been given the leadership among the Gentiles and Peter among the Jews, as is shown by Augustine's gloss on this passage.[41] This is again proved by what is written in Acts, Chapter 22; for while Paul was "in a trance," these words were spoken to him by revelation: "Depart, for I will send thee far hence unto the Gentiles." [42] Again, in Acts, Chapter 28, it is written: "And so we went toward Rome"; and a little below the Apostle says to the Jews at Rome: "Be it known therefore unto you, that the salvation of God is sent unto the Gentiles, and that they will hear it. And Paul dwelt two whole years in his own hired house, and received all that came in unto him, preaching the kingdom of God." [43] This is again brought out more particularly in Romans, Chapter 11: "For I speak to you Gentiles," said Paul, "inasmuch as I am the apostle of the Gentiles, I magnify mine office, if by any means I may provoke to emulation them which are my flesh"; [44] that is, although I may sometimes exhort the Jews also to do this, yet I am the apostle primarily to the Gentiles. And again in Galatians, Chapter 2, it is written: "James, Cephas, and John, who seemed to be pillars, gave to me and Barnabas the right hands of fellowship; that we should go unto the heathen," that is, the Gentiles, "and they unto the circumcision," [45] that is, that they should go to preach the gospel to the Jews. And finally, the same is written in I Timothy, Chapter 2, and II Timothy, Chapter 1; [46] from which I omit to quote for the sake of brevity.

16. Since, therefore, the Scripture clearly proves that Paul spent two years at Rome, and there received all the Gentiles who were willing to be converted, and preached to them, it is certain that he was the bishop of Rome in particular, because he there exercised the pastoral office, having from Christ the authority for this, commanded thereto by revelation, and

[39] Acts 9:15.   [40] Galatians 2:7.   [41] Peter Lombard *Collectanea* (PL 192. 108).
[42] Acts 22: 17, 21.   [43] Acts 28:14, 28, 30, 31.   [44] Romans 11:13, 14.
[45] Galatians 2:9.   [46] I Timothy 2:7; II Timothy 1:11.

elected by the other apostles. Concerning St. Peter—and here our second assertion will be made clear—I say that it cannot be proved through the holy Scripture that he was the bishop of Rome in particular, or, what is more, that he was ever at Rome.[47] For it seems most astonishing if, according to some saints' popular ecclesiastic legend, St. Peter preceded St. Paul at Rome, preached there the word of God, and was then seized; and after this, St. Paul arrived at Rome, and acting together with St. Peter had so many conflicts with Simon Magus, and with Peter fought so many battles against emperors and their deputies on behalf of the faith; and finally, according to the same story, both were beheaded at the same time because they confessed Christ, and slept in the Lord, and thus "they consecrated the Roman church"—if all this is so, then it seems most astonishing, I say, that St. Luke, who wrote the Acts of the Apostles, and Paul the Apostle, made absolutely no mention of St. Peter.[48]

17. Moreover, that St. Peter did not precede them at Rome seems very probable from what is written in the last chapter of Acts. For when Paul first addressed the Jews on his arrival, he spoke the following words, among others, wishing to indicate why he had come to Rome: "When the Jews spake against it, I was constrained to appeal unto Caesar. And they said unto him: We neither received letters out of Judea concerning thee, neither any of the brethren that came showed or spoke any harm of thee. But we desire to hear of thee what thou thinkest: for as concerning this sect, we know that everywhere it is spoken against." [49] Will anyone, therefore, who is seeking the truth and not merely looking for an argument, tell me whether it is at all probable that St. Peter preceded Paul at Rome, and dwelt there among the brethren, that is, the Jews, whose apostle he particularly and primarily was, and that he nevertheless made no statement concerning the Christian faith, which the Jews, speaking to Paul, called a "sect"? Moreover, when Paul took them to task for their lack of belief, if he had known that Cephas had been there and preached there, how would he have failed to mention him or refer to him as a witness for his endeavor, who had been a witness of Christ's resurrection, as is apparent from Acts, Chapter 3? [50]

18. And again, with reference to what we said before, who will think that Paul spent two years at Rome and had no meeting, conversation, or companionship with St. Peter? And if he did, that the writer of the Acts

---

[47] For an earlier denial that St. Peter was ever in Rome, see Moneta of Cremona *Adversus Catharos et Valdenses* v. ii. 1 (ed. T. A. Ricchinius [Rome, 1743], p. 411). See Vol. I, p. 274, n. 36.

[48] See above, i. xix. 7. The legend to which Marsilius refers is the *Acta s. Petri* (*Acta sanctorum* June 29 [VII, 387 ff.]). The story of the beheading of Peter and Paul may rest upon Marsilius' misinterpretation of Pseudo-Isidore *Decretales*, ed Hinschius, p. 635.

[49] Acts 28:19, 21, 22.   [50] Acts 3:15.

XVI: EQUALITY OF THE APOSTLES 253

would have made absolutely no mention of him? For in other less important places, when Paul met Peter, he mentioned him, and spoke with him, a. at Corinth (I Corinthians, Chapter 3) and at Antioch (Galatians, Chapter 2),[51] and so on in many other places. And if he had met him at Rome, which was the most famous of all cities, and the one where, according to the above story, St. Peter presided as bishop, why would Paul not have mentioned him? For these things are almost incredible, and hence it seems that that story or legend cannot with any probability be accepted on this point, and that it must be reckoned among the apocryphal writings. But according to the sacred Scripture we must hold beyond any doubt that St. Paul was the bishop of Rome, and that even if anyone else was with him at Rome, yet, for the above reasons, Paul was the particular and primary bishop of Rome, and St. Peter of Antioch, as is apparent from Galatians, Chapter 2. That Peter was at Rome I do not deny, but I hold it to be quite probable that he did not precede Paul there, but rather conversely.

19. But with reference to our main thesis, this must be noted most of all: that even though it may for some reasons seem fitting that certain men should be called the successors of St. Peter, because they are more reverent than the successors of the other apostles, and especially because they occupy the episcopal seat at Rome, yet the sacred Scripture shows no necessary reason why the successors of the other apostles should be regarded as subject to them in any power. And even if the apostles were unequal in authority, yet St. Peter or any other apostle did not, by virtue of the words of the Scripture, have the power to appoint or depose them, with reference either to the priestly dignity which we have called essential, or to their being sent or assigned to a certain place or people, or to the interpretation of the Scripture or of the catholic faith, or to coercive jurisdiction over anyone in this world, any more than, conversely, the other apostles had any such power over St. Peter or some other apostle. Whence it seems necessarily to follow that no successor of any apostle, whatever his particular title, has any of the above powers over the successors of the rest by virtue of the words of the Scripture. This conclusion can clearly be supported by the authority of Jerome, from whose epistle to Evander we have quoted in paragraph 8 of the preceding chapter.

[51] I Corinthians 3:22; Galatians 2:11–14.

CHAPTER XVII: ON THE AUTHORITY TO APPOINT
THE BISHOPS AND OTHER MINISTERS AND CURATES
OF THE CHURCH TO EACH OF THEIR DIGNITIES OR
OFFICES, THE SEPARABLE AND THE INSEPARABLE

W E have already discussed the efficient cause of the first priestly authority, which we have called essential. We now have to discuss the other, whereby some priests are put in charge of other priests, or of a people, or both, in a certain province or place;[1] and whence it pertains to them to dispense certain temporal goods called "ecclesiastic benefices";[2] and what is the source of the coercive jurisdiction which they, or some of them, have;[3] and to whom it pertains to define doubtful senses of the holy Scripture, especially on those points which concern what is necessary for salvation, and what is the most proper way to make such definition.[4] For when these questions have been made sufficiently clear, there will be manifest what it was the original intention of this work to make clear.

2. But before we take up each of these questions, it will be well to narrate first the method by which bishops or priests were appointed and assigned at the beginning of the primitive church, from which source the other practices were later derived. Now the principle of all these matters must be taken from Christ, who is the "head" and "rock" upon which the Catholic church was founded, as it is said by the Apostle in Ephesians, Chapters 4 and 5, and I Corinthians, Chapter 10,[5] and by the gloss on the words in Matthew, Chapter 16: "Upon this rock I will build my church."[6] Now this "head," "rock," and "foundation" of the church, namely, Christ, bestowed on all the apostles the priesthood and the episcopal authority over all nations and peoples, assigning none of them to a definite place or people in such a way that they were not allowed to preach anywhere else, although, by their own arrangement or by that of the Holy Ghost, some of them were assigned more particularly to the Gentiles and others more particularly to the Jews. This also seems to be the view of the gloss on the words in Galatians, Chapter 2: "And when they perceived the grace that was given unto me";[7] for the gloss says: "Christ entrusted to Paul the ministry of the Gentiles, just as he had entrusted to Peter the ministry of the Jews. But this dispensation was given them in such a way that Peter might

---

[1] See below, paras. 5–15.   [2] Paras. 16–19.   [3] II. xviii.
[4] II. xix–xx. I.   [5] Ephesians 4:15; 5:23; I Corinthians 10:4; cf. I Corinthians 3:11.
[6] Matthew 16:18; see *Glossa ordinaria, ad loc.*   [7] Galatians 2:8, 9.

preach to the Gentiles, if there was a reason, and Paul to the Jews." [8] The Apostle seems to have had a similar meaning in Romans, Chapter 11, when he said: "I magnify mine office, if by any means I may provoke to emulation them which are my flesh" ("that is, the Jews, of whom he was born" [9] in flesh, as the gloss thereon says). From these words it seems we must hold that by the power or character whereby a person is appointed a priest he has the power to minister everywhere and to every people without differentiation, although by divine revelation or by human arrangement some priests are assigned more to one place or people than to another, especially in modern times.

3. This seems to be in accord with the Scripture and with reason. For when Christ made a general grant of ministry to all the apostles, in Matthew, Chapter 28, he said to them all alike: "Go ye therefore, and teach all nations," [10] assigning none of them to any definite place or people. Sometimes, however, they seem to have been assigned to a particular nation or people by divine revelation, as when the Apostle said of himself, in Acts, Chapter 22: "And it came to pass that, when I was come again unto Jerusalem, even while I prayed in the temple, I was in a trance, and saw him," Christ, "saying unto me: Make haste and get thee quickly out of Jerusalem: for they will not receive thy testimony concerning me." And a little below is added what Christ said to him: "Depart, for I will send thee far hence unto the Gentiles." [11] So, then, Paul at one time received a definite assignment of place and people through revelation. So too did he receive such an assignment, together with the other apostles, by human arrangement. Whence in Galatians, Chapter 2, he said: "They," James, Cephas, and John, "gave to me and Barnabas the right hands of fellowship, that we should go unto the heathen, and they unto the circumcision." [12] So, then, the apostles were by immediate human arrangement assigned to a definite people and province. But it is certain that by such assignment, whether made by immediate revelation of God or by their own arrangement, they received no perfection through the Holy Ghost which they had not had before.

4. This is also to be seen by reason. For suppose that some bishop or other curate, assigned to a province or people, goes outside the province assigned to him (as we see happening more frequently than is necessary), and that he meets, either accidentally or intentionally, a person who is neither a believer nor baptized, but who asks to be baptized by him or by

[8] Pete. Lombard *Collectanea* (PL 192. 108).
[9] Romans 11:14, and Peter Lombard *op. cit.* (PL 191. 1485).
[10] Matthew 28:19.   [11] Acts 22:17–18, 21.   [12] Galatians 2:9.

someone else. If, then, the bishop baptizes this person while observing the proper form of the sacrament, it is certain that the person is indeed baptized, although a mortal sin may perhaps be committed by the bishop in thus baptizing someone in a province not subject or assigned to him. Therefore, the episcopal or priestly power which we have called essential assigns no one to a definite territory or people, but regards all priests alike. Sometimes, however, such assignments have been made by divine revelation, as in the primitive church, although more frequently by human arrangement, especially in modern times; and this for the purpose of avoiding scandal among bishops and priests, and for other evident advantages, which I shall indicate in the following pages.

5. Proceeding from these initial remarks to the particular questions set forth at the beginning of this chapter, we shall show first that the most proper immediate efficient cause whereby the apostles were assigned to certain peoples and provinces was the revelation of Christ or the harmonious arrangement of the apostles themselves; next, that the immediate efficient cause whereby their first successors were given definite assignments, before the conversion of the people, was the express will of all or most of the apostles, if all or most of them were present at the same time in the place or province in which a priest or bishop had to be appointed, or else it was just one of them, according to the circumstances of place, time, and people; and finally we shall show that after the apostles had died, or in their absence, the bishops and other spiritual or ecclesiastic ministers were given their secondary appointments through the most appropriate of the methods possible to human society, by the whole body of the believers in the place or province over which these ministers were to be appointed, but never by some individual group or person. The other questions will be answered later.

The first of the above statements is quite clear: namely, that no more appropriate cause of the secondary assignment of the apostles can be given than divine revelation, or their own deliberation; for in neither of these causes is malice or error seen to have entered. That this is true concerning divine revelation, there is no question; as for the apostles' own election, this also seems probable and must be believed, for they were inspired by the Holy Ghost, as we showed above from John, Chapter 20.[13]

6. Next I say that the immediate efficient cause of the secondary appointment or assignment of the first successors of the apostles, especially before the conversion of the peoples, was and ought to have been all or most of the apostles, or a single one of them, depending on circumstances as men-

[13] John 20:22-23. See above, II. xv. 3.

tioned above, such as, for example, whether all or most or only one of the apostles happened to be in the region. This is proved first from the Scripture, for in Acts, Chapter 6, we read that the apostles appointed deacons in this way, even with reference to the primary authority which we have called essential. Whence it is written: "They set them before the apostles, and when they," the apostles, "had prayed, they laid their hands on them." [14] They did not, therefore, bring them to Peter alone, but "before the apostles." Nor did Peter assume for himself alone special authority to lay his hands on them, but rather the apostles "laid their hands on them."

This is also in harmony with reason. For it is likely that the deliberations of all or most of the apostles together, with regard to promoting a person either to the priesthood or to some other holy order or secondary office, were more certain and less in error than were the deliberations of any one of them taken alone, just as we showed in the preceding chapter that for this reason they came together with other elders to settle the question of circumcision in the evangelic law. Again, this practice did away with a source from which scandal and strife might very likely have sprung up among the apostles, had one of them, in the presence of the others, desired to surpass the others in power or primacy; and when such strife did thus spring up among the apostles while Christ was living, he arrested it by showing that they were all equal, as we showed in the preceding chapter, from Matthew, Chapter 23, and Luke, Chapter 22,[15] and as we made even more clear by the words of the Apostle and the interpretations of the saints. Moreover, this method of common deliberation among the apostles was the most reasonable practice in order to remove from all their successors any pretensions to such special power, and to furnish an example for them to follow, as will be shown below in paragraph 9, from the gloss on Acts, Chapter 6.

7. If, however, all or most of the apostles were not present at the same time in the place where a bishop was to be put in charge of some multitude of believers to protect and maintain them in the faith, then it must soundly be said that such appointment could lawfully have been made by a single one of the apostles, especially where the believers were few in number, uneducated, and untrained to discern the most appropriate person for the episcopal office, and particularly so where there were very few persons fitted for this office. Bishops were often chosen in this way, and for these reasons, by Paul and his first successors, as is sufficiently clear from the Acts of the Apostles and from Paul's epistles to Timothy and Titus. But that a

[14] Acts 6:6.
[15] Matthew 23:8-11 (and 20:24-27); Luke 22:24-26. See above, II. xvi. 6, 11.

single apostle could and should lawfully make such an appointment can be shown from this, that the best and most appropriate pastor was thereby chosen. For either it was lawful for any person at his own pleasure to put himself in charge of other men as a minister of the gospel, or else such appointment had to be made by election of the subject multitude or by one of the apostles who was there present. The first method could have led to scandal and error: scandal, if two or more men had wanted to assume such authority for themselves; error, or the appointment of an inadequate pastor, because it is most usually the stupid and ambitious, rather than the virtuous and wise, who seek and try to assume high office. The second method, that of having a prelate elected by the multitude, might very likely have led to error and inadequacy because of that multitude's weakness in quantity and quality; for in the beginning they were uncultivated in most provinces, especially outside Judaea, and easily misled, as is quite clear from the whole epistle to the Galatians, and from many other writings. Whence the Apostle writes in I Corinthians, Chapter 3: "And I, brethren, could not speak unto you as unto spiritual, but as unto carnal. Even as babes in Christ I have fed you with milk, and not with meat: for hitherto ye were not able to bear it, neither yet now are ye able, for ye are yet carnal." [16] It was safer and wiser, therefore, that such appointment be made by the choice or decision of an apostle, who, because he had the Holy Ghost, outweighed in his life and wisdom a whole multitude of such uncultivated persons; although it is not to be denied that it would have been expedient for the apostle to have consulted the multitude about the morals of the man who was to be put in charge of them.

8. And now I wish to show that after the time of the apostles and of the first fathers who succeeded them in office, and especially now when the communities of believers have become perfected, the immediate efficient cause of the assignment or appointment of a prelate (whether of the major one, called the "bishop," or of the minor ones, called "curate priests," and likewise of the other minor ones) is or ought to be the entire multitude of believers of that place through their election or expressed will, or else the person or persons to whom the aforesaid multitude has given the authority to make such appointments. And I also wish to show that it pertains to the same authority lawfully to remove each of the afore-mentioned officials from such office, and to compel him to exercise it, if it seems expedient.

However, it must be noted that although it is in the power of every priest so to exercise his office as to promote to the priesthood any other

[16] I Corinthians 3:1–2.

believer who desires such appointment, the priest's ministry being as it were preparatory while God alone unqualifiedly and immediately imprints the essential priestly power or character, nevertheless, I say, in perfect communities of believers the priest is not allowed, either by divine or by human law, to bestow the priesthood at his pleasure upon any person at all, as we have said; indeed, the priest commits a grievous sin against divine and human law if he thus appoints a criminal or an otherwise unsuitable person. That he commits a grievous sin against divine law is apparent from the words of the Apostle in I Timothy, Chapter 3, and Titus, Chapter 1: "For a bishop must be blameless" [17] and must have the other qualifications there listed; and the same view must be held with regard to deacons, whence in I Timothy, Chapter 3, it is written: "Likewise must the deacons be grave," etc.[18] And that the priest commits a grievous sin against human law when he promotes to a holy order a thus unsuitable person, is clear from what was shown in Chapter VIII of this discourse.[19] For by so doing, the priest commits a transient act which harms someone else for the status of the present and the future world at once, and which he can be proved to have committed even if he denies it—the act, namely, of promoting to a public office a person of such qualities that he can corrupt the lives and morals of other persons of either sex, especially the female, or cannot give to men's morals so adequate guidance as is expedient and necessary for the status both of the present and of the future world—such a person as is a vicious or otherwise inadequate deacon or priest.

9. From the above statements, I now wish to give a necessary proof that in perfect communities of believers, the election, assignment, and presentation of persons to be promoted to ecclesiastic orders pertains only to the human legislator or the multitude of the believers in that place over which the minister is to care; and that no bishops or priests, individually or collectively, are allowed to appoint men to such orders without the permission of the legislator or of the ruler by its authority. First I shall demonstrate this by the holy Scripture, then I shall confirm it by reasoning.

10. This is quite clear by the authority of the Scripture in the Acts, Chapter 6. For when the holy apostles needed deacons to serve them and the people, they called on the multitude of believers as being the ones who had to elect and assign such deacons. Hence it is written in the above-named chapter that "Then the twelve called the multitude of the disciples," (that is, the believers, all of whom were then called "disciples," as it is written in the gloss),[20] "and said unto them: It is not reason that we should

---

[17] I Timothy 3:2; Titus 1:7.
[19] See above, II. viii. 5.
[18] I Timothy 3:8.
[20] Glossa interlinearis on Acts 6:1.

leave the word of God and serve tables. Wherefore, brethren, look ye out among you seven men of honest report, full of the Holy Ghost and wisdom, whom we may appoint over this business. But we will give ourselves continually to prayer, and to the ministry of the word. And the saying pleased the whole multitude: and they chose Stephen, a man full of faith and of the Holy Ghost, and Philip," [21] and similarly the other men. But if, while the apostles were present, such election was entrusted to an imperfect community in order to make it more certain that the fittest men would be elected, because the whole community can have knowledge, especially concerning the life and morals of one man, which a single very learned person frequently does not have; then how much more, when such prelates as were the apostles are absent and the community of the believers has become perfect, should the election of priests, for whom it is more necessary to be virtuous and wise than for deacons, be entrusted to the whole community, so that fuller and more certain report may be had about the persons to be elected. "Then the twelve called"; it was not Peter alone that called, so that the gloss thereon writes, "with their common consent." [22] They called "the multitude of the disciples," whereon the gloss writes: "They asked the consent of the multitude, which ought to be taken for an example." [23] Then the Scripture goes on to relate how they chose these men, whereon Raban writes: "This procedure must be observed in ordainments. Let the people elect, and the bishop ordain." [24] And this is what the Apostle clearly says in I Timothy, Chapter 3: "Moreover he," that is, the priest, "must have a good report of them which are without," [25] that is, outside the church, whence the gloss according to Jerome, "not only of the believers, but also of unbelievers." [26] And the same thing is said of deacons, a little below in the same book and chapter: "And let these also first be proved, and let them use the office of a deacon." [27]

11. And now I wish to show by probable reasoning, if one may call probable that which is necessary, that in perfect communities of believers the election and approval of any persons who are to be promoted to a holy order pertains to the judge in the third sense, that is, the sentence of the human legislator; so too does their secondary appointment whereby they are put in charge of some faithful people in a certain place, to be their bishops or curates, or as minor ecclesiastic officials; and the same is true with regard to their removal from that office, and their being compelled to exercise it, if such compulsion be necessary for ecclesiastic ministers. And after this, I shall

[21] Acts 6:1–5.
[23] *Glossa interlinearis, ad loc.*
[25] I Timothy 3:7.
[27] I Timothy 3:10.

[22] *Glossa interlinearis, ad loc.*
[24] *Glossa ordinaria, ad loc.*
[26] Peter Lombard *Collectanea* (PL 192. 345).

show to whom it pertains to distribute ecclesiastic temporal goods, called "benefices."

This assertion can be proved first by demonstrations identical with or similar to those whereby we showed, in Chapters XII, XIII, and XV of Discourse I, that the making of laws and the establishment of rulers pertain to the whole body of the citizens. All that must be done is to change the minor term of the demonstration, so that for the term "law" or "ruler" we substitute "the election or approval of a person who is to be promoted to a holy order, and his appointment or assignment to the headship of a certain people and province, and his removal therefrom because of a crime or for some other reasonable cause."

The necessity that such things be done by the legislator or the whole body of the citizens is so much the more evident, as any error made in appointing a person to a priestly or other ecclesiastic rank or office of headship is more dangerous than an error with respect to the human law or the appointment of a man to rule in accordance with it. For if a person who is promoted to the priesthood is morally vicious, or ignorant, or in both ways deficient, and is nevertheless made overseer and guide of a faithful people, then this people is faced with the danger of eternal death and grave civil harm. Eternal death looms because the priest has to give instruction and guidance in matters pertaining to what is necessary for eternal salvation. Whence in Malachi, Chapter 2: "The lips of the priest shall keep knowledge, and they shall seek the law at his mouth"; [28] by "the law" meaning the divine law containing the commands and prohibitions regarding what must be done or not done, the transgressor of which would not be excused because of the ignorance or malice of the priest. And therefore the people must discern what kind of pastor it is putting over itself, inasmuch as every person can be helped or harmed, or endangered, by the way in which the pastor's office is exercised. But such discernment is and reasonably ought to be in the power of the faithful people, for otherwise it could not avoid this evil.

What we have said is plainly the view of Augustine in his book *On Penance*, or rather it is the view of Christ, by whose authority Augustine speaks and confirms what he says. For he writes, and the Master of the Sentences quotes him in Book IV, Distinction 17, Chapter VI: "Whoever wants to confess his sins so that he may find grace, let him seek out the priest who knows how to bind and loose; lest, if he be negligent in his own regard, he be neglected by him," Christ, "who mercifully advises and entreats him; and lest both priest and penitent fall into the ditch which the

[28] Malachi 2:7.

stupid man was unwilling to avoid." [29] Every person, therefore, has or ought to have the power to choose for himself a suitable minister for penance, and similarly for the other sacraments, as the Master also says in the same place. Since, therefore, a better election can be made by the whole body of the faithful than by a single man, even a bishop, or by a single group, it is clear that such election or appointment of an overseer ought to pertain to the whole body of the faithful rather than to a single individual or group.

12. Moreover, a vicious or ignorant priest can lead to grave civil harm, since priests, through their authority as confessors, often have secret conversations with women. And since women are easily misled, especially young ones, whether virgin or married (as is clear from Genesis, Chapter 3, and as the Apostle shows in I Timothy, Chapter 2: for "Adam was not deceived, but the woman being deceived was in the transgression"),[30] it follows that a vicious priest will easily be able to corrupt their morals and modesty. We often see this happen nowadays because of the quality of the priests.[31] That this is a not inconsiderable civil evil can be seen by whoever is willing to consider its harmful consequences. For as Aristotle says in the first book of the *Rhetoric*, Chapter 8: "Wherever the condition of women is bad, as among the Lacedaemonians, almost half of life is unhappy." [32] For the wife is almost half of the home, as is shown in Aristotle's *Economics*.[33] Hence, if for the attainment of temporal welfare it is expedient that the legislator determine the persons who are to be named to the other offices of the state, and appoint or designate the person of the ruler, in order that the best election be made and the most suitable person be thereby named to office, as we believe we demonstrated in Chapter XV of Discourse I, then it seems that so much the more does it pertain to the same human legislator or the whole body of the faithful to determine who should be promoted to the priestly office, and to appoint priests in their pastoral office. For although a vicious ruler can inflict grave harm for the status of the present world, namely, temporal death, yet a vicious priest or ecclesiastic pastor can by his action inflict an even graver injury, namely, eternal death.

So too, because of this danger, the ecclesiastic minister must and reasonably can be compelled by the human legislator or the ruler to perform and administer the sacraments which are necessary for salvation, like baptism, if, being vicious, he refuses to do this. And what we have said above concerning promotion to holy orders, and appointments to major and minor

---

[29] Peter Lombard *Sententiae* Lib. IV. dist. 17. cap. v (PL 192. 883), quoting St. Augustine *De vera et falsa poenitentia* cap. x (PL 40. 1113).

[30] I Timothy 2:14 and Genesis 3.   [31] See Vol. I, p. 26, n. 24.

[32] Aristotle *Rhetoric* I. 5. 1361a 11.

[33] Pseudo-Aristotle *Economics* I. 2. See Aristotle *Politics* I. 13. 1260b 18; II. 9. 1269b 17.

cures of souls, can be confirmed by the passages from the *Codex* of Isidore quoted in Chapter XXI of this discourse, paragraphs 4 and 5.

13. Our words are also borne out by this, that the most renowned saints, like Saints Gregory and Nicholas and very many others, were appointed in the way we have said, as is clearly shown by their writings and accredited histories.[34]

14. Nor is any difficulty presented by the objection that priests, or a college of them, can better judge the qualifications of candidates for the priesthood and the pastorate and other, minor offices; and we can similarly dispose of the other objections which are like those presented in Chapter XIII of Discourse I, which seemed to prove that the making of laws or the establishment of rulers does not pertain to the whole body of the citizens.[35] For the objections here may be answered in the same way as were the objections there. For even if we assume that the priests can judge about such matters with greater certainty than can the rest of the citizens (an assumption which is often false nowadays), yet it cannot from this be inferred that the college of these priests alone has more certain judgment than has the whole multitude of which they are a part. And hence a judgment made by the college of priests together with the rest of the people will be more certain and more secure than a judgment made by the priests alone. For "the whole is greater than any of its parts taken separately." [36]

However, this must soundly be held, that a law which is well made in conformity with divine law ought to provide that the ruler must in this regard trust the judgment of the priests or teachers of divine law, and of other honorable men, just as he ought to make careful use of the judg-ment of expert and accredited men with regard to appointments in other disciplines, in order to gain information both as to the learning and as to the morals of the candidates. But when I say "judgment" of experts I use that word in its first sense, since it is the ruler by authority of the legislator who has to approve or disapprove persons by judgment in the third sense, and to establish them in, or remove them from, the exercise of their offices, as has been shown in Chapter XV of Discourse I. Otherwise, if the experts could make a judgment in the third sense, a single community would have as many supreme rulers as it would have persons who were judges, in the first sense, of adequacies or defects with respect to each of the offices of the state; but such a situation is inappropriate and impossible, if the state is to endure and be rightly ordered, as was demonstrated in Chapter XVII of Discourse I and in Chapter X of this discourse.[37]

15. It is the sentence or judgment, in the third sense, of the legislator,

[34] See above, p. 239, n. 26.   [35] See above, I. xiii. I.
[36] See above, I. xii. 5; I. xiii. 2.   [37] See Vol. I, p. 121.

or of the ruler by its authority, therefore, that must approve or disapprove candidates for ecclesiastic orders, and appoint them to a major or minor post or headship, and remove them therefrom or prohibit them to exercise it, or even, if out of malice they refuse to exercise their office, compel them to do so, lest by their wickedness someone incur the danger of eternal death, as for example through lack of baptism or of some other sacrament. This must indeed be understood to apply to perfect communities of believers. But in a place where the legislator and the ruler by its authority were infidel, as was the case in nearly all communities at the time of the establishment of the primitive church, the authority to approve or disapprove candidates for ecclesiastic offices (as well as to make the other appointments mentioned above and to regulate the exercise of these offices) would belong to the priest or bishop together with the sounder part [38] of the faithful multitude in that place, or else to the priest alone if he was the only believer there; and this without any consent or knowledge on the part of the ruler, in order that such promotion and appointment of prelates or curates might lead to the spreading of Christ's faith and salutary doctrine among the people—a result which would not be attained, but rather prohibited, by the authority, endeavors, and commands of an infidel legislator or guardian of the law. This was the procedure which the apostles followed at the time of the origin of the church of Christ, and which they were bound by divine command to follow, and which their successors would be bound to follow in default of the legislator. Whence the Apostle wrote, in I Corinthians, Chapter 9: "For though I preach the gospel, I have nothing to glory of: for necessity is laid upon me; yea, woe is unto me if I preach not the gospel!" [39] But when the faithful legislator and guardian of the law do want such things to be done, then, I say, to them belongs the authority for this in the way stated above, for the reasons or proofs already given, both from the holy Scripture and from probable and necessary human reasoning.

16. As for the distribution of temporal things, usually called "ecclesiastic benefices," it must be remembered that these things are set aside for the support of ecclesiastic ministers and other poor persons (which we discussed in Chapters XIV and XV of this discourse) either by the legislator or by some individual person or group. Now if such temporal goods have been thus set aside by the gift and establishment of the legislator, then, I say, the legislator can lawfully, in accordance with divine law, entrust to whomever it wants, and at any time, the authority to distribute these goods, and can, for cause, when it so wishes, revoke such authority from the in-

---

[38] *Saniori parte.* See above, II. vi. 12 and Vol. I, pp. 193–94.   [39] I Corinthians 9:16.

dividual or group to whom it has entrusted it. And this assertion, rather than the opposite, can be proved by the Scripture, as we showed above in Chapter XIV of this discourse by the authority of Ambrose from his epistle, *On Handing Over the Basilica*.[40] And not only can the faithful legislator lawfully, according to divine law, revoke the authority to distribute such temporal goods from the person or persons to whom it had entrusted it, but also it can sell or otherwise alienate these goods for a reasonable cause, since they belong to the legislator and are always rightfully in its power, unless perhaps it has transferred some thing, either with or without ownership, to the power of some other group or person. But to the above remarks it must always be added that in any event the faithful people, if it be able, is obligated by divine law to support ecclesiastic ministers with suitable food and clothing, wherewith the ministers ought to be content, as was shown from the first book of Timothy, last chapter.[41] But if, on the other hand, such temporal goods have been established for pious works by the gift or legacy of some individual person or persons, then, I say, such goods must be saved, kept, and distributed in accordance with the intention of the donor or the man who bequeathed them. But if any error appear in the distributors needing correction, such error must be corrected by the human legislator or the ruler by its authority, in accordance with the intention of the donor or bequeather. Indeed, if the legislator or the ruler know about such error, and are able to correct it, and yet fail to do so, then they sin, for such correction does not pertain to, nor ought to be made by, any other group or individual, unless the donor or bequeather has entrusted the authority for such correction to some particular group or individual, and the error, if any, of this latter party must finally be corrected by the ruler. However, no private individual or group can build a temple, and appoint a minister of the evangelic law therein, without the grant of the legislator, for the reasons given above.

17. I wish to show, moreover, that the authority of the catholic kings of France urges not the rejection but rather the upholding of my statements regarding the appointment of ecclesiastic ministers and the distribution or bestowal of temporal goods or benefices. For these kings assert rightfully (*de jure*), what in fact (*de facto*) they have up to the present time willed and caused immutably to be observed, that the authority to appoint men to ecclesiastic offices, and to distribute temporal goods or benefices, belongs to them in such a way that they do not derive this authority from any other mortal individual or group, of whatever condition. For such appointment, bestowal, or distribution is not prohibited to the legislator or ruler by

---

[40] See above, ii. xiv. 22.　　　　[41] I Timothy 6:8. See above, ii. xi. 4; ii. xiv. 6.

divine law; indeed, in perfect communities of believers, such authority, if it be lawful and not fraudulently usurped by individual priests or groups of them, is derived from the grant of the legislator. Hence in the laws of the Roman rulers there was established the manner and form of electing or appointing bishops, curates, deacons, and other ministers of temples with respect to the secondary appointments which were discussed in paragraphs 11 and 12 above, and the number of these ministers was fixed and determined.[42] For such determination pertains to the human legislator and the ruler, as was demonstrated in Chapter VIII of this discourse and in Chapter XV of Discourse I. Thus too laws were made with regard to the manner of handling ecclesiastic temporal goods or benefices, and with regard to contentious acts of priests both among themselves and towards others;[43] against which laws the first Roman priests did not rebel, but rather, being holy men and conscious, not ignorant, of their freedom, they were and wanted to be voluntarily subject to these laws, just as they rightly should have been, as will be more fully shown in Chapter XXI of this discourse, paragraphs 2 to 8. And we shall also show below how there has come about so great a change that now the priestly college not only claims exemption from the laws and customs of secular rulers, but even sets itself up as legislator over these rulers, and obstinately maintains and defends this position.

18. Another consequence of what we have said must also not be overlooked, namely, that if from the ecclesiastic temporal goods, and especially the proceeds of the immovable goods which we have called benefices, there remains a surplus over and above the needs of gospel ministers, then the human legislator or the ruler by its authority may lawfully, according to human and divine law, collect taxes and revenues therefrom for the defense of the country, or for the redemption of men taken captive in the service of the faith, or for the support of public burdens, and for other reasonable purposes, in accordance with the determination of the faithful legislator. For when a person has by gift or legacy set aside such temporal goods for pious purposes, entrusting them to some group or individual for distribution, these goods cannot have any greater immunity from taxation than they had when they were in the donor's power. But when they were in his power they were not exempt from public taxation, and consequently they are not so exempt after the donor or founder has transferred them to the power of any other party.

19. This view is upheld by Ambrose in his epistle *On Handing Over the*

---

[42] See *Corp. jur. civ., Codex Justinianus* I. iii. 41; XII. xxvi. See above, pp. 260–63.
[43] *Codex Justinianus* I. ii–iv.

Basilica, when he writes: "We give to Caesar the things that are Caesar's, and to God the things that are God's. That the tribute is Caesar's, is not denied." And again in the same epistle: "If he," the emperor, "demands tribute, we do not refuse it. The fields of the church pay tribute." [44] But Ambrose would have refused the emperor tribute if he had thought that it was not rightfully owed to him, just as he refused to let the emperor have the temples, or the authority over the appointment of priests therein, because he seemed to be favoring the Arians, even against the views of the people; but we shall discuss this in greater detail below. And Hugh of St. Victor also held this position with regard to taxation of ecclesiastic temporal goods, for in his book *On the Sacraments* he wrote:

Although the church receives for its use the fruits of earthly possessions, it cannot enforce justice through churchmen or through secular judgments. However, the church can have ministers, laymen, through whom the rights and judgments pertaining to earthly power may be exercised in accordance with the tenor of the laws and the duties of earthly right, but exercised in such a way that the church recognizes that it has power from the earthly ruler, and understands that it can never so remove its possessions from the royal power that, if reason and necessity demand, the royal power does not owe the possessions protection, and the possessions do not owe the royal power necessary tribute. For just as the royal power cannot fail to give the protection which it owes to someone else, so too a possession held by churchmen cannot rightfully refuse the tribute which is owed to the royal power in return for protection.[45]

CHAPTER XVIII: ON THE ORIGIN AND FIRST STATUS OF THE CHRISTIAN CHURCH, AND WHENCE THE ROMAN BISHOP AND CHURCH ASSUMED THE ABOVE-MENTIONED AUTHORITY AND A CERTAIN PRIMACY OVER THE OTHER BISHOPS AND CHURCHES

THE remaining aim which we now have to fulfill is to disclose the source and beginning wherefrom certain bishops or priests have come to have both coercive jurisdiction over all secondary priestly appointments, called non-essential, and the power to distribute all ecclesiastic temporal goods; and also wherefrom the Roman pope ascribes to himself the highest of all such powers. Following upon this, we must discuss to whom belongs the just power to interpret doubtful senses of Scripture, to hand down

---

[44] St. Ambrose *Sermo contra Auxentium* cap. xxxiii ff. (PL 16, 1060 ff.). See above, II. iv. 11.
[45] Hugh of St. Victor *De sacramentis* Lib. II. pars II. cap. vii (PL 176. 420).

these interpretations to the faithful, and to command that they be believed and observed. First, then, we assume from our conclusions in Chapters XV and XVII of Discourse I and in Chapters IV, V, VIII, IX, and X of this discourse, that coercive jurisdiction over anyone in this world belongs to no bishop, priest, or other church minister, as such; and again we have sufficiently shown in Chapters XV, XVI, and XVII of this discourse that no bishop or priest is by immediate decree of Christ subject to any other bishop or priest in any of the priestly powers mentioned above, essential or non-essential; and we have also said the same with regard to the distribution of ecclesiastic temporal goods, in the preceding chapter. Thus, anyone who considers the above sections could with sufficient clearness see the solutions of our proposed inquiries. Nevertheless, we prefer to proceed by answering these questions one by one, on account of the slowness of persons who have less acquaintance with such matters.

2. Attempting, then, to answer the proposed questions, we shall have to consider with regard to them: first, the origin of the above-mentioned powers, and how they have in fact (de facto) developed; next, how far such developed powers have been or should have been in conformity with divine and human right and with right reason, and how far in opposition and disconformity; so that, finally, we may know which of these powers, since they are in conformity, are to be approved and upheld, and which, the ones in disconformity, are lawfully to be denounced and shunned as harmful to the lives and peace of the believers. Now as for the actual development of these powers, and how far this development has been in accordance with right (de jure), the beginning must be sought in the holy Bible, and the later events we can gather from the approved histories, especially the above-mentioned *Codex* of Isidore; and, finally, we can cite some things which "experience, mistress of disciplines,"[1] has taught us.

3. Beginning, then, with the holy Bible as the fountain of the truth which we are seeking, we shall first consider Christ's words in John, Chapter 20, whereby he gave to all the apostles alike the priestly authority, or the power of the keys, or both, when he breathed on them and said: "Receive ye the Holy Ghost. Whosesoever sins ye remit, they are remitted unto them."[2] And to this we must add Christ's commandment whereby he ordered all the apostles alike to preach the gospel throughout the world, when he said to them, in the last chapter of Matthew: "Go ye therefore and teach all nations," etc.[3] To these apostles, Christ by his immediate call

---

[1] This echoes the maxim of canon law: "Experience is the efficacious mistress of things." See *Corp. jur. can., Sext.* Lib. I. Tit. 6. cap. 6; and also John XXII's *Ad conditorem canonum* (*Corp. jur. can., Extravag. Joh. XXII* Tit. 14. cap. 3).

[2] John 20:22–23.   [3] Matthew 28:19–20.

later added Paul as the chosen vessel of the Holy Ghost, as is sufficiently clear from the Acts, Chapter 9. And Paul together with the other apostles executed this command of Christ, as is plain from their acts and epistles: first in Judaea they preached and taught the gospel, or Christian faith, to which they there converted many men; and then, as a consequence of divine revelation and their own arrangement, some of them remained in Judaea, and the others separately betook themselves to various other peoples and provinces. Preaching the gospel there with faith and fortitude, each one made as much headway in converting persons of both sexes as his ability and God's pleasure allowed, as it is told in their writings and in the approved histories about them; although two among them were especially proficient in their preaching, namely, Saints Peter and Paul. This Paul, although he was not one of the twelve apostles, was called and sent by Christ no less immediately and primarily than was each of the other apostles, as is apparent from the Acts, Chapter 9, and as was sufficiently shown in Chapter XVI of this discourse from Galatians, Chapter 2, and the expositions of the saints.[4]

4. And so it was mainly from these two apostles, Peter and Paul, that the ritual of the Christian church was derived, although more manifestly from Paul, according to the Bible, and especially in relation to the Gentiles; for Paul was the first and principal apostle sent to the nations, or Gentiles or uncircumcision, just as Peter was to the circumcision, as is clear from Galatians, Chapter 2, and Romans, Chapter 11, and from the gloss of the saints thereon, as well as from many other passages of the Scripture.[5]

5. In imitation of their master, Christ, these two apostles, together with all the others, lived under the coercive jurisdiction of the secular rulers and taught others so to live, as was clearly shown in Chapters IV and V of this discourse. So too lived their successors, the priests or bishops, as well as their deacons and the other ministers of the gospel, to the time of Constantine I, emperor of the Romans, as is to be seen from the *Codex* of Isidore; so that throughout that whole period no bishop exercised coercive jurisdiction over any of the others. However,[6] since the bishops in many of the other provinces did not dare to come together publicly to discuss questions relating to the holy Scripture and to church ritual, they used to consult the bishop and church of the believers at Rome, because the congregation of the believers there was perhaps larger and more experienced, inasmuch as all the sciences were at that time vigorously pursued at Rome;

---

[4] See above, II. xvi. 2 ff. [5] See above, II. xvi. 2 ff., esp. 15.

[6] The passage from here to the end of paragraph 6 was quoted verbatim by John Rokycana at the Council of Basle, 10 March 1433, according to M. Bartoš, *Časopis Narodniko Musea*, 1928, p. 18, n. 14a (MS. of University of Cracow, 1760, fol. 416). See Scholz, p. 378, n. 2.

and hence the bishops and priests at Rome were more experienced, and their church had a greater number of such persons than had the other churches. And also the Roman believers were more reverent; for St. Peter, the oldest of the apostles, the most perfect in merit, and the most reverent, is recorded to have sat at Rome as bishop, and likewise St. Paul, of whom this is more certain, as was shown in Chapter XVI of this discourse; moreover, the city of Rome was the leading city and more famous than all the other provinces in the world. Hence too, the believers in the other provinces, lacking suitable men to govern their churches, appealed to the bishop and church at Rome to send persons to be their bishops, because the church of the believers at Rome had many more persons who were suited for such positions, as we have already said. And when the bishops and church at Rome were thus asked for counsel and assistance, with regard both to questions of faith and to ecclesiastic ritual and the provision of bishops, they charitably and fraternally supplied such aid to the believers who needed and requested it: they sent them bishops, who with difficulty were found willing to accept such calls; in a friendly manner they communicated to the other provinces the arrangements they had made with regard to ecclesiastic ritual; and sometimes too they lovingly admonished the believers of the other provinces on hearing that strife or schism had broken out among them.

6. This assistance and counsel were gratefully received by the churches of the other provinces, as is clear from the histories and the afore-mentioned *Codex*,[7] from the time of Pope Clement (who, as it is there written, was the first bishop to succeed Peter or Paul or both) to the time of Constantine I.

In the same or in a similar way, the Roman people of their own accord, and not by compulsion, received from the Greeks certain laws called the Laws of the Twelve Tables, which were the source of the other laws of the Roman people.[8] And yet it is certain that the Roman people were not on that account subject to any jurisdiction or authority of the Greeks. In a similar way, too, as the author of this book himself saw, heard, and knew, the scholars of the University of Orleans appealed by delegation and letter to the University of Paris, a more famous and venerable institution, to be allowed to have its rules, privileges, and statutes;[9] and yet the University of Orleans was not subject, either before or after, to any authority or jurisdiction of the University of Paris.

---

[7] See Pseudo-Isidore *Decretales*, ed. Hinschius, pp. 30 ff.

[8] See *Corp. jur. can.*, *Decret. Gratiani* Pars I. dist. 7. can. 1.

[9] This appeal probably occurred in 1312, when Marsilius was rector of the University of Paris. See M. Fournier, *Statuts et privilèges des universités françaises* (Paris, 1890–94), Vol. I, fasc. 1, p. 37.

7. Starting from the above-described priority which was based on custom and the voluntary consent of the other churches, the later Roman bishops, in the years down to the time of Constantine, came to assume a greater authority whereby they issued and commanded the observance of decrees or ordinances for the universal church, in matters pertaining to church ritual and to the acts of priests. But whether the Roman bishops could do this solely on their own authority, or whether the consent of the others was necessary, we shall say below.

As Isidore narrates in the *Codex*, in the chapter "On the Primitive Church in the Nicene Council," [10] and as is equally shown in the "Edict of the Lord Emperor Constantine" [11] which is contained in the *Codex*, the afore-mentioned Constantine was the first emperor who openly adopted the faith of Christ, this conversion being brought about through the ministry of St. Sylvester, the then Roman pope; and Constantine seems also to have been the first emperor who exempted the priesthood from the coercive jurisdiction of the secular rulers, and likewise, by the afore-mentioned edict, he gave to the Roman church and its bishop those authorities and powers over all the other bishops and churches which they now claim to belong to them from another source, as we have shown above in Chapter XIX of Discourse I, paragraphs 8 and 9; and together with these powers Constantine seems to have given to the Roman bishop and church coercive jurisdiction over the fields, estates, and most of the possessions of the other bishops and churches, as well as secular dominion over certain provinces, as can be clearly seen by anyone who reads the afore-mentioned edict. And also, as it is told in the above-mentioned source, Constantine was the first emperor who allowed the Christians to come together publicly and to build temples or churches; and it was at his command that the first Nicene council was held.[12]

This council, and the other events in the development of the church from the time of the apostles down to the present, will be discussed in their proper places, insofar as such discussion will be germane to our inquiry; and we shall narrate the history of these events, accepting those accounts which are consistent with divine law and right reason, and rejecting those which are inconsistent; and we shall give a clear account of how these things ought to have been done in order to be in accordance with the holy canon.[13]

[10] Pseudo-Isidore *Decretales*, ed. Hinschius, p. 248.
[11] The Donation of Constantine, *ibid.*, pp. 249 ff. See above, I. xix. 8, 9.
[12] Pseudo-Isidore *Decretales*, ed. Hinschius, p. 248.
[13] This project is taken up at II. xxii. 16. The intervening chapters deal with the indispensable preliminary question of the authority to interpret Scripture, as was indicated in the program set forth above, II. xviii. 1.

8. Having thus given a brief recital of the development of the matters under consideration from their origin, we now enter more fully upon a definitive discussion of them, first making, with the Apostle, this indubitable assumption: that the catholic faith is one, not many; whence in Ephesians, Chapter 4, it is written: "One lord, one faith." [14] And all the faithful must believe and profess this faith in unity, that is, according to the same meaning, as the Apostle shows a little below in the same book and chapter: "Till we all come in the unity of the faith, and of the knowledge of the son of God." [15] From which we shall with necessity infer,[16] first, that it is expedient to define doubtful meanings and sentences of divine law, especially the gospel, and to put an end to any adjustable disputes or controversies which may arise among its teachers [17]—such disputes as we read did arise owing to the ignorance, or viciousness, or both, of certain men, which was in accordance with the prophecy of Christ and the Apostle. And we shall show that from this it necessarily follows that this definition of meanings pertains only to a general council composed of all the believers or of those who have the authority of all the believers.[18]

Next I shall show, in accordance with divine law and right reason, that to call a general council, and to assemble it by coercive force if necessary, pertains only to the authority of the faithful human legislator which lacks a superior (*superiore carentis*),[19] and not to any individual person or group, whatever their dignity or condition, unless such authority shall have been granted to them by the legislator.[20]

Then I shall show with certainty that no ordinances regarding church ritual and human acts can be enacted, whose observance would be binding on all men under some punishment for the status of the present or the future world, unless such decrees are made by the general council or the supreme faithful legislator,[21] either directly or by authority previously received therefrom.[22] From which it will also be demonstrated that no ruler, province, or community can or ought to be put under interdict, or excommunicated, by any priest or bishop, whoever he be, except in the manner established by divine law [23] or by the aforesaid general council.[24]

Next it will be clearly shown that it pertains to the authority of no

---

[14] Ephesians 4:5.   [15] *Ibid.* 4:13.
[16] The following gives the contents of Chapters xx–xxiii.   [17] See below, II. xx. 1.
[18] II. xx. 2–*fin.*   [19] On this phrase, see Vol. I, p. 131.   [20] II. xxi. 1–3.
[21] This *supremus legislator fidelis* seems to refer to the universal authority of the Holy Roman Empire. See below, II. xxx. 8; also II. xxi. 8, 11; and Vol. I, pp. 130–31.
[22] II. xxi. 4–8.
[23] In suggesting here that divine law authorized the use of excommunication or interdict of rulers and peoples by the priesthood, Marsilius contradicts his own interpretation of divine law, probably inadvertently.
[24] II. xxi. 9.

single bishop, or of any other single individual or particular group, to appoint persons to all the church offices in the world, or to distribute or bestow on their behalf ecclesiastic temporal goods, called benefices; but that this authority belongs only to the founder or donor, or to the universal [25] faithful legislator, or to the person or persons to whom such power has been granted by the aforesaid donor or legislator, and according to the form and manner wherewith it has been so granted.[26]

Then it will be shown that it is convenient to appoint one bishop and church to be leader or head of the rest, and what qualities this head bishop and church should have, and by whose authority they ought to be appointed; and also that this leading bishop with his church will have to communicate to all the other bishops and churches the ordinances regarding church ritual and other human acts which have been enacted (or which it seems ought to be enacted) by the general councils for the common utility and peace of the faithful.[27]

And, finally, we shall draw this necessary inference from the above, namely, that the decisions with regard to the Scripture, the catholic faith, and church ritual, as well as the other decrees of the general council, can be altered, augmented, restricted, suspended, or totally revoked only by the authority of the general council, and not by any other particular group or individual.[28]

By all of these demonstrations every person will be made almost sensibly aware that the Roman bishop or his church, or any other bishop or church, as such, has none of the afore-mentioned powers or authorities over the other bishops and churches by divine or human right unless such power shall have been granted to him by the general council either outright or for a certain time. From this it will also be apparent that when the Roman or any other bishop ascribes to himself plenitude of power over any ruler, community, or individual person, such a claim is inappropriate and wrong, and goes outside, or rather against, the divine Scriptures and human demonstrations; [29] and that such claims on the part of the Roman or any other bishop must be completely stopped, through admonition and even through coercive power if necessary, by the human legislators or by the men who rule by their authority.

[25] See above, n. 21.   [26] II. xxi. 11–*fin*.   [27] II. xxii.
[28] II. xxi. 10.   [29] II. xxiii.

CHAPTER XIX: ON CERTAIN PRELIMINARY CONSID-
ERATIONS NEEDED FOR THE DETERMINATION OF
THE AFORE-MENTIONED AUTHORITY AND PRIMACY:
WHAT STATEMENTS OR WRITINGS IT IS NECESSARY
TO BELIEVE IN AND TO ACKNOWLEDGE AS TRUE FOR
THE SAKE OF ETERNAL SALVATION

BEFORE proceeding to the propositions which are to be demonstrated, we must note a consideration which is very useful, indeed necessary, for the certitude of all the statements to be made below. This consideration is the following: that for eternal salvation it is necessary for us to believe in or to acknowledge as irrevocably true no writings except those which are called "canonic," or their necessary consequences, or those interpretations or definitions of doubtful meanings of the holy Scriptures which have been made by the general council of faithful or catholic Christians, especially with regard to matters wherein error would lead to eternal damnation— matters such as are dealt with in the articles of the Christian faith.

2. That the holy Scriptures must be firmly believed and acknowledged to be true is assumed as self-evident to all Christians; but since it could be proved only by the authorities of these Scriptures themselves, I have omitted such proof for the sake of brevity. And that the same firm belief must be given to those interpretations of them which have been made in the way we have said, is clear enough; for it is apparent that it must be piously held that these interpretations were revealed to us by the same Spirit as were the Scriptures. This we can prove by Scripture and by an infallible deduction grounded in it. By Scripture we can show it from the words of the Truth contained in Matthew, Chapter 28: "And lo I am with you always even unto the end of the world." [1] Whereon Raban writes: "By this is meant that 'even unto the end of the world' there will not be lacking men on earth who are worthy of divine immanence and indwelling," [2] that is, men to whom, it must be piously held, the Holy Spirit is always present for the preservation of the faith. Whence Jerome writes: "Christ promises that he will be with his disciples even unto the end of the world, and shows that they will always live, and that he will never

---

[1] Matthew 28:20. On the difference between the interpretation of this text by Marsilius and by other medievals, see Vol. I, pp. 284–85, 288.

[2] In Thomas Aquinas *Catena aurea* (XI, 334).

depart from the believers." [3] And the same is clearly proved by the Acts, Chapter 15, where, after deciding some question, the congregation of the apostles and believers said: "It seemed good to the Holy Spirit and to us." [4] For they asserted, and Scripture asserts, that their decision on that question regarding the faith had been made by the Holy Spirit. Since, therefore, the congregation of the believers or the general council truly represents by succession the congregation of the apostles and elders and the other believers of that time, it is likely, or rather certain, that in the definition of doubtful meanings of Scripture, especially those wherein error would involve the danger of eternal damnation, the virtue of the Holy Spirit is present to the universal council, guiding its deliberations and revealing the truth.

3. This can also be seen by an infallible deduction which takes its force from Scripture: for Christ would have handed down the law of eternal salvation in vain if he did not reveal to the believers its true meaning, belief in which is necessary for their salvation, but instead allowed the majority of them to be in error regarding it, when they beg and invoke him for this true meaning. Indeed, not only would such a law be useless for salvation, but it might even seem to have been handed down for man's eternal perdition. And hence it must be piously held that the decisions of the general councils with regard to doubtful meanings of Scripture receive the origin of their truth from the Holy Spirit, the coercive authority for their observance and acknowledgment from the human legislator (as will be shown below), and their promulgation and teaching through the priests and gospel ministers, especially the one who has been made the leader for this purpose by the faithful human legislator which lacks a superior, or by the general council.

4. But as for other writings, which have been revealed and produced by the human spirit, it is clear that no one is obliged to believe in their certainty or acknowledge their truth. For one is not obliged to believe or to acknowledge as absolutely true any writing in which there is a possibility of falsehood. But such a possibility is incurred by writings which arise from the human contrivance of an individual or a partial group. For these writings may fall away from the truth, as experience shows and as is declared in Psalm 15: "I said in my haste, All men are liars." [5] But the possibility of such falsehood is not incurred by the canonic Scriptures, because they are not of human contrivance, but are given by the immediate inspiration of God, who neither can be deceived nor wishes to deceive.

5. This view of ours as to the difference between human writings and

the divine Scriptures is clearly confirmed by Augustine in his thirteenth epistle to Jerome, where he wrote:

I acknowledge your love. I have learned to pay honor and reverence only to the books of the Scriptures which are called canonic, so that I believe most firmly that no author of them has written anything false. And if I read anything therein which seems contrary to the truth, I shall be in doubt only as to whether the text is faulty, or the interpreter has not followed what was said, or I have not understood. But other authors I read in such a way that, however superior they may be in holiness or learning, I do not on that account consider their views to be true simply because they are the views of the authors, but rather because they have been able to persuade me, either through the canonic authors or by probable reasoning, that they do not wander from the truth.[6]

Augustine repeats and urges this same position in the prologue to the third book of the treatise *On the Trinity,* where he wrote: "Do not" (speaking to the reader) "show deference to my words as if they were the canonic Scriptures. In the latter," that is, the canonic, "believe without hesitation whatever you read, even if you have not believed it before. But in what I have written, do not firmly believe what you do not regard as certain, unless you have understood it to be certain." [7] He also said the same thing in his epistle to Fortunatus [8] and in many other places, from which I have omitted to quote for the sake of brevity. And Jerome also seems to have held this view in the *Exposition of the Catholic Faith,* where he said: "We accept the New and the Old Testament in that number of books which the authority of the holy catholic church has handed down." [9]

6. By "canonic Scriptures," therefore, St. Augustine meant only those writings which are contained in the volume of the Bible, and not the decretals or decrees of the Roman pontiff and his college of clergymen who are called "cardinals," nor any other human ordinances, contrived by the human mind, about human acts or disputes. For a canon is a standard and a measure, a measure because it is certain, which certainty is peculiar to the divine Scriptures alone from among all other writings, as we have shown from Augustine above. And hence Augustine distinguished his own writings from the canonic Scriptures; nor did he, whose holiness, authority, and knowledge were so great, presume to call his own writings canonic. For to do so is impious and sacrilegious, for in human accounts, spoken or written, error and falsehood can occur, which cannot happen at

---

[6] St. Augustine Epist. 82 (*Corpus scriptorum ecclesiasticorum Latinorum,* Vol. XXXIV [Vienna, 1895], Pars 2, p. 354; also in PL 22. 937).

[7] St. Augustine *De trinitate* III. Prooem. (PL 42. 869).

[8] St. Augustine *Acta contra Fortunatum Manichaeum* (PL 42. 111 ff.).

[9] Pseudo-Jerome *Symboli explanatio ad Damasum* (*Opera* [Paris, 1706], V, 124).

all in a canon truly so called, or in such an interpretation of the canonic Scripture as we have said to have been made by the general council.

7. For this reason we find that the third Council of Carthage very wisely prohibited that any writings other than the Bible be called canonic. Thus in the record of that council we read these words, which are contained in the above-mentioned *Codex* of Isidore: "Likewise it has pleased us that in the church no writings besides the canonic Scriptures should be read under the name of divine Scriptures. The canonic Scriptures are: Genesis," [10] and then the other books of the Bible are enumerated.

8. This view is not refuted by what Augustine writes against the Manichaeans in the *Epistle of the Foundation*. For Augustine says: "I would not believe in the gospel if I were not impelled to do so by the authority of the catholic church"; [11] wherein he seems to put human authority above the authority of Scripture; "for the cause of an attribute's inherence in a subject always itself inheres in the subject more firmly than does that attribute." [12] But we reply that it is one thing to believe that statements or writings have been made or written by some particular person, and it is another thing to believe that those statements or writings are true or false, useful or harmful, and must be obeyed or not. For a person may have the first belief on other men's testimony without the second, or the second without the first, or sometimes both at once. For example, a person will believe that a written document which is shown to him is the law of the land, from the common testimony of the inhabitants; but that this law is true and that it must be obeyed, not transgressed, he can learn through a sensible sign, such as punishment which he has seen inflicted upon its transgressors, or through his own right reasoning without any statement or persuasion on the part of other men. So too, conversely, when one sees a man writing a book or building a house or producing anything else, one will believe by oneself, without any testimony on the part of others, that the book or the house is the product of this man. But that the contents of the book are true or false, useful or harmful, and must be followed or shunned, one can believe by the testimony of other men, especially if they be trustworthy. And again, one may sometimes believe both at once through human testimony, as when a person who has never seen Hippocrates will believe, on men's testimony, that a book or a doctrine is by Hippocrates; and he will believe, on the testimony of experts, that the contents of the

---

[10] Pseudo-Isidore *Concil. Carthag.* Lib. III. can. 47 (*Decretales,* ed. Hinschius, pp. 297, 301).
[11] St. Augustine *Contra epistolam Manichaei quam vocant Fundamenti* V (PL 42. 176).
[12] Aristotle *Posterior Analytics* I. 2. 72a 28.

book are true or false, and that they must be heeded or not heeded in order to maintain health and avoid illness.

9. And in the same or in a similar way, one may believe, by the common testimony of the believers or the catholic church, that a certain writing which is contained in the Bible is the teaching or law of God which has been handed down or proclaimed by Christ, even though one has never seen or heard Christ, or perceived him by any other external sense. But that this writing is true, or that it must be obeyed, a person will believe by faith or by some sensible sign, such as a miracle, without testimony on the part of anyone else. Thus Paul believed that the law which he at first denounced was the teaching of Christ, by the testimony of the preachers whom he persecuted, but he did not on that account believe that this law contained the truth. Afterward, however, he came to believe that this law was true, first through a sensible miracle, and then by the faith which he had. And similarly, through human testimony one sometimes believes both that a document is by a particular author and that it is true, so that many persons, who have never seen Christ or known him by any external sense or perceived any miracle or sensible sign of him, nevertheless believe and have believed that this writing is the law made and handed down by Christ, and that its contents are true and must be observed in order to attain eternal salvation and avoid misery.[13]

10. In accordance with the foregoing, therefore, the statement of St. Augustine, that "I would not believe in the gospel if I were not impelled to do so by the authority of the catholic church," can have a double meaning. In one sense it can mean that Augustine believed this Scripture to be the gospel, that is, the teaching of Christ, by the testimony of the catholic or universal church, although that this Scripture or gospel was true he believed primarily through a miracle perhaps, or by some revelation, or by the faith which he had that Christ was true God and that consequently Christ's every teaching was true and had to be observed. But Augustine's statement can also have another meaning: that he accepted and believed, on the testimony of the catholic church, both that the Scripture is Christ's gospel and that it is true. The first meaning, however, seems more in accord with the doctrine of the Apostle in Galatians, Chapter 1; for the words of Christ or God are not true because they are upheld by the testimony of the catholic church, but rather the testimony of the church is true because, and when, it utters the true words of Christ, because Christ's words are true.[14] Hence the Apostle writes in the afore-mentioned place:

[13] See Thomas Aquinas *Summa theologica* II. ii. qu.6. a.1. Also Vol. I, pp. 67–68.
[14] See Dante *De monarchia* iii. iii.

"But though we, or an angel from heaven, preach any other gospel unto you than that which we have preached unto you, let him be accursed." [15] And similarly it must be understood that even if the whole church had preached something different, that is, contrary to the gospel, it would not have been true. And the reason is this, that it was certain that that gospel was the teaching or revelation of Christ, wherein there could be no falsity; although by the necessity of the consequent and by arguments from effect to cause (*a posteriori*) it does indeed follow that because the catholic church says that these words, "God is three in one," are true, therefore they are true, and similarly with any other statement or command of Christ which the church says must be observed. For it must be piously held, as was made clear by what we said above, that the statements of the catholic or universal church on matters of faith have been immediately revealed by the Holy Spirit. And hence, in whatever sense we interpret the above words of Augustine, they do not oppose the view which we have stated; for to believe what the church says on matters of faith is to believe the Holy Spirit rather than man. But the only reason why Augustine says that he believes in the gospel because of the authority of the catholic church is that his faith received its original stimulus from that church, which he knew to be guided by the Holy Spirit. For faith sometimes begins "from hearing." [16] And by catholic church I mean the church which is most appropriately and truly so called, in accordance with the last meaning of the word "church" given in Chapter II of this discourse, namely, the universal church.[17]

CHAPTER XX: TO WHOM BELONGS OR HAS BELONGED THE AUTHORITY TO DEFINE OR DETERMINE DOUBTFUL SENTENCES OF THE HOLY SCRIPTURE

HAVING made the above preliminary remarks, we now resume our discussion of the subjects set forth above. And first we wish to show that it is expedient and necessary to determine doubtful meanings or sentences of the holy Scripture, both those whose doubtfulness has already come to notice and those which will in the future, especially with regard to articles of the faith, commands and prohibitions. For that is expedient,

---

[15] Galatians 1:8.   [16] See Romans 10:17.
[17] See above, II. ii. 3. On this whole question of the relation between faith and authority or tradition, see also Vol. I, pp. 73–75.

or rather necessary, without which the unity of the faith would not be maintained, and lack of which would lead to error and schism with regard to the faith among Christian believers. But such a necessity is the determination of the doubtful and sometimes contrary views of learned men with regard to divine law. For diversities or contrarieties of opinion on this matter would cause diverse sects, schisms, and errors to arise, as is shown by the *Codex* of Isidore in the chapter entitled "Preface of the Nicene council." [1] For when a certain Alexandrian priest named Arius said that Christ was the Son of God in the sense that he was merely a creature born of God, and consequently unequal and inferior to God the Father, many Christians were shaken in faith by the dissemination of this error, and their number would have been greater, and they would have remained in error, if the true meaning of Scripture on this point had not been distinguished from the false. So too, when certain men gave utterance to unsound notions with regard to the Holy Spirit and the unity and plurality of person and essence in Christ, the first four synods, at Nicaea, Constantinople, Ephesus, and Chalcedon, were called and assembled in order to distinguish these notions from the true ones and to denounce and condemn them. For that such controversies would arise among the doctors of the Christian church, true or pretended believers, Christ prophesied in Luke, Chapter 21, and the Apostle in I Timothy, Chapter 4, and II Timothy, Chapter 3,[2] which I omit to quote because these passages are well known, and for the sake of brevity.

2. And now I am going to show that the principal authority, direct or indirect, for such determination of doubtful questions belongs only to a general council composed of all Christians or of the weightier part of them, or to those persons who have been granted such authority by the whole body of Christian believers. The procedure is as follows: Let all the notable provinces or communities of the world, in accordance with the determination of their human legislators whether one or many, and according to their proportion in quantity and quality of persons, elect faithful men, first priests and then non-priests, suitable persons of the most blameless lives and the greatest experience in divine law. These men are to act as judges in the first sense of the word, representing the whole body of the faithful by virtue of the authority which these whole bodies have granted to them, and they are to assemble at a place which is most convenient according to the decision of the majority of them, where they are to settle those matters pertaining to divine law which have appeared

---

[1] See Pseudo-Isidore *Decretales,* ed. Hinschius, p. 256. On Marsilius' conciliar doctrine, and its relation to that of his predecessors, see Vol. I, pp. 283–91.

[2] Luke 21:8; I Timothy 4:1–3; II Timothy 3:2–9, 13.

doubtful, and which it seems useful, expedient, and necessary to define. There too they are to make such other decrees with regard to church ritual or divine worship as will be conducive to the quiet and tranquillity of the believers. For it would be needless and harmful for the multitude of inexperienced believers thus to assemble: harmful, because they would be distracted from their tasks which are necessary for the sustenance of corporeal life, which would be burdensome or perhaps unbearable.

3. However, divine law lays upon all believers obligations toward such a council assembled for the afore-mentioned purpose, although the obligation takes different forms. The priests are obligated because their function is to teach the law in its true sense, to see to it that its integrity and truth are maintained, to condemn errors made regarding it, and to recall men from these errors by exhortations, arguments, and threats. Hence in the last chapter of Matthew, the Truth says to all the priests, in the person of the apostles: "Go ye therefore and teach all nations." [3] Hence too the Apostle Paul, speaking in the person of all the apostles, wrote in I Corinthians, Chapter 9: "Necessity is laid upon me; yea, woe is me if I preach not the gospel!" [4] Besides the priests, those persons who are learned in divine law are also obligated, more so than are the other believers, for they have to call upon the others and to come together with the priests, especially if they have been sufficiently requested or enjoined to do so; for "to him that knoweth to do good, and doth it not, to him it is sin," [5] as it is written in James, Chapter 4. Also, in order to settle other matters, outside divine law, which are important for the common utility and peace of the believers, persons who have been appointed for this purpose by the faithful human legislator can and must be present at the council. And the legislators also have obligations toward the council: namely, to elect suitable persons to make up the council, to provide them with the necessary temporal goods, and, if necessary, to compel, for the public welfare, the attendance of those who, although they are suitable and have been elected to this council, yet refuse to come, whether priests or non-priests.

4. That the aforesaid authority to make decisions and ordinances in the way we have stated belongs only to the general council, and not to any other particular person or group, can be proved by demonstrations and scriptural authorities similar to those whereby we showed, in Chapter XII of Discourse I and in Chapter XVII of this discourse, to whom belongs the authority to make the laws and to effect the secondary appointments to ecclesiastic offices. [6] All that need be done is to change the minor term

---

[3] Matthew 28:19. [4] I Corinthians 9:16. [5] James 4:17.
[6] See above, I. xii. 5 ff.; II. xvii. 9 ff.

of the demonstrations, so that for the term "law" or "secondary appointments to ecclesiastic offices" there is substituted "the determination or definition of questions about divine law, together with the other decisions which have to be made with regard to church ritual or divine worship and the peace and unity of the faithful." The necessity that this be heeded in these matters is so much the greater, as the more diligent is the discernment and care which must be had with regard to the law or the faith and those matters which can be of help or harm to all the faithful.[7]

5. It was in this manner that the apostles and the elders dealt with doubtful questions about the gospel, as is clear from Acts, Chapter 15, and as we showed at length in Chapter XVI of this discourse.[8] For the question of circumcision was not settled by St. Peter or any other apostle alone; but all the apostles and elders, or men more experienced in the law, came together for this purpose. A sign that what we have said is true is that Christian emperors and empresses with their officials were present at the leading councils and helped to settle doubtful questions about Scripture (as is clear from the oft-mentioned *Codex* of Isidore, in those passages which we shall quote in the following chapter, paragraphs 2 to 8), although in those days it was not so necessary that laymen be present as it is now, because nowadays far too many priests and bishops are ignorant of divine law. Hence, when the priests disagree among themselves as to what must be believed for eternal salvation, the weightier part of the believers must judge which side is the sounder; but when the priests all agree on a point which had seemed doubtful, their decision must be accepted. They will, however, have been appointed to orders in the way stated by us in Chapter XVII of this discourse.[9]

6. For this reason, too, I again wish to show that this determination of doubtful questions does not pertain to the Roman bishop, either alone or together with his college of cardinals; and consequently, that it does not pertain to any other one bishop, either alone or with some other particular group or college. For suppose, as has indeed happened, that a heretic is appointed to the Roman pontificate, or that the pontiff falls into this disgrace of heresy after his election, if not before, due to ignorance or malice or both; just as we read that such heretics have actually been named to the papacy, as for example Tiberius, "born a Roman." [10] Now if this pontiff has made a decision with regard to some doubtful passage of Scripture—regardless of whether he has made that decision alone or together with his

---

[7] See above, II. xvii. II.   [8] See above, II. xvi. 5–6.
[9] Note that by this last remark Marsilius safeguards the ultimate control of the "faithful legislator" over the determination of the meaning of divine law. See Vol. I, pp. 163, 286.
[10] See Martinus Polonus *Chronicon* (MGH, *Scriptores*, XXII, 416).

college. of cardinals (who will very likely share his error, because he chooses, and claims the power to choose, whichever men he wants, without designations being made by anyone else)—then will that decision have to stand, even though it has been made by this heretical bishop, whether alone or together with his college, or the majority of them, men who have perhaps been misled by ignorance or malice, cupidity or ambition, or some other vicious emotion?

7. Not to seek a distant example, we see that this is what has happened in the case of a certain Roman pope. For, wishing to avoid giving the impression that he was deserting Christ's supreme poverty and the status of perfection, and also desiring to retain the ownership of temporal goods, even real estate, and to exercise secular rule, this pope, either by himself alone or together with his college of cardinals, has issued an edict concerning the status of supreme poverty or perfection, which by its false interpretation contradicts the gospel of Christ,[11] as we have clearly shown in Chapters XIII and XIV of this discourse. Consequently, if this authority to settle questions of Scripture be granted to any bishop, either alone or together with his clerical college, then the whole body of the faithful will lie in danger of shipwreck with respect to the faith, as anyone of sound mind can understand from what we have already said and what we are going to say.

8. Moreover, if such authority belonged only to the Roman pope, or to any other bishop, in the way we have said; or if, as Isidore says (in the *Codex,* under the heading: "Preface of Isidore to the following work"),[12] the epistles or decrees of the Roman pontiff were equal or not inferior in authority to the decisions and definitions of the general council; then all secular governments, all the kingdoms and provinces of the world, and all individuals, whatever their dignity, preeminence, or status, would be subject to the coercive jurisdiction of the primary Roman prelate. For this was what Boniface VIII, Roman pope, asserted in his epistle or decree beginning: "One holy catholic church," and ending: "We declare, proclaim, and decree that henceforth it is absolutely necessary for salvation that every human creature be subject to the Roman pontiff."[13] Since, therefore, the decisions concerning Scripture which are made by a general council duly called, assembled, solemnized, and consummated, especially the decisions in whose truth it is necessary to believe for eternal salvation, are immutably and infallibly true, as was demonstrated near the begin-

---

[11] This is Pope John XXII's bull, *Cum inter nonnullos.* See above, II. xiii. 33, n. 65.

[12] Pseudo-Isidore *Decretales,* ed. Hinschius, p. 18.

[13] *Corp. jur. can., Extravag. commun.* Lib. I. Tit. 8. cap. I (Nov. 18, 1302). This is the famous *Unam sanctam.*

ning of Chapter XIX of this discourse,[14] it follows that this epistle of Boniface would obtain an indubitable, certain, and irrevocable truth. But to the contrary, it is clear, now and forever, that this epistle is from the very beginning false and erroneous, and that it is, of all imaginable falsehoods, the most harmful to all those who live a civil life, as was indubitably demonstrated in Chapters IV, V, and IX of this discourse.

9. The falsity of this epistle of Boniface, as well as of Isidore's statement (unless perhaps it be assisted by a pious interpretation), is clearly demonstrated by an epistle or decree of Clement V, the successor of Boniface, which begins: "It was deserving of our very dear son Philip, illustrious king of the French," and ends: "Both to the church, and to the king and kingdom named above."[15] For in this decree, Clement proclaims that the epistle of Boniface is in no way prejudicial to the afore-mentioned French king and kingdom. Since, therefore, according to the belief and knowledge of Clement and of all Christians, neither this king nor any of his successors nor any inhabitants of his kingdom believed or will believe that this epistle of Boniface is true but rather that it is openly false in that article in which he subjects to himself all governments and states; it necessarily follows that it is not necessary for salvation to believe in that article, for if it were, it would be prejudicial to anyone who did not believe in it.

10. Moreover, anyone who considers such epistles or decrees will see that they are unsound. For if Boniface's decree is true, then all the rulers and peoples of the world are obliged to believe it; but if Clement's is true, then not all are so obliged, because the king and people of France are specifically exempted from such belief. For some men, therefore, it is necessary for salvation, by the authority of Scripture, that certain things be believed, while for other men it is not necessary. Consequently, there is not "one Lord," nor "one faith," nor are "all" obliged to "come in the unity of the faith"[16] to Christ; the opposite of which is clearly stated by the teacher of the Gentiles in Ephesians 4.

11. Again, Clement should be asked by what sound understanding of his faith the French king and the peoples subject to him could be exempted from belief in that which it is necessary for salvation to believe in. Either they deserved to become heretics and unbelievers according to the faith, or else the epistle of Boniface contains an open lie, and thus "those things which do not come from truth very often overthrow themselves, even without being impelled by anyone,"[17] as Augustine says in *The City of God,* Book VII, Chapter XVI.

[14] See above, II. xix. 2–3.
[15] *Corp. jur. can., Extravag. commun.* Lib. v. Tit. 8. cap. 2 (Feb. 1, 1306, *Meruit*).
[16] See Ephesians 4:5, 13.   [17] St. Augustine *De civitate Dei* VII. xix (PL 41. 210).

12. Moreover, the other kings and peoples ought indeed to wonder and to ask what passage or sense of Scripture makes them all, except the French king, subject to the jurisdiction of the Roman pope; and why is belief in this more necessary for the salvation of one man than of another? For this is fantastic and ridiculous, and proceeds from the ambition of those who utter such words, from their ardent desire for secular rulership, and from their fear of the above-mentioned French king.

13. We have stated above that the general council can be made up also of non-priests, who will properly participate in the deliberations of the council together with the priests, and help formulate its decrees. We shall support this statement first by the *Codex* of Isidore, in the chapter entitled, "Beginning of the canons," that is, the rules of the church. For we find there these words among others: "Next let the laymen enter, who have earned seats by being elected to the council." [18] Much more, therefore, have they earned seats who are learned and skilled in divine law, even though they be not priests. For it was in this way that the apostles acted together with the elders, as we have shown above. Hence it must be noted that in the primitive church and in ancient times, especially before the time of Constantine, only the priests, and almost all of them, were teachers of divine law, just as they alone are obliged to be and ought to be, according to Malachi, Chapter 2: "The lips of the priest shall keep knowledge, and they shall seek the [divine] law at his mouth." [19] Hence too the Apostle writes in I Timothy, Chapter 3, and Titus, Chapter 1: "A bishop," that is, a priest, "must be apt to teach, holding fast the faithful word as he hath been taught, that he may be able by sound doctrine both to exhort and to convince the gainsayers." [20] Such being the qualities of the priests of that time, the priests were almost the only persons who came together to interpret and define difficult or doubtful questions of Scripture and faith. But now, because of the corruption of the ecclesiastic regime, the greatest part of the priests and bishops are slightly and, if one may say so, insufficiently versed in holy Scripture, because the temporal goods of benefices which accompany ecclesiastic offices are sought after and obtained by ambitious, lustful shysters, using servility, entreaty, bribery, or secular force.

14. And, invoking as witnesses God and the multitude of the faithful, I swear that I have seen and heard very many priests, abbots, and other church prelates who were so inferior that they could not even speak grammatically. And what is worse, in the church ritual I have known and seen

[18] See Pseudo-Isidore *Decretales*, ed. Hinschius, p. 22.
[19] Malachi 2:7.   [20] I Timothy 3:2; Titus 1:9.

a man less than twenty years of age, and almost totally ignorant of divine law, who nevertheless was appointed to the office of bishop in a large and famous city, when he not only lacked the priestly order, but had not even passed through the deaconate and subdeaconate. Such appointments the Roman bishop asserts he can lawfully make, and in fact he very often does make them and commits similar misdeeds in order to gain favor with the powerful, claiming that he, as Christ's vicar, has plenitude of power over appointments to ecclesiastic offices and the distribution of benefices. Whereupon he must properly be asked, why is such a mob of bishops and priests to be assembled in the general council, and how will such a council be able to distinguish the true senses from the false in doubtful passages of Scripture? Therefore, because of the inadequacy of these priests, it is very useful, or rather necessary, and in accord with divine law and right reason, that the general council include accredited, faithful non-priests (to be named by the faithful legislator), who are sufficiently learned in holy Scripture, and who surpass such bishops and priests in their lives and morals, so that by their deliberation together with the others doubts about the faith and other questions may be settled.

CHAPTER XXI: TO WHOM BELONGS OR HAS HITHERTO
BELONGED THE COERCIVE AUTHORITY TO ASSEMBLE
A GENERAL COUNCIL OF PRIESTS, BISHOPS, AND
OTHER BELIEVERS; AND TO WHOM BELONGS THE
AUTHORITY IN THE COUNCIL TO MAKE DECREES DIS-
OBEDIENCE TO WHICH WOULD RENDER BELIEVERS
LIABLE TO PUNISHMENT OR GUILT FOR THE STATUS
OF THE PRESENT OR THE FUTURE WORLD; AND
AGAIN, TO WHOM BELONGS THE AUTHORITY IN THIS
WORLD TO PUNISH ANY TRANSGRESSOR OF THE DE-
CREES OR DECISIONS OF THE GENERAL COUNCIL.
FURTHERMORE, THAT NO BISHOP OR PRIEST CAN
EXCOMMUNICATE ANY RULER OR PLACE ANY PEO-
PLE UNDER AN INTERDICT, OR BESTOW ON ANYONE
ECCLESIASTIC TEMPORAL BENEFICES OR TITHES OR
LICENSES TO TEACH, OR ANY CIVIL OFFICES, EXCEPT
BY THE DECISION AND GRANT OF THE GENERAL
COUNCIL OR THE HUMAN LEGISLATOR OR BOTH

NOW I wish to show that it pertains only to the authority of the faithful human legislator which lacks a superior, or to the person or
persons to whom it has granted such power, to call a general council, to
name suitable persons to it, to have it duly assembled, solemnized and
consummated, and to coerce lawfully, in accordance with divine and human law, those persons, whether priests or non-priests, clergy or non-clergy,
who rebel against coming to the council and accomplishing the necessary
and useful tasks listed above, or who transgress the decrees and decisions
of the council. Although these propositions were demonstrated in Chapter
XV of Discourse I and in Chapters IV, V, IX, and XVII of this discourse,
where we showed by demonstration, and confirmed by the authority of
Scripture, that it pertains only to the authority of the faithful human
legislator, and not to any priest or priestly college as such, to exercise coercive jurisdiction over all men without exception, priests and non-priests,
to make and approve appointments, and to establish all offices; neverthe-

less, we now wish to confirm these propositions by many passages of Isidore's *Codex,* especially those which recount proceedings that were in accord with divine law and right reason.

2. First, then, we quote from the chapter entitled: "Preface to the Nicene Council," where it is written as follows: "He," Constantine, "commands that Arius come together with the 318 bishops sitting there and that they," that is, the bishops, "judge about his propositions." [1] Note, then, that the bishops and priests were assembled in the aforesaid council by command of the legislator.[2] The same is again shown in the chapter entitled: "The Council of the 630 Bishops," where we find the following words: "The great holy venerable synod, which by the grace of God was assembled by the decree of the most devout emperors Valentinian and Marcianus." [3] Also in the chapter entitled: "Conclusion of the Seventh Council of Toledo, Beginning of the Eighth," where it is written as follows: "In the year of the orthodox and glorious king Receswinth, distinguished for the true dignity of his clemency, the ordinance of the divine will, through the most serene command of this prince, compelled us all to come together in the basilica of the holy apostles for the sacred assembly of the synod." [4] The same is again to be seen in the chapter entitled: "End of the Eleventh Council of Toledo, Beginning of the Twelfth"; [5] and in the "End of the First Council of Bracha, Beginning of the Second," [6] and in the epistle of the [Roman] Pope Leo to the synod of Ephesus; [7] also in the epistle of the [Roman] Pope Leo to the Emperor Theodosius,[8] again in the epistle of the Bishop Leo to Marcianus Augustus, which begins: "I asked"; [9] and likewise in the epistle to Marcianus Augustus, beginning "Many things to me in all." [10] The same is also to be seen from many other passages and epistles in the same *Codex,* which I have omitted to cite because the fact is well known, and for the sake of brevity.

3. That the aforesaid authority does not belong to the Roman bishop, either alone or with his college of cardinals, can be proved together with the foregoing by this, that if he, either alone or with his college, were accused of some crime which required the calling of such a council, it is very likely that he would delay calling it as long as possible, or would put it off entirely; which would be of grave harm to the believers. But such an eventuality cannot occur with the faithful legislator or the whole body of

---

[1] Pseudo-Isidore *Decretales,* ed. Hinschius, p. 256.

[2] It is to be observed that Marsilius here refers to Constantine as the "legislator." See Vol. I, p. 249.

[3] Pseudo-Isidore *Decretales,* ed. Hinschius, p. 283.   [4] *Ibid.,* p. 383.

[5] *Ibid.,* p. 411.   [6] *Ibid.,* p. 424.   [7] *Ibid.,* pp. 600–601.

[8] *Ibid.,* p. 576; see also pp. 601 ff.   [9] *Ibid.,* pp. 608–9.   [10] *Ibid.,* p. 582.

the believers, because they, or their weightier part, cannot be thus misled, either in civil affairs, as we showed in Chapter XIII of Discourse I, or in spiritual affairs, especially with regard to the faith, as was shown in Chapters XIX and XX of this discourse.

4. That to the faithful human legislator which lacks a superior belongs the authority to give a coercive command or decree ordering that all men alike, priests and non-priests, observe the general council's decisions, regulations, and other judgments (in the first sense of judgment), and to inflict punishment in person or in property, in this world, on transgressors of its command or decree, we wish to prove first by citing those proceedings which took place in due manner, as recounted by many passages of Isidore's *Codex*. First of all, then, this can plainly be seen in the chapter entitled: "Edict of the emperor Marcianus in confirmation of the Council of Chalcedon," where we find these words among others: "No one, whether he be clergyman, soldier, or of any other status, shall attempt henceforth to discuss in public, before an audience or assemblage, the decisions concerning the Christian faith, seeking thereby an opportunity for raising a tumult and accomplishing a perfidious purpose." And a little below these words are added: "For those who defy this law will not go unpunished." And again below: "If, then, it be a clergyman who dares to discuss religion in public, he will be removed from the company of the clergy. If he be a soldier, he will be divested of his shield"; [11] and similar decrees are made with regard to other groups. The same is again to be seen from the chapter immediately following, entitled: "The sacred decrees of the august emperors Valentinian and Marcianus, after the Council of Chalcedon, in confirmation of this council and in condemnation of heretics," wherein these words are found:

By this law we decree that if any persons are so deceived by the error of Eutyches that they follow the example of the Apollinarians, whom Eutyches followed, and who are condemned by the honorable rules of the fathers, that is, the canons of the church, and by the most sacred laws of the divine rulers, then such persons are to appoint or call upon no bishops, priests, or clergymen; and we also decree that Eutyches is to be completely deprived of the title "priest," because he has used it unworthily. But if, in opposition to our decrees, any such persons dare to appoint bishops, priests, and other clergymen, then we command that all who participate or attempt to participate in such appointments are to lie in danger of perpetual exile, by losing their good clergymen. [12]

From this is to be seen the truth of what we said in Chapter XVII of this discourse, that it pertains to the authority of the faithful legislator or ruler to make appointments to the priesthood and other holy orders.

[11] *Ibid.*, p. 288.   [12] *Ibid.*, pp. 288–89.

The same is shown in the chapter immediately following, entitled: "Another decree of the emperor Marcianus against the same heretics"; [13] and it is also to be seen in the chapter entitled: "Edict of the king in confirmation of the council," where among other statements we find this passage: "If any person refuses to obey these decrees, let him be excommunicated by every council, if he be a bishop, priest, deacon, or clergyman; if he be a layman and of honorable position, let him lose half his wealth, which is to go to the imperial treasury." [14] From this it is quite clear that the rulers or the human legislators lawfully can and once used to inflict on heretics penalties in person and in property, and exact these penalties, and appropriate them to themselves, as we said in Chapter X of this discourse. This is again to be seen in the chapter entitled: "Ending of the thirteenth Council of Toledo," which begins: "With the instinct of charity"; [15] and also in many other passages, which I omit to quote for the sake of brevity and because the above citations are sufficient.

5. It pertains to the human legislator, or to the ruler by its authority, not only to make coercive decrees concerning the observance of the decisions of the council, but also to establish the form and manner of appointing to the Roman apostolic seat or electing the Roman pontiff. Far from denying this, the Roman pontiff, we read, once eagerly requested that the emperor exercise this power, as the *Codex* relates in the chapter entitled: "Here begin the decrees of Pope Boniface: letter of appeal to Honorius Augustus, asking that the ruler appoint him in the city of Rome, inasmuch as the pontiff is never ordained by canvassing for votes." [16] This is also to be seen in the chapter immediately following, entitled: "Letter of Constantine Honorius the emperor to Pope Boniface: saying that if two bishops are again ordained at Rome, both will be driven from the city," and which begins: "The glorious and ever august emperor Victor Honorius to the holy and venerable Boniface, pope of the city of Rome." A little below in this decree the emperor writes as follows:

Know that it has pleased our piety that Your Holiness is solicitous regarding the disturbance of the churches or people. Our clemency believes that sufficient care has been taken that such disturbance can in no way occur. And when Your Holiness preaches, we wish this brought to the attention of the entire clergy, so that if by chance something happens to your pious self (which we do not hope), then they may all know that canvassing for votes must cease. And if it happens that two contestants are rashly and wrongly ordained, then neither of them will be priest [that is, Roman bishop], but only he will remain in the apostolic seat who is elected from among the clergy by the divine judgment and the consent of the whole body, and is then newly ordained. [17]

[13] *Ibid.*, pp. 289 ff.   [14] *Ibid.*, pp. 361–62.   [15] *Ibid.*, p. 419.
[16] *Ibid.*, p. 554.   [17] *Ibid.*, pp. 554–55.

From this can also be seen the truth of what we said in Chapter XVII of this discourse, that the secondary appointment of priests, bishops, and other church ministers in major or minor cures of souls pertains to the whole body of the believers or the faithful human legislator.

6. Our assertions can also be proved by the epistle entitled: "In Thanks to Marcianus Augustus: Because through His Diligence Peace Has Been Restored to the Church by the Council of Chalcedon," and which begins: "The Bishop Leo to Marcianus Augustus. I have great cause for rejoicing in all letters of Your Clemency." Near the end of this epistle we read the following words written by Leo: "Since the will of your very pious and religious self must in every way be obeyed, I have gladly added my official sentence to the synodic decrees, which were pleasing to me, regarding the strengthening of the catholic faith and the condemnation of heretics. That this official sentence may come to the attention of all priests and churches, may Your Clemency deign to give a command ordering it." [18] So, then, while the Roman pontiff added his official sentence or judgment (in the first sense) to the decisions of the council, he nevertheless begged the Roman ruler to issue a decree commanding the churches and priests to observe it; but the pontiff would not have made this request had not such authority belonged to the Roman ruler. From this can also be seen the truth of what we said in Chapters IV, V, and VI of this discourse: that to the human legislator, or to the ruler by its authority, belongs coercive authority over both priests and non-priests; and far from denying this, the Roman bishops in ancient times begged the emperors to give them such rules or laws.

7. The same point again clearly emerges from the chapter headed: "The Emperors Caesar Theodosius and Valentinian," near the beginning of which we find the following passage:

Since the guardianship of the catholic apostolic doctrine and of the faith is now suddenly being questioned and attacked by various arguments which disturb and confuse men's wits and souls, we have resolved to condemn such arguments as intolerable and sinful, lest by not doing so we should seem to affront God himself. And hence we order to assemble the men who are most pleasing to God, most devout, and most eloquent in defense of catholic piety and the true faith, that they may by their subtle inquiry destroy all such vain doubts, and strengthen the true catholic faith which is friendly to God. And therefore let Your Holiness choose ten very worshipful metropolitans residing in your diocese, and similarly ten other holy bishops distinguished in doctrine and in conduct, who excel all the rest in their knowledge and teaching of the true and immaculate faith; and do you all assemble next August at Ephesus, metropolis of Asia, without any delay or uncertainty, that is, with no one other than

18 *Ibid.,* p. 582.

the afore-mentioned persons in attendance at the holy synod; and when all these very holy and blessed bishops have assembled at the afore-mentioned city, as our sacred letters have ordered them, they are to conduct very subtle investigations and inquiries to destroy all errors which oppose the faith, and to strengthen the catholic doctrine which is in accord with the orthodox faith of our savior Christ, so that it may shine with its accustomed brilliance, and so that all men may henceforth preserve inviolate and unshaken their trust in loving God. If any one of these bishops or metropolitans, ignoring this synod which is so necessary and friendly to God, does not with all speed come at the appointed time to the place fixed upon, then he will have no excuse either from God or from our piety; for no one avoids a priestly assemblage unless he is oppressed by the consciousness of his own wickedness. Theodoretus, bishop of the city of Syria, whom we have previously ordered separated from his own church, we now command not to come to the holy synod unless and until the whole council in session agrees to have him join and participate as an equal. If any disagreement arises concerning him, then we command the holy synod to assemble without him and to make the regulations which have been ordered.[19]

Anyone who studies this edict will see that in it are propounded the three conclusions already set forth: first, that it is expedient to determine doubtful questions about divine law; second, that this determination pertains not to the authority of any one individual or group, but to the general council; and third, that only to the faithful human legislator, or to the ruler by its authority, belongs the authority to call or command such a council, to appoint and designate suitable persons to it, to order the observance of its decisions and decrees, and to punish transgressors thereof in and for the status of the present world.

8. And now we must show that no regulations concerning church ritual, whose observance is binding on men under some punishment for the status of the present or the future world, can be made by any one man, whatever his dignity or condition, but only by the general council, either directly or through authority derived from it, and with an intervening decree to that effect by the primary faithful human legislator or the ruler by its authority. And also we must show that without the authority of the legislator, no regulations can be made concerning other human acts, such as fasting, the eating of meat, abstinence, the canonization and veneration of saints, or marriage within certain degrees of relationship, nor can persons be prohibited or excluded from mechanical or any other work, nor can religious orders or groups be approved or disapproved, nor can any other regulations be made about similar matters which divine law allows or per-

---

[19] This is the letter to Dioscorus of Alexandria calling the so-called "Robber Council" of Ephesus (449). It is not contained in the printed text of Pseudo-Isidore, although Marsilius seems to cite it from Pseudo-Isidore. See J. D. Mansi, *Sacrorum conciliorum amplissima collectio*, VI (Florence, 1761), 587–90.

mits, if such regulations call for any ecclesiastic censure, like interdict or excommunication or any other similar penalty, major or minor; and still less can such regulations make anyone liable to punishment in person or in property, to be exacted in the present life, without the authority of the legislator, to whom alone belongs the lawful power to inflict and exact such penalties, as is sufficiently clear from Chapter XV of Discourse I and Chapter X of this discourse.

9. The above assertions, it is to be assumed, are proved by the same demonstrations and authorities whereby we showed above that it pertains to the general council to define doubtful senses of divine law, and to the faithful human legislator to regulate other human acts with respect to church ritual by coercive decrees; all that need be done is to change the minor term of the arguments. And another reason why these assertions are true is that things permitted by divine law can be prohibited or made unlawful only by the human legislator. Moreover, no bishop has immediately from Christ any authority over anyone else, as has been demonstrated in Chapters XV and XVI of this discourse, nor does any bishop have coercive jurisdiction over clergymen or laymen, as we showed above in Chapters IV, V, and IX of this discourse.

From the above it can fittingly be deduced that only the general council, and no bishop or priest or particular group of them, has the authority to excommunicate any ruler, province, or other civil community, or to forbid them the use of divine offices. For if a priest or bishop or some particular group of them, moved by ignorance or malice, excommunicates or lays under interdict a ruler or a province, there results great scandal to the peace and quiet of all the faithful. This was very recently shown by "experience the mistress of things," [20] when Boniface VIII, the Roman pope, tried to excommunicate Philip the Fair of bright memory, the catholic king of France, and to lay his kingdom and adherents under interdict, because this king protested against a written document beginning: "One holy catholic church," which was published by Boniface either alone or together with his coterie of cardinals, and which among its other assertions said, or rather concluded, that all the rulers, communities, and individuals in the world are subject in coercive jurisdiction to the Roman pope. And although at that time Boniface was aiming particularly against the afore-mentioned ruler and his subjects and adherents, yet his intention was to stir up against him as many of the other Christian rulers and peoples as he could, as is evidenced by the immortal truth and the memory of many persons still living; and Boniface would have succeeded in this aim, had he not been re-

[20] *Corp. jur. can., Sext.* Lib. I. Tit. 6. cap. 6. See above, II. xviii. 2.

moved from the ranks of mortals. But such a calamitous opportunity (rather than power) to stir up any other wickedness, which would inflict grave peril and schism on the believers, must be checked forthwith; and the procedure whereby such interdicts and excommunications are inflicted must be controlled and left only to the general council of Christians, whose judgment, under the guidance of the Holy Spirit, cannot be perverted by ignorance or malice.

10. From this it necessarily follows that no bishop or special group, council, or congregation, and still less any individual, whatever his status or dignity, can authorize or decree the alteration, augmentation, diminution, suspension, interpretation (especially on crucial points), or total revocation of the ordinances and decisions made by the general council, whether concerning the faith or the meaning of the evangelic law or concerning church ritual or divine worship, as well as all other ordinances made by the general council directly or indirectly, implicitly or explicitly, or in any other way. But if it clearly seems necessary to alter or totally to revoke such ordinances, they must be referred to a general council which is to be called for this purpose. This assertion is to be proved by the same reasonings and authorities whereby we have shown that such ordinances, decisions, and decrees are to be made only by the aforesaid council.

11. And again by the same scriptural authorities and human reasonings we can fittingly demonstrate that no one bishop or other individual or special group taken alone has the authority, without designation by the general council or the faithful human legislator, to assign or appoint persons to all the church offices in the world, or to distribute on behalf of these offices all ecclesiastic temporal goods, which are called "benefices," or to bestow on any persons licences to teach, notarial commissions, or any other public or civil offices, except by the aforesaid authority of the general council or the faithful legislator. Although these assertions have in a way been properly proved in Chapter XV of Discourse I and in Chapter XVII of this discourse, we have nevertheless decided to give further explanation and confirmation of them here through what we have said immediately above and through other probable arguments. For the Roman or any other bishop, or any particular clerical group together with the bishop, neither has nor ought to have the authority to do that which causes [21] all kingdoms and all polities, large and small, to be exposed to the danger of heresy and destruction. But this is what happens when the Roman or any other bishop is permitted to have such power of appointment, distribution, or bestowal apart from the decision of the universal

[21] Removing, with Scholz, period after *clericorum*.

legislator or the general council. For suppose, as we said above, that the Roman bishop is heretical, necromantic, avaricious, arrogant, or otherwise vicious, just as we have seen and read that some of them were.[22] Now if such a vicious pontiff has the authority, without any legal determination by the general council or the faithful mortal legislator, to appoint any persons he wishes to all the offices of the church, it seems very likely that he will choose for these offices, especially the major ones like cardinal or bishop, men whom he knows to be accomplices in his crimes and supporters of his every perverted wish. The result, therefore, will be that the whole flock of the believers will be exposed to the danger of subversion from the faith, as was to some extent shown in Chapter XI of this discourse; especially will this happen if the pontiff who has fallen into heresy because of ignorance or viciousness has the power to interpret divine law, as we have shown above in Chapter XX of this discourse, and as is clear to all men living today who remember or have actually witnessed the acts of two of the Roman bishops.[23]

Moreover, if it is found that divine or human law does not grant but rather denies to the Roman bishop the power to appoint his successor in the Roman episcopal seat, even though he can and should know best the qualifications of the men in that province and what is most suitable thereto, then why will this bishop be permitted to have the power or authority to name the successors of the bishops or other church prelates, curates, and ministers in foreign and distant provinces, when he has very little knowledge of what is suited to those provinces and the qualifications of the men therein?

12. Moreover, if any one bishop, either alone or together with some particular group of clergymen, has the power to bestow at his pleasure all of the world's ecclesiastic temporal goods, called benefices, without the aforementioned legal determination by the general council and the human legislator or the faithful ruler by its authority, then all kingdoms and all polities, large and small, will be put in danger of destruction. Furthermore, this practice will have the result that for the administration of churches and souls the richest, most influential, and most powerful men, no matter how ignorant or immoral, will be preferred over the poor, the just, and the humble, no matter how learned and upright these latter may be. For suppose that the Roman bishop is avaricious, arrogant, or otherwise vicious, and also that he is desirous of secular rule—just as we have seen many modern bishops to be of such character and to strive after such rule. Be-

---

[22] Sylvester II and Boniface VIII were charged with necromancy, Boniface VIII and John XXII with heresy, as also Liberius (see above, II. xx. 6).

[23] I.e., Boniface VIII and John XXII; see above, II. xx. 6.

cause of his insatiable avarice, then, and in order to satisfy his other vicious desires and to gain the favor and grace of the powerful, he will put ecclesiastic offices and benefices up for sale, and will also bestow them upon the powerful, the violent, and the pugnacious, or, at their request, upon their relatives and friends, whom he will believe to be able and willing to help him realize his vicious desires. Not only do arguments prove the possibility of such occurrences as we have mentioned, but "experience the mistress of things" [24] teaches that they have actually thus happened in the past and are still happening now, as is well known to practically all the faithful.

13. Furthermore, when the Roman bishop is permitted to have such general and unrestricted power to appoint officials and to distribute temporal goods and benefices, all kingdoms and polities are put in danger of destruction or violent turmoil, if such bishop seeks to subject secular governments to himself; and in a written document called a "decretal," which we have mentioned before, Boniface VIII did declare that all secular governments are subject in coercive jurisdiction to each successive Roman bishop, and he vehemently asserted that for the faithful, belief in this proposition was "necessary for salvation." [25] And the same position is implied in the edicts of a certain so-called Roman bishop directed against the noble Ludwig, duke of Bavaria, elected king of the Romans; for although this bishop seems to apply his statements only to the Roman kingdom or empire, [26] yet he therein includes all other states, inasmuch as among other considerations, he ascribes to himself the title "plenitude of power." For by this title he has as much coercive jurisdiction over the other kings as over the Roman ruler, as was clearly shown in the last chapter of Discourse I. [27] This bishop, then, is seeking, although wrongly, to have such coercive jurisdiction over all the rulers in the world; and by his distribution or donation of ecclesiastic temporal goods or benefices and tithes (of which an inestimable part have already come to belong to him, who has designs on all states), he can stir up great dissension, and has in fact done so hitherto and is still doing so, especially throughout the whole Roman Empire, as we shall show at greater length below.

14. Consequently, with regard to the reception or assumption of tithes and other ecclesiastic temporal goods, the human legislator or the ruler by its authority must note whether or not there is a surplus of such goods over

---

[24] See above, para. 9 of this chapter, n. 20.

[25] The bull *Unam sanctam*, in *Corp. jur. can., Extravag. commun.* Lib. I. Tit. 8. cap. 1.

[26] This refers to the bulls of John XXII against Ludwig of Bavaria, beginning with the one of Oct. 8, 1323, *Attendentes quod dum errori* (MGH, *Constitutiones*, Vol. V, No. 792, pp. 616–19).

[27] See above, I. xix. 9, incl. n. 15.

the needs of poor ministers of the gospel and other poor helpless men for whose sake such goods have been set aside; and also whether or not such surplus goods are needed to defend or otherwise to sustain the commonwealth. If they are needed for this latter purpose, then, regardless of any statements to the contrary by priests or other such ministers, the legislators or rulers can lawfully, in accordance with divine law, seize and use on their own authority all goods which remain over and above the needs of the aforesaid gospel ministers and poor men; not only tithes, but even quarters and thirds, and, in a word, whatever remains in excess of the needs of the priests and the helpless poor. For with food and raiment the priests should be content, as the Apostle says in I Timothy, Chapter 6.[28] But if legislators or rulers do not need such goods for the aforesaid use or purpose, they commit a mortal sin in consenting to receive them or in striving to obtain them. Therefore, the Roman bishop or any other single bishop, whether alone or with his college of clergymen, must not be permitted to have the power to distribute ecclesiastic temporal goods, lest by such power he be able to acquire secular influence to the detriment of rulers and peoples, and to stir up scandal and strife among the Christian believers. For this power of distribution is no slight but rather a great instrument for stirring up such strife, since very many men are misled into thinking that benefices can justly be distributed by the bishop and received by them, and hence they readily agree to accept and acquire such goods. For this reason, the general council and the human legislator must completely remove from the Roman or any other bishop this power which is so destructive of the peace of the believers, or else they must duly moderate such power, especially since it does not belong to the bishop by divine law, but rather was, just as it still is, forbidden to him, as has been sufficiently shown in Chapters XIII, XIV, and XVII of this discourse.

15. For the same reason, the power to bestow teaching licences ought to be and lawfully can be revoked from the Roman bishop or any other priest and his particular clerical college.[29] For the bestowing of such licences is the function of the human legislator, or of the ruler by its authority, since these matters can lead to the common benefit or harm of the citizens for the status of the present world, as was demonstrated in Chapter XV of Discourse I.

The same view must also be held with regard to instituting the canonization or veneratio of saints. For this can be harmful or helpful to the com-

---

[28] I Timothy 6:8. Cf. Vol. I, pp. 114–15.

[29] The papacy claimed sole power to authorize universities and bestow degrees. Philip the Fair overrode this claim in the case of Orleans; see Fournier, *Statuts*, as above, II. xviii. 6, n. 9, and also H. Denifle *Die Entstehung der Universitäten des Mittelalters* (Berlin, 1885), pp. 260 ff.

munity of faithful citizens. For a vicious bishop, if he were given such canonizing power, could pronounce certain men sanctified in order to confirm, by these men's statements or writings, his own vicious opinions, to the harm of other men; [30] consequently, this authority must be entrusted only to the general council of the believers. For it was in this way that Gregory IV, "with the consent of the emperor Ludwig and all the bishops, decreed that All-Hallows Day be celebrated"; [31] and hence a similar view must be taken with regard to all such matters.

Another reason why the power to grant teaching licences should be revoked from the bishops is the following. In ancient times the legislator granted this power to the bishops because of their saintly lives and wide learning, as is quite clear from the science of civil acts.[32] But at the present time the bishops, having the opposite qualities, subject to themselves colleges of learned men, taking them away from the secular rulers, and use them as no slight but rather very powerful instruments for perpetrating and defending their usurpations against the secular rulers. For since these learned men are unwilling to lose their professional titles, desiring the ease and glory resulting from possession of them, and believing that they have been obtained only by the authority of the Roman or other bishops, they carry out the bishops' wishes and oppose any persons, whether secular rulers or subjects, who contradict what they consider to be the authority of these bishops. But since such authority to bestow teaching licences belongs to the legislator or to the ruler by its authority, these alone should and lawfully can bestow, on their own authority, notary licences, professional titles, and the titles of other civil offices, in order that they may not lack but may rather acquire and preserve the favor of the learned and the wise, which favor must be considered to outweigh all other external aids for stabilizing and defending governments and constitutions.[33] For such authority to bestow licences and titles can belong to no private person, whatever his dignity or status, and to no particular group as such, but only to the ruler, as was demonstrated in Chapters XV and XVII of Discourse I.

[30] This may refer, as Previté-Orton suggests, to the canonization of St. Thomas Aquinas by John XXII on July 18, 1323.

[31] Martinus Polonus *Chronicon* (MGH, *Scriptores*, XXII, 427).

[32] I.e., *Corpus juris civilis.*   [33] Cf. Vol. I, pp. 113-15.

CHAPTER XXII: IN WHAT SENSE THE ROMAN BISHOP AND HIS CHURCH ARE THE HEAD AND LEADER OF THE OTHERS; AND BY WHAT AUTHORITY THIS HEADSHIP BELONGS TO THEM

NOW that we have determined these matters, we wish to show that it is expedient and very useful to appoint a single bishop and a single church or priestly college as the head or leader of the others. But first we must differentiate the ways or senses in which one church or bishop can be under ood to be the head of all the others, so that we may separate the proper way from the ways which are improper and inexpedient. [*i*] For one bishop and church to be the head of all the others can in one sense be understood to mean that all churches and individuals in the world are obliged to believe in their definitions or interpretations of doubtful senses of Scripture (especially with regard to what it is necessary to believe and observe for salvation), and to perform the church ritual or divine worship in accordance with their decrees. But in this sense no one bishop or church of any province, as such, nor any college of priests, is the head of the others, according to divine law, nor does the example of the primitive church show that it is expedient to have a head church of such a kind, nor, similarly, is such headship authorized by any decree of the faithful human legislator. For if there were such a head, one of the many evils that would follow therefrom would be this: that it would be necessary for salvation that all rulers, communities, and peoples believe, in accordance with the definition or decree of Boniface VIII, that they were all subject in coercive jurisdiction to the Roman pope,[1] and believe further, in accordance with the ordinances of a certain so-called Roman pope, that Christ did not counsel that the possession (in private or in common) of temporal goods in excess of present needs be spurned or renounced, and likewise the ownership of such goods, that is, the power lawfully to sue for them or to lay claim to them before a coercive judge.[2] The first of these assertions is the most horrible falsehood; and the second must de denied as heretical, as has been clearly shown above in Chapters XIII, XIV, XVI, XX, and XXI of this discourse.

2. [*ii*] Another sense in which one bishop and church or college can be

[1] See above, II. xxi. 13.

[2] This refers to John XXII's bulls *Ad conditorem canonum* (*Corp. jur. can., Extravag. Joh. XXII* Tit. 14. cap. 3) and *Cum inter nonnullos* (*ibid.*, Tit. 14. cap. 4). See above, II. xiii. 6, 10.

regarded as the head or leader of all the rest, is this: that all the clergymen or clerical colleges in the world are subject to their coercive jurisdiction. But this kind of headship belongs to no bishop or church according to divine law, but is rather forbidden by counsel or command, as has been adequately shown in Chapters IV, V, VIII, IX, and XI of this discourse.

3. [*iii*] This priority can be understood in still another sense: that to one bishop or church or college pertains the appointment of all church officials and the distribution, deposit, and withdrawal of temporal goods or benefices. But that some one bishop or church is in this sense prior to the others cannot be proved by divine law, but rather the opposite. And in a word, by virtue of the words of Scripture it cannot be proved that some one bishop or church is the head or leader of the others with respect to any authority or power, as has been shown in Chapters XV, XVI, XVII, XX, and XXI of this discourse.

4. Consequently, one bishop can no more excommunicate another than the other can excommunicate him; nor can one bishop interdict the reception of divine sacraments or services by the people or province entrusted to the care of another bishop, any more than the other bishop can do so to the former's people or province; nor, with regard to any other authority, does one bishop have more of it over another bishop, or over this other bishop's province, than the latter has over the former bishop or over his province, unless such authority or power shall have been granted by the general council or the faithful human legislator. For all bishops are of equal merit and authority insofar as they are bishops, as we showed in Chapter XV of this discourse from Jerome's epistle to Evander.[3] Nor is one bishop more perfect than another simply because a more perfect apostle or bishop laid his hands on him. For "let no man glory in men," wrote the Apostle; "for all things are yours, whether Paul, or Apollo, or Cephas, etc., and ye are Christ's."[4] Whereon the gloss: "'And ye are Christ's,' not man's, in creation or re-creation."[5] For this reason, it makes no difference with regard to any sacrament whether the priest who lays on his hands is more or less perfect, so long as he has the authority, because God alone gives the effect of a sacrament. And hence the Apostle, in the same chapter of Corinthians, settles this question by saying: "I have planted, Apollo watered, but God gave the increase."[6] For just as a tree's power of germination or of life-functioning is bestowed not by him who plants or waters the tree but rather by him who gives to the plant its vegetative soul, so too does the Apostle show that meritorious works are bestowed not by those who lay on their

---

[3] See above, II. xv. 8, 10.   [4] I Corinthians 3:21–23.
[5] See Peter Lombard *Collectanea* (PL 191. 1564).   [6] I Corinthians 3:6.

hands, and teach or give blessing, but rather by him who bestows the internal character or grace, God himself; although the former are of assistance, like those who water the plant. And since there is only one giver of internal authority, of character (of the same species), and of grace, namely, God himself, it follows that all bishops or priests are of equal authority and merit bestowed by God, which was the view held by Jerome.

5. By virtue of the words of Scripture, therefore, no bishop or church is the head or leader of the rest, as such. For the only absolute head of the church and foundation of the faith, by immediate ordainment of God, according to the Scripture or truth, is Christ himself, and not any apostle, bishop, or priest, as the Apostle very clearly says in Ephesians, Chapters 4 and 5, in Colossians, Chapter 1, and in I Corinthians, Chapter 10.[7] And hence he says that all the apostles, prophets, teachers, and other believers constitute the "body of Christ," which is the church as meaning the other members; but no one is the "head" except Christ alone. Whence in Ephesians, Chapter 4, it is written: "And he gave some, apostles; and some, prophets; and some, evangelists; and some, pastors and teachers; for the perfecting of the saints, for the work of the ministry, for the edifying of the body of Christ: till we all come in the unity of the faith,"[8] etc. And a little below the Apostle adds: "But speaking the truth in love, let us grow up into him in all things, which is the head, Christ: from whom the whole body fitly joined together and compacted by that which every joint supplieth, according to the effectual working in the measure of every part, maketh increase of the body unto the edifying of itself in love."[9] And again in Chapter 5 of the same epistle: "For the husband is the head of the wife, even as Christ is the head of the church: and he is the savior of the body. Therefore as the church is subject unto Christ, so let the wives be to their own husbands in every thing."[10] But never did Paul say that Cephas was the head of the church, or that the church was subject to him as its head, although such statements were made after Christ rose up from the dead and ascended the heavens. And hence the Apostle, speaking in the person of all believers, writes a little below in the same chapter: "For no man ever yet hated his own flesh, but nourisheth and cherisheth it, even as Christ the church, for we are members of his body."[11] Again, in Colossians, Chapter 1: "And he is the head of the body, the church: who is the beginning, the first-born from the dead; that in all things he might have the preeminence."[12] The same is clearly shown by St. Peter in his first epistle, Chapter 5: "And when the chief shepherd," Christ, "shall appear,

[7] See above, II. xvii. 2; also see below.　　[8] Ephesians 4:11–13.
[9] Ephesians 4:15–16.　　[10] Ephesians 5:23–24.　　[11] Ephesians 5:29–30.
[12] Colossians 1:18.

ye shall receive a crown of glory that fadeth not away." [13] But besides being the head, Christ alone is and was the foundation and rock of the church or faith. Whence in I Corinthians, Chapter 3, it is written: "For other foundation can no man lay than that is laid, which is Jesus Christ." [14] And again in Chapter 10 of the same epistle: "And that rock was Christ." [15]

6. [*iv*] There is another, and proper, sense in which a bishop or church can be understood to be or to have been made the head and leader of the other bishops and churches. This proper headship is derived from the authority of the general council or the faithful legislator, and is of the following kind: It is the duty of the head bishop, although together with his college of priests (whom the faithful human legislator or the general council has willed to associate with him for this purpose), to notify the faithful legislator lacking a superior if any emergency of the faith, or clear need of the believers, is brought to his attention which, after due deliberation, seems absolutely to require the calling of a general council. The general council must then be assembled by the coercive command of the legislator, in the way we have said. It is also the head bishop's duty to hold the leading seat or position among all the bishops and clergymen at the general council, to propose questions for deliberation, to review the discussions in the presence of the whole council, to have the proceedings recorded in writing under authentic seals and notarial stamps, to communicate and publish these proceedings to all churches which so request, to know and teach these results and answer questions about them; and also, if any persons transgress the council's decisions with regard both to the faith and to church ritual or divine worship, as well as the other ordinances for the peace and unity of the believers, the head bishop has to punish such transgressors by some ecclesiastic censure, like excommunication or interdict or other similar penalty, but in accordance with the determination of the council and by its authority, and not by any coercive power inflicting punishment in person or in property in and for the status of the present world. It is also the duty of the head bishop, acting together with the weightier part or majority of the college which has been assigned to him by the legislator, to sit in judgment over bishops and churches (not subordinated to one another) with respect to spiritual controversies properly so called, according to the second and third senses of the term "spiritual," as indicated in Chapter II of this discourse, in which class fall the ordinances concerning church ritual which the council has made and ordered to be observed. However, if the other churches with comparative unanimity clearly feel that it is likely that

---

[13] I Peter 5:4.   [14] I Corinthians 3:11.   [15] I Corinthians 10:4.

this duty is being abused or neglected by the head church's bishop [16] or college, then these other churches may lawfully appeal to the faithful human legislator, if the legislator, or the ruler by its authority, can conveniently correct such abuse or neglect; or else the other churches may request a general council, if, in the eyes of a majority of the other churches and in the judgment of the legislator, the case requires the calling of such a council.

I say, then, that only in this last way is it expedient, for the easier and more fitting maintenance of the unity of the faith, that some one bishop or church be made the head or leader of the others in the pastoral office, without coercive jurisdiction, although such headship is not commanded by divine law, since the unity of the faith would be preserved even without such a head, although not so easily.[17] We must next show what kind of bishop, church, or college of priests and clergymen, and from which diocese or province, it is more proper and expedient to name the head and leader of all the other bishops, churches, and clerical colleges; and finally we must show to whom belongs the authority to name this head, to correct him, and even to depose him if it seems expedient to do so.

7. The first proposition, that it is expedient to set up such a single head over the churches, can be proved once we grant the necessity of sometimes calling a general council of believers and priests for the sake of the abovementioned advantages with regard to church ritual, the faith, and divine worship. For many bishops or churches would in vain be occupied in a task which can equally conveniently be performed and completed by a single bishop or church. But the recommending that councils be called, together with the other functions which we said were to be the duty of this church head, can be performed equally conveniently by one man as by many, or even more conveniently.[18] Moreover, when such a head or leader is set up over the bishops and churches, a possible source of strife and scandal is removed. For in the assembled general council, it is necessary to establish the form and method of procedure. But if everyone alike could at will make such procedural decrees and commands, then scandal, strife, and confusion would in all probability arise among those present at the council. And again, inasmuch as in the general council assembled there are considerations of rank with respect to place, as in sitting or standing, and with respect to speech, as in proposing resolutions and debating, in addition to which it is sometimes necessary to give commands, as when one

---

[16] Removing, with Scholz, commas after *episcopo* and *ecclesiae.*
[17] See Vol. I, p. 279.   [18] See Vol. I, pp. 235, 278.

silences a too garrulous speaker; and also, inasmuch as it is necessary to sum up the decisions of the council, and have them recorded in writing by notaries under certified and authentic stamps and seals; for all these reasons it is expedient that one man be at the head of the rest, and that he have the authority to set the others in order and to command other expedient measures with regard to the solemnization and proper consummation of the council, lest the public welfare of the believers be disturbed or upset by a diversity, or sometimes even a contrariety, of such measures. Furthermore, such headship seems expedient because it is the custom of the Christian church, and because, being a sensible sign of the unity of the faith, it makes this unity more evident.

8. We now come to the questions of what bishop and church it is most proper to choose as head of the others, and from which province or diocese this head ought to be chosen. Discussing first the qualities of the head bishop, let us say, in accordance with the truth, that he ought to be the one who excels all others in the goodness of his life and in sacred doctrine, although the former qualification should be given more weight.[19] As to which place or province should have its church put over the others, it must be said that the headship should be given to that church whose college of priests or clergymen includes the most men who are most honorable in their lives and most pure in their sacred doctrine. But other things being equal, or not much different, it seems that the bishop and church of Rome (so long as that place remains habitable) deserves such headship for several reasons: first, because of the surpassing faith, love, and renown of the first bishop of Rome, who was St. Peter or St. Paul or both, and the great reverence paid to them by the other apostles; also, because of the venerable tradition of the city of Rome, its long leadership over the other cities, the great number of illustrious men, saints, and teachers of the Christian faith who lived at Rome in most periods from the very beginning of the established church, and the diligent care and assiduous labor which they exerted on behalf of the other churches to spread the faith and to preserve its unity; and again, because of the general monarchy and coercive authority which the people and ruler of Rome once exercised over all the rulers and peoples in the world, so that they alone had the power to make coercive commands binding on all men with respect to the observance of the faith and of the decisions of general councils, and to punish transgressors of these commands wherever they might be; and besides this, they greatly increased the size of the church, even though later on some of the Romans sometimes persecuted the Christians because of the malice of

[19] See Vol. I, p. 279, n. 63.

certain priests. And a final reason why it is appropriate that the bishop and church of Rome have the leadership is custom, inasmuch as all the believers have learned, or have become accustomed, to honor the bishop and church of Rome above all the rest, and to be stirred to virtuous living and the worship of God by their exhortations and admonitions, and to be recalled from vices and crimes by their reproofs, censures, and threats of eternal damnation.

9. As for the question of who has the authority to establish this leadership, the answer must be that this authority belongs to the general council or the faithful human legislator lacking a superior, to whom it also pertains to designate the clerical college or group which shall hold this leadership; and in accordance with this procedure, the city of Rome, so long as it endures and its people do not object, will lawfully and rightfully continue to hold the episcopal and ecclesiastic leadership, because of men's reverence for Saints Peter and Paul, and for the other reasons given above.

10. That this above authority to establish the leadership belongs to the legislator is borne out by an edict of Constantine I, the Roman emperor, which is included in the *Codex* of Isidore, and contains this passage among others: "We," that is, the Roman emperor, "decree that it," that is, the Roman church, "shall hold the leadership both over the four principal seats, at Antioch, Alexandria, Constantinople, and Jerusalem, and over all the other churches of God in the whole world; and that he who for the time being is the pontiff of the sacrosanct Roman church shall be the head and leader of all the priests throughout the world, and that all matters pertaining to the worship of God, or to the maintenance of the stability of the faith, shall be regulated by his judgment." [20] Note that Constantine clearly said that "the maintenance of the stability of the faith," or divine law, is to be regulated by the Roman pontiff; but Constantine did not say that the faith is to be determined in accordance with the views of the Roman pontiff or of his church or college alone. For, as we have said above, when there arise, with respect to Scripture and faith, opinions which can lead to schism, scandal, and the disturbance of the peace and unity of the believers, then it is the duty of the head pontiff to take account of such opinions, to inquire into them, to report them to the faithful legislator or to the ruler by its authority, and to ask it for a council to settle and, if expedient, to correct this situation. Thus, therefore, it was Constantine who gave to the Roman bishop and church this leadership or priority, and with this, because of his devoutness, Constantine granted them many other powers, which by divine or human right he was not at all obliged to grant.

[20] The "donation of Constantine," in Pseudo-Isidore *Decretales*, ed. Hinschius, p. 252.

And this leadership, which certain successors of Constantine perhaps revoked from the Roman bishop and church, was restored to this church by Augustus Phocas, as is clearly shown by Martinus' *Chronicle of the Roman Pontiffs and Emperors,* wherein these words are found: "Boniface IV, by birth a Marsian," etc., and a little below: "He obtained from Augustus Phocas, the emperor, a decree stating that the church of St. Peter the apostle was the head of all the churches, because the church of Constantinople was claiming this headship for itself." [21]

11. Furthermore, that this authority to establish the headship belongs to the faithful human legislator or to the ruler by its authority, in accordance with the advice and decision of the general council, can be proved by the same reasonings and authorities whereby we showed in Chapter XXI of this discourse that to the legislator or the ruler belongs the authority to call a general council and to punish by coercive force all those, whether priests or laymen, who refuse to come to the council and who transgress the council's ordinances. All that has to be done is to change the minor term of the reasonings. And from these propositions it necessarily follows that it pertains to the same authority lawfully to correct the head bishop and his church or college, to suspend him from office, and to deprive or depose him therefrom if such action seems reasonable and expedient.

12. But we must not omit to say that when believers, whether priests or laymen who are skilled in divine law, live under infidel legislators or rulers, then these believers are obliged by that same divine law to come together, if they conveniently can, to define and determine doubtful meanings of that law and to make other enactments which can advance the growth, the unity, and the common welfare of the faith and of the faithful; although this obligation is more binding upon the priests, who ought to arouse the other believers thereto, inasmuch as the priests' duty is to teach, exhort, reprove, and if necessary threaten others. But those men too have this obligation who are learned in divine law, and the priests must require them to fulfill it, for "to him that knoweth to do good, and doth it not, to him it is sin," [22] as it is written in James, Chapter 4. For just as by human law it is not only those who have been assigned to military duty, in infantry or cavalry, who are obliged to defend the civil liberty by physical combat in time of necessity, but also those who are in the other offices of the state, particularly those who are most suited to this task, and especially when their services have been requested by the soldiers or their leader; so too by divine law it is not only the priests who are obliged to defend and clarify the faith and to make regulations concerning church ritual, but also

[21] Martinus Polonus *Chronicon* (MGH, *Scriptores,* XXII, 422).   [22] James 4:17.

laymen, if they are skilled in divine law, especially when their services have been requested for this purpose by the priests, even though such functions are properly the duty of the latter.

13. At whose call shall the council of priests and of other suitable believers be assembled? This is a question which may well be asked, since no one of the priests or other believers is made leader of the rest, in the senses discussed above, by divine or by human law, because the human legislator is assumed to be everywhere infidel. We reply, in accordance with the sense of Scripture, that the general council is to be called or assembled by no bishop or priest having authority over the other priests and bishops, unless perhaps such authority may chance to have been granted to a priest by the above-mentioned majority of the believers. Suppose, then, that no one priest has thus been put at the head of all the rest by the multitude of priests and other believers, but that it is nevertheless expedient to choose such a head or to make some other regulation with regard to the faith or to church ritual. In such case I say that either the call for this council will come from all the priests, if by chance every one of them is of such great love as to wish to arouse the others for the sake of the preservation and growth of the faith, so that they will all unhesitatingly and readily agree and consent to assemble in a council; or else, if by chance they are not all so loving as to wish to induce the others to assemble with them in a council, then the call will come from those who are more fervent in divine love than the rest, whereupon the other priests or laymen will heed their words and recognize the rightness of their counsels.

In both these ways the apostles and elders were called in the past to assemble for the purpose of determining whether or not it was necessary for eternal salvation that uncircumcised brethren be circumcised, as is to be seen from the Acts, Chapter 15. For we nowhere read that the apostles assembled at the call of some one of them, by his own authority; but only this, that "the apostles and elders came together for to consider of this matter"; [23] and again, that "the twelve called the multitude of the disciples unto them." [24] The Scripture does not explicitly say which of the apostles was the first to arouse or call upon the others to assemble at these meetings. However, let us suppose that St. Peter was the first in this regard, because of his greater love; it would not then follow that he had any authority over

---

[23] Acts 15:6. From here until the end of the penultimate paragraph of this chapter, Marsilius' words are repeated in condensed form by Dietrich of Niem, *Circa convocationem generalium conciliorum* (1413/14), ed. H. Heimpel, "Studien zur Kirchen- und Reichsreform des 15. Jh.," I, 32-35, in *Sitzungsberichte der Heidelberger Akad. d. Wissenschaften*, Phil.-hist. Kl. (1929/30).

[24] Acts 6:2.

the other apostles, unless perhaps they had given him such authority by their own election, as has been shown above in Chapters XV and XVI of this discourse. For in cloisters and cities there are very many men who are more perfect in the meritoriousness of their lives and sacred doctrine, or more outstanding in political virtue, who yet are not the rulers or prelates of the less perfect, but most often their subjects; this situation frequently occurs nowadays with respect to priestly offices, through what baneful cause I do not know—or perhaps I do know.

14. Moreover, just as in the civil assembly the most conscientious, the oldest, and the most reputable men are sometimes given privileges with regard to sitting, speaking, and deliberating, and are paid many other honors by their fellow citizens, not because the latter are subject to their authority, but solely because reverence seems due to men of greater virtue and age; so too it is very likely and in harmony with Scripture that the other apostles deferred to Peter for these aforesaid reasons; for we read that he was the leader in making resolutions. And it was perhaps for this reason that some of the saints called him "the mouth and head of the company of apostles," [25] although the other apostles were not subject to him in any authority, unless, as we said before, such subjection was by their own election, by their having freely willed thus to put him at their head, just as the monks elect their abbot or prior and the people their leader.[26]

15. Hence, that the believers might have been called together and assembled in the aforesaid ways seems quite reasonable. For when men originally came together to establish the civil community and civil law, with the weightier part of them agreeing on matters pertaining to sufficiency of life, they were summoned not by the coercive authority of one or many persons, but rather by the persuasion or exhortation of prudent and able men. The latter, exceptionally endowed by nature with an inclination for this task, later through their own efforts made progress in their various pursuits and guided other men, either by successive stages or at one time, to the formation of the fully developed community, to which they were naturally inclined, so that they readily heeded this persuasion, as we have shown in Chapters III, IV, VII, and XIII of Discourse I from the *Politics*, Book I, Chapter 1, Book IV, Chapter 10, and Book VII, Chapter 12.[27]

[25] See St. Chrysostom, in Thomas Aquinas *Catena aurea* (XII, 462).

[26] By "people" (*populus*) Marsilius here seems to mean the *popolo* of an Italian commune, as distinct from the *magnati*, i.e., hereditary nobles and other very wealthy and powerful men (see Vol. I, pp. 28–29, 181). The "leader" (*praeses*) of the people is its own *podestà* or captain. See Previté-Orton, p. 353, n. 2.

[27] See above, I. iii. 3; I. iv. 3; I. vii. 2; I. xiii. 2. Also see Vol. I, p. 112.

Just so, analogously to this and in accordance with Scripture, we must reasonably hold that the multitude of the apostles and believers came together perhaps at the persuasion of one or more of the apostles whose love was more fervent, with the others readily heeding them, being filled with the grace of the Holy Spirit, and such being their inclination.

This too was perhaps the procedure followed after the time of the apostles by some of the bishops or priests who lived under infidel legislators or rulers and who were filled with the greatest love for Christ and for their neighbors; and it was with these men that Christ promised he would remain "even unto the end of the world," [28] the last words in the last chapter of Matthew. For it is of them that Raban writes, in his gloss on this passage, "that 'even unto the end of the world' there will not be lacking men on earth who are worthy of divine immanence and indwelling," [29] although every priest by his very office has this obligation to spread the faith, if he can properly do so. For in the last chapter of Matthew a command to this effect was given to all priests in the person of the apostles, when Christ said to them: "Go ye therefore and teach all nations." [30] Heeding this, the Apostle wrote in I Corinthians, Chapter 9: "Woe is me if I preach not the gospel, for necessity is laid upon me." [31] But his example, solicitude, and efforts on behalf of spreading the faith and preserving its unity are little heeded by the modern pastors of the Roman church, who stir up internal strife and discord among the Christian believers in order to be able the more securely, although wrongly and unlawfully, to exercise secular rulership over them.

16. And so from the above it is clear that the Roman bishop with his church has hitherto been the leader and head of all the other bishops and churches, and we have sufficiently shown in what this headship rightfully has consisted and consists. Reviewing [32] the source of this authority, the way in which he obtained it, and how far it was in fact, although wrongly and unlawfully, extended through fraud, let us say that from the beginning to the time of Constantine the Roman bishop with his church obtained this priority lawfully, through what was almost an election on the part of the other churches, offering him their consent and obedience; but this obedience was given voluntarily, not because the other churches were subject to the Roman bishop in any authority, but because of the preeminent love and constant faith of the apostles Peter and Paul, and because the Roman church had so many men of surpassing honor and learning, men

---

[28] Matthew 28:20.   [29] Raban, in Thomas Aquinas *Catena aurea* (XI, 334).
[30] Matthew 28:19.   [31] I Corinthians 9:16.
[32] Here Marsilius resumes his historical account of the development of the papal power which he interrupted at II. xviii. 7.

who, out of their boundless love, took pains to give instruction and fraternal advice to the prelates and believers of the other churches. And these other churches, regarding the Roman bishops as more learned, accepted their advice, and later they accepted their decisions on matters of church ritual because these decisions seemed useful and just, and finally they came to obey their commands under threat of an ecclesiastic censure of excommunication or interdict in order to preserve the unity of the faithful. This voluntary obedience through long custom obtained the force of an election. Hence, although at the beginning of the church obedience to the commands or decrees of the Roman bishop or church was not made obligatory upon the other Christian bishops and churches either by divine law or by any human law, any more than conversely, nevertheless, through the strengthening of this useful and reasonable custom whereby the unity of the faithful was more fully preserved (because they did not at that time have a faithful legislator to reduce them to order and to preserve them in unity), the faithful later on were obligated by divine law to be thus obedient in lawful and honorable matters, as if the Roman bishop with his church had been appointed by the believers through election to be their judge on questions of church ritual. Especially was this the case up to the time when they could publicly assemble and more adequately regulate the condition of the church.

17. With regard to contentious acts, however, the case is different. For the Apostle gave a different counsel as to how contentious acts among believers, whether priests or laymen, were to be judged, as we have shown from I Corinthians, Chapter 6, in Chapter IX of this discourse,[33] and as we shall explain more fully in Chapter XXIX.[34] For the Apostle did not wish that the judging of such acts be the function of any priest or bishop or particular group of them, as is quite clear from the Apostle's words, and from the expositions thereof by the saints.

18. Thus, then, at the beginning the Roman bishop and his church obtained the priority lawfully, through their loving solicitude; and later, because of their steadfast devotion, and the reverence and voluntary obedience which the other churches offered them, this priority assumed the force almost of an election. For it cannot be shown by Scripture that Christ or any of the apostles ever gave a command or counsel requiring the other bishops or churches to be subject to the Roman bishop or church, even in matters of church ritual. But if such subjection were necessary for the salvation of the believers (as certain Roman bishops now assert), not only in matters of church ritual but even in coercive jurisdiction, and not

---

[33] See above, II. ix. 13.   [34] See below, II. xxix. 4 ff.

only for clergymen but even for all secular governments, then how can it be thought that Christ and his apostles would have failed to teach the duty of such subjection? But since both Christ and his apostles openly decreed the opposite, especially with regard to coercive jurisdiction, as has been clearly shown from Scripture in Chapters IV, V, and IX of this discourse, such statements as those cited above must be reckoned among the apocryphal fables.

19. It was in the time of Constantine I, emperor of the Romans, who openly accepted the Christian faith and baptism, that the believers first began to assemble in public, to settle questions of faith and to regulate church ritual, as is to be seen from the *Codex* of Isidore, in the chapter, "On the primitive church in the Nicene Council." [35] Through an imperial edict of this Constantine, in harmony with the old praiseworthy custom which we have discussed above, the Roman bishop and church obtained that priority over the others which we have shown to belong to them, and also, besides this priority, they received the possession and ownership of certain provinces.[36] However, before the time of Constantine, and even after, certain Roman bishops wrote letters or decrees in which they claimed that the priority over the other bishops and churches, which we have shown to belong to them by election or by the ordinances of rulers, was owed to them by virtue of divine law, without the request or consent of the faithful human legislator or of any groups or individuals, whatever their preeminence or authority might be; but the opposite of this claim has been sufficiently proved in the preceding chapter.

20. After the time of Constantine I, and especially when the imperial seat was vacant, certain Roman bishops wrote letters declaring that this priority belonged to them now by virtue of divine law, now by the grant of rulers. As for the scope and nature of this priority, many of them suggested or declared that it extended to the interpretation of the evangelic law and the regulation of church ritual with regard both to divine worship and to ecclesiastic ministers, covering both kinds of their appointment, the inseparable or primary, which we have called essential, and also the secondary, which in Chapter XV of this discourse we called separable or accidental, together with the deprivation thereof. These Roman bishops asserted that this primacy extended over all other bishops, churches, peoples, and individuals, and they claimed that through it they had the authority to pronounce sentences of excommunication or of interdict of divine offices, or any other ecclesiastic censure, such as anathema, upon the afore-

[35] Pseudo-Isidore *Decretales,* ed. Hinschius, pp. 247 ff.
[36] The "donation of Constantine," *ibid.,* p. 252; see above, II. xxii. 10.

mentioned believers, both subjects and church ministers or prelates. Following upon this, other Roman bishops claimed to have complete jurisdiction or coercive power over all church ministers and groups of ministers in the world. So long as the Roman ruler remained powerful and his state was whole and his seat filled, these bishops exercised such coercive power on the ground that it belonged to them by grant of the rulers. But in the course of time, the Roman kingdom having been thrown into sedition, and especially while the imperial seat was vacant, the Roman bishops came to assert that this power was granted to them by divine law. In the following chapter we shall tell why the Roman ecclesiastic primacy has had such a varied history.

In the same way the Roman bishops have in their epistles declared that to them belongs the authority to dispense or distribute at will all the temporal goods of the church, without the request or consent [37] of any group or individual, of whatever dignity or authority. And not content with these excessive claims, the more modern Roman bishops have declared in their epistles or decrees that supreme coercive authority or jurisdiction over all the governments, peoples, and individuals in the world belongs to them by divine law, so that no ruler can lawfully exercise such coercive jurisdiction, which they call the "temporal sword," without or against their consent or dictate; and upon those rulers who do so, and upon the subjects of these rulers, the Roman bishops blatantly pronounce sentences of excommunication or interdict. For they assert that they alone in the world are the vicars of Christ, who was "king of kings and lord of lords," [38] and they secretly aim to attain such supremacy for themselves, through the title of "plenitude of power" which they claim belongs to them. For this reason, too, they say they have the lawful authority to bestow and to take away all earthly kingdoms and governments from kings or other rulers who disobey their commands, although these commands are in truth impious and frequently unlawful.

These claims have been expressed by Boniface VIII, among other Roman bishops, in statements which are no less reckless than they are harmful and contrary to the literal sense of Scripture, based upon metaphorical interpretations of it; [39] and he has gone so far as to decree that it is necessary for eternal salvation that all men believe and avow that this power belongs to the Roman bishops.[40] The men following Boniface—Clement V and the latter's so-called immediate successor—have reaffirmed his claim, although they seem to apply it explicitly only to the Roman empire.[41] But

---

[37] Reading, with Scholz and MSS, *sive consensu*.   [38] Revelation 19:16.
[39] See Vol. I, pp. 75–77.
[40] See *Unam sanctam;* see above, I. xix. 10; II. xx. 8; II. xxi. 9.
[41] See Clement V *Pastoralis cura;* see above, I. xix. 10. Also, the bulls of John XXII, *Si*

since their claims are based on the afore-mentioned title, namely, the plenitude of power given to them by Christ, it is certain that if any such power or authority belongs to them by grant of Christ, then it extends equally to all the states and governments in the world, like Christ's own power, as we showed at length in Chapter XIX of Discourse I.[42]

CHAPTER XXIII: ON THE MODES OF PLENITUDE OF POWER, AND THE MANNER AND ORDER OF THEIR ASSUMPTION BY THE ROMAN BISHOP, TOGETHER WITH A GENERAL STATEMENT OF HOW HE HAS USED AND STILL USES THEM

THE nature and extent of the priestly powers was determined in Chapters VI, VII, IX, and XI of this discourse; the equality or inequality of the priests in power and dignity was examined in Chapters XV and XVI of this discourse; and in the preceding chapter we discussed the proper and expedient priority or leadership of one bishop, church, or clerical college over all others, and the origin and development of this primacy, its secret and gradual transition into an improper form and species of priority, extending to so grave and unbearable an excess as the seizure of secular power, and the immoderate and completely intolerable desire of the Roman bishops for rulership, to which desire they have already given vocal expression.

2. In all the seizures of secular power and rulership which the Roman bishops have perpetrated in the past, and which, as everyone can plainly see, they are still striving with all their might, although wrongly, to perpetrate, no small role has been played in the past, and will be played in the future, by that sophistical line of argument whereby these bishops ascribe to themselves the title of "plenitude of power." This sophistry is also the source of the misreasoning whereby they try to prove that all kings, rulers, and individuals are subject to them in coercive jurisdiction. Hence it will be well to examine this plenitude of power, first by separating or distinguishing its various modes; next by inquiring whether in any one or more of these modes plenitude of power belongs to the Roman pontiff or to any other

---

fratrum et coepiscoporum, March 31, 1317 (*Corp. jur. can., Extravag. Joh. XXII* Lib. v. cap. 1) and the *monitorium* against Ludwig of Bavaria, Oct. 8, 1323 (MGH, *Constitutiones*, Vol. V, No. 792, pp. 616 ff.).

[42] See above, I. xix. 9–10.

bishop; then, by showing which meaning of this title the Roman bishop first claimed for himself; and finally by examining how this was transferred into other forms (would that they were not frauds!) harmful to all rulers and subjects living a civil life, and what use the Roman pontiff has hitherto made, and still makes, and unless he is prevented will most likely continue to make, of these forms of the title of plenitude of power.

3. Inasmuch as plenitude of power seems to imply a certain universality, and it is our purpose to deal only with voluntary powers, we must differentiate plenitude of power into its various modes or senses, according to the different kinds of universal voluntary power.[1]

[i] In [2] one sense, then, plenitude of power is and can be truly understood to mean, in accordance with the significance or force of the words themselves, the unlimited power to perform every possible act and to make anything at will. This power seems to belong only to Christ from among all men. Whence in Matthew, last chapter, it is written: "All power is given unto me in heaven and in earth." [3]

[ii] In a second sense, more pertinently, plenitude of power can be understood to mean that whereby a man is allowed to perform any voluntary controlled act upon any other man and upon any external thing which is in men's power or can be put to their use; or again, plenitude of power can be understood to mean that whereby a man is allowed to perform every act aforesaid, but not upon every other man or everything subject to human power; or, furthermore, plenitude of power can be understood as that whereby a man is allowed to perform not every act, but only a determinate kind or species of act, and yet following every impulse of the will, and upon every other man and everything subject to human power.

[iii] In a third sense, plenitude of power can be understood as the power of supreme coercive jurisdiction over all the governments, peoples, communities, groups, and individuals in the world; or again, over only some of these, but yet following every impulse of the will.

[iv] In a fourth sense, plenitude of power can be understood to mean the kind of power defined above, but over all clergymen only, and including the power to appoint them all to church offices, to deprive them thereof or depose them, and to distribute ecclesiastic temporal goods or benefices.

---

[1] See above, Introduction, pp. lxxxvii–lxxxviii. With the ensuing discussion compare the interpretations of plenitude of power given by Egidius of Rome in *De ecclesiastica potestate* III. ix–x (pp. 190 ff.) and by James of Viterbo in *De regimine Christiano* II. ix (ed. H. X. Arquillière [Paris, 1926], pp. 268 ff.). See Vol. I, pp. 8, 257; also above I. xix. 9, n. 15.

[2] Most of the remainder of this chapter as well as paragraphs 2–7 of the next chapter are reproduced verbatim by Philippe de Mézières *Somnium viridarii* cap. lxxxii (*Monarchia*, ed. Goldast, II, 87–88).

[3] Matthew 28:18.

[*v*] In a fifth sense, it can be understood as the power whereby priests can in every way bind and loose men from guilt and punishment, and excommunicate them, lay them under interdict, and reconcile them to the church, all of which was discussed in Chapters VI and VII of this discourse.

[*vi*] In a sixth sense, it can be understood to mean the power of the priests to lay their hands on all men so as to receive them into ecclesiastic orders, and the power to bestow or prohibit ecclesiastic sacraments, which was discussed in Chapters XVI and XVII of this discourse.

[*vii*] In a seventh sense, it can be understood as the power to interpret the meanings of Scripture, especially on matters which are necessary for salvation; and the power to distinguish the true meanings from the false, the sound from the unsound; and the power to regulate all church ritual, and to make a general coercive command ordering the observance of such regulations under penalty of anathematization.

[*viii*] In an eighth sense, and the last so far as our purposes are concerned, plenitude of power can be understood to mean a general pastoral cure of souls, extending to all the peoples and provinces in the world, which was discussed in Chapters IX and XXII of this discourse.

Plenitude of power might also be understood, in each of the senses given above, as that power which is limited by no law, so that non-plenary power would be that which is limited by the laws human or divine, under which right reason can also properly be placed. There are perhaps other modes and combinations of plenitude of power, but I think that we have enumerated all those which are pertinent for our purposes.

4. And so, having thus distinguished these modes of plenary power, I say that plenitude of power in the first two senses given above does not belong to the Roman bishop, to any other priest, or to anyone else except Christ or God. Because this fact is so evident, and is certified by divine and human wisdom and all moral science, I omit to discuss it, and also for the sake of brevity.

As to the third and fourth modes of plenary power, we have shown by demonstration in Chapter XV of Discourse I, and more fully confirmed by the infallible testimony of the sacred Scripture in Chapters IV, V, and VII of this discourse, and most firmly corroborated in Chapters XV, XVI, XVII, and XXI of this discourse, that in no way at all, let alone with plenitude, do these powers belong by divine law to any priest or bishop, as such, over any clergyman or layman. But as to whether human law has granted such plenitude of power to any clergyman, bishop or priest, or to any layman, in any way in which such power is capable of being granted and of being revoked by the judgment of the human legislator for a reasonable cause, this must be ascertained from the human laws and the rescripts or privileges of the human legislator.[4]

As to the fifth and sixth modes of plenary power, it has been shown in Chapters VI and VII of this discourse that the power to bind men to and loose them from guilt and punishment, and publicly to anathematize or excommunicate anyone, has not been granted to the priest absolutely or with plenitude, but rather this power has been so delimited by divine law that the priest cannot damn the innocent or loose the guilty with God. Also, the power of any bishop or priest publicly to excommunicate someone, and especially to lay a ruler or community under interdict, must properly be delimited by human enactment, as has been shown in Chapters VI, VII, and XXI of this discourse. Moreover, in Chapter XVII of this discourse it has been shown that the power to appoint ministers of the church by laying on hands, and to teach and preach, and to minister the ecclesiastic sacraments in communities of believers, does not belong to bishops or priests with plenitude, since the proper way to use these powers has been determined for bishops and priests by divine and human law.

As to the remaining modes of plenitude of power, the seventh and eighth, it has been shown in Chapters XX, XXI, and XXII of this discourse that they belong to no bishop or priest with plenitude, but in accordance with the determination of both divine and human law. Therefore, plenitude of power does not belong to the Roman bishop or to any other priest, as such, unless perhaps they mean by plenitude of power the priority or leadership which we have shown, in Chapter XXII of this discourse, to belong to the Roman bishop and his church over all other priests and churches, by authority of the faithful human legislator.

5. Now we must discuss what was the source of the Roman pontiff's original ascription to himself of the title of plenitude of power, and which mode of this title he first assumed, although such plenary power truly belongs to him in none of the senses given above. But this title seems to have been first assumed by the Roman pontiff in its eighth sense, and the original source wherefrom this title appeared to belong to him seems to have been the statement of Christ to St. Peter, in John, Chapter 21: "Feed my sheep"; [5] and also the words in Matthew, Chapter 16, spoken to Peter alone: "And I will give unto thee the keys of the kingdom of heaven"; [6] also the passage in John, Chapter 18: "Put up thy sword into the sheath"; [7] and again the reply of the disciples to Christ: "Behold, here are two

---

[4] See Vol. I, pp. 257–58.   [5] John 21:17.   [6] Matthew 16:19.   [7] John 18:11.

swords." [8] These passages are interpreted by some men as meaning that the whole body of sheep, that is, the Christian believers in the whole world, has been entrusted to Peter alone, and thus to every Roman pontiff as the particular vicar of St. Peter; and that the other apostles and the bishops who succeeded them were not entrusted with the guidance of all the sheep throughout the whole world, but to each of them was entrusted a particular determinate flock and province. St. Bernard, thus interpreting the words of Christ which we quoted above from John, Chapter 21, writes in his treatise addressed to the Roman pope Eugene *On Consideration,* Book II, as follows: "You are the one universal shepherd, not only of the sheep, but also of the shepherds. How do I prove this, you ask? By the word of the Lord. For to which, I will not say of the bishops, but even of the apostles, were all the sheep entrusted so absolutely and without differentiation? 'If you love me, Peter, feed my sheep.' Where no distinctions are made, no exceptions are made." And a little below, Bernard adds: "Hence, to each of the other apostles, who knew the sacrament, was allotted a particular flock. And thereupon James, 'who seemed to be a pillar' of the church, was content to serve only in Jerusalem, yielding to Peter the care of the whole." And then Bernard draws this pertinent inference: "According to your canons, therefore, the others have been called to take care of a part, while you have been called to plenitude of power." [9] At the beginning, then, plenitude of power was understood to mean the general administration or care of all souls.

6. While such was the meaning of this title when the Roman bishop first assumed it for himself, although it was not in harmony with the true sense of Scripture, as will be sufficiently proved in Chapter XXVIII of this discourse, this meaning was presumptuously transformed by him into a different one, perhaps for the sake of gain or other advantage, or in order to usurp preeminence over others. By this transformation, the Roman bishop claimed and publicly declared that he alone, by his own pronouncement or by the imposition of any this-worldly satisfaction which he might care to demand, could completely absolve sinners and exempt them from the penalties which they would be obliged to pay or suffer for the status of the future world in accordance with the demerits of their sins.

7. Having thus assumed these powers under a guise of piety and mercy (piety, that they might seem to have care and solicitude for all men by the

---

[8] Luke 22:38.

[9] St. Bernard *De consideratione* II. viii (PL 182. 751–52). There is an echo of Galatians 2:9 and the Epistle of Leo I to Anastasius of Thessalonica: Pseudo-Isidore *Decretales,* ed. Hinschius, p. 619.

motivation of charity; mercy, that they might be thought to have the power and the desire to take pity upon all men), the Roman bishops, supported by the privileges and grants of rulers, and especially when the imperial seat was vacant, then extended this title: first they made it apply to the regulation of church ritual by making certain laws over clergymen, which from the beginning were called "decrees"; and then they persuaded laymen to accept certain regulations which were made in the form of requests or exhortations, imposing fasts and abstinences from certain foods at fixed periods, for the purpose of obtaining divine suffrage and mercy so that the epidemics and the atmospheric tempests which then plagued men might be averted. All this is to be seen from the history of St. Gregory [10] and of certain other saints.

8. When the laymen in their devoutness voluntarily accepted and observed these regulations or requests, and such observance became an established custom, the Roman bishops began to proclaim them in the form of commands, and thus ventured, without leave by the human legislator, to frighten their transgressors with vocal threats of anathematization or excommunication—but all this under the guise of piety or divine worship.

9. But then the desire of the Roman bishops for domination grew even stronger. Seeing that devout believers, because of their foolishness and their ignorance of divine law, were frightened by such pronouncements, and that, from fear of eternal damnation, they believed they were obliged to obey the proclamations of the priests, the Roman bishops with their coterie of clergymen had the presumption to issue certain oligarchic edicts or ordinances concerning civil acts, declaring that they and the clerical order or office, wherein they also included any mere laymen they chose, were exempt from public burdens; and they promoted to the clerical order even married laymen, who readily joined in order to enjoy immunity from public burdens. In this way they have subjected to themselves a not inconsiderable part of the civil multitude, removing them from the power of the rulers. And again, desiring further to lessen the rulers' power, they have issued other edicts imposing the penalty of anathema upon those who have inflicted any personal injuries on men who were enrolled in a clerical group; similarly, they publicly defame them in their temples by excommunicating them, nonetheless demanding that such culprits be given the punishments fixed by human laws.[11]

10. But here is a still more detestable act, truly execrable in the priestly

---

[10] See "Vita Gregorii Magni," *Acta sanctorum* March 12 (II, 131–32). See also Johannes Diaconus (*ibid.*, II, 142 ff.).

[11] See *Corp. jur. can., Sext.* Lib. III. Tit. 2. cap. 1; Tit. 23. cap. 3; Lib. v. Tit. 9. cap. 5; Tit. 11. cap. 6, 8, 23; *Clem.* Lib. v. Tit. 8. cap. 1.

office: in order to expand their jurisdiction and thereby to increase their shameful gains, in open contempt of God and to the patent harm of rulers, the Roman and other bishops excommunicate and exclude from the ecclesiastic sacraments laymen and clergymen who neglect or are unable to pay certain pecuniary debts which it had been their civil obligation to discharge at the end of a certain time.[12] Christ and the holy apostles had brought these men into the church by means of many exhortations, hardships, and exertions, and finally through martyrdom and the spilling of their precious blood. For he who was "made all things to all men," in order that he might win over all men, did not act in the way these bishops do, but rather he wished that only grave crimes should cause sinners to be cut off from the company of the other believers, as we have shown from I Corinthians, Chapter 5, in Chapter VI of this discourse.[13]

11. Not content even with these acts, but seeking the highest degree of secular power, contrary to the command or counsel of Christ and the apostles, these bishops have rushed forth to make laws distinct from those of the whole body of citizens, decreeing that all clergymen are exempt from the civil laws and thus bringing on civil schism and a plurality of supreme governments, the incompatibility of which with the peace of men we demonstrated in Chapter XVII of Discourse I, adducing the sure testimony of experience. For this is the root and origin of the pestilence besetting the state of Italy; from it all scandals have germinated and grown, and so long as it continues, civil discord in Italy will never cease.[14] For the Roman bishop fears that this power into which he has gradually stolen through sly deception, and which custom (or rather abuse) has enabled him to retain, will be revoked by the ruler (which revocation he would richly deserve because of the excesses he has committed); and so by all kinds of malicious devices he prevents the appointment and inauguration of the Roman ruler. And a certain bishop has finally gone so far in his audacity as to issue edicts proclaiming that the Roman ruler is bound to him by an "oath of fealty," as being subject to him in coercive jurisdiction; this assertion can be found plainly expressed, by anyone who reads the document entitled *On the Sentence and the Thing Judged,* which is in the seventh ridiculous and despicable part of the statements which they call "decretals." [15]

12. Because Henry VII, of happy and divine memory, who occupies a

---

[12] See *ibid., Decretal. Greg. IX* Lib. III. Tit. 30. cap. 5; *Extravag. commun.* Lib. III. Tit. 6. cap. 1; *Clem.* Lib. III. Tit. 8. cap. 1.

[13] I Corinthians 9:21–22. See above, II. vi. 13.   [14] See above, I. i. 2; I. xix. 4, 11.

[15] See *Corp. jur. can., Clem.* Lib. II. Tit. 11. cap. 2, the bull of Clement V, *Pastoralis cura sollicitudinis,* March 14–19, 1314.

position of preeminence among the rulers of all ages, places, and conditions, refused to bow down before such headstrong rashness, this most Christian emperor and man of all the virtues is called a transgressor "who pretends to have forgotten" his sworn oath, in a certain document called a "decretal," which is as false as it is rash, entitled *On Oaths,* although its title might more appropriately be: on the wrongful injuries and insults inflicted upon the divine emperor, and upon all his successors, relatives, and allies. For this prince is defamed as a perjurer by the so-called "founders of the canons," [16] who strive to blacken his fair memory (if it could be stained by the words or writings of such calumniators).

13. Not daring to call these oligarchic ordinances "laws," the Roman bishops and their cardinals gave them the name "decretals" instead, although, like human legislators, they intend them to be binding on men for the status of the present world, with penalties to be inflicted for their transgression. From the very beginning they were afraid explicitly to express this intention by using the word "laws," for they feared resistance and correction by the human legislator, since by making such ordinances they committed the crime of treason against rulers and legislators; and so from the beginning they called these ordinances "canonic rights," [17] in order that by the coloring of the phrase (although it was used with impiety) they might better lead the faithful to regard such ordinances as valid and thus more fully to believe, respect, and obey them.

In this way, then, to conclude, the Roman bishops have gradually and secretly accomplished this transformation, and now openly claim for themselves plenitude of power in the last six senses, thereby committing very many monstrous crimes in the civil order against divine and human law and against the right judgment of every rational being. Of some of these crimes, although not all, we have made individual mention in the preceding chapter.

[16] See *ibid., Clem.* Lib. ii. Tit. 9. cap. 1, the bull of Clement V, *Romani principes;* and John XXII's bull, *Ad conditorem canonum* (*ibid., Extravag. Joh. XXII* Tit. 14. cap. 3. See above, ii. xiii. 6, n. 1.).

[17] *Iura canonica,* an expression usually rendered "canon laws."

CHAPTER XXIV: HOW IN PARTICULAR THE ROMAN BISHOP HAS USED HIS ASSUMED PRIMACY AND PLENITUDE OF POWER WITHIN THE LIMITS OF THE CHURCH OR THE PRIESTLY HOUSEHOLD

WE must now show how the Roman bishops have hitherto used, are now using, and, unless prevented, will most likely continue to use these modes of plenary power which they have assumed for themselves. We shall begin by discussing their use of these modes in the appointment of ecclesiastic officials and the distribution of ecclesiastic temporal goods or benefices, both to church ministers and to other poor persons, for whose sakes (as was shown in Chapter XIV of this discourse) these goods were given and set aside to be thus distributed by ministers of the church. Then we must show how the Roman bishops have hitherto used, are now using, and will continue to use these plenary powers in relation to those who live a civil life, both rulers and subjects.

2. By their past and present actions in accordance with this plenitude of power, the Roman bishops have contaminated and, if one may say so, destroyed the whole mystical body of Christ. For they have restricted, corrupted, and at length almost totally abolished the method of election, which is the best, indeed the only method wherein there is assurance of making an absolutely good appointment of any official; and they have done this notwithstanding that it was by the method of election that the apostles together with the other believers appointed the deacons, as it is told in the Acts, Chapter 6.[1] First of all, they have restricted this method, by turning over to the clergy alone what used to be done and ought to be done by the whole multitude of the believers, as was shown in Chapter XVII of this discourse. Moreover, they have corrupted this method by restricting it and by transferring the authority to select bishops to a group of inexperienced young men called canons, who are ignorant of divine law, so that the priests of the province have no voice in such appointments, unless perhaps the same person should happen to be both priest and canon (which is quite rare and unusual); and they have delegated to the clergy of only one church or temple in a province the authority to make appointments, which ought to be made by at least the whole clergy of the province, and especially by the priests, whose duty it is to be teachers of divine law, as we have shown

[1] Acts 6:2–6.

above.[2] And finally, they have almost completely abolished the method of election by reserving directly for themselves the power to bestow almost all ecclesiastic offices, high, middle, and low, including even those, like taking care of the temples, which mere laymen can perform; and not only this, but also the power to distribute temporal goods or benefices on behalf of these offices. By these reservations they declare null and void any elections they please, even though these elections have been duly performed and the men elected are adequate and approved; and in place of these men, the Roman bishops, using their plenary power (which is ignorant, or affected by bribery, importunity, like, dislike, fear, flattery, or desire for favor, or in some other way perverted), appoint persons who are ignorant of divine letters, uneducated and incapable, and very often men of corrupt morals and notorious criminals, who cannot even speak the language of the people over whom they are placed.

3. And so, let an answer to the words of Christ in John, Chapter 10,[3] be given by that Roman bishop who, among his other monstrous crimes, made official appointments in contravention or reversal of duly performed elections, by ordaining two bishops speaking his own Provençal tongue, one at Winchester in England, the other at Lund in Denmark, neither of whom could speak the language of the people entrusted to his charge, and the quality of whose doctrines and morals, while not my present concern, is illustrated by this (which is well known in Denmark), that the bishop at Lund despoiled the church and diocese of all the cattle needed for the cultivation of the fields, robbed the church treasury of the proceeds thereof, and fled back to his own country.[4] I repeat, let the Roman bishop answer: how will this shepherd "call his own sheep by name," when he has to know their morals by their confessions, and to censure and reprimand them; and how will the sheep follow him, when they have to understand the preaching and teaching of his voice?

4. Nor is there a lack of men eligible for the pastoral office, such as there was in ancient times, making it necessary to beg foreign provinces for pastors. For there were in England men far better in their lives and in knowledge of sacred doctrine than the man who was put over them, who was neither conversant with their language nor a doctor of the sacred Scripture, but merely a shyster lawyer; and the case was similar in Den-

---

[2] See above, ii. xvii. 8 ff.   [3] John 10:1-13.

[4] These bishops are Reginald Asser, papal nuncio in England, made bishop of Winchester by papal provision against the monks' election and the king's recommendation in 1320; and Isarn Morlane (alias Tacconi), similarly made archbishop of Lund in Denmark by Boniface VIII in 1302. Isarn laid the kingdom under interdict in 1299, and in that year there was a "grave pestilence of the cattle," according to Petrus Olaus *Annales* 1299 (ed. Jac. Langebek, in *Scriptores rerum Danicarum medii ævi* [Copenhagen, 1772], I, 189 ff.).

mark and in the other provinces, concerning which many testimonies of similar flagrant wrongs might be cited; but I pass them over for the sake of brevity.

5. Who will not be amazed or astounded that young men, ignorant of the divine Scriptures, lacking proper moral gravity, unlearned, untrained, and sometimes notorious criminals, are appointed to the major offices of the church through simoniacal corruption, or the importunities, not to say sometimes the fear, of the powerful, or flattery, or kinship, while doctors of the holy Scripture, men of proven honor, are rebuffed or overlooked? Am I telling fictions or falsehoods? If you add up the bishops or archbishops of the provinces, the patriarchs, and the lower prelates, you will find not one in ten who is a doctor of sacred theology or adequately trained therein. And, shameful to relate (but let us not hesitate, because it is true), modern bishops can neither preach to the people the word of God, nor refute the erroneous doctrines of heretics, if any appear; but when such occasions arise they shamelessly beg the doctrines of others, and this despite the words of the Teacher of the Gentiles in I Timothy, Chapter 3, and Titus, Chapter 1, that "the bishop must be apt to teach, holding fast the faithful word as he hath been taught, that he may be able by sound doctrine both to exhort and to convince the gainsayers." [5]

6. As for the lower prelates, the abbots and priors of monasteries and other ecclesiastic curates, I swear before God, the immortal truth, that large numbers of them are immoral and so poorly educated that they do not even know how to speak grammatically.

7. But the men who obtain most of the major offices of the church (again let me say, by means of plenitude of power), and who are considered capable of discharging the duties thereof, are shyster lawyers. These men the Roman pontiff appoints as being useful and defenders of the church, knowing how to argue at law in order to hold on to temporal goods or to usurp more of them. But doctors of sacred theology, on the other hand, the pontiff rejects as being useless. "For they are simple," as he and his college of cardinals say, "and they would allow the church to go under"; yet it is not temporal goods, but rather the believers of Christ, who are the "church," and it is on behalf of the latter, not for temporal goods, that the bishop ought to strive, in accordance with the counsel of Christ and of the Apostle, as given in John, Chapter 10,[6] and in the passage from the Apostle cited above, as well as in numerous other parts of Scripture, which I omit to quote because the fact is so clear, and for the sake of brevity.

8. For it is not temporal goods which are the heritage of the apostles,

which they bequeathed to their successors the bishops for safekeeping; nor
are the rights of Christ's bride the utmost limits of imperial and secular
lordship, which, under the sophistic pretense of such words, the modern
bishop of the Romans has so viciously set in opposition to the illustrious
Ludwig, duke of Bavaria, king of the Romans, in order to defend himself, or, rather, in order to attack Ludwig.[7] And hence Bernard, in his
treatise addressed to Eugene *On Consideration*, Book II, Chapter IV, after
speaking of the guardianship of souls or churches which was bequeathed
by the saintly apostles to their successors, writes as follows: "For what
else did the holy apostle bequeath? 'Such as I have,' he said, 'give I thee.'
What was that? One thing I know: it was not gold or silver, for he said:
'Silver and gold have I none.'" And a little below Bernard adds: "Even if
you lay claim to these things," that is, temporal goods, "by some other title,
you cannot do so by apostolic right." And still further below: "He gave
that which he had, namely, the guardianship, as I have said, of the
churches." But what about lordship or rulership? Hear Bernard's further
words: "Not lordship? Hear Peter: 'Neither as lording it over the clergy,'
he says, 'but being made a pattern of the flock.' And lest you think he spoke
only from humility, but not with truth, the voice of the Lord is in the
gospel: 'The kings of the Gentiles lord it over them, and they that have
power over them are called beneficent.' And then he adds: 'But you not
so.' It is quite plain, then, that lordship is forbidden to the apostles." [8]

9. But that which most merits the attention and astonishment of all,
and which ought to be duly reformed in the general council by the rulers
as ministers of God, is the appointment of the supreme pontiff and his
brethren, the cardinals, who we said were to be made the head and leaders
of the other clergy for the purpose principally of teaching and preserving
the truth and unity of the faith in accordance with the determination of
the general council. For not always, but only too rarely, is a doctor of the
holy Scripture elected to fill this highest dignity; most usually one of the
shyster lawyers is appointed, which is completely antithetical to the holy
Scripture, repugnant to right reason, and the most shameful of all practices in the eyes of all churches. And the same applies equally to the college of cardinals, for to it are often appointed lascivious youths ignorant of
divine letters, notwithstanding that this head bishop with his church or
college of cardinals ought to be the example or model for all the other
bishops and churches, and that the Roman pontiff has to guide the uni-

---

[7] See John XXII's *monitorium* against Ludwig (MGH, *Constitutiones*, V, No. 792, p. 617;
see above, II. xxii. 20, n. 41; also below, II. xxvi. 2).

[8] St. Bernard *De consideratione* II. vi (PL 182. 748). The passages quoted are Acts 3:6,
I Peter 5:3, Luke 22:25–26.

versal church with the aid and counsel of these cardinals, and not otherwise, especially when crucial questions arise.

10. But, to return to our previous subject, let us say that the Roman pontiff, through his plenitude of power, bestows the largest number of ecclesiastic offices, from the highest to the lowest, upon uneducated persons ignorant of divine letters (would that they were not criminals), both men known to himself and strangers, and even upon children and infants; and this practice derives additional support from the simoniacal corruption of the pontiff himself and his intermediaries, and from many other vicious emotions on their part. Now since the major, principal seats are thus contaminated by the appointment, or rather, intrusion, of such persons, the minor positions or offices, the bestowal of which pertains to the major officials, are polluted by the contagion. For these major prelates take pleasure in those who are like them, just as "man takes pleasure in man, and horse in horse," [9] according to the statement of the wise Gentile; and so they open to the ignorant and immoral that simoniacal or otherwise vicious door to church offices and benefices by which they themselves have entered. For, since they wish to act in accordance with their own habits, which their office has not changed, but rather more fully revealed, they hate, rebuff, and oppress, as being inimical to them, those men who are saintly, just, and learned, and who do not seek by such a path to enter the house of God. As the Truth says: "Everyone that doeth evil hateth the light." [10]

11. Nor shall I pass over in silence the fact that the Roman bishop, desiring to gain for himself the favor and influence of the powerful, and also, perhaps, because he has received money from them, has appointed to the episcopal seats in famous cities young men who are ignorant of divine law and other disciplines, and who have not been assigned to any holy order; such appointments he makes notwithstanding the statement of Jerome, in his epistle to Evander, that "the priest is contained in the bishop." [11] And since the ecclesiastic regime is thus contaminated, it is no wonder that the whole mystical body of Christ is ill. For the church prelates and other overseers omit to give exhortations, supplications, and rebukes in accordance with sound doctrine, but instead they openly commit foul and abominable crimes; and hence the people are scandalized by their example, for just as the target is to the archer, so are the church officials set up as an example to the common people.[12] Noting this, the Truth says, in Matthew, Chapter 5: "Let your light so shine before men, that they may

---

[9] Pseudo-Aristotle *Problems* x. 52.   [10] John 3:20.
[11] St. Jerome, Epist. 146 (PL 22. 1195).
[12] See Lamentations 3:12.

see your good works." [13] And this is the root and the primary evil of modern morals, which is finally culminated by eternal damnation; for as Christ says, in Matthew, Chapter 15: "If the blind shall lead the blind, both shall fall into the ditch." [14]

But what shall we say about the dispensation of temporal goods? Although the goods which remain over and above the needs of church ministers ought to be dispensed to the weak, the poor, and other unfortunate persons (as everyone knows), yet these goods are put to those uses (and, more truly, abuses) which we discussed in Chapter XI of this discourse. To this add the new way of giving subventions, whereby most of the temporal goods are consumed by mercenary soldiers, cavalry and infantry, in order to foment and nourish wars among the Christian believers, so that the pontiffs may in the end be able to subject these believers to their own tyrannical power. From what we have said it is clear, then, that because of plenitude of power the mystical body of the church is thoroughly contaminated and close to death in its matter or principal members, especially (in a word) the prelates.

12. But now, with respect to the form of this body, which ought to consist in the proper order and position of its parts, it will be seen, on close examination, to be like a deformed monster. For if an animal's body had its individual members directly joined to its head, who would not regard it as monstrous and useless for the performance of its proper functions? For if the finger or the hand were joined directly to the head, it would not have its proper position, and hence it would not have its proper power, movement, and action. But this does not happen when the finger is joined to the hand, the hand to the arm, the arm to the shoulder, the shoulder to the neck, and the neck to the head, all by proper joints. For then the body is given its appropriate form, and the head can give to the other members, one through the other, their proper individual powers in accordance with their nature and order, and thus they can perform their proper functions. And this form and procedure must be heeded in the ecclesiastic as well as in every civil regime. For the universal pastor or ruler cannot immediately inspect and direct the individual acts of all men in all provinces, so that if this inspection and direction are to be accomplished properly and adequately, he must have the assistance of special ministers and agents in proper order; only when the body of the church is thus ordered can it endure and grow. And this was the view held by the Teacher of the Gentiles in Ephesians 4, where he wrote as follows: "That we may grow up into him in all things, which is the head, even Christ; from whom the

[13] Matthew 5:16.   [14] Matthew 15:14.

whole body fitly joined together and compacted by that which every joint supplieth, according to the effectual working in the measure of every part, maketh increase of the body." [15]

13. But when the Roman pontiff is permitted to have plenitude of power, this whole form or order is destroyed; for he releases the lower officials and orders from the power, care, and correction of their superiors: the archbishops from control by the patriarchs, the bishops from the archbishops, the clerical groups or colleges from the bishops, as well as the abbots and priors of monasteries,[16] and finally (would it were not most viciously!) the religious groups called mendicant orders; and then, having destroyed the relative order of all of these, the Roman pontiff places them under his own immediate care and corrective power, not for the sake of any evident utility to be gained thereby, but rather because of his notorious avidity for heaping quarrel on quarrel in order to advance his own interests, aiming thereby to concentrate wealth into his own hands, to despoil the other prelates, and to subjugate them still further.

14. What great insolence follows from this, almost everyone knows. For the church officials, lacking supervision by their immediate superiors, become arrogant, disobedient, and disrespectful toward those whose inferiors they properly are, and convert this situation into a means whereby they as well as others may sin more freely. And those who should be their supervisors, deprived of their due power, are given the opportunity to become indolent and negligent. So many are the troubles and adversities which beset the believers because of this, and so incomprehensible is their variety and number, that I have omitted to discuss them individually, although most of them are readily apparent to anyone who desires to find them out.

I pass over the practice, which now from abuse bears the guise of rectitude, whereby the Roman bishop allows himself to put certain deacons called "cardinals," who are ministers of the tables, above bishops and priests in rank and dignity, not heeding the words of Scripture in this regard, nor caring how strongly this practice is condemned by Jerome in his epistle to Evander, as we showed in Chapter 15 of this discourse.[17]

And in addition there is this new germ of the same root: that the Roman bishop, by this plenitude of power, has forbidden all persons who hold ecclesiastic benefices anywhere to make wills without his consent, and he has decreed that the goods of intestates (complete or partial) devolve to himself and must be delivered immediately to his own seat.

---

[15] Ephesians 4:15–16. [16] See St. Bernard *De consideratione* III. iv (PL 182. 766).
[17] See above, II. xv. 5, 8.

And what is an even worse evil (since simony, although it is completed after the act, is the worst), the Roman bishop, by this same plenitude of power, reserves for himself the annates or first fruits of all benefices everywhere, in this way collecting all the treasures in the world for himself and stealing them from the states and provinces wherein they ought to be distributed to gospel ministers and other poor persons, or used, if necessary,[18] for the support of the commonwealth from which they are taken, inasmuch as they have been established and set aside for these purposes.

15. What is still more intolerable, the Roman bishop claims for himself, through this same plenitude of power, the authority to dispense legacies which Christian laymen have left in their wills to be used for overseas crossing or for other pious purposes, in accordance with the disposition of certain designated persons called "trustees." And such claims are not to be wondered at, for certain of these bishops have asserted that through this same plenary power they have lordship over all kings, princes, and states, as we have shown in Chapter XX of this discourse, although none of these powers belong to them, as has been shown in Chapter XV of Discourse I and Chapter XVII of this discourse.

From the same root will also come many other evils, even more vicious and grave than those cited above; but we cannot mention them all because they vary so in nature. For "if one wrong position is given," especially one in which are contained other thinkable wrongs with respect to human civil acts,[19] "then there is no difficulty in seeing how all the other wrongs follow,"[20] according to the statement of the wise Gentile. For if this plenary power belongs to the Roman bishop, it follows that he is allowed to do whatever he likes; hence he suspends and revokes, at his pleasure, all human ordinances and laws, even the decisions of the general council, a condition which both saints and philosophers loathed as the worst of evils in all earthly government, as we proved by demonstration in Chapter XI of Discourse I, and confirmed by the authority of Augustine in his gloss on I Timothy, Chapter 6, in Chapter V of this discourse.[21] Thus, therefore, when the Roman bishop is permitted to have plenitude of power, the whole body of the church becomes diseased, the whole order of the ecclesiastic household is disrupted, and all civil government is completely impeded or partially disturbed; and this notwithstanding that the words and deeds of this bishop and his church or college have been set up as an example for all the rest.

16. Let the believers do as I beg, and turn on these priests their eyes,

---

[18] Reading, with Scholz, comma after *oportet*.
[19] Reading, with Scholz, no comma after *humanos*, comma after *continentur*.
[20] Aristotle *Physics* I. 2. 185a 11.   [21] See above, II. v. 5, 8.

long duped by the veil of sophistic honorableness worn by most of them; then, when they have visited the Roman curia, or rather (to speak truthfully), the horrible house of hagglers and den of thieves,[22] they will clearly perceive that it has become almost entirely a retreat of men who are criminals and hagglers, in both spiritual and temporal affairs; and those believers who have not visited there will learn that this is so from many trustworthy persons. For what does one find there but a mob of simoniacs from everywhere? What but the shouts of shysters, the insults of slanderers, the mistreatment of just men? There justice for the innocent fails or is so long delayed, if they cannot buy it for a price, that finally, exhausted and worn out from innumerable difficulties, they are compelled to give up their just and pitiable claims. For there human laws are loudly proclaimed, but the divine teachings are silent or are rarely heard.[23] There careful plans are laid for the invasion of Christian provinces and their seizure by violent force of arms from those to whose custody they have lawfully been entrusted. But for the winning of souls there is neither care nor counsel. And, in sum, it is a place "without any order, and where the light is as darkness." [24]

17. I, who was personally there and saw the place with my own eyes, thought I was seeing that terrible statue which Nebuchadnezzar is said, in Daniel, Chapter 2, to have seen in his sleep, its head made of gold, its arms and breast of silver, its belly and thighs of brass, its legs of iron, its feet part of iron and part of clay.[25] For what does this huge statue represent but the status of the persons in the curia of the Roman or supreme pontiff, this image which once used to terrify the wicked, but now fills all virtuous men with dread? For the statue's upper members, the head, breast, and arms, what are they in appearance, in effect, and in meaning but gold and silver and the work of men's hands? Its belly and thighs, what are they but the sound and tumult of secular conflicts and controversies, and of abusive and simoniacal hagglings over both spiritual and carnal things; and shall I also say, the thunder and lightning of spoken and written excommunications and anathematizations pronounced against Christian believers who justly refuse to be subject in secular things to the Roman pontiff and his church, and to pay them temporal or material tribute?

[22] See Matthew 21:12–13.
[23] This echoes an old complaint against the papacy. Cf. Roger Bacon *Opus tertium* cap. xxiv (*Opera hactenus inedita*, Vol. I, ed. J. S. Brewer [London, 1859], p. 84): "In the church of God a civil lawyer, even if he knows only civil law and is ignorant of canon law and of theology, is given more praise and is sooner elected to high church offices than is a master in theology." See also Pierre Dubois *De recuperatione terre sancte* para. 29 (ed. Ch. V. Langlois [Paris, 1891], pp. 22–23).
[24] Job 10:22.   [25] Daniel 2:31–33.

What (tell me, I beg) are the brass thighs but the ostentatious display of all sorts of pleasures, luxuries, and vanities, unbecoming even to laymen, which are offered to men's senses by those who ought to provide examples of chastity and honorableness for others? Its iron legs, and its feet and fingers, made partly of iron and partly of clay, to what do they point but to the usurpation, invasion, and seizure of secular governments, states, and provinces by violent force of iron weapons, bearing with them in this pursuit the upper members of the statue, inviting the assistance of armed warriors by holding out gold and silver, and also the brass belly and thighs stridently promising such rewards, loudly (albeit falsely) granting absolution from sins and penalties, and unjustly (although completely without harm, because of God's protection) condemning and cursing those who defend their own liberty and wish to maintain due loyalty to their rulers? The clay pedestal and fingers, fictile and hence fragile, what do they represent but the inconstancy of the Roman curia? What do they denote but the weakness of the pretexts by which the Roman pontiff tries to uphold his oppressive hostilities against the Christian believers, not to mention the falsity and iniquity of these pretexts, which are manifest to all?

But the prophet Daniel also predicted that "a stone cut out of the mountain without hands" [26] was going to fall upon this statue, meaning by "stone" the king who has been elected by the whole body of men and whom God through his grace will arouse by bestowing power upon him, and whose kingdom will not be surrendered to anyone else. This king, more by the virtue or grace of the Trinity than by any deed or power of human hands, will first weaken and crush the clay part of this horrible, dreadful, monstrous statue, namely, the feet which improperly support it: that is, he will expose to all peoples and rulers the false and unjust claims of his opponents (or rather, as the poet truly says, their empty pretexts),[27] by unmasking the sophistry of these claims, refuting them by human demonstrations, and demolishing them by the truths of the holy Scripture. Next, this king will break the iron part of the statue, by curbing its atrocious and impious power. Then he will silence and stifle the brass, that is, the authority of malediction which the Roman pontiff has assumed over rulers and peoples, and the tumultuous usurpations of secular jurisdiction, with the resulting controversies and afflictions; and to the luxurious pleasures and licentious displays he will also put an end. And finally he will suppress the gold and silver, that is, the avarice and thievery of the Roman pontiff and the higher members of the Roman curia; and he will grant to himself the use of temporal goods in due moderation. And thus,

---

[26] Daniel 2:34, 35.   [27] See Pseudo-Cato *Disticha* II. 26; and Phaedrus *Fabulae* v. 8.

in accordance with the words of the prophet, "the iron, the clay, the silver, and the gold" will be crushed together; that is, all the vices and excesses of the Roman curia will be wiped out, "like the chaff of the summer threshing floors, carried away by the wind."[28] For what is so contrary to nature, to human and divine law, and to all reason, cannot long endure.[29]

CHAPTER XXV: HOW IN PARTICULAR THE ROMAN BISHOP HAS USED HIS ASSUMED PRIMACY AND PLENITUDE OF POWER OUTSIDE THE LIMITS OF THE CHURCH, WITH RESPECT TO LAYMEN OR CIVIL AFFAIRS

IT now remains for us to examine how the Roman bishops have hitherto used and are now using their assumed plenitude of power outside the limits of the church. First, however, we shall review the practice of the primitive church and its development from its founder and head, who is Christ, and from its first promoters, the holy apostles. Christ came into the world to establish and to exercise the priestly office, the pastoral care of souls. For he was the maker of the law of eternal salvation, and he included therein the provisions pertaining to sacramental ritual and observances, and also the commands and counsels regarding what must be believed, done, and avoided in order to be simply or eminently deserving of that happy or blessed life which we call eternal. Thus he gave up and explicitly renounced jurisdiction over civil acts, or this-worldly rulership, and he commanded or counseled that all the apostles and all their successors in the priestly office do likewise; and he expressly declared that he was subject by divine ordainment to the judgment or coercive power of the rulers of this world, and that his apostles were also; and the apostles, both by word and by deed, indicated the same thing with regard to themselves, as has been clearly shown from Scripture together with the authoritative expositions of the saints and doctors, in Chapters IV and V of this discourse, and as has also been proved by human reasonings in Chapters VIII and IX of this discourse. And also Christ exercised those powers which we discussed in Chapters VI, VII, XV, and XVI of this discourse,

---

[28] Daniel 2:35.

[29] Cf. the anti-papalist tract *Antequam essent clerici* (P. Dupuy, *Histoire du différend d'entre le pape Boniface VIII et Philippe le Bel* [Paris, 1655], "Preuves," pp. 21–23): "Hoc enim natura et ratio, ius divinum et humanum, pariter detestantur."

and he granted to the apostles and, through them, to their successors, the authority to exercise those powers. Moreover, he maintained supreme poverty, and taught, commanded, or counseled that the apostles and their successors do this also, in the way described and explained by us in Chapters XII, XIII, and XIV of this discourse.

2. This way of living and manner of exercising the priestly office in accordance with the above-mentioned powers was maintained by the apostles as "obedient children," [1] and also by the Roman bishops and by most, although not all, of the other successors of the apostles, until about the time of Constantine I, the Roman emperor. I say "not all," for some of the successors of the apostles possessed estates, of whom the first is recorded to have been Urban I, Roman bishop, but until his time the church or whole priestly college had maintained a way of living which was similar to that of Christ and the apostles,[2] and which we have called meritorious and supreme poverty. Although Urban may perhaps have possessed estates primarily for pious reasons, out of pity for the poor and a desire to aid them (to refer his motives to the good as much as we conscientiously can), yet if he assumed the power to lay claim to these estates or to their income before a coercive judge, or if, having the power to sell them and to distribute the receipts to the poor, he did not do so, then he undoubtedly deviated from the status of supreme poverty or perfection, regardless of whether or not he did this knowingly. And this course was also followed by several other Roman bishops up to the time of Constantine.

3. During this period, as we have said in Chapters XVIII and XXII of this discourse, the Roman bishops with their colleges established certain regulations for themselves with regard to church ritual, such as divine worship and the proper status of the priestly college; and they communicated these regulations to the other churches because they were useful and the other churches asked to know them. Also the Roman bishops, out of piety and love, assumed a diligent guardianship over the other churches in the world so far as they could, because the other churches very often did not have adequate rectors or pastors; and hence they gave advice and admonitions to the believers of these other churches on matters of faith and morals, which advice was voluntarily and gratefully accepted, for the reasons given in Chapters XVIII and XXII of this discourse. Also, when disputes occasionally arose among some of the priests, bishops, deacons, or other persons in these churches, and the fraternal warnings of members of their own congregation did not avail to make them stop disturbing the others in their morals or faith, then perhaps some of them, being more

---

[1] I Peter 1:14.   [2] See Martinus Polonus *Chronicon* (MGH, *Scriptores*, XXII, 413).

astute and piously desiring to live in Christ, induced the Roman bishop and his church (whose warnings were more greatly respected by the believers, for the reasons already given) to pronounce sentences of excommunication or anathematization upon those rebellious persons who were disturbing the others, and upon other criminals; or perhaps the Roman bishops in their religious zeal did this by themselves, without prior request. And hence the majority of those believers who lived in places other than Rome agreed to obey the Roman bishop and his church in order to preserve the unity of the faith and to maintain peace and quiet among themselves, because they could not attain these ends in any other more convenient way by coercive power, inasmuch as in those times the human legislator was almost everywhere infidel.

4. Then came the time of Constantine I, Roman emperor, who was the first Roman ruler to allow the Christian believers to assemble in public, and it was by his command and authority that the first general councils of priests or bishops were held. These councils defined and determined ambiguous meanings of the sacred Scripture, distinguishing the true ones from the false and erroneous ones which certain priests, sometimes from ignorance, more often through superstition and malice, spread among the Christian believers. Also, these general councils made regulations concerning matters of church ritual, such as divine worship and the rectitude and learning of deacons and priests, and they established the manner and procedure whereby priests were to be appointed to church offices in specified places or provinces, both the inseparable offices, which are called "orders," and the separable ones, which are called "prelacies" (*praelationes*) [3] or cures of souls, together with other such offices; and they further determined the manner of distribution of temporal goods or benefices, such as offerings and other things movable and immovable, which had been given to them on behalf of the ministry of the gospel. To enforce these regulations, the human legislator or the ruler by its authority laid down a coercive command or law making their observance obligatory for all priests and laymen in the way required of each, with transgressors to be given punishment in property or in person in and for the status of the present life. But these laws were made more for priests and bishops than for laymen, inasmuch as it was the former who most frequently gave cause for such edicts; nor did the Roman or any other bishops protest against the human legislator with the claim that they were not subject to the laws and edicts of the rulers, but rather they pressingly beseeched the rulers to make such laws, as can be seen from the *Codex* of Isidore and other accredited

[3] See Vol. I, p. 270.

histories, from which we quoted at length in Chapter XXI of this discourse.

5. The same rulers also established laws fixing the number of priests in each province, and regulating their temporal or carnal goods, both movable and immovable, which had been given to them by Constantine and other Roman rulers as well as by many private individuals; other laws, again, dealt with the civil or contentious acts of the priests, although these laws were moderated through special favors granted by grace of the human legislator. For the legislators noted the dignity and reverence of the priestly character, since it in truth represents the office of Christ, and they also noted the moral gravity, simplicity, and innocence of the persons who at that time ministered the gospel and held the priestly office; hence they made laws for the priesthood which were less rigorous than those made for laymen, even with regard to the same acts, and which granted many privileges to the priests, to prevent their being harassed by lay slanderers or being distracted from their divine duties. For the number of devout believers was then small, and out of humility they readily yielded to the insults of legal quibblers, nor did they resort to violence or the use of arms in order to defend themselves or to attack others. For in the old days it would have seemed a grave and monstrous civil crime for clergymen, especially priests and bishops, to take up arms, or to order others to take them up on their behalf. Hence Ambrose writes, as we have quoted above in Chapter IX of this discourse: "I shall be able to weep, I shall be able to lament, I shall be able to grieve; against arms, soldiers, and Goths, my tears are my weapons, for such are the munitions of the priest; in any other way I neither can nor should resist." [4] It was for this reason that the priests needed special favors and privileges in order to live in peace and safety and to avoid being harassed by slanderers, although in modern times their relation to laymen has in this regard been transformed into the opposite quality.

6. Thus, then, in ancient times and for a considerable later period the whole priestly college lived under the civil laws and ordinances of the rulers, and it was the rulers and the people who bestowed, confirmed, and invested the priests with their separable offices, such as the prelacies, the cares of souls, and other similar or lesser positions, as well as the power to distribute and dispense temporal goods or benefices. Nor did such subjection lead the ancient pastors or bishops of Rome to fight against the Roman rulers, the people, or individual church patrons, for they well knew that this subjection was binding upon them by divine and human law,

[4] St. Ambrose *Sermo contra Auxentium* cap. ii (PL 16. 1050). See above, II. v. 5; II. ix. 6.

as we have made sufficiently clear through Scripture and through human reasonings in Chapters IV, V, VIII, and XVII of this discourse. And thus we read concerning Symmachus, a native of Sardus, that when an election was contested between him and a certain Lawrence, "judgment was made, and Symmachus was confirmed" as Roman pope by Theodoric the king. This too is what Martin writes about St. Gregory, who, as he says, "is elected pope, and he," Mauritius the emperor, "expresses his consent in imperial documents." So too the Roman bishops used to beg the emperors to confirm their privileges, as we read concerning Vitalianus, a native of Signia, and Constantine, a native of Syros, as well as very many other Roman pontiffs; indeed, the pontiffs would very often come long distances in order to make these requests personally and have them confirmed by the emperors, as we read in the chronicles and approved histories.[5] And what is more, John XII because of his villainous acts was deposed as pope by Otto I, the Roman emperor, with the consent of all the people, both clergy and laymen. So too in the section of Martin's chronicle dealing with Benedict IX, we read that when two papal candidates contested an election, they were both "deposed by the imperial censure" of Henry, the then Roman ruler.[6] For that which has the primary authority to establish something also has the primary authority to depose it, when this is expedient; and hence since every bishop must be elected by the ruler and all the people, he can be deposed by their authority, as has been proved in Chapter XVII of this discourse.

7. Like Christ and the apostles, then, the Roman bishops and priests and the whole clergy of Rome and the other provinces used to live under the coercive governance of those who were the rulers by authority of the human legislator. But later on, certain Roman bishops succumbed to the persuasion and incitation of that ruler of this world, that first parent of arrogance and presumption, that inculcator of all vices, the devil; and they were led, or rather misled, to a path foreign to that of Christ and the apostles. For cupidity and avarice, invading their minds, expelled therefrom that supreme meritorious poverty which Christ had introduced and established in the church (in the third sense). And again, pride and ambition for secular rule, invading their minds, expelled therefrom that supreme humility which Christ had enjoined and commanded the church or whole priesthood to maintain. The first priest to undergo these vicious emotions, if no one else did so before him, was, we read, a certain Roman bishop Simplicius, also called Tibertinus. For this bishop, with authority taken

---

[6] See Martinus Polonus *Chronicon* (MGH, *Scriptores*, XXII, 420, 457, 423, 425).
[6] *Ibid.* (XXII, 431).

from I know not where (although I most certainly do know where he got his temerity, unless he be excused by ignorance), decreed that no clergyman must receive investiture "from a layman"[7] (meaning the investiture of benefices and offices, which we have discussed above), although his decree clearly indicates that his predecessors, wishing to show due humility and reverence to the rulers, used to receive their investitures from laymen. Again, Pelagius I, who was one of his successors although not the one immediately following him, decreed "that heretics were to be punished by the secular powers."[8] This decree is remarkable in that Pelagius was not unaware that such a law against heretics had been made in the time of Justinian the Roman ruler,[9] and in that it did not pertain to the authority of Pelagius, as bishop, to make such laws, unless he had perhaps received such authority from the human legislator, as we have shown in Chapters XII and XIII of Discourse I and in Chapter XXI of this discourse. And hence, like the above-mentioned Simplicius, he extended "his scythe to another's crop,"[10] for he usurped for himself authority which belonged to someone else. And this practice of usurpation was continued by Adrian III, who was another of his successors, although also not the one who came directly after him. For this Adrian decreed that no "emperor was to interfere with the election of the pope," to use the words of Martin.[11] But this decree was completely void, in that it emanated from a man who had no such legislative authority. Moreover, its content was patently wrong, as we have shown in Chapter XVII of this discourse, and the opposite practice had been confirmed by long and praiseworthy custom.

8. Now when Martin writes, in his section on Leo X, that "from foul custom the Romans petitioned the emperor to give them a pontiff,"[12] although he admits that it was a custom, which we grant to be true, he does not speak truly in calling that custom "foul" on his own authority, trying to justify so far as he can the usurpations of the Roman pontiffs, to obscure the rights of the rulers or the human legislator, and to please man rather than God[13] and truth; but he here shows that the origin and secret of this matter were hidden from him. For although to no ruler or other individual, as such, belongs the authority by divine or human right or by any honorable custom to make appointments to any office, especially that of Roman bishop, by following only his own impulse (as has been

---

[7] *Ibid.* (XXII, 419).   [8] *Ibid.* (XXII, 421).

[9] *Corp. jur. civ., Codex Justinianus* I. v, esp. 4, 5, 11, 12, 15, 16, 18, 20, 22.

[10] St. Bernard *De consideratione* I. vi (PL 182. 736), and Deuteronomy 23:25, Matthew 25:24. See above, II. v. 2.

[11] Martinus Polonus *Chronicon* (MGH, *Scriptores*, XXII, 429).

[12] *Ibid.* (XXII, 433). The reference should really be to Pope Leo IX (11th century).

[13] See I Thessalonians 2:4; Acts 5:29.

sufficiently shown in Chapter XV of Discourse I and Chapters XVII and XXII of this discourse); yet it could lawfully pertain to the ruler by authority of the human legislator to appoint the Roman pontiff by following a definite procedure and method fixed by law, namely, by obtaining the counsel of the priestly college and of other wise and virtuous men, and trusting the decision of the weightier part of these counselors. Nor should Martin be trusted on this point, for he with his order participated in a usurpation similar to that which we are now discussing; for through the Roman pontiffs the orders called "mendicant friars" obtained, or think they obtained, exemption from the jurisdiction of their pastors, the bishops and other superior prelates, although they can obtain exemption from the jurisdiction of rulers only through those privileges whereby the human legislator is found to have exempted the clergy.[14]

9. But as we were saying before, the custom whereby the pastors of the Roman church were appointed by the emperors, in the way we have said, was not foul or dishonorable. For we read (and it is granted by those who with you, Martin, try to oppose this truth) that the authority to make such appointments by that fuller method discussed above was granted by all the Roman people, including the bishop, the clergy, and the laity, to Charlemagne and to Otto I, king of the Teutons and later emperor of the Romans. And so in the approved histories we read, and it is true, that the following edict emanated from the common consent of the Roman people:

Leo, pope in the synod at Rome in the church of the Holy Savior, here follows the example of St. Adrian, bishop of the apostolic seat, who granted to Lord Charles, most mighty king of the Franks and Lombards, the patriarchal dignity and authority over ordainments and investitures in the apostolic seat. And so we, Leo, bishop and servant of God's servants, together with all the clergy and people of Rome, do proclaim, confirm, and establish this decree, whereby through our apostolic authority we do grant and bestow upon Lord Otto I, king of the Teutons, and upon his successors for all time in this kingdom of Italy, the power both to elect their own successors and to ordain the pontiff in the highest apostolic seat, and hence also the archbishops and bishops, so that these prelates are to receive their investiture from the king, but their consecration from the proper sources, with the exception of those cases where the emperor shall have made special concessions to the pontiff and archbishops. And from now on no person, whatever his dignity or religious merit, is to have the power to elect a patriarch or pontiff of the highest apostolic seat, or to ordain any bishop, without the consent of the emperor. This consent however, is to be given entirely without money, so that the pontiff may be patriarch and king. But if any bishop

---

[14] Martinus Polonus was a Bohemian Dominican and papal penitentiary. Gregory IX exempted the Franciscans and Dominicans from all but papal jurisdiction in 1231. Boniface VIII regulated their preaching and confessional privileges in the bull, *Super cathedram*, Feb. 17, 1300 (*Corp. jur. can., Clem.* Lib. III. Tit. 7. cap. 2).

is elected by the clergy, then, unless he be confirmed and invested by the afore-said king, he is not to be consecrated. And we decree that anyone who opposes this authority is to be excommunicated, and, unless he repents, he is to be punished by irrevocable exile or by the extreme penalty.

This edict was confirmed by Pope Stephen, successor of Leo, and by Nicholas, a successor of Stephen, who commanded that it be observed under pain of terrible anathematization, so that its violators or transgressors were to be reckoned "among the impious, who will not rise again." [15]

In this edict it is particularly to be noted that when the Roman bishop together with all the people transferred the authority over investitures to the emperor, this was on the part of the pope a kind of renunciation; for the primary authority over investitures belonged and still belongs to the ruler or the human legislator who had granted to the pope this authority to invest bishops and archbishops, inasmuch as all temporal things which have been transferred by anyone to any church, were and are subject to the human legislator of the province wherein they are situated. This is indicated in the above edict where it says, "with the exception of those cases where the emperor shall have made special concessions to the pontiff and archbishops." And similarly, the power to appoint the pontiff to the apostolic seat also belongs to the Roman ruler and people, as has been shown in Chapter XVII of this discourse; and from this people the clergy are not excluded but rather included, since they are a part of the people.[16] Now if in the past the people willed to transfer this power or authority to the ruler, either unreservedly or with legal limitation, then the Roman ruler lawfully received it, nor could it lawfully be revoked from him by a decretal or law of any Roman pontiff, unless there intervened a decree of the people to this effect. For to the Roman pope, either alone or together with the clergy, it does not pertain to make any laws or decretals which would oblige anyone in the community of the believers to be punished, as we have shown in Chapter XII of Discourse I and in Chapter XXI of this discourse. Nevertheless, certain Roman bishops, usurping the jurisdiction of peoples and rulers with regard both to the laws themselves and to the making of them, have ventured, although wrongly, to make and promul-gate such coercive decretals; and this practice has gradually been expanded, especially during vacancies in the imperial seat, as we have shown in Chapter XXIII of this discourse.

10. It was very largely because of these usurpations and the seizure of certain temporalities, so far as we can make out from the chronicles or

[15] Ivo of Chartres *Panormia* viii. cxxxvi (PL 161. 1337 ff.).
[16] See Vol. I, pp. 180–81.

approved histories, that strife arose between the emperors and bishops of
Rome, although by participating in such strife the bishops acted contrary
to the counsel or command of Christ and the apostles, whom they must
succeed in the apostolic or priestly office, for as bishops they ought to maintain supreme poverty and humility. But instead, deviating therefrom to
a different, opposite path through ignorance or malice, or both, they entered
upon ceaseless fighting and struggle against the Roman rulers. One of the
most aggressive of these Roman bishops was a certain Paschal, who fought
against Henry IV, king of the Teutons, prohibiting him, according to the
histories, from ascending the imperial throne, and stirring up the Roman
people against him, until finally Henry, in Tuscany, was practically forced
to write proclamations and letters granting to the bishop authority over
the investitures of bishops, abbots, and all other clergymen. But later,
Henry entered the city and seized the pope who was trying to extort an
oath from him, and also his college of cardinals; eventually the pope was
freed and had peace with the emperor. But then he renewed the old
warfare, and the final outcome was bitter struggle.[17]

11. Paschal's successor was a certain Calixtus, to whom, as Martin tells us,

the [aforesaid] emperor, experiencing a change of heart, freely resigned the
investiture of the bishops and other prelates by staff and ring, also empowering
him to choose officials for all the churches throughout the empire, restoring to
the Roman church the possessions and ornaments of St. Peter, which had been
taken away because of the quarrels which this emperor or some other one had
had with the church, and also conscientiously ordering the restitution of other
possessions, both of clergymen and of laymen, which had been seized on occasions of war.[18]

12. Later, perhaps for a legitimate reason, Otto IV and Frederick II,
Roman emperors, wished to revoke or did revoke these grants and privileges in whole or in part, and as a result they and some of their predecessors
were made the objects of many conspiracies, persecutions, and harassments
by the Roman bishops and clergy. The peoples subject to these emperors
gave them little help, perhaps because their rule or that of their officials
and ministers had sometimes savored of tyranny.[19]

13. This, then, as we have said, is and was the primary source of the
present strife and discord between the emperors and the Roman pontiffs,
since the controversies over divine law and over the heresies of certain rulers
have died out entirely. For the Roman bishops wrongly wish to possess

---

[17] Martinus Polonus *Chronicon* (MGH, *Scriptores*, XXII, 435). The reference should really
be to Henry V.

[18] *Ibid.* (XXII, 469).

[19] See Rolandinus Patavinus *Chronicon*, to 1260 (MGH, *Scriptores*, XIX, 32–147), and
Innocent IV's bull deposing Frederick II, July 17, 1245 (MGH, *Constitutiones*, II, 508 ff.).

excessive temporal goods, and refuse to be subject to the laws and edicts of
the rulers or the human legislator, thereby opposing the example and
teaching of Christ and the apostles, as we have shown above in Chapters IV, V, and XIV of this discourse; for with regard to things which are
not their own as well as with regard to things which are their own they
ought to yield rather than to fight, according to the counsel which the
Apostle gave to all believers in I Corinthians, Chapter 6, and which applies
especially to those who ought to imitate the life of Christ and the apostles,
as priests, bishops, and other spiritual ministers ought to do. "Why," the
Apostle says, "do ye not rather take wrong? Why do ye not rather suffer
yourselves to be defrauded?" And he adds these words, which may
appropriately be addressed to almost all Roman bishops and other clergymen: "Nay, ye do wrong, and defraud, and that your brethren. Know ye
not that the unrighteous shall not inherit the kingdom of God?" [20] But
the Roman bishops and the other priests little heed these words; and on
occasions when they have felt that the Roman rulers were oppressing them
by collecting tithes and other temporal tributes to take care of the pressing
needs of their soldiers in time of war in return for the benefits in the
form of material goods which the rulers had graciously bestowed on them,
these bishops and priests, swollen with pride, heedless of their status, the
most ungrateful of all ingrates, have with unbridled presumption rushed
forth to pronounce horrible blasphemies and anathemas upon both the
rulers and their subject Christian believers, although these curses revert
against the unhappy souls and bodies of those who utter them, rather than
affecting the rulers and the flock of innocent believers.[21]

14. Their insatiable appetite for temporal things causing them to be
discontented with the things which the rulers have granted to them, the
bishops have made many seizures of the temporalities of provinces belonging to the empire, such as the cities of Romagna, Ferrara, Bologna, and
many others, as well as estates and other possessions lying under imperial
jurisdiction, especially during vacancies of the imperial seat. And what is
the worst of all civil evils, they have set themselves up as rulers and
legislators, in order to reduce kings and peoples to intolerable and dis-
graceful slavery to themselves. For since most of these bishops are of humble
birth, they do not know what secular leadership is when they reach the
status of pontiff (just as the newly rich have no discernment with regard to
wealth),[22] and consequently they become insufferable to all the faithful.

---

[20] I Corinthians 6:7–8. See above, II. iv. 11.

[21] This refers particularly to Innocent IV's bull of deposition of Frederick II (see above,
n. 19); see also Boniface VIII's *Clericis laicos*.

[22] See above, I. xvi. 1, 15.

15. Moreover, believing that they may do anything they like through the plenitude of power which they assert belongs to them, they have issued and are still issuing certain oligarchic ordinances called "decretals," wherein they command the observance of whatever measures they consider favorable to their own temporal welfare and to that of their clergymen as well as of certain laymen (whose exemption we discussed in Chapter VIII of this discourse), although these ordinances are very harmful to the rulers and other believers. Those who disobey them they punish with anathemization oral or written, as we have said above, and some of them have even broken out with such great insanity that they have issued decretals proclaiming that all the rulers and peoples in the world are subject to them in coercive jurisdiction, and that everyone must believe in the truth of this proposition in order to obtain eternal salvation. But how ridiculous this is, we have shown above in Chapter XX of this discourse, paragraphs 8 to 13.

16. And so the Roman bishops with their clerical coteries have the firm desire and determination to maintain and defend these outrages which, as we said, they have perpetrated against all rulers and peoples, although most extensively and flagrantly against the Italian peoples and the Roman rulers. But this is not their only aim, for with all their resourcefulness they are scheming to perpetrate similar or greater outrages upon the other states, taking every external step they dare for the realization of this aim. Nevertheless, they well know (although they pretend it is not so and strive both to obfuscate and to deny it with poetic, shadowy words) that to the human legislator belongs the authority to bestow all privileges and concessions, and to take them away when such removal is judged by it to be expedient; and hence the Roman bishops go to all vicious lengths to prevent the election and inauguration of the Roman ruler, conscious as they are of their own and their predecessors' ingratitude and viciousness, and fearing that their privileges and concessions will be forcibly revoked by the Roman ruler, and that they will have to suffer well-deserved punishment.

17. And again because of this fear and because the aforesaid privileges would only through chicanery offer them the means to seize the powers, jurisdictions, and possessions of other states, since some rulers perhaps claim exemption from the authority of the ruler of the Romans,[23] the Roman bishops have sought to gain their ends through another crafty scheme. For they have assumed a title which they proclaim to be theirs and which they strive to make the instrument of these nefarious designs, the title of "plenitude of power," which they claim Christ gave to them in the person of

[23] See above, I. xix. 8; II. i. 3.

St. Peter, inasmuch as they are the particular successors of this apostle. And by means of this execrable title and these equivocally sophistical statements which all believers everywhere and always must deny as being false in every sense, the Roman bishops have hitherto misreasoned, and are now misreasoning, and are striving to continue to misreason and to cast into servitude to themselves all the rulers, peoples, groups, and individuals in the world. For they assumed the title of plenitude of power first of all in that sense in which it seems to mean the universal cure of souls or a universal pastorate, and then in that sense in which it means the power to absolve all men from guilt and punishment under the guise of piety, charity, and mercy; but then, as we showed in Chapter XXIII of this discourse, they gradually and secretly effected a transformation, and finally claimed the title in that sense whereby they understand plenitude of power to mean the universal authority and supreme jurisdiction or coercive rulership over all rulers, peoples, and temporal things; this transformation and the resultant presumptuous claim being based, although wrongly, upon their metaphorical expositions of the texts which we mentioned in Chapter XXIII of this discourse, paragraph 5. And here is a sign whereby everyone can see that the Roman bishops are claiming plenitude of power in this sense, that is, that they wish this plenary power to mean that to them belongs the authority of supreme jurisdiction or coercive rulership over all rulers, peoples, and individuals: in the seventh part of their statements which they call "decretals" is found a document entitled *On the Sentence and the Thing Judged,* wherein Clement V, the Roman pope to whom its authorship is ascribed, and his so-called successor, who later published it, revoked, so far as they could, a certain decree of the divine Henry VII, Roman emperor, addressing to him, both orally and in writing, the following words among others, delivered with their customary abusiveness, arrogance, and disrespect: "By that superiority which we undoubtedly have over the empire, and by that power in which we succeed the emperor when his seat is vacant, as well as by that plenitude of power which Christ, king of kings and lord of lords, granted to us, although we are undeserving, in the person of St. Peter, we, following the counsel of our brethren, declare the aforesaid decree and judgment, and whatever follows therefrom or is occasioned thereby, to be entirely null and void." [24]

18. That the deceptions of these bishops may no longer be hidden, I, as a herald of the truth, urgently proclaim and say to you, kings, princes, peoples, tribes, and men of all tongues,[25] that by this written statement of

---

[24] The bull *Pastoralis cura;* see above, I. xix. 10; II. xxii. 20; II. xxiii. 12. It was confirmed by John XXII and published July 16, 1317 (MGH, *Constitutiones,* Vol. V, No. 443, pp. 367 ff.).
[25] Omitting, with Scholz, the exclamation mark.

theirs, which is most clearly false in its every sense, the Roman bishops with their coterie of clergymen or cardinals do the greatest harm to you all. For they are striving to cast you into subjection to them, and they will succeed if you allow this statement to go unchallenged, and [26] especially if you allow it to have the force and validity of law. Note, thus, that if anyone has the primary authority to revoke the decree of any ruler or judge, then it necessarily follows that he has jurisdiction and coercive rulership over that ruler or judge, as well as the power to establish, disestablish, and depose his government. But this is the authority which the Roman bishop ascribes to himself over all rulers and governments alike throughout the world; for through that plenary power which he asserts Christ granted to him in the person of St. Peter, he has revoked a civil decree of that Henry whom we mentioned above. And also it necessarily follows that the Roman bishop has been given this plenary power as much over all the other kings and rulers in the world as over the Roman ruler; for Christ is, was, and will be king or lord over the other kings and rulers no less than over the Roman king or ruler. This is clearly indicated by the spoken or written statements of these bishops, when they say or write: "King of kings and lord of lords." [27] For if their words or writings applied only to a single ruler, so that they would say: through the plenitude of power granted to them by Christ, king and lord of the Roman king or emperor, etc., then it might be understood that the other kings and kingdoms were in some manner excepted from their sway. But now, inasmuch as they utter this phrase in the plural, without any qualification or differentiation, just as it is written in the gospel, although its meaning there is different from that intended by the Roman bishops, the consequence is that no king or ruler can be excepted therefrom, just as they intend no one to be excepted, but rather everyone to be included, as their predecessor Boniface VIII distinctly claimed elsewhere, and as we have shown in Chapter XX of this discourse, paragraph 8.

19. However, in order that the words or writings of the Roman bishops may no longer infect any person's mind, let us reiterate that although the gospel spoke truly in calling Christ "king of kings and lord of lords," and although it would still have been true to have added: "and of all creatures," nevertheless the person who asserted that any power of rulership or coercive jurisdiction, let alone plenary power, was given to the Roman or any other bishop in the person of St. Peter or of any other apostle, uttered a falsehood and an open lie which is contrary to the manifest doctrine of Christ, of the apostles Peter and Paul, and of James. For such power is,

---

[26] Reading, with Scholz, *et* before *praesertim*.   [27] Revelation 19:16.

was, and will be forbidden by Christ to the Roman and all other bishops in the person of every apostle, as we have established beyond a doubt through Scripture and the authorities of the saints in Chapters IV, V, and IX of this discourse.

20. And so by this new fiction, previously unheard of, the Roman bishop has the audacity openly to make an assertion which is as false as it is insolent, and which offends against his own mind as well as against that of almost all believers who consider it, when he pertinaciously asserts that he "undoubtedly" has "superiority" (he means in coercive jurisdiction or rulership) over the Roman emperor, and again that he "succeeds the [aforesaid] emperor when his seat is vacant." These assertions clearly reveal what vicious, unjust usurpations of imperial jurisdiction the Roman bishops have hitherto perpetrated and are still perpetrating, as we have said, especially during vacancies of the imperial seat. For who would have the effrontery to declare shamelessly that a proposition is undoubtedly true which was unheard of throughout the ages, which is confirmed neither by divine nor human law nor by right reason, and the opposite of which not only does have this confirmation but has always been conceived and asserted as an example of a truth believed by all men? And hence just as in the proverb about physicians it is said that "he heals most in whom most have confidence," so can we truly say: he wishes to mislead and deceive most in whom most belief is reposed in modern times.

CHAPTER XXVI: HOW THE ROMAN BISHOP HAS USED THIS PLENARY POWER AND PRIMACY STILL MORE PARTICULARLY WITH REGARD TO THE ROMAN RULER AND EMPIRE

THIS plenitude of power, then, has in its past development been used by the Roman bishops continually for the worse, and it is still being so used, especially against the Roman ruler and government. For most fully upon the latter can these bishops perpetrate this vicious outrage of subjecting governments to themselves, because discord and strife both among the Roman subjects themselves and against their ruler have been stirred up in the past, and are still being stirred up and nourished, by these so-called "pastors" or "most holy fathers." And another reason why their main efforts are directed against the Roman government is that when they have brought this government under their sway, they will easily (so they think) be able to subjugate the other states, although, as everyone knows, they are most greatly and particularly obligated to the Roman ruler and government for the benefits which they have received.

2. To make sure that the facts of which we are speaking are known to everyone, we declare that so thoroughly are the Roman bishops moved by cupidity, avarice, pride, and ambition that, made worse than bad by their ingratitude, they seek in every way to prevent the election and inauguration of the Roman ruler and are striving, finally, to destroy his government or to change it to another form so that it will be more completely subject to them, in order that the power of the aforesaid ruler may not correct the excesses which they have perpetrated against the empire and mete out to them well-deserved penalties. And although their intentions in obstructing the Roman ruler on all sides are clearly such as we have stated them to be, nevertheless they maintain a crafty pretense, saying their actions are motivated by the desire to "defend the rights of Christ's bride," [1] that is, the church, ridiculous though this sophistic piety is; for Christ's bride is not temporal goods or the desire for them or the striving after governmental jurisdiction, nor did Christ ever marry these, but rather he explicitly repudiated them as foreign to him, as we have shown from the divine Scriptures in Chapters IV, V, XIII, and XIV of this discourse. Nor are these the heritage which the apostles left to their true, not false, successors, as St. Bernard clearly says in his treatise addressed to Pope Eugene *On Consideration,* Book IV, Chapter IV; for Bernard writes: "This is Peter, whom no one ever saw bedecked with gems or silks or garments of gold, or mounted on a white horse, or attended by a soldier, or guarded by pugnacious servants. Yet even without these he considered himself sufficiently well equipped to observe the commandment: 'If you love me, feed my sheep.' For in these things," that is, in gold, gems, and other temporal goods, "you have succeeded not Peter but Constantine." [2] Thus, then, it is truly not Christ's bride that is defended by fighting over temporal goods. For Christ's true bride, the catholic faith and the multitude of the believers, is not defended but rather offended by the modern Roman pontiffs; and her beauty, that is, unity, is not preserved but rather defiled by them when they wound her and tear her members apart by stirring up feuds and schisms; and Christ's true companions, poverty and humility, they do not admit but entirely exclude, thus showing themselves to be not the ministers but rather the enemies of the bridegroom.

---

[1] See John XXII's decretals of Oct. 8, 1323, and March 23, 1324 (MGH, *Constitutiones,* V, 616, 617, 693).

[2] St. Bernard *De consideratione* IV. III (PL 182. 776).

3. And so, in their endeavor to overthrow the government of the Romans, the Roman bishops assume (as we have shown above from their written documents) that by divine or by human right or perhaps by both they "have superiority" over the Roman ruler or emperor, past, present, and future, and also that the imperial power or jurisdiction belongs to them "when the imperial seat is vacant." [3] But these assumptions are very clearly false and are confirmed neither by divine nor by human right nor by right reason; on the contrary, the very opposite of them has been demonstrated in Chapter XII of Discourse I and more fully confirmed through Scripture in Chapters IV, V, and IX of this discourse.

4. These assumptions, or rather presumptions, were occasioned (superfluously, let me add) by a certain devoutness, among other things. For some of the Roman rulers after the time of Constantine wished to give friendly notice of their election to the Roman pontiffs, in order that by paying to Christ in the person of the pontiffs this special respect, they might obtain from him through their mediation greater blessings and grace for their guidance of the empire; and likewise, in order to solemnize and herald their inauguration and to obtain more of God's grace, some Roman rulers had their royal crown placed on their heads by the Roman pontiffs. But who will say that such coronation gives any greater authority to the Roman pontiff over the Roman ruler than to the archbishop of Rheims over the king of the Franks? For such solemnities do not bestow authority; they only signify that authority is had or that it has been bestowed. But from this respect which was so willingly paid by the Roman rulers in their simplicity, not to say foolishness, the Roman pontiffs, who too frequently seek what is not theirs, have developed a custom, or rather abuse, of calling their commendation and benediction of an elected person their confirmation of his election. The Roman rulers of old did not see what harmful intent underlay this mode of designation, and so the Roman pontiffs continued to use it, at first secretly, but now openly, to mean that no person, regardless of how duly he has been elected king of the Romans, is to be called king, or to have or exercise the authority of the Roman king, unless he shall have been approved by the Roman bishop. And this approval consists in the mere will of the Roman bishop alone, as he says, inasmuch as he recognizes no one on earth who is superior or equal to him in such judgment, nor is he obliged in this or in any other matter to follow the counsel of his brethren, called the cardinals, although he may

[3] See above, II. xxv. 17.

use it; but through his plenitude of power he can, so he says, do precisely the opposite of what his cardinals advise in all things, if he so wills.[4]

5. But in this matter the Roman bishop, as is his custom, draws a conclusion which is false and bad from premises which are true and good. For from the fact that the Roman ruler in his devoutness has voluntarily paid respect to the Roman bishop, by giving him notice of his election and asking for his benediction and mediation with God, it does not follow that the election of the Roman ruler depends upon the will of the Roman bishop. For this would be none other than to destroy the Roman government and to prevent forever the election of the Roman ruler. For if the authority of an elected king depends solely upon the will of the Roman bishop, then the office of the electors is entirely an empty one, inasmuch as the man whom they elect is not king, nor is he to be so called, nor can he exercise any kingly authority, until he is confirmed by that bishop's will or authority, which he calls the "apostolic seat"; indeed (what is very oppressive even to hear, let alone to endure) the elected person will not even be allowed to draw from the revenues of the empire enough for his daily subsistence, without leave by this bishop. Hence, so far as the granting of authority to the king is concerned, what will his election by the princes amount to other than a nomination, since their designation of him will depend upon the will solely of one other man? For this much authority could be granted to the Roman king by seven barbers or blind men. I say this not in contempt of the electors but in derision of the man who wants to deprive them of their due authority. For he is ignorant of what is the force and meaning of an election, and why its authority depends upon the weightier part of those who have the right to elect; and he is also ignorant of the fact that the effectiveness of an election should not and cannot depend solely on the will of some one man, if it is to be reasonably instituted, but that it depends solely upon the legislator over whom the ruler is to be instituted, or upon those to whom this legislator has granted such authority, as we have demonstrated with certainty in Chapters XII and XIII of Discourse I.

6. Thus, therefore, the Roman bishop plainly wishes to destroy the office of the electors, although he strives with astounding subtlety to blind and deceive them as to this aim. For in certain of his speeches and writings he says that no person who is elected king of the Romans is king

---

[4] See the bulls of Boniface VIII, *Apostolica sedes* (MGH, *Constitutiones*, IV, 80) and *Romano pontifici* (*ibid.*, IV, 86); Clement V, *Romani principes* (*ibid.*, IV, 1207); John XXII's first *monitorium*, Oct. 8, 1323 (*ibid.*, V, 617).

or is to be so called before being confirmed, and he asserts that the authority for this confirmation belongs to his own free power, as does the
authority to appoint the electors; for, as he asserts, it was a Roman bishop
who transferred the empire "from the Greeks to the Germans in the person
of Charlemagne." [5] And in other edicts he declares that a man whom the
electors had chosen has been deprived, by Christ and by his own seat, of all
the authority that the electors could give him, and then he craftily adds:
"We wish no injury to come to the electors or to their office through this
edict," at the same time flagrantly injuring them, or rather completely
destroying their office: for he proclaims that "their election bestows no
kingly Roman authority upon anyone," and without their consent and
authorization he deprives the man elected by them of the right bestowed
by their election; and thus mocking them he injures them in the same way
that one man harms another when he takes out his eye even though he
protests that he means no harm.[6]

7. Again, to claim for himself the authority to confirm the elected
Roman king, and to decree that without such confirmation no one is or is
to be called king, or is to perform the kingly functions—this is none other
than to prohibit forever the effective appointment and inauguration of the
Roman ruler and to reduce the Roman government to total slavery to the
Roman bishop. For this bishop will not approve or confirm any elected
king of the Romans, if he does not wish to, since he asserts that he is
superior to everyone and is subordinate to no group or individual. But he
will never wish to confirm anyone, for before doing so he intends to exact
from the elected king certain oaths and agreements, among others an oath
whereby the Roman emperor swears fealty to the bishop and asserts that
he is subject to the bishop in temporal coercive jurisdiction. And the latter
also wants the elected king to promise and swear to uphold the bishop's
unjust and unlawful seizures of certain provinces. But since the royal
majesty cannot with a clear conscience take and fulfill such unlawful oaths
at the same time as the lawful oath, which he takes upon his inauguration,
to preserve the liberties of the empire, no elected king will ever take such
unlawful oaths or make such promises to the Roman or any other pontiff,
unless he is softer than a woman and is clearly perjuring himself in taking
such oaths or making such promises. Consequently, no elected king will
ever be inaugurated as king of the Romans or be entitled to speak for the
empire, if the royal or imperial authority of those who are elected depends

[5] See the bull of Innocent III, *Venerabilem* (MGH, *Constitutiones*, II, 509), and John XXII's
first *monitorium*, Oct. 8, 1323 (*ibid.*, V, 616).

[6] See the "Fourth Process" of John XXII against Ludwig of Bavaria, July 11, 1324 (MGH,
Constitutiones, V, 785, 787-88).

upon the Roman bishop; for this bishop will both in word and in deed oppose and prevent the royal accession as long as he possibly can, notwithstanding the utter viciousness of such action in seeking what does not belong to him.

8. But this leads to something even more gravely injurious and unbearably harmful to all rulers, communities, and individuals subject to the Roman empire. For since the Roman bishop asserts that during a vacancy in the imperial seat he succeeds the Roman emperor in office, it necessarily follows that he has the authority to compel all princes and other imperial feudatories to take oaths of fealty to him, and besides this the authority to demand and exact from them taxes and other forms of tribute, both such as the Roman rulers customarily received and also exceptional taxes which this bishop has wished to pretend are owed to him through the plenitude of power which he claims for himself; and also this bishop will have the authority, during an imperial vacancy, to bestow rulerships, fiefs, and other rights which the Roman ruler can bestow when a prince has died without leaving male heirs, or for some other reason. Moreover, and this is the most injurious and harmful of all, during an imperial vacancy, which, as we have said, the Roman bishop will strive to make permanent, all rulers, communities, groups, and individuals subject to the Roman empire will be compelled to bring their civil suits, real and personal, to the court of the Roman bishop by appeal or by delation, and to undergo civil judgment at his hands. And no ruler, community, or judge subject to the Roman empire will be able to command the execution of any civil sentence, for those whom their sentences condemn will always appeal from them to the court of the Roman bishop. But if subjects of the Roman empire refuse to obey this bishop or to be subject to him in the aforesaid ways, just as they are not obliged to, he will incessantly, viciously, and shamelessly persecute them by his so-called sentences of anathematization, malediction, excommunication, indictment for heresy, and interdict, and finally he will confiscate their temporal goods, granting these goods to whoever can steal them; also he will give pardons (although empty and false ones) to all those who incur any guilt or condemnation for persecuting or even killing the men who refuse to obey him, as well as their subjects or adherents, and he will absolve these men's subjects from their oaths of fealty, although to do this is heretical.

9. But if the Roman bishop, pretending as usual to be pious and solicitous for the people's welfare, says that this authority to confirm or approve the election of the Roman ruler belongs to him in order that no heretic may ascend the imperial throne, since such ascent would be to the grave

harm of the community of believers, this statement must fittingly be answered by saying that the election of the Roman emperor does not need this bishop's approval, for it is effected and solemnized by three devout Christian archbishops (each of whom has received from Christ episcopal or priestly authority equal to that of the Roman pontiff, as we have shown in Chapters XV and XVI of this discourse), as well as by four Christian secular rulers, by whom, coming together with the aforesaid religious pastors or prelates, the election of the aforesaid Roman ruler is consummated. And it is less likely that these seven men will err or succumb to vicious motives than that the Roman bishop will, believing as he does that the plenitude of power which he wrongly claims for himself gives him the rightful authority to follow only his own judgment. For by this authority he could at will judge anyone to be a heretic and deprive him of the right bestowed by his election, whereupon the function of the electing princes would be destroyed and the appointment and inauguration of the elected ruler would be forever prevented for the afore-mentioned reasons.

10. However, let us suppose, with our opponent, that the Roman ruler has fallen or falls into heresy before or after his election, and that the electing princes knew or did not know of it; then it must be said that the judgment or correction of this ruler does not on that account pertain to the Roman bishop either alone or together with his clerical coterie or council, but rather to the general council of those who live under the imperial rule, for the reasons given above and in Chapter XXI of this discourse. For the cardinals of the Roman bishop very often have acquiesced and still do acquiesce and participate in those usurpations of imperial authority which we have mentioned above, and hence it is unsafe for the election of the Roman ruler to be subject to such men's judgment. Furthermore, it must be asked, why do they not claim the power to judge and approve the personal qualifications of other kings? I answer for them that they do indeed intend to make this claim, although they have not yet dared attempt it, but they are awaiting a propitious occasion. We shall perhaps have something more to say about this later.

11. And so a certain modern so-called Roman pope, who through the above-mentioned false assumptions is the most recent entrant upon the path of error and iniquity, is now striving with might and main to hinder and prevent the peaceful accession of the noble Ludwig, duke of Bavaria, elected king of the Romans, to the imperial throne. For both by word and by deed Ludwig is destroying those assumptions, and properly so; for although he has not yet been confirmed or approved by this bishop, just as he does not need to be (as we have shown above), he nevertheless has

had himself addressed as Roman king, as in truth he was and is, ever since his election and proclamation by the electors, and also he has been administering all the imperial and royal functions, as it is his rightful obligation and power to do.

12. Hence, like the snake in Aesop's fable [7] (a story which is very relevant here), this so-called Roman bishop cares not that he and his predecessors were nourished in the bosom of the Roman rulers, and raised up by them from a condition of poverty, degradation, oppression, disrepute, and persecution to an exalted status where he now enjoys an abundance of temporal things, high office, honor, power, and tranquillity; heedless of this, he has turned against the Roman king, not like an heir of the apostles but like an unfeeling ingrate. First he spat out at this ruler in his usual vicious way, with disrespectful, insulting words; but then, mixing this with sweet poison, adopting a deceitful guise of piety, he writes in his letters, which he calls "edicts," that his vicious utterances are motivated by the desire to "recall the aforesaid Ludwig from the bypath of error to the narrow road of truth" [8] and salvation; he does not consider his own role, nor what he is saying, nor to whom he is saying it. To this bishop, as a wanderer from every path of truth and equity, the words in Matthew, Chapter 7, and Luke, Chapter 6, can most truly and fittingly be addressed:

And why beholdest thou the mote that is in thy brother's eye, but considerest not the beam that is in thine own eye? Or how wilt thou say to thy brother, Let me pull out the mote out of thine eye; and behold, a beam is in thine own eye? Thou hypocrite, first cast out the beam out of thine own eye; and then shalt thou see clearly to cast out the mote out of thy brother's eye. For a good tree bringeth not forth corrupt fruit; neither doth a corrupt tree bring forth good fruit. For every tree is known by his own fruit.[9]

Why, then, does this hypocrite, this vicious tree, bearing everywhere the fruits of malice, sedition, and discord, as everyone sees, strive under a false mask of piety and love to defame with his insulting words a virtuous, innocent, catholic, honorable man? Let him first remove the beam, that is, supreme ignorance and error, from his own dimmed, almost blind mind, and the malice and fury from his own wicked and obstinately shameless emotions; and then he will be able to discern the minutiae of the sins of other men, and to expurgate them more readily and effectively by his exhortations and admonitions.

Moreover, this bishop, whose false and crafty words are aimed to bring about not the correction but the civil death of the person to whom they are

[7] See Phaedrus *Fabulae* IV. 19.
[8] From the *monitorium* of Oct. 8, 1323 (MGH, *Constitutiones*, V, 617).
[9] Matthew 7:3-5, Luke 6:41-44.

addressed, has spat forth at this very Christian ruler poisons which he believes will destroy his civil life; for he has excommunicated him together with his adherents, and has interdicted the performance of divine services for communities of believers which give or which will give aid, counsel, or favor to him as Roman king.[10] Little or not at all does this bishop heed the warning which Ambrose gives in the book entitled *On the Priestly Dignity,* where, in his discussion of the passage in I Timothy, Chapter 3: "If a man desire the office of bishop," Ambrose in the eighth chapter writes the following words, among others: "Let the bishop not be quarrelsome, that is, let him not loosen his tongue for wrangling, lest the same tongue which praises God and offers divine services, spout forth the poisons of strife and dispute; for it is not fitting that blessings and curses come at the same time from the bishop's mouth, lest man be cursed by the same tongue which praises God; for one and the same fountain cannot pour forth both sweet and bitter water."[11]

And finally this bishop will perhaps give his malicious sting, which he considers death-dealing, and which he thinks and hopes will pierce the aforesaid ruler and bring about his final extermination. This culminating sting is a certain blasphemy, which he calls a "sentence," although in truth it is utter insanity, whereby the aforesaid ruler and all those who adhere to, favor, or obey him as king will be pronounced heretics and enemies or rebels against the church, and will be deprived of the right to all their temporal goods, movable and immovable. Through his misnamed sentence the bishop will confiscate these goods and grant them to anyone who wants them and seizes them; the lawfulness of such seizure will be upheld throughout all the provinces by proclamations either oral or written made either by the bishop himself or by various pseudo-preachers. Again, he will condemn the king and his followers to death, and will grant full pardon to those who assault or kill them; and if they are captured alive, wherever they be, he will make them slaves to their captors.[12] Moreover, for the purpose of inciting everyone to hate and rebel against the aforesaid ruler, the bishop bestows all the grades of ecclesiastic offices, from the highest (such as the bishopric, archbishopric, and patriarchate) to the lowest, and he pours forth ecclesiastic temporal goods, called benefices above, and treasures of money; and all this despite the fact that he has

---

[10] See the "Process" of March 23, 1324 (MGH, *Constitutiones*, V, 692 ff., 698).

[11] The treatise, attributed to St. Ambrose, of Gerbert (Pope Sylvester II) *De dignitate sacerdotali* cap. iv (PL 17. 573–74).

[12] As the future tense shows, this is an anticipation, based upon past condemnation proceedings by earlier popes, of the condemnations of Ludwig of Bavaria on April 3, 1327, and Oct. 23, 1327. See Previté-Orton's edition *ad loc.,* p. 409, n. 1.

no authority to make such sentences, as we have clearly shown in Chapters IV, V, VII, VIII, X, and XX of this discourse.

13. And in addition to these horrible evils, this bishop perpetrates a new kind of iniquity whose heretical viciousness is only too obvious. For he stirs up rebellion against the afore-mentioned catholic ruler by issuing various diabolic (although he calls them "apostolic") statements releasing this ruler's subjects and adherents from the oaths of fealty whereby they had been and in truth still are bound to him, and proclaiming these annulments everywhere through agents who hope that the bishop will reward them by giving them church offices and benefices.[13] But that this deed is not apostolic, but rather diabolic, is obvious. For when such action is carried on by this bishop and his accomplices, henchmen, adherents, and agents, working with tongue or pen, or through overt deeds (men blind with cupidity, avarice, and pride, and filled to the utmost with covetousness and viciousness, as everyone knows), the result is that the persons who believe their words and who carry them out in practice are led straight into the ditch of mortal sin. First they are led into manifest perjury, then into flagrant perfidy and injustice, and finally into rapine, homicide, and all kinds of crime, wherein they die unrepentant, misled by this most holy father and his agents; and since their crass ignorance does not excuse them before God, they are "cast into the everlasting fire," [14] that is, into the ditch of the everlastingly damned. For, as all persons possessed of reason and capable of using it certainly know and ought to know, neither the Roman bishop nor any other priest can without reasonable cause release anyone from any lawful oath which he has given or promised. But, now, as is certainly known by every person who wishes to stand on his own conscience and who is not moved by vicious emotions, the cause which the Roman bishop pretends against the pious prince Ludwig, or against any other ruler in similar circumstances, is not reasonable at all, but rather vicious, insolent, and unjust. And hence the leadership, teachings, and exhortations of this bishop and of his agents in these affairs must be avoided and utterly shunned as leading to the eternal destruction of men's souls; for such teachings are plainly repugnant to sound doctrine and to the words and convictions of the Apostle, as expressed in Romans, Chapter 13, Ephesians, Chapter 6, I Timothy, Chapter 6, and Titus, Chapters 2 and 3. For in these chapters the Apostle openly teaches that subjects ought "to be obedient to them that are their masters according to the

---

[13] See the excommunication proceeding against Ludwig of March 23, 1324 (MGH, *Constitutiones*, V, 692 ff.) and the directions for publication issued to bishops, March 28, 1324 (*ibid.*, V, 700–701).

[14] Matthew 18:9; see also Matthew 15:14.

flesh"; [15] "not only to the good and gentle, but also to the froward," [16] as St. Peter says in the second chapter of his first epistle. How much more, then, ought subjects to obey those rulers to whom they are bound by oath? This is brought out still more plainly by the glosses of the saints on these passages, which clearly state that subjects have the obligation and the duty to obey even infidel masters, however bad they may be: with the sound proviso, however, that this applies to those cases where obedience is not contrary to divine law in word or deed.[17] But there is no doubt that the words and deeds whereby the Roman bishop inveighs and proceeds against the Roman ruler are neither directly pursuant to commands of divine law nor harmonious therewith, but that they are rather inharmonious and manifestly contrary thereto, as we have shown through Scripture in Chapters IV, V, and IX of this discourse.

Moreover, to believe or to comply with these teachings or statements of the Roman or any other bishop is none other than to allow the root of all governments to be cut up, and the bond and nexus of every city and state to be destroyed. For I hold such root and nexus to be nothing other than the mutual allegiance and faith of subjects and rulers. For this faith, as Cicero says in his treatise *On Duties,* Book I, "is the foundation of all justice," [18] and he who strives to destroy it between rulers and subjects harbors no other design than to acquire for himself the ability to overthrow at his own pleasure the power of all governments, and hence to cast them into slavery to himself. And this also means that such a person disturbs the peace or tranquillity of all men who lead a civil life and hence deprives them of the sufficient life in the present world, and finally, as we have already said, leads those who subscribe to his doctrines straight to the eternal destruction of their souls. And hence let all Christians despise and fear, even more than they do the Pharisees' empty promise of pardon, the pernicious and insane doctrines, or rather, to put it more accurately, soul-seductions, of this bishop and his accomplices; by so doing the Christians will heed the counsel or command of Christ as given in Matthew, Chapter 15, where he says to all believers, although in the person of the apostles: "Let them alone," [19] by "them" meaning the Pharisees, who were then thought to be teachers of the Mosaic Law, although they interpreted it erroneously and were in continual opposition to Christ. By the Pharisees were signified and understood all false and sophistical teachers and

[15] See Romans 13:1–7; Ephesians 6:5–7; I Timothy 6:1–2; Titus 2:9, 3:1.

[16] I Peter 2:18.

[17] See *Glossa ordinaria* on I Peter 2, and Peter Lombard *Collectanea* on Titus 2 and 3 (PL 192. 391–92).

[18] Cicero *De officiis* I. vii. 23.   [19] Matthew 15:14.

preachers of the sacred Scripture, such as are these present persecutors of the Roman ruler and of other innocent, truly Christian men, in whose person Christ himself is persecuted and assailed. And the reason why we ought to let these false doctors alone is told by Christ when he adds, "They be blind leaders of the blind. And if the blind lead the blind, both shall fall into the ditch." [20] Thus, therefore, in accordance with the command of the Lord, these false teachers must be "let alone" and shunned as "blind" (from cupidity, avarice, pride, and ambition) "leaders of the blind," that is, of the avaricious, proud, and rebellious.

But in willful disregard of the apostolic or rather divine command which is clearly and unmetaphorically stated in Romans, Chapter 13: "Let every soul be subject unto the higher powers," [21] these false teachers by crafty, vicious persuasions teach and urge subjects to rebel against their rulers; and thus they resist "the ordinance of God." For in the above-named chapter the Apostle writes that "whosoever resisteth the power," that is, the secular ruler, "resisteth the ordinance of God." [22] And the Apostle also made a prophecy concerning these false teachers in I Timothy, Chapter 4, as well as in II Timothy, Chapter 3, when he said: "This know also, that in the last days perilous times shall come. For men shall be lovers of their own selves, covetous, boasters, proud, blasphemers, disobedient to parents"—under "parents" including rulers, whence Tully writes in the treatise, *On Duties,* Book I: "Foremost (*principes*) are our country and our parents, to whom we are obliged for the greatest benefits" [23]—"disobedient [then] to parents [or rulers], unthankful, unholy," faithless, not keeping their covenants, "without [supply: good] affection, truce-breakers, false accusers, incontinent, fierce, despisers of those that are good, traitors, heady, puffed up, lovers of pleasures more than lovers of God, having a form of godliness," that is, appearing to act out of worship, reverence, and love of God, "but denying the power thereof," [24] that is, of such godliness. All men can readily see the truth of this prophecy by considering the deeds of these false preachers, in accordance with the words in Matthew, Chapter 7: "Beware of false prophets, which come to you in sheep's clothing, but inwardly they are ravening wolves. Ye shall know them by their fruits." [25] And the Apostle, in conformity with the above-stated counsel or command of Christ, adds: "From such turn

[20] *Ibid.*   [21] Romans 13:1.   [22] Romans 13:2.

[23] Cicero *De officiis* I. xvii. 58. It will be noted that Marsilius' interpretation of *principes* as "rulers" instead of as "foremost" alters the meaning of the passage.

[24] II Timothy 3:1–5. The interpolated words "faithless, not keeping their covenants," are, as Previté-Orton says, an "inversion" of Deuteronomy 7:9.

[25] Matthew 7:15–16.

away," [26] that is, do not trust such men or obey them in such matters. But, sad to say, they now wield violent power, obtained partly through gift, because their specious godliness has enabled them to deceive so many men, but mainly seized through usurpations, at first hidden, but now flagrant and violent; and hence the Christian believers, made the objects of such men's violence, cannot turn away from them.

14. And in still another way is rebellion against faithful rulers stirred up among their subjects and allies by these false teachers, who are "unthankful, proud, truce-breakers, fierce," and indeed have all the other qualities named by the Apostle; "who call evil good, and good evil; who put darkness for light and light for darkness," as is said in Isaiah, Chapter 5.[27] This other means of rebellion is through the process of bestowing major, middle, and minor church offices, and of distributing or promising or corruptly trading temporal goods or benefices, both movable and immovable, and tithes, which were originally set aside for a good purpose. And although the bishop and his accomplices now seem to be directing such tactics against the Roman ruler alone, yet from the example of what happened to him, who was such a great benefactor of the Roman bishop and church, let the other rulers learn that the same evils may very likely befall them, and that the Roman bishop, devoid of good affection toward anyone, is planning to employ the same abusive tactics against them as soon as he gets the opportunity. For both in his speeches and in his writings he asserts that his plenitude of power, which he wrongly ascribes to himself, makes all rulers and peoples subject to his coercive rule or jurisdiction; eagerly striving to make this an actuality, he is watching out for the time when strife and schism will appear among Christian rulers or peoples, or when subjects will rebel against their masters. And he incessantly strives to stir up such conflicts in order that the weaker of the two opposing parties may be forced to beg him for help and to undergo his lordship. For although he wears a mask of piety and mercifulness, and seems at times to protect the weak and to give them material aid when they chance to be wrongly oppressed, yet he does this only when he is sure that those who need and implore his help will undergo his secular lordship or rulership thereafter; for he hopes that in this way both opposing parties, through their mutual violence and hatred, will be finally compelled to come under his power. And hence men must guard against all quarrels and actions which may make it necessary to seek this bishop's support, since the final outcome is loss of liberty and the slavery of those who receive such support.

[26] II Timothy 3:5.   [27] Isaiah 5:20.

15. In this way, then, the Roman bishop stealthily worms his way through all the states in the world, one by one, with the aim, which he incessantly strives to realize, of finally making all governments subject to his own power. For since he does not dare to attempt this process against all or most states at once, he intends gradually to acquire so much secular might that finally he will be able, as he thinks, to overcome without difficulty any governments which have not yet succumbed to his sway; for he would then confidently reveal to the other states the meaning of the title of plenitude of power which he has assumed, and would explicitly proclaim, by blasphemous decrees similar to those pronounced upon the Roman ruler and his loyal followers, that, just like the Roman government, so are the other rulers subject to his coercive lordship or jurisdiction. And their lawful refusals he would answer by violent force of arms, persecuting these rulers until they weakened and were exterminated.

By such ways and means, then, the Roman bishop and his accomplices have misled into schism and strife nearly all the governments, communities, and peoples of Italy, and now he is continually striving to do the same in Germany. For through such secular favors as the bestowal of church offices and benefices, and tithes and moneys, he has stirred up traitors and criminals among the subjects to rebel against the Roman ruler, and he relentlessly foments sedition whenever he can, among men from the highest to the lowest rank. Those who have followed this vicious leadership of his he calls "sons of the church" and "true believers"; those, on the other hand, who remain and wish to remain duly obedient and loyal to their ruler, he calls "schismatics" and "heretics," and persecutes them as enemies of the church, blaspheming them as much as he can, defaming and excommunicating them, and condemning their persons and property by secular decrees,[28] although neither divine nor human law gives to him, as such, any authority to make such judgments, as is clear from our earlier discussions, and as we have previously reiterated.

16. But now we come to what is the most vicious and most gravely harmful of all the acts of this present Roman bishop: an iniquitous practice which we have briefly mentioned above, and which no one who desires to cling to the law of love can pass over in silence. I refer to those acts of his whereby he brings about the eternal confusion and destruction of "all Christ's sheep," who he says were entrusted to him that he might feed them with salutary doctrine. For again putting "good for evil and light

---

[28] On John XXII's Italian politics, see K. Müller, *Der Kampf Ludwigs des Baiern mit des Römischen Kurie*, I (Tübingen, 1879); and also the bulls of John XXII (MGH, *Constitutiones*, V, 340, 696, 711).

for darkness," he has issued oral and written pronouncements "absolving from all guilt and punishment" every soldier, in cavalry or in infantry, that has waged war at a certain time against those Christian believers who maintain steadfast and resolute subjection and obedience to the Roman ruler; and by himself or through others this Roman bishop has issued oral and written proclamations making it lawful to attack in any way, to rob and even to kill these faithful subjects, as being "heretics" and "rebels" against the cross of Christ. And, what is horrible to hear, this bishop declares that such action is just as pleasing in God's sight as is fighting the heathen overseas, and he has this declaration published far and wide by false pseudo-brethren who thirst for ecclesiastic office. To those whom physical disability prevents from participating in such criminal action, he grants a similar fallacious pardon if they have up to that same time gotten others to perpetrate these outrages in their place or if they have paid to his vicious collectors a sufficient sum for this purpose.[29] But no one should doubt that, according to the catholic religion, this empty and ridiculous pardon is utterly worthless, nay, harmful, to men who fight in such a cause. Nevertheless, by vocally granting something that is not in his power, the bishop dupes simple men into carrying out his impious desires, or rather he seduces and misleads them to the eternal perdition of their souls. For when men, unjustly invading and attacking a foreign land, disturb the peace and quiet of innocent believers, and, even though they well know that their victims are true catholics, nevertheless rob and kill them because they are defenders of their own country and loyal to their true and legitimate ruler, then such aggressors are fighters not for Christ but for the devil. For they commit rapine, arson, theft, homicide, fornication, adultery, and practically every other kind of crime. And hence it is indubitably certain that the proper desert of such men is not pardon but rather prosecution and punishment by eternal damnation. And yet they are misled into perpetrating these crimes by the words and writings of the very man who calls himself (although he is not) Christ's vicar on earth.

Not content with these horrible crimes committed by laymen at his command and incitement, this "bloody and deceitful man" [30] chose a priest from among his brethren or accomplices (who are called cardinals) and sent him with a large body of cavalry and infantry into the province of Lombardy, for the purpose of attacking and killing Christian believers;

---

[29] The privileges and indulgences of crusaders to the holy land were given for the struggle against Recanati, Dec. 18, 1321 (G. Mollat, *Lettres communes de Jean XXII* [Paris, 1910], n. 16180), in accordance with the decretal of Innocent III, *Excommunicamus* (*Corp. jur. can., Decretal. Greg. IX* Lib. v. Tit. 7. cap. 13).

[30] Psalms 5:6.

and a monk, the abbot of the March of Ancona in Italy, was sent by him on a similar expedition.[31] Those believers who refuse to obey his vicious and impious commands against their ruler he relentlessly attacks with all sorts of persecution; and because their pious ruler Ludwig sympathizes with them and supports them as much as he can, this man has with his usual insolence gone so far as to call him, in speeches and writings, a "supporter of heretics."

Such are the purposes for which this bishop wastes the ecclesiastic temporal goods that devout believers, both rulers and subjects, communities and individuals, have put aside for the aid and support of gospel ministers and of the helpless poor; and he tries to make similar vicious use of the temporal funds which have been bequeathed for the cause of religion, such as for crossing overseas, ransom of men captured by infidels, and other such ends—to all such funds he unjustly lays claim as being subject to his own power. But to draw weapons, or to order weapons drawn, among Christian believers, especially for an unjust cause, is not an apostolic or priestly deed, nor does it befit a priest, or a man dedicated to God, to do such things. Rather, if disagreement or discord arises among Christians, the priest should by suitable exhortations recall them to harmony, as has been sufficiently shown in Chapters V and IX of this discourse through the words of the Apostle, Chrysostom, Hilary, and Ambrose.[32]

No bishop, therefore, should be permitted to have or be entrusted with such general, absolute, and far-reaching power to bestow and distribute temporal goods; but rather the rulers and legislators must either revoke such power entirely, or else so moderate it that goods which are set aside for the present and future welfare of the believers do not yield them continued temporal tribulations and finally eternal torment.

17. Such, then, are the methods (how honorable they are, and how pleasing to God, anyone of sound mind and unperverted emotions can comprehend) that have been employed, and are still being employed, by the modern so-called Roman pope and his ministers, whom he calls "legates," against Ludwig, king of the Romans, and against Ludwig's deputies and faithful subjects, especially in the provinces of Lombardy and Tuscany and in the March of Ancona. But persecution has particularly been visited upon that eminent, noble, illustrious catholic, Matteo Visconti of splendid memory, outstanding among the Italians for his up-

[31] The cardinal-priest was Bertrand du Pouget, nephew of John XXII, legate in Lombardy from July, 1320, to April, 1333, and charged with the war against the Ghibellines. The monk is Amèle de Lautrec, provost of Beaumont, abbot of St. Sernin of Toulouse, who was rector of the March of Ancona from August, 1317 to 1328, bishop of Castres from Dec., 1326.

[32] See above, II. v. 6; II. ix. 4–7.

rightness of character and his dignity, who was vicar of Milan by authority
of the emperor; and most of the faithful peoples who were his adherents
have been similarly persecuted. For the afore-mentioned bishop issues
profane statements wherein he proclaims, although with utter injustice,
that this noble Matteo led an accursed life and that he is "of cursed
memory." [33] But, in truth, the curse is not upon Matteo but rather upon
the bishop himself, through whom so many offenses come, and who always
"out of [his] evil treasure bringeth forth evil things"; [34] and his is the life
that God and men openly regard as accursed, and even more will he be so
regarded in the future, both before and after his death, in accordance with
the threat uttered by the Truth in Matthew, Chapter 18: "Woe to that
man by whom the offense cometh," and again: "But whoso shall offend
one of these little ones which believe in me, it were better for him that a
millstone were hanged about his neck, and that he were drowned in the
depth of the sea." [35] But the Roman bishop does not heed this threat, just
as he does not heed Christ's other warnings; obstinate and unrepentant,
he violently persecutes and blasphemes eminent men who maintain steadfast allegiance to their ruler, the king of the Romans, and he continually
strives by his profane, blasphemous utterances to stain their shining glory
before God and men. But in this he fails, for "God does not follow the
judgment" of this bishop and his church, because they "judge through
malice and ignorance," as the Master of the *Sentences* writes in Book IV,
Distinction 18, Chapter VI. And the reason why God does not follow this
bishop's judgment is given by Jerome in his commentary on the words in
Matthew, Chapter 16: "And I will give unto thee the keys of the kingdom
of heaven"; for Jerome writes, and his words bear repeating: "Some men,
not understanding this passage" (and it should be added, neither does this
bishop), "adopt the supercilious attitude of the Pharisees, thinking that
they can condemn the innocent and acquit the guilty"; and then Jerome
adds these pertinent words: "However, with God it is not the sentence of
the priests but rather the lives of the accused parties, that are inquired
into." [36] God, therefore, does not follow the vicious judgment of such a
priest or bishop or church. And therefore, as we have said, no believer
should respect or fear the blasphemies of this bishop and of his accomplices,
for these blasphemies do not affect the flock of the believers, but rather,
guided by the divine power, they strike back against the foul bodies and
the criminal, unhappy souls of those who rush forth to utter them.

18. We have now told the true origins of the matters under inquiry,

---

[33] See, e.g., MGH, *Constitutiones*, V, Nos. 897, 898, pp. 711 ff.
[34] See Matthew 12:35, 18:7.   [35] Matthew 18:6–7.   [36] See above, II. vi. 9.

and their proper and improper development thereafter, although the long intervening years, and human knavery and heedlessness, have caused this true history to be overlooked or forgotten, and in its place, because of the custom of listening to falsehoods or fancies, the opposite of the truth to be inserted in the minds of most believers.[37] This untruth had its origin and incitement in avarice or cupidity, and in ambition or pride, with more than a little aid and encouragement from that execrable opinion and assertion whereby the Roman bishop and the coterie or college of his clergymen declare that Christ gave plenitude of power to the Roman bishop, although in the person of St. Peter the apostle. But after long, diligent, and painstaking examination and study of the Scriptures, separating the divine Scriptures from human writings, which certain Roman pontiffs had confused, hoping through this confusion to impart to their own decrees that authority which belongs only to the sacred canon, we have determined the meanings of the aforesaid assertion or title; and in Chapter XXIII of this discourse we gave a proof, sufficiently convincing for all men who have the slightest use of reason and are not disturbed by vicious emotions, that the assertion of the Roman bishop's plenitude of power is false in all these meanings, especially the last one into which he transformed this title, whereby he ascribes to himself universal or supreme coercive jurisdiction, which he metaphorically calls the "temporal sword," [38] over all the rulers, communities, and peoples in the world. And although he now exploits this title only against the Roman ruler, for the reasons which we have given, yet he is going to do the same against all the other rulers as soon as he espies sedition arising in their kingdoms and sees that he has the power forcefully to usurp and seize them.

19. It is in this way, then, that the plenitude of power which knavery has permitted the Roman bishops to exercise has hitherto been used by them with regard to secular civil acts, and this is the way they are still using it, and will continue to use it, increasingly for the worse, unless they are prevented. For they have established oligarchic laws exempting the clergy and certain others of their allies from the civil laws duly made, to the gravest harm of rulers and peoples; and not content with this, they are having laymen cited to appear before their so-called officials or judges for trial, thereby completely destroying the jurisdiction of rulers.

And this is the singular cause, quite hidden in its origin, of civil war or discord—that cause which it has been our intention from the very outset

[37] See above, II. i. I.

[38] See Boniface VIII *Unam sanctam* (*Corp. jur. can., Extravag. commun.* Lib. I. Tit. 8. cap. I); also St. Bernard *De consideratione* IV. iii (PL 182. 776), and Egidius of Rome *De ecclesiastica potestate* II. xiv (pp. 132 ff.).

to reveal.[39] For many believers, misreasoning because of the confusing of
divine Scriptures and human writings, have been led to believe that the
Roman bishop and his clergymen, called cardinals, can make any decrees
they like over the believers, and that divine law binds all men to obey these
decrees, and that those who transgress them will be eternally damned. But
that this is not true, nor even close to the truth, but rather manifestly the
opposite of the truth, we have with certainty proved above, especially in
Chapters XII and XIII of Discourse I, and in Chapter XXI, paragraph 8,
of this discourse.

   This too is the cause, as we said in our prefatory remarks, of the travail
under which the Italian state has long been laboring, and is still laboring.
Extremely contagious, this cause is prone to creep up on all the other cities
and states; it has already infected them all to some extent, and unless
stopped, it will finally infect them totally, just as it has the Italian state.

   It will therefore be well for all the rulers and peoples, acting through a
general council to be called in the way we have said, to forbid and prohibit completely the use of this title by the Roman bishop or by anyone
else, lest otherwise the people be misled because of the custom of listening
to falsehoods; and the bishop's power of bestowing and distributing ecclesiastic offices and temporal goods or benefices must also be revoked, because
he abuses this power and thus causes the ruin of the bodies and the damnation of the souls of the Christian believers. Such revocation is a duty which
divine law makes binding upon all men who have jurisdiction, especially
kings; for they have been instituted for the purpose of making judgments
and doing justice, and their failure to do this in the present instance cannot be excused, because they well know what scandal arises from such neglect. And as for the Roman bishop and his successors, as well as all other
priests, deacons, and spiritual ministers (and may God be witness over
my soul and body that I address these words to them not as enemies but
rather as fathers and brothers in Christ), let them strive to imitate Christ
and the apostles by completely renouncing secular rulership and the ownership of temporal goods. For, as I have plainly proved, and as I have warned
them before all men, in accordance with the teaching of Christ and the
apostles, these bishops and priests are sinners; and as a herald of the truth
I have tried to lead them back to the path of truth through the harmony
of the divine Scriptures and human writings, so that they, and especially
the Roman bishop, who seems to have strayed most from the true path,
may beware of that "indignation of almighty God and of the apostles Peter

39 See above, I. i. 3.

and Paul" [40] with which this bishop in particular very often threatens others.

Hence let him first take heed and be personally mindful of the order of love, so that he may then teach others to be thus mindful. For he is not ignorant, or at least he will not henceforth be ignorant, that his unjust action in hampering, attacking, and distressing the Roman ruler and government is external, or rather contrary, to the counsel or command of Christ and the apostles. Nor, again, is he ignorant that bitter conflicts have arisen because of the scandals stirred up by himself and by certain of his predecessors in Italy, as a result of which violent deaths have been suffered by so many thousands of believers, whom we may with probability assume to have been sentenced to eternal damnation, because sudden death found them filled with hatred and malevolence for their brethren; while the rest of the believers are unhappy, expecting a similar perilous lot and miserable death, unless they are helped by the hand of the divine physician. For their minds have been invaded by hatred, strife, and conflict, whence wars follow after; and honorable persons of both sexes have been corrupted in morals and in intellect, so that their minds and bodies have been gripped by all kinds of vice, crime, error, and dissoluteness. Their offspring have been killed, their wealth consumed, their homes disrupted and destroyed, their cities, once great and famous, are now empty, bared of inhabitants, their fields lie untilled and deserted, having ceased to yield their accustomed fruits, and, what is the most deplorable of all, divine worship has almost entirely ceased in Italy, the churches or temples standing in solitude, stripped of rectors or those who have the cure of souls. And the miserable inhabitants, their minds blinded by their mutual hatred and discord, have been goaded on and are still being goaded on to all these misfortunes by "that great dragon, that old serpent," who is deservedly called "the devil and Satan," because with all his guile he "deceiveth" and strives to deceive "the whole world." [41]

20. Who, then, could be so rude a son of this father and mother land, once so beautiful and now so deformed and devastated, as to be silent and withhold the spirit of protest to the Lord when he sees and knows these things and can act against those who so unjustly betray and ruin her? [42] For of such a one will it most truly be said, with the Apostle, that "he hath denied the faith, and is worse than an infidel." [43]

---

[40] A reference to the *minatio* of papal privileges.   [41] Revelation 12:9.

[42] Previté-Orton points out the similarity of this passage to Machiavelli *Il principe* cap. xxvi.

[43] I Timothy 5:8.

In this way, then, let us conclude our discussion of plenitude of power, its various modes, its origin and development, which modes of it the Roman bishop assumed for himself, what his methods were, and what use he has made of it, both in the sphere of church ritual and with regard to men's secular civil acts.

CHAPTER XXVII: ON SOME OBJECTIONS TO THE CONCLUSIONS OF CHAPTER XV OF THIS DISCOURSE AND OF THE CHAPTERS FOLLOWING

BUT someone may well have doubts with regard to what we have said in Chapter XV of this discourse and in the chapters following. First of all it will be shown that the dignity of a bishop is greater than, and different in kind from, the dignity of a mere or simple priest—not only the dignity deriving from human appointment, which we have called "separable," but also that which is of divine ordainment, which we have called "essential." [*i*] It seems that this can be proved from Luke, Chapter 10, where we find this passage: "After these things the Lord appointed also other seventy-two and he sent them two and two before his face." [1] Whereon Bede writes: "Just as the twelve apostles undoubtedly presaged the bishops, so too did these seventy-two prefigure the elders (*presbyterorum*) of the second order of priests." [2] [*ii*] The same is also shown from I Timothy, Chapter 5, where the Apostle wrote: "Against an elder receive not an accusation, but before two or three witnesses." [3] Timothy, therefore, was superior to the other elders in dignity, but since this superiority was not bestowed by the election of the other elders or of the multitude of believers, therefore it was by divine ordainment. [*iii*] The same can again be seen from the epistle of Pope Clement, *To James the Brother of the Lord*.[4] [*iv*] And furthermore this seems to have been the view of almost all the bishops who are said to have succeeded St. Peter or St. Paul in the episcopal seat at Rome, as is plainly to be seen from the *Codex* of Isidore mentioned above.

2. And next it seems possible to show that in power or authority bestowed immediately by Christ, and not by man or men, St. Peter was superior to the other apostles, and that consequently his successors are superior to the successors of the other apostles. [*v*] This is to be seen first

[1] Luke 10:1.   [2] In Thomas Aquinas *Catena aurea* (XII, 114).   [3] I Timothy 5:19.
[4] Pseudo-Clement Epist. 1, in Pseudo-Isidore *Decretales*, ed. Hinschius, pp. 30 ff.

from Matthew, Chapter 16, where Christ said to St. Peter in particular: "And I say also unto thee, that thou art Peter, and upon this rock I will build my church; and the gates of hell shall not prevail against it. And I will give unto thee the keys of the kingdom of heaven," [5] etc. By these words Christ seems to have declared that St. Peter would be the head and foundation of the church, especially after Christ's death. Whereon the gloss writes: "He granted this [power] to a single man, Peter, in order to beckon us toward unity. For he made him leader of the apostles in order that the church might have one principal vicar of Christ, a vicar to whom the other members of the church might have recourse if they should chance to disagree among themselves. For if there were many heads in the church, the bond of unity would be broken." [6] [vi] The same is also shown from Luke, Chapter 22, where Christ said to Peter in particular: "I have prayed for thee, Peter, that thy faith fail not; and when thou art converted, strengthen thy brethren." [7] To St. Peter, then, was entrusted the primary pastoral care and strengthening of his brethren the apostles and of the other believers, because his faith was so strong; and it was for his faith that Christ seems particularly to have prayed, that it might not fail either in him or in any of his successors. Whereon the gloss writes: " 'Strengthen thy brethren,' since I have made thee leader of the apostles. And this strengthening by Peter must be understood to apply not only to the apostles of that day, but also to all the believers." And a little below the gloss adds: "Through his penance he," Peter, "obtained the leadership of the world." [8] [vii] The same is again shown from John, Chapter 21, where Christ said to Peter in particular: "Feed my lambs, Feed my sheep, Feed my sheep," [9] repeating the same phrase three times. And since no particular sheep were specified, it seems that Peter was immediately by Christ made the primary and universal pastor of all the sheep. Whereon Chrysostom writes as follows: "For Peter was the foremost of the apostles, the mouth of the disciples, the head of the college, and hence, after he had withdrawn his denial, he was entrusted with the leadership of the apostles by Christ." [10] [viii] And final confirmation of this view is given by the authority of many saints writing on the passage in John, Chapter 21: "If I will that he tarry till I come, what is that to thee? follow thou me." [11] For Augustine writes: "The church knew that it was endowed with two lives by the divine preachment, of which one is in faith, and the other in hope. The former," the life in faith, "was exemplified by the apostle Peter because

---

[5] Matthew 16:18-19. [6] Thomas Aquinas *Catena aurea* (XI, 199).

[7] Luke 22:32. [8] *Catena aurea* (XII, 230). [9] John 21:15-17.

[10] *Catena aurea* (XII, 462). [11] John 21:22.

of the primacy of his apostolate." [12] And also Theophylact writes thereon: "He made him leader of all the believers." [13] And Chrysostom: "If I am asked, 'In which wise did James mount the throne of Jerusalem?' I shall reply, 'Because he enthroned Peter as master of the whole world.'" And below, Chrysostom says the same thing: "To him," Peter, "was entrusted the leadership of his brethren." And again: "The Lord had given him," Peter, "important instructions, and had entrusted the entire world to his care." [14] And again on the words in John, Chapter 21, "If I will that he tarry," Theophylact writes as follows: "For now I send thee away to assume the pontificate of the entire world, and in this follow thou me." [15]

[ix] Another proof of this is that if Christ had not chosen a head for the church, he would have left it headless in his absence, and it would seem that he had not ordered the church according to the better or best arrangement. But on the other hand, it must be believed that Christ arranged and ordered the church in the best way. And therefore it must be held that Christ did choose a head. But no one was more suitable than St. Peter. Therefore, Peter was superior to the other apostles in authority by the direct designation of Christ.

3. Next we can prove the same thing specifically, by showing that Paul was not equal to St. Peter in dignity or authority. [x] For in Galatians, Chapter 2, we find this passage: "Then," writes Paul, "after three years I went up to Jerusalem to see Peter, and abode with him fifteen days." And a little below Paul goes on to say: "Then fourteen years after I went up again to Jerusalem with Barnabas, and took Titus with me also. And I went up by revelation, and communicated unto them that gospel which I preach among the Gentiles, but privately to them which were of reputation, lest by any means I should run, or had run, in vain." [16] Whereon the gloss writes: "He," Paul, "shows that he would not have had the care of the gospel, had it not been confirmed by the authority of Peter and corroborated by the others." [17] Since, then, according to the gloss, Paul received the care of the gospel from Peter, it is clear that he was not equal to Peter in authority. Whence it seems necessarily to follow, both from this and from the other passages cited above, that all the bishops in the world are subject by divine ordainment to the Roman bishop as St. Peter's particular successor; and also that the Roman church is the head and leader of all the other churches, because its bishop, being the successor of St. Peter therein, is the judge and pastor of all the other bishops. [xi] This is also shown by

---

[12] *Catena aurea* (XII, 463).   [13] *Ibid.*   [14] *Ibid.*.   [15] *Ibid.* (XII, 464).
[16] Galatians 1:18, 2:1–2.
[17] *Glossa ordinaria, ad loc.;* also in Peter Lombard *Collectanea* (PL 192. 103).

Isidore in his afore-mentioned *Codex,* in the chapter entitled "Preface of the Nicene Council." For Isidore there writes as follows: "All catholics must well know that the holy Roman church was not given the leadership through any synodic decrees, but that rather it obtained the primacy through the evangelic voice of our Lord and Savior, when he said to St. Peter the apostle: 'Thou art Peter, and upon this rock I will build my church, and I will give unto thee the keys of the kingdom of heaven.'" [18] This primacy, without any grant on the part of the rulers, was held by all the Roman bishops from the time of St. Peter to the time of Constantine I, the Roman emperor, and was used by them to lay down canons and command their observance throughout the whole church, as is quite clear from the above-mentioned *Codex.*

4. This same view I shall now confirm by reason. [*xii*] For there is "one faith," [19] according to the Apostle in Ephesians, Chapter 4, and therefore there is one church; but the church is one only because it has one head and leader, and in fitness for this head position no one surpasses or equals the Roman bishop, since he is the special successor of St. Peter, who was the rock on which Christ said he would found his church. [*xiii*] Another argument in confirmation of the same proposition is this: just as temporal things are placed under one leader, namely, the government, so too does it seem that spiritual things ought to be placed under one leader, namely, the bishopric. [*xiv*] Moreover, just as in a single temple or diocese there ought to be a single bishop, "lest the church of Christ be destroyed by each" of the priests therein "following his own will," as we quoted from Jerome's epistle to Evander in Chapter XV of this discourse; [20] so too it is even more necessary that there be a single head in the universal Christian church in order to preserve the unity of the believers. For the more common a good is than another of the same kind, the more divine and preferable it is.[21] [*xv*] Whence in John, Chapter 10, it is written: "And there shall be one fold and one shepherd." [22] But the most appropriate shepherd and head seems to be the Roman bishop, for the reasons given above.

5. From the foregoing it seems necessarily to follow that the Roman bishop is both directly and indirectly the sole primary efficient cause of the secondary appointment of all the other bishops, priests, and other ministers of churches or temples, because of his universal authority over them all. [*xvi*] This view is upheld by the authority of Ambrose in his book *On Handing Over the Basilica,* where he writes as follows: "The church is

---

[18] Pseudo-Isidore *Decretales,* ed. Hinschius, p. 255.   [19] Ephesians 4:5.
[20] See above, II. xv. 9.   [21] See Aristotle *Nicomachean Ethics* I. 2. 1094b 10.
[22] John 10:16.

God's, and hence it should not be given to Caesar. Caesar cannot have a right to the temple of God," [23] nor, consequently, can he have the right to appoint priests therein, which appointment gives what we have called the priests' secondary authority in Chapter XV of this discourse. But if Caesar cannot have the right to hand over the basilica, still less can any other ruler. And therefore, if no ruler can have a right to such authority, it will belong to him who is the head and first of all priests, the Roman pontiff, by divine authority.

6. [xvii] From this it also seems necessarily to follow that to the Roman pontiff belongs the authority to distribute or bestow benefices or ecclesiastic temporal goods, inasmuch as such goods are bestowed for the exercise of church functions.

7. From the above it also seems possible to infer that to the same head bishop belongs coercive jurisdiction over all the other bishops and temple ministers in the world. For they are subject to him by divine ordainment, as is clear from the previous reasonings. [xviii] This can also be supported by citing what is written in the *Codex* of Isidore, in the chapter mentioned above; for among others we find there this passage:

The ruler's admirable deed in this council should not, I think, be passed over in silence. For when the bishops had come together from all the territories, it happened, as usual, that quarrels arose among them for various reasons; accusations were frequently made, insults were exchanged, threats were uttered, and the bishops devoted their energies more to these disputes than to the purposes for which they had come. But the ruler, seeing that such quarrels were frustrating the main purposes of the assemblage, fixed a certain day on which each bishop was to present whatever grievances he fancied he had. And when they reconvened, the ruler collected from each one his charges. Gathering together all the complaints, and not revealing what they were, he said to the bishops: "God ordained you priests and gave you the power to judge us. And therefore we are rightly judged by you, but you cannot be judged by men. Consequently, you must expect God alone to judge you, and your quarrels, whatever they be, must be reserved for the divine scrutiny. For you are gods, given to us by God; and it is not proper that men should judge gods." [24]

And therefore to the Roman bishop, who, as it is said, is the god of such gods on earth, belongs the jurisdictional authority over them.

8. From the above it also seems that to the Roman bishop belongs the authority to command the convocation of general councils of priests, and to make whatever proposals and decisions he thinks should be made therein with regard to divine law and church ritual. [xix] Discussing the authority to call a council, Isidore in the preface to the afore-mentioned *Codex* writes

---

[23] St. Ambrose *Sermo contra Auxentium* cap. xxxv (PL 16. 1061).

[24] Pseudo-Isidore *Decretales,* ed. Hinschius, p. 256.

as follows: "The authority to call synods was entrusted to the apostolic seat. Canonic authority vouches for this, church history corroborates it, and the holy fathers confirm it." [25]

9. [*xx*] Concerning the power or authority to define or determine the meaning of Scripture, Isidore writes as follows in the same chapter of the *Codex:* "In this volume we have collected the proceedings of the various Greek and Latin councils, early and late, and have numbered and dated them so that they are ordered into distinct chapters. And we have also included the decrees of the Roman prelates up to St. Gregory, together with some of Gregory's letters, whose authority, as coming from the highest apostolic seat, was not unequal to that of the councils." [26] The supreme pontiff, then, can by his own authority make whatever decisions can be made by the authority of the general council, and hence his authority is "not unequal" to that of the general council, according to Isidore. But the general council has and should have the authority to determine, define, and interpret doubtful sentences of the sacred Scripture, as was shown in Chapter XX of this discourse. [*xxi*] And the same view in this regard seems to have been held by Jerome in his epistle entitled *On the Exposition of the Catholic Faith,* where he writes as follows: "This, most blessed pope, is the faith which we learned in the catholic church, and which we have always held. If we have included something therein which is unwise or ill-considered, we desire to be corrected by you, who hold the faith and the seat of Peter. But if this confession of ours is approved by your apostolic judgment, then whoever desires to besmirch me will prove, not that I am a heretic, but that he himself is unlearned, malevolent, or even uncatholic." [27]

10. [*xxii*] Concerning the power to make decrees regarding church ritual and eternal salvation, the same is to be seen from the utterance of Christ in Luke, Chapter 10. For Christ said to the apostles, and through them to all bishops or priests: "He that heareth you heareth me; and he that despiseth you despiseth me; and he that despiseth me despiseth him that sent me." [28] Therefore, it is necessary for salvation that the decrees of the priests be observed.

11. [*xxiii*] Summing up these powers, and greater ones, assigned to the Roman pontiff, St. Bernard in his treatise addressed to Pope Eugene, *On Consideration,* Book II, writes as follows:

Now we must see what remains, if anything, of the subject which we have been discussing. So, then, let us carefully consider who you are, that is, what role

---

[25] *Ibid.,* p. 19.   [26] *Ibid.,* pp. 17–18.

[27] Pseudo-Jerome *Symboli explanatio ad Damasum* (*Opera* [Paris, 1706], V, 124).

[28] Luke 10:16.

you play in the church of God on earth. Who are you? You are a great priest, the supreme pontiff. You are the ruler of the bishops, the heir of the apostles; in primacy you are Abel, in directorship Noah, in patriarchate Abraham, in rank Melchisedech, in dignity Aaron, in authority Moses, in judgeship Samuel, in power Peter, in unction Christ.

And a little below, Bernard continues in the same vein:

You are the one universal shepherd, not only of the sheep, but also of the shepherds. How do I prove this, you ask? By the word of the Lord. For to which, I will not say of the bishops, but even of the apostles, were all the sheep entrusted so absolutely and without differentiation? "If you love me, Peter, feed my sheep."

And a little below, Bernard adds:

Is it not clear that Christ designated, not some particular sheep, but all sheep, without qualification? For where no distinctions are made, no exceptions are made.

And a little further below:

Hence to each of the other apostles, who knew the sacrament, was allotted a single flock. And therefore James, "who seemed to be a pillar" of the church, was content to serve only in Jerusalem, yielding to Peter the care of the whole.

And then Bernard writes in conclusion:

According to your canons, therefore, the others have been called to take care of a part, while you have been called to plenitude of power. The power of the others is limited by certain restrictions, but yours extends even to those who have received power over others. Is it not in your power, for sufficient cause, to exclude a bishop from heaven, to depose him from his bishopric, and even to turn him over to Satan? Your privilege, therefore, stands unshaken, with regard both to the keys which you have been given, and to the sheep with which you have been entrusted.[29]

12. [*xxiv*] Not only did Bernard say that the Roman pontiff had authority over ecclesiastic ministers, such as bishops, priests, and the lower orders, but also he seems to have ascribed to this same bishop coercive jurisdiction over all rulers, which jurisdiction Bernard metaphorically called the "temporal sword." And hence in the same treatise addressed to Pope Eugene, in Book IV, Chapter IV, Bernard writes as follows:

Why do you attempt to usurp the sword which you were once ordered to replace in its sheath? And yet he who denies that this sword is yours, does not sufficiently heed, it seems to me, these words of the Lord: "Put back thy sword in its sheath." To you, then, belongs the sword, and it should be taken out of its sheath perhaps by your will although not by your hand. For otherwise, if this sword in no way belonged to you, then to the words of the apostles: "Be-

[29] St. Bernard *De consideratione* II. vii, viii (PL 182. 751, 752).

hold, here are two swords," the Lord would have replied not that "It is enough," but rather that it was too much. Both swords, therefore, belong to the church, both the spiritual and the material; the former, however, must be drawn by the church, and the latter for the church; the former by the hand of the priest, the latter by the hand of the soldier, but by the will of the priest and at the command of the emperor.[30]

[xxv] The above assertions are also confirmed by the authority of other saints. I have omitted to quote their words, however, because their arguments are to the same or similar effect as those which we have already cited and are to be refuted in the same way; and another reason for omitting them is for the sake of brevity. [xxvi] And also it would seem that these assertions can be confirmed by the decretals or decrees of the Roman pontiffs. For in these documents warning is given that ecclesiastic offices, and the benefices established on their behalf, must be awarded or bestowed by the Roman and other bishops, and not by the human legislator nor by him who rules by its authority. And also in these same decretals and decrees warning is given that priests and clergymen must not undergo the coercive judgment of the aforesaid legislator or ruler, but rather conversely. Furthermore, these documents assert that to the Roman pontiff belong all the powers which Bernard in his writings ascribes to this pontiff.

CHAPTER XXVIII: REPLIES TO THE FOREGOING OBJECTIONS

THE remainder of this discourse will be devoted to the proper exposition of the authorities of the Scripture or canon, and to the refutation of the human reasonings adduced in Chapters III and XXVII of this discourse, which seemed contrary to our own conclusions. But first it will be well to recall what we said in Chapter XIX of this discourse, in accordance both with the view of St. Augustine and with infallible reason grounded in Scripture, namely, that for salvation it is necessary for us to believe in or to acknowledge the certainty or truth of no statements or writings except those which are called canonic, that is, those which are contained in the volume of the Bible, and their necessary consequences, and those interpretations of doubtful senses of the sacred Scriptures which have been made by the general council of believers or catholics, especially in those clauses wherein error would lead to eternal damnation, such as are the articles of the Christian faith, together with the interpretations

[30] Ibid. IV. iii (PL 182. 776).

thereof made in general councils which have been duly called, attended, and consummated.[1] Consequently, those authorities of the sacred canon or Scripture which do not need a mystical exposition, we shall follow entirely in their manifest literal sense; but with regard to those which do need mystical exposition, we shall adhere to the more probable view of the saints. Those views which the saints have uttered by their own authority, apart from Scripture, and which are in harmony with the Scripture or canon, I shall accept; those which are not in harmony I shall respectfully reject, but only by the authority of Scripture, on which I shall always rely. For sometimes the saints disagree with one another in their views on Scripture and other matters, as, for example, Jerome and Augustine differ concerning the passage in Galatians, Chapter 2: "But when Cephas was come to Antioch, I withstood him to the face, because he was to be blamed," [2] and Ambrose and Jerome disagree regarding the virginity of Joseph; [3] and again, a saint sometimes makes statements which are inconsistent with other utterances of his own, as will be clearly seen below.[4]

2. We shall first answer the objections which were adduced in the preceding chapter. [i] The first objection, taken from Luke 10, was that bishops are of greater dignity than simple priests; for in Luke, Chapter 10, it is written that "after these things the Lord appointed also other seventy-two," and these seventy-two, according to Bede, prefigure the order of elders, which he calls the "second order," coming after the order of bishops.[5] To this it must be replied, in accordance with the views of the Apostle and of the saints as cited in Chapter XV of this discourse,[6] that by the seventy-two is more appropriately meant the order of deacons than the order of priests; or else we can fittingly reply that, even if the order of priests is meant, it does not follow that the bishop has a greater essential order than has the elder. Hence, when Christ sent them into the world, that sending signified the human election or appointment whereby one of them is put over the others in the ecclesiastic household. For when Christ said to them, "Go ye therefore and teach all nations," he did not bestow on them the essential dignity, for he had previously given them this. And even if he had given them both dignities at one and the same time, nevertheless I say that that sending did not give them any intrinsic perfection which they had not previously had when they received the

[1] See above, II. xix.

[2] Galatians 2:11, and see Peter Lombard *Collectanea* (PL 192. 110–14).

[3] See Peter Lombard *Collectanea* on Galatians 1:19 (PL 192. 101–2).

[4] On Marsilius' method of interpreting Scripture, and his position on traditional authorities, see Vol. I, pp. 73–77.

[5] See above, II. xvii. 1.   [6] See above, II. xv. 5.

priesthood through the Holy Spirit. And the reason why it was Christ who made this necessary human appointment whereby the apostles were placed over the other future priests, was that at that time there was no multitude of believers by whom such an election could be effected, and even if there had been, no multitude could have made such an appointment as appropriately as did Christ. Hence, after Christ's passion and resurrection, the apostles had recourse to the method of election in apportioning the provinces among them. For in Galatians, Chapter 2, we read: "James, Cephas, and John . . . gave to me and Barnabas the right hands of fellowship; that we should go unto the heathen, and they unto the circumcision." [7] And therefore, even if the appointment of the seventy-two had prefigured the status of the priests, as Bede asserted, nevertheless I say that the bishop does not have directly from God any greater intrinsic dignity, perfection, or character than does the priest, and the sufficient reason for this has been given in Chapter XV of this discourse.

3. [*ii*] To the next objection, from I Timothy, Chapter 5: "Against an elder," etc.,[8] I reply that the appointment whereby the Apostle elevated Timothy over the other priests in the province was a secondary, not an essential, one; for the will and appointment of the Apostle were then equivalent to an election because the multitude of believers were so few in number, and so inadequate and uneducated. Whence the Apostle in I Corinthians, Chapter 3, writes as follows: "And I, brethren, could not speak unto you as unto spiritual, but as unto carnal, even as unto babes in Christ. I have fed you with milk, and not with meat: for hitherto ye were not able to bear it, neither yet now are ye able. For ye are carnal." [9] We have discussed this more fully in Chapter XVII of this discourse, paragraph 7.

4. [*iii*] As for the objection drawn from Clement's epistle entitled *To James the Brother of the Lord*,[10] I do not accept it as valid, because a large part of this epistle's contents have made it extremely doubtful that it was written by Clement. Also suspect are the other decrees or epistles cited from Isidore's *Codex* in support of this objection, for in those which are entitled, *Epistle Concerning the Vestments and Vases: written to James the brother of the Lord,* and *Concerning the Common Life of the Apostles,*[11] the writer purports to be Clement telling James what Christ and the apostles did. But this would have been great ignorance, not to say presumption, on the part of Clement, for it would mean that he was trying to recount what he had merely heard (by way of teaching, as it were) to a

---

[7] Galatians 2:9.   [8] See above, II. xxvii. 1.   [9] I Corinthians 3:1–2.
[10] See above, II. xxvii. 1.   [11] Pseudo-Isidore *Decretales*, ed. Hinschius, pp. 46 ff., 65 ff.

person who had been present there and had actually seen Christ and the apostles, of whom he was one. For who was better able to instruct the disciples at Jerusalem concerning the life of Christ and the apostles: James or Clement? Who should have had greater knowledge of church ritual? As to whether it was the apostle or the successor of the apostle, there can be no doubt. Hence these epistles and decrees must be classed among the apocryphal fables. But suppose that Clement did write them, as some men assert, relying on fables and even rushing forth to make such a statement as that Clement, because he was a Roman bishop, had greater authority than the apostle James in the church of God. Those who make this assertion should properly be asked: Why are not Clement's epistles placed in the text of the sacred canon, as are those of James? The passages in these epistles which seem contrary to the views of Christ and the apostles will be dealt with by us when we discuss the scriptural authorities on which they seem to be based.

[*iv*] As for the statement that this view was held by all the bishops who succeeded St. Peter in the episcopal seat at Rome,[12] it must be replied that they understood this in the way indicated by us in our reply to the first objection; but if they understood it in a different way, then we, departing from them, follow the Apostle and Jerome as quoted in Chapters XV and XVI of this discourse.

5. Now we come to the canonic authorities which are held to prove that St. Peter was superior to the other apostles in dignity, not only by human election, but also by Christ's immediate ordainment. [*v*] The first citation was taken from Matthew, Chapter 16: "Thou art Peter, and upon this rock I will build my church . . . and I will give unto thee the keys of the kingdom of heaven," etc.; [13] which words are held to indicate that Christ appointed Peter to be the head and foundation of the church, at least during his (Christ's) absence. To this I reply that by God's immediate ordainment there is and was only one head and foundation of the church, namely, Christ, and not any of the apostles, even during Christ's absence, as we have with certainty proved through Scripture in Chapters XVI and XXII of this discourse. And so when the words of the canon, "Upon this rock," etc., are quoted, I reply, with the gloss, that " 'upon this rock' means 'upon Christ,' in whom you believe." Whereon the Interlinear Gloss adds: " 'Thou art Peter' means: thou art the rock made by me, but in such a way that I retain for myself the dignity of being the foundation." [14] Christ called him Peter, meaning "constant in faith," and we do not deny that

---

[12] See above, II. xxvii. 1.   [13] See above, II. xxvii. 2.

[14] *Glossa interlinearis,* and *Glossa ordinaria, ad loc.*

Peter was this. But even if Peter were more constant than the other apostles, and more perfect in merit, it does not follow that he was prior to them in dignity, unless perhaps by prior is meant prior in time, as we have clearly proved above through Scripture.[15] And that what we have said is the true meaning of Scripture is upheld by St. Augustine's interpretation of that passage; for in the *Book of Retractions* Augustine writes:

Concerning the apostle Peter I said somewhere that the church was built upon him as upon a rock. But since then, I know that in these words spoken by the Lord, "Thou art Peter, and upon this rock I will build my church," the phrase "this rock" has been most often interpreted by me as meaning him whom Peter acknowledged when he said: "Thou art the Christ, the son of the living God"; so that the man whom this rock called "Peter" presaged, as it were, the person of the church, which is built upon this rock. For Christ did not say to him, "Thou art the rock," but rather "thou art Peter"; the rock was Christ, who was acknowledged by Simon, just as he [Christ] is acknowledged by the whole church, which was signified by Peter." [16]

And the reason for this can be given in accordance with Scripture; for so long as Peter was a wayfarer, he could err and sin through his free will, just as we read that he denied Christ and that sometimes he did not walk straightly in accordance with the truth of the gospel. Such a person could not be the foundation of the church, but only Christ was this foundation, as is to be seen from I Corinthians, Chapter 3; for Christ alone could not err, inasmuch as he remained firmly impeccable from the moment of his conception. Whence the Apostle writes in the above-mentioned place: "For other foundation can no man lay than that is laid, which is Jesus Christ." [17]

6. And as for the words which were added by Christ: "I will give unto thee the keys of the kingdom of heaven," this utterance gave to Peter no authority over the other apostles, inasmuch as it gave this same judiciary power to the other apostles, according to Jerome and Raban, from whose glosses we quoted in Chapter VI of this discourse, paragraph 3. Moreover, it seems that it was not by these words that Christ gave to Peter the power of the keys. For Christ said, "I will give," which denotes the future; he did not say, "I give." But in John, Chapter 20, on the other hand, Christ said to all the apostles alike: "Receive ye the Holy Ghost, and whosoever sins ye remit," etc.[18] But even if Peter did receive the power of the keys through the above words, it does not follow that he was appointed the first pastor, unless we mean first in time; and the reason why Christ gave the keys

---

[15] See above, II. xvi. 10.
[16] St. Augustine *Liber retractationum* I. xxi, in Thomas Aquinas *Catena aurea* (XI, 198).
[17] I Corinthians 3:11. [18] John 20:22-23.

to Peter in particular was because Christ wished to indicate the unity of the church in faith, to which unity he beckoned the believers by that particular or single gift or promise of the keys, as the gloss says; [19] or perhaps the fact that Peter was the first to avow openly and steadfastly that Christ was the son of God, was the reason why Peter was first in time given the keys and honored, or promised to be honored, in order that by such gift or promise to Peter, others might be given an example to avow Christ so openly and steadfastly. But this does not prove that Peter was prior to the others in dignity or authority, although several of the glossators seem to make this assertion on their own authority, not having it from Scripture. But an infallible sign that our position is the true one is found in the passage of the gospel which we are now going to cite from Matthew, Chapter 20, and Luke, Chapter 22, where Christ, clearly settling this issue, said that none of the apostles was superior to the others. For "there was a strife among them, which of them should be the greater"; [20] and in Matthew, Chapter 23, Christ said to them: "But be not ye called Rabbi," that is, toward one another. "For one is your master; and ye are all brethren." [21] "Ye are all brethren," that is, equal; Christ, therefore, made no exceptions among them. And it is indeed remarkable if we are obliged to believe the authority of the glossators rather than Christ, whoever be that glossator, even a saint, and especially since he makes this assertion not as glossator but on his own understanding. For the scriptural passage is so clear on this point that it does not need a glossator. Moreover, the glossators themselves say the opposite, in their expositions of Galatians, Chapter 2, as has been shown in Chapter XVI of this discourse. But we have discussed this at sufficient length in Chapters IV and XVI of this discourse; [22] and we have not repeated all the proofs here because the fact is so well known, and for the sake of brevity.

7. [vi] Now we come to another canonic authority, Luke, Chapter 22. For Christ said to Peter: "I have prayed for thee," Peter, "that thy faith fail not; and when thou art converted, strengthen thy brethren." [23] From this passage some men draw two inferences, the first of which is that it is the faith of the Roman church alone which cannot fail, because by Peter's faith Christ meant also the faith of his successors, and consequently the bishop who succeeded Peter was superior to the others. The second inference is that by these words Christ put Peter at the head of the other apostles. Now I say that neither of these inferences follows from Christ's words. I prove this first in respect of logical necessity; for in these infer-

---

[19] See above, II. xxvii. 2.   [20] Matthew 20:24-28, Luke 22:24-30.
[21] Matthew 23:8.   [22] See above, II. iv. 3 ff.; II. xvi. 6 ff.   [23] See above, II. xxvii. 2.

ences the opposite of the consequent is consistent with the antecedent. Secondly I prove through Scripture, and through Christ's own words, not through any others, that neither of these inferences follows from Christ's words. The first inference does not follow because in the last chapter of Matthew Christ said to all the apostles: "Go ye therefore and teach all nations. . . . And lo I am with you always even unto the end of the world." [24] So, then, Christ promised that he would be with the others "always even unto the end of the world"; and therefore, if this is to be understood to apply to Peter's successors, Christ meant it to apply to the successors of the other apostles also. Moreover, even if the Roman bishop is called the successor of St. Peter in particular, yet it is certain that some of the men who held that office were heretics, as was shown in Chapter XX of this discourse with regard to Tiberius and several others.[25] Furthermore, the Roman bishop is not the particular successor of St. Peter, for the reasons given, in accordance with Scripture, in Chapter XVI of this discourse. The second inference likewise does not follow, and this too I prove through Scripture. For it was Paul who added to Peter in the gospel, and not conversely, as we have sufficiently shown from Galatians, Chapter 2, in Chapter XVI of this discourse.[26] And what is even more clearly destructive of this inference is that utterance of Christ which we have quoted above from Matthew, Chapter 20, and Luke, Chapter 22; [27] for by this utterance, taken in its open sense, Christ declared and decreed the opposite of the inference in question. And hence the gloss on this passage writes: "Just as I prayed for thee that thou shouldst not fail, so must thou, by the example of thy penance, strengthen thy weaker brethren, lest they despair of pardon," [28] understanding by "brethren" all believers alike. And when Christ addressed these words to Peter, he made the other apostles understand that they would do the same. Whence in Mark, Chapter 13, it is written: "What I say unto one" (or according to another reading, which is still the same in meaning: "What I say unto thee"), "I say unto all." [29] A possible alternative explanation, which the gloss seems to uphold, as to why Christ addressed his utterance to Peter in particular, is that Christ knew in advance that Peter would deny him. And hence he said to Peter in particular, "when thou art converted," that is, "by the example of thy penance," because it was more particularly by the words and example of Peter, who had merited pardon, that Christ could strengthen or confirm the weak in faith, "lest they despair of pardon."

[24] Matthew 28:19-20.
[25] See above, II. xx. 6-9.
[26] See above, II. xvi. 6.
[27] See above, para. 6 of this chapter.
[28] *Glossa interlinearis* on Luke 22:32.
[29] Mark 13:37.

8. [*vii*] As for the other canonic authority, John, Chapter 21, whereby some men try to draw the same conclusion as above, in that Christ said to Peter: "Feed my lambs, feed my sheep," etc.,[30] it must be replied, in accordance with the gloss, that the meaning of this passage is as follows: "To 'feed the sheep' is to strengthen the believers in order that they fail not, to lend them material support if necessary, to furnish an example of virtuous conduct, to withstand enemies," that is, of the faith, "and to correct sinners." And then the gloss adds: "And when Christ hears a third time that he is loved by Peter, he orders him to 'feed his sheep.' The triple denial is replaced by a triple avowal, in order that the tongue may not be less obedient to love than to fear."[31] Now all that this proves is that Christ appointed Peter pastor of the sheep. But it does not follow from this that Peter was placed over the other apostles, or was made prior to them in authority or dignity; nor, again, that the other apostles were not made pastors. For the opposite of each of these consequents is consistent with the antecedent, that is, with the above utterance of Christ. And what we say is borne out by this, that in the Mass of the catholic church, mention is made of all the apostles alike: "Truly it is worthy and just, right and beneficial, to pray to thee always, eternal Pastor, that thou shouldst not desert thy flock, but protect it continually through thy blessed apostles; that it may be guided by those same rectors whom thou gave to it to serve as supervisory pastors and vicars of thy work."[32] See, then, that the chant mentions "apostles," in the plural, and "rectors," "vicars," and "pastors," who were bestowed on the flock directly by Christ; but mention is not made of any one particular rector, vicar, or pastor appointed by Christ.

9. But if it be asked why Christ spoke these words to Peter in particular, the answer must be this: that in pardoning sinners, in cleansing the weak, and in reviving the dead, Christ at some times addressed a man in his own particular person while at other times he addressed a man in the person of all men or many men, as was the case in John, Chapter 5, where he said: "Sin no more, lest a worse thing come unto thee."[33] Hence, when Christ entrusted the pastoral office to Peter, he spoke to him in the person of all the apostles; and Christ himself showed in Mark, Chapter 13, that this was his way of speaking, when he said: "What I say unto one" (or "unto you"), "I say unto all."[34] But he addressed his words to Peter in particular because Peter was the oldest, or because his love was most ardent, or in

---

[30] See above, II. xxvii. 2. [31] *Glossa ordinaria* on John 21:15-17.
[32] *Missale Romanum, Praefatio solemnis de apostolis.* [33] John 5:14, 8:11.
[34] Mark 13:37; see above, para. 7 of this chapter.

order that the church of the future might be shown what qualities men ought to have in order to be appointed pastors, namely, they should be mature in age, which signifies prudence or scientific knowledge, and full of love, which signifies the care and diligence which pastors should have. Another possible reason why Christ spoke to Peter in particular was perhaps in order that Peter might not seem too downcast for having denied Christ; and this is the explanation which the gloss seems to uphold, when it says: "The triple denial is replaced by a triple avowal, in order that the tongue may not be less obedient to love than to fear." But regardless of which reason is most correct, it is most certain that Christ was addressing Peter in the person of all the apostles; for in the last chapter of Matthew he said to them all alike, "Go ye therefore, and teach all nations"; he did not say to Peter alone, Go thou, and send others; and thus Christ showed all the apostles that they were equal in authority, just as he also showed in the passage from Matthew, Chapter 13, quoted above, when he said to them: "Be not ye called Rabbi," that is, toward one another, or one over the other. "For one is your Master; and ye are all brethren." [35] But the explanation which to me seems most plausible and true as to why Christ said "Feed my sheep" to Peter in particular, is this, that because of Peter's steadfastness, Christ wanted to entrust to him in particular the care of the people of Israel, who were "a stiffnecked people" [36] toward God, as is said in Exodus, Chapter 33, and as the Apostle reiterates, quoting Isaiah in the last chapter of the Acts; [37] for the main purpose of Christ's coming had been the conversion and salvation of this people. Hence in Matthew, Chapter 15, it is written: "I am not sent but unto the lost sheep of the house of Israel." [38] That is, "I am not sent but" mainly—this qualification should be added. And this seems to have been the reason why the care of the people of Israel was entrusted to St. Peter in particular, when Christ said to him, "Feed my sheep." This clearly seems to have been the view of the Apostle, when he said: "When they saw that the gospel of the uncircumcision was committed unto me, as the gospel of the circumcision was unto Peter," [39] etc. Whereon the gloss according to St. Augustine writes: "'When they saw that the gospel of the uncircumcision was committed unto me,' as a believer, with as great primacy by the Lord 'as the gospel of the circumcision was unto Peter,' etc. For Christ entrusted to Paul the ministry of the Gentiles, just as he had entrusted to Peter the ministry of the Jews. But this dispensation was given them in such a way that Peter might preach to the Gentiles, if there was a reason, and Paul to the

---

[35] Matthew 23:8.
[36] Exodus 33:5.
[37] Acts 28: 25–28.
[38] Matthew 15:24.
[39] Galatians 2:7.

Jews." [40] Now I do not see from what words of Christ, other than "Feed my sheep," it could have been assumed by Paul or by any other saint that the care of the Jewish people had been particularly and primarily entrusted to Peter; for in Galatians, Chapter 2, Paul says that "the gospel of the uncircumcision was committed unto" him, "as the gospel of the circumcision was unto Peter." For if the gospel of the whole world had been committed to Peter more than to Paul or the other apostles, then it would have been improper for Paul to have written the above words; indeed, that entire statement of his, with the division expressed by him therein, would have been invalid.

The glosses or interpretations of the saints and other doctors on these three points of Scripture will be answered by us at the end of this chapter, in order that we may not have to reiterate the same assertions too often. [41]

10. [x] As for the statement of the Apostle in Galatians, Chapter 2, which seemed to indicate that he was inferior to the apostle Peter in authority, because he said: "I communicated unto them that gospel which I preach among the Gentiles, . . . lest by any means I should run, or had run, in vain," [42] reply must first be made in accordance with Augustine's gloss on this passage. For Augustine writes: "I did not learn from them as from greater men, but I 'communicated unto them' as friends and equals." [43] But our opponent cites Jerome's gloss on the words, "lest by any means I should run," etc., for Jerome here writes that "Paul shows that he would not have had the care of the gospel had it not been confirmed by the authority of Peter and corroborated by the others." [44] To this, however, I respectfully reply that either Jerome contradicts himself by what he writes below in the gloss, if his words are understood in the way our opponent seems to intend them; or else Jerome's gloss must be understood in accordance with the remarks of Augustine. For Paul communicated with the other apostles not because he was not sure that he was, or would be, entrusted with the gospel, but rather because he wanted his hearers to believe him more readily, which they would do if he told them that he had communicated with the apostles who had been with Christ, for their testimony was more acceptable to his hearers. And therefore his words, "lest by any means I should run, or had run, in vain," should not be interpreted as indicating any personal inadequacy on the part of the Apostle, or any doubts on his part with regard to the gospel, for he "neither received it of man, nor was [he] taught it, but by the revelation" [45]

[40] Peter Lombard *Collectanea* (PL 192. 108).

[41] The refutation of arguments (viii) and (ix) is thus postponed to paras. 28 and 29 of this chapter.

[42] See above, II. xvii. 3.

[44] *Ibid.*

[43] Peter Lombard *Collectanea* (PL 192. 103).

[45] Galatians 1:1, 11-12.

directly of God, as he himself says in Galatians, Chapter 1. Moreover, the Apostle wrote as follows in Galatians, Chapter 2, in reviewing that communication which he had with the other apostles: "But of these who seemed to be somewhat, they added nothing to me, but contrariwise." [46] Whereon the gloss according to Augustine:

> The Apostle in this passage, "these who seemed," etc., writes as if to say: I do not appeal to the earlier apostles, because I am sufficiently recommended by what has already taken place, so that those "who seemed to be somewhat," namely, Peter and the others who had been with the Lord, "added," that is, imparted, "nothing to me." Wherein it is clear that they are not superior to me, who have been made perfect by the Lord, so that there was nothing which they added to my perfection. For he who gave understanding to the three inexperienced men, gave it also to me.[47]

And a little below, the gloss according to Jerome writes as follows: "They 'added nothing to me,' but I 'added' to Peter." And further: " 'I opposed him,' as an equal. For Paul would not have dared do this unless he had known he was not unequal." [48] And therefore the words "lest by any means I should run, or had run in vain," should be understood as referring to the Apostle's listeners, who perhaps might not have believed him, or might not have believed him completely, and hence would have remained devoid of faith; and he similarly would have been devoid of success with regard to them, that is, his plans regarding those who heard him would have been frustrated, for he would not have aroused in them the faith which he intended by his preaching to arouse. This too is what the gloss according to Augustine says, further below:

> For if the apostle Paul, having been called upon from heaven after Christ's ascension, had not conferred with the apostles and communicated unto them the gospel, which showed that he was of the same company as they, then the church would not have believed him completely. But when the church saw that Paul was preaching the same gospel as the other apostles, and was living in their company and unity, and that through him the same sort of signs were being advanced as the others used, so that he was deserving of authority because he was commended by the Lord, then the church listened to his words, just as if it were Christ, as he most truly said, who was heard speaking in him.[49]

Paul, then, "was deserving of authority" simply because he was commended or approved by Christ; but Augustine did not write that Paul deserved his authority because he was commended by Peter or the other apostles. And a little below, Augustine's gloss adds: "And so he 'communicated unto them the gospel' and received 'the right hands of fellow-

[46] Galatians 2:6–7.
[48] Ibid. (PL 192. 108).
[47] Peter Lombard Collectanea (PL 192. 107).
[49] Ibid. (PL 192. 103).

ship,' because he had the same word as they, although he did not have it through them. For that communication with the apostles showed one uniform doctrine, from which all unsound divergences had been expunged." [50] This, then, was the purpose of that communication: to remove their listeners' doubts regarding doctrinal divergences. And this is what Augustine's gloss had said, previously:

"I went up again to Jerusalem," etc., writes Paul. "I went up with Barnabas," who was of the Jews, "and took with me also Titus," who was of the Gentiles; as if to say, I thus had with me two witnesses who could disprove the charge that I was preaching one doctrine to the Gentiles, and another to the Jews. "And I went up," not merely by my own inclination, but "by revelation" of God, and I was not taught by the other apostles as by greater men, but "I communicated unto them" as friends and equals "that gospel" of Christ "which I preach among the Gentiles." And the Apostle did this in order to fortify his preaching, because many persons, perturbed by the Jews, had doubts regarding the doctrine taught by him. [51]

These were the doubts which God wished to remove, and therefore it was not by human deliberation, but rather by revelation of God, that the Apostle said he had "gone up to communicate unto them" the gospel; not because the Apostle had any doubts regarding the gospel, but in order to remove from his listeners the aforesaid doubts.

11. To the statement of the glossator on Galatians, Chapter 2, that Paul the pastor was posterior to St. Peter the apostle, [52] it must be replied that the glossator's statement was correct, inasmuch as St. Paul was called to the apostolate at a later time than was St. Peter, and therefore he was posterior to him in time, but not on that account inferior in authority, nor did the gloss make this latter assertion, but rather the opposite.

From the above, therefore, it is clear that neither Peter nor any other apostle was greater than Paul, but rather they were all friends and equal in authority bestowed upon them immediately by Christ. If there was any priority of authority among them, this must have come through their own election perhaps, or else it must have been of the kind which we said, in Chapter XVI of this discourse, that St. Peter had over the other apostles.

12. [xi] We come now to the statement of Isidore's *Codex*, in the chapter entitled, "Preface of the Nicene Council," where it says: "All catholics must well know that the holy Roman church was not given the leadership through any synodic decrees, but that rather it obtained the primacy through the evangelic voice of our Lord and Savior," [53] understanding this to apply to the Roman bishop as well as to the Roman church. But we must

---

[50] *Ibid.* (PL 192. 104).   [51] *Ibid.* (PL 192. 103).
[52] See above, II. xxvii. 3.   [53] See above, II. xxvii. 3.

deny this assertion, whether it is made by Isidore or by any other extra-canonic authority. For the Roman church was made leader of the others through the decrees of the Roman rulers and by the consent of the other churches, amounting almost to an election arranged in the way described by us in Chapters XVIII and XXII of this discourse. Moreover, Isidore's inference does not follow from the canonic authority which he adduces, but rather, whether it be drawn by Isidore or by anyone else, that inference can be refuted through what we have said in Chapter XV of this discourse, paragraph 8, and in Chapter XVI, paragraphs 13 and 14. As for their attempt to support this inference through Matthew, Chapter 16: "Thou art Peter, and upon this rock," etc., we have already made clear the weakness of this position of Isidore in Chapter XXII of this discourse.

13. [*xii*] As for the argument that there is one church and one head bishop because of the unity of the faith, in accordance with what the Apostle writes in Ephesians, Chapter 4,[54] it must be replied that if we take "church" in its proper meaning, as standing for the multitude of the believers, then the church is one in the same way that the faith is one. And since the faith is not one in number in all believers, but rather is one in species or genus,[55] the argument does not prove that the church is one in any different way. And when it is added that the church is one only through the numerical unity of some bishop who is superior to the others, I deny this; and even if I were to grant it, I would deny the other inference which sought to prove that the Roman bishop has been made such head or leader of the church immediately through divine ordainment. For not Peter the apostle but rather Christ was the rock on which the church was built, as we have shown above in this chapter as well as in Chapter XVI of this discourse through Scripture. Moreover, the Roman bishop is not by God's immediate ordainment the particular successor of St. Peter or of any other apostle in such a way that superior authority over the other bishops belongs to him because of this, as we have shown above; but rather, if he does have any such special authority, it belongs to him through human appointment or election, as we have sufficiently shown in Chapter XXII of this discourse.

14. [*xiii*] As for the additional argument in confirmation of this, that there must be one bishop or bishopric as leader of spiritual affairs, just as there must be one primary ruler or government of all temporal affairs,[56] this analogy can be denied, because the numerical unity of the primary

---

[54] See above, II. xxvii. 4.
[55] See Thomas Aquinas *Summa theologica* II. II. qu.4. a.6. Resp. See also Vol. I, pp. 274–75.
[56] See above, II. xxvii. 4. On the reply, see Vol. I, p. 275.

ruler or government is necessary on account of men's contentious acts, as was demonstrated in Chapter XVII of Discourse I. But this unity is not necessary in any of the other offices of the city or state. Moreover, even if we grant the analogy with regard to the similarity or proportion which it initially assumes, yet to the added assertion, that the primary ruler or government is one, we can reply that this is true by human establishment, and not by any ordainment or decree made immediately by God or divine law. It was in this way, also, that we concluded in Chapter XXII of this discourse that it is expedient to establish, by a definite procedure and for a definite function, some one bishop and one church as head and leader of all the others.

15. [*xiv*] As for the other argument, that just as in a single temple there is a single bishop, so must it be in the entire world of the believers,[57] it must be replied first of all that it is neither necessary for salvation nor commanded by divine law that there be a single bishop in a single church; indeed, there could be many bishops, as we showed in Chapter XV of this discourse from the Acts, Chapter 20, and from many other passages by the Apostle, as well as from Jerome's epistle to Evander. And as for the practice in later times, whereby in a single temple or diocese there was appointed a single bishop by putting him antonomastically at the head of the household of the temple, this was directly of human establishment, and not, as we have said, a necessity imposed by divine law. But even if it were a necessity imposed by divine law, the analogy would still not hold. For the necessity that there be a single head in a single household is not the same as the necessity that there be a single head in a whole state or in several provinces, because those who are not members of the same familial household do not need the numerical unity of a single family head, since they do not mutually share with one another the food and other necessities of life (house, bed, and so on), nor do they associate with one another in such unity as do those who are members of the same familial household.[58] For our opponent's reasoning would conclude that it is equally necessary that there be a numerically single head in the entire world, which is neither expedient nor true. For in order that men may live together in peace, it is sufficient that there be a numerically single government in each province, as we have said in Chapter XVII of Discourse I.[59] But that it is necessary for eternal salvation that there be one coercive judge over all men does not yet seem to have been demonstrated, although this seems more necessary for the believers than that there be one

---

[57] See above, II. xxvii. 4.   [58] Cf. above, I. iii. 4; also Aristotle *Politics* II. 2. 1261a 15 ff.
[59] See above, I. xvii. 10; and Vol. I, pp. 128–29.

universal bishop, because a universal ruler can better preserve the believers in unity than can a universal bishop. For in ancient times the rulers used to coerce schismatics in order to preserve the unity of the faith, as has been shown in Chapter XXI of this discourse; but such compulsion could not have been exercised by the bishops, because they lacked coercive authority, which does not belong to them as such, as has been demonstrated in Chapter XV of Discourse I, and as has been more fully confirmed through Scripture and the authority of saints, as well as by rational arguments, in Chapters IV, V, VIII, IX, and X of this discourse. But what is the meaning of the numerical unity and leadership of a bishop and church or clerical college, and in what way it is expedient that this unified leadership be established, we have shown in Chapter XXII of this discourse, although, as we have said, no determinate priest or college is designated for this leadership by divine law, but rather such designation has be_n made by human election or appointment, as we have truthfully and clearly shown in Chapter XXII of this discourse.

16. [xv] As for the quotation from John, Chapter 10, "And there shall be one fold and one shepherd," [60] it must be replied that Christ was here speaking of himself. For he alone was the universal shepherd and leader of shepherds, and no one else after him; just as he alone was the head and foundation of the church, as we showed in Chapter XVI of this discourse, and repeated in many other places. And this was the open and literal view of St. Peter; for in his first canonic epistle, Chapter 5, he said: "And when the chief Shepherd," speaking of Christ, "shall appear, ye shall receive a crown of glory that fadeth not away." [61] This view was also held by the saints who wrote on this passage. For the gloss according to Gregory says: "From two flocks he makes one fold by joining together the Jews and the Gentiles in his faith." [62] See, then, how the flock is made one: they are joined in the unity of the faith. But Gregory does not say that the flock is made one because all the believers are placed under the Roman bishop or any other single individual except Christ. Moreover, the gloss according to Theophylact says: "For all have the same baptismal mark, one pastor, the word of God. Let the Manicheans therefore take heed, for there is one flock and one pastor of the New and the Old Testament." [63] Never was Peter or Paul or any other apostle named as the maker of this unity of the flock; but the only maker thereof is the unity of the faith and the person of Christ, who alone is the head and

[60] See above, II. xxvii. 4.   [61] I Peter 5:4.
[62] Thomas Aquinas Catena aurea on John 10:16 (XII, 374).
[63] Ibid.

foundation of the church and the leader of all the shepherds by God's immediate ordainment, as we have said above and as we have with certainty shown in Chapter XVI of this discourse.

17. [*xvi*] As for the other inference whereby it was concluded that the Roman bishop, either alone or together with his clerical college, is the primary efficient cause of the secondary appointment of all other church ministers, and has the power to assign or designate them to their temples, either directly or indirectly or in both ways,[64] I reply by denying this. And when it is confirmed by citing Ambrose, in his treatise *On Handing Over the Basilica,* where he writes that "Caesar cannot have the right" to appoint priests to temples or churches, because "the church is God's," it must be replied that the reason why Ambrose said this was because it was not safe in those days to allow the Roman rulers to bestow such offices, namely, cures of souls, inasmuch as those rulers were not yet sufficiently confirmed in faith; indeed, some of them sometimes favored heretical priests over true believers, as did that same emperor Valentinian to whom Ambrose addressed his epistle. But after the faith had taken root and become strong, both in subjects and in rulers, and the whole community was thus faithful, it was safer, more useful, and more in conformity with divine law for the bishops and others with the cure of souls to be elected or appointed by the authority of the whole body of the believers rather than by a single partial group of the state or community, or by only one man's will, which almost daily we see being easily perverted by bribery, entreaty, love, hate, or some other vicious emotion. And therefore we agree with Ambrose in this, that the right to appoint men with the cure of souls, bishops or priests and the other temple ministers, belongs not to Caesar in his own person nor to any other individual, but rather to the whole body of the believers or to the person or persons to whom the whole body of the believers has freely given such authority. Nor did Ambrose himself deny this. Hence he often appealed against the emperors to the faithful people by whom he himself had been elected bishop in the way described by us in Chapter XVII of this discourse. Nor did he say that this authority belonged to the Roman or any other pontiff, but rather, for the reason given above, he said that the church or temple belongs only to God and to the multitude of believers as being the church in its principal and primary sense, whose head is Christ; and to this church "Caesar cannot have a right," that is, rightful possession. For all temporal things, whatsoever they be, can be the possession of Caesar, whether Christian or infidel.[65] But the temple, or the appointment of

[64] See above, II. xxvii. 5.
[65] See *Corp. jur. civ., Codex Justinianus* VII. xxxvii. 3. Also Vol. I, p. 114, esp. n. 144.

priests therein, pertains only to the authority of the multitude of the believers, as has been shown in Chapter XVII of this discourse; nor did Ambrose say or think the opposite of this. A sign of this was given by Ambrose in his first epistle to Valentinian when he said that the only reason why he had engaged in dispute, as shepherd of the believers, had been in order to prevent the flock of believers from being entrusted to the supervision of a bad or heretical priest. For Ambrose wrote: "Would that I might clearly see that the church was not being handed over to the Arians! I would freely offer myself to the will of your piety." [66] And he clearly demonstrates that his meaning with regard to handing over the basilica must have been such as we have said it to be here and in Chapter XVII of this discourse. For if the basilica in a community of believers were held by a heretical bishop or priest who was unwilling to give it up, it is clear that he could justly be compelled to do so by the coercive judge using armed force in accordance with the human laws. But this coercive judgment and force belong to the authority of no priest, as the same Ambrose truly attests in his epistle entitled *To the People*. For he writes: "Against Goths and soldiers, my tears are my weapons; for such are the munitions of the priest; in any other way I neither can nor should resist"; [67] and of course this proposition has been demonstrated in Chapters XV and XVII of Discourse I, and has been confirmed by the authority of Scripture and the saints, as well as by other proofs, in Chapters IV, V, VIII, and X of this discourse. And therefore Ambrose's meaning must soundly be held to have been such as we have said, for the Apostle also appealed to Caesar, as we have shown above from Acts, Chapter 25. Hence, either this position must be taken in communities of believers, or else individuals must be permitted to teach what they wish concerning the faith, as Hilary seems to have thought in his epistle to Constantius.[68] Thus, therefore, it seems that to the whole body of the believers, or to the ruler in accordance with its ordainment, belongs the authority to hand over the basilica or temples and to appoint priests therein. And this is what is done in certain churches by the catholic kings of France, who recognize no priest or bishop from whom they derive this authority. And we believe that this, too, was and must have been the meaning of Ambrose; but if his view was contrary to this one which we know and believe to be the meaning of the canon, then we depart from his opinion (which we are not compelled to believe in order to attain salvation, since his writings are not canonic), and, adhering to

[66] St. Ambrose Epist. 21. 19 (PL 16. 1049).
[67] St. Ambrose *Sermo contra Auxentium* cap. ii (PL 16. 1050).
[68] See above, II. ix. 5; also Vol. I, p. 166.

the canonic Scriptures, we uphold the view which we have stated as the true one.

18. [*xvii*] As for the inference which seemed to be drawn from the same epistle of Ambrose, that the supreme jurisdiction over ecclesiastic temporal goods which are bestowed on gospel ministers for the exercise of their offices pertains to the Roman bishop directly by divine authority,[69] it is clear from the foregoing that this inference is invalid, as we have also sufficiently proved in Chapter XVII of this discourse, and as Ambrose also confirms in his afore-mentioned epistle *On Handing Over the Basilica*, where he writes as follows: "If he," the emperor, "demands tribute, we do not deny it. The fields of the church pay tribute. If the emperor desires the fields, he has the power to claim them; no one of us intervenes. What the people bestow can redound to the poor. Let there be no ill-will over the fields; let him take them if such is his pleasure; I do not give them to the emperor, but neither do I deny them." [70] But he who always seeks to defend the fields will perhaps object to this, saying that these fields are "rights of Christ's bride," little caring about defending the true bride, that is, the catholic faith, as the king and kingdom of Armenia can manifestly testify; [71] and he will also say that St. Ambrose made the above statement not because the fields of the church rightfully owe tribute, but because the emperors exact tribute from the fields by force and oppression. It is this obviously false interpretation of Ambrose's words which is frequently used by some Roman bishops and their accomplices in order to avoid and escape the coercive jurisdiction of the rulers, for these bishops assert that it is in fact (*de facto*) by violence, and not by right (*jure*), that they are brought to the judgment of secular rulers. But the opposite of this was stated by Christ in John, Chapter 19, which we quoted above in Chapter IV of this discourse; [72] and this view, which is the one we hold in accordance with the canon, was set forth by Ambrose when he wrote: "We pay to Caesar the things that are Caesar's, and to God the things that are God's. The tribute is Caesar's, it is not denied. The church is God's, and it ought not to be ascribed to Caesar," but rather (one should add) it ought to be ascribed to the faithful priest in accordance with the judgment of the faithful multitude, as we have said above and as we have clearly confirmed in Chapter XVII of this discourse. Therefore, the tribute and jurisdiction over

---

[69] See above, ii. xxvii. 6.

[70] St. Ambrose *Sermo contra Auxentium* cap. xxxiii (PL 16. 1060–61).

[71] This refers to John XXII. See above, ii. xxvi. 2. Oshin and Leo V, kings of Little Armenia (Cilicia), had made vain appeals to John XXII for help against the attacks of the Moslems. In 1337 John did give subsidies, but to no avail.

[72] See above, p. 123.

ecclesiastic temporal goods belong to the ruler not through force, but by right.

19. As for the other inference whereby it seemed to be concluded that every clerical college is subject to the coercive jurisdiction of the Roman bishop, because he is the ruler of all by divine ordainment,[73] the antecedent must be denied. For we have shown above that no bishop or priest is by God's immediate ordainment, or by divine law, subject or inferior to the Roman bishop in any authority which essentially or accidentally belongs to a priest. [xviii] And as for the words of Constantine which are quoted from Isidore's *Codex*,[74] it must be replied that they were words of exhortation and admonition, whereby the devout Constantine showed what qualities bishops and priests ought to have. For they ought to act in such a way toward one another and toward others that they would not have to quarrel and appeal to secular judgment, just as the Apostle teaches in I Corinthians, Chapter 6, where he says: "Why do ye not rather take wrong? why do ye not rather suffer yourselves to be defrauded?" rather than "to go to law with one another?"[75] And as for Constantine's added statement, that "God gave you the power to judge us," etc., it must be replied that this statement is true if by "judge" it means the first sense of judgment, coercive of no one in this world, which we have sufficiently discussed in Chapters VI, VII, VIII, and IX of this discourse. But from the afore-mentioned words quoted by Isidore, regardless of whether or not they were spoken by Constantine, it does not follow that the other bishops are subject in jurisdiction to the Roman bishop. For Constantine said: "You must expect God alone to judge you, and your quarrels, whatever they be, must be reserved for the divine scrutiny"; he did not say, for the judgment or scrutiny of the Roman pontiff.

As for the added assertion that the Roman bishop is God's representative on earth,[76] it must be replied that the Roman bishop is immediately by divine ordainment no more God's representative than is any other bishop, as we have often stated and proved above. And even if the Roman bishop were God's representative on earth in respect of spiritual teaching and ministry, it would not follow that he is God's representative in respect of coercive judgment over any clergyman or layman, as we have shown above in Chapters IV and V of this discourse and in many other places; but in coercive judgment it is the rulers who are the ministers of God, as the Apostle Paul said in Romans, Chapter 13, and as St. Peter wrote in his first canonic epistle, Chapter 2.[77]

---

[73] See above, II. xxvii. 7.   [74] See above, p. 368.   [75] I Corinthians 6:7.
[76] See St. Bernard, above, II. xxvii. 11.   [77] Romans 13: 1–7; I Peter 2:13–15.

Moreover, even if Constantine had openly asserted that the Roman bishop is God's representative in respect of coercive judgment, I would deny his assertion, because it is neither canonic nor a consequence of a canonic statement. But if Constantine had decreed this by way of an edict, then it would be expedient to observe it like the other human laws, but not as having been decreed by immediate ordainment of God. However, from that very passage of Isidore's *Codex* it is clearly to be seen that all the bishops are subject in coercive jurisdiction to the Roman ruler. For freely, and not under compulsion, the bishops brought their quarrels and disputes to be judged not by the Roman pontiff but by the Roman ruler, requesting that he examine and judge them, as Isidore narrates in the above-cited passage.

20. And when it is further inferred from the same antecedents that to the Roman bishop, either alone or together with his priestly college, belongs the authority to convoke general councils of priests and other believers, and therein to make the ordinances which we have discussed above, this inference must be denied together with its antecedent. For the opposite both of the antecedent and of the consequent in this inference has been demonstrated in Chapters XVI and XXI of this discourse. [*xix, xx*] As for the supporting arguments based on the authority or opinion of Isidore [78] (for the arguments do not undergo interpretation, inasmuch as it was Isidore himself who expressed this opinion), I deny all of them as being inconsistent with the sacred canon and with demonstration grounded therein, as we have clearly and lengthily proved in Chapters XX, XXI, and XXII of this discourse, and as we have also shown from the documents cited by Isidore himself in the *Codex*.

[*xxi*] As for the words of Jerome in the *Exposition of the Catholic Faith,* where he says to the Roman bishop, "We desire to be corrected by you, who hold the faith and the seat of Peter," in which words Jerome seems to affirm that the Roman bishop is St. Peter's particular successor,[79] it must be replied that the reason why Jerome said that the Roman bishop "holds the faith and the seat of Peter" was because St. Peter is recorded to have been in charge of the Roman church as bishop; and inasmuch as this church is the head of the others by human statute, Jerome calls this church and its bishop the successor of the most worthy or eminent apostle, although by God's immediate ordainment the Roman bishop neither is nor was superior to the others with respect to any authority bestowed immediately by Christ, as we have shown above and have fully proved in Chapter XVI of this discourse.

[78] See above, II. xxvii. 8, 9.   [79] See above, II. xxvii. 9.

And as for Jerome's added words, "If this confession of ours is approved by your apostolic judgment," etc., wherein Jerome seems to affirm that only the Roman pontiff has the authority to define and determine doubtful senses of divine law, even in the articles of faith, it must be replied that this was not Jerome's meaning, but the reason why he wrote these words was rather because the Roman bishop had to answer questions concerning the definitions or decisions which the general council had made with regard to the catholic faith and church ritual. For it was for the performance of this function that the Roman bishop and his church had been appointed head or leader of the others, in the way stated by us in Chapter XXII of this discourse. And a proof that Jerome's meaning was such as we have said is given in his epistle to Evander where, condemning certain practices of the Roman church with regard to deacons, he explicitly said: "If authority be in question, the whole world is greater than the city," [80] that is, the authority of all the churches in the world is greater than the authority of the church of the city of Rome. Therefore, it is only by that authority which is the greatest and most certain of all that doubts concerning the faith ought to be settled, as has been shown in Chapter XX of this discourse. Thus too the same Jerome in the *Exposition of the Catholic Faith* plainly follows the interpretations approved by the general councils, and shuns and condemns those which the general councils have condemned. But if, on the other hand, Jerome had thought that the Roman bishop alone has the authority to define doubtful senses of Scripture, then I shun his view as being neither canonic nor a necessary consequence of a canonic statement. For, as we have stated and proved above (and it bears repeating), neither St. Peter nor any other apostle assumed for himself alone the authority or power to settle doubtful questions concerning the faith; but for this purpose "the apostles and elders came together," [81] as is explicitly said in the Acts, Chapter 15.

21. [*xxii*] As for the quotation from Luke, Chapter 10, "He that heareth you heareth me," etc.,[82] it must be replied that these words are true, for by "ye " is meant the general council, which alone represents Christ, the maker of the eternal law, or the congregation of the apostles and their church. And again these words are true if we interpret "you" distributively, as meaning those persons who speak in accordance with divine law and do not indulge in unjust blasphemies. It was in this sense that Christ said of the Pharisees: "Whatsoever" they say, "that observe and do," meaning whatsoever they say in accordance with divine law, as Jerome writes in

---

[80] See above, II. xv. 8. St. Jerome Epist. 146, *Ad Evangelum* (PL. 22. 1194).
[81] Acts 15:6.   [82] See above, II. xxvii. 10.

his commentary on these words of Christ in Matthew, Chapter 23.[83] Or else the passage, "He that heareth you," etc., must be interpreted to mean that he that hears commands or prohibitions of divine law is obliged to obey them; but he that hears counsels, such as the one relating to fasting, is not obliged to obey them unless there intervenes the consent of all the believers or of the weightier part of them in the general council.

22. [*xxiii*] Now we shall discuss the statements which Bernard makes in his treatise addressed to Eugene, *On Consideration*, Book II.[84] And first, as for Bernard's question, "Who are you?" and his own answer, "A great priest, the supreme pontiff," it must be replied that Bernard's answer must be denied, if he meant that Eugene was the supreme pontiff by immediate ordainment of God or by command of divine law, for such a view would be neither consistent with the sacred canon nor a necessary consequence thereof, as we have shown in Chapters XVI and XXII of this discourse. But on the other hand, Bernard's reply must be upheld if he meant that this primacy belongs to the pontiff by human election or appointment in the way stated in Chapter XXII of this discourse. And as for Bernard's additional statement, "You are the ruler (*princeps*) of the bishops," this is true if we take "ruler" in its broad sense, as meaning that the pontiff has been made the foremost of the bishops in the aforesaid way, by human appointment. But Bernard's statement must be denied if the word "ruler" is taken in its strict sense, for even Bernard himself denies that Pope Eugene, and consequently any other bishop, has rulership (*principatum*), as he writes in the same treatise addressed to Eugene, Book I, Chapter V, from which we have quoted above in Chapter V of this discourse.[85] And as for what Bernard says further, "You are the heir of the apostles," so too are the other bishops, although the Roman bishop is the foremost heir, in the way stated by us in Chapters XVI and XXII of this discourse. "In primacy you are Abel"—it is true that the Roman bishop was given the primacy, but this was by human election, either directly, or indirectly out of reverence for him who was the first of the apostles in point of time. "In directorship Noah"—it is true that he is, by human appointment, among clergymen and over clergymen. "In patriarchate Abraham"—it is true that the Roman pontiff is the father of all spiritual fathers, but only in spiritual ministry, and only by human appointment. "In rank Melchisedech"—this is true with respect to priesthood, in which Melchisedech foreshadowed Christ, although in this regard all other priests are also "in rank Melchisedech"; but the Roman pontiff is not "in rank Melchisedech" with respect to kingship, for in this regard Melchisedech, who was at once

[83] See above, II. v. 6.   [84] See above, II. xxvii. 11.   [85] See above, II. v. 2, 3.

priest and king, foreshadowed only Christ, and not any other priest. But on the other hand, neither did Melchisedech foreshadow Christ with respect to earthly kingship, for Christ did not come for the purpose of exercising such kingship, nor did he wish to do so, as we have shown in Chapter IV of this discourse; but it was Christ's priesthood and heavenly, not earthly, kingship, that Melchisedech, who was at once priest and earthly king, foreshadowed. And still less did Melchisedech foreshadow earthly rulership in some priest or bishop; for Bernard in his treatise most explicitly denies such rule to the Roman bishop. Nor did Melchisedech prefigure anyone other than Christ with respect to priestly primacy; but such primacy, as we have said, is held by others only through human appointment. "In dignity Aaron"—it is true that the Roman bishop is like Aaron in holding the primacy among priests, but there is also a difference, as we have said, in that Aaron held his primacy through immediate appointment by God, but this is not the case with the Roman or any other bishop who succeeded the apostles. "In authority Moses"—the very opposite of this was clearly stated by Bernard earlier in his treatise *On Consideration*, Book I, Chapter V, and also in Book III, Chapter I.[86] For Moses was ruler in accordance with coercive law, as is apparent from the Acts, Chapter 7; but in the afore-mentioned places Bernard denied that any successor of the apostles was such a ruler. Moreover, Moses was ruler by immediate ordainment of God, and over all of Israel; but the Roman bishop holds his primacy directly by human grant alone, and only over gospel or temple ministers. "In judgeship Samuel"—it is true that the Roman bishop is a judge like Samuel, but there is a double difference: first, the Roman bishop does not have his judgeship by immediate ordainment of God, as did Samuel; and second, the Roman bishop is judge only over priests and lower gospel ministers, while Samuel was judge over all the people of Israel without any differentiation. "In power Peter"—it is true that he is, in essential power, through immediate action of God, and so too is every other bishop or priest. But his primacy over the other bishops and priests is directly obtained in only one way by any Roman bishop, namely, by human appointment; and this is so regardless of whether St. Peter held this primacy through direct appointment by God or whether it was not in this way but rather through election by the other apostles, as we believe in accordance with Scripture, and as has been shown in Chapter XVI of this discourse (assuming, of course, that even such primacy was held by Peter). "In unction Christ"—this is true, if it means the unction of grace or of the Holy Spirit, which is given with the priestly character, and which every

[86] St. Bernard *De consideratione* I. vi; III. i. (PL 182. 735 ff., 757-60).

priest receives. But on the other hand, if by unction is meant primacy over
the whole church by immediate appointment of God, not of man—such
primacy as Christ alone had over all priests—then I deny his statement because the Apostle says the opposite in many passages of Scripture, as has
been shown in Chapter XVI of this discourse.

As for Bernard's added statement, "You are the one universal shepherd,
not only of the sheep, but also of the shepherds," if Bernard meant that
the Roman bishop's pastorate was derived directly through human appointment, I would grant his words; but if through ordainment of God or
through decree of divine law, as he seems to intend, then I deny his statement, because it is neither canonic nor a necessary deduction from the
canon, but rather the opposite. And as for his attempt to base this assertion
upon the canon, when he writes: "How do I prove this, you ask? By the
word of the Lord: 'If you love me, Peter, feed my sheep.' For to which, I
will not say of the bishops, but even of the apostles, were all the sheep entrusted so absolutely and without differentiation? Is it not clear that Christ
designated, not some particular sheep, but all sheep, without qualification?
For where no distinctions are made, no exceptions are made"—to this it
must be replied, always respectfully, that one must indeed marvel at this
question of Bernard's whereby he asks "to which of the apostles" (he does
not merely say of the bishops) "were the sheep entrusted so absolutely and
without differentiation?" To this question I answer that the sheep were
entrusted to all the apostles, collectively and distributively. How do I prove
this, you ask? By the word of the Lord, more clearly than does Bernard.
For in the last chapter of Matthew, these words, as the last of all the commands, were spoken by Christ to all the apostles: "Go ye therefore and
teach all nations," etc.[87] And I say that my proof is clearer than Bernard's,
because in John, Chapter 21, when Christ said, "Feed my sheep," he did
not add the word "all." But it is certain that he comprehended more sheep
when he handed over all of them universally, than when he merely said,
indefinitely, "Feed my sheep." Consequently (we still speak respectfully)
it seems that the scriptural passage which Bernard cites is susceptible of a
different interpretation, more in harmony with Scripture. This interpretation is the one which we mentioned above in paragraph 9, and it bears repeating. For in Matthew, Chapter 15, we read that Christ said: "I am not
sent but unto the lost sheep of the house of Israel." [88] And this utterance,
according to the interpretation of the saints, must be understood to mean,
as Jerome writes, "Not that Christ was not sent also to the Gentiles, but
rather that he was sent primarily to Israel." [89] Further, Remigius writes,

[87] Matthew 28:19.   [88] Matthew 15:24.
[89] Thomas Aquinas *Catena aurea, ad loc.* (XI, 191).

more pertinently and with greater literal accuracy: "Particularly was Christ sent to save the Jews, in order that by his corporeal presence he might teach them." [90] Therefore, according to the interpretation of the saints, although Christ was sent for the salvation of all people, yet he was particularly and primarily sent for the salvation of the Jews, as is also borne out by his words according to Matthew, "I am not sent but unto the lost sheep of the house of Israel." Therefore, the care of these sheep, from among the others, he appropriated to himself when he said, "the lost sheep of the house of Israel." And since this people was always "stiffnecked" as is shown in Exodus, Chapter 32,[91] as well as a killer of prophets, as the Truth itself stated in Luke, Chapter 13,[92] and since, furthermore, Christ knew that Peter was most steadfast in faith and most fervent in love of God and of his neighbor, Christ recommended the sheep of Israel in particular to Peter's care, when he said, "If you love me, feed my sheep," that is, take particular pains to teach the people of Israel. And a proof that this is true is given in Galatians, Chapter 2: "When they saw that the gospel of the uncircumcision was committed unto me, as the gospel of the circumcision was unto Peter," etc.; and [93] the Apostle's statement could be confirmed by other passages of the gospel. And again: "They gave to me and Barnabas the right hands of fellowship, that we should go unto the heathen, and they unto the circumcision," [94] that is, to the Jews. Therefore, by these words, "Feed my sheep," Christ did not entrust to St. Peter a more general cure, but rather a more particular one over a particular people. For there can be no more general cure than that which he gave to all the apostles, when he said, in the last chapter of Matthew and in John, Chapter 20: "Go ye therefore, and teach all nations," etc., and "Receive ye the Holy Ghost, and whosesoever sins ye remit, they are remitted unto them," etc.[95] For by these words, all the apostles received the pastoral authority and cure, and over all people alike, just as Augustine said in the ninety-fourth of the *Questions on the New Testament,* from which we quoted above in Chapter XVI of this discourse.[96] And then again (let Bernard answer), what more general cure did Christ entrust to anyone than the one to Paul, when he said, in Acts, Chapter 9: "He is a chosen vessel unto me, to bear my name before the Gentiles, and kings, and the children of Israel"? [97]

And as for Bernard's further statement, that "to each of the other apostles

---

[90] *Ibid.* [91] Exodus 32:9. [92] Luke 13:34.
[93] Reading, with Bigongiari (p. 43), *et* for *nec.* [94] Galatians 2:7, 9.
[95] John 20:22–23.
[96] St. Augustine *Quaestiones veteris et novi testamenti* qu.95 (PL 35. 2292). See above, II. xvi. 8.
[97] Acts 9:15.

was allotted a single flock," this is clearly not in harmony with Scripture; Paul's epistles do not bear it out, nor can it be proved from Scripture, but rather the opposite, as we showed above. And as for the additional assertion, that "according to your canons, the others have been called 'to take care of a part,' [while you have been called to 'plenitude of power,']" if it was meant that such guardianship had been bestowed by direct designation of God, then I deny these statements, both those written by Eugene and those of Bernard agreeing therewith; for no writings are or ought to be called canonic except such as we said in Chapter XIX of this discourse, and moreover, the opposite of these statements has been repeatedly proved by us through Scripture. But if, on the other hand, what was meant was that such plenary power had been bestowed directly by human appointment, in the way we said in Chapter XXII of this discourse, as a universal care of the churches, then we grant Bernard's statement.

And as for Bernard's still further words: "The power of the others is limited by certain restrictions, but yours extends even to those who have received power over others. Is it not in your power, for sufficient cause, to exclude a bishop from heaven . . . ?", it must be replied, as above, that by God's immediate ordainment the Roman or any bishop has no more authority over the others than the others have over him. For the Roman bishop, through authority immediately bestowed on him by Christ, can no more excommunicate or depose another bishop because of a crime, than the other can do so to him, as we have proved through Scripture and also reiterated above in Chapters XV and XVI of this discourse. But if Bernard means that this primacy is held directly by human grant, then in spiritual ministry and guidance the Roman bishop has over the other bishops such primacy as the general council has granted to him, and in temporal affairs such primacy over the others as the mortal legislator has granted to him.

And as for Bernard's final statement in this passage: "Your privilege, therefore, stands unshaken," etc., it must be replied that this is true, for the Roman bishop has the power to loose men from and bind them to sins, to teach them, and to minister the sacraments of the law of eternal salvation, and similarly every other bishop and priest has these powers by divine law. But if by "privilege" Bernard means some primacy over the other bishops which belongs to the Roman bishop by divine law or by immediate ordainment of God, then I decline, as above, to accept his views, for the aforementioned reasons.

23. [*xxiv*] As for the other passage from the same treatise of St. Bernard addressed to Eugene, Book IV, Chapter IV, where Bernard seems to affirm that to the Roman bishop belongs coercive jurisdiction, metaphorically

called the "temporal sword," not only over clergymen but also over laymen, when he writes: "And yet he who denies that this sword is yours, does
not sufficiently heed, it seems to me, the word of the Lord," etc., and then,
in conclusion: "Both swords, therefore, belong to the church, both the
spiritual and the material," etc.[98]—to this it must be replied, as much with
wonderment as with respectfulness, that Bernard himself made a statement in this connection which is clearly not in accord with, indeed it is
contrary to, the view expressed in the above passage; for immediately
above in the same chapter, discussing this authority or power, Bernard
wrote: "Why do you attempt to usurp the sword which you were ordered
to replace in its sheath?" But it is obvious that what a person usurps does
not pertain to his own authority.

24. But in reply to this criticism of ours, Bernard or someone interpreting
him will say, in accordance with his statement made at the end of the
above passage, that although the aforesaid authority belongs to the priest,
yet the execution of it must not be done by him, which execution he called
the drawing of the material sword.[99] However, this reply is not in harmony
with the meaning of Scripture. For Christ denied of himself not only this
drawing of the material sword, but also the judgment and command as
to its being drawn, when he said, in Luke, Chapter 12, to the man asking
him for such judgment, "Man, who made me a judge or a divider over
you?"[100] This utterance, together with certain others both of Christ and
of the apostles, is discussed by Bernard in his treatise addressed to Eugene,
On Consideration, Book I, Chapter V, from which we have quoted above
in Chapter V of this discourse; and this discussion of Bernard destroys that
interpretation of his above-cited statement which we have just mentioned.
For Bernard wrote to Pope Eugene: "Hear what the Apostle thinks" (and
it is written in I Corinthians, Chapter 6) "on such matters," namely, the
authority to judge temporal affairs.

"Is it so, that there is not a wise man among you," he says, "that shall be able
to judge between his brethren?" And he adds, "I speak to your shame. Set them
to judge who are the most despised in the church." And so, according to the
Apostle, you, a man of apostolic rank, usurp a lowly office, the rank of the
"most despised." [Note that he is speaking about the office, not about the execution thereof.] Hence too the bishop [Paul] instructed another bishop [Tim-
othy]: "No soldier of God entangleth himself with secular affairs." But I spare
you. For I do not wish to speak strongly, but to point out what is possible. Do

[98] See above, II. xxvii. 12.

[99] For this distinction between "authority" and "execution," see Egidius of Rome *De ecclesiastica potestate* III. v (p. 173); James of Viterbo *De regimine Christiano* II. x (ed. H. X.
Arquillière [Paris, 1926], p. 289). See also Vol. I, p. 233, incl. n. 48.

[100] Luke 12:14.

you think these times would continue if the men who fight over earthly heritage and ask you for judgment were answered by you with the words of the Lord: "O men, who has made me a judge over you?" What kind of judgment would soon be pronounced over you? Something like this: "What says this rustic, untutored man? You do not know your primacy, you dishonor your high, preeminent seat, you lower the apostolic dignity." And yet they who would say this will not, I think, show where any apostle ever sat as judge over men, or adjuster of boundaries, or distributor of lands. For I have read that the apostles stood to be judged themselves, but not that they sat to judge others. That will be in the future, it did not so happen in the past. Does the slave lower his dignity so greatly if he does not wish to be greater than his master, or the disciple if he does not wish to be greater than he who sent him, or the son if he does not transgress the bounds set by his father? "Who has made me judge?" asks the Master and Lord. And will the servant or disciple feel wronged unless he is able to judge the whole world?

Therefore, Bernard (or rather Christ and the apostles) removes from his successors, the priests and bishops, not only the execution of secular judgment, but also the office or authority of judging about such things. Hence Bernard adds below: "These lowly earthly affairs have their own judges, the kings and princes of the earth. Why do you invade foreign territory? Why do you extend your scythe to another's crop?" [101]

This view is again reiterated and confirmed by Bernard in Book II, Chapter IV (from which we have quoted above in Chapters V, XI, and XXVI of this discourse), where he makes the following pertinent remarks: "Not lordship?" that is, was not lordship left by Peter to his successors? "Hear him" (Peter).

"Neither as lording it over the clergy," he says, "but being made a pattern of the flock." And lest you think he spoke only from humility, but not with truth, the voice of the Lord is in the gospel: "The kings of the Gentiles lord it over them, and they that have power over them are called beneficent." And he adds, "But you not so." It is quite plain, then, that lordship is forbidden to the apostles. Go, then, if you dare, and usurp either the apostolate if you are a lord, or lordship if you are an apostle. You are plainly forbidden to have both [that is, both at once; and this is what Bernard himself adds]. If you wish to have both at once, you shall lose both. In any case, do not think you are excepted from the number of those about whom God complains in these words: "They have reigned, but not by me: they have been princes, and I knew not." [102]

The same view is also set forth by Bernard in his epistle to the archbishop of Sens, where he writes as follows: "This is what is done by these men," that is, the men who suggested disobedience.

101 St. Bernard De consideratione ii. vi (PL 182. 735). See above, ii. v. 2, 3.
102 Ibid. ii. vi (PL 182. 748). See above, ii. iv. 13; ii. xi. 7; ii. xxiv. 8.

But Christ ordered and acted otherwise. "Render," he said, "to Caesar the things that are Caesar's, and to God the things that are God's." What he spoke by word of mouth, he soon took care to carry out in deed. The institutor of Caesar did not hesitate to pay the tax to Caesar. For he thus gave you the example that you should do likewise. How, then, could he deny the reverence due to the priests of God, when he took care to show it even for the secular powers? [103]

Christ, therefore, wanted not to exercise temporal dominion over the rulers of this world, but rather to be subjected to them and to pay them due tribute and respect, so that he might furnish an example of such conduct to all his successors, first to the apostles, and then to the priests and bishops.

Expressing the same view even more explicitly, Bernard adds further:

Why, then, O monks, does the priestly authority trouble you? Do you fear harm? But if you suffer for the sake of justice, you will be blessed. Do you despise worldliness [that is, the rulers of this world]? But no one had a more worldly function than Pilate, before whom the Lord stood to be judged. "Thou shouldest not have any power over me," said the Lord, "unless it were given thee from above." He was already then saying and undergoing in his own case what he afterwards proclaimed in the churches through the apostles: "for there is no power but of God," and "whosoever resisteth the power resisteth the ordinance of God." So go now, if you dare, and resist Christ's vicar, even though Christ did not resist his adversary; or say, if you dare, that God does not know the decree of his legate, even though Christ avowed that even over himself the power of the Roman ruler had been ordained by heaven.[104]

And therefore the bishop usurps a foreign office, and extends his "scythe to another's crop," when he undertakes to judge the secular acts of men, whatever their status.

And as for Bernard's further assertion in the above-cited objection: "He who denies that this sword is yours does not sufficiently heed, it seems to me, these words of the Lord," etc., I reply that no one whom I have seen or heard has denied this or can deny this more explicitly than did Bernard himself, as is clear from those utterances of his which we have quoted above. To which it must be added, always respectfully, that this passage which Bernard cites has been more appropriately interpreted by other saints. For, as they all agree, Christ was speaking metaphorically when to his disciples' words, "Behold, here are two swords," the Lord replied, "It is enough." Whereon Chrysostom writes: "If he wanted them to use human power a hundred swords would not be enough. But if he did not

[103] St. Bernard *De moribus et officio episcoporum* cap. viii (PL 182. 829). See above, II. iv. 11.

[104] *Ibid.* cap. ix (PL 182. 832). Cf. above, II. v. 4.

want them to use human aid, even two swords are too much." [105] From this it is apparent that Christ's words had a mystical meaning; and this is also clearly indicated by his utterance in Matthew, Chapter 26, and John, Chapter 28, when, on being defended by the sword, he said to Peter: "Put up again thy sword into its place," or, "into the sheath," [106] wherein he showed that he had not commanded the apostles to defend him by such swords, but rather had been speaking mystically. And it is in this mystical sense that St. Ambrose properly understands and interprets the aforesaid words of Christ, when he writes as follows: "Two swords are permitted, one of the New Testament, the other of the Old, by which we are defended against the plots of the devil. And Christ says, 'It is enough,' because he who is defended by the doctrines of both Testaments lacks nothing." [107] Now by those priests who strive and strain with all their might, although wrongly, to usurp secular governments, wandering expositions of Scripture are gladly accepted when such expositions seem to savor of their corrupt opinion and perverted emotions. But if Christ's words be taken literally, they are not in opposition to our view, for the material sword is not rulership or the judgment of secular acts; and if Christ's words be taken metaphorically, then what he entrusted to Peter or any other apostle cannot signify, according to Christ's own view, secular rulership or judgment, as has been clearly proved elsewhere by St. Bernard (quoted by us above), and as we have indubitably shown through Scripture in Chapters IV and V of this discourse.

And as for what Bernard adds, that "To you belongs the sword and it should be taken out of its sheath perhaps by your will," I reply that Bernard wrote "perhaps," although he should have had no doubts on this point, unless perhaps he soundly meant that when the ruler draws his sword in an emergency, such as in starting a war, and he is not sure whether he is acting justly in accordance with divine law, then he ought to act "by the will of the priest" in the sense that he ought to make use of the counsel of the priests in a general or special council, in order to avoid incurring mortal sin. And the ruler should thus proceed in his other individual and civil acts as well, especially when he fears that he may incur mortal sin through ignorance; although not because he is subject to the priest in such a function. For in this same way, when the ruler has to bestow teaching licences or expel lepers from the city, he ought to make use of the counsel of experts, although he is not subject to them in jurisdiction, as we have said in Chapter X of this discourse. Hence, when Bernard

[105] In Thomas Aquinas *Catena aurea* on Luke 22:38 (XII, 232).
[106] Matthew 26:52; John 18:11.
[107] *Glossa ordinaria, ad loc.* See also Thomas Aquinas *Catena aurea* (XII, 232).

at the end of his above-quoted passage says that the temporal sword must be drawn "by the will of the priest and at the command of the emperor," he means by "will" not command or coercive authority, but rather counsel; for command was expressly said by him to pertain to the emperor or ruler, although frequently the Roman bishop unjustly commands the Christian believers to draw swords against one another. And, to sum up, if Bernard by the above words means that such office or judgment pertains to the authority of any priest or bishop, as being superior to any ruler in secular judgment, in the third sense of judgment, then I say that Bernard openly and manifestly contradicts both himself and the sacred Scripture which he quotes, as is to be seen from the foregoing. Consequently, if such was his view in this passage, then I absolutely refuse to accept it, for it is not canonic but rather inconsistent with and contrary to the canon.

25. [*vi, vii, xxv*] We come now to the statements of the saints and doctors, especially in their glosses on the scriptural passages in Matthew, Chapter 16, "Thou art Peter, and upon this rock," etc.; again in Luke, Chapter 22, "I have prayed for thee, Peter," etc.; and also in John, Chapter 21, "If you love me, feed my sheep"; by which statements the glossators seem to hold that Christ directly gave to St. Peter power or authority over the other apostles; for these writers call Peter "leader of the apostles" and "universal pastor," and some of them also call him "head of the church." [108] To these statements it must be replied, but respectfully, that Christ directly gave to St. Peter no essential authority, which we have called priestly, nor any accidental pastoral preeminence over the other apostles, but rather he removed from Peter and the others such authority and preeminence over one another, as we have clearly proved in Chapter XVI of this discourse through Scripture and the interpretations of the saints and teachers, and as we have also reiterated at the beginning of this chapter. Hence, following Christ and the Apostle, as well as other utterances of the saints, I refuse to accept the view concerning pastoral primacy or leadership which the above-mentioned interpretations of Scripture and other similar ones seem to uphold, in opposition to the position stated by us in Chapters XVI and XXI of this discourse; for that view is not canonic, nor does it follow from a canonic utterance, and indeed some of the writers who uphold it have elsewhere urged the opposite position in their interpretations of Scripture. But here they go outside Scripture to base such statements on their own views, following custom and familiar sayings rather than the words of Scripture.

26. For if Christ intended St. Peter to be the head and leader of the

[108] See above, II. xxvii. 2, 12.

apostles, then who will not wonder that when the apostles quarreled over which of them was the greatest, Christ always replied that they were all equal, and denied that any of them was prior to the others in authority? And why did not Christ command the other apostles to subordinate themselves to Peter in the pastoral office, in order to prevent so important a ministry as the headship of the church from being unknown to them and their successors? But we never read in Scripture that Christ gave such a command to the apostles. And why did Peter give to Paul "the right hand of fellowship"? Rather should he have given him a command, as being his superior. And, in a word, the entire Scripture, wherever it touches upon this subject, clearly proclaims the opposite of the view held by our opponents.

But let us suppose (what we have denied in accordance with Scripture) that Christ had directly entrusted St. Peter with the pastoral care of the other apostles. Even so, it could not on that account be proved through Scripture that the Roman or any other bishop after St. Peter's death is pastor of all the others by immediate ordainment of Christ, but rather such authority belongs to the head bishop directly through human election, as we have shown above in Chapters XVI, XVII, and XXII of this discourse.

27. [ix] And when it is objected that the church would be headless and would not have been ordered according to the best arrangement by Christ if he had left it without a head in his absence,[109] we can reply, with the Apostle as above, that Christ has always remained the head of the church, with all the apostles and church ministers as the other members, as is clear from Ephesians, Chapter 4, and many other passages which we have sufficiently cited in Chapter XXII of this discourse, paragraph 5. And this was also clearly indicated by Christ himself in the last chapter of Matthew, when he said: "I shall be with you even unto the end of the world." [110]

And let our opponent answer: Is not the church without a mortal head whenever the Roman bishop's seat is vacant? Obviously yes. But it must not on that account be granted that the church was left unordered or poorly arranged by Christ. Consequently, we must return to what we have said above and to what we are going to say in refuting the next objection. But the more fully to satisfy our current objector, let us formally answer his apparent reasoning.

When it is deduced and inferred that Christ would not have ordered the church according to the best arrangement if he had left it without a definite mortal head in his absence, this inference must be denied. And

[109] See above, II. xxvii. 2.   [110] Matthew 28:20.

when it seems to be supported by the argument that the church is arranged for the best through the appointment of such a head, I believe it must be granted that the best arrangement for church ritual and the observance of the faith is attained by the appointment of such a mortal head; but I think it must be added that it does not from this follow that any particular mortal has been designated for such headship immediately by Christ, but rather that it was better to have the head designated and elected by the believers, and that this was the best arrangement given by Christ to the church militant.[111] For the clergymen of Rome or of any other city are perhaps not always superior in sacred Scripture and in morals to clerical colleges in other parts of the world, as is sufficiently clear from a comparison of them with the university and clergy of Paris. Consequently, by leaving to the believers the appointment of such a head of the church, in the way stated by us in Chapter XXII of this discourse, paragraphs 8 and 9, Christ left the church with the best arrangement appropriate to human society; and it was in this way perhaps that the apostles appointed Peter the head of the church, as we have shown from the decree of Anacletus in Chapter XIV of this discourse, paragraph 12.

28. [*viii*] We come next to Augustine's statement on the passage in John, Chapter 21: "I will that he tarry," to the effect that "the life which is in faith was exemplified by the apostle Peter because of the primacy of his apostolate." [112] To this I reply that Augustine meant primacy with respect to time, for Peter was the first to be called to the apostolate by Christ, just as he was the first in time to receive the promise of the keys, according to Augustine's gloss on the words in Matthew, Chapter 16: "I shall give unto thee the keys of the kingdom of heaven." [113] For the life which is in faith, that is, the corruptible life of this world, precedes in time the life which is in hope, that is, the incorruptible life of the other world.[114]

[*xxvi*] As for the citations from the decrees or decretals of the Roman pontiffs in confirmation of the various objections,[115] it must be replied in general to all such writings and utterances, which are not of the kind described by us in Chapter XIX of this discourse, that we are not obliged to believe them to be true; nor do we believe those of them which contain views opposed to those which we have set forth above and which we hold with Scripture, but rather we shun and openly deny them, although respectfully.

And as for the conclusion which they particularly urge, that to the Roman bishop, either alone or together with his clerical college, belongs the

---

[111] See Vol. I, p. 282.   [112] See above, II. xxvii. 2.   [113] See above, I. xix. 7.
[114] See Augustine on John 21:22, in Thomas Aquinas *Catena aurea* (XII, 463).
[115] See above, II. xxvii. 12.

authority to appoint persons to church offices and to bestow temporal goods
or benefices on behalf of these offices, it must be replied that if by church
offices are meant holy orders and the accompanying characters which are
impressed on the soul as habits, then these offices can be bestowed only by
the bishops and priests, or by God through the ministry of the bishops and
priests alone, and not through the ministry of any other group or individual; and belief in this, rather than the opposite, is necessary for salvation, for the reason that this is found to be the ordinance of divine law,
but not because it is a statute established by human decretals or decrees.
However, the qualifications of candidates for these church offices ought not
to be examined or determined without the authority of the faithful legislator or of its ruler, as we have said in Chapter XVII of this discourse,
and as we have also proved in Chapter XV of Discourse I. But on the
other hand, if by church offices are meant assignments or appointments
of priests and the other afore-mentioned officials to major or minor cures of
souls in definite places for the guidance of definite peoples, then appointments to such offices, and the distribution or bestowal of ecclesiastic temporalities on their behalf, pertain to the faithful legislator, in the way stated
by us in Chapter XVII of this discourse; and we make the general assertion
that such authority neither belongs nor ought to belong to any single
bishop or college of priests anywhere, as has been shown in Chapters XVII
and XXI of this discourse.

29. Therefore, with regard to any objections to our statements which
are based upon the decrees or decretals of the Roman pontiffs, it must be
said that although such decretals or decrees, and any other similar writings
and utterances (which are not of the kind described by us in Chapter XIX
of this discourse), may contain very many teachings and counsels which are
even useful for the status both of the present and of the future world, yet
inasmuch as such statutes come from the Roman bishop and his clerical
college without authorization by the faithful legislator or ruler, and by a
procedure different from or opposed to the method stated in Chapter XXI
of this discourse, they are obligatory upon no one with respect to any
guilt or punishment, especially temporal. For this is the status which is
accorded those who compose such documents, as was the case with the
Pharisees and Scribes, to whom Christ said, in Mark, Chapter 7: "Howbeit
in vain do they worship me, teaching for doctrines the commandments of
men. For laying aside the commandment of God, ye hold the tradition of
men"; and further: "Full well ye reject the command of God, that ye may
keep your own tradition," [116] that is, the decretals and decrees aiming at

[116] Mark 7:7–8, 9.

the usurpation of temporal goods. For these decretals, as such, are not laws divine or human, but merely documents or statements, and, in most cases, oligarchic ordinances.[117] Consequently, those persons who make such ordinances by a procedure opposed to the one stated by us above and without the above-mentioned authority; and who induce anyone to observe them by making unauthorized assertions, almost using coercion by threatening simple transgressors of them with eternal damnation; or who pronounce verbal or written blasphemies, anathematizations, or other maledictions upon anyone—such persons must be given the extreme corporal penalty as conspirators and fomenters of civil disunion. For this is the gravest species of the crime of treason, since it is committed directly against the government, leading to multiplicity of even the supreme government and thus necessarily to the destruction of every polity.

CHAPTER XXIX: REFUTATION OF THE OBJECTIONS WHICH WERE ADDUCED FROM SCRIPTURE IN CHAPTER III OF THIS DISCOURSE FOR THE PURPOSE OF SHOWING THAT COERCIVE JURISDICTION BELONGS TO THE BISHOPS, AND THAT THE SUPREME COERCIVE JURISDICTION BELONGS TO THE ROMAN BISHOP AS SUCH

WE must now reply to the objections which were adduced from Scripture in Chapter III of this discourse, and which might perhaps lead someone to think it possible to prove that the Roman pope or any other bishop is judge in the third sense over all clergymen, or over all men without differentiation; and that such judicial power is derived not by appointment of the human legislator, but by immediate ordainment of God. And first, as to the objection drawn from Matthew, Chapter 16, when Christ said to St. Peter, "I will give to thee the keys of the kingdom of heaven," etc.,[1] it must be replied that by these words Christ gave to St. Peter or any other apostle no power other than that of binding men to and loosing them from sins, as St. Bernard explicitly says in his treatise addressed to Eugene, *On Consideration*, Book I, Chapter V (from which we have quoted above in Chapter V of this discourse),[2] and as we have also shown at length in Chapters VI and VII of this discourse; nor was any plenitude

---

[117] See Vol. I, p. 143, also p. 73.   [1] See above, II. iii. 2.   [2] See above, II. v. 2.

of power given in this connection in any way other than what was said in Chapter XXIII of this discourse. Hence by the above-cited words of Christ, the Roman or any other bishop or priest in the person of an apostle or apostles received from Christ no coercive authority or jurisdiction in this world over any clergyman or layman. For Christ said, "I will give to thee the keys of the kingdom of heaven," as distinct from the earthly kingdom. For from earthly governance Christ showed by his example that each of the apostles and their successors, the bishops or priests, were excluded, when he said, in Luke, Chapter 12: "Man, who has made me judge [that is, over earthly affairs]?" [3] and the same is also proved by the other passages cited in Chapters IV and V of this discourse.

The same reply, or a similar one, must be made with regard to the canonic utterances of Christ in Matthew, Chapter 18, and John, Chapter 20, where he said to the apostles: "Whatsoever ye shall bind on earth," etc., and "Whosesoever sins ye remit," etc.[4] For by these words Christ gave to the apostles no power other than the one mentioned above, and in the way we have stated.

2. As for the other citation from Matthew, Chapter 11, where Christ said, "All things are delivered to me by my father," [5] it must be replied that from this it does not follow that "I have delivered the power over all things to any apostle or apostles," as we have stated in Chapter IV of this discourse. For the point at issue here is not what power or authority Christ was able to give to any apostle or apostles and their successors, but rather what power he wanted to give and in fact (*de facto*) did give them, and from what he excluded them by counsel or command.[6] And this question has been adequately settled in Chapters IV, V, VI, and IX of this discourse. Whence Bernard, upholding this view in his treatise addressed to Eugene, *On Consideration,* Book III, Chapter I, writes as follows: "For I do not think that you were given stewardship over it," that is, the world, "unqualifiedly, but rather with certain restrictions: you were not given possession. If you go on to usurp the world, you are contradicted by Him who says, 'The world is mine, and the fullness thereof.' You are not he of whom the prophet says, 'And all the earth shall be his possession.' This is Christ, who claims possession both by right of creation and by the merit of redemption." [7] And Bernard adds many other pertinent remarks which I have omitted to cite because the above is sufficient, and for the sake of brevity. It is not the case, therefore, that all the things which were given

---

[3] Luke 12:14.   [4] Matthew 18:18; John 20:23.
[5] Matthew 11:27.   [6] See above, II. iv. 2.
[7] St. Bernard *De consideratione* III. i (PL 182. 758). The texts cited are Psalm 49:12 and perhaps Ezekiel 45:8 mingled with Numbers 24:18.

to Christ were in turn given by him to an apostle or apostles, and without any [8] restrictions, but rather Christ gave only certain things, and with certain definite restrictions. Moreover, according to the glosses of all the saints on this passage, Christ meant that this bestowal was made upon himself in accordance with his divinity whereby he was the eternal son of God; [9] which could not possibly be an attribute of any of the apostles or their successors. Consequently, the above utterance of Christ implies nothing that can even superficially oppose the view which we hold.

3. To the objection based upon Christ's statement in Matthew, Chapter 28: "All power is given to me in heaven and in earth," [10] the same reply must be made as to the objection immediately preceding. For from this it does not follow, even if we assume that Christ received all power on earth in accordance with his humanity, that he gave all power to an apostle or apostles, but rather he gave only that power which he mentioned in Matthew, Chapter 28, and in John, Chapter 22,[11] and which we have described in Chapters VI and VII of this discourse; for it was only with this power that Christ came to reign. Whence Jerome writes on the above passage: "Power was given to him in heaven and in earth so that he who had previously reigned in heaven might reign on earth through the faith of the believers." [12]

4. As for the objection based upon Matthew, Chapter 8, and Mark, Chapter 5: "And the devils besought him, saying," etc.,[13] it must be replied that this text does not oppose the view which we hold. For suppose, as is true, that if Christ had so willed, he could have had complete lordship and power over all temporal things, even in accordance with his humanity; yet from this it cannot be necessarily inferred that he gave similar power to an apostle or apostles, or to their successors. Rather, Christ by word and by deed taught them to shun the possession and ownership of temporal goods, as well as coercive jurisdiction or judicial authority over anyone in this world, as has been shown in Chapters IV and V of this discourse, and reiterated in the preceding chapter. Now although Christ sometimes exercised power or ownership over such things, yet on those very rare occasions when he did so he acted not in the manner of a human ruler or judge, but through miracles and by divine rather than human power, such

---

[8] Inserting, with Scholz and mss., *omnem.*

[9] See the glosses on Matthew 11:27, especially in Thomas Aquinas *Catena aurea* (XI, 148). On this distinction between what belongs to Christ *qua* God and *qua* man (*secundum divinitatem* and *secundum humanitatem*), to which the following paragraphs also refer, see Vol. I, pp. 17–18, n. 20.

[10] See above, II. iii. 3.　　　　[11] Matthew 28:19–20; John 20:23. See above, II. vi. 2.

[12] *Catena aurea* on Matthew 28:19 (XI, 333).　　　　[13] See above, II. iii. 4.

as when he made the fig tree wither away,[14] his purpose being to show to his apostles the nature of his divinity, so that he might make them stronger in faith; or else it was for some even better purpose, unknown to man but known to him, as it is said by Chrysostom [15] and Jerome in their glosses on the passage cited above. "The purpose of killing the pigs," writes Jerome, "was to furnish men with an opportunity for salvation." [16] Therefore, Christ did not teach the apostles to perform miracles, as we have shown above in Chapter IV of this discourse from Augustine's tenth sermon *On the Words of the Lord in Matthew;* [17] and still less did Christ want them to exercise power in such a way as to harm others and cause scandals. Hence, when Christ exercised power over temporal things, his purpose was not to show the apostles that they should exercise similar power, but rather to show them that he was truly God.

5. To the objection based upon Matthew, Chapter 22, Mark, Chapter 11, and Luke, Chapter 19: "Then Jesus sent two disciples, saying to them, Go ye into the village that is over against you, and immediately you shall find an ass tied," etc.,[18] the reply must be like the one immediately preceding.

As for the passages about the two swords, from Luke, Chapter 22, and the feeding of the sheep, from John, Chapter 21,[19] they do not contradict, or necessarily imply anything that contradicts, the view which we hold, as we have shown at length in the preceding chapter.[20] For by these utterances Christ did not give to St. Peter or any other apostle, or to any of their successors, coercive jurisdiction or judicial authority over anyone in this world, but merely the pastoral office, which we have sufficiently discussed in Chapter IX of this discourse.

6. As for what the Apostle writes in I Corinthians, Chapter 6, "Know ye not that we shall judge angels? how much more secular things?," [21] this does not contradict, or imply anything that contradicts, the view which we hold. For in this passage the Apostle was warning or addressing not only the priests but all the believers of Corinth; for he addressed his epistle to all of them in general, as is clear from the salutation, because they were quarreling with one another over secular and civil matters, and summoning one another to trial before infidel judges. Hence the Apostle, counseling them as their pastor, warned them to appoint their judges from among the faithful; not, indeed, priests or bishops, but other believers. Thus, immediately after the words quoted above, the Apostle

---

[14] Matthew 21:19–21; Mark 11:13, 20–1.   [15] Thomas Aquinas *Catena aurea* (XI, 116).
[16] *Ibid.*   [17] See above, II. iv. 2.   [18] See above, II. iii. 5.
[19] See above, II. iii. 6, 7.   [20] See above, II. xxviii. 9, 22–24.   [21] See above, II. iii. 8.

adds: "If then ye have judgments of things pertaining to this world, appoint them to judge who are the most despised in the church. I speak to your shame. Is it so that there is not among you any one wise man that is able to judge between his brethren? But brother goeth to law with brother, and that before unbelievers." [22] These words of the Apostle are interpreted in the gloss according to Augustine, Ambrose, and Gregory, as follows:

"If then ye have judgments of things pertaining to this world," etc. Just as the Apostle had previously reproved them for going to law before infidel judges, despising judges who were believers, so now he reproves them for appointing as judges those who were "the most despised," although believers; as if to say, Ye too ought to judge. So the Apostle writes: "If then ye have judgments of things pertaining to this world," meaning that they should not have such judgments, but should rather despise them. "If ye have judgments . . . set them to judge who are the most despised," that is, undiscerning and lowly, "in the church"; as if to say: This is what ye have done. For the brethren were forced to have recourse to infidel judges. The Apostle reproves them for this practice, speaking to them ironically; and because this practice should not be followed, he adds: "I speak to your shame"; as if to say: I do not command you, but I remind you that you will be ashamed, and you ought to blush because "there is not among you any one wise man . . . that is able to judge between his brethren," so that you have to appoint stupid men for judges. And yet it is better to appoint stupid men, if wise ones are lacking, than to go before infidel judges. "It is so," then, "that there is not among you any one wise man . . . but brother goeth to law with brother," which is bad, "and that before unbelievers," which is worse. Or else the Apostle's meaning is as follows: having said that they could judge about these lowly things, the Apostle designates what persons should be appointed to settle such matters, namely, "those who are the most despised in the church"; for the more worthy persons ought to deal with spiritual affairs. This was as if to say: Since you have to judge, do it in this way: "if ye have" affairs "of things pertaining to this world, appoint them to judge who are the most despised in the church," that is, men who are wise, but yet of lesser merit; for the apostles, having to preach, traveled too much to have time for such matters. Therefore he wanted that such affairs be judged by those wise men, faithful and holy, who remained at home, and not by those who roamed hither and thither to spread the gospel. From such tasks we cannot excuse ourselves even if we want to. For Christ is my witness that I would prefer to do manual labor for a certain number of hours every day, and have the remainder of the day free for reading and prayer or for the study of divine letters, than to undergo the tumultuous perplexities of lawsuits concerning secular affairs, whether in a judicial or in an interlocutory capacity. I say, "appoint them to judge who are the most despised," but this "I speak to your shame," namely, in order that those men may try earthly disputes who have perceived the wisdom of exterior things. But those who are endowed with

[22] I Corinthians 6:4–6.

spiritual gifts ought not to become entangled in earthly affairs, so that, not being compelled to deal with lesser goods, they may be able to serve greater ones. But nevertheless great care must be taken that those who shine with spiritual gifts do not turn their backs on the problems of their weaker neighbors, but they ought to entrust them to others who are capable of dealing with them, or else they themselves should handle them.[23]

7. These words written by the Apostle and the saints must be given careful attention. For they clearly show, first, that all disputes among any persons whatsoever, over matters which do not pertain to divine law, are secular and non-spiritual, and pertain to secular judgment. For the Apostle in the above passage, and the saints in their interpretations thereof, spoke in general terms, and made no distinction (just as none should be made) between those temporal or civil disputes which are among priests or clergymen alone, or among priests and laymen, and those which are among laymen alone.[24] For let answer be given, I beg, by that sophist and abuser of words who calls spiritual what is unqualifiedly secular according to the usage of the Apostle and the saints—let him answer this question: If a priest does injury by word or deed to a brother, whether priest or layman, is this injury any more spiritual than that inflicted by a layman?[25] To reply in the affirmative is ridiculous, and to believe it is utter insanity; for an injury done by a priest is certainly more carnal or secular and more detestable than that which is inflicted by a layman. For he sins more gravely and more shamefully who is obligated to teach others, both by word and by deed, not to do injury, as was shown at length in Chapter VIII of this discourse.[26] That such acts of clergymen are and ought to be called secular, not spiritual, is clearly affirmed by Ambrose[27] in his gloss cited above, when, discussing the contentious lawsuits of priests and clergymen, which were being tried before him who was a bishop, he calls them "tumultuous perplexities of lawsuits concerning secular affairs," not differentiating between these lawsuits or disputes because of the status of the persons involved. For the distinction between priest and non-priest is in this respect accidental, like the distinction between circles of gold and circles of silver, a distinction drawn by no artisan, because it makes no essential difference in what he produces.[28]

A second conclusion which clearly emerges from the above passages of the Apostle and the saints is that the authority to judge contentious acts does not belong to the priests, and that the authority to appoint such judges belongs not more, but rather less perhaps, to the priests than to the other be-

[23] In Peter Lombard *Collectanea, ad loc.* (PL 191. 1576–77).
[24] See Vol. I, pp. 120–21.   [25] Cf. II. ii. 7; and Vol. I, pp. 102–3.
[26] See above, II. viii. 7.   [27] A slip for Augustine.
[28] See above, II. viii. 7; II. x. 7.

lievers; but this authority belongs to the whole body of the believers, as has been proved in Chapter XV of Discourse I. And hence the Apostle wrote, "Appoint [ye] them to judge," using the plural (*Constituite*); he did not say to some one bishop or priest, Appoint thou them to judge, in the singular (*Constitue*). For whenever some task had to be performed which pertained to the office of the priest or bishop, the Apostle directed his command to the individual clergyman involved, and not to the multitude of the believers, for example, with regard to such tasks as the appointment of priests, bishops, or deacons, or the preaching of the gospel, and the other functions which are peculiar to the priest or pastor. And hence in Titus, Chapter 1, the Apostle wrote: "For this cause left I thee in Crete, that thou shouldest set in order the things that are wanting," namely, with regard to salutary doctrine and morals, "and shouldest ordain priests in every city, as I also appointed thee." [29] But the Apostle did not say to Titus, Appoint thou someone to be judge of secular affairs; nor did he write to the Corinthians, The bishop or priest will appoint someone to be your judge; but rather the Apostle said to the whole body of the believers: "Appoint [ye] them to judge," not indeed commanding them, but counseling or reminding them; whence the gloss on the words, "I speak to your shame," states, "This was as if to say: I do not command you, but I remind you that you will be ashamed." For the Apostle well knew that the appointment of such judges did not pertain to his office, and still less to that of any other priest or bishop. Nor again did he counsel that any priest or bishop be appointed to exercise such judicial office, but rather the opposite, as he said, "no soldier of God entangleth himself with secular affairs." [30] But he did counsel that those persons should be appointed judges who were "the most despised in the church," that is, those of the believers who were not suited for preaching the gospel; however, not all such believers were to be named judges, but the Apostle, according to the gloss of the saints, wished or counseled that only those believers should "try earthly disputes who have perceived the science of external things. But those who are endowed with spiritual gifts ought not to become entangled in earthly affairs." [31] And this was also clearly said by St. Bernard in his treatise addressed to Eugene, *On Consideration*, Book I, Chapter V, from which we have quoted above in the preceding chapter. [32]

8. But against this view an objection will be raised, based upon a statement of Ambrose [33] which we quoted above among the glosses. For in discussing the judgments of secular contentious acts, he wrote: "From such

[29] Titus 1:5. [30] II Timothy 2:4. [31] See above, II. v. 2.
[32] See above, II. xxviii. 24. [33] A slip for Augustine.

tasks we cannot excuse ourselves even if we want to." And in confirmation of this, Gregory adds: "But nevertheless great care must be taken . . . but they," the bishops, "ought to entrust them," that is, the judgments of secular acts, "to others who are capable of dealing with them, or else they themselves should handle them." [34] And therefore it seems that the judging of such matters, and the appointment of such judges, pertain to the bishops or priests as such, for, as the saints themselves hold, they cannot be excused from these tasks and must exercise "great care" with regard to them.

9. But to this objection based upon the above passages and upon other similar utterances of the saints and doctors, we must reply that in ancient times when these saints lived, because of the respect accorded the priestly status and the confidence that was felt in their moral virtue, as well as for the other reasons mentioned by us in Chapter XXV of this discourse, paragraph 5, the faithful legislators and rulers granted to the bishops and to the leading pastors of souls the function of being judges in the third sense over the persons and temporal goods of the clergymen, in order that these latter might not be distracted or disturbed from their divine functions, and might meet with more honorable treatment in secular affairs. And inasmuch as some of the above-mentioned saints had been appointed bishops in provinces or territories whose rulers or inhabitants had bestowed on them the aforesaid judicial office, these saints could not have been excused from the task of judging secular lawsuits between clergymen unless they had given up their bishoprics.

10. But again, someone may well ask why it was that holy men like St. Sylvester and very many others assumed judicial authority and secular powers, and possessed and administered temporal goods, if such functions did not and do not pertain to the office of priests, bishops, and other ministers of the gospel.

11. To this it must, I think, be replied, in accordance with the truths cited above, especially in Chapters XVII and XXV of this discourse, that because the church or multitude of the believers was small at the beginning and for a long time thereafter, it was frequently made to undergo persecution and even martyrdom at the hands of the infidel rulers and subjects, and it lived in great poverty. For this reason, when the emperors later became Christian, devout, and friendly to the holy bishops, these latter, being true pastors and desiring to secure the safety, increase, preservation, and sustenance of their flock, obtained from the emperors favors, grants, and privileges, not in order to advance themselves, but rather for the purpose of being able to help, protect, and nourish the faithful people.

[34] See above, para. 6 of this chapter.

It was in this way, then, and for these reasons, that the holy bishops undertook to judge secular acts, especially among clergymen. Thus too they accepted the task of administering certain temporalities, without possession or ownership thereof or the power to claim them for themselves, in order that this might redound to the advantage of the poor believers. Hence Ambrose in his treatise *On Handing Over the Basilica* writes: "If the emperor desires the fields, he has the power to claim them for himself; no one of us intervenes. What the people bestow can redound to the poor." [35] None of the priests or bishops, then, intervened to claim the fields, for they renounced the ownership thereof, in imitation of Christ and the apostles; they steadfastly endured suffering even to the point of death on behalf of the faith. But the modern bishops, on the other hand, especially those of Rome, engage in bitter conflicts over the ownership of the fields and other temporalities, and they foment such conflicts among the Christian believers everywhere, asserting that they thus "defend the rights of Christ's bride," [36] although these are not her rights, but rather wrongs; and they neglect almost entirely the defense of the true bride, that is, the faith, the teaching thereof, and morals, taking no measures to prevent her from being destroyed through vicious practices or acts, or through attack by infidels, as we have said in Chapter XXVI of this discourse.

It was for the reasons given above, then, that some of the saints accepted such offices and benefices in ancient times. But such things could appropriately be renounced by modern clergymen, at least in communities of believers; for now the rulers adequately defend the clergy against oppression, indeed the clergy can hardly be restrained from attacking others. But modern pastors aim not to renounce secular offices and possessions and the ownership of temporal goods, but rather to fight for them even with armed force, not merely in order to hold on to what they already have, but to usurp all the rest, as can be learned by any person no matter how undeveloped he is in understanding, so long as nothing else is wrong with him. By this display of covetousness the clergy very frequently scandalize the whole body of the believers, not heeding Christ's threat in Matthew, Chapter 18: "Whoso shall offend one of these little ones," etc.[37] Whereon the gloss according to Jerome: "While this may be a general statement expressing opposition to all those who scandalize someone, yet by implication it can be understood to apply even against the apostles, who in asking which of them was greatest, seemed to be quarreling with one another over authority. And if they had persisted in this vicious conduct,

---

[35] St. Ambrose *Sermo contra Auxentium* cap. xxxiii (PL 16. 1060). See above, II. xiv. 22.
[36] See above, II. xxvi. 2.   [37] Matthew 18:6.

they might by their scandal have lost those persons whom they were calling to the faith, when these saw the apostles fighting with one another over glory." [38] And what Jerome wrote concerning the apostles must be understood to apply also to all their successors, bishops or priests. But if these refuse to give up voluntarily such judicial functions and the authority to distribute temporal goods, and instead continue to abuse them, then the rulers or faithful legislators lawfully can and must, in accordance with divine and human law, revoke these powers from them, as has been demonstrated in Chapter XV of Discourse I and in Chapters XVII and XXI of this discourse.

12. As for the objection which was based upon the words of the Apostle in I Corinthians, Chapter 9, and in II Thessalonians, Chapter 3: "Have not we power," etc.,[39] this was refuted in Chapter XIV of this discourse.[40] For the power which was there mentioned by the Apostle is not the power of jurisdiction, but merely the power lawfully (in accordance with divine law) to request, although not in coercive judgment, the food and clothing which ought to be given to a minister of the gospel by those who are able to do so.

As for the objection which was based upon the passage in I Timothy, Chapter 5, where the Apostle said, "Against a priest receive not an accusation," etc.,[41] it must be replied that the Apostle meant these words to apply in cases where the priest had to be publicly corrected by his superior, pastor or teacher. For the Apostle did not command any priest or bishop to exercise coercive jurisdiction over anyone, inasmuch as he knew that such authority did not belong to him or to any of his successors. But he showed that the only way in which it pertains to a pastor to correct others is by words, for he added: "Them that sin rebuke before all, that the rest also may have fear"; [42] he did not say: Seize or imprison them, but rather he taught that those who cannot be corrected by words should be avoided. Whence in Titus, Chapter 3, he wrote: "A man that is a heretic, after the first and second admonition, avoid, knowing that he that is such an one is subverted and sinneth, being condemned by his own judgment." [43]

---

[38] Thomas Aquinas *Catena aurea, ad loc.* (XI, 211).   [39] See above, II. iii. 8.
[40] See above, II. xiv. 7.   [41] See above, II. iii. 9.   [42] I Timothy 5:20.
[43] I Titus 3:10–11.

CHAPTER XXX: REFUTATION OF THE RATIONAL AR-
GUMENTS PRESENTED IN CHAPTER III OF THIS DIS-
COURSE FOR THE SAME PURPOSE; AND ALSO CON-
CERNING THE TRANSFER OF THE ROMAN EMPIRE
AND OF ANY OTHER GOVERNMENT: HOW IT SHOULD
AND CAN BE DONE ACCORDING TO RIGHT REASON

THE last remaining task of this discourse is to refute the arguments presented in Chapter III of this discourse for the purpose of supporting the error of those who assert that coercive jurisdiction belongs to priests or bishops, and that the supreme of all such jurisdictions in this world belongs to the Roman bishop, as such.

As for the first argument, that as the body is to the soul, so is the ruler of the body to the ruler of the soul,[1] this proposition, taken universally, is false. For although the soul is distinguished from the body inasmuch as the soul is not the body, yet if we take the word "ruler" in its proper sense, there is no ruler of the body who is not also in some way ruler of the soul, and conversely,[2] as is clear from Chapters VIII and IX of this discourse.

But if by "ruler of the body" is metaphorically meant a physician, who takes care of the body as a practical teacher concerned with the acts of the irrational and nutritive faculty, and if by "ruler of the soul" is meant a physician and practical teacher or instructor concerned with the acts of the rational and appetitive faculties, not only in and for the status of the present world, such as teachers of the human sciences or disciplines, but also for the status of the future world, such as pastors and priests, then the aforesaid proposition could be granted if it were taken indefinitely, but it it were taken universally it would always be open to many objections. For between the soul and the body, and again between the rational and the irrational faculties, there are many differences which do not exist between those persons who are teachers or caretakers of the one and those who are teachers or caretakers of the other. For the rational faculty, in the image of the Trinity, composes syllogisms, while the irrational does not; but there is no such difference between the teachers or caretakers of these respective faculties; and so on with the rest. Hence the above proposition may be granted if it is understood in a certain qualified sense: namely, that just

---

[1] See above, II. iii. 10.

[2] For earlier versions of this reply to the soul-body argument, see Vol. I, p. 101, n. 62.

as the rational and appetitive soul is nobler than the body, that is, than that which is ensouled in accordance with the nutritive faculty, so is the teacher or caretaker of the rational soul more worthy than the teacher or caretaker of the irrational; or else this comparison may be made between the teacher of the rational soul for the status or purpose of only the present world, and the teacher of the rational soul for the status or purpose primarily of the future world. But even if the one teacher is in this way more perfect than the other, it does not follow that the more perfect one is judge over the less perfect by coercive judgment; for if this were so, then the mathematician would be coercive ruler over the physician, and very many would be the manifest evils which would follow from this.[8]

But if, as our opponent seems to intend, by "ruler of bodies" is meant the coercive ruler or judge (in the third sense) of men in and for the status or purpose solely or primarily of the present world; and if by "ruler of souls" is meant the person who is judge (in the third sense) for the status or purpose primarily of the future world, then this comparison or proportion could be granted if taken in a certain qualified sense or indefinitely; but if it were taken universally, it would be open to many objections, as we said before. And when it is assumed in the minor premise that the body is subordinate to the soul, or that the irrational is entirely or in some manner subordinate to the soul, that is, to the rational; then, even if we unqualifiedly grant that the body is subordinate with respect to perfection, it does not follow that the body is subordinate with respect to jurisdiction; for to argue in this way would be to draw an invalid inference. But yet let us suppose, although it does not follow from this argument, that the ruler of bodies, that is, the coercive judge over men for the status of the present world only, is subordinate in jurisdiction to the coercive judge of souls for the status of the future world. From this it does not follow that any ruler or coercive judge of this world is subordinate in jurisdiction to some bishop or priest. For no bishop or priest, as such, is a ruler or coercive judge over anyone for the status of the present or the future world, as has been shown in Chapters IV, V, and IX of this discourse. For the coercive judge of souls, or for the status of the future world, is Christ alone. Whence in James, Chapter 4, it is written (and it bears repeating): "There is one lawgiver and judge, that is able to destroy and to deliver."[4] But Christ decreed that not in this world, but only in the future world, would he irrevocably judge, punish, or reward any mortal, as we have said and

---

[8] See Vol. I, p. 228. For a similar argument, see John of Paris *De potestate regia et papali* cap. v, xvii, xviii, xix (ed. D. J. Leclercq, *Jean de Paris et l'ecclésiologie du XIIIe siècle* [Paris, 1942], pp. 184, 225–26, 227, 229–30, 234).

[4] James 4:12.

proved through Scripture in Chapter IX of this discourse. But the Roman bishop, with the other pastors,[5] is a teacher of souls, like a physician, and not a coercive judge or ruler, as we have shown above through the gospel, through the Apostle, Hilary, and Chrysostom, and by cogent reasoning.

2. As for the further argument, that as corporeals are to spirituals, so is the ruler of corporeals to the ruler of spirituals,[6] this is to be refuted in the same or in a similar way as the preceding argument, because it is based upon almost the same root. For the major premise, if taken universally, is open to very many objections. As for the minor, which asserts that corporeals are subject to spirituals, this is to be granted if "subject" is taken to mean "less perfect," and if the words "temporal" and "spiritual" are taken in their proper meanings. As for the added statement, that the Roman bishop is ruler or judge of spirituals, if "judge" is taken in its first sense, as meaning a theoretic or practical judge of spiritual things, then it is true that the Roman and every other bishop is or ought to be such a judge; and from this the conclusion is that he is more perfect than the person who judges by such judgment about corporeal things only, mainly because of the relative goodness of the things judged.[7] But from this it does not follow that such a judge of spiritual things is superior in jurisdiction or in coercive judgment to the judge of corporeal things. For if this were so, then the zoologist would be ruler or coercive judge over the astronomer or geometer, or conversely;[8] yet neither of these consequences is either necessary or true. On the other hand, if it is meant that the Roman or any other bishop is judge of spiritual things in the third sense of judge, that is, as coercive, then it must be denied as manifestly false, as we have shown above from James, Chapter 4, as well as in Chapter IX of this discourse. For Christ alone is such a judge, and we have never denied, nor do we now deny, that the judge of this world is subject to Christ with respect to coercive jurisdiction for the status of the future world. Hence the Apostle in Ephesians, Chapter 4, and in the last chapter of Colossians writes, "The Lord both of them and of you is in heaven";[9] but no apostle or priest of the New Law other than Christ was then in heaven. Consequently, the judges of this world will be judged by this judge alone with coercive judgment, and those who have demerits will be punished by coercive force, but in the other world and in accordance with its law, as was shown in Chapter IX of this discourse. The above-stated misreasoning, then, was fallacious because of the equivocal use of the word "judge."

3. As for the argument that, as end is to end, and law to law, etc., so is

[5] Reading, with Scholz, *pastoribus* for *pastor*.
[7] See Aristotle *De anima* I, 1, 402a 1–3.
[9] Ephesians 6:9; see Colossians 4:1.

[6] See above, II. iii. 11.
[8] See Vol. I, p. 228.

judge to judge,[10] this could be denied if taken universally. But if it is taken indefinitely, with the minor premise added, then the conclusion follows, perhaps because of the matter of the premises, that the coercive judge in accordance with divine law is superior to the coercive judge in accordance with human law; this we have granted before. But if it be assumed that the Roman or any other bishop is judge in accordance with divine law, then a distinction must be drawn because of the equivocal meanings of the word "judge," and the argument must be denied in that sense whereby our opponent seeks to conclude that the Roman or any other bishop is coercive judge in this world or in the future world in accordance with divine law.

4. The next argument was that he whose action is nobler or more perfect ought not to be subject in coercive jurisdiction to him whose action is less noble or less perfect, and that this relation holds between the action of the bishop or priest and that of the ruler, for to consecrate the eucharist and to minister the other ecclesiastic sacraments, which is the function of the bishop or priest, is nobler and more perfect than to judge and command concerning men's civil or contentious acts, which is the function only of the ruler [11] or of him who has coercive [12] jurisdiction, as such.[13] But in this argument the major premise is false and must be denied if taken universally; and if it is not taken universally, then the argument will not have the required form. Objection would similarly be made to the minor premise if it were taken universally, that is, as holding for any priesthood or priest. For in laws [14] other than the Christian, the action of the priests is not nobler than the action of the ruler, for the opposite of this has been shown in Chapter XV of Discourse I, but only in the law of the Christians is the action of the priests the most perfect of all; this, however, we hold by faith alone.[15]

The first premise of this argument, therefore, is false. For there is nothing to prevent that which has an absolutely nobler or more perfect action from being dependent in some respect upon that which has a less perfect action, and thus being less perfect in that respect. For example, the human body, which is absolutely more perfect than any other body, simple or composite (at least, any generable body), is in some respect potential to and less perfect than many other bodies, simple and composite.[16] This is also to be seen in the parts of the same composite body. For although the

---

[10] See above, II. iii. 12.   [11] Reading, with Scholz, *principantis* for *principatus*.
[12] Reading, with Scholz, *coactivam* for *activam*.   [13] See above, II. iii. 13.
[14] On this use of the term "law," see Introduction, above, pp. xc–xci.
[15] See Vol. I, pp. 69–70.
[16] See Aristotle *De caelo* II. 12. 292b 1 ff.; *De partibus animalium* II. 10. 656a 6 ff.; *Nicomachean Ethics* VI. 7. 1141a 21 ff.

eye is a more perfect member or part than the hand or foot, because it performs a more perfect action, nevertheless it is dependent upon them and receives some action or motion from them; and, conversely, they are also dependent upon the eye, for it guides them toward the goal to which they move or are moved. Thus too the Apostle in I Corinthians 12 wrote: "And the eye cannot say to the hand, I need not thy help." [17]

In the same or in an analogous way, therefore, the government is dependent upon, and receives some things through, the actions of some of the lower parts of the state, which we discussed in Chapter V of Discourse I, although this dependence is not in respect of coercive judgment; and yet these other parts of the state are in some respects dependent in a better and more perfect way upon the government, such as in respect of coercive judgment, as was shown in Chapter XV of Discourse I. Thus, therefore, the priesthood is dependent upon and receives some things from the government, and conversely. For the priesthood receives from the government the bringing of its civil acts to justice, and protection from injury, in order that the priests may neither harm nor be harmed by others in and for the status of the present life; for this is the function of the ruler and of no other part of the state, as has been demonstrated in Chapter XV of Discourse I. This was also expressed by the Apostle in Romans, Chapter 13, from which we quoted above in Chapter V of this discourse.[18] And this was also his view in I Timothy, Chapter 2, when he wrote: "I exhort, therefore, that first of all supplications . . . be made for kings, and for all that are in authority, that we may lead," that is, have, "a quiet and peaceful life." [19] And conversely, the government needs and is dependent upon the action of the priesthood, for it receives from it the teaching together with the sacraments whereby men in this world are prepared for salvation or eternal beatitude for the status of the future world, and what is contrary thereto is removed.

But the government and the priesthood do and receive these actions to and from one another in different ways. For since the ruler is coercive judge in this world by ordainment of God, although immediately by appointment of the human legislator or of some other human will, it follows that if the priest transgresses a human law which is not contrary to divine law, the ruler can lawfully impress his action upon the priest through coercive force, by inflicting pain or punishment, even if the priest be unwilling, as has been demonstrated in Chapters V and VIII of this discourse, and in Chapter XV of Discourse I. But the bishop or priest, on

---

[17] I Corinthians 12:21.   [18] Romans 13:1–7. See above, II. v. 4.
[19] I Timothy 2:1–2. See above, II. v. 7.

the other hand, is not a coercive judge over anyone in this world in accordance with divine law, as has been shown in Chapter XV of Discourse I and in Chapters IV, V, and IX of this discourse, but rather he is a judge in the first sense of "judge," a practical teacher, as it were, like a physician; and consequently through his action or command he neither can nor should coerce anyone by pain or punishment, in property or in person, in the present life.

Thus, then, we have revealed the falsity of the first proposition of the argument stated above, which asserted that all that which performs a more perfect action must not be subject in jurisdiction to that which performs a less perfect action. For from this proposition there also necessarily follows another manifest absurdity, namely, the falsehood that no theoretic artificer, or at least no first philosopher or metaphysician, is subject to the jurisdiction of the ruler in accordance with human law, since none of the operative habits other than faith, which are in the ruler or in anyone else, and none of the actions which emerge from these habits, are equal in perfection to the habit of the first philosopher or to the action emerging through this habit; and yet it is possible that an adequate and rightly appointed ruler lack this habit.[20]

5. As for the subsequent objection that it seems improper for Christ's particular vicar, the Roman bishop, or for any other successor of the apostles, to have to be subject to the coercive judgment of the ruler in accordance with human law,[21] it must be replied that it is no impropriety that someone's vicar be subject to that judge (or a similar one) to whom that vicar's lord voluntarily subjected himself for the purpose of maintaining the proper order of this world. For Christ, God and man, voluntarily underwent the coercive judgment of Pontius Pilate, the ruler in accordance with human law, the vicar of Caesar;[22] and so too did the holy apostles, and in accordance with divine law they commanded others to do the same, as has clearly been shown through Scripture and the statements of the saints and other doctors in Chapters IV and V of this discourse, and as was reiterated in Chapter XXVIII. Hence, since "the servant is not greater than his lord; neither is the apostle greater than he that sent him," as we quoted in Chapter XXVIII of this discourse from Scripture through Bernard,[23] it is not improper but rather quite proper, indeed it is necessary for the peace of the state or polity that every bishop, priest, and clergyman be subject to the coercive judgment of the rulers in accordance with human law. The contrary of this is entirely improper and

---

[20] See above, I. xv. 1.   [21] See above, II. iii. 15.
[22] Removing, with Bigongiari (p. 48) and Scholz, parentheses around *Caesaris*.
[23] John 13:16; see above, II. xxviii. 24.

unbearable, as has been demonstrated in Chapter XVII of Discourse I, and as has been confirmed above in this discourse by the eternal testaments.

Moreover, the Roman or any other bishop is not the vicar or minister of Christ for the exercising of every office in this world, but only for a determinate office, namely, the priesthood, in which, as such, there is to be found no coercive judgment, nor superiority or inferiority with respect to such judgment, as we have plainly proved from Aristotle in Chapter IX of this discourse, paragraph 8. But the ruler in accordance with human law, on the other hand, is the vicar or minister of God with respect to the office of government, in which there are to be found superiority and subjection with respect to coercive power. And hence in Romans, Chapter 13, the Apostle wrote as follows, making no exceptions of bishops or priests: "Let every soul be subject to the higher powers"; and then he told the reason why: "For he is the minister of God." So, then, the ruler is the vicar of God, not for every kind of function indiscriminately, but for the purpose of coercing those who do evil in this world. Whence the Apostle adds: "A revenger to execute wrath upon him that doeth evil"; [24] but evil can be done by bishops or priests, and no judge other than the ruler was ever assigned to them by Christ or any of the apostles, by word or by deed or example, as we have shown in the afore-mentioned chapter of this discourse. [25]

6. We come now to the objection which was put in the form of a question, that if it is expedient that the rulers according to human authority be corrected when they sin against divine or human law, it nevertheless does not seem that they can appropriately be corrected, since the primary ruler or rulers, at least, have no superior in the polity; and consequently they ought to be subject to the coercive judgment of the priests or bishops. [26] To this it must be replied that the ruler who sins against divine or human law can and should appropriately be corrected by the ecclesiastic minister, the bishop or priest, through words of exhortation or censure, although the words should be mild, according to the teaching of the Apostle in II Timothy, Chapters 2 and 4, and the explication of Chrysostom, which we cited in Chapter IX of this discourse. [27] But the correction should not be through coercive power, for such power over anyone in this world does not pertain to the bishop or priest, as such, as has been frequently proved and reiterated above. But if the ruler commits excesses against the laws, then insofar as he does so against human law as we defined it in Chapter X, [28] the authority

---

[24] Romans 13:1, 4.　　　[25] See above, II. ix. 1 ff.　　　[26] See above, II. iii. 15.

[27] II Timothy 2:24; 4:2. Chrysostom *De sacerdotio* II. iii, iv (PG 48. 634 f.). See above, II. ix. 4.

[28] See above, I. x. 3–6.

to correct him and also to inflict temporal pain or punishment upon him, if necessary, pertains only to the human legislator or to the persons whom it has appointed for this purpose, and the correction must be in accordance with human law, as we think has been sufficiently shown in Chapter XVIII of Discourse I.

7. The final argument was that that person is superior to the Roman emperor in jurisdiction, and can rightfully appoint and depose him, who "transferred the empire from the Greeks to the Germans in the person of Charlemagne"; but this person is the Roman pope; therefore the Roman pope is superior to the emperor, and can rightfully appoint and depose him.[29] To this it must be replied that if the major premise be taken indefinitely, then from it together with the minor premise no conclusion can be drawn, because a syllogism cannot be made from an indefinite and a particular premise.[30] But if, on the other hand, the major premise were taken universally, so that it said: Every person who has transferred the Roman empire from the Greeks to the Germans is superior, etc., then this proposition would have several true objections against it unless the subject were made determinate. For if a person had transferred the empire in fact (*de facto*), but not rightfully (*de jure*), or if he had made this transfer by using power which was not his own or which someone else had on that occasion given to him as a deputy for that purpose, then such a person, who had in this way transferred the empire, would not on that account by himself alone have superior jurisdiction over the Roman ruler or the just power to appoint and depose him. On the other hand, the aforesaid major premise is granted if it is made determinate as follows: Every mortal who has justly transferred, or who can justly transfer, the Roman empire from the Greeks to the Germans by authority which is his own and is not granted to him by someone else, is superior in coercive jurisdiction to the Roman ruler, and can justly appoint and depose him. But as for the subjoined minor premise, which says that the Roman bishop or pope is the person who has transferred the empire in the way we have said, this must be denied as completely false. For the opposite of this proposition has been demonstrated in Chapter XV of Discourse I, and has been confirmed, together with the opposite of the conclusion which is drawn from it, in Chapters IV and V of this discourse, through Scripture and the statements of the saints and catholic doctors, and we have reiterated this in many other passages; and in Chapter XXI of this discourse we have proved, from approved histories, that the opposite of that conclusion was in fact ob-

---

[29] See above, II. iii. 14. The order of the last two arguments is here reversed.

[30] See Aristotle *Prior Analytics* I. 4. 26b 21–24.

served without protest by the ancient fathers and pastors who were Roman bishops.

We come now to the assertion which is made in the document entitled *On Oaths* (which is in the seventh part of certain statements called *Decretals*) [31] and also in an epistle written by a so-called Roman pope to the noble Ludwig, duke of Bavaria, elected king of the Romans [32]—the assertion, namely, that "the Roman empire was" reasonably or justly "transferred from the Greeks to the Germans in the person of Charlemagne, by the apostolic seat" or Roman pope, either alone or together with his clerical college. Let us grant this assertion for the present, because in a separate treatise we are going to discuss this transfer with respect to how it in fact proceeded.[33] Let us assume, then, that the empire was justly transferred from the Greeks to the Germans; I declare, nevertheless, that this was not done by the authority of the Roman pope, either alone or together with his clerical college, as we have said above.

8. And hence it must be noted, in accordance with the demonstrations given in Chapters XII, XIII, and XIV of Discourse I, and in accordance with right reason, that to the same body belongs the primary authority to make human laws, to establish the government, to elect the ruler, to grant him authority, and, with regard to all these matters, to make any changes, cancellations, additions, subtractions, suspensions, corrections, removals, transfers, revocations, or anything else which the aforesaid body, having such authority as principal and not from anyone else, has deemed expedient and has expressed through its will. As to what is the body to which the aforesaid authority belongs, this has been determined in Chapters XII and XIII of Discourse I. Consequently, wherever a statement is made by anyone that the pope or any other individual person or particular group of the province or state has transferred the empire, or has established any other government or ruler who is designated by election, if such statements or writings are to be true, and if such establishment or transfer is to be valid or just, then it must be made or have been made by the authority of the primary legislator in the province or provinces over which, from which, and to which such establishment or transfer is to be made or to have been made. Therefore, if a statement is made, orally or in writing, to the effect that the transfer of the Roman empire, or the appointment of some

---

[31] *Corp. jur. can., Clem.* Lib. II. Tit. 9. cap. 1. See above, II. xxiii. 12.

[32] This is John XXII's *monitorium* of Oct. 8, 1323 (MGH, *Constitutiones*, V, 616). See above, II. xxvi. 6.

[33] This refers to the brief tract *De translatione imperii* (*Monarchia*, ed. Goldast, II, 147–53), which is an abbreviation of Landulfus of Colonna's treatise of the same name (in *ibid.*, II, 88–95) with interpolated contradictions some of which are explicitly taken from the *Defensor pacis*.

emperor, has been duly made by the Roman pope either alone or together with his clerical college, and if such statement is to be true, then it must be understood to mean that the pope and the cardinals made this transfer or appointment by virtue of the authority granted to them for this purpose by the supreme human legislator of the Roman empire, either directly or indirectly; or else that the aforesaid transfer or appointment was made by them not in an unqualified sense, but in some special sense, as, for example, that they proclaimed or announced (but still by virtue of the above-mentioned authority) that the transfer or appointment had been made. For the aforesaid legislator may perhaps have made some transfer or appointment with respect to the empire, the announcement or proclamation of which it later entrusted to the Roman pope alone, as being the most reverent of all human beings, or to the pope together with his priests, as being the most venerable college of clergymen—not, indeed, because such announcement was necessary to the validity of the transfer or appointment, but only for the sake of solemnizing it. For the transfer of governments, the establishment of laws and appointment of rulers, and similarly all other civil functions, as such, depend for their validity upon the election or ordinance of the aforesaid legislator alone, as has been demonstrated in Chapters XII and XIII of Discourse I, and as has been reiterated with some clarification, not altogether uselessly, in Chapter XXVI of this discourse, paragraph 5. And a similar view must be taken throughout with regard to the establishment of the office of the princes who elect the Roman emperor; for these electors have in this regard no other authority, and from no other source, than that which is given to them by the aforesaid supreme human legislator of the Roman empire, nor can this authority be revoked or suspended by anyone other than that legislator.

Let it suffice, then, to have discussed in this way the doubts which were raised in Chapters III and XXVII of this discourse, and to have put an end to the questions.

DISCOURSE THREE

CHAPTER I: REVIEW OF THE PRINCIPAL AIMS AND CONCLUSIONS OF DISCOURSES I AND II, AND THEIR CONNECTION WITH WHAT IS TO FOLLOW

IN the foregoing we have set forth the singular cause which has hitherto produced civil discord or intranquillity in certain states and communities, and which will go on to do the same in all the other states unless it is stopped. This cause is the belief, desire, and undertaking whereby the Roman bishop and his clerical coterie, in particular, are aiming to seize secular rulerships and to possess excessive temporal wealth. In his endeavor to obtain the supreme of all rulerships, this bishop bases his claims upon that plenitude of power which he asserts Christ granted to him in particular in the person of St. Peter, as we have said in the last chapter of Discourse I and as has been reiterated, not inappropriately, in many chapters of Discourse II. However, no rulership or coercive judgment over anyone in this world, let alone the supreme one of all, belongs to him or to any other bishop, priest, or clergyman, as such, collectively or distributively, as we have demonstrated by sure human methods in Chapters XII, XIII, and XV of Discourse I, and as we have confirmed in Chapters IV and V of Discourse II by the testimonies of the eternal Truth, as well as by the expositions of its saintly interpreters and of very many of its approved teachers. In Chapters VI and VII of Discourse II we have indicated, through the Scriptures and by sure reasonings, what is the nature and extent of the power of the priests or bishops. And in Chapter XXIII of Discourse II we have shown that to none of these, either collectively or distributively, belongs the plenitude of power which they, and especially the Roman bishop, had assumed for themselves. It seems, therefore, that the roots of that singular evil which we mentioned so often in our prefatory remarks have been adequately cut out. Now, in order that the sprouts and offshoots of the strife or discord which this pestilence has hitherto brought and is still bringing to states and communities may the sooner wither up and be incapable of further propagation, we shall write this third and last discourse. This discourse will consist only in certain conclusions which will be explicitly and necessarily inferred from the self-evident or demonstrated propositions set forth above. Through these conclusions, if they are diligently studied and acted upon, the afore-mentioned pestilence and its sophistic cause will without difficulty be excluded from states, and will henceforth be denied entry both to these and to all other civil communities.

CHAPTER II: IN WHICH ARE EXPLICITLY INFERRED CERTAIN CONCLUSIONS WHICH FOLLOW NECESSARILY FROM THE RESULTS SET FORTH IN THE FIRST TWO DISCOURSES. BY HEEDING THESE CONCLUSIONS, RULERS AND SUBJECTS CAN MORE EASILY ATTAIN THE END AIMED AT BY THIS BOOK

OF the conclusions to be inferred, we shall place this one first:

1. For the attainment of eternal beatitude it is necessary to believe in the truth of only the divine or canonic Scripture, together with its necessary consequences and the interpretations of it made by the common council of the believers, if these have been duly propounded to the person concerned. The certainty of this is set forth in, and can be obtained from, Discourse II, Chapter XIX, paragraphs 2 to 5.

2. Doubtful sentences of divine law, especially on those matters which are called articles of the Christian faith, as well as on other matters belief in which is necessary for salvation, must be defined only by the general council of the believers, or by the weightier multitude or part thereof; no partial group or individual person, of whatever status, has the authority to make such definitions. The certainty of this is to be had in Discourse II, Chapter XX, paragraphs 4 to 13.

3. The evangelic Scripture does not command that anyone be compelled by temporal pain or punishment to observe the commands of divine law: Discourse II, Chapter IX, paragraphs 3 to 10.

4. For eternal salvation it is necessary to observe only the commands of the evangelic law, and their necessary consequences, and the dictates of right reason as to what should be done and not done; but not all the commands of the Old Law: Discourse II, Chapter IX, paragraph 10 to the end.

5. No mortal can dispense with the commands or prohibitions of the divine or evangelic law; only the general council or the faithful human legislator, and not any partial group or individual person, of whatever status, can prohibit things which are permitted by that law, by obliging transgressors of this prohibition to incur guilt or punishment for the status of the present or of the future world: Discourse I, Chapter XII, paragraph 9; Discourse II, Chapter IX, paragraph 1, and Chapter XXI, paragraph 8.

6. Only the whole body of citizens, or the weightier part thereof, is the human legislator: Discourse I, Chapters XII and XIII.

7. The decretals or decrees of the Roman or any other pontiffs, collectively or distributively, made without the grant of the human legislator, bind no one to temporal pain or punishment: Discourse I, Chapter XII; Discourse II, Chapter XXVIII, paragraph 29.

8. Human laws can be dispensed with only by the human legislator or by someone else acting by its authority: Discourse I, Chapter XII, paragraph 9.

9. An elective ruler, or any other official, is dependent only upon election by the body having the authority therefor, and needs no other confirmation or approval: Discourse I, Chapter XII, paragraph 9; Discourse II, Chapter XXVI, paragraphs 4 to 7.

10. The election of any elective ruler or other official, especially if such office carries coercive force, depends upon the expressed will of the legislator alone: Discourse I, Chapter XII; Chapter XV, paragraphs 2 to 4.

11. The supreme government in a city or state must be only one in number: Discourse I, Chapter XVII.

12. Only the faithful ruler in accordance with the laws or approved customs has the authority to appoint persons to the offices of the state and to determine their quality and number, as well as all other civil affairs: Discourse I, Chapter XII; Chapter XV, paragraphs 4 and 10.

13. No ruler, and still less any partial group or individual person of whatever status, has plenitude of control or power over the individual or civil acts of other persons without the determination of the mortal legislator:[1] Discourse I, Chapter XI; Discourse II, Chapter XXIII, paragraphs 3 to 5.

14. A bishop or priest, as such, has no rulership or coercive jurisdiction over any clergyman or layman, even if the latter be a heretic: Discourse I, Chapter XV, paragraphs 2 to 4; Discourse II, Chapters IV, V, IX, and X, paragraph 7.

15. Only the ruler by authority of the legislator has coercive jurisdiction

[1] See Vol. I, p. 257.

over the person and property of every individual mortal person, of whatever status, and of every group of laymen or clergymen: Discourse I, Chapters XV and XVII; Discourse II, Chapters IV, V, and VIII.

16. No bishop or priest or group of them is allowed to excommunicate anyone without authorization by the faithful legislator: Discourse II, Chapter VI, paragraphs 11 to 14; Chapter XXI, paragraph 9.

17. All bishops are of equal authority immediately through Christ, nor can it be proved by divine law that there is any superiority or subjection among them in spiritual or in temporal affairs: Discourse II, Chapters XV and XVI.

18. By divine authority, accompanied by the consent or concession of the faithful human legislator, the other bishops, collectively or distributively, can excommunicate the Roman bishop and exercise other authority over him, just as conversely: Discourse II, Chapter VI, paragraphs 11 to 14; Chapters XV and XVI.

19. No mortal being can give a dispensation with respect to marriages prohibited by divine law, while those prohibited by human law pertain only to the authority of the legislator or of him who rules through the legislator: Discourse I, Chapter XII, paragraph 9; Discourse II, Chapter XXI, paragraph 8.

20. Only the faithful legislator has the authority to legitimize illegitimate children so that they may succeed to their inheritances and receive other civil and ecclesiastic offices and benefits: same passages as immediately above.

21. It pertains only to the faithful legislator to exercise coercive judgment with regard to candidates for church orders and their qualifications, and no priest or bishop is allowed to promote anyone to these orders without authorization by this legislator: Discourse I, Chapter XV, paragraphs 2, 3, and 4; Discourse II, Chapter XVII, paragraphs 8 to 16.

22. Only the ruler in accordance with the laws of the believers has the authority to regulate the number of churches or temples, and of the priests, deacons, and other officials who are to minister therein: same passages as immediately above.

23. Only by the authority of the faithful legislator can and should separable church offices be bestowed and taken away, and similarly benefices and other things established for religious purposes: Discourse I, Chapter XV, paragraphs 2 and 4; Discourse II, Chapter XVII, paragraphs 16 to 18; Chapter XXI, paragraphs 11 to 15.

24. No bishops, as such, collectively or distributively, have the authority

to appoint notaries or other civil public officials: Discourse I, Chapter XV, paragraphs 2, 3, and 10; Discourse II, Chapter XXI, paragraph 15.

25. No licence for the public teaching or practice of any art or discipline can be bestowed by any bishop, collectively or distributively, as such; but this pertains only to the legislator, at least the faithful one, or to the ruler by its authority: same passages as immediately above.

26. Persons appointed to the diaconate or priesthood, and others who are irrevocably dedicated to God, must be given preference in church offices and benefices over persons who are not thus dedicated: Discourse II, Chapter XIV, paragraphs 6 to 8.

27. Ecclesiastic temporal goods which remain over and above the needs of priests and other gospel ministers and of the helpless poor, and which are not needed for divine worship, can lawfully, in accordance with divine law, be used in whole or in part by the legislator for the common or public welfare or defense: Discourse I, Chapter XV, paragraph 10; Discourse II, Chapter XVII, paragraph 16; Chapter XXI, paragraph 14.

28. All temporal goods which have been set aside for religious purposes or for deeds of mercy, such as legacies bequeathed for overseas crossing to resist the infidels, or for the redemption of captives, or for the support of the helpless poor, and for other similar purposes, are to be distributed only by the ruler in accordance with the designation of the legislator and the intention of the donor: same passages as immediately above.

29. Only the faithful legislator has the authority to grant exemption to any group or religious body, and to approve or institute such exemption: Discourse I, Chapter XV, paragraphs 2, 3, 4, and 10; Discourse II, Chapter XVII, paragraphs 8 to 16; Chapter XXI, paragraphs 8 and 15.

30. Only the ruler in accordance with the designation of the human legislator has the authority to exercise coercive judgment over all heretics, criminals, and other persons subject to temporal pain or punishment; to inflict on them penalties in person, to exact penalties in property, and to dispose of these latter penalties: Discourse I, Chapter XV, paragraphs 6 to 9; Discourse II, Chapter VIII, paragraphs 2 and 3; and Chapter X.

31. No one who is subject and obligated to someone else by lawful oath can be released by any bishop or priest without reasonable cause, which cause is to be judged by the faithful legislator by a judgment in the third sense; and the opposite of this is contrary to sound doctrine: Discourse II, Chapters VI and VII; and Chapter XXVI, paragraphs 13 to 16.

32. Only the general council of all the faithful has the authority to designate a bishop or any metropolitan church highest of all, and to deprive

or depose them from such position: Discourse II, Chapter XXII, paragraphs 9 to 12.

33. Only the faithful legislator, or the ruler by its authority in communities of believers may assemble through coercive power a general or partial council of priests, bishops, and other believers; and if a council is assembled in a different way, then decisions made therein have no force or validity, and no one is obliged under temporal or spiritual guilt or punishment to observe such decisions: Discourse I, Chapter XV, paragraphs 2, 3, and 4; Chapter XVII; Discourse II, Chapter VIII, paragraph 6 to the end; and Chapter XXI, paragraphs 2 to 8.

34. Fasts and prohibitions of food must be imposed only by the authority of the general council of believers, or of the faithful legislator; if divine law does not prohibit the practice of mechanical arts or the teaching of disciplines on any day, then these can be forbidden only by the aforesaid council or legislator; and only the faithful legislator or the ruler by its authority can enforce the observance of such prohibitions by temporal pain or punishment: Discourse I, Chapter XV, paragraphs 2, 3, 4, and 8; Discourse II, Chapter XXI, paragraph 8.

35. The canonization and worship of anyone as a saint must be established and ordained only by the general council: Discourse II, Chapter XXI, paragraph 8.

36. Only the general council of believers has the authority to make decrees forbidding bishops, priests, and other temple ministers to have wives, as well as other ordinances with regard to church practice; and such decrees may be dispensed with only by that group or person to whom the authority for this has been given by the aforesaid council: same passages as immediately above.

37. From the coercive jurisdiction granted to a bishop or priest a litigant may always appeal to the legislator or to the ruler by its authority: Discourse I, Chapter XV, paragraphs 2 and 3; Discourse II, Chapter XXII, paragraph 11.

38. A person who is to maintain the evangelical perfection of supreme poverty can have no chattels in his power without the firm intention of selling them as soon as possible and giving the price received to the poor; of no thing, movable or immovable, can he have the ownership or power, that is, with the intention of laying claim to that thing before a coercive judge from anyone who seizes or wishes to seize it: Discourse II, Chapter XIII, paragraphs 22 and 30; Chapter XIV, paragraph 14.

39. Communities and individuals are obliged by divine law to contribute, so far as they can, the food and clothing which are needed, at least on each

successive day, by the bishops and others who minister the gospel to them; but they are not obliged to give tithes or anything else over and above the needs of the aforesaid ministers: Discourse II, Chapter XIV, paragraphs 6 to 11.

40. The faithful legislator, or the ruler by its authority in a province subject to it, can compel bishops and other gospel ministers, who have been provided with sufficient food and clothing, to perform the divine functions and to minister the ecclesiastic sacraments: Discourse I, Chapter XV, paragraphs 2, 3, and 4; Discourse II, Chapter VIII, paragraph 6 to the end; Chapter XVII, paragraph 12.

41. Appointments of the Roman bishop and of any other ecclesiastic or temple ministers in accordance with divine law to separable ecclesiastic offices, as well as suspensions and removals therefrom because of delict, must be effected only by the faithful legislator, or the ruler by its authority, or the general council of the believers: Discourse I, Chapter XV, paragraphs 2, 3, 4, and 10; Discourse II, Chapter XVII, paragraphs 8 to 16; Chapter XXII, paragraphs 9 to 13.

42. We might infer many other useful conclusions which necessarily follow from the first two discourses; but let us be content with those deduced above, because they afford a ready and sufficient entering wedge for cutting away the afore-mentioned pestilence and its cause, and also for the sake of brevity.

CHAPTER III: ON THE TITLE OF THIS BOOK

THIS treatise will be called *Defender of Peace*, because it discusses and explains the principal causes whereby civil peace or tranquillity exists and is preserved, and whereby the opposed strife arises and is checked and destroyed. For this treatise makes known the authority, the cause, and the concordance of divine and human laws and of all coercive governments, which are the standards of human acts, in whose proper unimpeded measure civil peace or tranquillity consists.

Moreover, this treatise enables both rulers and subjects, who are the primary elements of every state, to comprehend what must be done in order to preserve their own peace and freedom. For through the human and divine truths written in this book, the first citizen or part of the civil regime, the ruler (whether one man or many), will comprehend that to him alone belongs the authority to give commands to the subject multitude collectively or distributively and to mete out punishment to any person when it is expedient, in accordance with the established laws. And the ruler will also learn that he must do nothing apart from the laws, especially on important matters, without the consent of the subject multitude or legislator, and that the multitude or legislator must not be provoked by injury, because in its expressed will consists the virtue and authority of government. The subject multitude, and each individual member thereof, can in their turn learn from this book what sort of person or persons should be appointed to rule, and that for and in the status of the present world they are obliged to obey only the commands of the ruling part as coercive, and then only when those commands are in accordance with the established laws, while those which are not thus in accord must be dealt with in the manner described in Chapters XIV and XVIII of Discourse I. And the subject multitude will also learn the extent to which it is possible to see to it that the ruler or any other part of the community does not assume for itself the arbitrary discretion [1] to make judgments or to perform any other civil acts contrary to or apart from the laws.

For when these truths are comprehended, retained in mind, and diligently heeded and observed, the state or any other temperate civil community whatsoever [2] will be preserved in peaceful or tranquil existence; through this, men who live a civil life attain a sufficiency of worldly life, while without it they are necessarily deprived of such sufficiency and are poorly disposed for eternal beatitude as well. That these are the ends and the best objects of human desire, although in two different worlds, we have assumed in our preceding statements as being self-evident to all men. And to what we have written above we now add that if there happens to be found in this treatise any statement, conclusion, or other utterance which is not catholic, then such has not been made pertinaciously, and we leave its correction and determination to the authority of the catholic church or the general council of faithful Christians.

On Baptist's Day, 1324,[3]

The *Defender* is finished.

Praise and glory to thee, Christ!

---

[1] *Arbitrium.* See above, I. xi. 1, 3, 5, 7; I. xiv. 5, 6. See also Vol. I, pp. 24, 144, 243–44; and Introduction, p. xc.

[2] See Vol. I, p. 128.   [3] That is, June 24, 1324.

APPENDIX I

ON MARSILIUS' MISINTERPRETATIONS OF SOME
TEXTS OF ARISTOTLE

THE misinterpretations of Aristotle found in Marsilius' crucial argument in proof of the necessary impervertibility of the people's will (I. xiii. 2, pp. 50–51) are important enough to require a separate discussion. Among other things, these misinterpretations provide a cardinal example of the way in which Marsilius substitutes necessities for Aristotle's practical contingencies.[1]

Consider the statement which Marsilius here quotes from Aristotle: "that part of the state which wishes the polity to endure must be weightier than the part which does not wish it": *oportet valentiorem esse partem civitatis volentem non-volente manere politiam; δεῖ γὰρ κρεῖττον εἶναι τὸ βουλόμενον μέρος τῆς πόλεως τοῦ μὴ βουλομένου μένειν τὴν πολιτείαν (Politics* IV. 12. 1296b 14 [Sus. p. 425]).[2] This statement is presented by Aristotle as the general principle for dealing with the question of "what kind of constitution is beneficial to what kind of persons" (*ibid.* IV. 12. 1296b 12). Hence the quoted statement means for Aristotle that *if* a constitution is to be beneficial for the persons living under it, *then* "that part of the state which wishes the constitution to endure must be stronger (κρεῖττον) than the part which does not wish it." The necessity (δεῖ, *oportet*) of the statement is thus entirely hypothetical: it sets forth the condition required for a desired end. Marsilius not only changes "stronger" to describe a quantitative majority ("in most of its individual members," *secundum eius plurimum*), but he changes the statement into one of an absolute necessity, which "necessarily follows" from the natural impulse, itself viewed as a necessarily existing fact, of all men to live in the state.

A similar misinterpretation marks the next quotation from the *Politics* (VII. 14. 1332b 30 [Sus. p. 303]). Marsilius makes two interpolations in this quotation, which are introduced in the translation by the phrase "that is" each time, while in his own Latin text his interpolations are given in parentheses: " 'It is impossible that there be so many persons in the government,' that is, rebellious, or not caring to live a civil life, 'that they are stronger than all the others,' that is, than those who want to carry on a political life": *totque multitudine esse eos in politeumate (insolentes scilicet, seu non curantes civiliter vivere) ut sint valentiores hiis omnibus (videlicet politizare volentibus) unum impossibilium est;*[3] τοσούτους τε εἶναι τοὺς ἐν τῳ πολιτεύματι τὸ πλῆθος ὥστ' εἶναι κρείττους πάντων τούτων ἔν τι τῶν ἀδυνάτων ἐστίν. Marsilius' interpretation is here precisely the opposite of Aristotle's meaning. Aristotle has said, in the sentence preceding this one, that "it is difficult for a constitution to endure

---

[1] See Vol. I, pp. 208–9; also pp. 48–51, 57–59, 61–63, 106–7, 255–56.

[2] Marsilius' quotation omits *enim* after *oportet*, in Moerbeke's translation as given in Susemihl.

[3] Marsilius' quotation omits *qui* after *eos*, and *aliquod* after *unum*.

which is framed contrary to justice. For everyone in the country stands with the persons governed in desiring to rebel, and [here begins Marsilius' quotation] it is impossible that there be so many persons in the government that they are stronger than all of these." Marsilius has interpreted Aristotle's "persons in the government" (*eos in politeumate*) to mean those who are "rebellious, or not caring to live a civil life"; and he has interpreted "all of these" (i.e., the governed, who *are* in revolt) to mean "those who want to carry on a political life." Aristotle's discussion of the dynamics of particular constitutions is thus made by Marsilius into a discussion of the citizens' desire for civil life as such. Moreover, Aristotle's "impossible" in this sentence means nothing more than "difficult," as the preceding sentence shows (cf. also *Metaphysics* v. 12. 1019a 12–21, on this meaning of "impossible"); but Marsilius has transformed it into an impossibility of physical nature, as the remainder of the paragraph shows, with its references to "nature" and "natural science." (On the "nature" to which he here refers, cf. Aristotle *Physics* II. 8. 198b 10 ff.; *Parts of Animals* I. 1. 639b 23 ff.; also above, pp. lxix–lxx; and Vol. I, pp. 54–59.)

APPENDIX II

NATURAL DESIRE, THE UNITY OF THE INTELLECT, AND POLITICAL AVERROISM

MARSILIUS' argument in i. xiii. 2 brings to a focus some concepts and problems which have an important bearing on the philosophic bases of his entire politics. Three points in particular deserve special attention: the doctrine of the non-futility of natural desire, the Averroist doctrine of the unity of the intellect in all mankind, and the relation of Marsilius to "political Averroism."

(1) *The non-futility of natural desire.* The argument of i. xiii. 2 [1] holds that since all men have a natural desire for sufficiency of life, they necessarily desire also whatever is necessary for such life. If they did not desire these necessary means, then the initial natural desire would be "futile," and this in turn "would mean that nature errs or is deficient for the most part."

The premise which Marsilius here invokes—that a natural desire cannot be futile or in vain [2]—was quite common among the scholastics. It was explicitly invoked, for example, by Averroes, Albert the Great, Thomas Aquinas, Siger of Brabant, and John of Jandun in their commentaries on the first sentence of Aristotle's *Metaphysics:* "All men have a natural desire for knowledge." The non-futility of natural desires was, however, susceptible of two different interpretations: as Siger pointed out, it could mean either that natural desires are *capable* of fulfillment or that they are *actually* fulfilled. Siger chose the former alternative,[3] and this too was the interpretation of Aristotle's sentence given by Averroes,[4] Albert,[5] and Thomas,[6] the latter two adding that

---

[1] In Vol. I, pp. 203–12 (where I called it "the argument from will"), I have examined this argument in some detail.

[2] i. xiii. 2: "inane namque foret tale desiderium."

[3] Siger of Brabant *Quaestiones in Metaphysicam* Lib. ii. qu. 3 (ed. C. A. Graiff [Louvain, 1948], pp. 38–40): "*Utrum naturale desiderium possit esse otiosum.* . . . Solutio. Distinguendum de otioso. Uno modo est otiosum quia impossibile, alio modo quia non includit finem. Primo modo non potest esse otiosum . . . ratio desiderii naturalis non est nisi ex potentia ad desideratum, ideo non potest esse ad impossibile. Secundo modo potest esse otiosum."

[4] *Commentarium in libros Metaphysicorum* Lib. ii. cap. i (in *Aristotelis opera cum Averrois commentariis* [Venice, 1574], viii, fol. 28 K): "si comprehensio esset impossibilis, tunc desiderium esset ociosum. Et concessum est ab omnibus, quod *nulla res est ociosa in fundamento naturae et creaturae.*"

[5] *Metaphysicorum libri XIII* Lib. i. Tr. i. cap. iv (in *Opera,* ed. Borgnet [Paris, 1890], VI, 7–8): "Subjiciatur ergo a nobis primum, quod *non potest esse vanum naturale et toti speciei conveniens desiderium.* Hoc enim supposito, probabimus quod omnes homines natura scire desiderant . . ." See also *ibid.* cap. v (VI, 9–10).

[6] *In Metaphysicam Aristotelis commentaria* Lib. i. Lect. i (ed. M. R. Cathala [Turin, 1935], n. 4, p. 6): "Quaerere scientiam non propter aliud utilem, qualis est haec scientia, non est vanum, cum *naturale desiderium vanum esse non potest.*" See also *In Eth.* Lib. i. Lect. 2. n. 21 (p. 8), where an infinite regress of desired ends is refuted through the impossibility that "naturale desiderium sit inane et vacuum."

pleasures and other influences may prevent the actual fulfillment of man's natural desire for knowledge. John of Jandun, on the other hand, took the latter alternative. This, however, required a new distinction. For if the natural desire of all men for knowledge is actually fulfilled, then a distinction must be drawn between "all men" (or "most men") taken *distributively* and taken *collectively*. That all or most men taken distributively do actually fulfill their natural desire for knowledge is obviously false, John pointed out, for such desire entails that men desire all the sciences equally, since all the sciences are of equal perfection; but so far is it from being the case that *every* man has all the sciences, that it is scarcely the case that *any* man has them all. The "all men" of Aristotle's sentence must, therefore, "be understood collectively, as meaning that philosophy and science are perfect in the majority of men taken together, so that men collectively have every science, one man having one part, another another, and so forth. *And in this sense a natural desire is not futile in the whole species and in most men.*" [7]

Now Marsilius' insistence on the non-futility of natural desire, in his argument from will, is clearly in the tradition we have been examining; even its terminology is similar. Like Albert the Great and John of Jandun, Marsilius views natural desire and its non-futility within the context not of individuals but of the whole species; thus his argument, like that of John, applies to the desires of "the same specific nature in most of its individual members," viewed collectively.[8] Yet on this point Marsilius' doctrine exhibits a corporatism which is more rigorous in the impingement of the whole on the parts than is the case in the collectivism of John. Both Marsilius and John conceive the species as composed of individuals each of whom makes his contribution to the desires and achievements of the whole. But for John this contribution occurs through each individual's fulfilling separately his own natural desire for knowledge, without any great degree of contact of each with all the others.[9] For Marsilius, on the other hand, the contribution of the individual, if it is to fulfill the natural desire of "all men" taken collectively, can operate only through each individual's acting as an organic part of the whole *universitas*. It is still individuals who act; the "specific nature" which characterizes them does not remove their literal numerical diversity,[10] so that Marsilius is not

---

[7] *Quaestiones in duodecim libros Metaphysicae* (Venice, 1525), Lib. 1. qu. 4 (fol. 4 P-Q).

[8] Note the striking similarities among Albert, John, and Marsilius on this point. Albert (*loc. cit.* above, n. 5): "non potest esse *vanum* naturale et *toti speciei* conveniens desiderium." John (*loc. cit.* in preceding note): "appetitus naturalis non est *ociosus in tota specie et in pluribus hominibus.*" Marsilius (1. xiii. 2): "nihil desideratur per eandem *naturam specie secundum eius plurimum* et immediate cum ipsius corruptione simul; inane namque foret tale desiderium." The text of John of Jandun here quoted, as well as another text from John's *Quaestiones de Anima* Lib. III. qu. 10, is cited by B. Nardi to show "the Averroist influence on Marsilius." See Nardi's article, "La filosofia del medio evo nel pensiero di Giovanni Gentile," *Giornale critico della filosofia italiana*, XXVI (1947), 223-24. Nardi does not, however, take account of the differences between Marsilius and the other Averroists which are indicated on our following pages.

[9] See in this connection the analogy which John draws of men's collective attainment of all knowledge, to the fact that "tota pecunia mundi habetur ab omnibus hominibus" (*loc. cit.* in n. 7).

[10] Cf. the discussion of the unity of the state, 1. xvii. 11; and Vol. I, pp. 116, 209-10, 217-18.

here repeating some of the more extreme versions of the organic analogy. Yet the fitting of the individual into the "specific nature" is not merely the addition or combination at some late stage of previously isolated units; it is rather a chemical composition in which the individuals, if left to operate by themselves, will have desires and acts quite different from what they will have as members of the *universitas*.[11] This difference is important for the philosophic bases of Marsilius' republicanism. It helps account for its corporatist rather than individualist character.

Not only does Marsilius make, for the first time, a political application of the premise of the non-futility of natural desire, but in this application it receives a scope and detail which it had not previously attained. Where all his predecessors had said that the object of man's natural desires is something as general as "knowledge" or "the good," Marsilius, as we have seen, holds that this object is, successively, the sufficient life, the state, whatever is necessary for the state's preservation, and finally good laws. Moreover, in support of this necessary sequence of natural desires, Marsilius' argument reintroduces the Aristotelian concept of "deformity" which carries on the specifically biological context of his political philosophy, whereas his predecessors had appealed only to such general dicta as that "God and nature do nothing in vain,"[12] and that "natural desire is nothing other than the inclination inhering in things from the ordering of the prime mover, which cannot be frustrated."[13] And finally, Marsilius, like John of Jandun, interprets the non-futility of natural desire to mean that the object of this desire is actually attained, not merely that its attainment is possible. For John this had meant that all or most men taken collectively, or as a species, actually have all the sciences. For Marsilius, however, it means that the *universitas civium* or its weightier part, which is the legislator of the state, is all but infallible both in will and in execution: "election is always made for the common benefit, which the human legislator almost always aims at *and achieves.*"[14] Both John and Marsilius thus exhibit a kind of optimism about the collectivity of men, in the realms of the theoretic and the practical, respectively, which is as utopian as it is extreme. Yet in the political sphere it is this same doctrine, expressed as faith in the natural good-

---

[11] See I. xii. 5; I. xiii. 4–6; and Vol. I, pp. 194–95, 205, 215–18. This difference is also seen in John's discussion of the question "Utrum omnes homines appetunt unam scientiam" (*Quaest. in Metaphys.* I. qu. 5 [fol. 5] ff.]). He replies by distinguishing in men two "forms," a *forma communis* and a *forma individualis*. All men desire by the "common form" the one science "quae maxime satiat appetitum," because "in omnibus hominibus est idem principium appetendi secundum formam communem." But all men do not desire this one science "ex parte naturae individualis, quia secundum diversitatem complexionis diversificatur appetitus." Hence too, because of intellectual difficulties, bodily pleasures, and other reasons, all men do not pursue or attain the one science which they desire *ex parte naturae communis.* This distinction between the desires which men have from their individual and their common "forms" or "natures" is analogous to Marsilius' sharp separation between men's individual and corporate wills; but for Marsilius the corporate will is a "common form" which characterizes men not severally but only collectively.

[12] John of Jandun *Quaest. in Metaphys.* I. qu. 4 (fol. 4M): "natura nihil facit frustra, et deus in primo Caeli." The reference is to Aristotle *De caelo* I. 4. 271a 34. See also *De anima* III. 9. 432b 21.

[13] Thomas Aquinas *In Eth.* Lib. I. Lect. 2. n. 21 (p. 8).

[14] I. xvi. 19. For other similar statements, see I. xii. 8; I. xvi. 11, 21; and Vol. I, pp. 57–58.

ness of man, which animated many of the republican and democratic move-
ments in modern times. In any case, the upshot of Marsilius' naturalist-
corporate interpretation of desire is that nature operates as an efficient cause
within the wills of all or most men taken together, driving them from one
desire to the next until the state and all its laws and institutions are established,
thereby fully satisfying the original desire. Nature hence gives a sanction to
corporate majoritarian republicanism which is completely denied to all other
kinds of state.[15]

(2) *The unity of the intellect.* Analogues of Marsilius' general doctrine
might be found in many earlier phases of medieval thought, especially in the
theory of the *universitas* as developed by legists, canonists, theologians, and
philosophers.[16] In none, however, is the political application of natural desire
developed with the biological literalness which Marsilius effects on the basis
of Aristotle's "natural science."

With respect to this basis, some scholars [17] have suggested that Marsilius'
republican theory of the single will of the *universitas civium* for good laws is
derived from the Averroist doctrine that there is a single intellect in all men.
The source of this famous doctrine was in Aristotle's brief discussion of the
distinction between the "passive" and the "active" intellects, the former being
that which, like matter and potentiality, can "become all things," while the
latter is that which acts upon the passive intellect to make it operate.[18] According to Aristotle, the passive intellect is perishable while the active intellect
is "separable, impassive, and unmixed . . . immortal and eternal." From this
Averroes, followed by Siger of Brabant and John of Jandun, concluded that
since matter is the principle of numerical multiplicity, the active intellect,
being an immaterial "nature" or "form," cannot receive such multiplicity, so
that there is a single active intellect for all mankind.[19]

---

[15] A similar point was subsequently made by Nicholas of Cusa, who like Marsilius argued
from the premise that a natural desire cannot be futile to the conclusion that the majority of
the people will not fail to achieve what is right and useful: "Major pars populi . . . a
recta via ac pro tempore utile non deficiet, *alioqui contingeret naturalem appetitum frustrari*
. . . Videmus enim hominem animal esse politicum et civile et naturaliter ad civilitatem
inclinari" (*De catholica concordantia* Lib. III. Praefatio. Ed. S. Schard [Basel, 1618], p. 354).

[16] The authoritative discussion of the development of the theory of the *universitas*, despite
various well-founded criticisms of its philosophic thesis, is still the masterly third volume of
O. von Gierke's *Das deutsche Genossenschaftsrecht* (Berlin, 1881), unexcelled for its wealth
of footnote material. The "second chapter" (pp. 186–644) is on "Die mittelalterliche Staats-
und Korporationslehre," and its first three sections deal with the *Korporationstheorie* of,
respectively, the glossators on Roman law, the canonists, and the legists to Bartolus of Sassoferrato.

[17] E. Troilo, "L'Averroismo di Marsilio da Padova," in A. Checchini and N. Bobbio, eds.,
Marsilio da Padova: Studi raccolti nel VI Centenario della morte (Padua, 1942), pp. 64 ff.;
B. Nardi, *op. cit.* (above, n. 8), p. 224. The same derivation is also suggested in general terms
by J. H. Randall, Jr., in *The Renaissance Philosophy of Man*, ed. E. Cassirer, J. H. Randall,
Jr., P. O. Kristeller (Chicago, 1948), p. 264.

[18] *De anima* III. 5. 430a 10–25.

[19] Averroes *De anima* Lib. III. Com. 5 (in *Aristotelis de Anima libri tres cum Averrois commentariis* [Venice, 1574], fol. 148C ff.). Siger of Brabant *Quaestiones de anima intellectiva*
(in P. Mandonnet, *Siger de Brabant et l'averroïsme latin au XIII⁰ siècle*, 2d ed. [Louvain,
1911], II, 165). John of Jandun *Super libros Aristotelis de Anima subtilissimae quaestiones*
Lib. III. qu. 7 (Venice, 1519), fol. 54r. In the present connection there is no need to go into

Between this unitary intellect and the corporate will posited by Marsilius, there seem to be some affinities. The *universitas* which he takes as the subject of his argument in I. xiii. 2 and elsewhere is a corporate "whole" (*totum*), an identical specific nature (*eandem naturam specie*), whose desires are necessarily had by most of its members (*secundum eius plurimum, ut in pluribus*) only as parts of that nature, or whole, and not otherwise. Marsilius thus seems to make that nature a single will which is as determinative of its collective "parts" as is the single intellect posited by Averroes.[20] Indeed, since Marsilius' argument that the whole is superior to the part [21] applies to both the understanding and the will of the *universitas*, it achieves a similar unifying effect for both.

In saying that the intellect and the will of the whole body of citizens are qualitatively superior to the intellect and will of any part of that whole body, Marsilius is saying that when individuals think and desire as parts of the whole, their thoughts and desires necessarily receive from that context a beneficent character which they would otherwise lack. To be sure, Averroes and his followers explicitly applied their doctrine only to the intellect, not to the will nor to morals and politics; but as Thomas Aquinas pointed out, since the will is in the intellect, the numerical unity of the latter for all mankind entails a similar unity of the former, with corresponding moral and political repercussions.[22]

A further point closely related to the political perspective of Marsilius consists in the fact that Averroes and John of Jandun gave a majoritarian interpretation of the intellect's eternity, which they held to be a necessary consequence of its unity. Averroes declares that the intellect's philosophic knowledge, far from ceasing with individual cognitive acts, "is found perfect in

---

the vexed questions of the distinctions among the various kinds of intellect differentiated by Averroes and others—active, passive, possible, material, "acquired" (*adeptus*)—or of the shifts in the position of Siger. For a recent summary of some of the scholarly controversies on the latter point, with references to the writings of Grabmann, Van Steenberghen, Nardi, and others, as well as a discussion of the scholastics' polemics over the unity of the intellect, see S. MacClintock, "Heresy and Epithet: An Approach to the Problem of Latin Averroism," *Review of Metaphysics*, VIII (1954–55).

[20] There is a decided difference in this respect between Marsilius' collectivism and the purely distributive sense in which Thomas Aquinas upholds the natural necessity of the will for the ultimate end of man. Likewise different is Thomas' postponement to the future life of the necessary sequence of volitions for whatever is necessarily connected with the ultimate end. Cf. *S. theol.* I. qu.82. aa.1, 2; also Vol. I, p. 56, n. 25.

[21] I. xiii. 2, 4. Cf. Vol. I, pp. 194–95, 212–19.

[22] Aquinas, of course, held, as against Marsilius, that the unity of the intellect could not be a beneficent doctrine because it annihilated individual personality and responsibility. See *De unitate intellectus contra Averroistas Parisienses* (in *Opuscula omnia*, ed. P. Mandonnet [Paris, 1927], I, 56): "Si igitur intellectus non est aliquid hujus hominis, vel non est vere unum cum eo, sed unitur ei solum per phantasmata, non erit in homine voluntas, sed in intellectu separato, et ita hic homo non erit dominus sui actus, nec aliquis ejus actus erit laudabilis vel vituperabilis: quod est divellere principia moralis philosophiae." Cf. *Cont. gent.* II. lxxvi (fin.), where a similar argument against the active intellect's being a separate substance outside man is concluded with these words: "periebit tota scientia moralis et conversatio politica." Cf. also Albert the Great *De quindecim problematibus* I (ed. Mandonnet, *Siger*, II, 33).

the greater part [*in maiori parte*] of the subject in every time"; [23] and John of Jandun expounded this doctrine as meaning that "each man has some part of philosophy, one man one part, another man another part . . . and thus in all those men taken together philosophy is perfect, and those are the greater part [*major pars*] of men. For there are few men who have absolutely no part of philosophy. . . . And thus in all those men collectively [*conjunctim*] and not in each one distributively [*divisim*] philosophy is found perfect." [24] This point is similar to the application which Marsilius makes of the whole-part principle to prove the greater intellectual adequacy of the *universitas* or its *pars valentior* in comparison with any smaller number of men. Moreover, Marsilius, like Averroes and John, applies this majoritarian doctrine to men's judgment and possession of the various arts.[25]

While these points are quite suggestive of the philosophic lineage of Marsilius' corporate republicanism, it must be noted on the other side that the literal terminology of the doctrine of the single intellect is nowhere found in the *Defensor pacis*. He is far from saying that the state is "a species . . . of active intellect, immanent in the form of collective understanding and will." [26] The "identical specific nature" which he holds to characterize the wills of all or most men is not regarded by him as *numerically* one, even in the sense in which the Averroists viewed this numerical unity as somehow constituting the intellects of all men collectively while yet not removing the numerical diversity of men themselves. These, to be sure, are technical points, and one should not perhaps expect too literal an observance of them in a political treatise, although the literalness of Marsilius' political adaptations of Aristotle's "natural science" suggests an opposite interpretation.

The most telling argument, however, against the derivation of Marsilius' corporate republicanism from the doctrine of the single intellect is that, in consequence of the contrast between his voluntaristic emphasis and the intellectualism of the other Averroists, his political doctrine is radically divergent from that of the earlier "political Averroists," Averroes himself and John of Jandun.

(3) *Political Averroism.* The concept of "political Averroism" is a recent construct of historians of medieval thought. They have used it to characterize the political attitude resulting from the emphases implicit in the Averroists' doctrines of the contrariety between reason and faith: skepticism about the ability of faith and religion to correspond to the demands and results of rational inquiry; veneration for Aristotle and denigration of traditional religious authorities; religious indifferentism; secularism and anti-clericalism; determinism.[27] Most of these emphases are also to be found in Machiavelli, and

---

[23] Averroes *De anima* Lib. III. Com. 5 (fol. 150E).

[24] John of Jandun *Quaest. de Anima* Lib. III. qu. 10 (fol. 59r-v). John also makes the same point *ibid.* III. qu. 29 (fol. 80r) in discussing the question "Utrum intellectus est perpetuus." Cf. B. Nardi, *op. cit.* (above, n. 8), p. 224.

[25] See *Defender of Peace* I. xiii. 3, 7; and the pages of Averroes and John cited above, notes 23, 24.

[26] E. Troilo, *op. cit.*, pp. 64–65.

[27] See Vol. I, pp. 39–44, 56–57, 78–84; cf. also the references cited in Vol. I, p. 40, n. 38. See also G. de Lagarde, *La naissance de l'esprit laïque au déclin du moyen âge*, III (Saint-Paul-Trois-Châteaux, 1942), Chap. III.

accordingly it has been suggested that the close affinity between Marsilius and Machiavelli has this common Averroist source. But much further research must be undertaken in the political writings of the Averroists before it can be established what was the relation between their philosophic emphases and their specifically political doctrines. However, it seems clear that the former are logically compatible with quite different political doctrines. That the political Averroists would be anti-clerical is to be expected. But whether this anticlericalism would eventuate in a general republican suspicion of all attempts to obtain political supremacy for one or a few men, or whether it would lead instead to setting up an absolute secular ruler in opposition to the clergy; whether its disdain for the traditional religious authorities would involve contempt for the masses who accepted such authorities, or would lead instead to an exaltation of the people's insight in independence of the traditional authorities—on these and similar questions much flexibility was possible.[28] And, a fortiori, from the doctrine of the unity of the intellect no single kind of political doctrine necessarily followed. This emerges clearly through reference to the political writings of Averroes and John of Jandun, the two "political Averroists" who seem to have written most on politics prior to Marsilius.[29]

Both Averroes and John of Jandun upheld a strongly aristocratic conception of political authority. As against Marsilius' emphasis on the volitional and intellectual competence of the *universitas civium* and his defense of the *vulgus,* Averroes distinguished sharply between the masses of men, who are amenable only to rhetorical arguments, and the philosophers, who alone can follow demonstrative arguments.[30] Justice requires that the latter alone rule over all other men for their own good,[31] employing for this purpose, as rhetorical devices, the medicinal lie [32] and religion.[33] The political orientation of John of

[28] The point is related, of course, to the more general question of the relation between philosophies and political doctrines. That the relation is not one of necessary entailment seems clear; yet it would be hasty to conclude that there is no logical connection, in some "weaker" sense, at all.

[29] The political writings of Averroes are contained especially in his *Paraphrasis in libros de Republica Platonis* (in *Aristotelis opera . . . cum Averrois commentariis* [Venice, 1552–60], Vol. III); his *Commentarius in Moralia Nicomachia* (in *ibid.,* Vol. III); and his *Traité décisif sur l'accord de la religion et de la philosophie,* tr. L. Gauthier (Algiers, 1942) (this translation is preferable to the English rendition by Mohammad Jamil-Ur-Rehmann: *A Decisive Discourse on the Delineation of the Relation between Religion and Philosophy,* in *The Philosophy and Theology of Averroes* [Baroda, 1921]). The chief source for John of Jandun's political doctrines is his *Quaestiones in duodecim libros Metaphysicae* (Venice, 1525), esp. Lib. I, qus. 1, 17, 18, 21, 22; Lib. II, qus. 4, 11; Lib. XII, qu. 22. See also his *Tractatus de laudibus Parisius,* ed. Le Roux de Lincy and L. M. Tisserand, in *Paris et ses historiens aux 14ᵉ et 15ᵉ siècles* (Paris, 1867), pp. 32–78. I have examined John's *Quaestiones* briefly in "John of Jandun and the *Defensor Pacis,*" *Speculum,* XXIII (1948), pp. 267–72.

[30] *Traité décisif,* pp. 8, 26; *Paraphrasis . . . de Repub.* Tr. I (fols. 491F, 493F).

[31] *Paraphrasis . . . de Repub.* Tr. I (fol. 492B, D).

[32] *Ibid.* Tr. I (fol. 494F).

[33] *Traité décisif,* pp. 17 ff. Cf. *Destructio destructionum* Disp. VI (in *Aristotelis opera* [Venice, 1560], X, 208E ff.). It is impossible to see the grounds on which M. M. Gorce declares that Averroes was "fort démocrate" (*L'essor de la pensée au moyen âge* [Paris, 1934], p. 32). In support, Gorce refers to E. Renan, *Averroès et l'averroïsme,* 3d ed. (Paris, 1882), pp. 161–62; but no democracy is necessarily implied in Renan's statements there that, according to Averroes, the army must protect the people and that "le tyran est celui qui gouverne pour lui et non pour le peuple." It is also to be noted that the *Paraphrasis* on Plato's

Jandun was strikingly similar to that of Averroes. Although John did not make the philosophers rulers, he insisted that the philosophers are the "final cause" of all the parts of the state, because the whole state, and "political happiness," are ordered toward the "theoretic happiness" which consists in this-worldly "knowledge of God," which the philosophers alone possess.[34] Without this knowledge good action is impossible; [35] hence the philosophers must function as teachers of the rulers.[36] While John declared that most men have a natural inclination to this knowledge of God, he added that most men have "unordered desires" and hence are held back from such knowledge.[37] Moreover, he frequently repeated Aristotle's distinction between natural slaves and natural rulers,[38] and he also distinguished, in a manner analogous to that of Averroes, between the faith of the *vulgus,* which is directed to false religions rather than to philosophy, and the faith of the philosophers.[39]

Thus, while Averroes, John, and Marsilius all set up a politics characterized by secular values and secular authority,[40] the practical, voluntarist emphasis of Marsilius' values yielded a republicanism strikingly different from the aristocratic doctrine which was the outcome of the intellectualism of the others. It is possible that Marsilius for the first time saw the political implications of the Averroist unity of the intellect. But if so, he was also unique among the Averroists in his republican disposition of what for the others had been hierarchic gradations requiring an exclusive monopoly rather than an inclusive sharing of authority.

Republic is to be taken as expressing Averroes' own political doctrine, not only because of his many supporting interpolations of details explicitly reflecting his personal observations and ideas (many of these interpolations refer to what occurs "nunc nostris in civitatibus," e.g., *Paraphrasis* Tr. III [fol. 513B]), but also because of the remarkable agreement of the *Paraphrasis* with Averroes' political conceptions in the *Traité décisif,* the *Destructio destructionum,* and the commentary on Aristotle's *Metaphysics.* Averroes tells us that he wrote his *Paraphrasis* on the *Republic* to take the place of a commentary on Aristotle's *Politics,* which he had "not yet seen" (*Paraphrasis* Tr. I [fol. 491B]; see also *Comm. in Moralia Nicomachia* Lib. x. cap. ix [in *Aristotelis opera,* Venice, 1560, III, 317E]). See, however, L. Gauthier, *Ibn Roschd* (Paris, 1948), p. 14.

[34] *Quaest. in Metaphys.* I. qu. 18 (fol. 15K).
[35] *Ibid.* I. qus. 1, 21, 22 (fols. 2A, 17Q, 18Q).
[36] *Ibid.* I. qus. 1, 22 (fols. 2A, 19B-C).
[37] *Ibid.* II. qu. 4 (fols. 25J, 26B).
[38] *Ibid.* I. qus. 21, 22; XII, qu. 22 (fols. 17N, 18J, 144D). See Vol. I, pp. 177–78.
[39] *Quaest. in Metaphys.* I. qu. 17 (fol. 14E). See Vol. I, pp. 83–84, esp. n. 45.
[40] Although John of Jandun occasionally declares that his statements apply specifically to Christianity, in that perfect "knowledge about God" will be had only in the future world (*Quaest. in Metaphys.* II. qu. 4 [fol. 25O]), and that the supreme pontiff should be *princeps* over the whole world (*ibid.* XII. qu. 22 [fol. 144C-D]), the pervasive tenor of his whole doctrine shows that no such restriction is essential to it. The theological virtues as such play no part in his doctrine, and the "knowledge of God" is described almost exclusively in the terms of Aristotle's "theology," that is, the latter half of Book XII of the *Metaphysics.* See also Vol. I, p. 78, n. 8; and above, p. 24, n. 5.

AFTERWORD

THE PUBLICATION in 1956 of Alan Gewirth's English translation of the complete text of Marsilius of Padua's *Defensor pacis* (together with his companion study, *Marsilius of Padua and Medieval Political Philosophy*, published five years earlier) heralded the beginning of a remarkable renaissance in Marsilian studies that continues to the present day. In the decades (indeed, centuries) before Gewirth's germinal accomplishment, Marsilius (sometimes known by the non-Latinized version of his name, Marsiglio) had been largely dismissed as a crackpot, a heretic, or an anomaly—in all cases, someone whose thought was entirely out of step with his time. Perhaps Gewirth's greatest achievement was to render Marsilius's magnum opus accessible to a large English-speaking audience in a manner that was true to the historical character of the text, while also revealing the considerable philosophical depth and scope of the work. Although Gewirth's translation was not the first English rendering of the treatise—a carefully expurgated version had been produced by William Marshall for King Henry VIII in 1535—it set a standard to which other modern translators of the *Defensor pacis* into German, Italian, French, and Spanish aspired.

In the half-century since the translation was first published, under the title *The Defender of Peace*, the body of scholarly literature on Marsilius has advanced considerably in a number of ways, due in no small measure to the intellectual vigor of Gewirth's contribution. While Gewirth has gone on to establish himself as one of the preeminent moral and political philosophers of the late twentieth century—returning to the study of Marsilius only on rare occasions—his English version of the *Defensor pacis* has remained more or less continuously in print. Over the years, it has been reprinted by Harper and Row, Arno, and the Medieval Academy of America's Texts for Teaching series published by University of Toronto Press—and now, its original publisher, Columbia University Press. If only as a result of this longevity, the body of scholarship on Marsilius's thought that the translation (and companion monograph) did so much to pioneer and promote continues to build on foundations that may be traced back to Gewirth.

The *Defensor pacis* is equally famous as a work of temporal political theory and as a contribution to ecclesiology. Approaching it from such a dual perspective is hardly anachronistic: by dividing the two primary sections of the tract (known as Discourse I and Discourse II) according to matters of secular and of church government respectively, Marsilius encouraged a dichotomous reading. Indeed, the thematic and conceptual gulf between the two discourses once seemed so wide that scholars commonly supposed Marsilius's colleague John of Jandun to be the coauthor of the *Defensor pacis*, until Gewirth himself proved in a classic article that the treatise was the work of a single hand.[1] The structural division of temporal from spiritual matters perhaps constitutes the single most distinctive feature of the tract, in comparison with other scholastic and polemical writings of the later thirteenth and fourteenth centuries, which tended to address directly the issue of ecclesiastical versus secular power.

When the *Defensor pacis* first circulated following its completion in 1324, it caused an immediate scandal in Paris, where its author served on the faculty of the University. The main source of this scandal—not only in the fourteenth century but into the Reformation and even more recent times—was the work's ecclesiology: specifically, its ringing denial of the papal plenitude of power and its assertion of the supremacy of the General Council of the Church in the full range of ecclesiastical and theological affairs, conjoined with its apparent subordination of the clergy to the control of secular rulers. When Pope John XXII condemned the *Defensor pacis* and its author in 1327 (on the basis of second-hand reports), it was the ecclesiological claims of Discourse II that he singled out as the basis for anathematization.

Perhaps the single most noteworthy change to occur in the wake of Gewirth's scholarship has been the deflection of attention away from the second discourse and toward the first. In *Marsilius of Padua and Medieval Political Philosophy*, Gewirth devoted five chapters to Discourse I and only one chapter to Discourse II, in spite of the fact that Discourse II runs three times the length of Discourse I. This shift in focus heralded a dramatic transformation in the way that scholars have approached the *Defensor pacis*. Unlike a hundred (or even fifty) years ago,[2] the work is now viewed primarily (if not quite exclusively) as a contribution to the political theory of the secular community. Specifically, Gewirth's contribution has been to associate Marsilius's thought with the perennial philo-

---

[1] Alan Gewirth, "John of Jandun and the *Defensor Pacis*," *Speculum* 23 (1948): 267–272.

[2] In 1902, William A. Dunning spoke the received opinion when he remarked, "The full import of Marsiglio's theory of the state only appears when he presents his theory of the church, which is really the chief topic of the book" (*A History of Political Theories: Ancient and Medieval* [New York: Macmillan, 1902], p. 241).

sophical problems and classic "canon" of the Western political tradition by employing these as the measures by which to evaluate both the innovations and the adherence to convention contained in the *Defensor pacis*.

The leading principles of Discourse I may be summarized as follows. Marsilius advocates a normative conception of the foundations of a healthy or well-ordered temporal community, irrespective of its institutional arrangements. The chief benefit of temporal life, the peaceful enjoyment of the material and moral fruits of earthly existence, is best realized when human beings are joined together into a fully perfected political society. To achieve this, however, it is necessary for humans to exercise their reason and free will in order to consent to the communal arrangements under which they live. What distinguishes citizens from noncitizens for Marsilius is primarily the ability of citizens to give assent to the laws and governors to which they are subject, or to refuse such approval.

The *Defensor pacis* thus declares that the human legislator, or source of supreme authority, within the political community is the whole body of citizens, or its greater part (*valentior pars*). The meaning of the latter phrase has been widely debated, but it ought to be construed neither as an early statement of the principle of majoritarian democracy nor as a version of the aristocratic doctrine that the views of the "better" citizens should predominate in public decision-making. Marsilius instead lays stress upon consensus; he permits each and every citizen the opportunity to consent to, amend, or even disapprove of legislation and other common affairs. Yet he expects that most citizens who share the same powers of reason will be in agreement about matters pertaining to the public welfare. Only a contentious few, whom he describes as possessing "deprived natures" (*naturam orbatam*), will refuse to join in accepting the determinations of the civic body. The term *valentior pars* seems to denote all but the minuscule number of such demented souls.

Marsilius's normative theory has immediate implications for his critique of papal pretensions. The establishment and perpetuation of the political community derives from the exercise of the natural human faculties of reason and volition rather than from any form of direct divine concession. Hence, the pope, or indeed any priest, enjoys at best the same status as the other parts of the civic body. Should some member of the clergy interfere with the orderly operation of temporal government or legislation on noncivil grounds—for example, because he claims to have special power as God's ordained servant—he denies to the rest of the citizens their place within the communal association and, in effect, enslaves them by reducing their wills to his own. Consequently, all citizens are under a duty to uphold the just organization and peace of their own communities that requires them to repel the incursions of popes and clerics into the temporal sphere.

One of the primary concerns of recent scholarship has been the identification of the appropriate historical and intellectual contexts in which to place the ideas propounded in Discourse I. Chief among the topics of investigation in this regard is the relation between the *Defensor pacis* and its sources. Marsilius has customarily been classified as a quintessential medieval Aristotelian. It is true that the text of the *Defensor pacis* is littered with quotations from the writings of Aristotle—not only the *Politics* and *Nicomachean Ethics* but also the *Rhetoric* and various works on natural philosophy (recalling Marsilius's training as a physician). But authoritative citation ought not to be confused with philosophical influence.[3] Marsilius fails to cite or employ some of the most conventional ideas associated with medieval Aristotelianism (such as the teaching that man is a "political animal"). Moreover, he frequently distorts the meanings of the passages from Aristotle to which he refers (as in the case of claiming the authority of the Philosopher for a theory of consent that is manifestly non-Aristotelian). Additionally, in Marsilius's later writing, the *Defensor minor*, which purports to be a restatement and application of the basic principles of the *Defensor pacis*, Aristotle's work is cited only once in passing. In view of such factors, many scholars have begun to propose alternate ways to characterize Marsilius's thought in relation to its predecessors: strong echoes of Augustinian, Ciceronian, and Averroistic doctrines have been detected in the pages of the *Defensor pacis*, for example. Yet the sheer range of Marsilius's sources, not to mention the iconoclasm of their deployment, suggests that his political theory is simply too *sui generis* to be adequately classified as adhering any single philosophical school.

Another contextual dilemma posed by the *Defensor pacis* arises from the question of whether Marsilius intended to advocate the values or institutions of any specific exemplar of political arrangements. Some have discerned in his teachings an articulate defense of the communal liberty so cherished by the Italian cities during the Latin Middle Ages. According to Quentin Skinner's influential interpretation, for instance, the *Defensor*

---

[3] A point underscored by Conal Condren, "Marsilius of Padua's Argument from Authority: A Study of Its Significance in the *Defensor Pacis*," *Political Theory* 5 (May 1977): 205–218; Cary J. Nederman, "The Meaning of 'Aristotelianism' in Medieval Moral and Political Thought," *Journal of the History of Ideas* 57 (October–December 1996): 563–85.

pacis afforded "exactly the sort of ideological backing which the City Republics of the *Regnum Italicum* needed most . . . in order to defend their traditional liberties."[4] Marsilius is said to hearken back to the political organization of medieval communes along the lines of his native Padua to such a degree that, in the estimation of certain scholars, his account of popular, consensual government in the first discourse offers a precise blueprint of the Italian constitutional systems with which he was familiar.[5] By contrast, Marsilius's appeal to the condition of the Italian cities that pervades Discourse I has been balanced by other scholars against his evident devotion to the German Empire under the rule of would-be Emperor and King Ludwig of Bavaria, to whom the *Defensor pacis* is dedicated. Not only do the details of Marsilius's biography suggest a long-standing active commitment to the imperial cause, but his overt appeal to the conditions of the German Empire in the second discourse seems to undercut the devotion to Italian republicanism ascribed to Discourse I. Pointing to the resemblance between Marsilius's extensive discussions of elective monarchy in the first discourse and the elective nature of German kingship, for example, these commentators claim that the doctrines of the *Defensor pacis* are thoroughly imbued with imperialist ideology.[6] Although the dichotomy between so-called republican and imperialist interpretations of the text may seem irresolvable, some scholars have suggested that there may be no conflict between the two perspectives. Rather, if one keeps in mind the primacy of Marsilius's polemical goal—to defeat the papacy's interference in all forms of temporal affairs—it becomes possible to understand him as designing a set of political doctrines that would suit all European regimes regardless of scale or constitutional arrangement.[7] The theory of the *Defensor pacis* is intended to be "generic" in quality, just in order to achieve the overarching aim of defeating papal pretensions to political power, which Marsilius believes to be at the root of social conflict throughout Europe.

[4] Quentin Skinner, *The Foundations of Modern Political Thought*, 2 vols. (Cambridge: Cambridge University Press, 1978), 1.19; cf. 1.52–65 passim.

[5] J. K. Hyde, *Society and Politics in Medieval Italy. The Evolution of the Civil Life, 1000–1350* (London: Macmillan, 1973), pp. 187–195; also see J. K. Hyde, *Padua in the Age of Dante* (Manchester: Manchester University Press, 1966).

[6] Jeannine Quillet, *La Philosophie Politique de Marsile de Padoue* (Paris: J. Vrin, 1970), pp. 19, 84–88 passim; Georges de Lagarde, *La naissance de l'esprit laique au déclin du moyen age*, new ed., vol. 3, *Le Defensor Pacis* (Louvain-Paris: Nauwelaerts, 1970), p. 268; Michael Wilks, *The Problem of Sovereignty in the Later Middle Ages* (Cambridge: Cambridge University Press, 1963), pp. 110–113, 186.

[7] Antony Black, *Political Thought in Europe, 1250–1450* (Cambridge: Cambridge University Press, 1992), pp. 60–67; Conal Condren, *The Status and Appraisal of Classic Texts* (Princeton: Princeton University Press, 1985); Cary J. Nederman, *Community and Consent: The Secular Political Theory of Marsiglio of Padua's Defensor Pacis* (Lanham, Maryland: Rowman and Littlefield, 1995).

Given the apparent distance between Marsilius and his intellectual and political circumstances, it might be tempting to treat his work as completely novel and out of step with its time—in particular, as "anticipating" features of modern political thought. Gewirth himself encouraged such an approach to the *Defensor pacis* by highlighting its supposedly secularist and populist tendencies. For example, Gewirth propounded the notion that Marsilius's concept of law approximated the doctrine of modern legal positivists, for whom the validity of statute is entirely a matter of its promulgation in accordance with preexisting procedural standards. Hence, legitimate legislation does not depend upon its congruence with some "higher" standard of justice or rectitude, whether natural or supernatural. Inasmuch as Marsilius insists that human law is the result of the will of the civic body expressed by an act of overt consent, he would seem to subscribe to the position that public approval is the sufficient, as well as necessary, condition of legislative authorization. Such a claim would certainly place him at odds with the entire medieval tradition of legal and political thought. Yet the ascription to the *Defensor pacis* of legal positivism is not entirely convincing.[8] In a key passage, Marsilius in fact denies that human laws inconsistent with "true cognitions" of justice can be regarded as worthy of obedience, even if they adopt the proper "form" of law. He thus reveals himself to be more consistent with conventional medieval teachings about the inherently moral and religious bearing of law than is sometimes posited.

"Modernizing" interpretations of the *Defensor pacis* also place heavy emphasis upon its apparent advocacy of "popular sovereignty" and even of democracy.[9] The most extreme expressions of this thesis tend to explain Marsilius's "radical" populism as a kind of knee-jerk reaction to the hierocratic doctrines of his papal opponents. By insisting upon the finality of the popular will, Marsilius postulated the complete sovereignty of the people and thus constructed an image of the source of political authority that ran directly contrary to the plenitude of power claimed by the papacy.[10] Certainly, Marsilius seems at times to take the act of consent to law and to leadership as an individual and inviolable duty incumbent upon each citizen, stressing the necessity of public discussion and decision-making in order to guarantee civil liberty and common good. Yet the

---

[8] Ewart Lewis, "The 'Positivism' of Marsiglio of Padua," *Speculum* 38 (1963): 541–582.

[9] These are documented by Conal Condren, "Democracy and the *Defensor Pacis*: On the English Language Tradition of Marsilian Interpretation," *Il Pensiero Politico* 8 (1980): 301–316.

[10] Walter Ullmann, *Medieval Political Thought* (Harmondsworth, Middlesex: Penguin, 1975), pp. 204–214; Arthur Stephen McGrade, *The Political Thought of William of Ockham* (Cambridge: Cambridge University Press, 1974), pp. 82–83.

Defensor pacis still follows ancient and medieval custom in the refusal to include democracy among the healthy or well-ordered forms of constitution, and it organizes political institutions along "functional" lines (resembling the medieval guild structure) rather than according to strictly individual rights.[11] Indeed, some scholars have reacted so stridently to the "democratic" interpretation of Marsilius's thought that they have proposed that his populism is wholly illusory. In fact, this antimodern reading contends that the ostensive commendation of popular consent in the *Defensor pacis* is really nothing more than a restatement of conventional medieval corporatism, in which the assent of the governed to their rulers and laws is purely formal and without effect.[12] But this framework, too, seems to overlook important dimensions of Marsilius's writing, in particular, his insistence that the individual consent of citizens is to be preferred, even when seeking it is manifestly less efficient. Perhaps the most satisfactory conclusion is that the generic character of the Marsilian theory is again in evidence: he believed in the consent of the governed as the criterion for legitimate rule but was prepared to accept that a range of political mechanisms might be consonant with that basic principle.

A few scholars have been inclined to reject entirely Gewirth's emphasis on the first discourse of the *Defensor pacis*, preferring instead to revive the earlier view that the important elements of Marsilius's thought are to be found in the ecclesiology of Discourse II. In part, a case is made that the supposedly innovative doctrines ascribed to the initial section of the treatise are in fact rooted not in a "secular" argument but in Christian patristic and canon law sources that are employed in the second discourse to bolster the teaching about conciliar supremacy within the Church.[13] On this account, the theory of temporal government presented in the first discourse is merely a sort of logical extension and elaboration of the theory of Church government that Marsilius articulated in Discourse II. Once again, the ideas of *Defensor pacis* may be placed nearer to the core of the Christian intellectual tradition than they have commonly been located.

Failure to attend to the second discourse has also been blamed for a lack of appreciation for Marsilius's contribution to the growing late-medieval debate about natural rights. In his own interpretation of Marsilius's

[11] Antony Black, *Guilds and Civil Society in European Political Thought from the Twelfth Century to the Present* (Ithaca: Cornell University Press, 1984), pp. 86–95.

[12] Michael J. Wilks, "Corporation and Representation in the *Defensor Pacis*," *Studia Gratiana* 15 (1972): 251–294; Arthur P. Monahan, *Consent, Coercion, and Limit: The Medieval Origins of Parliamentary Democracy* (Montreal and Kingston: McGill-Queen's University Press, 1987), pp. 209–229.

[13] Brian Tierney, *Religion, Law, and the Growth of Constitutional Thought 1150–1650* (Cambridge: Cambridge University Press, 1982), pp. 48–50.

thought, Gewirth had explicitly denied the presence of rights language in the *Defensor pacis*.[14] This is only true, however, of the discussion in Discourse I. When one turns to Marsilian ecclesiology, we find a lengthy and careful examination of the concept of rights, couched in the terminology of the Spiritual Franciscan controversy about the poverty of Christ.[15] The Spiritual wing of the Franciscan Order had been vocal in its defense of its right to renounce worldly possessions—a right that had been denied by the papacy, which set out to suppress the majority Spirituals and to reintroduce a more moderate understanding of Franciscan teaching. Arguably, Marsilius's employment of Spiritual Franciscan vocabulary reflected his polemical aims, affording yet another stick with which to beat the papacy. For he derives from his analysis of human rights the conclusion that a clerical community genuinely devoted to the imitation of Christ would cheerfully surrender all its earthly goods and live in perfect poverty, as the Spiritual Franciscans wished to do. Once again, Marsilius's reliance upon authoritative argumentation may be in evidence; in the later *Defensor minor*, the rights vocabulary of the Franciscans (like the terminology of Aristotelianism) is nowhere on display. Yet this does not undermine the view that Marsilius contributed an important advance—especially, in framing the distinction between so-called objective and subjective conceptions of rights—to the late medieval debate about rights theory.

The revival of interest in Discourse II indeed provides a useful corrective to extensive concentration on the doctrines of the first discourse. But to insist upon the primacy of the former over the latter is to repeat the same mistake that has been criticized by promoting another one-sided interpretation of the *Defensor pacis*. In Marsilius's own view, the contents of both discourses were important to his principal aim, albeit for different reasons. This is evident from a consideration of the brief and seldom examined Discourse III of the work, which contains a summation and conclusion of its arguments. Marsilius asserts there that his primary goal in composing the treatise was pedagogical: to teach subjects as well as rulers how to conduct their affairs in order to achieve and preserve peace and liberty, particularly to eliminate the causes of intranquillity and civil strife. Of the forty-one main conclusions that Marsilius highlights in the third discourse, five are explicitly ascribed solely to Discourse I, thirteen to Discourse II, eighteen to both discourses, and five to neither discourse.

14 Alan Gewirth, *Marsilius of Padua: The Defender of Peace*, vol. 1, *Marsilius of Padua and Medieval Political Philosophy* (New York: Columbia University Press, 1951), p. 225.
15 Brian Tierney, *The Idea of Natural Rights* (Atlanta: Scholars Press, 1997), pp. 108–118.

In Marsilius's own mind, then, neither portion of the treatise deserves to be privileged to the exclusion of the other. Each section contributes a number of important elements to the overarching argument of the *Defensor pacis*, and in many cases, the two parts of the whole directly complement one another. Certainly, the specific arguments proposed in each discourse may be treated separately, since they focus on different ends of human life. Still, the dual discourses must ultimately be read together if one is to grasp the full force of the *Defensor pacis* as a coherent and integrated unity.

The unity of the argument in the *Defensor pacis* may perhaps be appreciated more completely by turning to Marsilius's own supposed restatement of his doctrines in his later treatise, the *Defensor minor*. The *Defensor minor*, which was only identified as Marsilius's work in the late nineteenth century, had been composed sometime between 1339 and 1342, in part at the request of King Ludwig, and in part as a reply to critics and reaffirmation of the principles contained in the *Defensor pacis*. The *Defensor minor* is, structurally speaking, a more conventionally medieval work than the *Defensor pacis*, in the sense that it does not introduce a cleavage between its discussion of temporal government, on the one hand, and ecclesiology, on the other, and, by inference, between the natural and supernatural realms or between reason and revelation. Rather, Marsilius's later work concentrates directly upon the relationship between earthly jurisdiction and spiritual authority.

Marsilius focuses in the *Defensor minor* upon the particular circumstances of the Empire and Ludwig's claim to the imperial title. This does not signal, however, a reorientation or departure from the *Defensor pacis*. The "generic" approach to the political community adopted in the *Defensor pacis*, explicitly declining to privilege any constitutional system or geographic unit of association, is translated in the *Defensor minor* into the concrete terms of an imperial regime, in contrast to a city or "national" kingdom. Marsilius contends that the Roman Empire, just like any other earthly polity, has an independent foundation stemming from the consent of its corporate community (or "human legislator"). The papacy enjoys no greater right to interfere in the affairs of the Empire than in any other form of political association.

Consequently, many of the characteristic doctrines of the *Defensor pacis* are reencountered in the *Defensor minor*. Because the *Defensor minor* operates at a level of greater specificity than the *Defensor pacis*, it erases several of the ambiguities of the earlier work and affords further insight into Marsilius's fundamental intellectual and political commitments. One of the most ill-defined aspects of the *Defensor pacis* was the exact composition of the "human legislator" or "people" or "civic body," that is, the original, supreme, and final authority within the political community. At times, the *Defensor pacis* seems to adopt a highly inclusive conception of citizenship (at least when judged by late medieval standards), which grants equal political standing to all free male adults regardless of social or economic status. Commentators have occasionally attempted to diminish or deny the implications of such a broad definition of entitlement to full civic rights through the citation of apparently mitigating or countervailing passages. But the *Defensor minor* leaves no doubt about Marsilius's confidence in the competence of ordinary persons to exercise the responsibilities associated with citizenship. Referring to his own comments in the first discourse of the *Defensor pacis*, he asserts that the correction of negligent or harmful rulers pertains to the human legislator, which he then defines with reference to "workmen" (*fabris*), "craftsmen," and "other mechanics," as well as men of prudence or learning. In fact, he declares that if correction has to be undertaken by any single segment of the civic body, rather than the whole, it is preferable to assign this task to the laboring part. This confirms his intention in the *Defensor pacis* to uphold that all citizens, regardless of their station in life, enjoy sufficient powers of reason to judge for themselves whether laws or rulers serve the common good.

The *Defensor minor* also explicates with greater precision Marsilius's view about the foundations of law. Like *Defensor minor*, the *Defensor pacis* argues that there are two basic kinds of law: divine law, ordained by God, who, along with His son, judges in accordance with it; and human law, established by the human legislator and imposed by those persons to whom the legislator assigns the judicial role. Marsilius insists in the *Defensor pacis* that no human law merits obedience which has not first been expressly authorized by the earthly legislator, leading to the charge discussed previously that he advocates legal positivism. In the *Defensor minor*, however, Marsilius proclaims that human and divine laws should be consistent and mutually reinforcing: God-given law decrees obedience to all human legislation which is not incompatible with divine dictates; human law must promulgate nothing which conflicts with God's will. He adds that, should a case arise in which some human statute commands what is opposed to divine law, the latter takes absolute precedence over the former. Marsilius thus embraces a version of the traditional Christian doctrine that all duly ordained human power must be obeyed unless its commands conflict with God's law, at which time the Christian must refuse to submit. But he denies one prominent feature of this doctrine: it is not for priests or prelates to decree such resistance—in as much as they may only advise but never command—but for the Christian believer to decide. In turn, since the whole civic community propounds human law, it seems unlikely that such conflicts of divine with temporal law will emerge in the first place, since the earthly legislator is coextensive with the body of the faithful.

Futhermore, the *Defensor minor* permits a more thorough understanding of the nature and operation of the General Council of the Church. According to the *Defensor pacis*, the purpose of such a Council is the canonical interpretation of Holy Scripture. Although the Church elects the members of this Council as a whole, Marsilius does not construe it as a representative body in a modern, political sense. Rather, since the truths of Scripture are fixed for all time, the Council's duty is solely to discover and articulate such truths with reference to the Holy Spirit instead of an earthly constituency. In this sense, the General Council is infallible in a way that individual priests or prelates, or their various groupings, cannot be; the Council alone had access to eternal truth. During the 1330s, Marsilius's fellow exile and antipapal propagandist, William of Ockham, had launched a stinging attack on this doctrine of conciliar infallibility by claiming that since individual members of the Council were not capable of unerring insight into God's wisdom, neither could the Council as a whole know unequivocally what is true. Ockham appeared to regard the Marsilian view as unvarnished mysticism. Marsilius responds in the *Defensor minor* that what cannot be accomplished by one person may often be achieved by the cooperation of many. In the case of a General Council, this cooperation occurs as the result of discussion and mutual edification, by means of which a consensus about the truth is eventually attained. The Holy Spirit is infused in individual members of the Council as a result of their reciprocal interaction, through a process analogous to that described in the *Defensor pacis* by which civil communities reach agreement about legislation.

As befits an author who generated such great controversy in his own lifetime, the story of the reception and interpretation of Marsilius's thought prior to the twentieth century forms a complex and difficult tale. Echoes of his teachings have been detected in most of the canonical figures of modern political thought—from Machiavelli and Hobbes to Rousseau and Marx—yet there is little compelling evidence that the *Defensor pacis* was read by any of them. More certain is that a number of later medieval and early modern thinkers of slightly less exalted reputation may be counted among the audience for Marsilius's text. Marsilian ideas about government, secular as well as ecclesiastical, were incorporated (often without mention of their source) into the works of such important leaders of the conciliar movement as Dietrich of Niem and Nicholas of Cusa. The Counter-Reformation brought renewed interest in the *Defensor pacis*, as defenders of Roman orthodoxy detected strains of Marsilius's teachings about the papacy in the writings of Luther (a charge which seems more fanciful than true). Marsilius was especially well received in early modern England, where the publication of Marshall's strategically edited translation of the text during the reign of Henry VIII renewed its author's original polemical aim of opposing papal interference in public affairs. Among Marsilius's sympathetic English readership may be counted Richard Hooker, Thomas Starkey, and George Lawson. On the Continent, the eminent and influential Protestant theorist Johannes Althusius also found intellectual stimulation in the *Defensor pacis*. Given these historical connections, it is hardly surprising that scholars have consistently emphasized how Marsilius's writing constitutes an important precursor of, if not source for, the Reformation.[16]

This is not to suggest that the story of Marsilius's significance ought to be confined to his early modern readership or his intellectual resemblance to the reformers of the sixteenth and seventeenth centuries. As Gewirth emphasized in the concluding chapter of his 1951 study, Marsilius continues to speak to many of the salient issues of modern political life, expressing his doctrines in a language that has resonance and relevance. Whether in addressing the role of citizenship as a buffer between individual and community or in explicating the foundations of religious toleration, the *Defensor pacis* and Marsilius's other writings afford a distinctive theoretical perspective that rivals any of the great thinkers of the Western political tradition. Thus, the *Defensor pacis* should be approached not as an artifact or curiosity of a past age but as a living document that still offers considerable and original insight into the enduring problems posed by politics, in the twenty-first century as well as in the fourteenth.

Cary J. Nederman

16 Steven Ozment, *The Age of Reform, 1250–1550: An Intellectual and Religious History of Late Medieval and Reformation Europe* (New Haven: Yale University Press, 1980), pp. 149–155.

BIBLIOGRAPHY, 1950–2000

A VERY THOROUGH BIBLIOGRAPHY, covering literature in all languages during the period from 1960 to 1994, may be found in Carlo Dolcini, *Introduzione a Marsilio da Padova* (Rome and Bari: Editori Laterza, 1995), pp. 85–112. The bibliography below covers editions of Marsilius's writings and surveys of his thought published after Alan Gewirth's germinal 1951 study, *Marsilius of Padua and Medieval Political Philosophy* (New York: Columbia University Press, 1951). It also includes some important specialized research, as well as work published too late to be included in Dolcini's bibliography.

EDITIONS AND TRANSLATIONS OF MARSILIUS'S WRITINGS

Le Défenseur de la Paix. Ed. Jeannine Quillet. Paris: J. Vrin, 1968.

El Defensor de la Paz. Ed. L. Martinez Gomez. Madrid: Tecnos, 1989.

Il Difensore della Pace. Ed. Cesare Vasoli. Turin: Unione Tipografico-Eeditrice Torinese, 1960.

Il Difensore Minore. Ed. Cesare Vasoli. Naples: Guida, 1975.

Oeuvres Minueres. Ed. Colete Jeudy and Jeannine Quillet. Paris: Editions CNRS, 1979.

Der Verteidiger des Friedens. Ed. Walter Kunzmann and Horst Kusch. Berlin: Rutten & Loening, 1958.

Writings on the Empire: Defensor Minor and De Translatione Imperii. Ed. Cary J. Nederman. Cambridge: Cambridge University Press, 1993.

SECONDARY WORKS

Baernstein, P. Renée. "Corporatism and Organicism in Discourse 1 of Marsilius of Padua's *Defensor pacis*." *Journal of Medieval and Early Modern Studies* 26 (Winter 1996): 113–138.

Black, Antony. *Guilds and Civil Society in European Political Thought from the Twelfth Century to the Present*. Ithaca: Cornell University Press, 1984.

———. *Political Thought in Europe, 1250–1450*. Cambridge: Cambridge University Press, 1992.

Blythe, James M. *Ideal Government and the Mixed Constitution in the Middle Ages*. Princeton: Princeton University Press, 1992.

Burns, J. H., ed. *The Cambridge History of Medieval Political Thought*.
Cambridge: Cambridge University Press, 1988.

Canning, Joseph. *A History of Medieval Political Thought 300–1450*.
London: Routledge, 1996.

Coleman, Janet. "Medieval Discussions of Property: *Ratio* and *Dominium*
According to John of Paris and Marsilius of Padua." *History of Political
Thought* 4 (Summer 1983): 209–228.

Condren, Conal. "Marsilius of Padua's Argument from Authority: A
Study of Its Significance in the *Defensor Pacis*." *Political Theory* 5 (May
1977): 205–218.

———. "Democracy and the *Defensor Pacis*: On the English Language
Tradition of Marsilian Interpretation." *Il Pensiero Politico* 8 (1980):
301–316.

———. *The Status and Appraisal of Classic Texts*. Princeton: Princeton
University Press, 1985.

Damiata, Marino. *Plenitudo Potestatis e Universitas Civium in Marsilio da
Padova*. Florence: Edizioni "Studi Francescani," 1983.

De Rossi, Guido. *Marsilio de Padoue, Profeta de la Politica Moderna*. Lima:
Mosca Azul Editores, 1976.

Di Vona, Piero. *I Principi del Defensor Pacis*. Naples: Morano Editore,
1974.

Gewirth, Alan. "Republicanism and Absolutism in the Thought of
Marsilius of Padua." *Medioevo* 5 (1979): 23–48.

Grignaschi, Marc. "La Rôle de l'aristotélisme dans le 'Defensor Pacis' de
Marsile de Padoue." *Revue d'Histoire et de Philosophie Religieuse* 35
(1955): 310–340.

Grogacz, Mieczyslaw. "L'homme et la communauté dans le *Defensor Pacis*
de Marsile de Padoue." *Medioevo* 5 (1979): 189–199.

Hyde, J. K. *Padua in the Age of Dante*. Manchester: Manchester
University Press, 1966.

———. *Society and Politics in Medieval Italy: Civil Life, 1100–1350*. London:
Macmillan, 1973.

Koch, Bettina. "Zum mittelalterlichen Politikverständnis: Die *Civitas* als
Fokus des Politischen im *Defensor pacis* des Marsilius von Padua?" In
Hans J. Lietzmann and Peter Nitschke, eds., *Klassische Politik*.
Opladen: Leske & Budrich, 2000.

Lagarde, Georges de. *La Naissance de l'Esprit Laïque au Déclin du Moyen
Age*. 5 vols. New ed. Louvain and Paris: Éditions Nauwelaerts and
Béatrice-Nauwelaerts, 1956–1970.

Lewis, Ewart. "The 'Positivism' of Marsiglio of Padua." *Speculum* 38
(1963): 541–582.

Lewis, Ewart, ed. *Medieval Political Ideas.* London: Routledge and Kegan Paul, 1954.

Monahan, Arthur P. *Consent, Coercion, and Limit: The Medieval Origins of Parliamentary Democracy.* Kingston and Montrèal: McGill-Queens University Press, 1987.

Morrall, John B. *Political Thought in Medieval Times.* New York: Harper & Row, 1962.

Mulcahy, Daniel G. "The Hands of Augustine but the Voice of Marsilius." *Augustiniana* 21 (1971): 457–466.

Nederman, Cary J. "Nature, Sin and the Origins of Society: The Ciceronian Tradition in Medieval Political Thought." *Journal of the History of Ideas* 49 (1988): 3–26.

——. "Nature, Justice and Duty in the *Defensor Pacis*: Marsiglio of Padua's Ciceronian Impulse." *Political Theory* 18 (November 1990): 615–637.

——. "The Union of Wisdom and Eloquence Before the Renaissance: The Ciceronian Orator in Medieval Thought." *Journal of Medieval History* 18 (1992): 75–95.

——. "Freedom, Community and Function: Communitarian Lessons of Medieval Political Thought." *American Political Science Review* 86 (December 1992): 977–986.

——. *Community and Consent: The Secular Political Theory of Marsiglio of Padua's* Defensor Pacis. Lanham, Maryland: Rowman & Littlefield, 1995.

——. *Worlds of Difference: European Discourses of Toleration, c.1100–c.1550.* University Park: Pennsylvania State University Press, 2000.

Offler, H. S. "Empire and Papacy: The Last Struggle." *Transactions of the Royal Historical Society Series* 6, no. 5 (1956): 21–47.

——. *Church and Crown in the Fourteenth Century: Studies in European History and Political Thought.* Ed. A. I. Doyle. Aldershot: Ashgate/Variorum, 2000.

Pincin, Cailo. *Marsilio.* Turin: Edizioni Giappichelli, 1967.

Quillet, Jeannine. "L'Aristotèlisme de Marsile de Padoue." *Miscellanea Medievalia* 2 (1963): 696–706.

——. *Le Philosophie Politique de Marsile de Padoue.* Paris: J. Vrin, 1970.

——. "*Universitas Populi* et Representation au XIV Siécle." *Miscellanea Medievalia* 8 (1971): 186–201.

——. "L'aristotèlisme de Marsile de Padoue et ses rapports avec l'averroïsm" *Medioevo* 5 (1979): 124–142.

——. "Nouvelles Études Marsiliennes." *History of Political Thought* 1 (Autumn 1980): 391–409.

Rubinstein, Nicolai. "Marsilius of Padua and Italian Political Thought of His Time." In J. R. Hale, J. R. L. Highfield, and B. Smalley, eds.,

Europe in the Later Middle Ages. Evanston, Ill.: Northwestern University Press, 1965.

Segall, Hermann. *Der Defensor Pacis des Marsilius von Padua: Grundfragen der Interpretation.* Wiesbaden: Franz Steiner Verlag, 1959.

Skinner, Quentin. *The Foundations of Modern Political Thought.* 2 vols. Cambridge: Cambridge University Press, 1978.

Spiers, Kerry E. "The Ecclesiastical Theory of Marsilius of Padua: Sources and Significance." *Il Pensiero Politico* 10 (1977): 3–21.

Struve, Tilman. *Die Entwicklung der Organologischen Staatsauffasung im Mittelalter.* Stuttgart: Anton Hiersemann, 1978.

Tierney, Brian. *Religion, Law, and the Growth of the Constitutional Thought, 1150–1650.* Cambridge: Cambridge University Press, 1982.

———. "Marsilius on Rights." *Journal of the History of Ideas* 52 (1991): 3–17.

———. "Political and Religious Freedom in Marsilius of Padua." In Noel B. Reynolds and W. Cole Durham, Jr., eds., *Religious Liberty in Western Thought.* Atlanta: Scholars Press, 1996.

Turraco, Stephen F. *Priests as Physicians of Souls in Marsilius of Padua's Defensor Pacis.* San Francisco: Mellen Research University Press, 1992.

Ullmann, Walter. *Principles of Government and Politics in the Middle Ages.* London: Methuen, 1961.

———. *The Individual and Society in the Middle Ages.* London: Methuen, 1967.

Vasoli, Cesare. "La *Politica* di Aristotele a la utilizzazione de parte di Marsilio da Padova." *Medioevo* 5 (1979): 237–252.

Webb, Diana. "The Possibility of Toleration: Marsiglio and the City States of Italy." In W. J. Sheils, ed., *Persecution and Toleration.* Oxford: Blackwell, 1984.

Wilks, Michael J. *The Problem of Sovereignty in the Later Middle Ages.* Cambridge: Cambridge University Press, 1963.

———. "Corporation and Representation in the 'Defensor Pacis.'" *Studia Gratiana* 15 (1972): 251–292.

INDEX

Aaron, 393

Abel, 392

Abraham, 392

Acts: contentious, 107; controlled and uncontrolled, 156-73; cognitive, 157; *see also* Immanent acts; Transient acts

Acts of the Apostles: concerning coercive judgment of priests, 139, 179, possessions, 193, 212, 215, 219, 222, 223, deacons, 235, 257, 259-60, bishops, 236, circumcision, 244, plenitude of power, 245, Paul as apostle to the Gentiles, 251, authority of congregation, 275, 391

Adrian III, 336

Affections, 157

Agriculture, 15, 17

Albert the Great, 24n, 190n, 191n

Alcuin, 209n

Aliens, 46, 66

Altopascio, knights of, 162

Alvarus Pelagius, 112n, 249n

Ambrose, Saint: quoted in Peter Lombard *Collectanea*, 103, 105, 106, 127, 130-31, 135, 137, 165, 207, 243, 409-10, in Thomas Aquinas *Catena aurea*, 118, 119, 400, in Peter Lombard *Sentences*, 143, 153, 154; cited, 174, 180-81; difference in interpretation of Scripture from Jerome, 372; *see also On Handing Over the Basilica; To the People*

Anacletus, pope, quoted, 249

Animals, 63-64

Apostle, the, *see* Paul, Saint

Apostles, 91-92; writings of, 127-41; priestly keys given by Christ to, 140-52; as judges, 168; and status of supreme poverty, 187-233; equality of, 241-53; assignment to certain peoples and provinces, 256-58; *see also* under individual names, e. g., Matthew

Apostolic seat, 347

Aristocracy, 27, 59, 81

Aristotle, 4-5; on monarchies, 8-9, 68-71 *passim*; on government, 9-20 *passim*, 25, 27, 30, 31, 33, 62-65 *passim*; on civil communities, 10, 11, 12, 50; on qualities of rulers, 26, 56-60 *passim*, 65, 72-80 *passim*, 88-89, 108; on law, 35-52 *passim*, 160, 163; on beginnings, 54; on revolutions, 66; on cause of strife, 90-91; on the priesthood, 96, 169, 183, 421; on opposition to truth, 99; on the meaning of words,

102, 195, 226, 422n; on justice, 159, 190-93 *passim;* on temporal welfare, 262, 367

Armenia, 388n

Artisan, 15, 17, 20

Arts, 17; *see also* Artisan

Asser, Reginald, 322n

Astrology, 39n

Augustine, Saint: on keys to the kingdom, 93, 142, 143, 150, 151; on the church, 102, 365-66, 375; on equality of priests and bishops, 114-18, 127, 130-32, 136-38, 168, 242-43, 245, 246, 251, 261, 408-12 *passim;* on human and divine laws, 170; on status of supreme poverty, 198-99, 221, 222, 224; on canonic writings, 276-78, 284; difference in interpretation of Scripture from Jerome, 372; on apostleship of Peter and Paul, 379-82 *passim*, 403

Augustinus Triumphus, 34n, 140n, 236n, 244n

Augustus Phocas, 306

Authority, congregational, 244-45, 275; *see also* Coercive authority

Avarice, 203

Averroes, quoted, 40; doctrine of unity of intellect, 51n

Avicenna, 13n

Bacon, Roger, 329n

Baptism, 141; *see also* Sacraments

Basil, quoted, 126, 202

Basilica, 387

Bede, quoted, 223-24, 364; cited, 372

Beguins, 162

Benedict IX, 335

Benefices, concerning distribution of, 264-67, 273, 285-86, 287, 294, 295-96, 312-13, 314, 321, 326, 327, 388-89, 404-5, 428-29

Bernard, Saint, in *De moribus et officio episcoporum*, 121, 124, 131; in *On Consideration*, 126, 128, 129-30, 186, 236n, 317, 324, 345, 361n, 369-70, 392-401 *passim*, 406

Bible, *see* Scriptures

Bigongiari, D., 20n, 28n, 85n, 182n, 225n, 226n, 237n, 395n, 420n

Biological basis of Marsilian politics, 50-51

Biological needs as generating society, 13

Bishop of Rome, *see* Pope

Bishops: origin of office, 93; coercive authority of, *see under* Coercive authority; the "spiritual" and, 105-7; power of excom-